Racial and Ethnic Relations in America

SEVENTH EDITION

S. Dale McLemore
University of Texas at Austin

Harriett D. Romo
University of Texas at San Antonio

PEARSON

Boston   New York   San Francisco
Mexico City   Montreal   Toronto   London   Madrid   Munich   Paris
Hong Kong   Singapore   Tokyo   Cape Town   Sydney

Senior Editor: Jeff Lasser
Editorial Assistant: Sära Owen
Marketing Manager: Krista Groshong
Production Administrator: Marissa Falco
Editorial-Production Service: Colophon
Electronic Composition: Omegatype Typography, Inc.
Composition and Prepress Buyer: Linda Cox
Manufacturing Buyer: JoAnne Sweeney
Cover Administrator: Kristina Mose-Libon

For related titles and support materials, visit our online catalog at www.ablongman.com

Library of Congress Cataloging-in-Publication Data

McLemore, S. Dale.
    Racial and ethnic relations in America / S. Dale McLemore, Harriett D. Romo.—7th ed.
        p.   cm.
    Includes bibliographical references and index.
    ISBN 0-205-38197-9
    1. Minorities—United States. 2. United States—Ethnic relations. 3. United States—Race relations.   I. Romo, Harriett. II. Title.
    E184.A1M16 2004
    305.8'00973—dc22

                                                                        2004040983

Printed in the United States of America

10   9   8   7   6   5   4   3   2   1   RRD-VA   07   06   05   04

Dedicamos este libro a nuestras queridas familias.
This book is dedicated to our families.

Contents

Preface   xvii

1 Natives and Newcomers   1

An Overview of Assimilation in America   3
  A Popular View   3
  Some Non-European Instances   5
  Some Factors Affecting Assimilation   6
    Differences in Social Power 6 ◆ *Voluntary or Involuntary Entrance* 7 ◆
    Group Size, Concentration, and Time of Entry 7 ◆ *Ethnic and Racial
    Similarity* 8
Development of Assimilation Theory   8
Race and Ethnicity   11
  Race   11
  Ethnicity   13
Discussion Questions   14
Key Ideas   15
Key Terms   16
Notes   18

2 Together or Apart?
Some Competing Views   20

Subprocesses of Assimilation   22
Gordon's Theory of Assimilation Subprocesses   25
Three Ideologies of Assimilation   27
  The Anglo-Conformity Ideology   27

The Melting-Pot Ideology   30
The Ideology of Cultural Pluralism   31
An Antiassimilationist View: Blauner's Theory of Internal Colonialism   33
Two Antiassimilationist Ideologies: Separatism and Secessionism   35
Using the Models as Descriptions   38
REALITY CHECK: INTERVIEW WITH CURTIS   42
Discussion Questions   44
Key Ideas   45
Key Terms   47
Notes   49

3 The Rise of Anglo American Society   51

The English Legacy   52
Indian–English Relations   55
Servants and Slaves   59
The Colonial Irish   63
The Colonial Germans   65
The Revolutionary Period   66
REALITY CHECK: INTERVIEW WITH PAM   69
Discussion Questions   71
Key Ideas   72
Key Terms   74
Notes   74

4 The Golden Door   76

The First Great Immigrant Stream   79
The Nineteenth-Century Irish   79
The Potato Famine   80 ◆ *Natives' Reactions   82* ◆ *Women Immigrants   83*
The Nineteenth-Century Germans   84
Political Participation   86
Changing Patterns of Immigration   87
The Second Great Immigrant Stream   89
The Italians   90
Natives' Reactions   92 ◆ *Ethnic Identity   93*
Sephardic and Ashkenazaic Jews   94
German Jews   94 ◆ *Russian Jews   95*

Italians and Russian Jews   95
Immigration Restriction: A Preview   98
The Third Great Immigrant Stream   98
Rejection of the National-Origins Principle   100
Some Sociocultural Effects of the New Laws   101
Increasing Racial and Ethnic Diversity   101 ◆ *Settlement Patterns   102* ◆
Time of Arrival   102 ◆ *Undocumented Workers   103*
Flashpoint 1: Are Immigrants Good for America?   104
The Economic Question   105 ◆ *The Ethnic Absorption Question   106*
REALITY CHECK: INTERVIEW WITH AMANDA   108
Discussion Questions   110
Key Ideas   110
Key Terms   111
Notes   112

5 Nativism and Racism   113

Nativism   114
Scientific Racism   117
Racial Differences   117
Mental Testing and Immigration   118
The Rise of Environmentalism   119
Comparing Races   119 ◆ *Testing Theory   120*
Flashpoint 2: Hereditarianism Revisited   120
Immigration Restriction   123
The Chinese Exclusion Act of 1882   123
The Immigration Act of 1924   124
Contemporary Racism   126
Prejudice and Discrimination   128
Theories of Prejudice   128
Cultural-Transmission Theories of Prejudice   128 ◆ *Group-Identification Theories
of Prejudice   130* ◆ *Personality Theories of Prejudice   131*
Theories of Discrimination   132
Situational Pressures Theories of Discrimination   132 ◆ *Group Conflict Theories
of Discrimination   134* ◆ *Institutional Discrimination Theories   136*
REALITY CHECK: INTERVIEW WITH JANA   138
Discussion Questions   141
Key Ideas   142
Key Terms   144
Notes   145

6   African Americans:
    From Slavery to Segregation   149

The Period of Slavery   150
    The Impact of Slavery on Its Victims   152
        The Profitability of Slavery   152
Immigrant or Colonized Minority?   153
Emancipation and Reconstruction   153
    Freed African Americans   154
    White Hostility   155
The Restoration of White Supremacy   156
    Economic Slavery   157
    Jim Crow Laws   157
    Voting Restrictions   158
    Separate but Equal   159
Migration and Urbanization   160
The Civil Rights Movement   162
    Separate and Subordinate   162
    The Niagara Movement   163
        The NAACP   164
    Continued Racial Violence   164
    Separatism   165
        Back to Africa   165   ◆   *Black Muslims   167*
    Strategy, Tactics, and Conflict   168
        CORE: The Expansion of Nonviolent Protest   169   ◆   *The Decline of Colonialism   170*
    Victories in the Courts   170
        Brown v. Topeka Board of Education   171
    REALITY CHECK: INTERVIEW WITH CARLA   172
Discussion Questions   175
Key Ideas   175
Key Terms   176
Notes   177

7   African Americans:
    Protest and Social Change   178

The Rise of Direct Action   179
    Increasing Militancy   179
    Civil Rights Legislation   181

Black Power   181
   Renewed Black Nationalism   182   ◆   Violent Protests   182   ◆
   Declining Momentum   184
Renewed Visibility of Black–White Conflict   184
   The Beating of Rodney King   185
   The O. J. Simpson Trial   186
   Racial Profiling   187
   Some Corporate Cases of Discrimination   188
African American Assimilation   189
   Cultural Assimilation   189
    *The Moynihan Report   189   ◆   An Ethnic-Resource Model   190   ◆   Contemporary
    Families   190   ◆   The "Million Man March"   191*
   Secondary Structural Assimilation   191
    *Occupations   192   ◆   Incomes   193   ◆   Growing African American Affluence   194
    ◆   Education   195   ◆   Residential Assimilation   196*
   Primary Structural Assimilation   199
   Marital Assimilation   201
   Other Forms of Assimilation   202
   Flashpoint 3: The Affirmative Action Debate   203
    *Early Legal Challenges   204   ◆   The Bakke Decision   204   ◆   Salient Issues   205
    ◆   The Hopwood Decision   205   ◆   Percent Plans   206   ◆   The Michigan Law
    School and Undergraduate Admission Decisions   207   ◆   The Effectiveness of Affirma-
    tive Action   209   ◆   A Final Consideration   210*
African American "Success"   211
   The Cultural View   212
   The Structural View   214
    Middleman Minorities   214   ◆   A Social Class Analysis   215
   Black Immigration   217
    REALITY CHECK: INTERVIEW WITH JEFFREY   219
Discussion Questions   221
Key Ideas   221
Key Terms   223
Notes   224

8 Mexican Americans: From Colonized Minority to Political Activists   226

Early Indian–Spanish Relations   227
The Texas Frontier   229

Conflict in the Borderlands 230

The Immigrant Model 232

Mexican Immigration and Native Reaction 236
   The Great Depression 237
   The Bracero *Program* 238
   The Zoot-Suit Riots 239
   The Mexican American Civil Rights Movement 242
   The Post-Chicano Era 245

   REALITY CHECK: INTERVIEW WITH EDDIE 246

Discussion Questions 248

Key Ideas 249

Key Terms 250

Notes 251

9 Puerto Ricans and Mexican Americans: Identity and Incorporation 253

Identification and Diversity 256

The Colonization of Puerto Rico 258

Cultural Assimilation: English and Spanish 259
   Flashpoint 4: Bilingual Education 261
      Historical Perspectives 262 ◆ *Legal Developments* 263 ◆
      ASPIRA of New York, Inc. v. Board of Education of the City of New York 264 ◆
      Long-Term Implications 266

Cultural Assimilation: Family Patterns 267

Secondary Structural Assimilation 269
   Occupations 269
   Incomes 270
   Education 271
   Residential Assimilation 273

Primary Structural Assimilation 275
   Friendship Patterns 275

Marital Assimilation 276

Other Forms of Assimilation 277

Mexican American and Puerto Rican "Success" 278

   REALITY CHECK: INTERVIEW WITH JOHNANA 281

Discussion Questions   283

Key Ideas   283

Key Terms   284

Notes   285

10   Native Americans   288

The English Penetration of the Continent   290
    The French and Indian War   290
    The Proclamation of 1763   291
    Enforcing the Treaties   291

Indian Removal   292
    Legal Issues   292
        The Indian Removal Act   293
    The Trail of Tears   293

Plains Wars and Reservations   294
    Increased Warfare   294
    Violations of the Treaties   295
    The Battle of Little Bighorn   296

From Separatism to Anglo Conformity   296
    The Bureau of Indian Affairs   297
    The End of Treaty Making   297
    The Dawes Act   298
    Indian Education   299
    The Ghost Dance and Wounded Knee   299

Cycling between Anglo Conformity and Cultural Pluralism   300
    The Indian Reorganization Act   301
    The "Termination" Policy   301

Pan-Indian Responses and Initiatives   303
    Protest Organizations   303
        The Society for American Indians   304   ◆   *The National Congress of American Indians (NCAI)*   305
    The New Tribalism   305
        The American Indian Movement   306   ◆   *Games of Chance*   307   ◆   *Sovereignty for Alaskan Tribes*   307

Immigrant or Colonized Minority?   308

Native American Assimilation   310
    Cultural Assimilation   311
        Language Maintenance   312   ◆   *Indian Religious Freedom*   313   ◆   *Traditions*   315   ◆   *American Indian Ethnic Renewal*   316   ◆   *Pan-Indian Identity*   316

        Secondary Structural Assimilation   317
            Education 317 ◆ Occupations and Incomes 318 ◆ Life Chances 322
        Primary Structural Assimilation   322
        Marital Assimilation   323
        Other Forms of Assimilation   325
    American Indian "Success"   327
        REALITY CHECK: INTERVIEW WITH JEAN WILMA   328
    Discussion Questions   330
    Key Ideas   330
    Key Terms   332
    Notes   333

11   Japanese Americans   335

    Japanese Immigration and Native Reactions   337
        Anti-Japanese Protest   337
        The School Board Crisis   338
        The "Picture-Bride Invasion"   339
    The Japanese Family and Community in America   340
        Family and Community Cohesion   340
        Japanese Occupations and Alien Land Laws   342
        Exclusion   343
        The Second-Generation Period   344
    War, Evacuation, and Relocation   345
        The Relocation Program   347
        Life in the Camps   348
        Legal Issues   350
    Japanese American Assimilation   352
        Cultural Assimilation   352
            Intergenerational Differences 352 ◆ The Sansei 353
        Secondary Structural Assimilation   354
            Education, Occupation, and Income 354 ◆ Organizational Membership 355 ◆
            Residential Assimilation 355
        Primary Structural Assimilation   356
        Marital Assimilation   356
        Other Forms of Assimilation   358
    Japanese American "Success"   358
        The Cultural View   358
        The Structural View   360
        Consequences of Issei Success   360
        A Comparison of Success Theories   361

The "Model Minority" Stereotype   362

Discussion Questions   365

Key Ideas   365

Key Terms   366

Notes   367

12 Chinese, Korean, Filipino, and Asian Indian Americans   369

Chinese Americans   371
Roots of the Chinese American Family and Community   373
Chinese American Assimilation   376

Korean Americans   380
Roots of the Korean American Family and Community   382
Korean American Assimilation   384

Filipino (Pilipino) Americans   385
Roots of the Filipino American Family and Community   388
Filipino American Assimilation   391

Asian (East) Indian Americans   392
Roots of the Asian Indian American Family and Community   395
Asian Indian American Assimilation   397

Some Additional Observations on Asian American Assimilation   399

Discussion Questions   400

Key Ideas   401

Notes   402

13 Vietnamese Americans, Arab Americans, and Resurgent Racism   407

Refugees: An International Issue   409

Vietnamese Americans   410
The Thirty Years War in Vietnam: 1945–1975   411
The War and the Boat People   411
Roots of the Vietnamese American Family and Community   412
Refugee Resettlement 412 ◆ The Refugee Camps 413

Vietnamese American Assimilation 414
  Cultural Assimilation 414 ◆ *Secondary Structural Assimilation 415* ◆
  Primary Structural Assimilation 416 ◆ *Marital Assimilation 417* ◆
  Conclusion 417

Arab Americans 418
  Roots of the Arab American Family and Community 420
  Arab Immigration between 1948 and 1965 422
  Arab American Assimilation 423

Resurgent Racism 428
  REALITY CHECK: INTERVIEW WITH THU 432

Discussion Questions 433

Key Ideas 434

Notes 435

14 The Future of Ethnicity 439

Further Reflections on Assimilation and Ethnicity 440
  In Retrospect 441
    The Colonial Immigrants 441 ◆ *The First-Stream Immigrants 441* ◆
    The Second-Stream Immigrants 442 ◆ *Some Other Indications of Assimilation 442*
  White Ethnic Identity 443
    An Interpretation 444
  The Non-White Experience 445

Consequences of Colonization and Immigration: An Alternative View 447
  Early Stages of Ethnic-Group Formation 447
    Immigrant Groups 447 ◆ *An Important Implication 448*
  A Dynamic View of the Colonial and Immigrant Models 448

Some Applications of the Alternative View 449
  Mexican Americans, Puerto Rican Americans, and Native Americans 449
  African Americans 451

Some Tentative Conclusions about Racial and Ethnic Relations
in the United States 452

The Future of Ethnicity in the United States 454

Across National Boundaries 455
  Sweden 455
  South Africa 456
  Canada 457
  Brazil 458
  Kosovo 459

Discussion Questions 460

Key Ideas 461

Key Terms   462
Notes   463

Appendix 1   465

Appendix 2   467

References   477

Name Index   520

Subject Index   527

Preface

Ethnic tensions are prevalent throughout the world and, in many cases, are accompanied by open conflicts, including wars. Tensions and conflicts between Arabs and Jews, Russians and Chechens, and various ethnic groups in the Balkans and Africa remind us that many countries throughout the world are characterized by racial and ethnic diversity. We are reminded, too, that, although the specific history of ethnic groups in the United States is unique, some aspects of the fascinating and important problems we will study are common to humankind.

This volume continues the basic strategy of discussion and analysis that was used in the previous editions. It focuses on interracial and interethnic relations in the United States and rests on ideas derived from (1) the sociological analysis of intergroup processes and (2) the history of the interactions of American racial and ethnic groups. We take this approach because the study of social processes—such as competition, conflict, segregation, stratification, accommodation, fusion, and separation—is inherently temporal. We believe that an understanding of the interactions of different racial and ethnic groups is most effectively grasped through an examination of the history of their relations with one another.

Our processual-historical approach moves, broadly speaking, from the beginnings of contact among different groups in North America to the pressing racial and ethnic problems of the contemporary United States; but as we discuss various groups and issues, we must focus on more limited spans of American history. Along the way we consider a wide range of sociological issues such as racial and ethnic differences, various processes through which one group may be included within another, the reactions of natives to foreigners, various aspects of racism, racial and ethnic prejudice and discrimination, class and ethnic stratification, vertical mobility, stereotyping, social distance, authoritarianism, the effect of social pressures on behavior, segregation, desegregation, variations in economic adaptations to discrimination, and the processes through which ethnic groups form, organize, and disappear. Each of these topics, as well as a number of others, is introduced to advance the central ideas of the book.

We have maintained assimilation theory as the basis for our discussion of the experiences of different groups, but our analysis of new variations of assimilation theory has been given greater emphasis than previously, allowing us to illustrate more fully the complexity of the incorporation process. Following brief discussions in Chapters 1 and 2 of some fundamental ideas and theories, we present examples in Chapters 3 through 5 of the experiences of several groups of White immigrants who were mainly voluntary entrants into the country and arrived before the twentieth century. These discussions also contain some preliminary analysis concerning two groups who entered the country involuntarily—Africans and Native Americans. The consequences for the members of an ethnic group of being brought into the country involuntarily are then explored in Chapters 6 through 10. These chapters are devoted to African, Mexican, Puerto Rican, and Native Americans.

Chapters 11 through 13 explore the experiences of seven racially distinctive groups that entered the United States more or less voluntarily or were refugees. These chapters focus on the experiences of Japanese, Chinese, Korean, Filipino, Asian Indian, Vietnamese, and Arab Americans. The final chapter closes the presentation with some conjectures about the future of racial and ethnic relations in the United States that are suggested by our analysis and, also, looks briefly at the experiences of several other nations in dealing with racial and ethnic issues.

The main differences between the seventh edition and the sixth edition are as follows:

- **Chapters 6 and 7** concerning African Americans have been substantially rewritten and moved forward in the presentation.
- **Chapters 8 and 9** on Mexican and Puerto Rican Americans and **Chapter 10** on Native Americans also have been substantially rewritten.
- Sections on Chinese, Korean, Filipino, and Asian Indian Americans in **Chapter 12** and on Arab Americans in **Chapter 13** are entirely new.
- **Chapter 11** on Japanese Americans now follows the chapters concerning the main groups of involuntary entrants and contains a new section on the "model minority" concept.
- The material concerning the reduction of prejudice and discrimination has been abridged and now appears as **Appendix 2.**
- All of the book's chapters have been reviewed and updated.

The choice of groups to be discussed is not intended to slight the members of the many other groups that might have been studied and have contributed in many different ways to the development of the United States. We have not intended to present a complete profile of any given group. The choices were dictated chiefly by our desire to highlight the main racial and ethnic dilemmas faced by the United States as seen through the lenses of a given set of Key Ideas. For this reason, you may find it is helpful to read the Key Ideas and Key Terms pertaining to a given chapter both before and after reading the chapter itself. This procedure may help you to distinguish between the central points of the discussions and the many details that are useful in understanding those points.

We are indebted to many people, the first of whom are the many scholars whose efforts have produced the rich literature on which this volume is based and whose continued research is rapidly increasing our knowledge of racial and ethnic relations in the United States and throughout the world. We are also indebted to the students in Dr. Romo's classes who gave their time for the interviews and shared their thoughts and experiences with us. We are grateful to Dr. Ricardo Romo and Dr. Jack Gibbs for their interest, encouragement, and suggestions and, also, to the reviewers of the sixth edition who provided thoughtful comments and suggestions concerning this revision: Emma G. Bailey, St. Cloud University; Robert L. Boyd, Mississippi State University; Jessie Ruth Gaston, California State University Sacramento; and George Yancey, University of North Texas. We wish to express special thanks to Patsy McLemore for her assistance in manuscript preparation, to Jeff Lasser, our editor, and to the staff at Allyn & Bacon for their support throughout the writing and preparation of this book.

Natives and
Newcomers

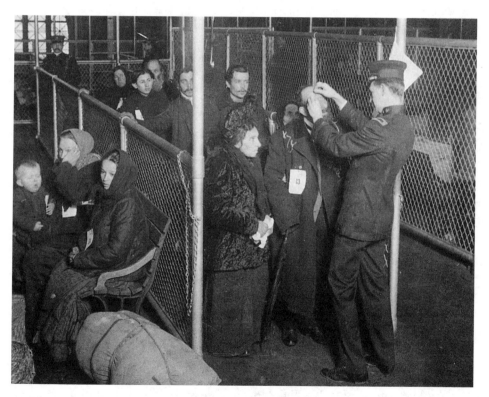

On Ellis Island customs officials registered immigrants, attached labels to each one, checked heads for lice, and referred those who might be unacceptable for health or other reasons for further screening. Many were denied entry into the United States.

Send These, the homeless, tempest-tost, to me:
I lift my lamp beside the golden door.

—Emma Lazarus

E pluribus unum.

—Motto on the Great Seal of the United States of America

The United States of America is often described as a nation of nations. Contemporary illustrations of the meaning of this statement abound. For instance, a manager of a new housing complex in downtown Los Angeles, California, discovered that those living in the apartments spoke at least twelve different languages, including Tagalog, Vietnamese, Thai, Zapotec, Indonesian, and Laotian. A San Antonio, Texas, newspaper found that one of the most popular names for boys in Texas and California is the Spanish name José. In addition, Americans are increasingly likely to be of a mixed racial heritage. Since 1960, the number of interracial couples in the United States has grown more than tenfold, and the rate of intermarriage is expected to increase in the coming years. And since the attacks of September 11, 2001 on New York and Washington, DC, America has been wracked with numerous controversies and confusions concerning the Arab American, Arab, and Muslim people in our population. As often happens during periods of national crisis, people focus renewed attention on the racial and ethnic differences that exist within our diverse and changing society.

The cultural and racial diversity of the American people increased appreciably during the last decade of the twentieth century. Within that time the United States received more newcomers, representing nations from all over the world, than during any other decade in its history. While the presence of so many new arrivals may stimulate racial and ethnic antagonisms, it also may remind us that most Americans are descended from people who arrived here within the last five or six generations.[1] Only the American Indians can claim to have been here for more than five centuries. The recency of the arrival of most American groups is suggested by the fact that many Americans still think of themselves as having a "nationality" in addition to their identity as Americans. Every day we are reminded that cultural and racial diversity exists in America, and that cultural and racial identities are sources of both pride and conflict.

These realities raise a number of important questions: Is the cultural makeup of American society undergoing a radical change? How do newcomers see their new land and their place in it? How do long-time residents react to the newcomers? If Americans trace their national origins to other countries, do they think of themselves first as Americans and only then as members of an **ethnic group** (a term emphasizing cultural heritage) or a **racial group** (a term emphasizing physical appearance)? Should multiple loyalties be encouraged as sources of variety and strength or discouraged as sources of disunity and distrust? Some of these perplexing questions call for factual answers. Others are concerned mainly with the goals, values, and purposes of American society as a whole and each of the various groups within it.

In this book we explore various aspects of these and other questions as we analyze the experiences of different groups that form the fabric of American society. We are especially interested in the following questions: Is there a uniform social process through which all groups of newcomers and their descendants must travel to become established in the economic and social "mainstream" of American life? Is American society actually becoming more diverse ethnically, as our examples have suggested, or are the forces that promote group mergers and decrease diversity moving at an even faster pace?[2] If America is becoming more diverse ethnically, how will the social characteristics of the American "mainstream" be affected? These questions have aroused debate throughout American history. For the most part, people have generally believed that there is a single, basic route to **Americanization** or **assimilation** into American society. The leading idea of assimilation theory has been that new immigrant groups are transformed from outsiders into full members of American society by giving up their previous ways of life to embrace an Anglo American cultural core. The experiences of various groups who have, nonetheless, maintained their ethnic or racial identities in the face of pressures to assimilate core Anglo American norms and values have tested this notion. American society is far from homogeneous, and immigrant ethnicity has affected American society as much as American society has affected it (Alba 1999a). From this perspective, assimilation can take place as two or more groups, or parts of them, diminish the cultural and social distance between them (Alba and Nee 1997).

An increasing number of people maintain that there is more than one social process that operates to change groups of newcomers and their children into Americans. Portes and Rumbaut (1990:7–8), for example, argue that the ethnic diversity among newcomers is greater now than ever before. They find the idea that there is a uniform process leading to Americanization "increasingly implausible" and state that "there are today first-generation millionaires who speak broken English, foreign-born mayors of large cities, and top-flight immigrant engineers and scientists in the nation's research centers. There are also those, at the other extreme, who cannot even take the first step [toward Americanization] because of the insecurity linked to an uncertain legal status."

We begin our exploration of these ideas by sketching very briefly the general social process most Americans have assumed is the basic route to Americanization for individuals and groups. This popular image is based heavily on the experiences of certain groups of newcomers who arrived during a particular period of U.S. history and has been the focus of fierce debate. As we proceed, we introduce a number of important competing ideas to help us understand fully how a group's identity and various individuals' identities may be transformed to that of being "Americans."

An Overview of Assimilation in America

A Popular View

The principal stages through which an immigrant is generally presumed to travel on the road to Americanization have been portrayed in many biographies, novels, plays, movies, and scholarly books and articles. Both in fact and in legend, millions of people have come to the United States in search of economic, religious, and other opportunities. Those who arrived earlier may already have established "national churches, immigrant-aid societies, foreign-language newspapers, and other institutions" (Petersen 1980:239) to form an immigrant community within the new homeland.

In the popular view, the life of the newcomer is filled with problems to solve and obstacles to overcome. He or she must find a place to live, find a job, cope with learning a new language, and adopt a new way of living. The old ways and ideas are no longer appropriate. The newcomer must rapidly learn the "American way" to speak, dress, think, and act. As the newcomers make choices seeking to take advantage of opportunities to improve their social situations, assimilation is likely to take place despite the intentions of the immigrants to resist it. But even the **first generation** immigrant who wishes to do so probably will not be able to make a complete transition to the new way of life. His or her name, patterns of speech, dress, manners, religion, food preferences, place of residence, or type of occupation may continue to mark him or her as an "outsider." In most cases, the newcomers do not want to give up the old ways entirely. They may wish to be accepted as Americans in all ways that are essential to their livelihood and immediate welfare and to participate as fully as they like in the mainstream of American life. But they may prefer the sights, scents, sounds, and friendships that exist only in the ethnic community—the Chinatowns, Little Italys, Latino barrios, African American neighborhoods, and Little Saigons—that the members of their national group have developed.

The immigrants' children, the **second generation,** may learn many of the old-country ways from their parents and also may be unable or unwilling to drop all vestiges of their parents' culture and behavior. They may attend public schools and become more fluent in English than their parents; and they may fail to learn, or may actively reject, many of their parents' ways. These Americans may achieve greater economic success than their parents and may move out of the old neighborhood, marry someone of a different **ethnicity,**[3] or change their name to something that seems more "American." Still, these individuals may regard themselves or be regarded by others as remaining in some significant ways "**ethnics.**" On the positive side, a person who is bicultural may enjoy the "best of both cultural worlds"; on the negative side, the individual may not feel completely "at home" in either culture.

Finally, according to the familiar image being sketched, the grandchildren of the immigrants, the **third generation,** may move completely into the mainstream of American life. Although their parents will not have socialized them into the old culture, they may have learned to speak a few words of the grandparents' native language and they may have learned certain old-country recipes, folk songs, and proverbs. They also may feel a strong sense of attachment to their ethnic heritage, but they will speak mostly English, and questions concerning their nationality will seldom arise.

According to the traditional assimilation model, the individual has now become a full member of the host society, sharing equally with the other established members in the distribution of social rewards. He or she may "rise" to any position the society has to offer. This image of the **assimilation process**—called by some scholars "straight line theory"— is highly controversial. It assumes, among other things, that newcomers look forward to "progressing" in American society rather than looking back to life in the homeland. It assumes also that, on the average, each generation will reach a higher level of social and economic standing than the preceding generation. Stated differently, the longer a group has been in the United States, the more successful it will be in social and economic terms (Suarez-Orozco 2000:6).[4] As applied to European immigrant groups, this line of thought has been generally correct (Glazer and Moynihan 1964:313; Levitt and Waters 2002:15), but the description we have offered so far overlooks many complications.

Consider, for instance, the different life experiences of the children of immigrants who arrive in the United States with their parents in comparison to the experiences of their siblings who are born in the United States. Those in the former group (increasingly called the *1.5 generation*) are, strictly speaking, first-generation immigrants; but depending on their ages when they arrive, the course of their adaptation to the culture of the new country may be more-or-less similar to that of their brothers and sisters. Consider, too, the much broader question of how well the **three-generations process** describes the experiences of non-European groups in America.

Some Non-European Instances

If we were to attempt to explain what has happened to American Indians during the past four centuries in terms of the popular image of Americanization, it would be clear that the three-generations description simply does not fit this case. The complex societies of Indians preceded the first English settlements. For the most part they did not enter American society voluntarily through immigration but, rather, through conquest and the occupation of their territories. In the process, however, historians have found that Indians often incorporated "foreigners," including many African Americans, into their families and communities. By the end of the American Revolution, Indian–African American intermarriage resulted in a substantial and visible "mixed population in a number of areas" (Mandell 1998). Some were clearly Indian, some were African American, and others maintained dual identities. During a later period of relocation to reservations and antiassimilationist policies toward Indians, further ethnic divisions occurred. During the civil rights movement, Indians expressed renewed pride in their ethnic identities. In the decennial census of 1990 the numbers of persons identifying themselves as American Indian increased rather than decreased, as is expected in traditional assimilation theory. Moreover, as American Indians have increased their incomes through gambling casinos and other enterprises on the reservations, some tribal members living in urban areas have moved back to the reservations and worked to reclaim their Indian culture and language.

The African ancestors of most Black Americans came to the United States as bonded servants or slaves. They, too, obviously did not emigrate to the United States in the traditional way we have discussed. Although much human migration involves, to some degree, both voluntary and involuntary elements, it is clear that the involuntary element was enormously greater in the migration experiences of most Black Americans than was true of any other group that has come to the United States.[5] Recent scholarship has suggested that there were many nonmarital as well as marital sexual relationships among Blacks and Whites and that some prominent American leaders fathered children with slave women. Thus, there may have been more "racial mixing" than the strict laws in many states that prohibited interracial marriages and relationships would lead us to believe.[6] It is clear, also, that after many more than three generations, Black Americans, on average, have not entered fully into the mainstream of American life and become simply "Americans."

Mexican Americans present a somewhat more complicated case. Like the American Indians, the ancestors of some Mexican Americans were brought into the United States involuntarily through conquest. The ancestors of some others, however—and this is by far the largest category—have migrated more or less voluntarily to the United States from Mexico. Many of those in the latter group did not consider the border between the two countries to be very important culturally and did not think of themselves as immigrants to a foreign country (Alvarez 1985). Like American Indians and Black Americans, most Mexican Americans have not completed the process of **inclusion** within three generations.

Why have some groups long present in the United States not merged uniformly into American society? Is it likely, given still longer periods of time, that the groups that have not gone through the three-generations process will gradually be assimilated fully? Will the newcomers who now are reaching America follow the three-generations pattern? Stated more generally, the primary question we consider here and throughout the book is this: *What factors affect whether the members of a given group assimilate into various aspects of American life and the rate at which various types of assimilation occur?*

Some Factors Affecting Assimilation

Differences in Social Power.   Throughout most of the history of the United States White Americans have been not only the largest group, but also the most *powerful* group. Their members have been more highly represented in positions of authority within the government, military services, and economic and educational organizations of the society than any other group. In these positions, they have played the greatest role in making decisions that affected the relations among different groups. The many other racial and ethnic groups that have been represented in our society have been both smaller in size and less powerful. In all human societies, some group or groups will have greater social power than others and, therefore, a greater capacity to *control* than others; and the kinds of relations these groups have with one another represent a vital element in the operation of the society.[7] Racial and ethnic relations, not only in the United States but throughout the world, may be viewed as revealing some of the social consequences that may arise when one group is more powerful than, and dominates, another.

Often the power of a **dominant** (most powerful) **group** is accepted as legitimate by **subordinate** (less powerful) **groups**, and the commands of its members are willingly obeyed. Sometimes, however, the subordinate groups do not wish to obey and, then, the dominant group may rely on coercion, leading to overt or covert conflicts between the groups. *The relative power or degree of dominance of various racial and ethnic groups, rather than their sheer size, is of paramount sociological significance.* We note in passing that all segments of a dominant group do not necessarily share the group's power equally. In our society, for instance, men and members of the upper socioeconomic classes generally have wielded greater power than women and members of the lower classes.

Throughout American history, the most powerful group also has been the largest group; but in many societies that is not the case, and it is the differences in social power that are of greatest significance in our analysis. We use the terms **majority** and **minority,** therefore, to indicate differences in group power rather than merely to indicate differences in size. Our concern is *the extent to which the minority group's behavior and life circumstances are related to the greater power exercised by the majority.*

But a majority-group's power is always limited in some respects. Minority-group members, even those who are extremely oppressed, do exert some influence, however small, over the development of intergroup relations; hence, although the rate of a group's assimilation within American society may be affected strongly by the extent to which the White Americans desire or resist their inclusion, the rate also is affected by the extent to which a minority-group's members desire or resist inclusion. For example, the existence of neighborhoods that are settled primarily by one ethnic group or another does not by itself demonstrate either that the concentrations have arisen primarily because the majority has enforced separation (**segregation**) or the minorities have chosen separation (**congregation**). *It is absolutely essential in any case that we study the historical sequences that have created the dominant-subordinate group relations of interest to us.*[8]

Voluntary or Involuntary Entrance.

Our discussion has indicated that the members of groups who choose to become a part of American society are more likely to follow the three-generations process than those who enter the society involuntarily. Those who enter voluntarily may seek full inclusion, make great efforts to learn English, and be willing to alter many ways of acting that were customary in their former homeland. People who are enslaved or conquered, on the other hand, may be reluctant to become members of the society that is responsible for their enslavement. Their goal may be to escape from the new society that has been imposed on them or to drive the invaders out and return to their former way of life.[9] Please note, however, that even though a voluntary entrance into American society may initially lead people to be more favorable toward the adoption of its culture, and an involuntary entrance may favor the rejection of Americanization, the possibility exists that the two types of entrance may not necessarily lead to different results.

Americanization may be viewed, even by those who migrate voluntarily, as having both desirable and undesirable aspects. For example, if the members of a racial or ethnic group view full inclusion within American life mainly as a process whereby a cherished way of life is gradually eroded or destroyed rather than as progress, they may struggle to maintain a separate ethnic identity. From this standpoint, a major problem for newcomers is the difficulty of *resisting* assimilation. Frequently, too, the members of an immigrant group may be uncertain regarding whether, or in what ways, inclusion should be sought. Nearly all Jews, for instance, may agree that the members of their group should learn English and be permitted to attend the public schools, but they may disagree sharply concerning the extent to which their religious ceremonies should be conducted in English.

Group Size, Concentration, and Time of Entry.

It is well known that majority-group members are much more concerned about the presence of minority-group members and give much more evidence of rejecting them in those locations in which the minority is relatively large and in which the minority group has grown rapidly in size.[10] If the minority group actually becomes larger than the majority group, the concern of the dominant group probably will escalate. This situation has been common in the experience of Black Americans in many towns in the southern United States and of Mexican Americans and American Indians in many towns of the southwestern and western portions of the United States. When the minority is the larger group, the majority may erect many types of social barriers between itself and the minority. In these circumstances, the majority may be particularly sensitive, and may react violently, to even the slightest sign that these barriers are being eroded.

The economic conditions within the receiving country at the time a group arrives are critical factors affecting the group's reception. During periods of economic expansion when more "hands" are needed to do the work, immigrants are encouraged to move to the United States and are accepted more readily than during periods of economic downturns. When many Americans are out of work, the fear that "they" are taking "our" jobs away provides a powerful motive to resist the inclusion of newcomers. In addition to the timing of a group's entry, the length of time that has elapsed since the members of a group first arrived also is an important factor affecting inclusion. Lieberson and Waters (1988:43) found that among those who described their ancestry as "American" in the decennial census of 1980, 98 percent had "at least three generations' residence" in the United States.

Ethnic and Racial Similarity.   Another factor affecting the rate of assimilation of a minority group within the United States is the similarity between the culture (ethnicity) of the minority and the culture of the majority. People whose native languages are Chinese, Korean, or Japanese, for instance, may experience more difficulty in mastering the speech patterns and inflections of the English language than those whose native languages are Dutch, German, or Spanish. And since Judeo-Christian beliefs are dominant within the United States, those who have been raised in a different religious tradition may find many "American" ways offensive and may resist them. Much the same may be said concerning American approaches to politics, education, courtship, marriage, and many other aspects of life.

A final factor affecting assimilation to be mentioned here—though many others will be uncovered in the course of our analysis—is the racial (physical) identification of the individual or group. Although White Americans generally have shown some hostility toward all foreigners, they have been more willing to accept the members of some groups than others. The history of the United States shows, in particular, that White resistance to the inclusion of different groups is greater for groups considered to be "non-White" than for groups considered to be "White."[11]

 # Development of Assimilation Theory[12]

The most influential theory based on the three-generations idea was developed primarily by the American sociologist Robert E. Park. Park's theory, called the **cycle of race relations,** focused on four processes or stages: contact, competition, accommodation, and eventual assimilation. According to Park these stages represent "the processes by which the integration of peoples and cultures have always and everywhere taken place" and are "apparently progressive and irreversible" (Park [1926]1964:104).* Since Park (1964:205) thought of assimilation mainly as a process that "erased the external signs . . . which formerly distinguished the members" of the smaller group, he gave little attention to how the characteristics of the receiving society might affect the assimilation of newcomers or how the society itself might be changed by their assimilation. Park did later concede that the cycle could end in a society that included a permanent racial minority (Kazal 1999).

During the late 1930s and early 1940s, historians Marcus Hansen and Oscar Handlin made notable contributions to assimilation theory. Hansen (1938) found that among some groups the grandchildren of the immigrants experience a revival of interest in the culture of the old country that fosters a reemergence of ethnic consciousness just when, according to Park's theory, ethnic ties should be disappearing. In a study that focused on the assimilation of the Irish into the social, cultural, economic, and political life of Boston, Handlin (1941) found a pattern that largely conformed to the expectations of the cycle of race relations; however, the Irish stopped short of full assimilation. They did not melt into the core Anglo culture and society but, rather, remained "outsiders" who were "beneath" the native residents and various groups of more assimilated immigrants.

In another important contribution, Kennedy (1944) studied the patterns of intermarriage among various European ethnic groups. She found that although ethnic intermarriage was increasing, as expected under the race cycle theory, the religious barriers among the groups remained strong. Irish, Italian, and Polish Catholics preferred to intermarry among themselves; British, German, and Scandinavian Protestants preferred Protestant spouses; and Jews preferred to marry other Jews. Thus assimilation occurred within the various religious groups—Jewish, Catholic, and Protestant—and not indiscriminately (Kennedy 1944).

During a peak of ethnic and racial unrest in the 1960s, theories of assimilation fell out of favor as scholars noted that ethnic groups appeared to be persisting and reviving rather than declining as had been expected (Olzak and Nagel 1986:1–2). Many people had assumed that the passage of time would automatically erase group differences, but this assumption was increasingly called into question, especially as it applied to racial minorities. Ethnic groups and identities were sustained by common interests, ethnic networks, family ties, and a strong ethnic organizational life. Many scholars attacked the idea that American society was unified by a consensus on Anglo American values and norms. They presented instead a picture of a fragmented American society filled with intergroup conflicts. An increasing emphasis on **ethnic pluralism** and ethnic conflict shifted the focus away from assimilation, which was said to emphasize interethnic consensus.

In contrast to the growing sentiment against assimilation theory, however, Milton Gordon (1964) presented at this time a new and valuable approach advocating a much more specific analysis of the structure of American society and the general process of assimilation than had been done previously. According to Gordon, U.S. society consisted

---

*When the work of an author was originally published at an earlier date we have included that date for historical reference. The later publication date is a more recent edition and is cited in the references. These dual dates appear throughout the text.

of a number of **subsocieties,** each with its own **subculture.** These subsocieties might be based on ethnic, racial, religious, or social class affiliations. The core subsociety of the United States, with a subculture derived from the culture of England, was described as being White, middle class, and Protestant. Racial groups, non-European immigrant groups, and some religious groups retained their own organizational networks and their own primary group contacts within specific ethnic enclaves. Gordon (1964:71) proposed that an understanding of assimilation among American groups could be advanced by an analysis of seven specific **subprocesses of assimilation,** which we consider in detail in Chapter 2.

Gordon also noted that socioeconomic class status and group identity play a vital role in the process of assimilation and the operation of American society. Instead of simply losing their ethnic memberships and identities, individuals form networks with co-ethnics of the same social class. The resulting subsocieties, called **ethclasses,** constitute the basis for the functioning and persistence of ethnicity in American life (Gordon 1964:51).

In the 1980s and 1990s, historians and sociologists noted an increase of common feeling among European ethnics based on "whiteness." They also became more aware that individuals may have multiple ethnicities and began to focus attention on assimilation between groups of immigrants as well as on assimilation between newcomers and Americans. Additionally, there was an increasing awareness that assimilation theory should take into account the **transnational** character of much contemporary immigration. Modern means of communication and transportation enable recent immigrants to the United States to maintain strong ties with friends and families in their countries of origin more easily than ever before and to remain at home, in a psychological sense, even while they are physically in the new country.

Still further, within various social settings, assimilation processes may affect different portions of a group in different ways, leading to **segmented assimilation.** Several of the largest recent immigrant groups have included both people with high educational and occupational skill levels and people with little education and occupational skill. The process of becoming an American may be a very different experience for the members of these two immigrant subgroups. For example, the members of the higher socioeconomic segment may experience rapid adaptation and movement into the mainstream, while the members of the lower socioeconomic segment may find the American dream to be out of reach (Levitt and Waters 2002:2; Zhou 1997:979). Together these considerations have stimulated a renewed appreciation of the manifold ways that assimilation may act as a powerful and variable force (Kazal 1999:298; Nagel 2002:259).

Many questions that intrigued Park and the other theorists early in the twentieth century were revived. What social forces hold a diverse country together? How do immigrants come to see themselves as Americans? Is there such a thing as an American identity? What is the nature of American pluralism? But this revival was accompanied by a much more complex and flexible vision of ethnicity than had existed previously. To illustrate, Kazal (1999:298) described ethnicity as a "process of construction or invention which incorporates, adapts, and amplifies preexisting communal solidarities, cultural attributes and historical memories." This process—which is a form of **ethnogenesis**—is thought to involve continual negotiation among various racial and ethnic groups and the dominant group (Nagel 2002:264). An ethnicity may disappear, be reinvented (sometimes as a pan-ethnic identity, such as Asian or Hispanic), or become a double identity (such as African American). In addition, individuals may choose to emphasize one or more aspects of their ancestry and to emphasize different identities in different contexts (Waters 1990).

In this book we have chosen to use many of Gordon's concepts and his theory of assimilation to describe and understand the experiences of different ethnic groups in American life, but we have done so with an awareness that the various processes of intergroup adjustment may not operate uniformly during one period or another or in the same ways for all groups.

 # Race and Ethnicity

The terms *race* and *ethnicity* have been assigned a variety of meanings and are the subjects of continuing debate. Each term refers in part to the fact that people may believe they and certain other people are the descendants of related ancestors and, further, that those of related ancestry comprise natural social groups or categories.[13] Among those who perceive that they share with others some trait that is taken to denote common ancestry, there may develop a sense of "interconnectedness," "peoplehood," or group identification.

Race

As we have noted, racial group or category designations refer mainly to aspects of a person's physical heritage, whereas ethnic group or category designations refer mainly to aspects of a person's sociocultural heritage. People tend to *assume* that groups based on physical and social inheritance are natural and of special importance (Allport 1958:106; Petersen 1980:239). The plausibility of this viewpoint rests primarily on the centuries-old observation that family members usually resemble one another more in both appearance and behavior than do unrelated individuals.[14]

The practice of distinguishing between people's heritages primarily in physical terms or primarily in sociocultural terms is widely accepted. Its common acceptance, indeed, and the social groupings that are generally recognized thereby, provide the underpinnings for the analyses within this book; but let us note that *the boundaries between and within racial and ethnic groups are not sharp and fixed.* They in fact overlap, are blurred, and may change.

To illustrate, let us consider briefly some issues that arise in the process of attempting to determine a person's racial group membership. In everyday situations, most people are defined by themselves and others as belonging to a particular racial group even when they are aware that some racial "mixing" has occurred. They are thought to *be* (and are treated as being) members of this race *or* that race. Under these circumstances it is easy to assume that the boundaries of this system are "real" and have been imposed on us by nature. In fact, however, the conclusion that a person is a member of a single race involves a much larger element of choice and social agreement than may be apparent. The most frequently chosen defining trait, skin color, obviously varies by degrees and cannot be used to establish sharp boundaries. Since all of the other visible traits (e.g., eye shape, nose shape) that are commonly employed suffer this same defect, any effort to establish sharp boundaries among the races on the basis of any one of these commonly used physical traits is bound to be imperfect.[15]

The problem of overlapping boundaries cannot be surmounted by combining the various traits, either. It is true that in the United States people who trace their origins to Europe are more likely to be called and to call themselves "White" than are people who trace their origins to Asia and Africa (i.e., there is a **correlation** between geographical origin and skin color), but some people who trace their origins to Europe have darker skins than some people who trace their ancestry to Asia and Africa (i.e., the correlation of geographical origin and skin color is not perfect). As additional traits are added, the probability that all of them will lead to the same racial assignments declines.[16] The low levels of correlation among clusters of these different socially accepted criteria of racial grouping have led scholars to disagree concerning how many human races there are, with ranges running from only a few to very many.[17]

Blurred boundaries among races is not the only problem. As we discuss later, several groups of Europeans who came to the United States and who today are unquestioningly accepted as White were not considered to be White at the time they arrived (Jacobsen 1998) but were thought, instead, to be "members of 'degenerate races' " (Nagel 2002:265). These changes in the racial designation of some groups show clearly that *although people commonly think of races, and sometimes ethnic groups, as sharply distinguishable and fixed biological entities, their boundaries, in fact, are set by social agreement.*

Two dramatic illustrations of this point have received widespread attention. In 1998 researchers reported they had found almost conclusive DNA evidence that Thomas Jefferson fathered at least one child with his slave, Sally Hemings. The descendants of this union have always been considered to be Black, even though Jefferson was White and Hemings was, by the reckoning of the times, "three-fourths" White. Then in 2003, it was revealed that Strom Thurmond of South Carolina, a prominent U.S. Senator and at one time a leading segregationist, was the father of his Black housekeeper's daughter. The senator's family confirmed that the daughter, who was 78 years old in 2003, was the child of the senator, and his housekeeper was 16-years old at the time of the birth. In reporting the story, many journalists noted that African Americans and Whites are so intertwined genetically that conventional racial categories are meaningless. Such findings make clear that the apparent sharpness of racial and ethnic boundaries reflects the fact that people react to the members of these socially recognized groups in quite different, socially important ways.

The logic of this conclusion has led some students of racial and ethnic groups to argue that race is a sociopolitical rather than a scientific concept and to recommend that it be abandoned completely as a scientific term (Littlefield, Lieberman, and Reynolds 1982:644).[18] It also led to a demand, primarily by interracial couples and those with multiethnic children, that people should be allowed to select one or more racial categories that reflect the complexities of their lives and heritages. Consequently, for the first time, the census of 2000 allowed people to check more than one racial identity on the census survey form.

Given this new option, 6.8 million of the 281.4 million Americans counted in the 2000 census marked two or more boxes or wrote a Hispanic-origin term as their second race. The most popular combination was "White" and "Some other race," which was reported by one-third of those who checked more than one race. The second most popular response was White and American Indian representing 16 percent of those reporting more than one race.

This change in the way racial information is gathered represents a radical shift away from the assumption that each individual has only one racial identity and, in Prewitt's (2002) opinion, is the greatest change in the measurement of race in the history of the Unites States. He believes, too, that it will take some time for the consequences of using the multiple-race category to become clear. On one hand, the use of multiple designations may increase the difficulty of interpreting the statistics on race and make it more difficult to demonstrate the existence of discrimination. Governmental agencies may adopt apparently "colorblind" policies that would permit policy makers to ignore major inequalities among racial and ethnic groups in areas such as wealth, education, health, and health care (Murguia and Forman 2003). On the other hand, the blurring of racial categories in political, legal, and social affairs, Prewitt speculates, may lead racial categories to disappear not only in the legal and political spheres but also perhaps even in the public's consciousness.

Ethnicity

Although the concept of ethnicity usually emphasizes a person's sociocultural heritage, "a biological connotation sometimes adheres still to 'ethnic' " (Petersen 1980:235);[19] but even when a person's appearance or behavior is generally acknowledged to derive exclusively from culture, there is a common tendency to treat the characteristic as a fixed, all-or-none matter and to miss entirely the flexibility of the group boundaries thus created.

In addition, there is a strong tendency to create derogatory images of members of various groups, a subject that we pursue in Chapter 5. Both majority-group and minority-group members may well believe that "we" who share certain sociocultural characteristics are more honest, or skillful, or loyal, or humane than "they" who share other sociocultural traits. Such judgments about **in-groups** and **out-groups** are made with little reflection in our daily lives, and they seem to rest on hard experience and firm foundations. Even when such views are poorly founded, they nevertheless exist as social realities and guide social behavior. They also create formidable barriers to intergroup understanding and the full inclusion of minority groups within a society.

As we analyze racial and ethnic relations in America, then, we must recognize the social reality of the racial and ethnic categories that exist in our society and, simultaneously, maintain an awareness that these categories have not been imposed on us by nature. They are created by the members of social groups (even when physical traits are used as building materials) and they are subject to reconstruction. Since there is no firm line of division between the concepts of race and ethnicity, we often use ethnicity as a general term that includes race.

Some scholars have argued that alterations in our existing racial and ethnic categories will occur naturally with the passage of time. The argument is that racial and ethnic distinctions are inherently at odds with the demands of a modern urban, scientific, society and that, consequently, "the forces of history" are against the maintenance of such distinctions. Americans generally believe that an individual's rewards and place in society should depend heavily on his or her **achieved characteristics,** such as educational level and occupational skill (the **principle of achievement**) rather than on **ascribed characteristics,** such as race, ethnicity, family status, sex, and age (the **principle of ascription**). Hence, social distinctions based on racial and ethnic differences are considered to be inconsistent with modern life and ought automatically to decline.

But if racial and ethnic distinctions have been declining, why have civil rights activities become more prominent in the United States since the 1950s? And why is it true that "Everywhere one looks, ethnic division persists" (Spickard 1989:11)? These questions suggest that we may not take for granted the idea that racial and ethnic differences automatically will decline. As a society reorganizes along new lines, numerous conflicts almost certainly will arise between dominant and subordinate groups; nevertheless, even if the process is not automatic, should not the passage of time generally lead interacting racial and ethnic groups gradually to adjust to one another and become more alike? The implications of various answers to this question must be examined in detail. We begin this examination in the next chapter.

Discussion Questions

What does it mean to be an American today?

Who wishes to be considered, and will be accepted, as full participants in American society?

How is the question of race dealt with in the assimilation process? If assimilation means becoming American, who are the non-Americans?

What kinds of interactions are occurring among the various ethnic groups in the United States?

Will ethnic and racial differences disappear with the passage of time?

To what degree are the newest immigrants assimilating?

What keeps people together in this nation and what keeps them apart?

Is there a dominant group in American society?

Why do sociologists continue to use racial and ethnic categories?

Key Ideas

1. Many people assume that the usual and normal course of Americanization requires three generations. In this view, the adult grandchild of the immigrant generally is, and should be, fully Americanized.

2. A basic sociological task is to try to understand the factors affecting whether, to what extent, and the rate at which the members of a particular group have been included within a given society.

3. Many factors may affect the rate at which different groups move toward full inclusion within a society. Some of the most important of these are (a) the attitudes and relative power of the majority and the minority, (b) whether the group's entry into the society was largely voluntary or involuntary, (c) the relative size, rate of increase, and degree of concentration of the minority, (d) the time at which the minority entered the society, (e) the cultural similarity of the majority and minority, and (f) the racial similarity of the majority and minority.

4. Several scholars have maintained that when racial or ethnic groups come into contact, a specific sequence of events is set into motion. Robert E. Park's theory, the cycle of race relations, holds that racial and ethnic contact leads to competition, accommodation, and eventual assimilation. Park's theory assumes that these processes always occur in that order. The sequence is thought to be universal, inevitable, and irreversible, ending with the disappearance as a separate group of the less powerful of the two groups.

5. Many studies of the race cycle idea found that it seemed to fit many cases, at least partially; but it also failed fully to forecast the results of intergroup contact. By the 1960s, the theory had attracted many critics and was largely discredited. Many scholars argued, for instance, that the smaller ethnic groups founded by immigrants had not merged completely with the majority group. Others argued that the process of merging was often interrupted by a resurgence of ethnic awareness, group pride, and ethnic group reconstruction. During this same period, however, a new theory, presented by Milton M. Gordon, provided the basis for an improved analysis of assimilation processes.

6. Numerous problems exist in the effort to classify people as members of specific racial and ethnic groups. The boundaries between racial and ethnic groups overlap and, in many ways, are blurred. Even though people commonly think of races, and sometimes ethnic groups, as sharply distinguishable biological entities, their boundaries are not set by nature but are set, rather, by social agreement; hence, these boundaries are flexible rather than fixed.

7. Judgments about in-groups and out-groups are made routinely and may rest on poor foundations. Such judgments, nevertheless, exist as social realities and guide social behavior. They serve as significant barriers to intergroup understanding and the inclusion of minority groups within a society.

8. Americans generally believe that an individual's place in society should not be determined by ascribed characteristics (such as race, ethnicity, or sex) but, rather, should depend on the individual's achievements; hence, an individual's rewards should be based on the principle of achievement rather the principle of ascription. To the extent that these ideas are translated into action, the ties that bind individuals to racial and ethnic groups in American society should become progressively weaker; but the history of the past four decades of the twentieth century raise questions about this view.

 Key Terms

achieved characteristics   Those characteristics of a person, such as his or her educational level and occupation, that may be acquired through the efforts and performance of the individual.

Americanization   The accumulated changes in the culture, occupations, friendship patterns, marital patterns, and identities of those who are not Americans as they become Americans.

ascribed characteristics   Those characteristics of a person that are assigned to him or her by birth, such as gender role, race, or ethnicity.

assimilation   The general process through which newcomers to a group are transformed from outsiders into full members of a group or society.

assimilation process   The specific, continuous changes that occur in different aspects of life as newcomers to a group are brought into the group.

congregation   The concentration of a group of people within a particular area primarily because they wish to be together.

correlation   The strength of the tendency of two or more variables to occur together.

cycle of race relations   Robert E. Park's theory stating that when groups come into contact with each other they set into motion an inevitable and irreversible chain of events leading to intergroup competition, accommodation, and the eventual assimilation of the smaller group into the larger group.

dominant group   The most powerful group within a society.

ethclasses   Subsocieties that form within ethnic groups comprised of people of similar social class position.

ethnic group   A group or category of people whose inclusion in the group or category is based primarily on similarities of nationality, religion, language, or other aspects of a person's sociocultural heritage. The term also may be used more broadly to include racial groups.

ethnic pluralism   A condition of intergroup adjustment in which the members of ethnic groups are successful in maintaining their preferred degrees of separation from the majority.

ethnicity   The "sense of peoplehood" shared by those who believe they are members of a given ethnic group; a person's ethnic identification.

ethnics   People who are identified as members of a particular ethnic group.

ethnogenesis   The social processes through which people (1) from the same geographic regions join together to form a new ethnic group within a different society; (2) revive the functions of an ethnic group that has lost all or most of its previous role; or (3) bring together in a new, broader ethnic group several groups that are thought to be related.

first generation   People of foreign birth who have emigrated to the United States.

inclusion   A general term used to designate all social processes that lead to the merger of a minority group with a majority group.

in-group   A group of people who share certain traits and characterize themselves as "we."

majority   See "dominant group."

minority   See "subordinate group."

out-group   The members of any group that lies beyond the circle of those who characterize themselves as "we" and are referred to as "they."

principle of achievement   The belief that individuals should be rewarded on the basis of their individual efforts and performances rather than on the basis of inheritance.

principle of ascription   The belief that certain inherited characteristics should determine their holder's share of society's rewards.

racial group   A group or category of people whose inclusion in the group or category is based primarily on inherited physical characteristics such as skin color, hair form, and facial form.

second generation   People who are born in the United States and whose parents were immigrants.

segmented assimilation   The effects of the subprocesses of assimilation on the different members of a group will vary. Although a majority of the members of a group may adopt the culture of Anglo American society, some groups of immigrants may adopt the standards of other groups within the society; hence, the general pattern of assimilation for an immigrant population will not be uniform.

segregation   The concentration of a group of people within a particular area primarily because the majority group has left them little choice.

subculture   The patterns of culture that emerge within an ethnic group as the old-country ways are transplanted and modified through contact with the host country's culture.

subordinate group   A group that is less powerful than the most powerful group in a society.

subprocesses of assimilation   Specific types, levels (or components) of the general process of assimilation. The subprocesses identified by Milton M. Gordon are defined in Chapter 2.

subsocieties   Social networks and formal organizations within a group that are the source of group identification and enable the group's members, if they so wish, to confine all of their primary social relationships to other group members.

third generation   People who are born in the United States and whose parents are second-generation Americans.

three-generations process   An intergenerational sequence through which an ethnic group loses its distinctiveness within three generations.

transnational   Refers to the fact that many individuals have a sense of identity rooted in more than one society. They may live and work in the United States, but they maintain close ties with the place in which they, their parents, or their grandparents were born.

Notes

1. Social demographers estimate that a generation is approximately 25 years.

2. For instance, Farley (1966:108–214) argues that for Whites ethnicity already has lost much of its meaning and that "potentially" race also could follow this path. We explore these crucial, and explosive, questions more fully in later chapters.

3. "A convenient term for [a] sense of 'peoplehood' is 'ethnicity' " (Gordon 1964:24).

4. Suarez-Orozco refers to these ideas as the "clean break" assumption and the "uniform progress" assumption.

5. Schermerhorn (1970:98) presented a classification of migrations according to the amount of coercion involved. Slave transfers are the most coercive type.

6. Four important legal cases debated the racial issues surrounding miscegenation law (laws against interracial marriages or sexual relationships). These cases were *Kirby v. Kirby* (1922), *Estate of Monks* (1941), *Perez v. Lippold* (1948), and *Loving v. Virginia* (1967). The arguments in these cases reflected the social and scientific ideas about race that were dominant at the time (Pascoe 1996). Alba (1999a) points out that racial/ethnic boundaries blur, stretch, and move, as the current emphasis on the social construction of race implies.

7. For a comprehensive treatment of the concept of control and of its importance in sociological analysis, see Gibbs (1989).

8. Heraclitus, a scholar of ancient Greece, put it this way: "He who watches a thing grow has the best view of it."

9. An influential analysis of minority groups in terms of their goals was presented by Wirth (1945:347–372).

10. As (1) the ratio of the incoming minority to the resident population increases and (2) the influx becomes more rapid, the probability of conflict increases (Williams 1947:6–7). This viewpoint has been referred to as the visibility-discrimination hypothesis, the competition hypothesis, and the minority-size hypothesis (Burr, Galle, and Fossett 1991:833).

11. Distinctions also are made within the White group. Dark-skinned Whites are generally less acceptable to the dominant group than are Whites of lighter skin (Warner and Srole 1946:285–286).

12. This section is heavily indebted to the valuable work of Russell A. Kazal (1999).

13. *Social groups* are small aggregates of people who know one another and interact on a personal level. *Social categories* are large aggregates of people who share one, or several, social characteristics.

14. The idea that clans, tribes, nations, and races owe their resemblances to shared blood was discredited by the discoveries of Mendel and others. A person's characteristics result from the operation of separate parti-

cles ("genes") of the germ plasm of the parents (Dobzhansky 1962:27). The genetic elements are either present or absent; they do not "mix." An element may be present within the gene structure of an individual (the genotype) but find no expression whatever in the visible characteristics of the individual (the phenotype). The unexpressed characteristic is nonetheless still there.

15. Blumenbach, an early anthropologist, appreciated this point far better than many later observers. In his words, the "innumerable varieties of mankind run into one another by insensible degrees" (Quoted by James C. King 1971:113).

16. Swedes typically are thought to be tall, long headed, blond, and blue eyed; but a study of Swedish people found that only 10.1 percent of those studied had *all four* of these

traits (Loehlin, Lindzey, and Spuhler 1975: 22).

17. Linnaeus distinguished 4 races, Buffon distinguished 6, Deniker concluded there are 29, Coon et al. constructed 30, and Quatrefages listed 150 (Dunn and Dobzhansky 1964:110; Loehlin, Lindzey, and Spuhler 1975:33).

18. Among anthropologists the concept of race has been passé since the end of World War II, but some anthropologists wonder whether it should be revived (see, e.g., Keita and Kittles 1997; Mukhopadhyay and Moses 1997; Visweswaran 1998).

19. "Ethnic" comes from the Greek *ethnikos,* meaning a nation or race, and "nation" comes from the Latin *nasci,* meaning "to be born"; hence, both ethnicity and nationality are derived from terms that originally referred to a group's biological heritage (Petersen 1980:234).

Together or Apart?

Some Competing Views

The process of assimilation is complex. Some people favor a complete merger of the majority and the minority. Others advocate lower levels of merger. Defining a group's goals allows for a better understanding of what assimilation means to them.

They must cast off the European skin, never to resume it. They must look forward to their posterity rather than backward to their ancestors.

—John Quincy Adams

America is God's crucible. The great melting pot where all the races of Europe are melting and reforming!

—Israel Zangwill

Thus "American civilization" may come to mean the perfection of the cooperative harmonies of "European civilization" . . . a multiplicity in a unity, an orchestration of mankind.

—Horace Kallen

The Indians are not willing to come to live near to the English. . . . A place must be found somewhere remote from the English, where they must have the word constantly taught, and government constantly exercised.

—John Eliot

We saw in Chapter 1 that the path immigrant groups generally are thought to travel as they move from the status of foreigners to that of Americans is supposed to be completed in about three generations. We saw, too, that Robert E. Park's theory of assimilation is consistent with this view but that Milton Gordon's theory includes the possibility that cultural assimilation may not lead to other forms of assimilation. Gordon's theory does agree, however, that if the assimilation of a group reaches a certain point, the completion of the assimilation process becomes inevitable. Park's and Gordon's theories, and assimilation theories in general, are consistent with the idea that as ethnic differences decline the society's underlying order and unity rest increasingly on agreements concerning values and norms among the different groups. For this reason, assimilation theories generally are referred to as **consensus** or **order theories.**

We also noted in Chapter 1 that people who enter U.S. society voluntarily ordinarily have different experiences and goals than those who enter involuntarily. Involuntary inclusion (the inclusion of slaves, for example) is likely to be accompanied by much more conflict between groups than is voluntary inclusion; hence, if one group lives involuntarily in the same territory with another for three or more generations, the result may be high levels of intergroup tension and disunity rather than order and consensus. Theories predicting that intergroup association over long periods of time will generate lasting hostility are examples of **conflict theory.**

Conflict theorists attack assimilation theories for (1) giving insufficient attention to the power differences and social conflicts that exist among racial and ethnic groups, (2) confusing the idea of assimilation as an historical reality or matter of fact with the idea of assimilation as a desirable condition that groups should work to achieve, (3) being in-applicable to the experiences in America of non-Whites and those who have entered the society involuntarily, and (4) recommending or requiring that people sacrifice their indi-viduality and group heritage. These and other criticisms have stimulated the development of a number of alternative theories that we will discuss at pertinent places throughout the book. The most important of these alternatives for our purpose is the **theory of internal colonialism.** This theory plays an important role in our discussions of the experiences of African Americans, Mexican Americans, and Native Americans.[1]

The implications of the major ideas introduced so far must be examined in much greater detail. We begin with a brief discussion of the subprocesses of assimilation de-scribed by Gordon (1964). To illustrate the ideas being presented, we refer to certain events drawn from the early colonial period of American history; in so doing, we make certain statements concerning colonial American society that will be discussed further in Chapter 3. We also present a brief summary of the main features of Gordon's **theory of assimilation subprocesses.**

 # Subprocesses of Assimilation

The European "discovery" of the Western Hemisphere near the end of the fifteenth century was followed by a long period of competition among several European nations for control of the land and resources of the new territories. By the time the English es-tablished their first successful colonies in Jamestown, Virginia (1607) and Plymouth, Massachusetts (1620), the Spanish and Portuguese had been colonizing the New World for more than a century; the Spanish had already established permanent settlements in what are now Florida, New Mexico, and California. All of the territories claimed and occupied by these and other European powers had been held previously by various in-digenous "Indian" peoples. As the Jamestown and Plymouth colonies expanded—by armed conquest and other techniques—the English became the dominant or occupy-ing group in an increasingly large territory. The Native Americans gradually were forced either to retreat to lands that the English did not occupy or, if they wished to be included in English colonial society, to remain where they were on terms set by the English.

This process of expansion and domination by the English led, in time, to the seizure of New Netherland, which had been established earlier by the Dutch. New Am-sterdam (1626) became New York (1664), giving the English tentative control of a strip of coastal territory stretching from Massachusetts to Virginia. During the next three dec-ades, the mainly English population of this still-expanding territory became much larger in size, gained a stronger grip on the land, and came increasingly to think of itself as comprised of "Americans." As this sense of "Americanness" developed, the established Anglo Americans drew sharper lines between themselves and more recent newcomers, whom they regarded as "foreigners."

These considerations support a very important point: *By the last quarter of the sev-enteenth century, the Anglo Americans had become established as the "native" group along the Atlantic seaboard from Massachusetts to Virginia.* Now, obviously, this statement does not mean the Anglo Americans were natives in exactly the same sense as the Indians. Anglo Americans who were born in the colonies were natives in the literal sense of the word—America was their native land; but, unlike the Indians, they had not been on the land before the European invasion began. They and their ancestors had displaced the Indians as the principal occupants of the land and had established their own ways of living as dominant. In this way, the Anglo Americans established their culture and institutions as the basic elements of American life. From their perspective, then, the more nearly a person approximated the Anglo American pattern the more nearly "American" he or she was judged to be.[2]

Let us examine more closely "the Anglo American pattern" and attempt to describe some of its component parts. Consider, for instance, some of the main features of Anglo American culture. English was the accepted language, and foreigners were expected to learn and use it; Protestant religious ideas were dominant, and non-Protestant practices were discouraged; and the system of law and government that was being established throughout the territory clearly was imported from England, as was the system of business practices that was established. It is true, of course, that various non-English elements were being added to the culture of the Anglo Americans. Many foods, planting practices, hunting methods, and other knowledge that were crucial to survival in North America were being borrowed from the Native Americans; and many other cultural items were being contributed by other groups. Dutch place names, for example, already had supplanted Native American names in some parts of New York and continue to be used there even now. Moreover, many aspects of English culture had been affected by the "long intimate and cranky relationship" (Tuchman 1988:57) that had existed between the English and the Dutch prior to 1664; and, in addition to the Dutch, New Amsterdam contained people of Swedish, French, Portuguese, Jewish, Spanish, Norwegian, Polish, Danish, African, German, and several other ethnicities when the English arrived there.[3] Given this diversity, the culture of the Anglo *Americans* was no longer identical to that of the English. In its major contours and social structure, nevertheless, it was distinctively English.

Within this context, we may say that if the Native Americans or the Dutch or the members of the many other groups that already were present in the English colonies abandoned their previous cultural practices and took up those of the colonists, they were undergoing a form of cultural assimilation. In this case the term refers to the subprocess of assimilation through which the members of a subordinate group gradually relinquish their own culture and, *at the same time,* acquire that of the dominant group.[4] Since this subprocess of inclusion involves the *substitution* of one heritage and behavior pattern for another, we will refer to it as **cultural assimilation by substitution.** We also will examine cases of cultural assimilation in which the subordinate group keeps most, or a significant portion, of its own heritage (McFee 1972). In those cases we will use the term **cultural assimilation by addition.** Obviously, when this type of cultural assimilation occurs, the subordinate group remains distinguishable.

The complete merging of one group into another requires more, however, than cultural assimilation by substitution. It also requires what Gordon calls structural assimilation, which focuses on the type of human relationships sociologists call **primary relationships.** These relationships are predominant within families, friendship groups, and "social" clubs but are not typical of relationships at work, in schools, in commercial transactions, at political meetings, and in places of public recreation. The latter are called **secondary relationships.**

Our analysis will be aided greatly by dividing Gordon's structural assimilation into two subprocesses, one for social settings in which secondary relationships are paramount and one for settings in which primary relationships are paramount. **Secondary structural assimilation** refers to equal-status relationships between subordinate- and dominant-group members in the public sphere. **Primary structural assimilation** refers to close, personal interactions between subordinate- and dominant-group members in the private sphere.[5]

The next step of ethnic assimilation to be included in our analysis is **marital assimilation.** This subprocess refers to the gradual merging of subordinate and dominant groups through intermarriage. In many cases, merging takes place directly as members of the dominant group marry partners from various subordinate groups; often, however, it takes place less directly as out-group marriages occur between the members of more or less assimilated groups.[6] To continue our previous illustration, the Native Americans, Africans, Dutch, and others could be considered fully assimilated at the most personal levels of association only when friendships and marriages among these groups and the dominant group were taking place without regard to racial or ethnic distinctions.

Even groups within which high levels of intermarriage exist, however, still may not be merged in several important respects. People whose parents or more distant ancestors came to America from another country—for instance Germany or Ireland or Italy—may continue to consider themselves to be in some degree German or Irish or Italian even though they were born in America and never lived in the ancestral homeland; or members of the dominant group may continue to think of the descendants of these groups as in some way not yet fully "American." Until the members of both the majority and the minority share the view that they are part of the same ethnic group **identificational assimilation** is incomplete. Moreover, when the descendants of immigrants think of themselves or are perceived by members of the majority as retaining in some measure a foreign identity, majority and minority members may feel prejudice toward one another and may discriminate against one another. Although there is widespread agreement that the term *prejudice* refers to an attitude, it has been argued that an attitude concerning a person or group should be considered a prejudice only if it is a judgment that is not based on fact or experience. Similarly, most people agree that the term *discrimination* refers to an overt action, but it is used by some to refer only to actions that spring from prejudice. And, although these terms generally connote an unfavorable attitude or action, they are sometimes also used to refer to attitudes and actions that are favorable to a particular person or group. In short, there are no precise or universally accepted definitions of prejudice and discrimination. For our purposes **prejudice** is an unfavorable attitude toward people because they are members of a particular racial or ethnic group and **discrimination** is an unfavorable action toward people because they are members of a particular racial or ethnic group. Both prejudice and discrimination may vary by degrees and, therefore, their levels may range from extremely high to extremely low.[7]

The presence or continuation of prejudice and discrimination against the members of another group or their descendants shows that a *complete* merger of the groups has not occurred and that some further assimilation is possible. Gordon refers to the subprocess through which intergroup prejudice disappears as **attitude receptional assimilation** and to the subprocess through which discrimination disappears as **behavior receptional assimilation.** But even the disappearance of ethnic prejudice and discrimination does not mark the complete merger of the groups. There may still remain conflicts between the groups over values and power; and only the elimination of these remnants of group differences results in **civic assimilation**, which, in Gordon's terms, means that the separate groups now have become one group. Those who previously were English or Native American or Dutch or Irish are now simply "Americans."

For the present, we list eight subprocesses of assimilation that may lead to a situation in which subordinate and dominant groups become indistinguishable from one another: (1) cultural assimilation by substitution,[8] (2) secondary structural assimilation, (3) primary structural assimilation, (4) marital assimilation, (5) identificational assimilation, (6) attitude receptional assimilation, (7) behavior receptional assimilation, and (8) civic assimilation. We generally refer to the third and fourth subprocesses simply as secondary and primary assimilation and to the sixth and seventh subprocesses as attitudinal and behavioral assimilation. Note that in the list *secondary assimilation appears ahead of primary assimilation.* The reasoning is that since in modern societies people typically meet and interact with one another in impersonal settings before they become close friends, secondary assimilation into jobs, schools, political parties, elected offices, and neighborhoods might be expected to precede primary assimilation.

Our discussion takes place primarily at the group level and, therefore, refers to the effects of the subprocesses of assimilation on the majority of the members of the various groups. In reality, the assimilation of some members of each group, for different reasons, will diverge from the group's average. Instead of adopting the culture of the Anglo American group or "mainstream," some individuals adopt the standards of other groups within the society. The resulting pattern is one of **segmented assimilation** rather than uniform assimilation. The meaning and value of these distinctions will become progressively clearer as we move through our analysis.

Gordon's Theory of Assimilation Subprocesses

In the theory embodying these ideas and concepts, all of the eight subprocesses contained in our list may occur simultaneously and "may take place in varying degrees" (Gordon 1964:71); however, the rate of change expected at each level depends on its place in the list; hence, cultural assimilation by substitution should proceed more rapidly than secondary assimilation, and so on through the list; however, the various subprocesses do not identify distinct and inevitable stages of assimilation. According to Gordon's theory, as noted in Chapter 1, *a group may assimilate culturally without necessarily proceeding through the remaining levels of assimilation.* The condition of "cultural assimilation only" may "continue indefinitely" (Gordon 1964:77). Past a certain point, however, assimilation in all respects becomes inevitable. The crucial point in the process for Gordon is *the formation of primary group relations*. Once the minority group enters "into the social cliques, clubs, and institutions of the core society at the primary group level," marital assimilation will follow. As marital assimilation advances, identificational assimilation will take place, intergroup prejudice and discrimination will decline, and, eventually, "the descendants of the original minority group become indistinguishable" from the majority group (Gordon 1964:80).[9] To summarize, Gordon's theory of assimilation subprocesses states (or implies) the following:

1. Each type (subprocess) of assimilation occurs at a different rate, though all of the types may be occurring simultaneously in some degree. Cultural assimilation by substitution occurs most rapidly, followed, in order, by secondary assimilation, primary assimilation, marital assimilation, identificational assimilation, attitudinal assimilation, behavioral assimilation, and civic assimilation.
2. The movement of interacting groups through the various steps toward a full merger, however, is not inevitable. A group may complete cultural assimilation only or cultural assimilation and secondary assimilation only without completing the remaining subprocesses. It may remain at the level of either cultural assimilation or secondary assimilation indefinitely, provided primary assimilation does not occur.
3. If primary assimilation does occur, marital assimilation, then identificational assimilation, attitudinal assimilation, behavioral assimilation, and civic assimilation are inevitable.

These ideas permit us to delineate more sharply the degrees and types of assimilation that have occurred, have not occurred, or are occurring between a given dominant group and any given subordinate group. If we compare the Native Americans and Dutch, for example, we may now say that although most of the Anglo Americans expected these ethnically distinctive peoples who lived among them to undertake cultural assimilation by substitution, this task posed greater problems for the Native Americans than for the Dutch. For one thing, the "distance" between the ideas, beliefs, manners, and physical appearance of the Native Americans and those of the Anglo Americans was far greater than the distance between the Anglo Americans and the Dutch; so for Native Americans cultural assimilation (if they chose to undertake it) involved greater change. For another thing, and partly as a consequence of cultural differences and similarities, the dominant group was more willing to accept the members of some groups than of others; so from the beginning as a group the Dutch were more acceptable to Anglo Americans than were the Native Americans.

These same considerations apply to the ease or difficulty with which secondary assimilation occurred among Native Americans. Any efforts they might have made to participate in the schools, jobs, or public life of American communities may well have been met by rejection and hostility; and, in many cases, they were expected to remain on reservations or beyond the frontier of settlement. Even more emphatically, primary assimilation and marital assimilation generally were opposed actively. The White, Protestant, European, Dutch, on the other hand, faced no insuperable barriers to a steady movement through the remaining levels of assimilation. Even so, we must conclude—*in direct opposition to the three-generations idea*—that many of the Dutch did *not* move through all of the subprocesses within three generations and, also, that many did not wish to do so. Even though the Anglo Americans and the Dutch were able to understand one another fairly easily and to establish many forms of cooperation, the Dutch language was maintained in some families far beyond three generations, as were preferences for Dutch friends and marriage partners.

In addition to various concepts and a theory of assimilation, Gordon also presented a description of three systems of belief (or ideologies) concerning assimilation. *An understanding of these ideologies is crucial to our analysis of the processes through which groups come together, partially or completely, or remain apart.* It is also important that in passing we note a problem that lies at the center of many debates but that raises issues going far beyond our present concerns. Our discussion necessarily involves considerations of both (1) the beliefs different people hold concerning how the ethnic groups of our society *ought* to relate to one another and (2) the beliefs that are presented in competing theories that are meant *to explain the actual relationships* that now exist, have existed, or may exist between the various groups. The problem is that although it is easy to state the distinction between these two matters, it is by no means easy (some would say impossible) to maintain it in our thinking.

The assimilationist ideologies and **antiassimilationist ideologies** we will discuss are intended to be statements of the first type, that is, sets of beliefs concerning what various people think *ought* to be; but these sets of beliefs also afford valuable frameworks within which to organize the evidence that people use to help them decide whether interethnic relations are getting better, worse, or remaining the same, and, beyond that, to reach decisions concerning the kinds of actions or social policies that might be of value in the effort to change the way ethnic groups relate to each other. Additionally, many of the concepts comprising these statements also appear as elements of the theories that are constructed to help us understand the realities of social life.

With these points in mind, we turn now to a consideration of the ideologies of assimilation outlined by Gordon.

 # Three Ideologies of Assimilation

The Anglo-Conformity Ideology

We have said that from the standpoint of the Anglo American ethnic group in colonial America, an American was someone who fitted exactly (or closely resembled) the pattern of life, standards of behavior, and racial type the Anglo Americans preferred. He or she spoke English, was of a Protestant religious persuasion, was of the so-called White physical type, had an English surname, and practiced the customs, behavior, and manners of the Anglo Americans. This definition of the term *American* fostered the idea that to assimilate into Anglo American society foreign individuals and groups should accept the society and merge completely into it. This belief has been labeled the **Anglo-conformity ideology** of assimilation.[10]

From this perspective Native Americans and Africans were considered to be racially non-White and *could never satisfy all of the requirements of complete assimilation even if they were disposed to try*. Although the dominant group exerted pressure on all subordinate groups to adopt Anglo conformity, only the members of White ethnic groups were considered eligible candidates for full inclusion into the society. The members of non-White groups who conformed to the expectations of the dominant group by adopting the Anglo American culture still were not permitted, as a rule, to move freely into the economic and political life of the Anglo Americans, let alone into their private social gatherings and families. Anglo-conformity assimilation, therefore, always has been more difficult for non-Whites than for Whites.

But any individual or group wishing to complete Anglo-conformity assimilation must go beyond intermarriage. They also must think of themselves only as Americans and give their undivided allegiance to the United States. They must no longer be the objects of prejudice and discrimination by the majority or harbor prejudicial thoughts or engage in discriminatory actions directed toward the majority. Finally, their group must no longer be engaged in conflicts with the majority over values or power. These points are summarized in Table 2.1.

We note again that in the **Anglo-conformity model** cultural assimilation occurs by the *substitution* of the majority-group's culture for the native culture rather than by the *addition* of the former to the latter. In a slightly moderated form of Anglo conformity, some vestiges of the native culture may be acceptable to the majority group and may even be viewed as positive characteristics. These cultural remnants include things such as special holiday celebrations, ethnic foods and recipes, and folk costumes, dances, and songs. These elements may, in fact, become a part of the dominant culture. In any case, the minority's members exhibit a very high degree of secondary assimilation in education, occupations, places of residence, political participation, and mass recreation (i.e., in the *public sphere* of secondary relations), and they participate little or not at all in activities organized specifically for members of their own ethnic group (i.e., the *private sphere* of secondary relations). Intergroup friendships and marriages take place without regard to ethnicity, and ethnic prejudice, discrimination, and conflict over values and power are no longer problems.

This **model of assimilation** represents a mental image of the ideal solutions the members of any group—majority or minority—may prefer to the problems of intergroup relations. The Anglo-conformity model describes a set of ideal goals or *standards* toward which out-group members may elect, or be expected, to move. Those who accept this model may measure any given group's "progress" in American society by comparing the group's actual location in regard to each subprocess of assimilation to the ideals set forth in the model.

The general argument presented so far is that the English colonial efforts during the seventeenth century created an Anglicized version of *the very meaning of the word "American"* and that Anglo conformity was established tentatively as the accepted way for outsiders to achieve full inclusion. Those who championed this view looked down on members of any group who departed very much from the Anglo American ideal or who appeared not to wish to become Americans. Using Anglo conformity as the ideal, groups could be graded as more or less desirable according to how closely they

TABLE 2.1   Anglo-Conformity Model

Group	Goals Concerning Assimilation
Majority and minority	**Cultural** Both groups agree that the minority will give up its culture and substitute the dominant culture. The minority's cultural distinctions will gradually disappear.
Majority and minority	**Secondary** Both groups agree that the minority will be accepted as equals in the educational, occupational, residential, and mass recreational spheres of society. The minority's separate secondary structures will gradually disappear.
Majority and minority	**Primary** Both groups agree that the other group's members will be accepted as close friends and members of their primary groups. The selection of friends primarily from their own group will gradually be discontinued.
Majority and minority	**Marital** Both groups agree that the other group's members will be accepted as marriage partners. They will gradually discontinue selecting partners primarily from their own ethnic group until mate selection will occur without regard to ethnicity.
Majority and minority	**Identificational** Both groups agree that the minority will accept the general society they are entering as their society. They will identify completely with it and give it their undivided loyalty.
Majority and minority	**Attitudinal** Both groups agree that they should drop all prejudices toward one another and learn to judge one another's members as individuals rather than as representatives of different groups.
Majority and minority	**Behavioral** Both groups agree that they should not discriminate against one another's members and should learn to judge one another's members in terms of their individual merits and achievements.
Majority and minority	**Civic** Both groups agree that the individual members of the two groups should participate on an equal footing in the civic life of the community. As the minority is assimilated into the majority, no basis will remain for intergroup conflict over power or values.

resembled the Anglo American pattern at the outset, how rapidly they departed from their own cultural and social patterns, and how "successfully" they came to resemble the Anglo Americans. From this viewpoint, American nationality did not arise as "a blending of all the people" in the colonies; an " 'American' was a modified English-man" (Schwarz 1995:62).

This view of Americanization was not accepted by all members of the dominant group, of course; but by the end of the first century of English colonization, it had become paramount. Its continued force into the second century of colonization depended on the continuing dominance of the Anglo American group itself, and that dominance was threatened in some ways we will discuss in Chapter 3. We turn first to two other major assimilationist alternatives to the ideology of Anglo conformity. The first of these to develop in American society was the ideology of the melting pot.

The Melting-Pot Ideology

In 1783, J. Hector St. John Crevecoeur ([1782]1976:25–26) asked, "What, then, is the American, this new man?" and proposed the following answer: "He is neither a European nor the descendant of a European. . . . Here individuals of all nations are melted into a new race of men." The basic belief lying behind the **melting-pot ideology** is that the culture and society of each ethnic group should be blended with the culture and society of the host group to produce a new and different culture and society. The **melting-pot model** is depicted in Figure 2.1.

As is true of Anglo conformity, the melting-pot view embraces the idea that minority groups in America should become indistinguishable from the majority. It adds to Anglo conformity, however, the further idea that the host culture and society also will "melt" so that the new society will reflect the proportionate influences of the groups that have gone into its making. The melting-pot ideology is thoroughly assimilationist but rejects the idea that the Anglo American core should remain as it was before assimilation occurred. Although a complete merger of groups would occur under this model of assimilation, as in the Anglo-conformity model, the Anglo American core also would be substantially changed. Advocates of this ideology believe the new host society resulting

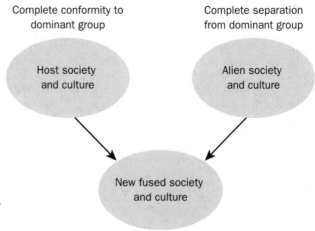

FIGURE 2.1   A Model of Assimilation: The Melting Pot
(Arrows indicate the preferred direction of social and cultural change)

from the blend of the previously separate groups would be most consistent with the fundamental ideals of the United States.

The Ideology of Cultural Pluralism

Although the idea of cultural pluralism is quite old in American thought, its formulation as an explicit ideology is usually traced to the writings of the Jewish philosopher Horace Kallen (Gordon 1964:141; Meister 1974:53–61; Newman 1973:67). Beginning in 1915, Kallen attacked the idea that it was necessary for ethnic groups to give up their distinctive cultures or lose their distinctiveness in order to be *completely* American. Kallen argued in favor of an **ideology of cultural pluralism** based on the belief that the members of every American ethnic group should be free to participate in all of the society's major institutions (e.g., schools, jobs, politics) while simultaneously retaining or elaborating their own ethnic heritage.

In Kallen's view, neither the Anglo-conformity nor the melting-pot ideologies outlined acceptable goals for America. True Americanism, he thought, required us to protect and nurture the various distinctive cultures that exist within the United States. Unlike the other two assimilationist ideologies we have discussed, which assume (or hope) that intergroup relations will end in a merger in which the distinctive groups become indistinguishable, pluralist ideology is based on the idea that the members of minority groups should be accepted as *completely Americanized and assimilated without being required to disappear as distinctive groups.* Since groups may remain more or less distinctive, depending on how fully they assimilate in terms of each of the eight subprocesses of assimilation, many different models of pluralism may be visualized.

We use the **model of cultural pluralism** summarized in Table 2.2 as our reference point in this book. Here we see that the minority group's members exhibit a very high degree of cultural assimilation but possess a distinctive heritage for use within the group. They are bilingual and bicultural. Cultural assimilation has occurred through the *addition* of the majority's culture to the minority's culture rather than by the *substitution* of the former for the latter. The differences of the majority and minority are mutually accepted and respected. The minority's members exhibit a very high degree of structural assimilation in education, occupations, places of residence, political participation, and mass recreation (i.e., desegregation in the *public sphere*); but they also remain very highly segregated in the religious, health care, welfare, and "social" recreational activities of their ethnic group (i.e., the "ethnic group" or *private sphere* of secondary relations). Ethnic preferences remain important factors in the choice of friends and marriage partners, and minority group members maintain a high level of ethnic pride while, simultaneously, giving their primary allegiance to the overall society. Intergroup prejudices and discrimination still exist but are subdued. Majority and minority groups have equal civil standing, and intergroup conflicts over values or power are expressed entirely through the established legal and political framework of the society (Gordon 1964:158).[11]

The goals of some versions of cultural pluralism include the acceptance of the Anglo American culture as the "standard" pattern of the country but present *a different*

TABLE 2.2   A Model of Cultural Pluralism

Group	Goals Concerning Assimilation
Majority and minority	**Cultural** Both groups agree that the minority will accept and practice the culture of the majority; however, the minority will retain and elaborate a large portion of its own cultural heritage. The cultural assimilation of the minority will occur through the *addition* of the dominant culture to the minority culture rather than through the *substitution* of the former for the latter.
Majority and minority	**Secondary** Both groups agree that the minority will be accepted as equals in the educational, occupational, residential, and mass recreational spheres of society. Members of the minority will be free to choose whether to enter fully into the secondary structures of the majority or to live mainly within separate secondary structures.
Majority and minority	**Primary** Both groups agree that although the other group's members will be acceptable as close friends and members of their primary groups, each group nonetheless will select friends primarily from within their own group and intergroup friendships will not be actively encouraged.
Majority and minority	**Marital** Both groups agree that they will select marriage partners primarily from within their own group and intergroup marriages will be less prevalent.
Majority and minority	**Identificational** Both groups agree that the minority will accept the general society they are entering as their own, will give it their primary allegiance, and will derive their main ethnic identification from it; however, it is agreed that if they wish to, minority group members may also continue a secondary identification with their own group and its heritage.
Majority and minority	**Attitudinal** Both groups agree that they should drop all prejudices toward one another and learn to judge one another's members as individuals rather than as representatives of different groups. Each group, nevertheless, will encourage its members to take pride in their own group, its heritage, and their membership in it.
Majority and minority	**Behavioral** Both groups agree that they should not discriminate against one another's members and should learn to judge one another's members in terms of their individual merits and achievements. Each group, nevertheless, is free to give special recognition to exceptional achievements by its members.
Majority and minority	**Civic** Both groups agree that the individual members of the two groups should participate on an equal footing in the civic life of the community. All conflicts between the groups over power or values must be solved through peaceful, legal, and democratic processes.

model of intergroup merger—one that rejects Anglo conformity and the melting pot but emphatically accepts the desirability of complete Americanization. It is vital to grasp the idea that from this perspective, if a group were to achieve the goals outlined here, it would have completed the requirements of assimilation. Its members would be viewed *as being as completely American as if they had lost their distinctiveness in accordance with the goals of Anglo conformity or the melting pot.* Advocates of this view wish to be an integral part of the society's cultural, educational, occupational, and political mainstream.[12]

Those who favor pluralism, Anglo conformity, or the melting pot specify different degrees and methods of intergroup merger while envisioning high levels of similarity and cooperation in regard to the mainstream of the culture and society. Both pluralists and Anglo conformists expect high levels of assimilation along the cultural dimension (though differing on whether it is desirable for this to occur by addition or by substitution) and in the public sphere of secondary assimilation. The aim of the pluralist model is to show that individuals and groups may become "one hundred percent Americans" without following the paths of Anglo conformity or the melting pot. Pluralists believe that high levels of societal unity and harmony are consistent with the maintainence of ethnic diversity in the cultural, personal, and marital arenas.

Since pluralism offers a broader range of possible models than either Anglo conformity or the melting pot, it also raises a major question: How much diversity is compatible with national unity? Many people who wish to live in a culturally diverse society may reject the model of cultural pluralism we have described as containing a dangerous degree of separation; hence, they may prefer a model of pluralism in which the groups may be distinguishable but nevertheless be more nearly alike in some respects than we have outlined.

 # An Antiassimilationist View: Blauner's Theory of Internal Colonialism

The models of assimilation we have described assume that as time passes the members of dominant and subordinate groups become more nearly alike in various respects, while the intensity of interethnic conflict declines. The models assume, too, that when conflict does arise it generally will be settled peacefully through negotiation, the courts, and the political process. Many theorists believe such views are unrealistic and, especially, that they ignore or downplay the long-term effects on people's social position and motivations of being forced to enter a society. You may easily imagine that when people are enslaved or conquered by the members of another group, their overriding reaction is to resist the dominant group, overthrow it, or try to escape from it rather than to strive to become a part of it.

To gain some appreciation of the importance of this point, consider the situation of the groups in Africa who were conquered as various European countries divided up the continent among themselves. Blauner (1972) has noted that in contrast to the more or less voluntary movement of the **immigrant minorities** to America, the **colonized minorities** of Africa generally were indigenous to the areas in which they resided and were forced to "join" the society of the colonizers. Furthermore, the colonized minorities of Africa typically were not numerical minorities. They had less power, of course, which is why we call them minorities; but by sheer weight of numbers they have been in a better position than immigrant minorities to maintain and elaborate their cultures in the face of the dominant group's efforts to establish its own culture as the only acceptable one (Blauner 1972:53).

The economic situation of the colonized minorities of Africa also has differed noticeably from that of the immigrant minorities in America. Although the American immigrant minorities usually have had to take whatever kind of work they could get, at least initially, they frequently have been able to move on to something more desirable and to exercise some degree of choice in what they would accept. Even their first jobs were likely to be ones that some Anglo Americans were doing or had done recently. The complaint that "they" are undercutting us economically and are taking "our" jobs away has been heard monotonously in America. But this kind of labor difficulty did not arise in the African colonies. There the indigenous populations usually were required to engage in only the hardest, most menial kinds of tasks. The better jobs were reserved for members of the dominant group. Ordinarily, the opportunity to move around and compete freely with the members of the dominant group did not exist or was very limited (Blauner 1972:55).

Under these conditions, the colonized minorities in Africa did not usually come to think of themselves as French or Dutch or English, and they did not typically move into the mainstream of the dominant group's social life. Instead, the colonized minorities of Africa looked forward to the day when the European invaders could be annihilated or forced to leave and return to their own countries. When these circumstances are viewed within the context of Park's race-cycle theory, we see that race relations were not characterized by a steady movement forward out of the stage of accommodation into the final stages of assimilation. Rather, it was primarily a back-and-forth movement between the stage of accommodation and the prior stage of conflict. In its main or "classical" form, which was witnessed repeatedly in Africa after World War II, this oscillation continued until the dominant White group, in most instances, was thrown out of power and the previously colonized minorities became majorities. In many of these cases large numbers of the dominant White group fled or were driven out of the country. The final stage of relations between dominant Europeans and colonized Africans, then, was a conflict (usually violent) followed by separation rather than an accommodation followed by assimilation. With these points in mind, Blauner (1994:159) argued that "the communities of color in America share essential conditions with Third World nations abroad: economic underdevelopment, a heritage of colonialism and neocolonialism, and a lack of real political autonomy and power." Blauner added that colonization has taken different forms in the history of different American ethnic groups and that variations in time, place, and the manner of colonialization have affected the character of racial domination and the responses of the dominated group.

The three American ethnic groups that best illustrate the **colonial model** are American Indians, African Americans, and Mexican Americans. As we shall see, the history of American Indians since 1492 clearly illustrates the consequences for indigenous peoples that follow being overrun by invaders and forcibly drawn into a society through conquest. The history of African Americans clearly illustrates the consequences for people of being subjected to a rigid system of slavery; and the history of Mexican Americans presents a complicated mixture of the consequences that may arise from both colonization and immigration. We consider these issues more fully in later chapters.

Our discussion of assimilation theory provides the basis for a description of three **assimilationist ideologies**—Anglo conformity, the melting pot, and cultural pluralism—that outline alternative goals for groups that are, through time, moving toward the creation of a single group. We turn now to a description of two antiassimilationist ideologies that draw their inspiration from conflict theories such as the theory of internal colonialism. While assimilation theories forecast some form of intergroup merger between majorities and minorities, conflict theories forecast that colonized minorities, and perhaps others as well, either will remain substantially apart from the majority for an indefinite period of time or will withdraw from the society altogether.

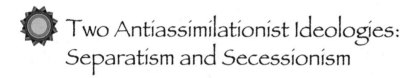

Two Antiassimilationist Ideologies: Separatism and Secessionism

We noted that the model of cultural pluralism we have outlined is only one of many possible versions of pluralism. We now consider an ideology that represents the view of pluralists who desire a still higher degree of separation than that described so far. Some pluralists suggest that separate school systems, separate economies, and even separate states or autonomous regions within the United States should be established. They may believe also that whenever such separate institutions cannot be organized, the rights of the minority should be legally protected through the establishment of proportionate quotas in schools, jobs, and political offices. Pluralists of this type may object to the idea that only members of minority groups should be bilingual. Perhaps English should not be the general language in all parts of the country or within every institutional setting; and perhaps the members of the majority should also be expected to be bilingual. Equality of results, not of opportunity, is the goal.[13] We will simplify the problem of discussing innumerable possible pluralisms by distinguishing only one other model of pluralism as a contrast to cultural pluralism. Our second model emphasizes separation and is generally antiassimilationist in tone and intent.

For our purposes, in a society having pluralism *of this second type* only some members of the group master the dominant culture and become bilingual and bicultural. Among these, cultural assimilation takes place *by addition* rather than *by substitution*. Both groups formally accept the culture of the other but strive nevertheless to restrain its influence. The minority's members exhibit a low degree of secondary assimilation in both the *public* and *private* social spheres. Their education, occupations, places of residence, political participation, recreation, religious observances, and health and welfare activities are separated from those of the broader society insofar as that is possible within the framework of a single society. The minority's members are legally protected against coercive efforts to force them to assimilate in any respect. *Each group's share of public offices and benefits depends on the group's relative size.*

Out-group friendships are strongly discouraged by both groups, and out-group marriage is strongly discouraged. The minority's members think of themselves primarily as members of their original group and only nominally as members of the broader society. Strong feelings of prejudice exist between the majority and minority, acts of discrimination between the majority and minority are common, and conflicts concerning differences in power and values frequently lead to intergroup violence. Since this second form of pluralism espouses a high degree of separation in the cultural, public, and social lives of the dominant and subordinate groups, we will refer to it as the **ideology of separatism** or simply as separatism. Our **separatist model** is summarized in Table 2.3.

Please note, however, that separatism in this sense still is not based on a desire to bring about a complete separation. A separatist view that advocates a group's complete separation or withdrawal from the society is called an **ideology of secession.** Secession is well illustrated by the withdrawal of the southern states from the United States in 1861 and by the breakup of the Soviet Union in 1991.

Our discussion has attempted to show that the ideology of pluralism embraces varying degrees of merger and separation. One view proposes a form of pluralism that is decidedly assimilationist in tone and intent. Even though this, the cultural, form of pluralism contains certain separatist elements, these are present mainly in the sphere of private relations. Advocates of this kind of separateness emphasize that it does not detract from the unity of the nation but instead, by permitting different racial and ethnic

Table 2.3   A Model of Separatism

Group	Goals Concerning Assimilation
	Cultural
Majority	The majority expects the minority to adopt and practice the culture of the majority.
Minority	The minority adopts and practices the culture of the majority only insofar as is necessary for survival. The minority practices and elaborates its own culture insofar as is permitted.
	Secondary
Majority	The majority will not accept the members of the minority as equals in the educational, occupational, residential, political, and mass recreational spheres of society.
Minority	The minority attempts to participate in the secondary institutions of the majority only insofar as is necessary to survive. The minority elaborates and lives mainly within its own secondary structures. It struggles to reduce the influence of the majority on minority members' lives.

Table 2.3   Continued

Group	Goals Concerning Assimilation
	Primary
Majority	The majority does not consider the minority group's members to be acceptable as close friends and members of the majority's primary groups.
Minority	The minority does not consider the majority group's members to be acceptable as close friends and members of the minority's primary groups.
	Marital
Majority	The majority does not consider the minority group's members to be acceptable as marriage partners. Intermarriage is strongly discouraged, often through legal prohibitions and other barriers.
Minority	The minority does not consider the majority group's members to be acceptable as marriage partners. Intermarriage is strongly discouraged.
	Identificational
Majority	The majority expects the minority to accept the general society as their own, to identify themselves primarily in terms of it, and to give it their undivided loyalty.
Minority	The minority identifies primarily with its own group and grants the general society only limited allegiance and loyalty.
	Attitudinal
Majority	The majority maintains a high level of prejudice toward the members of the minority and disapproves of any majority member who expresses tolerant views toward the minority.
Minority	The minority maintains a high level of prejudice toward the members of the majority and disapproves of any minority member who expresses tolerant views toward the majority.
	Behavioral
Majority	Majority group members often discriminate against minority group members. Many forms of discrimination are integral parts of the folkways and laws of the general society.
Minority	Minority group members discriminate against majority group members insofar as is possible for members of a subordinate group. The minority struggles to decrease the level of discrimination to which it is subjected.
	Civic
Majority	The majority works to maintain the existing value system of the society and to monopolize social power. Minority group members are allowed into positions of power only when it is expedient for the majority.
Minority	The minority resists the dominant value system wherever it conflicts with their own value system; it struggles to attain social power. There is frequently intergroup conflict, often violent, over power and values.

groups to retain their distinctiveness without discrimination, creates especially loyal citizens. The second form of pluralism we have outlined, however, is antiassimilationist. Here the separatist elements are much more significant than in the cultural form and are definitely a challenge to the unity of the nation and the loyalty of its citizens. Indeed, this form of separatism may precede or lead to the secession of disaffected groups.

The three ideologies of assimilation and two ideologies of separation we have presented offer alternative sets of goals that individuals and groups may choose to pursue and, also, to prescribe for others. Although they are not commonly referred to by the names we have given them, or in such detail, aspects of these models often are brought to public notice and enter public debate. For example, in speeches given on national holidays or at patriotic celebrations speakers often say that "America is a melting pot" or may celebrate the fact that millions of immigrants have reached our society over the years and found the opportunities needed to enter the mainstream and live "the American dream." For example, in his famous "I Have a Dream" speech, Dr. Martin Luther King, Jr. outlined his vision (or assimilation model) for future relations among the races.

Although assimilationist images are by far the most widely accepted in our society, separatist or secessionist views have always been present; and some of the advocates of these views are prominent in American history. Various representatives of the Native American peoples, Tecumseh for example, presented eloquent defenses of the desires of these groups to leave American society and to regain their former independence. As we shall see later, Marcus Garvey played a similar role among African Americans, and Malcolm X argued during a portion of his life for a type of separatism.

Using the Models as Descriptions

Recall that in addition to affording statements of what one may think *ought* to occur, the models we have presented also may be used as frameworks for *describing* the relations that have existed in the past or currently exist between groups. When they are used in this way, the models suggest the following interesting and debatable question: To what extent do these competing views afford accurate descriptions of what *actually has occurred* in American society during the past two or three centuries? Since we will be reviewing various kinds of evidence bearing on this question throughout the remainder of this book, our comments at this point are only preliminary.

We have asserted that by the end of the colonial period, Anglo conformity was the most widely accepted ideology within the dominant Anglo American group; and our previous examples of the way English culture became Anglo American culture through innovation and the adoption of Native American, African, Dutch, and other cultural elements during the colonial period illustrated the operation of social processes that led to the fusing of many cultural elements. Some other examples showed that the fusing process has continued in American society since that time. But since a fusing of cultural elements is expected to occur in both the Anglo-conformity model and in the melting-pot model, these examples may be cited as evidence that we have been moving toward either of these two sets of goals.

Persuasive arguments have been presented on both sides. Park's theory states that "eventually" subordinate groups take on the characteristics of the dominant group, which is what one would expect on the basis of Anglo conformity. But the melting pot also has had strong advocates. For instance, the **frontier thesis** was presented by the historian Frederick Jackson Turner (1920). According to Turner, the Western American frontier functioned as a great leveler of persons and a blender of cultures. On the frontier, people had to adapt to the harsh conditions confronting them by devising and sharing solutions to the problems they faced. People borrowed freely from the various cultures there and, in the process, developed a new American culture that contained significant contributions from the various participating cultures and societies but was distinctly different from any of them.

The process of cultural accumulation that started on the Atlantic seacoast during the seventeenth century has continued as American society has grown and changed. For example, many types of previously foreign foods, beliefs, words, phrases, and various styles of dress, music, and dance gradually have become accepted as "American." In addition, when U.S. citizens are today asked to name their "nationality," an increasingly large proportion of them say "American." Consider additionally that the "English" culture on which the early Anglo American culture rested was itself the product of an extremely long period of cultural merging; hence, the Anglo American culture that developed during the colonial period consisted not only of English, Dutch, Native American, African, and many other elements then present in North America, but, also, of the fused elements of thousands of other cultures that existed during a period of several millennia before Europeans were even aware of the existence of the Western Hemisphere. The English language of today, for instance, reflects the fact that tens of thousands of words taken from the Celts, Romans, Danes, and Norman French, among others, were organized around an Anglo-Saxon core, which, in turn, consisted of elements borrowed from many additional languages (Bryson 1990:46–47). In the long view of history, *all* modern cultures and societies are constructed from a vast accumulation of sociocultural elements from the past.[14]

These examples introduce a point we stress in Chapter 14. It is vital that analyses of intergroup relations include clear statements concerning the *lengths of the periods of time* that are assumed to be needed for given sociocultural changes to take place. We may accept, for example, that the English culture of 1600 consisted of fused elements from a large number of other cultures and also that the processes of melting continued in America during the colonial period without necessarily accepting the idea that the melting-pot model affords the best description of the actual effects of assimilation in America during the years since 1776.

Consider some points that have been raised in favor of the claim that contemporary American society is not mainly a product of a melting-pot fusion of various societies and cultures during the past two or three centuries. Although we have noted that vast sociocultural changes certainly have taken place in American society since colonial times, this society has continued to consist of a variety of different racial and ethnic groups. As we shall see, many minority groups either did not wish to "melt" into the "mainstream" of the society or were prevented from doing so. Many groups remained distinctive even after they adopted high levels of cultural assimilation; consequently, several scholars have argued that despite the profound changes that have occurred in, and enriched, American culture and society, the Anglo American foundation that initially defined the society's basic characteristics and structure (e.g., its language, laws, commercial organization, and basic values) has not thus far been altered markedly by the melting process.

From this perspective, changes in the defining features of Anglo American society have been comparatively small. The argument here is that although a high level of melting has taken place, it has been mainly in the direction of Anglo conformity. This view proposes that those who adopt the melting-pot metaphor usually are referring, in fact, to the processes that lead to Anglo conformity. As expressed by Herberg (1960:21), "Our cultural assimilation has taken place not in a 'melting pot,' but rather in a **'transmuting pot'** in which all ingredients have been transformed and assimilated to an idealized 'Anglo-Saxon' model" (emphasis added). In a similar vein, Glazer and Moynihan (1964:v) observed in relation to New York City that "The point about the melting pot . . . is that it did not happen;" and, in Hirschman's (1983:398) opinion, the melting-pot metaphor has been significant mainly as "a political symbol used to strengthen and legitimize the ideology of America as a land of opportunity where race, religion, and national origin should not be barriers to social mobility."

At least three reservations are crucial in relation to these judgments. First, the Anglo American framework underlying American society certainly has not been static; second, if the processes of change continue for an indefinite period into the future, they "eventually" may well transform even the basic structure of the society; and third, the melting process may have produced a higher degree of mutual blending in some areas of the country than in others (Adams 1934). These valid considerations do not, however, afford a sufficient basis for stating conclusively that the fusion of the cultures of the natives, the later newcomers, and the indigenous population has significantly altered the foundations of the dominant culture thus far.

Whatever interpretation of the past a person favors, the coming chapters will make clear that sociocultural diversity has existed in America from the first; and, as is true for nearly all modern societies, America is still a multicultural society. Given these facts, the advocates of pluralism maintain that despite the dominant group's continuous pressures on them, most subordinate-group Americans have given only lip service to the two ideologies favoring sociocultural fusion and that, in fact, some unarticulated form of pluralism has had many more adherents than is generally acknowledged. They argue that the time has now come for the American people to synchronize their ideology with social reality. Let us now, they say, recognize and promote our diversity instead of continuing to place pressure on the members of subordinate groups to move toward a single social pattern.

Critics of pluralism, of course, do not agree that pluralist ideology (as distinct from the fact of sociocultural diversity) has played a significant role in our history; but even if that were true, they question the wisdom of endorsing pluralism as an accepted way to become an American and they raise questions that point to some important theoretical objections. For instance, will the acceptance of pluralism lead to a hardening of the group divisions that exist among us, promote intergroup hostility and conflict, and threaten the unity and stability of American society? Can the members of a subordinate group maintain their balance between the social forces pressuring them toward fusion, on the one hand, and separation, on the other? Won't they, perhaps over a period of several generations, be drawn inevitably toward one or the other of these competing poles?

These questions pose serious problems for pluralist theory. The existence of constantly opposing pressures favoring either total conformity to the dominant group, at one extreme, or secession, at the other, suggests that cultural pluralism is inherently unstable. No group, critics say, can stop just at the point of assimilation defined by cultural pluralist philosophy. The group must continue through the exact point of merger it prefers toward one or the other of the two opposing poles. Either the submersion of the minority within the dominant group or the separation (possibly accompanied by open warfare) of the groups is the inevitable result. Contemporary examples of the latter outcome include the ethnic conflicts between Azerbaijan and Armenia accompanying the dissolution of the Soviet Union and between Serbia and Bosnia-Herzegovina and Serbia and Kosovo accompanying the dissolution of Yugoslavia.

The main reasons for supposing that pluralism will not necessarily collapse under either the centripetal pressures of conformity or the centrifugal forces of separation are derived from America's political experience as the world's oldest democracy. The framers of the U.S. Constitution recognized that many different groups would struggle to gain control of the society; so they sought to write a legal document that would achieve a balance of social forces by providing ample checks against dangerous accumulations of power. To help reach this goal, they divided power among the three main branches of government, between the central government and the states, and between the large states and the small. The extent of the framer's success is a complex subject with a long history of debate behind it, and some skeptics doubt that American democracy could continue under an explicit policy of pluralism.

We have seen already that the Anglo Americans became the most powerful group in American society during the colonial period; but, as we will see in Chapters 3, 4, and 5, the fluctuating levels of immigration during the eighteenth, nineteenth, and twentieth centuries periodically raised the fears of natives that newcomers would gain control of the system and replace them as the dominant group. The struggle for political power in America, therefore, has taken place to some extent along ethnic lines; and, as a part of this struggle, the dominant group frequently has used ethnic discrimination to prevent "domination by ethnic strangers" (Horowitz 1985:188). An important issue for a pluralist social policy therefore is that since ethnic groups would continue to be distinctive and visible, the dominant group might continue to fear losing control and might continue to practice exclusion and oppression.

The pluralist position in political theory, however, is that the competing interests of groups embedded within an explicitly plural ethnic system may be stable for an indefinitely long period of time. This position is based on the idea that since many different types of interest groups, including ethnic groups, seek out government officials and attempt to influence the officials' actions, the resulting decisions reflect the balancing of many different points of view (see, e.g., Riesman, Glazer, and Denney 1950).[15] Ethnic diversity, not uniformity, is seen to be the key to the maintenance of a vigorous democracy. As stated by Wirth (1945:355), the advocates of pluralism believe it is "one of the necessary preconditions of a rich and dynamic civilization under conditions of freedom."

To summarize, each of the models presented in this chapter helps us to state clearly, and to compare, both the *goals* different individuals and groups in American society believe they and others *ought* to pursue (i.e., they may serve as ideologies) and the *actual location* of any given individual or group (on average) in regard to the eight subprocesses of assimilation in our analysis (i.e., they may serve as descriptions). Stated differently, the models help us to specify both (1) what the members of any group, individually or collectively, *want* and (2) *how near to or far from those goals* any individual or group actually is. The theories of assimilation we have presented are efforts to explain how assimilation occurs and to forecast the probable future of intergroup relations in America. The value of these theories depends on how closely their explanations correspond to social reality.

Two of the ideologies of assimilation—the melting-pot ideology and the ideology of cultural pluralism—emerged in reaction to the demand by the dominant group that ethnic groups should rapidly fuse with the existing society. Both of these alternatives to Anglo conformity have emphasized the advantages of accepting diverse elements into the mainstream of American life. In its cultural form, pluralism holds that minority groups may retain or construct distinctive heritages and, at the same time, live in harmony and equality with the dominant society. In its separatist form, pluralism doubts the good will of the majority and focuses on what it believes to be basic flaws in the society. It sees majority and minority groups more as adversaries than as cooperating partners in a joint venture. Separatists do not accept the basic values of the dominant group, and they consider the levels of distinctiveness permitted under cultural pluralism to be unsatisfactory. True democracy, from the separatist perspective, cannot occur when the majority has the power to control the destiny of a minority group's members. A minority's ability to protect its rights depends, according to this line of reasoning, on a high degree of independence in the economic, political, and educational arenas, as well as in more personal matters. Separatism shades into the more extreme position of secessionism, which represents the ultimate challenge to the goals of all three assimilationist ideologies.

The implications of the major ideas introduced so far must be examined in much greater detail in relation to the actual experiences of different groups within American society. We begin this effort in Chapter 3 by expanding our discussion of the way the Anglo Americans consolidated their power on the Atlantic Coast of North America.

 Reality Check

INTERVIEW WITH CURTIS

Curtis is a White American of German descent. He is married, has two young daughters, and is a sixth grade teacher who is working on a graduate degree. His wife's father was White and her mother was Mexican American. Curtis's family lives in an ethnically mixed neighborhood. The school in which Curtis teaches has a diverse student body, although most of the teachers are White.

How do you refer to yourself in terms of racial and ethnic relations?
I don't think about it a lot but I'm sure that the answer to your question would be that I consider myself just White.

When did you first become aware of your racial and ethnic identity?
My parents were both raised in East Texas, so they had some prejudicial attitudes about minority groups; but that never seemed to rub off on me and my siblings. I think my last name is German, but we never really talked about coming from a German background, and there wasn't really any German culture infused into my upbringing; however, in high school I developed an interest in German culture. As far as being White, it was never talked about very much; it was just kind of taken for granted.

Would you tell me about the high school you attended?
The high school I attended in the late 1970s was a real diverse south Texas school. We had a large Hispanic as well as African American population. Everyone in my class and at my high school seemed to get along pretty well. Things that we did in high school, the activities that we participated in, were very integrated. We were friends, and I don't recall any disagreements at all that happened at the school that were centered around ethnic and racial groups.

Tell me about your family.
I would say that my children probably identify themselves as White. My wife probably identifies herself as a "coconut" because her mom was Mexican American and her dad was a White from Appalachia. She felt really uncomfortable growing up in San Antonio, because, although she looked Hispanic, she didn't speak Spanish; so she wasn't quite a part of either the majority group or the Hispanic group. Still, our family's activities, birthday parties and stuff, all have an Hispanic flavor to them. There are a lot of other customs that we practice around these types of holidays.

Does your family talk about race and ethnic relations?
I have been known to talk about things like that for the whole trip to school in the morning with my two young daughters, and it's about a 20-mile journey. Once one of my daughters was at a neighboring girl's birthday party and I don't know exactly what happened, but my daughter said something to a little Black girl about "we don't wanna play with you because you're Black." The girl's mom called over—she's real good friends with my wife—so my wife and I sat Alison down and talked about how that should not be an issue, that it was inappropriate for her to say that.

What stands out as most important to you about being White?
I don't know if I attach any kind of significance to it. You know, maybe I haven't had a whole lot of time recently to really reflect on it. I have small children at home, a full-time job, and graduate school. I guess the most important thing about it is that there are a whole lot of issues that I guess people in other ethnic

(continued)

and racial groups have to deal with that I don't. So I do recognize there is some privilege about being White. That's the only significance that I can attach to it.

How does your racial or ethnic background affect you in your life?
Other than having an interest in German, being of German heritage does not affect me. There is very little from my ethnic heritage that is a part of my household. We do more things that are part of the Hispanic culture than we do anything else as my wife is half Hispanic. In my job at school, when I'm interacting with students of different ethnic or racial groups, sometimes there is a barrier there, and until I have an opportunity to be around these kids for a while I feel there is some distrust because I'm White.

Have you ever experienced an uncomfortable situation because of your race or ethnicity?
I guess I'm uncomfortable when I find myself in a crowd where I'm the minority. When I'm in those situations I feel that I'm perceived as a stereotypical White male, with maybe some preconceived attitudes about being in a group of minorities; so it takes a while before I feel comfortable. After you interact with people for a while and they see how you really are, the discomfort goes away.

Would you tell me about your friends?
I have friends who are White, certainly; and I have friends who are Black and Hispanic. I think it is pretty proportionate to the makeup in this area. I live in a very diverse neighborhood, so I have neighbors that are Black and Hispanic; but I think I would probably have some reservations if my daughters were to come to me someday and say they wanted to be romantically involved with someone of a different race. I think I'd feel that way because I recognize it's going to be an added burden to be dealt with, rather than because I hold that group in negative regard.

Discussion Questions

In regard to aspects of secondary assimilation—education, occupation, residence, and so on—is Curtis highly integrated into the majority?

How did Anglo conformity become the dominant ideology of assimilation in the United States?

Why are assimilation theories opposed by conflict theorists?

Do you favor an ideology of assimilation or of separation? Why?

What practical problems are presented by each of the ideologies of assimilation or separation?

Which model of assimilation or separation best describes the existing group relations in the United States today? Give examples.

 # Key Ideas

1. Assimilation theories generally are consistent with the idea that as ethnic differences decline, the society's underlying order and unity rest increasingly on a consensus among the different groups concerning basic values and norms. For this reason, assimilation theories generally are referred to as consensus or order theories. Conflict theories, in contrast, emphasize that the inclusion of foreign groups is likely to be accompanied by and lead to high levels of intergroup tension and hostility rather than order and consensus.

2. The subject of assimilation is complex. It is important to think separately about *the facts* of assimilation and *the goals* that may be pursued. In regard to facts, it is helpful to focus on a set of specific subprocesses of assimilation rather than on a single general process. In regard to goals, it is helpful to identify competing ideologies.

3. Milton M. Gordon has identified seven subprocesses of assimilation: (1) cultural assimilation, (2) structural assimilation, (3) marital assimilation, (4) identificational assimilation, (5) attitude receptional assimilation, (6) behavior receptional assimilation, and (7) civic assimilation.

4. Our analysis identifies two additional subprocesses by dividing cultural assimilation into two subprocesses (cultural assimilation by substitution and cultural assimilation by addition) and by dividing structural assimilation into two subprocesses (secondary structural assimilation and primary structural assimilation).[16]

5. According to Gordon's theory of assimilation, each of the subprocesses listed in Key Idea 3 may occur simultaneously and in varying degrees, and the rate of change in each one will correspond to its position in the list. In contrast to Robert E. Park's view, *a group may assimilate culturally without necessarily proceeding through the remaining stages.* As primary assimilation advances, however, Gordon's theory agrees with Park's *that assimilation in all respects becomes inevitable.*

6. Gordon also specified three main assimilationist ideologies that favor different goals: Anglo conformity, the melting pot, and cultural pluralism. The models of assimilation based on these ideologies do not represent the actual levels of assimilation of any particular group or groups; they represent, rather, *the goals* toward which a group may elect or be expected to move. The models also may be used to help specify how near to or far from the goals an individual or group actually is.

7. Anglo Americans had become established as the dominant group along the Atlantic seaboard from Massachusetts to Virginia by the end of the seventeenth century. They had displaced the Native Americans and established their own ways of living as dominant. The more nearly a person approximated the Anglo American ethnic model, the more nearly "American" he or she was judged to be. This perspective on assimilation is called the Anglo-conformity ideology.

8. The melting-pot ideology and the ideology of cultural pluralism are prominent assimilationist views opposing the idea that Anglo conformity is the *only* way to become a "100 percent" American and also the idea that people of White, Anglo-Saxon ancestry necessarily make the most desirable citizens.

9. The melting-pot ideology, like the ideology of Anglo conformity, favors a complete merger of the majority and the minority. Unlike Anglo conformity, the melting-pot model states that both the majority and the minority should change, creating a new society and cultural identity.

10. The ideology of cultural pluralism opposes the complete merger of minorities with the majority. It seeks instead various degrees of merger and separation depending on the type of assimilation under consideration. Many pluralist models may be constructed. One example, which we refer to as cultural pluralism, stresses equality of opportunity for minority-group citizens plus the right to retain their cultural and social distinctiveness. In this form, the minority seeks to master the culture of the dominant group without losing its own culture. It also seeks secondary assimilation *in the public sphere.* This approach, therefore, is decidedly assimilationist with respect to the nation's central institutions even though separation in the private spheres of life is preserved.

11. The extent to which a person voluntarily enters a new society may be a crucial factor in determining the way the person reacts to that society. Members of immigrant minorities are more likely to wish to adopt an assimilationist strategy than are members of colonized minorities. Prolonged conflicts between the host group and colonized minorities are likely and may promote separatist and secessionist ideologies and movements.

12. The most extreme antiassimilationist view is secessionism. Secessionists advocate a total separation of ethnic groups, through violence if necessary.

13. The models presented in this chapter help us to specify both (1) what the members of any group, individually or collectively, *want* and (2) *how near to or far from those goals* any individual or group actually is. The theories of assimilation are efforts to explain how assimilation occurs and to forecast the probable future of intergroup relations in America.

14. An important issue for theories of pluralism is whether any group can resist the centripetal social forces favoring full merger at one extreme or the centrifugal social forces favoring complete separation at the other.

 Key Terms

Anglo-conformity ideology   A set of beliefs based on the idea that non-Anglo individuals and groups should accept Anglo American society and conform to its patterns of culture, social institutions, and social and private life.

Anglo-conformity model   A specific vision of complete assimilation in which subordinate groups accept and conform to the Anglo American patterns of culture, social institutions, and social and private life.

antiassimilationist ideologies   Systems of beliefs that oppose assimilation.

assimilation ideology   Systems of beliefs concerning how society should bring minority groups within it into full participation in society.

attitude receptional assimilation   The subprocess through which ethnic prejudice declines.

behavior receptional assimilation   The subprocess through which ethnic discrimination declines.

civic assimilation   The subprocess through which intergroup conflicts over values and power decline.

colonial model   A perspective that analyzes intergroup relations in terms of the ways colonization has affected racial domination and the responses of the dominated group. When applied to U.S. racial and ethnic relations, the model assumes that persons of color in America share many of the same experiences that conquered people in Third-World nations have experienced.

colonized minorities   Ethnic groups, generally indigenous to an area in which they become minorities, who are forced to become a part of the society of colonizers.

conflict theory   A theory emphasizing that power and value differences exist between dominant and subordinate groups and that social conflicts are normal consequences of these differences.

consensus (order) theories   Theories emphasizing that the underlying order and unity of society rest on a consensus concerning basic values and norms of behavior among the different groups within it.

cultural assimilation by addition   The subprocess of inclusion through which the members of a subordinate group acquire the culture of the dominant group but retain or elaborate most, or a significant portion, of their own culture.

cultural assimilation by substitution   The subprocess of inclusion through which the members of a subordinate group gradually relinquish their own culture and acquire that of the dominant group.

discrimination   An unfavorable action toward people because they are members of a particular racial or ethnic group.

frontier thesis   Frederick Jackson Turner's theory stating that the Western American frontier functioned as a great leveler of persons and a blender of cultures to create a social melting pot.

identificational assimilation   The subprocess through which both minority group members and majority group members come to identify the minority group members as full members of the larger society.

ideology of cultural pluralism   A set of beliefs based on the assumption that the members of every American ethnic group should be free to participate in all of the society's major institutions (e.g., schools, jobs, politics) while simultaneously retaining or elaborating their own ethnic heritage and social institutions.

ideology of secession   A system of beliefs based on the assumption that ethnic groups within a society should separate completely and form new, independent societies.

ideology of separatism   A system of beliefs based on the assumption that there should be a high degree of separation in the cultural, public, and social lives of dominant and subordinate groups.

immigrant minorities   Minority groups that were created through voluntary immigration.

marital assimilation   The subprocess of inclusion through which the dominant and subordinate groups gradually merge through intermarriage.

melting-pot ideology   A set of beliefs based on the assumption that the culture and society of each subordinate group should be blended with the culture and society of the host group to produce a new and different culture and society.

melting-pot model   A specific vision of complete assimilation shared by those who accept the ideology of the melting pot.

model of assimilation   A hypothetical conception of the specific way in which a smaller group that is outside a larger group becomes an integral part of the larger group.

model of cultural pluralism   See "pluralist model."

pluralist model   A specific vision of complete assimilation proposed by advocates of the ideology of pluralism.

prejudice   An unfavorable attitude toward people because they are members of a particular racial or ethnic group.

primary relationships   Warm, close human relationships that are regulated mainly by sentiments of liking and affection and are characteristic of small, tightly knit groups such as the family.

primary structural assimilation   The subprocess of inclusion through which dominant and subordinate group members engage in close, personal interactions with members of the other group.

secondary relationships   Human relationships that take place outside of small, tightly knit groups such as the family and are regulated mainly by conventional social roles and norms, administrative rules, and laws.

secondary structural assimilation   The subprocess of inclusion through which dominant-group and subordinate-group members engage in nondiscriminatory interactions within occupational, educational, civic, neighborhood, and public recreational settings.

separatist model   A specific pluralist vision of intergroup relations in which the cultures, institutions, and social lives of subordinate groups are highly separated from those of the dominant group.

theory of assimilation subprocesses   Gordon's theory of assimilation. It identifies seven subprocesses of assimilation, operating simultaneously and at varying rates of speed, to bring about various types of intergroup merger. The theory states that cultural assimilation may occur without necessarily leading to the remaining forms of assimilation; however, once primary assimilation occurs, the other forms inevitably follow.

theory of internal colonialism   Maintains that if a group enters a society involuntarily, power and value conflicts will characterize the relations between the dominating and dominated groups until social conflicts between the groups result in their eventual separation.

transmuting pot   The idea that the melting pot metaphor is often used to describe the social processes that lead, in fact, to Anglo conformity.

 # Notes

1. Some additional theories center on concepts such as ethnogenesis, ethnic enclaves, middleman minorities, social class conflict, dual labor markets, split labor markets, and intergroup competition.

2. Although it is useful for comparison to think of Anglo Americans as sharing a single set of standards, there is a substantial diversity within this "host," "charter," or "core" group. Gordon (1964:74) employed one term, the core subsociety, to refer to middle-class Anglo American standards and another term, the core group, to refer to the standards of the entire Anglo American group.

3. Eighteen languages were spoken in New Amsterdam at the time it was annexed by the English (Hansen 1945:39).

4. To be sure, this process operates in both directions. As the subordinate group acquires the culture of the dominant group, the dominant group also will acquire some aspects of the culture of the subordinate group. For the

sake of clarity, we defer a consideration of such important complications.

5. Gordon's (1964:31–38) analysis clearly recognized the importance of the distinction between secondary and primary relationships, but he did not carry the terms over into the naming of the subprocesses of assimilation.

6. We consider in later chapters some problems in assessing various aspects of marital assimilation.

7. We explore these concepts more fully in Chapter 5.

8. We do not list cultural assimilation by addition here because it does not lead to the disappearance of the groups; however, we soon discuss the crucial role this subprocess of assimilation plays in our analysis. In later chapters, we introduce additional subprocesses.

9. Gordon's theory specifies that cultural assimilation only may last indefinitely and also that primary assimilation is the watershed point in the movement toward full merger, but

the status of secondary assimilation in the theory is to some extent unclear. We interpret the theory to mean that the process of merger may stop indefinitely either after cultural assimilation or after secondary assimilation.

10. This term is generally accepted and will be used in this book. Gordon (1964:85) attributed it to Cole and Cole (1954).

11. For a related effort to describe an ideal or perfect cultural pluralism, see Murguía (1989: 109–111).

12. This view of pluralism has also been called "consensual pluralism" (Horton 1966: 708) and "liberal pluralism" (Gordon 1964:88).

13. Scholars who focus on interethnic relations in Third World countries generally refer to this form of pluralism as cultural pluralism (Horowitz 1985:135–139).

14. Linton (1936:326–327) commented, for instance, that the "solid American citizen" may thank "a Hebrew deity in an Indo-European language that he is 100 percent American."

15. In contrast, Mills (1956), among others, maintained that a relatively small number of people actually make the decisions that appear to be made through democratic procedures.

16. Tables 2.1, 2.2, and 2.3 distinguish between cultural assimilation by substitution and cultural assimilation by addition in the descriptions of the goals concerning assimilation rather than in the headings.

The Rise of Anglo American Society

George Washington presided at the Constitutional Convention of 1787 where those present debated who should be counted as citizens. The Anglo American group became dominant and established its standards as paramount. This group's legacy in the United States has been the dominance of the English language and customs as well as English ideas of commerce, law, government, and religion.

*You will do well to inoculate the Indians by means of blankets, as well as
to try every other method that can serve to extirpate this execrable race.*

—Sir Jeffrey Amherst

*. . . all children born of any negro or other slave, shall be slaves as their
fathers were for the term of their lives.*

—Maryland Law of 1664

The process through which many immigrants and their descendants appear to have passed to become full members of American society was described briefly in Chapter 1. For those considered to be members of the "White race" this process appears frequently to have required a period of about three generations. In Chapter 2 we sketched some of the events that, by 1700, enabled the English to gain control over a strip of land along the Atlantic seacoast of North America and to generate and adopt the Anglo conformity ideology of assimilation. We also reviewed two additional ideologies of assimilation—the melting pot and cultural pluralism—and an antiassimilationist ideology—separatism.

This chapter has two main purposes. First, we discuss further how the Anglo American group came into existence in the seventeenth century and established its standards as paramount. Second, we describe certain crucial variations in the operation of the processes of intergroup adjustment during the colonial period. Some groups (for example, the Dutch, the Scotch-Irish, and the Germans) were propelled more or less strongly toward a merger with the Anglo American group; but two other prominent groups, the Native Americans[1] and Africans as noted in Chapter 2, generally were held at or desired to remain at a distance. The varying degrees and qualities of assimilation and separation experienced by different groups during these formative years left a lasting imprint on the social order of the Anglo Americans. This imprint continues even now to affect intergroup relations in the United States.

The English Legacy

Hardly more than a century after their successful beginnings at Jamestown, Virginia (1607), and Plymouth, Massachusetts (1620), the 13 American colonies of the English were well established. By that time, the English language, English customs, and English ideas of commerce, law, government, and religion were predominant throughout the region. The conditions in the New World promoted, and sometimes required, new ways of doing things; so the various elements of English culture and society had been modified in myriad and complex ways to produce the complicated mixture of peoples and cultures of the new "American" society and culture. A consideration of some early developments within this new society—English in broad outline but with many non-English elements—is crucial to an understanding of racial and ethnic relations in America today. To illustrate, we first review how certain legal and political traditions were transplanted from Europe to America.

Both Jamestown and Plymouth were founded by commercial companies that hoped to establish profitable businesses in America. These companies, operating under a charter granted by King James I, worked with varying degrees of success to colonize the territories granted to them. The London Company landed 104 men and boys in 1607 to construct a trading post that was named Jamestown. When the second boatload of settlers arrived early in the next year, the original group had been reduced by disease and conflicts with Indians to less than half of their original number. The next several years were filled with misery and discouragement for these early settlers, and their suffering was made worse by the seeming pointlessness of their efforts (Burner, Fox-Genovese, and Bernhard 1991:34; Morison 1972:87–90). As employees of the company, most of these unfortunates had little stake in the enterprise. As would be true later for hundreds of thousands of others, they were expected to work as bonded servants for a specified number of years (usually seven) in order to pay for their passage and keep. Moreover, little was produced in the colony during the early years that could be sent to England for sale; consequently, the investors in the London Company were not making the profits they had hoped for; and, unless changes were made, the entire enterprise was in danger of failing.

Three important changes were made in the organization of the Jamestown colony. First, the king for a time discontinued his direct control of the colony. Second, the company (now the Virginia Company) began to grant settlers land and stock in the company so that they, too, would have a stake in its success. Third, in 1619, the company permitted a representative assembly to be established. This assembly, which has been widely hailed as the beginning of representative democracy in America, could enact any law that was not contrary to the laws of England. The king retained veto power, but the Virginia settlers had a great deal of control over their own affairs.

Like most other Europeans, the investors in Jamestown thought it possible that gold and silver would be discovered by the expeditions they financed. They also hoped to establish a profitable trade in furs and other goods with the Indians and to use products from the forests to supply England's navy. No riches in precious metals were to be found in the Chesapeake Bay area, however, and factionalism threatened the very existence of the colony; but the discovery that Virginia was an excellent place to grow tobacco provided the economic foundation that was needed for the colony to survive. In Morison's (1972:90) words, "Virginia went tobacco-mad" and by 1618 "exported 50,000 pounds' weight of tobacco to England."

Many investors in the London and Virginia companies suffered financial losses; so, understandably, they may have considered their efforts in America to be a failure. Yet from the vantage point of the present, the events at Jamestown were of the greatest significance in establishing the social and cultural framework of the English colonies and of their descendant, the United States.

The second early success in the colonization of English America also occurred under the sponsorship of the Virginia Company: the founding of Plymouth by the Pilgrims. In this case though, as is well known, the 102 Pilgrims who agreed to cross the

Atlantic on the *Mayflower* sought to separate themselves from the Church of England in order to practice their own version of the Protestant faith, as well as to find improved economic conditions. And so it is not surprising to learn that the variation of English life they founded emphasized not only English ideas and ways but also those of their particular Protestant religious group. This fact played an extremely important role in the subsequent English immigration to America and in shaping the value system that became predominant in colonial American society.

Another group of dissenters from the Church of England also gained a charter to establish a colony in New England; and in 1630 some 800 members of this group, who wished to practice a "purified" version of Protestantism, emigrated to Massachusetts Bay. There they established several colonies (including Boston) that were more religious than commercial in nature, which attracted many people to them for religious reasons. During the first ten years, between 15,000 and 20,000 more Puritans reached the Massachusetts Bay Colony (Burner, Fox-Genovese, and Bernhard 1991:37; Jordan and Litwack 1987:25). Possibly twice that number had arrived in other portions of the lands claimed by England, making this the first period of heavy immigration to America.

The comparatively large size of the English immigration at this time is significant. Consider, by contrast, what happened in New Netherland. The Dutch companies that founded New Netherland were attempting to colonize at roughly the same time as the English, but their efforts to increase the population were not as successful. At one point, the Dutch West India Company offered large grants of land along the Hudson River to members of the company who would finance the passage of fifty families. This inducement did not, however, lead to the volume of immigration that was taking place in the English colonies. When the English occupied this territory (1664), the population of the English colonies may have been six or seven times as large as that of New Netherland. The task of conquest, therefore, was greatly simplified, and New Netherland was captured without a struggle. English control of the coast now stretched without interruption from Massachusetts through Virginia. These considerations remind us again that as Anglo American society expanded, the *standards* of the new society were being established. The very meaning of the terms *American* and *foreigner* was coming into being, as was the idea that the metamorphosis of the latter into the former required conformity to the Anglo American pattern of living.

These newly established standards involved more than ethnicity, however. Europeans had been taught throughout the Christian era that all people are brothers, but they nevertheless considered some peoples to be inferior to others (Gossett 1963:8–11). To illustrate, each European national group exhibited **ethnocentrism**—the practically universal tendency to consider one's own society to be superior to all others (Sumner [1906]1960:27). Consequently, this attitude resulted in more favorable treatment for members of the in-group than members of the out-group. Despite their ethnocentrism, however, the European nationalities shared many **folkways,** customary practices that regulate every aspect of life, ranging from what kind of clothing is acceptable to how many spouses a person may have, and **mores,** which are folkways that concern society's welfare (Sumner [1906]1960:18). On the basis of their shared folkways and mores (centered on Christianity), the European groups distinguished themselves as "civilized" and the Indians as inferior "savages." Although some individual Europeans considered the

Indians' ways of life to be pure and noble, the belief grew and spread during the seventeenth century that the cultural differences between Europeans and non-Europeans were so great that neither the Indians nor the Africans were suitable materials for complete assimilation into the developing society of the Whites.

The ethnocentrism of the English at the beginning of the colonization period may have included some hostility based on differences in skin color; however, as we shall soon see, Indian–White relations and Black–White relations in the English colonies appear not to have been shaped markedly by the **doctrine of White supremacy,** which was based on the belief that Whites were becoming dominant because they were biologically superior to other racial groups (Fredrickson 1971:242–252). This doctrine (to which we return in Chapter 5) has been elaborated mainly in the last two centuries and, thus, is a product of the modern era.

Indian–English Relations

To understand the past and present experience of the American Indians, we must begin with two central facts. First, the Indians discovered America. Archaeological evidence indicates that there were people in Alaska by 25,000 B.C.; they had reached South America by 15,000 B.C. (Spencer, Jennings et al. 1977:6–12). Thus, when the ancestors of some Anglo Americans disembarked from the *Mayflower,* the ancestors of some American Indians were already there to meet them. From the time of the early contacts to the present, the Indians' lands gradually have been occupied by invaders.

The second fact to be noted concerns the diversity of societies and cultures among the Indian tribes. At the outset, at least two hundred different tribes or bands stretched across the continent (Spicer 1980a:58). These societies possessed cultures that varied in many significant ways. Consider, for example, the diversity of languages. At least two hundred separate languages (not counting dialects) were spoken among the Indians at the time of first contact.[2] Although the members of these societies could communicate with one another through interpreters and sign language, their languages sometimes differed from one another as much as English and Chinese. Even closely related languages might differ as much as French and Spanish (Spencer 1977a:37–39).

The Indian societies differed also in the way they made their living and the manner in which they were organized. Many of the tribes were hunting and gathering societies; others lived primarily from small-scale gardening; still others had developed more advanced agricultural methods. These societies ranged from very small, simply organized groups to comparatively large, highly organized groups. The diversity of Indian cultures and societies was so great, as we shall see, that they were seldom able to lay aside their differences in order to face the invaders in a unified way; hence, the interactions among the different groups resulted in a bewildering array of changing relationships.

The Iroquois Confederacy, for example, consisted of an alliance of five tribes: Cayugas, Mohawks, Oneidas, Onondagas, and Senecas. This organization probably was formed before the arrival of the Europeans as a defensive measure in a longstanding conflict between the Iroquois and the Algonkians. By the time the Europeans arrived, the

Iroquois were among the most politically and militarily active people in the Northeast. They had achieved dominance over a large region and had established an active trading network throughout it (Nash 1974:13–25).

A different confederation of Indian tribes was present in the Chesapeake Bay area when the English founded Jamestown. This confederation, named "Powhatans" after their leading chief, already had had some unpleasant contacts with Europeans and was therefore somewhat suspicious of these newcomers. The Powhatans did not, however, attempt immediately to expel the English settlers, although they greatly outnumbered them. Since the Powhatans were engaged in warfare with other Indian tribes, they hoped to form an alliance with the English. Besides, the Indians had no way of knowing about the dangers of European diseases or the size of the immigration to come.[3] Had the Indians wished to end Jamestown, they could have done so easily. In fact, the colony would not have survived its first winter without the Powhatans' help.

During the early years, the Jamestown settlers did not have a fixed policy toward the Indians. The king had given the land to the Virginia Company, but he had left the problem of dealing with the Indians to the colonists. The colonists knew that the Indians might reject their efforts to make use of the land or take possession of it; consequently, it was not at all clear how this delicate matter was to be handled. The ethnocentrism of the English, of course, led them to hope that the Indians would recognize the "superiority" of English culture, welcome its "benefits," cede their lands, become converted to Christianity, and serve willingly as a labor force for the colonists. The Indians, however, soon made it plain that they saw their own culture as superior and were not going to volunteer to perform the hard labor that would be required to make Jamestown a self-sustaining enterprise. When the colonists attempted to force the Indians to work, conflict between the two groups erupted.

Despite a slow start, the population of Jamestown grew rapidly after tobacco production commenced. Beginning with the struggling survivors of the first three years (about 60 people), the population reached 1,200 in 1624 (Jordan and Litwack 1987:21). This rapid increase in population created a great demand for additional land for tobacco plantations, which in turn led to increased friction with the Indians. By 1622, the Powhatans realized they had made a serious mistake; so they launched a full-scale effort to drive the colonists out. They killed almost one-third of the invaders but did not succeed in ending the colony. They did succeed, however, in convincing this particular group of English people that there could be no lasting accommodation between the groups. The hope of Christianizing and "civilizing" the "savages" was abandoned as an official policy.[4] Beyond this point, the English generally sought to seize the Indians' lands and to subjugate or eliminate the Indians themselves.

The Indians responded in kind. In 1644, they tried again—though by now they were much weaker—to drive the English into the sea. Again, they inflicted heavy casualties on the Whites but could not end English colonization. At the conclusion of this conflict, the English signed a treaty with the Powhatans that, in effect, initiated the reservation system. The treaty, in Nash's (1974:65) words, "recognized that assimilation of the two peoples was unlikely and guaranteed to the indigenous people a sanctuary from white land hunger and aggression." In this way, the Whites set into motion a method of conquest that was used repeatedly for more than two centuries. As a rule, major conflicts were ended through the signing of treaties that assured the Indians certain "reserved" lands, which, after a while, would be infiltrated, seized, and occupied. Each time, new reservations would be created over which the Indians would be guaranteed permanent control. Soon, however, a new round of encroachments would begin.

The relationships between the Puritans and the Indians of several tribes in the Massachusetts Bay region were similar to those that developed in Virginia. The initial contacts, made with the Wampanoags, generally were friendly; and, as in Virginia, the assistance of the Indians proved to be essential to the survival of the colonists.[5] The Indians of Massachusetts also were eager to establish trade relations and military alliances with the colonists; and, in fact, an alliance between the Puritans and Massasoit, Chief of the Wampanoags, was kept in force for over forty years.

The alliance with Massasoit did not prevent the colonists from occupying Indian lands, however. At first this practice caused little difficulty because the Indian population in eastern Massachusetts already had been greatly reduced by epidemics introduced by European fishermen and explorers (Snipp 1989:20–21). But as the main Puritan immigration commenced in the 1630s, the desire for land mounted and so did friction between the groups.

To an even greater extent than in Virginia, the policy of the English toward the Indians in New England was ambivalent. The English definitely wished to occupy the Indians' land, which might have the effect of driving the Indians away, but they also were eager to force the Indians to discontinue their "heathenish" beliefs and rituals and adopt the "civilized" religion and culture of the English, which required that they remain close at hand.

The Puritans' ambivalence may be seen in the arguments that arose among them concerning their right to occupy the land. Roger Williams, for example, maintained that the king had no right to give away the Indians' land and that the colonists were occupying it illegally. Although the leaders of the Plymouth colony considered Williams to be a radical, his belief that the Indians' land should be purchased from them already had become the basis for the official American Indian policies of Spain and Holland. Most of the English, though, did not accept the idea that the Indians were the true owners of the land. Various legal doctrines were advanced to justify taking the land, the most important of which was the doctrine of *vacuum domicilium*.[6] According to this view, the land claimed by the American Indians was in reality "unoccupied." This curious contention rested on the conviction that, to be occupied, land had to be put to "civilized" uses. Civilized uses, in turn, were the very ones to which the Puritans wished to put the land. One passenger of the *Mayflower*, argued as follows: "Their land is spacious and void, and they are few, and do but run over the grass, as do also the foxes and wild beasts. They are not industrious . . . to use either the land or the commodities of it, but all spoils . . . for want of manuring, gathering, ordering, etc. . . . . So it is lawful now to take a land which none useth" (Quint, Cantor, and Albertson 1978:11).[7]

In short, the "failure" of the indigenous population to use the land in ways that the settlers deemed appropriate was interpreted by many Puritans to mean that the land was "unoccupied" and could be used as they saw fit. As the settlers acquired additional land, either by seizure or through some form of purchase, they encountered the Indians of various tribes and attempted to bring them under English rule. As the frontier moved south and west, various small groups of Indians were left behind in "reserved" areas and "praying" villages. The English expected these Indians to adopt English culture in every particular way as rapidly as possible and, simultaneously, to discontinue all of their Indian ways of thinking and acting. This did not mean that the English were prepared to permit the Indians who succeeded in mastering English culture to occupy positions of leadership and wealth within Puritan society, to enter into their homes as equals, or to marry into their families. It meant that the Indians were to be tolerated within the physical limits of New England, provided they appeared to the eye to be "civilized."

The Indians, for their part, had shown strong resistance to becoming a part of Anglo American society. They wished to retain their own tribal identities, traditions, and institutions. From their viewpoint, they were the civilized hosts whereas the Whites were the barbaric invaders. Consequently, some Indian leaders, such as the Wampanoag Chief Metacom (whom the English called King Philip), mounted several unsuccessful attempts to unite the tribes in the region and to drive the English out.

By the last quarter of the seventeenth century, the Anglo American colonists of Virginia and New England had devised a two-pronged policy toward the Indians. The Indians were expected either to give up whatever lands the colonists wanted and to move peacefully beyond the frontier, or they were to remain within the confines of Anglo American settlement under watchful eyes. A refusal by the Indians to accept one of these alternatives could lead to their annihilation or forcible removal from the area. In this way, the Indians either were excluded physically from participation in Anglo American society or were permitted to cling to the lower rungs of the social ladder. Despite the numerous differences that existed among the various tribes, including such things as the extent to which they had allied themselves with the colonists, all of those in America at the time of the "discovery" soon were considered by the majority of the English to be essentially alike. The label "Indian" was applied to all of the indigenous people. Eventually, they came to be regarded as unassimilable and ineligible for full membership in the new host society being created. This view was not shared by all of the Anglo Americans, however. Even though the ideology of separatism was paramount for more than two centuries, some members of the dominant group continued to hope to "civilize" and assimilate the Indians; and during the latter third of the nineteenth century, the ideology of Anglo conformity regained supremacy in Indian affairs.

The situation of Indian–English contact, first in the Northeast and then later in other parts of North America, illustrates clearly the way interracial and interethnic contacts may lead to repeated and persistent conflicts as the participants struggle to gain control of land and other resources and to establish themselves as the dominant group. Indian–English contacts also represent our first illustration of a vital point to be developed in Chapters 6 through 13: *Minority groups that have a strong sense of group identity and are socially self-sufficient at the time they become subordinate are likely to resist assimilation strongly for long periods of time.* Minorities of this type are highly unlikely to pass, in only a few generations, through the process of assimilation described by Park's race-cycle theory or Gordon's assimilation theory. After three generations, most Indians exhibited low levels of cultural assimilation into Anglo American society; and they exhibited very low levels of secondary, primary, and marital assimilation.

Servants and Slaves

African or Black people were represented among the first groups to arrive among the Spanish explorers in the New World, but the initial instance of Black "immigration" to what is now the United States occurred in Virginia in 1619.[8] It is recorded that the Virginia settlers bought "twenty Negers," who arrived on a Dutch warship (Frazier 1957:3). Although not much is known about the treatment of these 20 people, one thing appears to be established: They "were not slaves in a legal sense" (Franklin and Moss 1988:53). They were purchased as indentured or bonded servants rather than as absolute slaves. As we have noted, many of the White people who were a part of the English colony in Virginia also had come there under a similar arrangement.

Englishmen who were impoverished or had been convicted of a crime sometimes were sold into bondage for a specified number of years. Even free men sometimes were willing to accept a period of servitude in return for their passage to the New World. This system was recognized in England as legal and profitable to all parties, and the servants under this arrangement were sometimes referred to as slaves (Handlin 1957:7–9). Through such contracts, England profited by reducing the number of people who were public charges; the purchaser of the servants profited by having cheap, "slave" labor available for a fixed period; and the servants profited by having the opportunity to escape their unpleasant circumstances at home and, perhaps, to get a new start in life. Even during the period of indenture, a slave had certain rights and was, therefore, legally protected from excessive harshness by the master. Initially, these protections apparently applied to the Black bonded servants as well as to the Whites. English law during this period provided that "a slave who had been baptized became infranchised" (Frazier 1957:23). Those who were so treated might then become free. Although it is probable that Black servants were not treated in exactly the same way as White servants, even in the early years, much evidence favors the view that the laws regulating the rights and obligations of servitude applied to the members of both races and all nations.[9]

The main issues that provoked racial distinctions in legislation were the question of the length of the term of service, the problem of the standing of Christianized slaves, and the legal position of the children of slaves. For at least 20 years after Black servants were introduced into Virginia, many employers had a definite preference for White laborers and were also unwilling to commit themselves for long periods to the support of servants. As time passed, however, the profitability of Black labor increased and so, understandably, did the masters' desire for it; hence, by the 1660s, both Maryland and Virginia had taken legal steps to make the attainment of freedom more difficult for Black slaves. For example, in 1664, Maryland's legislature passed an act that required all non-Christian slaves, especially "Negroes," to serve for life (Degler 1972:71). This particular law was later repealed to prevent unscrupulous masters from marrying their White female servants to Black male servants in order to force the women into longer periods of servitude and to gain possession of their children. In the meantime, however, the noose around the freedom of Black people was permanently tightened. Since the law of 1664 had left open the possibility that Christianized Blacks might someday become free, a new law was passed stating that baptism did not amount to manumission (i.e., being freed).

A similar process of legalizing lifetime slavery for Blacks, even those who were Christians, occurred in Virginia. In 1661, a law imposing penalties on runaway slaves distinguished clearly between Black and White runaways and implied that the period of indenture for at least some Blacks was forever (Franklin and Moss 1988:54). Another law passed in the same year made this racial distinction hereditary. The ability of any Black person to gain freedom in Virginia seems to have ended by 1682. In that year, a law was passed establishing Black slavery for life, whether an individual had been baptized or not. In hardly more than 60 years, then, the Africans who had entered the colonies of Maryland and Virginia descended from a legal position similar to that of the indentured servants from other nations to a status of lifelong bondage. But the gap in status was not yet absolute. The terms *servant* and *slave* were still sometimes used interchangeably.

The possibility remained that at least some White people also might be reduced to the type of slavery that had been forced on Blacks, which in return influenced the choices of Whites who might otherwise have chosen to come to Maryland and Virginia. White servants frequently wrote letters to their relatives and friends back home warning them not to come to these colonies and, in some cases, begging for help. One Richard Frethorne ([1623]1988:36), for example, wrote his parents that "there is nothing to be gotten here but sickness and death." He pleaded with them to redeem his debt. Travelers also told of the harshness of White servitude.[10] Such places as Pennsylvania and New York, therefore, frequently were more attractive to free-born immigrants who feared they might be bound over as servants if they went to Maryland or Virginia. In the latter colonies, the masters' desire to encourage the immigration of White settlers and an increasing preference for Black labor on the plantations led to a gradual strengthening of the position of the White slaves (Handlin 1957:15). The Blacks, who had come to the colonies involuntarily and who did not write horror stories to those back home, were unable to benefit from this small source of protection. Neither were they able, at this point, to become enfranchised through baptism and thus claim the protection of the laws of England. In this way, the condition of the White servants gradually improved whereas the condition of the Black slaves slowly became worse.

The spread of the plantation system of agriculture increased the width of the status gap between Black and White servants. Black laborers could not desert the plantation and disappear among the citizenry nearly so easily as could White laborers. Therefore, the masters' investment in Black laborers was protected. Furthermore, Black women and children could be used in the fields along with the men, thus decreasing the number of unproductive hands at the masters' disposal (Frazier 1957:29–30).

As the plantation economy developed throughout the South, it was obvious to the members of the planter class that the fewer rights laborers had and the harder they were required to work, the lower would be the cost of their labor and the larger would be the planters' profits. Thus, the planters encouraged measures that moved the Blacks further from the status of human beings and closer to the status of mere property. Under these conditions, the Blacks had descended, by the beginning of the eighteenth century, into a state of complete, legally defenseless bondage. The term *slave* became unambiguous. The conclusion now had been reached that to be a slave *meant* that a person was of African descent. An African heritage, and particularly black skin, had become its symbols. The equation of "Black" with "slave" became fixed, making it impossible even for "free" Blacks to enjoy their legal rights.

The relegation of the African slaves to the status of property also increased the masters' desire to own more of them; and the increasing size of the slave population brought with it some new problems for the Whites. The importation of slaves increased so rapidly that in some places the planters became alarmed by the possibility that the slaves would become too numerous to control. Georgia, for example, attempted at first to prevent the importation of Black slaves entirely so that rebellions would be less likely to occur and the colony would be easier to defend. In South Carolina, the number of Black slaves had become so large by 1700 that the planters were permitted to have no more than six adult Black males for each White servant (Frazier 1957:32). Nevertheless, the White–Black ratio throughout the southern colonies declined sharply. In 1670 it was higher than 14 to 1; but by 1730, it had declined to less than 3 to 1; and by 1750, it had reached 1.5 to 1.[11]

The concern of the dominant group was well placed. Despite the fact that the masters took extraordinary precautions to keep the slaves under their dominion, slave resistance was a problem from the first. This fact frequently has been obscured by the claim that as long as they were well fed and were not treated harshly, the Black slaves were usually happy, contented people—what Jacobs and Landau (1971:100) called the *Gone With the Wind* version of slavery. This view of Black people was used to justify slave-holding; but a closer inspection of the historical record contradicts the thesis that Black slaves were happy and did not resist their enslavement. At the time of their acquisition—usually by purchase from African slave traders who captured their victims in the valleys of the Gambia, Niger, and Congo rivers—many slaves resisted vigorously. Frequently, as they were being transported through the infamous "Middle Passage" to the New World, many incidents occurred aboard ship. There were instances in which the slaves overcame the crews and captured the ships on which they were imprisoned. These revolts were so common that "they were considered one of the principal hazards of the slave trade" (Frazier 1957:85). Moreover, when escape or attack seemed impossible, many slaves jumped overboard to their deaths.[12]

The resistance to slavery by no means ended after the slaves arrived in America. Throughout the nearly two and one-half centuries of American slavery, most of the main forms of overt and covert resistance known to mankind were employed. From the beginning, individual slaves revolted against the system by running away. Considering the difficulties of all other forms of resistance, this may have been the most effective way to strike back. But even running away presented great difficulties of survival for one person alone. Some slaves were convinced that such an effort was hopeless (Rawick 1996:61). In many cases, fugitive slaves banded together and established independent "maroon communities" in various inaccessible places. They also sometimes were able to find protection and long-term sanctuary within Indian societies. Probably the most famous instance of maroon communities being established in conjunction with Indian societies is that of the Black Seminoles.[13] Black slaves in South Carolina and Georgia learned that they could escape across the border into Florida and enjoy either full freedom under the Spanish or an extremely favorable form of vassalage with the Seminoles. Among the Seminoles, the fugitive slaves typically established separate communities, adopted many aspects of Indian culture and, in some cases, intermarried with the Indians (Mulroy 1993:6–21).

The likelihood of escape by running away was dramatically improved near the beginning of the nineteenth century. At this time, the existing arrangements for assisting fugitive slaves, primarily those in the northern states, were enlarged and made more efficient as the complicated network of people and facilities known as the **Underground Railroad** gradually took form. Several "tracks" to the North developed; however, during the decades immediately preceding the Civil War, the center of the Railroad's activities was Ohio. Hundreds of "stations" and "conductors" assisted the fugitives in their long journey to havens in the North and in Canada.

Also during the nineteenth century, individual forms of resistance to slavery were supplemented by organized resistance. As a preventive measure, the Whites often separated slaves of the same tribe. Most slaves were not permitted to speak their native tongues or to retain their African names; and they were permitted to travel only for short distances and under careful surveillance. White slave patrols were used extensively to police the activities of Blacks and to interfere with any disapproved organizational efforts. In most places, it was illegal for a slave to learn to read or write or for anyone to teach a slave these skills. News of slave unrest was suppressed to diminish the possibility that such news might generate or strengthen resistance in other places. In brief, the masters were at great pains to keep the slaves in a state of ignorance and to disrupt communications among them. Under such circumstances, planning and executing a revolt were no easy matter.

We return to the issue of slave resistance in Chapter 6. For the moment though, we emphasize that the relations of Blacks and Whites during the period discussed illustrates the process through which the White American majority came into being and placed non-White people into a subordinate position. By the beginning of the eighteenth century, the Blacks as a group were physically within the developing Anglo American society and played an absolutely vital economic role there; but they were not candidates for full membership in the society. They were not encouraged, in many cases not permitted, to undergo cultural assimilation; and after three generations they certainly exhibited low levels of secondary, primary, and marital assimilation. As was true for the Indians, the human interactions and acceptance that are necessary for the "eventual" assimilation of Park's race-cycle theory to take place did not exist. The statuses of Indian and Black groups had been degraded during the seventeenth century. Therefore no one knew where or when the descent would end. To the questions, "What is an American?" and "How does a person become an American?" a majority of the members of the dominant group had adopted one answer—Anglo conformity. They also had established policies that raised barriers in the paths of any Indians and Africans who might also wish to adopt that same answer.

The eighteenth century created some challenges to Anglo American dominance. The first test came from a very heavy immigration to America of the Irish, particularly the so-called Scotch-Irish of Ulster.[14] A second test came from a heavy immigration of

Germans; and the revolutionary war of 1776 represented a third. Let us turn first to the immigration from Ireland.

 The Colonial Irish

The Irish began to arrive in the English colonies almost at once. By 1610, according to Adamic (1944:315), hundreds of the Irish had reached Jamestown. Throughout the seventeenth century, many more fled from the troubled Emerald Isle to the Atlantic colonies.

The largest and most discussed prerevolutionary immigration from Ireland to colonial America, however, consisted mainly of people from Northern Ireland (Ulster). Many people living in Ulster at this time were descendants of immigrant Scots who had been brought to Northern Ireland by the English early in the seventeenth century to work the Plantation of Ulster.[15] In contrast to the other citizens of Ireland, who were predominantly Catholic, the Irish of Scots descent were mainly Presbyterians. Although the Presbyterianism of these people was involved in their departure from Ireland, economic reasons were probably much more important. Presbyterians, as well as Catholics, were the targets of new laws passed by the Protestant English rulers of Ireland. One law permitted absentee English landowners, who owned the lands on which most Irish lived and worked, to raise rents as high as they wished. As the landowners raised the rents, the Irish were reduced to a state of poverty. Greeley (1971:28) quoted Jonathan Swift as stating that "The rise of our rents is squeezed out of the very blood, and vitals, and clothes, and dwellings of the tenants, who live worse than English beggars." Under these conditions, a large number of the Irish, particularly those of Scots descent, decided to go to America, beginning markedly around 1717.

More pertinent to our present discussion than their reasons for leaving, however, is the reception that awaited them in the colonies. At first, the Scotch-Irish headed mainly for New England where, in general, they were met with reserve. Although these people were from the British Isles, were mainly Protestants, and were needed to help settle the frontier, they definitely were not accepted wholeheartedly by the now-native Americans. They clearly were regarded as "foreigners" who deviated in certain undesirable ways from the Anglo American ideal pattern of behavior. They were said to drink too much, to fight too much, and to be generally ill-tempered, troublesome, and coarse of speech. Ulstermen generally were regarded "as illiterate, slovenly, and filthy" (Burner, Fox-Genovese, and Bernhard 1991:72). These presumed differences created friction between the Americans and the Scotch-Irish. In one case, for example, a Scotch-Irish Presbyterian meeting house was destroyed (Hansen 1945:49). In another instance, "a mob arose to prevent the landing of the Irish" (Jones 1960:45). In 1718, the Scotch-Irish were blamed for a shortage of food in Boston (Seller 1984:141); and a Boston newspaper stated in 1725 that the difficulty created by the newcomers "gives us an ill opinion of foreigners, especially those coming from Ireland" (Jones 1960:46).

Pennsylvania soon became the most frequent destination of the Scotch-Irish immigrants. Not only did the way they were treated in New England have something to do with this, but also William Penn was actively advertising in Europe for settlers, especially for the frontier areas. So the Ulster Irish were greeted in a much friendlier way in Pennsylvania. Even here though, as the number of Irish immigrants mounted, certain interethnic problems arose. For example, it was said that unless something was done, the Scotch-Irish would "soon make themselves Proprietors of the Province" (Jones 1960:46).

The newcomers apparently were not great respectors of property; they frequently "squatted" on land without paying for it. There was also a strong mutual antagonism between the German and Scotch-Irish settlers of Pennsylvania that led to numerous disturbances. Before long, the Pennsylvania authorities began to discourage the continuation of the Scotch-Irish immigration, so this particular immigrant stream began to move heavily into the frontier regions of Virginia and the Carolinas (Jones 1980:899–900) where they were in constant conflict with the Indians (Burner, Fox-Genovese, and Bernhard 1991:72).

The case of the Scotch-Irish affords an early example of the mixed reactions exhibited by Americans toward most later arrivals. On the one hand, immigrants frequently have been actively recruited to meet labor shortages and populate frontier areas; but, on the other hand, Americans have been afraid the newcomers would compete for land and jobs and would not conform to Anglo American folkways and mores. Perhaps they would, instead, establish an alternative pattern of life or, worse yet, establish themselves as a new dominant group. This ambivalence usually has been displayed in various acts of violence and other forms of hostility against members of the minority ethnic groups. Some of the difficulties encountered by the colonial Scotch-Irish require us to consider them the first large American immigrant minority group.[16]

The feelings of rejection and the acts of hostility were not onesided, however. The Scotch-Irish came to America mainly in groups and tended to stick together after they arrived. They were quite conscious of themselves as a distinctive nationality group and did not mingle easily with the host Anglo Americans. Indeed, they "nurtured a profound hatred for the English" (Burner, Fox-Genovese, and Bernhard 1991:94); and, as mentioned previously, they surely did not get along well with the other noticeable immigrant minority group of the day—the Germans. They were "avid politicians" who "demanded a voice in the lawmaking process" but who "totally disregarded the law if it did not suit them" (Burner, Fox-Genovese, and Bernhard 1991:72).

Given this outline of the entry of the Scotch-Irish into American society, what may be said concerning the course of their inclusion into American life? As Park's formulation of the cycle of race relations would lead us to expect, the contacts between the Scotch-Irish and the other main groups in American society at that time—majority and minorities alike—produced a certain amount of competition and conflict. A gradual accommodation was achieved, however, aided by the migration of the Scotch-Irish to the frontier areas in large numbers. So far, so good. But how rapidly did the Scotch-Irish move toward the fourth stage of Park's race cycle, *eventual* assimilation? To expand our understanding here, we refer to some of the subprocesses of assimilation derived from Gordon's theory that were presented in Chapter 2.

By the standards of Anglo conformity, the Scotch-Irish were good candidates for complete assimilation in three generations. They were White Protestants from the British Isles; and, although the research evidence on these matters is far from complete, most writers agree that those elements of culture (e.g., speech, dress, manners) that served readily to distinguish them from the Anglo Americans were fairly rapidly laid aside. This cultural transformation, however, does not mean that the second-generation

Scotch-Irish (or even the third) became socially indistinguishable from the dominant group. Many, if not most, were likely to select working partners and friends who were Scotch-Irish, and they were likely to marry someone who was Scotch-Irish; hence, secondary, primary, and marital assimilation were still incomplete when cultural assimilation (primarily by substitution) was well advanced. Even though by the time of the Revolutionary War the descendants of the early Scotch-Irish immigrants were for most practical purposes a functioning part of the Anglo American host group, it still is not correct to state, as many writers have, that the Scotch-Irish were at this point assimilated into American society in the Anglo conformity style.[17]

We conclude, then, that the Scotch-Irish were not completely assimilated into the Anglo American majority, even culturally, by the end of the eighteenth century; nevertheless, the various types of assimilation leading toward Anglo conformity were all underway.[18] The main result of these different processes was to help solidify the American majority as a White, Protestant group of British origin. Even though the Scotch-Irish had created certain difficulties for the dominant Anglo Americans, there was never any widespread doubt that the Scotch-Irish could and, given time, would conform to the Anglo American pattern. Moreover, in the opinion of some scholars, even the increased immigration of Catholic Irish before the Revolution did not seriously slow the movement of the Irish into American life (Diner 1996:163). The case of the colonial Germans, however, presented a more serious problem to the majority.

 The Colonial Germans

At approximately the same time that the Scotch-Irish settlers were coming to New England and Pennsylvania, a large number of Germans and German-Swiss were moving to America.[19] As was true for the Scotch-Irish, Pennsylvania proved to be the most popular destination, although some members of the German group went originally to New York, Virginia, the Carolinas, and Georgia. These people, generally referred to as the "Dutch" (from *Deutsch*) or the "Palatines," were quite noticeable to the Anglo Americans. Many of them were members of various Protestant religious sects (e.g., the Mennonites), who dressed distinctively, settled together in rural areas, and did their best to maintain the language and customs of the old country. Although the majority of those who came later were less militantly Protestant, they still usually clustered in farming regions and held themselves apart from all other groups.

The primary area of settlement lay to the west of Philadelphia. Here the Germans, or "Pennsylvania Dutch" as they still are called, established prosperous and well-managed farms. They quickly earned a reputation for thrift, diligence, and farming skill that has continued to the present. And their numbers grew rapidly. By 1766, Benjamin Franklin estimated that one-third of the colony's people were German (Wittke 1964:71).[20]

This large immigration of people who spoke German, who differed clearly from the Anglo Americans in culture, and who tended to settle cohesively in isolated areas aroused a strong antipathy among many of the "old" Americans. Some of the complaints against the Germans were identical to some lodged against the Scotch-Irish. They were said to "squat" illegally on other people's land, and their manners and morals were frequently thought to be rude and unseemly. To a much greater extent than the Scotch-Irish, however, the Germans posed an apparent threat of disloyalty. It was feared that they might set up a separate German state or even, as Benjamin Franklin put it, "Germanize us instead of our Anglifying them, and will never adopt our Language or Customs" (Kamphoefner 1996:152). At one point, a law was passed requiring immigrant Germans to take an oath of allegiance and, during the French and Indian War, many among the Anglo American and Scotch-Irish groups suspected the Germans of sympathizing with the French.

An important result of these differences and suspicions was to intensify the Germans' determination to survive as a group and, thereby, to slow the rate at which they and their descendants adopted the traditions of the Anglo Americans. The German language, only slightly modified by contact with English, was transmitted quite faithfully from the first to the second generation and even from the second to the third. The Germans did not wish to attend English-speaking schools or to participate in the political affairs of the dominant group. The sect Germans, such as the Mennonites, refused to bear arms, to hold public office, and sometimes even to pay taxes.

Since German farmers tended to build stone and heavy wood houses and barns, to buy adjacent lands, and to establish orchards and raise large families, they did not move readily; hence, they were likely to remain in close contact with others of their nationality. They organized publishing houses, German-language newspapers, and fairs and other celebrations to bring their people together on a regular basis. Although the sect Germans were more cohesive than the church Germans (such as the Lutherans), by the end of the eighteenth century, a German's friends still were likely to be Germans; and intermarriage, though increasing, was still low. Consequently, the Germans, especially in Pennsylvania, maintained their sense of ethnic distinctiveness beyond the third generation.

It seems fair to say that in terms of each of the subprocesses we have identified, the assimilation of the Germans into the majority group was slower than that of the Scotch-Irish and was accompanied by greater friction and hostility. This resistance to assimilation meant that the Germans were viewed with greater suspicion by the Anglo Americans. Nevertheless—and this is an important qualification—the German presence in large numbers in American society *did* strengthen further the dominant position of the White Protestants. Suppose, for example, that the Germans had succeeded in "Germanizing" the Anglo Americans and the Scotch-Irish. The dominant group in American society still would have been White and Protestant. It also still would have been European in culture, even if not of British origin. This is another way of noting that there were important similarities as well as differences between the Anglo American and German groups, similarities that, through time, enabled the Anglo American majority to maintain its basic pattern of life as the "standard" pattern.

The Revolutionary Period

Some interesting evidence bearing on the group cohesiveness of the colonial Germans and the Anglo Americans as well as on the group cohesiveness of the Anglo American group itself is provided by the alignments that took place during the Revolutionary War.

Although many claims have been made that particular ethnic groups were solidly behind Washington and the Congress, it appears that the lines of cleavage varied from colony to colony.

The Scotch-Irish of Pennsylvania, for instance, evidently were strongly behind the patriot cause, but in New England the Scotch-Irish served on both sides; and in the back-country of the southern colonies, some were on the loyalist side and some fought at one time or another for both sides (Jones 1980:901–902). The Germans also present a mixed picture. In Pennsylvania, many of the Germans subordinated their dislike of the Scotch-Irish and joined with them against the local loyalists. In Georgia, on the other hand, most of the Germans supported the British. In all probability, the majority of the ordinary German settlers were largely indifferent to the Revolution.

The cleavages within the Anglo American group were regional to some extent, but there also were important social and economic lines of demarcation. The decisive point for the present discussion, however, is this: The majority of those who actively participated in the Revolution, who led the Revolution, and who held the reins of government when the Revolution ended were members of the Anglo American group. This group had become dominant during the seventeenth century and had successfully met the challenges posed by the Scotch-Irish and the Germans during the colonial period. Now a sizable portion of this group had gained full control of the political institutions of the country, thus strengthening still further their claim to represent the ideal pattern for all Americans to follow. More than ever before, to be accepted as fully American one had to conform to the Anglo American model of behavior and appearance.

The events of the first three decades of the existence of the United States worked generally in the direction of consolidating the acceptance of Anglo American ethnicity as the "standard" or "semiofficial" ethnicity of America. One important factor in this trend was a greatly decreased flow of immigrants to the United States between 1793 and 1815. The Napoleonic Wars in Europe interfered markedly with the free flow of international traffic and were the primary cause of the decline in immigration. Since the existing ethnic groups were not being reinforced by sizable infusions from their homelands, the pressures on them to conform to the dominant Anglo American pattern were more effective than might otherwise have been the case.

Another important factor that reinforced the dominance of the Anglo Americans was that by 1790 four out of five Americans were immigrants from the British Isles or their descendants (Easterlin 1980:479). Moreover, and despite the fact that more immigrants had arrived during the eighteenth than in the seventeenth century, most of the American population by this time was native born (Easterlin 1980:477); hence, people who were "native Americans" were becoming an increasingly large proportion of the population.

A third significant factor aiding the consolidation was the success of the Anglo American leaders in strengthening the powers of the postrevolutionary central government. The colonial immigrants from the British Isles were accustomed to the existence of social class differences in wealth and prestige, and these differences were present from the earliest days of the colonization; but these immigrants also believed in democracy and became accustomed to having a share of the power that was vested mainly in a comparatively few wealthy people. Those in the "lower orders" respected wealth but they also respected education and favored as leaders men like Washington, Adams, Jefferson, Franklin, and

Madison who were both wealthy and educated (Sydnor 1965:60); consequently, many of those who led the Revolution and the formation of the American government were men of property. These men also felt a strong central government was needed to protect their interests. In *The Federalist Papers,* Hamilton ([1787]1961:66) argued that unless the national government was strengthened, the states would soon become separate nations. Concerns of this sort led Congress to convene a meeting of leaders in 1787 to amend the Articles of Confederation. Early in the convention, however, the delegates decided to draft a new document—the Constitution.

Practically all of the delegates who came to the convention represented the dominant White Protestant Americans, in general, and were members of the wealthier portion of that group, in particular. They were an aristocracy of wealth, education, and social position. The Constitution that was finally approved by the states benefited many groups that were not specifically represented in the convention. Still, there were economic tensions between Americans who were property owners or merchants, on the one hand, and those who were poor and in debt, on the other; and these economic differences led to some lengthy, occasionally violent, conflicts (Rubenstein 1970).

But this is not the place to engage in the debate over the motives of the framers of the Constitution.[21] The point, rather, is that during the first five years of the postwar period, many internal divisions threatened the very existence of the United States and, simultaneously, the shaky dominance of the White Protestant Americans over a vast territory. The ratification of a new Constitution, written and supported by wealthy representatives of the White Protestant group, was an important step in the direction of consolidating in law the dominant position of this group.

Let us review the argument that has been presented. The effects of the events commencing with the original settlement of Jamestown and Plymouth by people of English ethnicity combined to establish an American nation that was primarily a "fragment" of English culture and society. Outstanding among these events were the conquest of New Netherland; the exclusion of the Indians and Africans from full participation in the developing society; the assimilation of various types and degrees of a large number of Scotch-Irish and German immigrants; the successful Revolutionary War against Britain; the successful beginning of Constitutional government; and the decreased flow of immigrants following the Revolution.

We emphasize again that although the social order that had been established by the end of the eighteenth century was decisively patterned after English society and culture, the pattern itself was not inflexible. The developing *American* society and culture not only affected the immigrants, Indians, and Africans who were in contact with it but was, in return, to some degree affected by them. The crucial argument being presented is that the transformations taking place within this dynamic setting were predominantly toward the fixed Anglo American sociocultural pattern. The upshot was that, by the end of the Napoleonic Wars in 1815, the Anglo-conformity ideology was more firmly established as the normal and accepted view of assimilation than ever before. At this point, the White Protestant Anglo Americans were the unquestioned majority in American society. On the surface at least, it may have seemed only a matter of time until practically all of the Europeans and their descendants would be culturally assimilated by substitution and, perhaps, in every other way.[22]

The Indians and Blacks, of course, were still very visible, and there was no prospect that they would soon disappear. These groups simply lay beyond the practical scope and intentions of the Anglo Americans; they were not genuine candidates for Anglo conformity. The assumption of the dominant group was that America was to be "a White man's country." Fully assimilated Americans and potential Americans were *by definition* White and Protestant.

Much more difficult for the dominant group to accept was the continuing visibility of certain European groups, such as the sect Germans. As stated earlier, a number of the Mennonite groups lived largely apart from all others and clung jealously to their own traditions, language, and religious observances. One who believed in the goals of the Anglo-conformity ideology could argue, of course, that it was wrong for these groups to resist assimilation. The resistors could argue, in turn, that it would be wrong not to maintain their own group life and culture. Here we see an example of the way some groups worked to find an alternative to Anglo conformity as the solution to the problem of intergroup adjustment in America. These groups were dissatisfied with the idea that they should "melt" into the Anglo American majority, but they were unable to present a different view that would be accepted by the dominant group. Their inability to *state* such a view, however, did not prevent them from attempting to *live* along different lines. *Pluralism and separatism, thus, were realities in America long before they were expressed systematically as ideologies.*

We have seen that the Anglo-conformity ideology encountered, survived, and ultimately was strengthened by the challenges of eighteenth-century immigration and the American Revolution; however, the seeds of three rival ideologies—the melting pot, cultural pluralism, and separatism—already were present in American thought. The first two ideologies reached maturity during the first and second halves of the twentieth century, respectively; whereas the third has appealed more or less strongly to different groups at different times. In Chapter 4 we develop these thoughts further against the background of the additional challenges to Anglo conformity that were presented by the heavy immigrations of the nineteenth and twentieth centuries.

 ## Reality Check

INTERVIEW WITH PAM

Pam grew up in Illinois. Both parents have graduate degrees. She is of Irish and German heritage but identifies more with being White than a particular ethnic heritage. Her family relatives have lived in the United States since the early 1800s.

How do you refer to yourself?
I usually just use White or Caucasian. My mom says she is Anglo American. The actual term isn't a big deal because my family is so mixed. I can't really say I'm one ethnicity or another but just a mix of European and everything. White or Caucasian, either one is just fine with me. Sometimes when I'm around relatives who

(continued)

have a strong German background, I can see this is where certain family traits come from. Or when other members of my family can trace back to Ireland, I can feel the identity with that. But it's just kind of a jumbled mess. I think of myself as Caucasian; it just embraces it all for me.

What stands out as most important in your ethnicity?
I think they've been very important to the country—good and bad. I think that for the Caucasian or the Anglo American, the most important thing that they've done is forming the society we live in today and the democracy. Other things have been important but wrong, such as slavery and other such things. When I think about my race, I guess I can identify it with the things that they've done for our nation.

How does your background affect you in your daily life?
It affects me that there are so many people like me. I mean I'm just this Anglo American blonde, very White, complete American. In some ways maybe it makes it easier for me to get certain things than it would be for other people. When I think about my identity, I identify more with being not just a White or Caucasian individual, but also a Caucasian female individual and how that defines my identity more than just my racial group.

When did you first become aware of your ethnicity?
When I was younger. I grew up in a very small farming community in Southern Illinois and it was almost completely White. Then my parents got divorced and my mom and my sister and I moved to an urban area in suburban St. Louis. I began learning about other cultures and making friends from different ethnic groups. I became more aware of my identity and my distinction from other people.

Have you ever been in an uncomfortable situation because of your ethnicity?
Sometimes when I was the actual minority and all my other friends were from other ethnic groups, and people would talk about their experiences and what united them. They shared the same background and I was different. I began to feel uncomfortable, but I also began to realize that this was because typically it would be the other way around. In most cases, it would be mostly White people with just a few other people of different ethnic groups, and I began to understand what people must be going through. Although we were friends and we had a lot in common, there was some distinction.

Tell me about your family.
Everybody has been in the United States for at least a hundred years on either side of the family. They became farmers in Illinois and that's where they lived ever since. Both my parents, especially my mom, always made an effort to try and teach us about different cultures. It's very important to my parents that I get an education and do well and work hard throughout my life. What I respect about my parents is that they are very hard-working individuals. They taught me to be the same way, to just work as hard as I can and do the best I can.

Tell me about your friends.

My closest friends are White, but I also have a lot of friends from different ethnic backgrounds. It's interesting to learn about their cultures too. We go to the movies, go out to a party or a club or something like that with friends from either background. The only thing that maybe we would do separate is that I have friends who go to the historically Black fraternities. Sometimes I go to stuff with them, but sometimes I can understand that it's best that I don't go. There is some separation. But for the most part, I would do the same things with them that I do with my White friends.

Is marriage or a romantic relationship with someone outside your ethnic group acceptable to you?

It's never really come up. I couldn't really say for sure, but I don't think I'd have a problem dating somebody if it was the right person. I'm more concerned that the person I marry have the same aspirations that I have and the same goals and desires for the future that I have, than their race or ethnic group. Some of the older people in my family, like those of my grandparents' age, they might question it a little bit but I think my parents would probably be just fine because they love me enough and they know who I am, that I have certain feelings about racial and ethnic issues, and so I don't think they'd be totally surprised if something like that happened.

Tell me about your high school.

My high school was in a university town, a small university, but close enough to the city so there were a lot of different ethnicities. There was a certain amount of segregation between the races, but there was a lot of mixing too. A little of both. . . . My high school was probably about two-thirds White. The rest was probably Black and Asian. They were so into hiring minority administrators and teachers that the number of minority administrators was high in our school compared to the student population. It was one of the most mixed schools in the area. Even other areas had very high minority populations, they probably had around the same figures that we did, and we lived in the suburbs.

Discussion Questions

Pam has Irish grandparents and German grandparents, but she has developed a different identity that is neither Irish nor German. How did she come to refer to herself as White Anglo American?

Using the subprocesses of assimilation discussed in Chapter 2 as a framework, identify the ways that Pam has assimilated.

What indicators of cultural assimilation are evident in Pam's profile?

How has secondary structural assimilation affected Pam's life?

Do her personal interactions reflect a high degree of primary structural assimilation?

Is she likely to marry someone from another racial or ethnic group?

In what ways might gender influence the extent to which a person assimilates?

How has family background influenced Pam's experiences with other racial and ethnic groups?

What factors facilitated or slowed the assimilation of the Scotch-Irish and German immigrants?

 # Key Ideas

1. The dominant group in American society was created as people of English ethnicity settled along the Atlantic seacoast and gradually extended their political, economic, and religious control over the territory. This group's structure, folkways, and mores may be traced to (a) the English system of law, (b) the organization of commerce during the sixteenth century, and (c) English Protestant religious ideas and practices, especially Puritanism.

2. By 1700, the Anglo Americans had replaced the American Indians as the "native" American group along the Atlantic seacoast. Those who came from the outside were regarded as "foreigners." The more nearly newcomers resembled the Anglo Americans in appearance and in patterns of behavior, the more nearly "American" they were thought to be. The Indians and Blacks had been defined as ineligible to participate fully in the developing society. Although Indians often could choose to remain physically within the boundaries of English colonial society, they usually chose not to. Blacks, on the other hand, were required to remain within those boundaries. In both cases, however, their physical inclusion was combined with social exclusion.

3. The Indian tribes were present for thousands of years before the arrival of the European explorers and colonists. This land belonged to them.

4. There were at least 200 tribes in what is now the United States. The tribes spoke at least two hundred mutually unintelligible languages and exhibited varying levels of social, economic, and political organization. The tribe was the social unit to which the Indians gave their primary allegiance. Larger confederations of tribes were rare and only loosely organized.

5. Indian–English relations illustrate the point that minority groups that are cohesive and self-sufficient at the time they are brought into a society are likely to resist assimilation for a long time.

6. Africans in the English colonies did not at first occupy the status of chattel slaves. Their status was similar to that of the White bonded servants. In little more than half a century, however, their social position was that of mere property and slaves for life. African ancestry had become synonymous with the status of slave.

7. The argument that the slaves were generally happy and contented ignores many facts. They used every conceivable form of resistance to oppression. Given the oppressiveness of the slave system, however, most of the resistance was unorganized.

8. The position of the Anglo American majority and, consequently, the preeminence of its pattern of living were challenged during the eighteenth century by heavy immigrations from Northern Ireland (Ulster) and from the German states of central Europe. Even though these groups exhibited many of the cultural and social characteristics of the Anglo American majority, to some extent they both became the objects of hostility and discrimination. They were the first large immigrant minorities in American history.

9. The complete assimilation of the Scotch-Irish and German groups did not occur within three generations. Each subprocess of assimilation—cultural (by substitution or addition), secondary, primary, and marital—probably occurred more rapidly among the Scotch-Irish than among the Germans; however, the Scotch-Irish were still a fairly distinct group late into the nineteenth century, and some would argue that they have not completely lost their distinctiveness even today.

10. The experience of the Scotch-Irish and Germans illustrates the point that groups may reach a high level of cultural assimilation but remain incompletely assimilated in some other respects.

11. Although the Scotch-Irish and German groups posed challenges to the Anglo Americans and their version of the "semiofficial" pattern of American life, the outcome served to strengthen the main features of the ideology of Anglo conformity. The experience seemed to prove that White Protestant Europeans could and would conform to the Anglo American pattern.

12. The results of the Revolutionary War and, later, the Constitutional Convention left the Anglo American majority in firm control of American society. This position was strengthened further by a decrease in European migration during the period between 1793 and 1815.

13. By 1815, the Anglo-conformity ideology was practically unchallenged. To become "fully American," one had to be White and had to be, or become, Protestant. By this definition, non-White peoples such as Blacks and Indians were not, and could not become, full-fledged Americans.

Key Terms

doctrine of White supremacy   The belief that the growing dominance of the Whites throughout the world was a result of biologically inherited differences in ability among racial groups.

ethnocentrism   The tendency to consider one's own society to be superior to all others.

folkways   The customs or practices the members of a society have adopted as answers to life's problems.

mores   Those folkways that concern society's welfare.

Underground Railroad   An elaborate network of people who used their resources and homes to help Southern slaves flee to the North and freedom. Both White abolitionists and free Blacks helped in these efforts.

Notes

1. Some descendants of the indigenous population of the United States prefer to be identified by specific tribal names or the term *Native American*. Snipp (1989:5) stated that this term appears to be declining in popularity among Indians and that the term *American Indian* is preferable. We use *Indians, American Indians, Native Americans*, and various tribal names as identifiers.

2. Some writers say there was an even greater diversity of cultures and languages. Cook (1981:118) stated that there were approximately 400 different cultures and 500 languages. Jordan and Litwack (1987:2) stated there were "some twelve hundred different dialects and languages."

3. There is disagreement concerning the size of the American Indian population at this time in various parts of the New World. Scholars have presented estimates of the total number of Indians north of Mexico ranging between 900,000 and 18 million (Snipp 1989:6). Snipp concluded that the Indian population of North America probably was no smaller than 2 million and no larger than 5 million (Snipp 1989:10, 63). Estimates for Mexico and the rest of the Western Hemisphere also vary widely. Embree (1970:18) estimated there were around 10 million in all; Wagley and Har-

ris (1958:15) stated there may have been as many as 20 million; and Thornton (1996:44) estimated the total at around 75 million.

4. The Spanish, in contrast, maintained a major missionary effort for over three centuries.

5. Governor William Bradford claimed that Squanto (Tisquantum) had been sent by God to help the settlers (Jordan and Litwack 1987:25). Squanto had been kidnapped and taken to England by Captain George Waymouth in 1605 and had learned to speak English (Dennis 1977:4).

6. Two other popular legal theories were "the right of just war" and "the right of discovery" (Fredrickson 1971:35).

7. We thank W. Allen Martin for suggesting this quotation.

8. The term *African American* seems currently to be preferred by more Americans of African descent than any other. Many people, however, prefer the term *Black*; and we use the terms interchangeably.

9. Jordan (1972:86) stated "that there is simply not enough evidence" to settle the question.

10. Migration is strongly influenced by information that is distributed through social networks of relatives and friends (Bodnar 1985: 57–84).

11. Calculated from Burner, Fox-Genovese, and Bernhard (1991:74).

12. Bennett (1964:41) reported that "So many dead people were thrown overboard on slavers that it was said that sharks would pick up a ship off the coast of Africa and follow it to America." Burner, Fox-Genovese, and Bernhard (1991:78) estimated that about 10 million slaves embarked on the Middle Passage and that about 2 million of these "died in transit."

13. This group is also known as Seminole Blacks, Indian Blacks, Seminole freedmen, and Afro-Seminoles (Mulroy 1993:1).

14. There is general agreement that around 250,000 Ulstermen of Scots descent and between 100,000 and 200,000 Germans came to America before the Revolution (Conzen 1980:407; Dinnerstein and Reimers 1975:2; Greeley 1971:31; and Jones 1960:22, 29).

15. This group traditionally has been referred to as Scotch-Irish (or Scots-Irish). Although we treat them as Irish, many of its members may have been more Scot than Irish. Present-day demographers estimate that by 1790 more than 8 percent of the U.S. population was Scottish, while about 6 percent was from Ulster (Lieberson and Waters 1988:39). At the same time, nearly 4 percent of the Irish population of the United States was not from Ulster. This sizable population was predominantly Catholic, and some scholars say that by the time of the American Revolution, there were more Catholic Irish than Protestant Irish in America (Diner 1996:163). Some also argue that the emphasis on the Ulster Irish creates the impression that the Catholic Irish contributed little to the development of colonial America. No such implication is intended here.

16. In Leyburn's (1970:65–76) opinion, the Scotch-Irish were "full Americans almost from the moment they took up their farms in the backcountry."

17. Dinnerstein and Jaher (1970:4–5) stated that "Within three generations . . . (the) Scotch-Irish dropped their 'foreign' characteristics, assimilated to the dominant culture, and disappeared."

18. As recently as 1972, a number of seemingly assimilated groups (including the Irish Protestants) still differed from one another in regard to certain basic values (Taylor 1981).

19. The *Mayflower* of German immigration, the *Concord,* arrived in Philadelphia in 1683. The small group of immigrant families aboard was led by Franz Daniel Pastorius, an able and well-educated man who was the first to issue a public protest against slavery in America (Adamic 1944:168–169).

20. Franklin's estimate appears to have been accurate. Present-day demographers estimate that in 1790 the English comprised around 35 percent of Pennsylvania's population and that the Germans comprised around 33 percent (Lieberson and Waters 1988:39).

21. For discussions see Lutz (1987) and Middlekauff (1987).

22. Although we assume from this perspective that the majority pattern remained essentially unchanged, we also assume that, as the minority groups adopted the host culture, they made enormous contributions to the development of the society (Gordon 1964:73; Lipset 1979:103).

The Golden Door

Southern European immigrants worked in crowded, unsanitary conditions for long hours and little pay. They encountered difficult economic conditions and few opportunities to interact as equals with members of the dominant Anglo American society. As greater numbers of immigrants from diverse ethnic and racial groups came to the United States, they encountered heightened discrimination.

. . . the Great Migration was not only one of people but of talents, skills, and cultural traditions.

—Max Lerner

A nation in a state of peace and safety, ought not to deny a hospitable reception to the fugitive from oppression or misfortune at home.

—William Rawle

People do not cross continents and oceans without considerable thought, nor do they uproot themselves from family, friends, and familiar terrain without significant strain.

—Leonard Dinnerstein and David M. Reimers

No one wants to be a Know-Nothing. Yet Uncontrolled immigration is an impossibility.

—Arthur M. Schlesinger, Jr.

The greatest human migration in the history of the world has occurred since 1815. Uncounted millions of people have left their ancestral farms and villages to live in cities and cross the oceans. Although the specific reasons for migration varied substantially according to the time and place, the main factors contributing to this great movement of people were rapid changes in agriculture, population size, and industrial production. A significant effect of the workings of these three great factors was to reduce large numbers of farmers to a condition of poverty and thus, simultaneously, to "push" them off the land and "pull" them toward jobs in other places.[1]

Two results of the improvement of agricultural methods were especially important. First, during the seventeenth and eighteenth centuries, the population of Europe more than doubled. Second, the new methods made possible and profitable the farming of larger areas of land with fewer workers. These facts increased the efforts of the more powerful landowners to enlarge their lands. Consequently, many small private farms and much land held in common were gradually "enclosed" by the large landowners. With their farms gone, many people faced the choice of remaining as paupers where they were or moving in the hope of finding work and better living conditions elsewhere.

The choice was by no means easy. In many cases, people did not have the money required to make the journey and stay alive until work was found. Even if there were enough money to send one person ahead (usually a young male), the family members left behind frequently remained in desperate condition. To be sure, the increasing numbers of factories and the growth of cities created jobs for large numbers of the rural poor. But the growth of the population was so rapid that there were seldom enough jobs for those who wished to work. In addition, just as is true today, the number of jobs available fluctuated with the ups and downs of business activity.

The millions of people who were uprooted by these great changes from a preindustrial to an industrial form of social organization comprised the migrant "streams" or "waves" that flowed out of their native lands and into other countries. The United States has been, overall, the most popular destination. Between 1820 (when the U.S. government began keeping official records on immigration) and 1994, more than 61 million newcomers to this country were counted; and by the year 2000 the number had exceeded 66 million (Table 4.1). This number does not include the large number of immigrants who entered the United States without official documents. Many other countries—Russia, Canada, Argentina, Brazil, and Australia, to name only a few—also have received millions of immigrants. Whether people chose to go to one country or another depended to a large extent on such things as the likelihood that work would be found, the availability of transportation, and the presence of friends and relatives in the country of destination.

TABLE 4.1   Immigration to the United States, 1820–2000

Years	Number	Rate*
1820–1830	151,824	1.2
1831–1840	599,125	3.9
1841–1850	1,713,251	8.4
1851–1860	2,598,214	9.3
1861–1870	2,314,824	6.4
1871–1880	2,812,191	6.2
1881–1890	5,246,613	9.2
1891–1900	3,687,564	5.3
1901–1910	8,795,386	10.4
1911–1920	5,735,811	5.7
1921–1930	4,107,209	3.5
1931–1940	528,431	0.4
1941–1950	1,035,039	0.7
1951–1960	2,515,479	1.5
1961–1970	3,321,677	1.7
1971–1980	4,493,314	2.1
1981–1990	7,338,062	2.9
1991–2000	9,095,417	3.2
Total	66,089,431	

* Per 1000 U.S. population.
Source: U.S. Immigration and Naturalization Service, *Statistical Yearbook of the Immigration and Naturalization Service, 1998,* 2000:20–22; U.S. Immigration and Naturalization Service, *Statistical Yearbook of the Immigration and Naturalization Service, 2000,* 2002:7–10.

The waves of immigrants arriving at America's shores have tended to peak when economic conditions within the United States were good and to recede when there were economic downturns (Olzak 1986:25). But, as has been suggested already, much more than the "pull" of the American economy was involved in the uprooting and movement of so many people. The convergence of many different forces has led to three fairly distinct and astonishingly large immigrant streams to the United States. During the period of the **first great immigrant stream** (1820–1889), people from countries located in western and northern Europe were predominant; during the period of the **second great immigrant stream** (1890–1924), people from southern and eastern Europe were predominant; and during the period of the **third great immigrant stream** or the **new immigration** (1946–present), people from Latin America and Asia have thus far been predominant. The decade from 1880 to 1889 combined high immigration from both of the first two great streams and was a period of transition from the first to the second. For reasons to be discussed later, immigration dropped dramatically after 1924, resumed after 1946, and assumed some new and distinctive traits after 1965.

The First Great Immigrant Stream

America was not really a very popular destination for emigrants during the decade of the 1820s. An economic panic destroyed many of the opportunities the emigrants were seeking, so immigration into the United States was comparatively low; however, the number of immigrants almost quadrupled within the next 10 years. As the number of immigrants increased, the number of letters that were exchanged between Europe and America also increased. The newcomer's letters described their travels and new lives in America, leading to increases in the number of people who wished to come here and to increases in the number of agencies to help people arrange their travel and find employment. These changes helped make America more attractive to the millions of people who left Europe in the next two decades. During that period, more than 4 million people swelled the ranks of the first great stream. Although even larger numbers of people arrived in some later periods, the number arriving in the 1850s was the largest ever in comparison to the existing total population of the United States.

As was true of the colonial immigration, more people in the first stream came from Ireland, Germany, and the United Kingdom than from any other countries. With only one exception,[2] these three countries were among the top three until the last decade of the nineteenth century. The largest absolute number of first-stream immigrants arrived during the 1880s (see Figure 4.1).

The Nineteenth-Century Irish

As had been true earlier, the large immigration of the Irish preceded that of the Germans. For 30 years the Irish continued to arrive in larger numbers than the Germans, though the

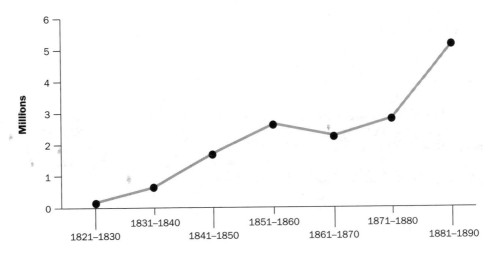

FIGURE 4.1   The First Great Immigrant Stream
Number of Immigrants by Decade, 1821–1890

Source: U.S. Immigration and Naturalization Service, *Statistical Yearbook of the Immigration and Naturalization Service, 1994,* 1996:26.

totals for both groups rose sharply. As this movement of people reached a peak during the 1850s, however, the German immigration became heavier than the Irish; and it remained so throughout the following decades of the nineteenth century. Table 4.2 shows Irish immigration figures from 1820 to 2000.

To understand these large migrations, it is necessary to consider what was happening to many small farmers in Europe during this time. The basic problem consisted of a combination of a high population density, an unsound system of land tenure, and a high reliance on the potato.

The Potato Famine.   In 1815, Ireland was the most densely populated country in Europe (Jones 1976:69). The end of the Napoleonic Wars brought about a deflation of land values, a decline of foreign markets for wheat, and a decrease in the number of jobs available. The saving feature in the situation for the Irish was the potato. It was fairly easy to cultivate, and it took only an acre or so of land to support a family. As future events proved, however, this heavy reliance on the potato was ill advised. The potato could not be preserved, it was hard to transport, and it was hard on the soil.

A foreshadowing of later events occurred in the early 1820s when the potato crop failed and famine followed. Although this famine was not nearly so severe as the one that led to the heaviest Irish immigration, many people left the country at this time. Despite this famine (and a relaxation by England of restrictions on immigration from Ireland), the vast majority of the Irish preferred to remain in Ireland. For the moment, there was enough food to go around. But a series of disagreements between landowners and tenants made it more difficult for people to lease land on which to support their families,

TABLE 4.2   Irish Immigration to the United States, 1820–2000

Years	Number
1820–1830	54,338
1831–1840	207,381
1841–1850	780,719
1851–1860	914,119
1861–1870	435,778
1871–1880	436,871
1881–1890	655,482
1891–1900	388,416
1901–1910	339,065
1911–1920	146,181
1921–1930	211,234
1931–1940	10,973
1941–1950	19,789
1951–1960	48,362
1961–1970	32,966
1971–1980	11,490
1981–1990	31,969
1991–2000	56,950
Total	4,782,083

Source: U.S. Immigration and Naturalization Service, *Statistical Yearbook of the Immigration and Naturalization Service, 1998,* 2000:20–22; U.S. Immigration and Naturalization Service, *Statistical Yearbook of the Immigration and Naturalization Service, 2000,* 2002:7–10.

leading to an increase in the tempo of out-migration. During this period, a substantial proportion of the Irish immigrants to America still, as in colonial times, were Protestants; however, during the 1830s, an important change occurred in the character of the movement. By the latter part of that decade, most of the immigrants were Roman Catholics from the south and west of Ireland.

Two decisive blows came in the mid-1840s. A particularly virulent form of potato rot struck the Irish crop, destroying not only the potatoes in the ground but also many of those already stored. Between one-third and one-half of the Irish potato crop was destroyed by the disease. Then the potato gardens all over Ireland withered and died in the space of a few days. At this point, people finally realized that Ireland simply could not support so large a population. Therefore, many people left in what soon became a general "flight from hunger." Those who could arrange passage to England or America did so. Within a year, at least a half million people had starved to death, while perhaps a million more had died of fever. Those who survived were in desperate condition (Jones 1960:109; 1976:67). During the next several years, the total number of Irish emigrants—the so-called famine Irish—reached unprecedented figures. By the mid-1850s, approximately 2 million people representing all social classes had left Ireland (Jones 1976:69). "The famine," wrote Diner (1996:164), "swept up Irish people, regardless of age, gender, or skill level." For a vast segment of the population, forced emigration became "the only alternative to death" (Greeley 1975:31).

Natives' Reactions.   Most of the Irish who arrived in America were poverty stricken. They had no money to proceed westward on their own, and they usually got out of the coastal cities only when they were needed in inland factories and mines and to help construct canals and railroads. Consequently, the conditions in the "little Dublins" and Irish "shanty towns" that sprang up along the East Coast were very poor (Wittke 1964:134). People were crowded together in tenements, and sometimes 20 or more families lived in a single house or apartment. The houses tended to be poorly lighted and ventilated; diseases such as cholera were rampant. Amidst all this, the "drink menace" increased in severity, the Irish reputation as ruffians and brawlers grew, and family ties were weakened. Although there was little serious crime among the Irish, they nevertheless were arrested frequently for minor offenses. These characteristics contributed to many native Americans' view of the Irish as an ignorant, practically barbaric, people. Cartoons often depicted them as apes "with a shillelagh in one hand and a pint of booze in the other" (Greeley 1975:6). All of these things contributed to the Americans' hostility toward the Irish and made their task of getting established in America still more difficult. Employers often preferred workers from other groups, resulting in many posted notices saying "No Irish Need Apply" (Jones 1976:78–79).

Aside from their high concentration in the eastern cities and towns and the behavior that the dominant group found to be offensive, two features of the social organization of the Irish worried the native Americans. The first of these was their conspicuous Roman Catholicism. During the eighteenth century, the Irish founded the first Catholic churches in the United States (Diner 1996:163); and the spread of Catholicism in the United States between 1825 and 1855 was due primarily to them. Subsequently, the Irish dominated the Catholic hierarchy in America. Wittke (1964:152) reported that "in 1836 the diocese of New York and half of New Jersey contained about 200,000 Catholics and of the 38 priests 35 were Irish and 3 were German." As Irish laborers were drawn from the East Coast to work on canals and railroads, new Roman Catholic parishes were created to serve them.

The Irish attracted the unfavorable notice of the native Americans in still another way. They were very active in politics. The Irish peasants had a history of conflict with their English overlords and were well acquainted with many of the techniques of organizing and carrying through political campaigns. The Irish, said Adamic (1944:344), "took to politics like ducks to water." In most cities, they were solidly behind the Democratic Party and tended to vote as a bloc on critical issues. In cities like New York and Boston, the "Irish vote" became increasingly important. As their numbers grew, the Irish became especially visible in various public service jobs and political offices. Angry natives frequently claimed that the Irish sold their votes to the Democratic city political machines in return for jobs and other favors. As we shall see, the fears of the natives led to various organized efforts to regulate and curb immigration.

The Irish reacted to the hostility of the Protestant Americans and to the problems of adapting to their new environment in much the same way as most immigrants before and after them. The ethnic communities they established arose in part because of, and were strengthened by, the rejection they faced in their interactions with members of the host society. Immigrants need, first of all, to solve the problem of making a living; to do that, they frequently rely on others of their nationality group for help. Moreover, the strange and hostile world of the natives typically stimulates the immigrants' desire to associate in a reassuring and friendly way with others of the same nationality—to eat together and engage in familiar recreational or religious activities. These forces encourage the members of a given nationality group to congregate to form benevolent societies, churches, patriotic organizations, newspapers, and social clubs. The ethnic group that is formed through this process, in the words of Francis (1976:169), is "exclusively the result of processes originating in the host society itself." The group is dependent on the host society for the satisfaction of almost all its basic needs and is under strong pressure to move toward a mastery of the host group's culture. Although the ethnic society that has been constructed within the host society is intrinsically valuable to its members, and although they make vigorous efforts to retain it, its major purpose is to establish a place for its members *within* the host society.

Women Immigrants.   The Irish who immigrated in the nineteenth century shared many experiences with their compatriots of the eighteenth century. For example, both groups responded in large numbers to economic pushes in their homeland and sought a better life in America; both groups joined with others of their nationality to construct ethnic communities; and both groups were subjected to hostility and rejection by Americans. They did differ, though, in the strength of the incentive for single men or women to leave the country. During the early decades, most immigrants were single, able-bodied males; but with the onset of the great famine, the number of women fleeing Ireland became roughly equal to the number of men. As the century advanced, the proportion of women became steadily larger (Diner 1996:163–167). By the first decade of the twentieth century, approximately 109 Irish women arrived for every 100 Irish men (Steinberg 1989:162).

This shift in the relative proportions of women immigrants was related to shifts in English colonial policy in Ireland. By the nineteenth century, control of most of the land had been placed into the hands of the English government and a few Protestant and absentee landowners. This policy greatly reduced the amount of farming land available to the Irish, especially the Catholics, and strengthened their tradition of permitting only eldest sons to inherit lands and leases. Subdividing land among all heirs was resisted because smaller plots simply could not support families. As a result, younger sons were left with few economic options. The main alternatives were to find work on someone else's farm or to migrate. Frequently men were forced to delay marriage or to remain unmarried. But the effect of these changes on women was even more profound. Faced with few opportunities to marry and even fewer employment opportunities than the men, "young women, even more often than men, decided to emigrate" (Steinberg 1989:164).

Under these conditions, domestic service in America—an occupation shunned by the women of most ethnic groups—became an attractive option for Irish women. Employers of domestic servants preferred single women and women who could speak English. Large numbers of Irish women met both of these qualifications. For their part, the single Irish women wanted jobs that assured them of food, shelter, and protection in an alien environment. These factors combined to stimulate an active commerce on both sides of the Atlantic to bring employers of domestics and "Bridgets" together in America; consequently, Irish women were much more likely than the women of the other main groups to go into domestic "service" when they reached the United States. According to Steinberg (1989:163), among "immigrants arriving between 1899 and 1910, 40 percent of the Irish were classified as servants."

The nineteenth-century immigration of the Irish illustrates how the industrialization of western Europe led to a rapid growth of population, the consolidation of land holdings, widespread food shortages, and a massive flight from hunger. It shows, too, how the capitalist economies increasingly operated across national borders. To a larger extent than previously, the destinations and patterns of settlement of the Irish immigrants were affected by the efforts of growing American industries to meet their needs for labor. Most of the Irish men were manual laborers who were forced to take whatever work was available; large numbers of Irish women had little choice but to accept domestic service. The revolutionary effects of industrialization, only barely noticeable before the 1840s, became increasingly visible later in the century.

The Nineteenth-Century Germans

As was true for the Irish, the majority of German immigrants were small farmers who had been driven from their lands by widespread crop failures and financial difficulties. By the 1840s, the situation of many small farmers in Germany had become desperate. Weather conditions had been poor; the price of food was rising. Many small farmers were deeply in debt. According to Hansen (1945:225), "overpopulation, hunger and employment were the topics that dominated all discussions of social conditions."

The potato crop failed in Germany in the 1840s, just as it did in Ireland. Although the crop failure created a social crisis in Germany, the situation was not as bad as in Ireland because the Germans had not relied so heavily on a single crop. Nevertheless, many people were eager to leave before things became still worse. The fear that waiting longer might be a mistake was heightened by a widely circulated rumor that the United States was on the verge of prohibiting immigration. This rumor encouraged many people to leave immediately. Hence, even though hunger was involved, the "America fever" that developed in Germany at this time was not so directly a flight from famine as was the case in Ireland. During this period, the number of Germans emigrating to America jumped very sharply. Table 4.3 shows German immigration figures from 1820 to 2000.

As large numbers of people in Germany became interested in emigrating to the United States, several colonization societies were formed on both sides of the Atlantic. One of the most famous of these organizations made an effort to settle German immigrants near St. Louis in the 1830s (Jones 1976:125). In the 1840s, another organization

TABLE 4.3   German Immigration to the
United States, 1820–2000

Years	Number
1820–1830	7,729
1831–1840	152,454
1841–1850	434,626
1851–1860	951,667
1861–1870	787,468
1871–1880	718,182
1881–1890	1,452,970
1891–1900	505,152
1901–1910	341,498
1911–1920	143,945
1921–1930	412,202
1931–1940	114,058
1941–1950	226,578
1951–1960	477,765
1961–1970	190,796
1971–1980	74,414
1981–1990	91,961
1991–2000	92,606
Total	7,176,071

Source: U.S. Immigration and Naturalization Ser-
vice, *Statistical Yearbook of the Immigration and
Naturalization Service, 1998,* 2000:20–22; U.S. Im-
migration and Naturalization Service, *Statistical
Yearbook of the Immigration and Naturalization
Service, 2000,* 2002:7–10.

sent thousands of German settlers to Texas with the "avowed object of peopling Texas
with Germans" (Hansen 1945:231). And, in the 1850s, an effort was made to settle Germans in Wisconsin. Altogether, Germany contributed more immigrants to America during the nineteenth century than any other country. By the end of the century, Germans
were "the single largest ethnic minority in 27 states" (Dinnerstein and Reimers 1975:25).

During this time, travel literature concerning America had become especially popular in Germany. In addition to guidebooks, periodicals, and pamphlets published and
disseminated by travel agents, there were books written by those who had traveled in
America or had already migrated. Most important of all were personal letters. When letters arrived, they frequently were read aloud in the midst of audiences. Their impact on
the listeners ordinarily was great. The widespread interest in America within Germany
and the increasing availability of travel literature led to the formation of village reading
clubs. In this way, many people received information concerning the United States and
became interested in moving there.

As in the eighteenth century, the Germans were comparatively unfamiliar with the language and institutions of the Anglo Americans; and their efforts to preserve their ethnic distinctiveness in America were very noticeable. Although the Germans were widely distributed throughout the United States, they built up large concentrations in cities like Chicago, Milwaukee, St. Louis, Cincinnati, and New York. For example, by the middle of the nineteenth century most of the large German population of New York lived in an area lying just north of the Irish district. Within this area, nearly all of the businesses were owned and operated by Germans, and German was the principal spoken language. There were in this district German schools, churches, restaurants, saloons, newspapers, and a lending library; and the Germans, no less than the Irish, formed numerous mutual-aid societies and benevolent associations to assist the immigrants to deal with the complexities of the strange new environment.

The German language became so prominent in many communities that the public schools either offered bilingual instruction in English and German or German was offered as an optional course of study, sometimes from the earliest grades. In some instances where the German population predominated, German was the language of instruction and English-speaking students—as a report from Missouri stated—either were "deprived of school privileges or else (were) taught in the German language" (Kloss 1977:89). During the 1840s, Cincinnati placed German and English on an equal footing as languages of instruction (Wittke 1964:229). The growth of German as a spoken language and as a language of instruction led to conflicts between German and English speakers. For instance, in 1875 the Germans of New York City staged "a great protest demonstration" following an announcement that German instruction in the schools was to be abolished (Kloss 1977:91). In subsequent years, some Germans fought for the continuance of German instruction in the schools and against the teaching of many other foreign languages. They maintained that German should have a favored status because it was an especially important language of science, literature, and international communication. At the same time, German theories of education also were playing a central role in the development of American public school systems.

Political Participation.   Another important feature of German immigration during the nineteenth century concerned politics. Germany at this time was still not a unified nation. The governments of the separate states were controlled by numerous princes. As the economic conditions of Germany worsened, there was an increasing desire, especially among intellectuals and young people, for large-scale reforms. The demands for solutions to the problems of hunger and unemployment and for a more democratic form of government led to revolutions in 1848 and 1849. These uprisings were crushed but clearly "highlighted the severity of social problems" (Weggert 1992:228) The revolutionary leaders, many of whom were distinguished people of property, education, and high social standing, fled from the country and eventually made their way to the United States. These so-called Forty-eighters numbered only a few thousand and represented only a small proportion of the German immigration to the United States during this period, but they played an important role in determining the reaction of native Americans to the entire German immigration.

Many of the Forty-eighters were radical reformers who were disappointed to find that the United States was not a democratic utopia They were shocked by slavery, corrupt political machines, the lack of civil rights for women, American Puritanism, and many other aspects of American life. In general, American life seemed to them to be "half-barbarian" (Wittke 1964:193). They openly criticized the shortcomings of American democracy, advocated the abolition of slavery and the U.S. Senate, as well as the office of President; and they hoped to transform the United States into a land of complete freedom of thought, rationality, and high culture (Jones 1960:155; Wittke 1967:8). They also founded athletic organizations (called *Turnvereine*) that became known as centers of radical reform and sponsored numerous newspapers to circulate their views.

The Republican Party (formed in 1854) attracted many of the Forty-eighters. The Republicans' stand against slavery and in favor of foreign-born citizens was especially appealing to many German idealists. Germans, such as Carl Schurz, were so conspicuous during Lincoln's campaign for the presidency in 1860 that many observers have claimed his victory in the midwestern states was due to a bloc vote by the Germans. Although this claim underestimates the deep divisions between and within the German American and German immigrant communities, it highlights the extent to which the Forty-eighters contributed to a sharp increase in German political participation in the United States and, perhaps, in the other main spheres of secondary assimilation as well (Conzen 1980:421; Jones 1960:162).

The radicals within the German immigrant group were sharply opposed by the large majority of German Americans who reached the United States before the 1840s. Many of the German Lutheran immigrants of the preceding century had moved very noticeably in the direction of Anglo conformity in their church services. The American Lutheran church had substituted English for German as the language of worship, and the traditional Lutheran beliefs and practices had been modified accordingly. The Missouri Synod, formed by the more recent Lutherans, emphasized the preservation of the German language and traditional beliefs and practices. These modifications led to acrimonious feuds between colonial and nineteenth-century German Lutherans.

Changing Patterns of Immigration

The Civil War created a comparative lull in immigration but certainly did not stop it. Over 2.3 million immigrants arrived during the 1860s, and still more arrived during the succeeding 10 years (refer back to Table 4.1 and Figure 4.1). More significant than the sheer numbers, however, is that during the 1871–1880 period, a noticeable change began to occur in the national origins of the newcomers. Before the war, the largest numbers of immigrants were from Germany, Ireland, and the United Kingdom. During and after the war, these groups continued to grow rapidly and, in time, were augmented by large numbers of northwestern Europeans from Scandinavia. Immigration from Scandinavia during the decade preceding the war was about 21,000; but during the 1861–1870 decade, the number of newcomers from Norway and Sweden increased more than fivefold. In the years between 1871 and 1880, the number almost doubled again. However, the comparative increases among those arriving from southern and eastern Europe—particularly from Italy, Austria-Hungary, and Russia—were still more dramatic. By the 1890s, these countries were the leading countries of origin for immigrants to America.

As time passed, it became obvious that the federal government ultimately would be required to assume a major role in the control of immigration. The shift to federal control was launched in 1875 when the U.S. Supreme Court ruled that only the U.S. Congress was empowered by the Constitution to regulate immigration (Bernard 1980:489). In contrast to an earlier ruling, the Court now said that all of the regulations that had been enacted over the years by the states and cities were unconstitutional. As if to stress the point, Congress passed the 1875 Immigration Act that sought to bar various types of "undesirable immigrants," such as those who engaged in "lewd" or "immoral" conduct (Abrams 1984:108; Cafferty, Chiswick, Greeley, and Sullivan 1983:43).

The 1880s were very significant both for the absolute number of immigrants arriving then and because that decade was the high point of the first immigrant stream. More immigrants came from Germany, the United Kingdom, and Scandinavia than ever before or since, and more came from Ireland than at any time since the peak in the 1850s. At the same time, however, the immigrant stream from southern and eastern Europe continued to increase rapidly.

As time passed, the receiving facilities in New York—located at the southern end of Manhattan Island in a former place of amusement called Castle Garden—became increasingly crowded. New York was by far the most popular landing site for European immigrants. During the years Castle Garden served as the city's port of entry (1855–1891), more than 7.5 million aliens were received there (Bolino 1985:3). At the end, however, the overcrowded conditions at Castle Garden and the misuse of the depot for political purposes led the federal government to take control of immigration and to open a new receiving station just offshore on Ellis Island. The new facility "was officially dedicated on New Year's Day, 1892" (Bolino 1985:4).

For more than 30 years, Ellis Island served as the "golden door" for approximately 16 million immigrants and became, along with the nearby Statue of Liberty, a symbol of hope, freedom, and opportunity. The island also developed a somewhat sinister reputation. Many people who attempted to enter the country there were detained and were subsequently deported. For the many who were denied entrance and were sent back to their homelands, Ellis Island became "The Isle of Tears" (Bolino 1985:44).[3] Kraut (1982:55) states that even those who were admitted after only a few hours on Ellis Island frequently considered the experience "the most traumatic part of their voyage to America." The immigrants feared being detained or separated from their families, and they feared the physical examination to discover contagious diseases. They also had difficulty communicating with the inspectors and, when the immigrants could not spell their names, they often entered the United States with new, "Ellis Island" names (Kraut 1982:54–57). It is estimated that more than 100 million Americans today are descended from those whose first taste of their adopted land took place at Ellis Island (Horn 1988:63).

During this period, the number of immigrants arriving from each of the main countries of the first stream declined from their high levels during the 1880s; and, for the first time, more newcomers arrived from Italy, Austria-Hungary, and Russia than from Germany, Ireland, and the United Kingdom (see Figure 4.2). This second immigrant stream continued and increased during the first two decades of the twentieth century. So the first decade of the twentieth century proved to be the high point of immigration not only of the second stream but also of any decade thus far. Immigrants from Italy, Russia,

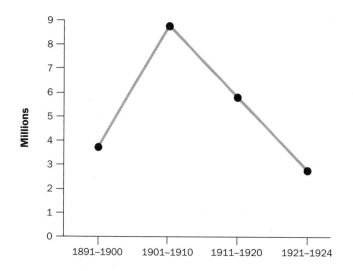

FIGURE 4.2   The Second Great Immigrant Stream
Number of Immigrants by Decade, 1891–1924

Source: U.S. Immigration and Naturalization Service, *Statistical Yearbook of the Immigration and Naturalization Service, 1994,* 1996:27; U.S. Bureau of the Census, *Historical Statistics of the United States, Colonial Times to 1970,* 1975.

and Austria-Hungary were the most numerous in all but the three years preceding 1924. By that year, three laws aimed at restricting immigration from southern and eastern Europe (discussed in Chapter 5) had taken effect; and as immigration from Europe ebbed, Canada and Mexico became the leading countries of origin for immigrants.

The Second Great Immigrant Stream

Soon after Ellis Island opened, officials began to comment on the change in the "types" of newcomers who were arriving. In addition to the Austrians, Hungarians, Italians, and Russian Jews, the second immigrant stream contained significant numbers of Bohemians, Bulgarians, Croatians, Greeks, Lithuanians, Moravians, Poles, Serbs, Slovaks, Slovenes, and others from southern and eastern Europe. These newcomers seemed even more foreign to Americans than the earlier foreigners from northern and western Europe. Many of the "old" first-stream foreigners, now in their second or third generation as Americans, had assimilated culturally by substitution, were well represented in the economic and political mainstream, and appeared to be moving toward complete Anglo conformity assimilation; consequently, there was no longer any real question of their "assimilability." But these "new" second-stream immigrants appeared to pose a more difficult problem.[4]

What was so unusual about the second-stream immigrants? Their languages, of course, were further removed from English than was true of most of the first-stream immigrants. Some of their religious practices, too, contrasted strongly with the prevailing Protestant and Anglicized Catholic services. Their dress, manners, and foods also seemed especially strange; but, in addition to these cultural differences, many Americans soon came to believe that there was something "artificial" about the second immigrant stream. American employers were eager to tap the large pools of cheap European labor, so they sent recruiting agents to whip up interest in American jobs. At the same time, rapid improvements in ocean travel greatly increased competition for passengers among steamship lines. Specialized agents also encouraged people throughout the southern and eastern European areas to emigrate. The changes in the organization of the global economic system that we first noted in our discussion of the nineteenth-century Irish were now well underway. The second-stream immigrants were, like most of their predecessors, poverty-stricken peasants who were being forced off the land by industrialization; but these people, accustomed to life in small villages and farms, arrived in an America that was now well along the road of change from an agrarian to an industrial and urban nation.

The frontier had been declared officially "closed" after the census of 1890. There was no more free land for immigrants to clear and settle. As the demand for land increased, so did its price; and the immigrants increasingly could not escape the port cities in which they had landed. Given the location of Ellis Island, the city of New York, in particular, was flooded with immigrants. Even when they were able to leave port cities like New York, Boston, Baltimore, Philadelphia, or New Orleans, the immigrants usually wound up in inland cities like Cleveland, Chicago, Pittsburgh, or St. Louis (Novotny 1974:133).[5] The main jobs available were as unskilled laborers on the railroads or in factories; and by 1900, second-stream immigrant groups were the main source of workers for nearly all segments of industrial production (Kraut 1982:86). Since in nearly all cases the immigrants could afford only the least expensive housing, ethnic slums developed in all of America's major cities. Disease was rampant. Novotny (1974:138) reported that "nearly 40 percent of the slum dwellers suffered from tuberculosis." The promise of a new life in America thus became a shattered dream for large numbers of immigrants. Not surprisingly, many of these disappointed people returned to their homelands at the first opportunity.

We should note though that despite the hardships and disappointments, many of those who went back home—especially young, single, men—later returned to the United States. The emergence of a pattern of two-way or cyclical migration represents another important distinction between the first and second immigrant streams (Portes and Bach 1985:31).

The Italians

Probably the most prominent group of newcomers and urban dwellers at this time were the Italians. Several factors made this group particularly conspicuous. First, of course, were their sheer numbers and the rate at which they arrived (see Table 4.4). Well over 3 million Italians reached the United States during the 30-year period beginning in 1890.[6] Second, a large majority of the Italians arriving at this time were from the southern regions. The people from these regions were overwhelmingly illiterate, landless peasants who were escaping from a harsh physical climate, overpopulation, economic dislocations, and an oppressive social class structure (Alba 1985:23–27, 38–40; Lopreato 1970:25–33).

Third, and somewhat surprising, these agricultural people did not move in large numbers directly into farming occupations when they reached America. To be sure, the

TABLE 4.4   Italian Immigration to the United States, 1820–2000

Years	Number
1820–1830	439
1831–1840	2,253
1841–1850	1,870
1851–1860	9,231
1861–1870	11,725
1871–1880	55,759
1881–1890	307,309
1891–1900	651,893
1901–1910	2,045,877
1911–1920	1,109,524
1921–1930	455,315
1931–1940	68,028
1941–1950	57,661
1951–1960	185,491
1961–1970	214,111
1971–1980	129,368
1981–1990	67,254
1991–2000	62,722
Total	5,435,830

Source: U.S. Immigration and Naturalization Service, *Statistical Yearbook of the Immigration and Naturalization Service, 1998,* 2000:20–22; U.S. Immigration and Naturalization Service, *Statistical Yearbook of the Immigration and Naturalization Service, 2000,* 2002:7–10.

changing American economy offered fewer encouragements than previously for those wishing to leave the cities; however, despite their lack of urban and industrial skills, the southern Italians generally preferred to remain in the cities (Alba 1985:47). But they were "too many and too late" (Schermerhorn 1949:232); so the men of this group frequently had to accept the pick-and-shovel jobs at the bottom of the occupational hierarchy that few others wanted. They also were drawn to occupations that required little in the way of initial capital. For instance, Italian men were nearly eight times as likely as other White workers to be "hucksters and peddlers" (Lieberson and Waters 1988:126). Nevertheless, despite these problems, possibly 40 percent of the men found work in skilled blue-collar and lower white-collar jobs (Alba 1996:173).

Comparatively few Italian women made the journey to America during this period. Among Italians arriving between 1899 and 1910, there were "only 27 women for every 100 men" (Steinberg 1989:162). In most cases, fathers, husbands, or other male family members left their families behind as they traveled to the new country; so most of the women who made the crossing were going to join other family members who already were established abroad. Under these circumstances, separated families were reunited, new families were formed readily, and Italian women were not pressured to enter the paid labor force; hence, unlike Irish women, only a small proportion of them accepted paid employment. Those who did went mainly into the "needle trades."[7] Few were forced to accept domestic service (Steinberg 1989:165).

A fourth way in which the southern Italian immigrants stood out was that, to an unusual degree, this group contained a large proportion of males who did not intend to remain in America—so-called **sojourners** (or **birds of passage**). These immigrants, rather, wished to make their fortunes and return with honor to the homeland (Lopreato 1970:14–15; Piore 1979). Jones (1976:196) quoted a successful Italian American, Stefano Miele, as follows: "If I am to be frank, then I shall say that I left Italy and came to America for the sole purpose of making money." Lopreato (1970:110) observed that the Italians' "zeal for assimilation in American life left something to be desired." And Caroli (cited by Alba 1996:173) reported that approximately 1.5 million Italians returned to Italy between 1900 and 1914.

A final, though hardly unique, characteristic of the Italian immigration is that a large proportion of the group's members were obliged to occupy housing that was in many instances unfit for human habitation. The conditions in the Italian slums were frequently so terrible that they were widely publicized. Since many Americans did not understand the circumstances giving rise to the squalid conditions in the slums, the residents themselves, or their culture, often were blamed. As had been true of the Irish in an earlier period, it was assumed that the Italians were "just naturally" depraved.

Natives' Reactions.   Among the Americans' mental images of the Italians, one received special notoriety. The Italians acquired a reputation for criminality. Newspapers throughout the country described in lurid detail extortions and murders attributed to the "Mafia" (or "Cosa Nostra"). Many Americans feared that a notorious criminal organization had been imported by the southern Italians and now posed a serious foreign threat to democratic methods of assuring law and order. Although there is little doubt that Mafia-like organizations did develop among the Italians at this time, there is substantial disagreement concerning the reasons for it and the extent to which there was anything peculiarly Italian about it. Among the first-generation Italians, for example, crime rates were no higher than among other immigrant groups; and they were actually lower than those of native Americans (Schermerhorn 1949:250). A study in Massachusetts in 1912 showed that the Italian born were greatly underrepresented in the prison population of the state (Jones 1976:213). In Alba's (1985:36) opinion, most accounts of organized crime among Italian Americans mistakenly dwell on events in Sicily and on southern Italian culture; and they falsely portray "organized crime as an alien and almost accidental growth in American soil . . . rather than as a native product that demanded the energies of numerous ethnic groups." He argued further that the criminal gangs that operated within Italian American communities probably were not organized at a higher level and "had essentially died out by 1920" (Alba 1985:62–63). The higher levels of organization did not occur until the 1930s, with Prohibition, and were not confined to people of Italian ancestry.

Peculiarly Italian or not, the idea that America's Little Italys were "seething hotbeds of crime" (Schermerhorn 1949:250) was commonly believed.[8] This belief helped to fuel a rising level of native hostility during this period. It also had another effect of considerable interest to us. It helped to awaken among the Italians a sense of ethnic identity.

Ethnic Identity.   As in the cases of the Indians and Blacks (and later the Asians), Americans tended to lump all people from Italy into the same category. But the immigrants themselves had a very different view of the matter, at least at first. The immigrants who left Italy came not as Italians but as representatives of particular villages, cities, or regions. The cleavages among the "Italians" themselves were very deep. Since Italy had only recently become united, the cultural and economic differences between the northerners and southerners were wide. The people in the north felt and acted superior to the people in the south. And even among the southerners, the social differences among the peoples from different villages and regions were pronounced. Consequently, as Lopreato (1970:104) stated, "When the Italians came to the United States they imported a pitiful tendency to mistrust and avoid all those who did not share their particular dialect and customs." This identification of the individual with groups smaller than the Italian nation was evident in the residential patterns in New York (Alba 1996:174).

Various Little Italys developed along separate streets or city blocks, each one exhibiting village, provincial, or regional loyalties (Wittke 1964:441). Neapolitans, for instance, gathered around Mulberry Bend; Sicilians clustered on Elizabeth and Prince Streets; and Calabrians lived on a portion of Mott Street (Alba 1985:48–49; Riis [1890]1957:41–52). As had been true for immigrant groups to America from the earliest days, this method of organizing enabled the immigrants to give and receive help from people like themselves and to bask in the warmth and security of their friendship. Here people could speak their native language, eat food prepared in the "proper" way, and escape the insults and inconveniences encountered in the "outside" world. The ethnic slum, for all its terrible faults, served in certain ways to shield and protect the immigrant. But, to repeat, the Americans did not usually recognize the distinctions that existed among the immigrants from Italy. Consequently, hostility and rejection were directed at the "Italians." They were called "wops," "dagos," "guineas," and "the Chinese of Europe" (Dinnerstein and Reimers 1975: 40); hence, in Schermerhorn's (1949:250) words, "The Sicilians, the Neapolitans, and Calabrians thus became conscious of their common destiny as Italians in America." The hostility of the dominant group "Italianized them" (Lopreato 1970:171).

The process, illustrated by the Italians, by which people from the same geographic regions join together to form a new ethnic group within a different society is a form of **ethnogenesis** (Greeley 1971; Singer 1962).[9] This process may occur initially because the members of a group share certain historical and cultural characteristics. From this perspective, the importance of these shared characteristics derives from the common experiences of the group's members in the new society, especially the experience of rejection by the dominant group (Portes and Bach 1985:25). This common experience in turn provides a basis for a *transformed* ethnicity, one that is not a simple derivative of the society from which the immigrants came (Alba 1985:9; Geschwender, Carroll-Seguin, and Brill 1988:516). As Lurie (1982:143) expressed it, "Immigrant communities usually were not communities when they came; their ethnic identities were, to a surprising extent, constructed in America."

Sephardic and Ashkenazaic Jews

If the Italians were the most conspicuous portion of the second immigrant stream, the Jews were only slightly less so. Although Jews had been present in the United States since the colonial period, the largest wave arrived from Russia during the period of the second immigrant stream. The earliest Jews, the **Sephardim,** were from Spain, Portugal, and Holland. The Sephardim were few in number, but they played an important role in establishing Jewry in America. A second and much larger wave of Jewish immigrants originated in Germany and areas dominated by German culture (Sklare 1975:263). The same forces that led the other large groups of nineteenth-century Germans to come to the United States stimulated the immigration of German Jews as well. Many of the Forty-eighters were representatives of this group. The German Jews, the first of several Jewish groups from countries in central and eastern Europe (the **Ashkenazim**), so outnumbered the Sephardim that they soon became the primary force within Jewish American life.

German Jews.   The rise of the German Jews was not due entirely to their numbers, however. Of great importance also is that the German Jews had undergone a comparatively high level of cultural assimilation by substitution in Germany. The identification of the German Jews as Germans continued in the United States. According to Wittke (1964:329), the Jews participated in the activities of the *Turnvereine* and generally supported German cultural activities. Hence, the political and social characteristics of the German Jews were more prominent than their religion; and their religious practices were themselves much less distinctive than those of the Orthodox Jews who arrived both before and after them.

Most of the German Jews were participants in the Reform movement. The Reform synagogue differed from the Orthodox in such things as using little Hebrew in religious services, seating men and women together, celebrating Sunday as the Sabbath, approving intermarriage, and omitting prayers for the restoration of the Jewish state (Schermerhorn 1949:391). When combined, these factors stimulated a comparatively rapid cultural assimilation by substitution and a very rapid secondary structural assimilation of the German Jews in the United States. As the members of this group spread out across the country, many of them rose rapidly into the middle and upper classes. One of the most celebrated occupations of both first- and second-stream Jews was that of itinerant peddler. This line of work appealed to Jews, as it did Italians, because the cost of going into business was so low (Gold and Phillips 1996:189). Lieberson and Waters (1988:126) reported that in 1900 Russian men (most of whom presumably were Jewish) were over 23 times as likely to be "hucksters and peddlers" as were other White men in the labor force. "The new immigrant who was fired with ambition to succeed but hamstrung by limited capital," Kraut (1982:95) observed, "took up the peddler's . . . pushcart." Some of America's great department stores—including Macy's, Gimbel's, Bloomingdale's, Filene's, Goldwater's, and Sears Roebuck—grew from such beginnings (Jones 1976:164–165). By the time the Russian Jews began to arrive in significant numbers, the German Jews al-

ready were established as the elite of American Jewry (Sklare 1975:263)—a status reflected by a strict pattern of within-group and intercity marriage alliances (Baltzell
1964:57). The rapid movement of the German Jews toward the mainstream of American
cultural and secondary structural life suggested that in time—perhaps the fabled three
generations—they would proceed through the remaining phases of assimilation and
would disappear as a distinctive group.

Russian Jews.   That the full Anglo conformity assimilation of the German Jews did
not occur may be due to the arrival of the extremely numerous and culturally distinctive
Jews of the second immigrant stream. Between 1.5 and 2 million Russian Jews arrived in
the United States as a part of the second immigrant stream.[10] Like the German Jews, the
Russian Jews had at one time lived in Germany; and their main language was Yiddish, a
mixture of Hebrew and German. Because of this historical unity, these two groups are
both considered to be Ashkenazaic Jews; but after centuries of separation, the German
and Russian groups were markedly different. Unlike German Jews, Russian Jews had
been forced to live apart from the dominant group in certain parts of the country known
as the Pale of Settlement. They had been oppressed by various restrictive laws (such as
the military draft) and by organized violence (pogroms). Under these conditions, they
had remained strongly united and had maintained their native culture and language to a
high degree. Moreover, in contrast to the German Jews, the Russian Jews had every intention of keeping their culture intact in the New World. Most of the men wore beards,
they organized Jewish schools to teach the ancient religious ways, they held strictly to the
Sabbath and the dietary laws, and they dressed in distinctive ways. Even the German Jews
considered these newcomers to be social inferiors and did not wish to associate with
them (Schermerhorn 1949:393). It was, Glazer wrote, "as if a man who has built himself
a pleasant house and is leading a comfortable existence suddenly finds a horde of impe-
cunious relatives descending upon him" (quoted by Baltzell 1964:58). But the German
Jews were concerned about the welfare of their co-religionists and also feared that their
unusual manner of dress and other folkways might stimulate anti-Semitism among native Americans. For these reasons, the German Jews extended a broad range of assistance
to the Russian Jews (Gold and Phillips 1996:188–189).

Italians and Russian Jews

Like the Italians, the Russian Jews were largely trapped in the port cities of the East, especially the Lower East Side of New York. Despite the efforts of Jewish Americans to assist
the newcomers in relocating to other parts of the country, most of them remained in the
newly formed urban ghettos. The Russian Jews also resembled the Italians in having had
little previous experience in urban living. Most of them had come from small villages.
Finally, the members of these two second-stream immigrant groups did not come to
America with the desire to assimilate.

These similarities between the Italians and the Russian Jews do not mean that their
reactions to the new environment were identical. For example, although neither group
wished at first to assimilate in America, their reasons were quite different. The Italians, as

we noted previously, typically did not bring their families, planning instead to make a fortune and return with it to the homeland. Although the Russian Jews brought their families and planned to remain permanently in America, they did not wish to give up the ancient culture they had so zealously defended in eastern Europe.

Two other differences between the Italians and the Russian Jews are noteworthy. The first has to do with the psychological impact of American urban living on the members of the two groups. It is an understatement to say that thousands of people in all of the second-stream groups were bitterly disappointed by the conditions they found in the New World. They were exploited at every turn, not only by the Americans but also by many of their own countrymen who "knew the ropes." They were forced to work at unfamiliar jobs, at low wages, and with no job security. Usually, they had no choice but to move into the tenement slums with their crowding, noise, filth, lack of sanitation, and crime.[11] Understandably, many people felt defeated, homesick, and lonely. Both the Italians and the Jews were subject to these tremendous pressures. The Jews, however, were somewhat more insulated than the Italians. As bad as the conditions were, the Jews found in America a degree of freedom from persecution unimagined under the rulers of eastern Europe. Moreover, since the Jews had come over in families, including an unusually high proportion of children under the age of 14, they had quickly erected a cultural tent, so to speak, which gave them added protection against the insults and deprivations that were common in the lives of immigrants. They were extremely eager to make use of their new freedom and, consequently, embraced the opportunities that existed in public education and politics much more rapidly than did the Italians.

The second notable difference between the two largest groups of the second immigrant stream concerns the types of skills they possessed and the economic possibilities that were available to them. Although neither group was really familiar with the requirements of urban-industrial living, more Jews than Italians happened to possess occupational skills that could be put to quick use in such a setting. Ironically, some of the varied restrictions that had been placed on the Jews in eastern Europe had forced them into activities that now were of some value. An example of the way some of their previous skills helped the Jews to develop a distinctive wedge into the economy was their heavy concentration in the needle trades (Novotny 1974:138). By 1900, Russian (probably mostly Jewish) men were over 30 times more likely to be tailors than were other White men in the labor force (Lieberson and Waters 1988:126). They began making all types of clothing. Soon the garment industry in New York was run disproportionately on Jewish labor (Kraut 1982:82). Their concentration in this industry became so great that they effectively monopolized it in a short time (Gold and Phillips 1996:189). In addition, though, many of the Jews were experienced merchants and were especially resistant "to serving as a mere source of labor power" (Portes and Bach 1985:38). The Russian Jews, as had the German Jews, sought to establish themselves as entrepreneurs and owners of property. For instance, to return to the "huckster-and-peddler" example, although both the Italians and the Russian Jews were attracted disproportionately to these occupations, the latter were much more likely to be found there than the former.

Although it was advantageous to the Jews, relative to the other immigrant groups, to have some readily saleable skills, they nonetheless worked under poor and oppressive conditions. The garment industry was so competitive that it was very difficult for its workers, large numbers of whom were women and children, to eke out a living. They worked extremely long hours, for very low wages, under unsanitary conditions; and they encountered vigorous, sometimes physical, resistance when they organized labor unions to represent their interests. Moreover, the garment shops frequently were extremely dangerous places to work. In one notorious instance, 146 workers were killed when the Triangle Shirtwaist Company's factory in New York was gutted by fire (Burner, Fox-Genovese, and Bernhard 1991:647–650).[12]

There was another deplorable side to all of this that affected the members of many immigrant groups at that time and, in fact, continues to affect immigrants even in the present period.[13] Several industries, including the garment industry, subcontracted or "farmed out" sizable shares of their work to people who labored in their homes; so large numbers of Jewish homes became "sweatshops." Jacob Riis ([1890]1957:80) observed in 1890 that "the homes of the Hebrew quarter are its workshops also." Not only were the working conditions in these home sweatshops frequently worse than those in the factories, but also the contractors often exploited an especially vicious aspect of the piecework payment arrangement. They gradually reduced the prices paid for each piece of work, thereby forcing the workers to increase their productivity in order to keep their earnings at the same level. A frequent result of this method was to force women and children to work as many as 18 hours a day (Novotny 1974:141–142). As Riis ([1890]1957:80) noted, all of the members of the family, young or old, helped with the work "from earliest dawn until mind and muscle give out together."

Our comparison of some of the differences between the way the Italians and Jews responded to the American setting illustrates a very important point: Although the members of these groups came to America as immigrant laborers and constructed ethnic communities in response to native hostility, their communities nevertheless may have represented significantly different modes of adaptation. The neighborhoods of both groups served residential and economic functions; but the economic function appears to have played a more decisive role in shaping the character of the ethnic neighborhoods established by the Jews. Although these neighborhoods resembled one another in appearance and served to shield their residents from the indignities heaped upon them by the dominant group, the Jewish neighborhoods are frequently cited as examples of an entrepreneurial approach by immigrants to the problems of adapting to a new setting. A number of other American ethnic groups—including the Asian Indians, Chinese, Cubans, Greeks, Koreans, and Japanese—also are named frequently as examples of this mode of adaptation.

Whether the immigrants of the second stream worked mainly as common laborers for members of the dominant group or for others of their own ethnicity, the human suffering engendered among all of them by the conditions of slum life in America at that time is truly incalculable. Despite great odds, the various second-stream immigrant groups endured and gradually made niches for themselves in American society, though not necessarily through the three-generations process. But, they were neither "a cluster of creative, ambitious, and optimistic individuals on the path from rags to riches" nor "a faceless mass of unskilled labor, sadistically exploited by robber barons" (Kraut 1982:75). In time, as the story of their courage, determination, and success became widely known, they became models of what one may accomplish in America through hard work and perseverance; but when their struggle was most intense, native Americans generally did not see the second-stream immigrants as a confirmation of the American dream. They saw instead a massive renewal of the assault by strangers on the folkways and mores of American life. Once again, as in the earlier peak periods of immigration, the Americans increasingly feared that their social dominance and well-being were threatened; and, as a remedy, they increasingly demanded various forms of restrictions on immigration.

Immigration Restriction: A Preview

Various arguments and studies alleging that the immigrants of the second stream were inherently inferior to those of the first stream led Congress to pass a series of laws that, by 1924, effectively closed the golden door. The 1924 law introduced the use of the **national-origins principle** in the calculation of immigration quotas. This principle was based on the idea that the members of some racial or ethnic groups are inherently superior and preferable as immigrants to those of other groups. Its application had the effect of granting preferences to immigrants from countries of the colonial and first immigrant streams. The national-origins principle became the subject of angry political debate and, in time, the cornerstone of American immigration policy. The effects of the important law of 1924 were reinforced by the Great Depression during the 1930s and again by World War II in the 1940s, producing during those two decades the lowest rate of immigration in American history.

The United States faced a dilemma throughout the twentieth century in its efforts to regulate the flow of immigration while, at the same time, honoring its historic commitment to accept the "huddled masses" of the world. This dilemma intensified as the forces of industrialization and urbanization "shrank" the world dramatically. By the end of World War II, these forces had encircled the globe, and their influences strongly shaped the character of international migration. As the world changed, so did the United States. In contrast to the "open door" of the nineteenth century, a proliferation of laws, regulations, and legal agencies were created to deal with the increasing complexities of immigration.

The Third Great Immigrant Stream

By the end of World War II, a large number of people had been displaced from their homes and had become **refugees**.[14] Another important development following World War II was a worldwide increase in labor migrations from the poor to the rich nations (Massey 1981:58). These developments were joined by important changes in the immigration policies of the United States that favored the admission of refugees, the members of new immigrants' families, and skilled and technical workers. Taken together, these events helped produce a third great immigrant stream to the United States or the new immigration.

The third immigrant stream started slowly at the end of World War II but gathered steam in each subsequent decade (see Figure 4.3). By 2000, the number of immigrants in the third stream had reached a level not seen since the earliest decade of the twentieth century, and 1991–2000 witnessed the largest number of newcomers of any decade in our history. Please notice though that, in relation to the total population of the United States, these massive increases in the foreign-born population still are well below those produced by the second immigrant stream (refer back to Table 4.1).

Figure 4.3 and Table 4.1 show in different ways that the third immigrant stream increased in volume more sharply after the 1960s than it had up to that time. The main reason for this large shift is that in 1965 the U.S. government made some far-reaching changes in the country's basic immigration law, the Immigration and Nationality Act of 1952 (INA). The new law, the Immigration and Nationality Act Amendments (INAA), was passed in 1965 and went into effect in 1968. Its purpose was to make America's immigration law more democratic, more humane, and fairer to all of the world's countries. To make entry into the United States more democratic, the INAA discarded the system of quotas that gave preference to immigrants from the countries of the colonial and first immigrant streams.

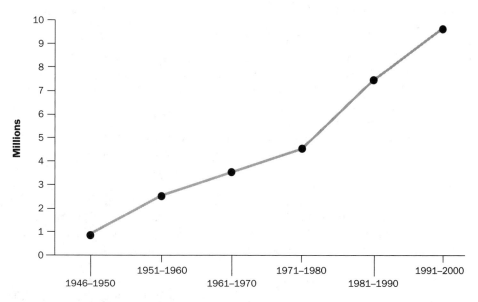

FIGURE 4.3   The Third Great Immigration Stream
Number of Immigrants by Decade, 1946–2000.

Source: U.S. Immigration and Naturalization Service, *Statistical Yearbook of the Immigration and Naturalization Service, 1994,* 1996:26; 2002; U.S. Bureau of the Census, *Statistical Abstract of the United States, 1995,* 1996:9.

Rejection of the National-Origins Principle

The legal changes that laid the groundwork for these basic shifts in the character of American immigration began during World War II. In 1943, a program to admit temporary agricultural workers from Mexico was initiated;[15] and in 1948 Congress passed the Displaced Persons Act. It was clear by then that the patchwork of immigration laws adopted during the preceding decades needed to be put into better order.

Legislation designed to systematize, and to some extent liberalize, the existing laws was introduced into Congress. The result of this effort, the INA of 1952 (McCarran-Walter Act), continued the established quota approach for the nations of the Eastern Hemisphere and, consequently, was severely criticized by those who wished to do away with the national-origins principle. The INA, however, provided that members of all races could become citizens, eliminated sexual discrimination in admissions, introduced "special preference" designations for people who had talents or skills that were needed in the United States, and increased the number of relatives of citizens and permanent residents who could be brought into the country above the quota limits (U.S. Immigration and Naturalization Service 1996:A.1–12). And it granted the government the power to admit additional people as "parolees" (Reimers 1985:26). In 1953, Congress passed the Refugee Relief Act; and in 1957 it passed the Refugee Escape Act (U.S. Immigration and Naturalization Service 1996:A.1–12, A.1–13).

Despite the loosening of restrictions permitted under the INA, the various refugee and displaced persons acts, and the government's parole power, criticisms of the national-origins principle of admission continued to mount. Consequently, in 1965, the INA was amended (the Hart–Cellar Act). This act broke sharply with the idea that the members of some racial or ethnic groups were inherently superior to those of other groups and were, therefore, to be preferred as immigrants. The national-origins quota system was abolished "eliminating national origin, race, or ancestry as a basis for immigration to the United States" (U.S. Immigration and Naturalization Service 1996:A.1–14). The new quota system raised the total who might be admitted annually from 150,000 to 290,000 people, beginning in 1968. A ceiling of 170,000 was set for all countries outside of the Western Hemisphere; no single country was assigned more than 20,000 visas per year. In addition, for the first time, an upper limit of 120,000 people annually was set on the entire Western Hemisphere, though no limits were set on any given country within it. As the volume of immigration from Mexico, Central America, the Caribbean, and South America rose, however, the pressure to assign limits to specific countries of the Western Hemisphere also rose. So, in 1976, the Western Hemisphere Act established a 20,000-visa-per-year limit for each country in this hemisphere (U.S. Immigration and Naturalization Service 1996:A.1–15).

The 1965 INAA also established a new preference system aiming first to reunite family members; second, to permit certain professional and skilled workers to enter the country; and third, to provide a place of asylum for refugees (Seller 1984:156). For example, among the seven preference categories listed, preferences one, two, four, and five (74 percent of the total) were allocated to family members. Preferences three and six were allocated to professional and skilled workers (20 percent of the total), and preference seven was reserved for refugees (6 percent of the total) (Keely 1980:17; Maldonado and Moore 1985:14). Of special importance was that the immediate relatives of U.S. citizens (i.e., spouses, children, and parents) were eligible to enter above the existing numerical limits. A summary of these laws is presented in Appendix 1.

Some Sociocultural Effects of the New Laws

An important post-World War II responsibility of the United States was to assist in the rebuilding of Europe and the relocation of the hundreds of thousands of people who had been displaced by the war. The United States at that time also was entering a new period of high international tension in which the country engaged in a global effort to "contain communism." Large numbers of World War II refugees and refugees from countries with communist governments sought asylum in the United States. The laws concerning refugees and displaced persons, and also the government's parole authority, were responses to these new global realities; and, as we have seen, refugees have been an important part of the third stream.

Since most of the refugees entering the United States in the decades immediately following World War II came mainly from countries represented in the first and second immigrant streams, the third immigrant stream seemed at the outset—with one major exception, Mexicans—to be mainly a resumption of the first and second streams. As had been true in the earlier periods, Germany, Canada, the United Kingdom, and Italy were among the countries that were most prominently represented (see Figure 4.3). But this pattern was altered markedly as wars in Southeast Asia and the Middle East created large refugee populations in those parts of the world. We return to this topic in a later chapter.

Increasing Racial and Ethnic Diversity.   The changes contained within the INAA of 1965, in combination with economic and political problems in third-world countries, stimulated a sharp increase in the volume of immigration from Mexico, Central America, the Caribbean, South America, and Asia and altered the sociocultural composition of the immigration flow that had commenced immediately following World War II. These changes in the new immigrant stream became more pronounced in the following decades of the twentieth century with the largest numbers of newcomers coming from Mexico. The other leading countries of origin have been, in order, the Philippines, Korea, China (including Taiwan), India, the Dominican Republic, Vietnam, and the countries of Central America (U.S. Immigration and Naturalization Service 1996:28). In addition, around 400,000 new immigrants have arrived from the countries of Africa since 1965.

The new immigration was enlarged and accelerated as new residents became citizens and exercised their right to bring in members of their immediate families above the quota limit. This pattern, in which the members of an ethnic group encourage and assist co-ethnics to migrate and join them, is an example of a **chain migration.** The overall result was that European immigrants, who comprised the overwhelming majorities of the colonial, first, and second immigrant streams declined sharply as a proportion of the total number of immigrants, whereas the proportion of those from Latin America and Asia rose to become, by 1980, the largest share. In addition, by far the largest numbers of refugees, who—like immediate family members—were eligible to enter above the quota limits, came from these same regions of the world.

These latest newcomers have exhibited a much wider variety of social, educational, and occupational backgrounds than those in the previous immigrant streams, greatly increasing the sociocultural diversity of the United States. Both the INA of 1952 and the INAA of 1965 included preference categories for those who had scarce job skills. These provisions have enabled a sizable group of professionals to join the third stream. To illustrate, in fiscal year 1994 among the immigrants admitted who listed a previous occupation, nearly one-third described themselves as having worked either in "Professional speciality and technical" or in "Executive, administrative, and managerial" jobs. People in these categories came from all over the world, but almost three-fourths of them were from Asia and Europe (47 percent and 27 percent, respectively) (U.S. Immigration and Naturalization Service 1996:68–69). In the same year, more than one-fifth of those admitted with a stated occupation were listed in the category "Operator, fabricator, and laborer." These workers, too, came from all over the world; but their origins were more concentrated in the Western Hemisphere, with over 50 percent of them coming from Mexico and the countries of the Caribbean.

Settlement Patterns.   The immigrants of the third stream also have been more diverse in their places of destination than were the immigrants of the first two streams. Although some states that traditionally have received large numbers of immigrants, such as New York, have continued to be popular destinations, some additional states and regions of the country have received a large proportion of the third-stream immigrants. The Vietnamese refugees, for instance, were intentionally resettled by the government in various parts of the country. They are concentrated mainly in California, Texas, Pennsylvania, and Louisiana (Montero 1979:8; Wright 1980:511). The Cubans, who also were intentionally resettled in different parts of the United States, have migrated in large numbers to southern Florida and southern California. Cubans remain in sizable numbers, however, in northern metropolitan areas with large Spanish-speaking populations. Koreans are concentrated in Los Angeles, New York, and Chicago; and East Indians are concentrated in California and New York (Mogelonsky 1996:133). The majority of Mexicans have settled in the border states of the Southwest, particularly in California and Texas (Perez 1980:257; Portes and Rumbaut 1990:46).

Time of Arrival.   Still another source of diversity among the new immigrants stems from the length of time the members of each group have been represented in significant numbers within the U.S. population. Substantial numbers of Mexicans, Chinese, Japanese, and Filipinos reached the United States before 1924. Although the range of differences in education and job skills within these groups was large, most of the nineteenth- and early twentieth-century immigrants from these groups were fairly similar to one another; they were mainly manual laborers with little education. Nevertheless, despite high levels of prejudice and discrimination against them and imbalances in the numbers of men and women, these groups weathered the initial difficulties and successfully established families and lasting communities in different parts of the United States.

As we have seen, however, these groups' compatriots in the third immigrant stream, though still exhibiting a wide range of social characteristics, have tended on the average to be of much higher initial educational and skill levels than were their co-ethnics from the earlier period. In addition, the descendants of the earlier immigrants are now highly assimilated culturally and structurally into American society. The presence of third-, fourth-, or even later-generation descendants of the earlier immigrants enables new immigrants to take advantage of the established institutional and social life of the ethnic communities that already exist within American society. The presence of both old-timers and newcomers creates a much more diverse ethnic situation within these groups, and within the United States as a whole, than existed before 1965.

Several of the new immigrant groups, however, have found few co-ethnics awaiting them in the United States. For example, there were very few Koreans in America until the Korean War started in 1950. Since that time over 800,000 Korean immigrants have been admitted. A very similar pattern may be seen among people from India, the Arab countries, the Dominican Republic and the other Caribbean countries, and El Salvador and the other countries of Central America. Following the passage of the INAA of 1965, the populations of people from each of these countries and regions have risen by hundreds of thousands.

Undocumented Workers.   The many pressures faced by poor people throughout the world generate a strong "push" that encourages them to migrate from their home countries, while the economic opportunities that exist in the world's richer countries provide an enticing "pull" for them to migrate to those countries. Although the changes in America's immigration policies initiated by the INAA were viewed as liberalizing the law—particularly the rejection of the national-origins principle and the emphasis on family reunification—there still existed quota limits. Additionally, the labor certification procedures established by Congress made the entrance of many types of workers more difficult. Many of the people who wished to enter the United States in pursuit of work therefore were excluded by the visa limits or were unable to find a job in advance (as required by law); consequently, many of these workers found ways to enter without acquiring the proper papers. The combined force of the economic gap that exists between the rich and poor nations of the world and the changes that were made in America's immigration laws resulted in a large increase in the number of "undocumented" or "illegal" immigrants. The exact size and impact of the undocumented immigrants has been the subject of furious debate.

There is controversy, too, over the proper terminology to be used in referring to these newcomers. The term "illegal immigrant" may suggest unfairly that the typical undocumented worker is a person of criminal tendencies who schemes to remain permanently in this country, but many observers believe the undocumented worker is generally "positively self-selected in terms of ambition and willingness to work" (Portes and Rumbaut 1990:11) and is usually a person who is seeking honest work. The undocumented worker also frequently is a sojourner and may soon return to his or her home.

The multiple entrances and exits of particular workers have established a cyclical migration flow that has complicated the problem of estimating how many undocumented immigrants are actually in the country at a given time. News stories frequently have raised the specter of an "invasion" of undocumented immigrants and have suggested that there could be as many as 15 million such persons in the United States; but, based on several studies employing different research methods, researchers concluded that in 1980, the number of undocumented workers in America was probably no more than 4 million (Bean and Tienda 1987:119–120; Massey 1981:61); however, by 2000, U.S. Census figures suggested there may have been as many as 8 million undocumented workers in America (Jencks 2001a:61). Mexico is the largest source of these workers but significant numbers also come from Canada, Central America, the Caribbean nations, Europe, and Asia (Lapham 1996:58).

In any event, there has been a widespread *perception* that undocumented immigration is an important problem and that something must be done to bring it under control. Undocumented immigrants were said to be displacing U.S. workers, undermining wages and working conditions, and receiving social services illegally (Papademetriou 1987:325).

The addition to the American population of so many people from so many different countries has altered the ethnic landscape of the United States, affecting practically every aspect of life ranging from the foods Americans eat to the languages that are spoken in the schools to the variety of religions that are practiced. Whether these changes are, on balance, a boon or a bane has become a widely debated subject throughout the country. The new immigration—called by some commentators "the browning of America"—has once again aroused the same fears expressed by natives during the previous periods of high immigration.

Flashpoint 1: Are Immigrants Good for America?

From the earliest days of colonization, the dominant group encouraged voluntary immigration with alternating enthusiasm and resentment. Even though the colonists created systems of bonded servitude and slavery to help them clear the land, till the soil, and produce raw materials for the mother country, these sources of labor alone were never sufficient. Large numbers of newcomers were required. Some Americans have always questioned the desirability of an open-door policy, however, and, as we have seen, various restrictions on immigration have been imposed in the past.

The magnitude and diversity of the third immigrant stream have revived the debate over immigration. Opinion polls show that many people believe the United States is being inundated by immigrants and some writers have stated that immigration either should be sharply curtailed or stopped altogether (Brimelow 1995). At the center of this volatile debate are two questions: (1) Is immigration *economically* desirable? (2) Is the United States *capable of absorbing* so many ethnically diverse new immigrants? Since answers to these questions involve complex technical issues and judgments, our aim here is only to outline briefly a few important ideas presented in the debate.

The Economic Question.   Whether the economic benefits of immigration out-weigh its costs is hotly debated. Consider the frequent claim that immigrants take jobs away from citizens and depress wages. We may begin to assess the validity of this claim by noting that research concerning the second immigrant stream appears to support the idea that immigration did not create unemployment among natives between 1890 and 1924, though it may have depressed their wages (Borjas 1996:74; Jencks 2001a:57). Even if these findings were true in the past, we cannot safely assume that they apply without alteration to the present. For one thing, the findings do not distinguish among different segments of the labor force. For another, there are important differences to consider between the economic and demographic circumstances of the past and present immigrant streams.

To illustrate how immigration may lead to gains and losses for different groups of Americans while benefiting the society as a whole, Borjas (1996:76–77) invites us to think about the presumed gains of international trade. When we purchase a particular product made by low-wage workers in another country, higher-paid American workers who also make that product may suffer wage cuts or lose their jobs; however, those who buy the lower-cost item may, as a group, save more money than is lost by the workers. Similarly, when immigrants compete for jobs with native workers and drive the wages of the native workers down, native consumers benefit from lower prices and employers benefit from lower costs. Under these circumstances, the net gain for the society—including the creation of more new jobs—may be greater than the monetary losses suffered by the native workers. The native workers who lose through increased competition, therefore, may favor greater immigration restriction while the consumers and employers who gain may favor less restriction.

After the Civil War, for instance, many African American leaders argued that immigrants were taking jobs that rightfully should go to African Americans. Between 1900 and 1935, many African American newspapers strongly endorsed proposals to ban Mexican immigrants from the United States and warned that immigrants would steal jobs from African Americans (Fuchs 1990:296). A study by Muller and Espenshade (1985), however, showed that Mexican immigrants in Los Angeles did not increase the aggregate level of unemployment among non-Hispanic Whites or among African Americans and, in fact, may have facilitated upward job mobility among African Americans. Similarly, studies by Vernez and McCarthy (1990) and Fix and Passel (1994) found that immigration increased the number of jobs without any serious long-run displacements of native-born workers. The latter view apparently was accepted by many African American leaders who urged Congress to approve the legalization of undocumented Mexican immigrants.

Another aspect of the economic debate concerns the claim that, even though immigrants pay taxes, their heavy use of public services results in an overall monetary loss to American society. Huddle (1993), for instance, concluded that immigrants cost the country's taxpayers more than $42 billion per year. In a detailed critique of Huddle's work, however, Passel (1994) concluded there is no evidence that immigrants cost the United States more than they contribute in taxes. In fact, according to his calculations, the immigrants of the third stream generate a surplus of at least $25 to $30 billion per year. Borjas (1996:77) argued, instead, that although there is a net gain (or "immigration surplus"), it is much smaller than Passel calculated. Borjas stated that the net gain is about $7 billion, or less than $30 per year for each native worker. Borjas concluded that if we could accurately calculate the total cost to taxpayers of services to immigrants, we would find the monetary benefit of immigration to be small at best.

Bean (1993:1F) proposed a middle ground between those who believe continued immigration is basically good for America and those who believe continued immigration is a luxury America can no longer afford. Bean suggested that whether the economic effects of immigration are mainly positive or negative depends on the economic conditions of the country. "In good economic times," he stated "immigrants may be helpful"; but he cautioned that "it may be wise to devise policies to slow unskilled immigration during periods of stagnant economic growth" (Bean 1993:5F).

Vernez and McCarthy (1996:45–46) presented still another view. They stated that the existing studies prove little more than that the most recent immigrants have low incomes and that families with low incomes contribute less in taxes than families with high incomes. They argued that instead of focusing on short-term policy issues, immigration research should examine long-term issues such as the overall effects of population growth, the environmental costs of a growing population, and ways to develop the U.S. economy.

The Ethnic Absorption Question.   We argued previously (1) that the basic framework of American society and culture was established during the colonial period primarily by people from England, with numerous borrowings and innovations, and (2) that Anglo conformity became the accepted, semiofficial pattern that immigrants were expected to adopt. Nevertheless, this dominant conception of Americanism has never been accepted by all citizens; and, as we have seen, it has been challenged periodically though, so far, never overturned.

Since the 1960s, however, Anglo conformity increasingly has given ground to the pluralist belief that *people of every racial and ethnic group may become "100 percent Americans" without changes in their physical appearance or a complete substitution of Anglo American ways for those of their own cultures.* As stated by President Franklin D. Roosevelt, "Americanism is a matter of the mind and heart; Americanism is not, and never was, a matter of race and ancestry" (Schlesinger 1992:37).

Those who favor Anglo conformity oppose the pluralist view of Americanism. They are aware that if the new immigration continues at its present level, by 2050 the White majority will have declined to around 53 percent (U.S. Bureau of the Census 2001:17). Brimelow (1995:9, 216), for instance, agreed that American immigration has been a "triumphant success" but expressed doubt that America can now successfully absorb the new immigrants unless its admissions policies are sharply altered. We must at least have a lull, he said, similar to the ones that took place in the periods 1776 to 1815 and 1924 to 1965.

A different reservation about present immigration policies has been expressed by Borjas (1996:74). He has calculated that the average skill level of immigrants to America has been declining and that a continuation of this trend suggests that immigrants will experience increasing problems as they try to enter fully into American life. To illustrate, in 1970 the average educational level of newcomers was 0.4 years of schooling lower than that of natives, and newcomers earned 83 percent as much income as natives. By 1990, the average educational level of newcomers was 1.3 years of schooling lower than that of natives, and newcomers earned 68 percent as much income as natives. These declines in education and income levels have led, said Borjas, to increased welfare assistance among immigrants such as participation in cash-assistance programs, Medicaid, and food-stamp relief. These trends, he stated, mean that, on the average, the American-born children of the new immigrants may face even greater hardships than those of the past.

Under these circumstances, members of the second generation may experience downward mobility—as suggested by the segmented assimilation hypothesis. As Jencks (2001b:94) noted, second-generation members typically are better educated and earn more than do their parents. Still, he echoes Borjas's concern and states that millions of poor, second-generation immigrants may not achieve even the socioeconomic level of their parents. In response to this pessimistic assessment, Alba (2002) criticized Jencks's "unjustifiably gloomy tenor" as well as the strong reliance of both Borjas and Jencks on economic data. Alba stated that an analysis of demographic data for the period 1998 to 2000 "shows unmistakable socioeconomic advance in the second generation. . . ."

We close this brief consideration of the contemporary immigration debate with one last question: Could the present levels of immigration lead to separatism? In a comparison of the past and present periods of high immigration, Kennedy (1996) suggests that the most important difference between the new immigration and those of the past is the heavy concentration of a single large ethnic group (Mexicans) in a single region of the country (the Southwest). In addition to the concentration and size of the Mexican American population is its proximity to the mother country. The combination of these factors, Kennedy (1996:68) suggested, opens to Mexican Americans a new option—the possibility of preserving "their distinctive culture indefinitely." Kennedy argued that America's response to this unprecedented possibility should be to help new immigrants to make their way into American society. To accomplish that, he said, we must not choose the heavy-handed tactics of the past but, rather, be "less confrontational, more generous, and more welcoming than our current anxieties sometimes incline us to be."

The vigorous debate over the new immigration and the ethnic diversity it has helped create in the United States illustrates the continuing conflict between the ideologies of Anglo conformity, cultural pluralism, and separatism in American life. The size and ethnic composition of the third immigrant stream have added to the heterogeneity of American society. Whether this increasing diversity is, on balance, desirable or undesirable is at the center on an ongoing, often emotional debate concerning alternative visions of what kind of country America ought to be.

The appeal of pluralism as the preferred route to Americanization has been greatly enhanced by the increasing ethnic diversity of the United States, but the danger that pluralism may slide into separatism also has increased, and this increase has been accompanied by a rise in hostility toward immigrants. In the next chapter we discuss some of the roots of people's beliefs about immigrants, some of the political consequences of these beliefs, and some of the theories that have been presented to explain them.

☀ Reality Check

INTERVIEW WITH AMANDA

Amanda is a college freshman. She grew up in Houston, Texas. Both of her parents have B.A. degrees in accounting. Her grandparents experienced the Holocaust and were sent to death camps in Poland. She attended private Jewish schools until eighth grade. Her mother's family came to the United States in the early 1900s and her father's family immigrated after World War II.

How do you refer to yourself?
I refer to myself as being Jewish before I would refer to myself as being White or American. Probably because it was a really big part of my life growing up. I was always in religious youth groups. I always went to Synagogue with my parents. Not just on holidays but on a regular basis. I never really refer to it as ethnic. More as a religion. I went to a Jewish private school; most of my friends are Jewish also so that's how they refer to themselves and probably how they refer to me.

What stands out as most important about your culture?
My parents have stressed that they want me to continue our religion and I've never even thought about marrying someone out of my religion. It's always been like I knew I was gonna marry someone that was Jewish. I was never going to date anyone that wasn't Jewish. I was going to raise my kids as Jewish. Probably the same way that my parents raised me. My kids would always go to a Jewish day school like I did. My culture is very family oriented. Spending holidays was always spending it with my family.

How has your background affected your daily life?
It hasn't had any negative effects so far. Only positive things. I've been to Israel many times. I think another big part is that my grandparents are survivors of the Holocaust so because of that my background has always been a really big part of me.

When did you become first aware of your ethnicity?
I don't think it was ever a case that I was first aware. It was just always like that. I was aware of other religions since I was always surrounded by other people who were in the same background as I was. We'd see Christmas lights and my house didn't have that. We'd see Easter Egg hunts but I'm not doing that. My school was all Jewish and it was like that until eighth grade. I guess when I was younger everybody was like that too because we were all alike.

Have you ever experienced an uncomfortable situation because of being Jewish?
Never. So I guess I have to be lucky because of that.

Tell me about your family.
Being Jewish is a big part of my family. My parents raised us to know that being Jewish was very important. And it is going to continue with me and I think the

only big thing that my parents stress is that it's very important to date Jewish people because you never know who you're gonna fall in love with. If you only date Jewish people you know that it's going to be someone Jewish. I have a younger sister who is 10. We always spend the holidays with my family. It's always been a big part of our life, for Passover or Rosh Hashanah and Yom Kippur we're always with our family. My dad's parents are survivors of the Holocaust. They didn't talk about it when we were younger in order to like protect us from the truth but it's amazing how they have such positive outlooks on life. They stress how important it is to be free and live every moment as the best and not to be upset. They are positive influences and role models on my life.

Last year I took a trip to Poland and Israel. We went to the concentration camps and marched the same march that the prisoners marched from one death camp to the other. It was hard for me to grasp what actually took place there. When I came home and showed my pictures to my mom and my dad and my grandparents, the whole effect of my week in Poland hit me. Now I know everything that happened. I'm glad I did it.

Tell me about your friends.
All my friends are Jewish. I'm in a Jewish sorority and we mix with fraternities that are all Jewish. I don't know if that is necessarily a good thing but that's just how my course in life has taken me. . . . My sorority took a lot of time first semester so I've done nothing else yet. It's a Jewish sorority but I wouldn't necessarily say that it's a religious sorority. You're not supposed to eat bread for eight days during Passover and they were serving bread at my sorority house.

Is marriage outside your background acceptable?
I wouldn't even know how to approach my parents with something like that. It's always been that I was going to marry Jewish. It's never a question. It's like what is. There are no interracial, interreligion marriages in my family and we have a big family. The marriage thing is a really big part with being Jewish.

Did you speak another language besides English before entering school?
I took Hebrew every day. I should speak it fluently right now but I can't, but there's no reason that I shouldn't. It's more of a written language. We're taught that in elementary and middle school and high school but I can't speak it fluently.

Tell me about your high school?
I went to public high school in ninth grade. It was my first experience with the real world. It was an extremely diverse high school. I think that the reason that my parents decided to do that was to give me a real taste of the world. You need to know what's out there. The school was probably a third Hispanic, a third African American, and a third White. There was a big Jewish population. I was always in Honors classes and in class I would always feel like I was in the majority but walking down the hall I would feel like a minority.

Discussion Questions

What role does Amanda's family play in maintaining her Jewish identity?

In what ways has Amanda assimilated?

How have family and community supports helped Amanda maintain her identity?

Describe the three great immigrant streams. In what important ways have they differed?

What have been the main sociocultural effects of the third great stream?

Should America's immigration policies be revised? In what ways?

What are the social pressures to assimilate that Amanda has experienced?

 Key Ideas

1. The greatest human migration in history has occurred since 1815. Millions of people have come to the United States as parts of three great immigrant streams. The first two great streams, which overlapped in the nineteenth and early twentieth centuries, were completed by 1924. The largest groups of immigrants in the first stream originated in Ireland, Germany, the United Kingdom, Canada, and Scandinavia. The largest groups in the second stream originated in Italy, Austria-Hungary, and Russia.

2. The immigrants from every country have tended to cluster together with others from their land of origin. In the process, they have formed ethnic communities for mutual aid and the reconstruction of their ethnic institutions and heritages.

3. During times of famine or economic or political disruption, large numbers of people were "pushed" from their homes and "pulled" toward opportunities in new lands.

4. The Irish and German emigrations were precipitated by rapidly growing populations and crop failures. Both groups were politically active and aroused the hostility and fear in native Americans.

5. Industrialization on both sides of the Atlantic brought great numbers of immigrants from southern and eastern Europe. The second-stream immigrants seemed to threaten the integrity of Anglo American society and culture. Demands for immigration restriction rose.

6. The experiences of the Italians illustrated the process of ethnogenesis. People from Italy became "Italian" in response to the pressures existing within American society.

7. The experiences of the Jews illustrated some of the important factors that affect the adjustment of immigrants to a new society. Important are whether individuals or family groups are most prevalent, whether men or women are more numerous, the extent to which the group already shares a common identity, and the kinds of skills they possess.

8. Political disturbances, wars, and changes in America's immigration laws have helped stimulate the third great immigrant stream.

9. The immigrants of the third stream differ from those of the first and second streams not only in their countries of origin but also in the diversity of their socioeconomic backgrounds and in their destinations. They have come mainly from Asia and Latin America and represent a broad range of educational and occupational levels.

10. The third immigrant stream has caused many people to wonder whether the newcomers will fit into the existing structure of American society or will alter it fundamentally.

 Key Terms

Ashkenazim   Jews from countries in central and eastern Europe.

chain migration   A pattern of migration of any size that is initiated by individual immigrants whose communications with family members and other co-ethnics lead additional immigrants to move to the new location over some period of time.

ethnogenesis   The social processes through which people (1) from the same geographic regions join together to form a new ethnic group within a different society; (2) revive the functions of an ethnic group that has lost all or most of a previous role; or (3) bring together in a new, broader ethnic group several groups that are thought to be related.

first great immigrant stream   The large emigration to America between 1820 and 1889 of people who originated primarily in the countries of western and northern Europe.

national-origins principle   Previously applied to the calculation of immigration quotas; based on the idea that the members of some racial or ethnic groups are inherently superior and, therefore, preferable as immigrants to those of other groups.

refugees   People who are outside of their country of nationality and are unable or unwilling to return to that country because of persecution or a well-founded fear of persecution.

second great immigrant stream   The large emigration to America between 1890 and 1924 of people who originated primarily in the countries of southern and eastern Europe.

Sephardim   Jews from Spain, Portugal, and Holland.

sojourners (birds of passage)   People who are, or intend to be, in a country temporarily.

third great immigrant stream (the **new immigration**)   The large emigration to America between 1945 and the present comprised of people who originated primarily in the countries of Latin America and Asia.

Notes

1. We rely on the "push–pull" image to help identify some important factors that encourage migration but do not imply that human beings are robots "drawn from their homes against their wills, as if by a 'distant magnet' " (Kraut 1982:9). The decision to emigrate is based on many factors (see also Portes and Rumbaut 1990:8–14, 223–224).

2. More immigrants arrived from France than Germany during the 1820s.

3. After 1924, Ellis Island was no longer used to receive immigrants. It became a detention center and point of deportation. In 1965, President Lyndon B. Johnson declared Ellis Island to be a part of the Statue of Liberty National Monument (Bolino 1985:42, 52); in 1989 the Ellis Island Immigration Museum was opened to the public.

4. A congressional commission (the Dillingham Commission) portrayed the immigrants of the second stream as something "new" in American history who could not be expected to become good Americans, as had the "old" immigrants.

5. Approximately 75 percent of the residents of Boston, Chicago, Cleveland, Detroit, and New York in 1910 were immigrants or the children of immigrants (Kraut 1982:77).

6. The United States was not the only destination of Italian immigrants. Many sought work in other European countries and millions went to Argentina and Brazil (Alba 1985: 39).

7. These trades include "dressmakers, milliners, seamstresses, and tailoresses, and could be stretched to include workers in textile mills" (Steinberg 1989:153).

8. Baltzell (1964:30) reported that when New York's Mayor Fiorello La Guardia criticized his fellow Republican President Herbert Hoover, Hoover wrote to him saying "You should go back where you belong. . . . The Italians are preponderantly our murderers and boot-leggers."

9. This process also has been called "emergent ethnicity" (Yancey, Ericksen, and Juliani 1976).

10. The official statistics concerning the Jews are less reliable than for many other groups because some Jews are listed only as nationals of the particular countries from which they came (Schermerhorn 1949:398).

11. Notorious Jewish gangsters included "Bugsy" Siegel, Meyer Lansky, and Arnold Rothstein; but, according to Gold and Phillips (1996:183), "Jewish criminality was generally of the nonviolent type."

12. The "shirtwaist" was a fashionable blouse that had a high collar, full bosom, and narrow, pleated waist. Most of the 500 employees of the factory were young Jewish and Italian women (Burner, Fox-Genovese, and Bernhard 1991: 647–648).

13. See, for example, Jane H. Lii, "Week in Sweatshop Reveals Grim Conspiracy of the Poor," *New York Times* (March 12, 1995:1); "7 Thais Plead Guilty in Sweatshop Slavery Case," *New York Times* (February 11, 1996:12).

14. Refugees apply for admission while they are outside of the United States; asylees apply from within the United States (Immigration and Naturalization Service 1996:76).

15. This "temporary" program continued until 1964 (see Chapter 8).

Nativism
and Racism

Prejudice may arise from many sources, including the views of family or peers, or it may come from strong identification with a particular group. Groups that promote hatred and discrimination continue to recruit members in the United States.

As a nation we began by declaring that "all men are created equal." When the Know-Nothings get control, it will read "all men are created equal except Negroes and foreigners and Catholics."

—Abraham Lincoln

. . . it is on the moral qualities of the English-speaking race that our history, our victories, and all our future rest.

—Henry Cabot Lodge, Sr.

 # Nativism

The host group's reaction to immigrants, as discussed previously, depended on things such as the size of an incoming group, the rate at which they arrived, their concentration, and the similarity between their culture and the Anglo American culture. If a group arrived in large numbers and behaved in ways that the members of the host society regarded as "too" different, the Anglo Americans became alarmed and reacted in hostile ways. Under such conditions, the usual levels of antiforeign activity increased greatly. Despite their fluctuating views, Americans generally preferred policies that encouraged a heavy flow of White immigrants from western Europe. After the United States gained independence, an "open-door" immigration policy was adopted. The basic assumption behind this policy was that immigrants helped the country economically.

The door to America was never entirely open, however. The fear that foreigners would not understand or respect democratic institutions or would in some way work to undermine them was voiced during the debates over the Constitution. In the first flush of their new-found freedom, the Americans suspected that Catholics might be monarchist subversives and that immigrants from France might attempt to foment the kind of unrest that had led to the French Revolution. These and other concerns about foreigners created a widespread **xenophobia.**

The first federal laws concerning naturalization, passed in 1790, provided that "any free white person" who had lived in the United States for 2 years could apply for citizenship (Ueda 1980:737). By implication, of course, Black slaves, Native Americans, and indentured Whites were excluded as potential citizens. These laws also ruled out applicants who were not of "good moral character" (Cafferty, Chiswick, Greeley, and Sullivan 1983:40). For the most part during this time, immigration and naturalization were left to state and local governments.

With the onset of the first great immigrant stream, many Americans were convinced that foreigners represented a serious threat to their way of life. Their hostile reactions, called **nativism,** included vitriolic attacks on Catholicism and the Pope, on the pauperism and illiteracy of the immigrants, and on the political rights of naturalized citizens. It also included an increasing number of proposals that laws be passed to restrict immigration, limit the rights of immigrants, and increase the length of time needed to become a naturalized citizen.

As the Irish population in America grew, and many of its members moved into various political and municipal jobs, there was an outburst of anti-Catholic propaganda. Many Americans believed the authoritarian organization of the Catholic church was incompatible with the democratic institutions and ideals of American society. Many newspaper accounts, books, pamphlets, and speeches claimed that the Irish Catholics were emissaries of the Pope who were working to undermine American traditions and overthrow the government of the United States. In 1834, for instance, the famous inventor Samuel F. B. Morse wrote several widely publicized statements claiming that the papal conquest was underway (Morse [1835]1976:61).[1] In 1836, an infamous tract, *The Awful Disclosures of Maria Monk,* portrayed monasteries and convents as dens of immorality (Monk [1836]1976:77). Anti-Catholic sentiments also were expressed in conflicts over the Catholics' opposition to the use of the King James version of the *Bible* in public schools and to their demands that state funds be used to support parochial schools.

The opposition to Catholicism was fused with a frequent, and not completely untrue, complaint that Europe was using America as a "dumping ground" for its paupers and criminals. There was widespread fear that the immigrants did not understand the American political system and could easily be manipulated by corrupt leaders. The Irish were accused of using rough, "un-American" methods to rig the outcomes of elections. Instances of bloc voting, electoral fraud, and voter intimidation were cited to show that the very foundation of American democracy was being undermined. Apparently, in some large cities, it was a common practice to illegally naturalize immigrants the day before an election (Jones 1960:154). Moreover, the continued interest of the Irish in the political affairs of Ireland increased the fear that they were not loyal to the United States.

The Germans also were targets of the growing xenophobia of the native Americans. The Germans were feared because they were presumed to be revolutionaries. Even Americans who did not accept the exaggerated charges against immigrants and naturalized citizens did not like the German revolutionaries who fled to America in 1848. As noted earlier, the members of this group were thought to be atheists and radicals who were contemptuous of American traditions.

The idea that immigrants were destroying the basic fabric of American society seemed even more plausible because of the rising controversy between the North and the South over slavery, westward expansion, and economics. As the possibility increased that the Union would collapse, various political parties were formed to protect the rights and privileges of natives and to combat immigration and immigrants. For example, in 1845 the Native American Party was formed. The purpose of this new party was to devise "a plan of concerted political action in defense of American institutions against the encroachments of foreign influence" (Feldstein and Costello 1974:147). The Native American Party's Declaration of Principles argued that the natives were rapidly becoming "a minority in their own land." And it recited some of the charges mentioned previously: The newcomers were working for foreign governments; they were mainly Europe's unwanted criminals, paupers, and imbeciles; they sought unfair political advantage by organizing along ethnic lines; and they "offered their votes and influence to the highest bidder" (Feldstein and Costello 1974:153).

The Native American Party did not succeed on a national scale; but it was soon followed by one that did—the American or "Know-Nothing" Party. The name of the party came from the fact that its members answered "I know nothing" whenever people sought information concerning its principles (Faulkner 1948:345). The party's slogan was "America for the Americans" (Jones 1960:157), and its platform urged that only native Americans be permitted to hold public office. The Know-Nothings opposed the admission of paupers into the country and believed that the period required for naturalization should be extended to 21 years. By 1854, the Know-Nothings had gained enough strength to elect a number of state governors and U.S. congressmen and to dominate several state legislatures. But by the election of 1856, conflicts between the North and the South overshadowed immigration as a threat to national life; the Know-Nothings' presidential candidate, former President Millard Fillmore, was soundly defeated.

The Civil War gave numerous foreigners a chance to demonstrate their loyalty either to the Union or the Confederacy. "In both sections of the country," according to Jones (1960:170), "immigrants responded to the call to arms as readily as did the natives." But the immigrants' loyalty had not removed all antialien sentiments. For example, in 1863 the Irish in New York staged 3 days of violence to protest the practice of permitting rich draftees to avoid military service, which the largely poor Irish were unable to do. Although these Draft Riots were fueled by anger at the White Republican establishment, most of the rioters' attacks were on Blacks. A wave of anti-Irish reaction followed the Draft Riots, suggesting again that the war had not submerged all nativism.

The conflicts between the native Americans and the peoples of the first great immigrant stream subsided markedly immediately following the Civil War. Most Americans still believed that immigrants should discard their foreign ways and adopt the basic pattern of American life as soon as possible. The people from northern and western Europe had proven that they could and would fit into the dominant Anglo American mold, that they were assimilable. Indeed, many of those whose parents had arrived during the 1840s and 1850s now exhibited high levels of cultural and secondary structural assimilation and had, for many practical purposes, joined the ranks of the natives; at the same time many of those whose grandparents had arrived during the 1820s and 1830s were undergoing primary structural, marital, and identificational assimilation. Although these changes increased the willingness of Americans to accept the later arrivals of the first immigrant stream, these immigrants still faced prejudice and discrimination. The levels of hostility were lower than they had been before the Civil War, however, which increased the probability of the civic assimilation of the first-stream immigrants.

The beginning of the second immigrant stream, however, aroused new doubts. As its volume overtook, and then surpassed, that of immigration from northern and western Europe, xenophobia mounted. As noted previously, the peoples of the second immigrant stream seemed to many Americans to be even more foreign than those of the first immigrant stream. Many Americans feared that the manners and customs of the most recent groups would threaten the very basis of Americanism, and their arrival in large numbers as a part of America's shift from an agrarian to an industrial economy made it seem that the newcomers were directly responsible for the many problems associated with industrialization. For example, during this period, workers began to organize labor unions in an attempt to ensure employment and decent working conditions. These organizational efforts were, to put it mildly, not well-received by the owners and managers of industry. Strikes and picket lines by working men were met by private armies and strike-breakers. Sabotage, assassinations, and open warfare were increasingly common in coal mines, steel mills, and railroads (Rubenstein 1970:29). Since many of these conflicts involved immigrant workers, xenophobia increased. These events in the East added strength to a movement initiated by conflicts between native workers and Chinese immigrants on the West Coast to end America's open-door policy and to establish legal restrictions on immigration into the United States.

The charges against the Chinese emphasized the usual economic and political claims relating to the disadvantages of accepting immigrants; but now prominently added to these arguments were certain pseudoscientific claims about the nature of racial differences. Immigrants were to be hated and excluded, according to this new theory, because they were presumed to represent the "defeated" and, therefore, biologically "unfit" portions of their respective races. This new line of thought—called **scientific racism**—developed rapidly during the last quarter of the nineteenth and the first quarter of the twentieth centuries.

 # Scientific Racism

Racial Differences

We noted in Chapter 1 that many people believe racial categories are specific, unvarying entities. In fact, however, the boundaries of races (and, more obviously, ethnic groups) are set by social agreement. The traits ordinarily selected to form the basis of the social definitions of race are, of course, visible and biological. Visible traits such as skin color, head shape, eye form, hair texture, and so on are biologically inherited. As we emphasized, however, none of the traits that most people view as "racial" can be used to establish clear-cut lines of division among the races. The apparent sharpness of racial boundaries in the United States stems from the fact that Americans believe race to be important and generally follow established folkways in identifying people as members of particular racial groups. After people have been classified, the members of each group generally will treat in-group members more favorably than out-group members.

The fusion of several intellectual trends during the latter half of the nineteenth century fueled the dispute concerning racial differences. Ideas from Charles Darwin's theory of organic evolution were used to argue that individuals, nations, and races were engaged in a struggle to select the "fittest" and that, therefore, social dominance was a sign of natural superiority. The advocates of **social Darwinism** believed that socially dominant groups are groups that have demonstrated their biological "fitness" in the struggle for survival.

Darwin's ideas also were compatible with an influential, now discredited, interpretation of European and American history that claimed the tall, blond, blue-eyed peoples of northern and western Europe were the modern remnants of a talented race called the Nordics (or Teutons), who were descended from the ancient Aryans of India (Gossett 1963:84–122). The Nordics were said to have a special talent for political organization that enabled their members to form representative governments and create just laws (Higham 1963:137); hence, the Nordic portion of the White race was destined to rule over all races, including the shorter "Alpine" and the darker-skinned "Mediterranean" portions of the White race.

Social Darwinism also held that White people were more intelligent than other people, which strengthened a line of argument that has always been at the core of the race-differences controversy. The dispute over racial differences in intelligence gained momentum throughout the nineteenth century and, as we soon discuss, is still with us today. But the argument today revolves around evidence based on standardized tests of mental ability. Let us examine briefly the role of these tests in the continuing debate on racial differences in mental ability, and their effects on American immigration policies.

Mental Testing and Immigration

The main line of division on the issue of differences in mental ability lies between the competing ideas of **hereditarianism** and **environmentalism.** Francis Galton (1869), who initiated the field of mental testing in his studies of British men of distinction, argued that nature (heredity), not nurture (environment), was responsible for the rise of people to eminence. From Galton's perspective, no social barriers could suppress the naturally talented person, and no social enrichment could cause an untalented person to become successful. He accepted the doctrine of White supremacy but feared that the "Anglo-Saxon race" was degenerating genetically.[2] Galton and his followers assumed that each person was endowed at birth with a certain intellectual capacity that could be measured with appropriate types of mental tests. In 1905, Alfred Binet and Thomas Simon produced the first "scale" of intelligence (Klineberg 1937:323);[3] however, *they did not believe their scale was a measure of innate intelligence.* It was intended originally to be used only as a tool to assist in identifying children with learning problems.[4]

The Binet–Simon scale was developed near the peak of the second immigrant stream to the United States during a time of mounting pressure to adopt policies restricting admissions of new immigrants on the basis of racial or ethnic identity. The restrictionist's efforts were aided greatly by the evidence from a massive mental testing program conducted by the American Army during World War I. This program tested over 1.7 million men and was the first large effort at mental testing. It also stimulated a period of intense scholarly and public interest in some pertinent questions. What, exactly, is "intelligence"? Does the ability to answer the questions and tasks used in intelligence testing depend on experience? Is human intelligence a unitary thing, or is it composed of different elements?

The results of the Army's studies had a profound impact on scholars, policymakers, and the lay public.[5] In general, Black people and immigrants did not score as well on the tests as native Whites, even when efforts were made to take into consideration group differences in schooling and experience. In terms of the average (median) scores, White recruits of native birth ranked first, foreign-born White recruits ranked second, northern Black recruits ranked third, and southern Black recruits ranked fourth.

In an important contribution to the developing controversy concerning racial and ethnic differences in intelligence, C. C. Brigham (1923) analyzed the Army data further and presented them in *A Study of American Intelligence,* "a companion volume" to *America, A Family Matter* by C. W. Gould (1922). Gould's book argued for restrictions on immigration to the United States and against "racial mixing." Brigham's analysis strengthened the case for special restrictions on immigrants from the countries of southern and eastern Europe. The book showed that the foreign-born recruits from countries representing the first immigrant stream exceeded the average for foreign-born recruits from countries representing the second immigrant stream. Brigham (1923:182) concluded that the results support "the thesis of the superiority of the Nordic type."

The Army's test program results seemed overwhelmingly to support the hereditarian perspective on group differences in intelligence. Most psychologists at this time were "of the opinion that the inherent mental inferiority of [immigrants and non-Whites] had been scientifically demonstrated" (Thompson 1934:494); and most ordinary citizens were convinced the matter had been settled once and for all. Indeed, the hereditarian view seemed so compelling at this point that the nation's immigration policies were radically altered to reflect what was taken to be established fact.

The Rise of Environmentalism

As the number of studies comparing the IQ scores of different racial and ethnic groups continued to mount, many scholars concluded that the effects of people's backgrounds— such as a person's social status and test experience—had been underestimated. Even Brigham reconsidered the matter and retracted his previous conclusion.[6] Certain questions of method were explored more fully, and the Army data were subjected to further analyses.

By the beginning of World War II, scholarly opinion (though not that of the general public) had reached a position far removed from the dominant opinion of the early 1920s. Although some scientists still accepted the hereditarian thesis, most agreed that both heredity and environment affected an *individual's* mental test scores in some complicated, poorly understood way. For most researchers, the question was no longer, "Is intelligence determined by heredity *or* environment?" The question was, rather, "How do heredity and environment combine to affect the scores obtained on intelligence tests?" Environmentalists had shown clearly that factors such as the test taker's previous experience, socioeconomic status, self-esteem, and motivation can influence test results.[7]

In the ensuing debates among scholars surrounding the proper interpretation of these points, the weight of informed opinion continued to shift toward an emphasis on the role of environmental factors in producing group differences in intelligence test scores. A further consequence of the years of study and debate was that the key issues became more technical. For this reason, we focus on only a few important points and, especially, on some statistical arguments that lie at the heart of the contemporary controversy.

Comparing Races.   Consider again the view presented in Chapter 1 and earlier in this chapter that although people commonly think of races, and sometimes ethnic groups, as sharply distinguishable biological entities, their boundaries, in fact, are set by social agreement. There is massive evidence showing that the visible (phenotypic) races are highly intermixed and that, therefore, no strong claim can be made that a given difference between these groups (such as in average IQs) reflects biological differences (Ryan 1995:27).[8]

From this perspective, unless a valid *biological* method of setting racial boundaries is discovered, *no statistical argument,* however sophisticated, can demonstrate that an average difference between races has a genetic basis. Nevertheless, statistical arguments are still widely used and often are accepted as demonstrating that average group differences in IQs have a genetic basis. For this reason, it is essential that we be conversant with the main statistical arguments.

Testing Theory.   The statistical arguments begin with the finding that people who do well on one test are likely to do well on another. Charles Spearman (1904) stated that this finding shows each individual possesses a general intellectual ability (intelligence) that is inherited and unchangeable; and he devised a statistical procedure to isolate and measure this ability.[9] In a severe criticism of Spearman's theory of intelligence and testing, L. L. Thurstone (1935) showed, with a different statistical technique, that there are several different types of intelligence instead of only one and that the various types are measured differently by different tests.[10]

The main question then, as expressed by Gould (1981:253, 302), is this: "How can the claim be made that general intelligence is biologically fixed if an alternative, but equally accurate, method of computing factors shows there are several different types of intelligence rather than a single type?" Researchers who follow Thurstone's lead search for patterns of differences among intellectual functions rather than for a way to rank racial and ethnic groups on a single scale of general intelligence (Loehlin, Lindzey, and Spuhler 1975:177–188).

By the late 1960s, public discussions of intelligence had shifted toward devising ways to improve intellectual achievement through deliberate changes in people's environments. Many studies and demonstration projects provided evidence that better nutrition, living conditions, and educational methods could bring about dramatic improvements in academic achievement and in IQ scores. As we discuss later, large government programs, such as the Head Start preschool program for low-income children, were launched to achieve these purposes. Public policy at this point seemed no longer to rest on the belief that mental ability is fixed by nature but, rather, on the belief that it can be molded substantially by improving our knowledge and our environment.

Flashpoint 2: Hereditarianism Revisited

During the last third of the twentieth century, those who were confident that the nation's educational and other social problems could be solved primarily through environmental changes were outraged by the publications of three scholars: Arthur R. Jensen, Richard J. Herrnstein, and Charles Murray. The first publication, by Jensen (1969:79), acknowledged that "no one . . . questions the role of environmental factors" on intelligence test scores, but he argued that the environment's role was comparatively small. In his view, better schools and social programs can do little to raise IQs.

Jensen relied on **estimates of heritability** to calculate the relative contributions of heredity and environment to an individual's mental ability. These estimates are based on comparisons of the IQ test scores of people who are genetically related or unrelated and are raised in similar or dissimilar environments. Jensen (1976:103) concluded that about 80 percent of the differences in IQ scores among *individuals* are due to their genetic endowments. He went on to state, however, that average *group* differences also are best explained in genetic terms.

Jensen's review was criticized vigorously. Some authors argued that his estimates of heritability are much too high, which may well be correct.[11] A more damaging criticism, however, is that the foundations for such estimates are studies of *specific* populations at particular times. If the estimates are accurate, they may be used properly to study differences *only within that population;* hence, even if the estimates Jensen used were accurate for one group, they still could not be used correctly to study differences *between* that group and any other group.[12]

The problem here lies in the fact that many *highly heritable characteristics may develop differently in different environments.* Consider this hypothetical example: If seeds of grain are planted in rich soil, they will be taller at maturity, on the average, than if they had been planted in poor soil. In both cases, however, there would have been *individual* variations in height. The individual variations in height would in either case be a result of genetic differences, but the *average* difference in height between the two groups would be due *entirely* to different environments.[13] When we apply this reasoning to average differences among the IQ scores of human groups, we see that *all* of the average difference between the groups may be due to different living conditions *even if* IQ is highly heritable.

In another explosive publication, Herrnstein (1971) added fuel to the fire in an exploration of some possible implications of the hereditarian thesis for the future of American society. If differences in intelligence are mainly inherited, Herrnstein said, and if educational and occupational success require intelligence, then a person's general social standing will be determined to some extent by his or her inherited intelligence.

Given this chain of reasoning, Herrnstein argued that one of American democracy's most cherished principles—the principle of achievement—is leading toward a strange result. In a society in which **vertical social class mobility** is affected substantially by individual ability, the more intelligent members of the lower classes will rise in the social hierarchy, leaving the less talented behind. Ironically, therefore, the ultimate effect of weakening the barriers to social mobility—of increasing what most Americans consider to be "fairness"—may be the creation of an "hereditary meritocracy." Because such a **stratification system** would be based increasingly on genetically inherited intelligence, children born into rich and powerful families of high standing generally would become rich and powerful adult members of the upper class; children born into poor and downtrodden families of low standing generally would remain members of a lower class throughout their lives.

In *The Bell Curve,*[14] Herrnstein and Murray tried to prove that this dismal scenario is becoming a reality in America. They argued that as occupational specialties become more technical and colleges increasingly base admissions on individuals' ability to do well on standardized tests, those who succeed in college are increasingly channeled into "high IQ professions" having high pay and prestige.[15] This educational and occupational stratification, they claim, will gradually lead to the isolation of the "cognitive elite" from the rest of American society (Herrnstein and Murray 1994:25, 91).

Had the authors limited their analysis to this highly debatable thesis, perhaps the book would not have generated such a heated controversy; but they did not. Eight of the first 12 chapters explored the relationship of IQ to a number of social problems among *White* Americans; but in Chapter 13 they introduced the incendiary subject of ethnic differences in IQ. They argued that the inequalities in IQ among ethnic groups are not due to biases in the tests or to differences in socioeconomic status (SES).[16] They argued further that the higher prevalence of problem behaviors among some minorities may be traced to their lower average IQs and that the lower average IQs are due in part to genetic differences. We highlight only three of the many issues raised by these inflammatory claims.

First, several critics focused on Herrnstein's and Murray's misuse of statistics (see e.g., Cole 1995; Kamin 1995; Suzuki 1995). Herrnstein and Murray claimed that group differences in undesirable behaviors were caused by differences in "intelligence itself, not just its correlation with socioeconomic status . . ." (Herrnstein and Murray 1994:117);[17] yet on the same page, they conceded that the amount of variation explained by IQ is "usually less than 10 percent and often less than 5 percent." How can such weak statistical connections be held to support their strong claim (Gould 1994:146)?

Another statistical problem concerns the important question, "Can intelligence be raised?" Herrnstein and Murray (1994:389–416) argued that "the story of attempts to raise intelligence is one of high hopes, flamboyant claims, and disappointing results." When Hauser (1995) reanalyzed their data on changes in IQ scores among Blacks and Whites, however, he discovered that Herrnstein and Murray (1994:389) had underestimated the actual amount of change by perhaps as much as 50 percent. He concluded that academic achievement can be improved and that *The Bell Curve* is a "flawed and destructive" work (Hauser 1995:153).

A *second* criticism of the book is less clear-cut and more debatable than the first, but it may be more important. Many outraged commentators argued that *The Bell Curve* was a cleverly written political brief presented in the guise of dispassionate science. The entire work seemed to be aimed mainly at supporting the authors' attack on the federal government's immigration, education, welfare, and affirmative-action policies and programs. For instance, Herrnstein and Murray agreed that Flynn's (1987)[18] discovery that IQ scores have risen throughout the world during the last generation "should caution against taking the current ethnic differences as etched in stone" (Herrnstein and Murray 1994:309); yet the primary message of the book was that these differences *are* "etched in stone." They might have given greater weight, instead, to the fact that such a large and rapid change in IQ scores could not have been caused by genetic changes (Fischer et al. 1996:52).[19]

Consider now a *third* issue raised by Herrnstein and Murray. In many ways *The Bell Curve* was a contemporary version of the social Darwinism of the nineteenth century. At the time *The Bell Curve* was published, people from Latin America and Asia comprised the bulk of the third immigrant stream, and the book echoed the fears of the nativists of the nineteenth and early twentieth centuries that the rising tide of non-Nordic immigrants was intellectually inferior to the native population and would lower America's mental level. In a short section on immigration that was reminiscent of the work of the early advocates of intelligence testing and immigration restriction, Herrnstein and Murray (1994:359) raised anew the specter of racial deterioration, arguing that the average IQ of Americans may be dropping. They recognized that in the past America has been very successful in attracting immigrants "who were brave, hard-working, imaginative, self-starting—and probably smart" (Herrnstein and Murray 1994:361); but they then advanced reasons for thinking that, overall, the contemporary period of immigration may be less successful than the previous periods.

As we have seen, this type of reasoning was very prominent during the second immigrant stream. Recall that this period was rife with nativist and racist ideas. These elements combined with the findings of the mental testing movement to prepare the way for large-scale restrictions on immigration in America. In the period immediately following World War I, all of the needed ideological and political forces coalesced in support of the Immigration Act of 1924. The passage of this law took place after decades of agitation in favor of restrictions on immigration. We now examine briefly the major events that culminated in the 1924 Immigration Act, beginning with the campaign that began in 1882 to exclude the Chinese.

 Immigration Restriction

The Chinese Exclusion Act of 1882

Few Chinese immigrants had reached America before the California gold rush began; but in the three decades following 1849, more than 228,000 Chinese arrived. As we discuss more fully in Chapter 12, these immigrants were part of a much larger emigration from China that was precipitated partly by deteriorating economic conditions in China and partly by the opening of employment opportunities in other parts of the world. The immigrants were attracted to the United States at first by the reports of fabulous wealth to be gained in gold mining, but later they responded to a joint effort by the United States government and railroad owners to attract low-wage workers to build the Central Pacific Railroad.

The presence of the Chinese in California soon became the subject of political debate and public protest. White miners in many of the camps passed resolutions excluding the Chinese and, in some cases, launched physical attacks against them (Boswell 1986:356). In 1852, the governor of California recommended that some action be taken to stem the "tide of Asiatic immigration" (Daniels 1969:16), and during the next three decades hundreds of Chinese people were harassed, expelled, and sometimes slaughtered (tenBroek, Barnhart, and Matson 1954:15).

In 1854, a former U.S. Commissioner to China expressed the fear that America faced an "inundation of oriental barbarism" in the form of Chinese "coolie" labor (Curran 1975).[20] Anticoolie clubs were organized beginning in 1862—the same year in which Governor Leland Stanford argued that the Chinese immigrants represented "an inferior race" and would "exercise a deleterious influence upon the superior" natives (Curran

1975:81). It was also in this year that Congress authorized the construction of a transcontinental railroad. This project required a large number of laborers to do hard and dangerous work; so the Central Pacific Company recruited and hired thousands of Chinese workers. When the railroad was completed in 1869, the railroad workers (most of whom were Chinese) were thrown out of work and into direct competition with native workers for other jobs.

Native workers and small businessmen considered the Chinese workers to be the "slave laborers" of big business, and they deeply resented what they considered to be unfair competition (Boswell 1986:357–358; Hirschman and Wong 1986:5). This resentment led to the formation of a Workingman's Party that campaigned with the slogan "The Chinese Must Go!" (McWilliams 1949:174). A statement by this party in 1877 claimed that "white men, and women, and boys, and girls . . . cannot compete with the single Chinese coolie in the labor market" and, further, that "none but a degraded coward and slave would make the effort" (Kitano and Daniels 1988:22–23). The clamor for action, especially in California, became so strong that by 1880 both major political parties came out against permitting the Chinese to come to America to work, adding impetus to a trend toward restrictions on immigration.

The year 1882 was a watershed year in the history of American immigration. The number of immigrants reaching the United States in that year exceeded all previous years. Also in 1882, Congress enacted a comprehensive immigration law that prohibited the admission of convicts, lunatics, idiots, and people who were deemed likely to become public charges (Abrams 1984:108). Of special relevance to us here is that in the Chinese Exclusion Act of 1882 Congress voted to suspend for 10 years the entrance of Chinese workers and, also, to declare them to be ineligible to become citizens of the United States. The previous exclusions of immigrants had been based on the personal characteristics of different individuals but now, for the first time, American policy endorsed the idea that an entire group of people might be undesirable as immigrants and unfit for citizenship because of their race or nationality! As Reimers (1985:4) expressed it, "With the passage of this act the Chinese became the first and only nationality to be barred by name."

The Chinese Exclusion Act sharply reduced the number of Chinese coming into the United States.[21] It did not, however, stop discrimination and violence against them; and the pressure to impose even greater restrictions on them was maintained. Within the next two decades, the rights of the Chinese in this country were sharply curtailed. In 1892, the laws preventing the entrance of Chinese laborers into the United States were extended and, in 1902, they were made "permanent" (Lai 1980:221). The period of the most rapid growth of the Chinese American population was yet to come, however, as we discuss in Chapter 12.

The Immigration Act of 1924

The second great immigrant stream reached its peak in the decade before World War I, although it continued at a high level during the 1911–1920 period. Numerous accumulated dissatisfactions among Americans (many of whom were themselves recent arrivals)

led to an almost continuous agitation to push Congress into passing laws that would restrict, or halt entirely, the immigration of members of various national groups.

By 1917, pressures from those who feared racial deterioration and the inundation
of American institutions by "hordes" of European and Asian immigrants had reached a
high level. In that year the federal government passed an Immigration Act that barred al-
coholics, stowaways, vagrants, and people who had had an attack of insanity (Cafferty,
Chiswick, Greeley, and Sullivan 1983:44).[22] The most controversial portion of the Act of
1917, however, was the requirement that all immigrants must pass a literacy test before
entering the country. President Woodrow Wilson vetoed the bill stating that it embodied
"a radical departure from the tradition . . . of this country," but his veto was overturned
by Congress (Jones 1976:228).

The Immigration Act of 1917 did little to reduce the flow of immigration. In 1921,
the Emergency Quota Act (the Johnson Act) for the first time introduced a quantitative
formula placing a general limitation on the number of immigrants who could be admitted in a single year; consequently, this act represented an historic departure from the
open-door policy (Abrams 1980:27). The basic strategy of the law was to increase the
proportion of all admittees who would be from the European countries that contributed
most heavily to the colonial and first immigrant streams, while simultaneously decreasing the total number of legal immigrants. This dual result was obtained, moreover,
without legislating specifically against particular nationalities. To produce this diplo-
matically tricky outcome, the act restricted immigration from Europe, Africa, the Near
East, Australia, and New Zealand to 3 percent of the number of foreign-born members
of each nationality counted in the United States census of 1910. Since a larger number of
foreign-born immigrants in 1910 were from the countries of northern and western Europe than from any of the other places of origin, this legislation favored the countries of
the colonial and first immigrant streams. At this point, immigration from other countries of the Western Hemisphere was not of great concern, so no quotas were set for
these nations.[23]

The application of the quantitative formula of the 1921 law to the calculation of
quotas had a dramatic effect on the size and sources of American immigration. Previously, the annual immigration from all nations averaged over 850,000 people, around 79
percent of whom came from countries such as Italy and Russia; after the 1921 act, annual
immigration was reduced to around 355,000, about 44 percent of whom came from
countries of the second stream. Still, these changes did not satisfy the strongest advocates
of restrictions on immigration; consequently, the restrictionists continued to press for a
stricter law. The Immigration Act of 1924 (the Johnson–Reid Act) was the result.

This law continued the quota strategy of the Act of 1921 but altered it in four main
ways. First, it changed the "base" year initially from 1910 to 1890; second, the annual
quota for all countries was set at 165,000 for the period 1924–1929; third, beginning in
1929 the annual quota for all countries was lowered to 150,000; and fourth, beginning in
1929 (using 1920 as the base year), the national-origins principle was to be used in the
calculation of the annual quota of each country. For instance, if 30 percent of the Americans in 1920 were of English origin, then the annual quota for English immigrants would
have been 45,000 (i.e., 30 percent of 150,000). Because in both 1890 and 1920 most
Americans either were from Ireland, Germany, the United Kingdom, Canada, France,

and Scandinavia or were descended from people from those countries, the 1924 law led to a still higher proportion of admissions for the people of the countries of the colonial and first immigrant streams than had the 1921 law (Cafferty, Chiswick, Greeley, and Sullivan 1983:53). In short, with the quota formulas that were adopted, the limits of overall immigration were lowered while the proportions set for the more "desirable" immigrants were increased, as was intended. The Immigration Act of 1924 resulted in a dramatic change in America's historic "open-door" policy by implementing restrictions that permitted close control over immigration. Many of the details of implementation were set through legal cases brought by ethnic groups whose members wished to become citizens (Ngai 1999). These cases often turned on the question of who is to be defined as White. Appendix 1 presents a summary of some of the important immigration and naturalization legislation passed since the first federal law in 1790.

We have seen thus far that the members of the dominant Anglo American group in the United States have exhibited strong views concerning the desirability of various groups of outsiders and that these views have been defended in economic, political, cultural, and racial terms. These views have been accompanied by different types and degrees of physical, social, and legal reactions. In all of the circumstances we have considered, greater or lesser degrees of conflict have been present. Two main assumptions have guided much of the research concerning the factors determining these patterns of prejudice and discrimination. The first assumption is that a central aspect of racism is discrimination by the dominant group. The second assumption is that discrimination by members of the dominant group is caused by each individual's level of prejudice.

 Contemporary Racism

We have seen that people from countries of the first immigrant stream generally have been more acceptable to Anglo Americans than those from countries of the second immigrant stream. And regardless of their place of origin, Whites have been more acceptable than non-Whites. Our analysis has shown that the historical sequence of intergroup contacts in America created a particular pattern of social "layers" among America's ethnic groups, a stratification system based on ethnicity, in which the groups differed in power and prestige. Although the members of the dominant group have rated all other groups as "beneath" them socially and have tried to keep each group "in its place," the doctrines of scientific racism provided the rationale for directing the greatest hostility toward groups that were deemed to be racially different.

Our brief review of the IQ controversy showed, however, that the ideas of scientific racism were under strong attack throughout most of the twentieth century. By the time Jensen published his defense of the hereditarian view, the climate of opinion was such that most scholars believed the analysis was anachronistic and badly informed. By that time also, as we discuss later, the Supreme Court of the United States had ruled in the famous case *Brown v. Board of Education of Topeka* (1954) that segregation in the public schools was unconstitutional; and the Congress of the United States had passed the sweeping Civil Rights Act of 1964. These landmark legal and legislative events reflected important changes in the attitudes of Americans toward racist ideas, and they encouraged citizens to adopt more tolerant attitudes and behavior toward the members of other groups.

Public statements by members of the dominant group, for whatever reason, did in fact become less strident and, apparently, more sympathetic to minority groups. For example, a study conducted by the National Opinion Research Center (NORC) found that public approval for the principle of school segregation had declined from 68 percent in 1942 to 7 percent in 1985 (Bobo, Kluegel, and Smith 1997; Hyman and Sheatsley 1964; Schuman, Steeh, and Bobo 1997). The level of Whites' acceptance of the idea that they should be given preference in the job market has also declined sharply, from 55 percent in 1944 to 3 percent in 1972 (Bobo, Kluegel, and Smith 1997). By the 1980s, the overall level of anti-Black prejudice had declined to very low levels (Firebaugh and Davis 1988:261).[24]

These shifts in attitudes may have been part of a general shift among Americans in the direction of greater tolerance (Williams, Nunn, and St. Peter 1976). Alternatively, the decline in prejudice revealed by public opinion polls may be an illustration of a phenomenon known as **social desirability bias.** This term refers to the fact that to present ourselves to others in a favorable light, we often give the answers we believe are expected rather than our true opinions (Dovidio and Gaertner 1993:188; Lobel 1988:30). The apparent gains in tolerance displayed in opinion polls, therefore, may have meant that "old-style bigotry" or "old-fashioned racism" had been superseded by a much more guarded "modern racism" (McConahay 1986). Although the majority-group members who were polled generally rejected blatant forms of prejudice and discrimination, they still opposed fundamental changes in race relations (Bobo 1988:88–91; Bobo, Kluegel, and Smith 1997). The targets of their opposition apparently had not changed, but these targets now were attacked indirectly rather than directly (Pettigrew and Martin 1989:171–172).

Opponents of school desegregation, for instance, might agree with the abstract principle that school desegregation was desirable but, at the same time, insist that this objective should be reached through neighborhood desegregation rather than through busing. In the meantime, most actual efforts to expand either busing or neighborhood desegregation were opposed. In addition, although many dominant-group members rejected the idea that Whites are genetically superior to other groups, they often still argued that the problems faced by minority-group Americans are evidence of insufficient effort on their part (Kluegel 1990:513); therefore, even though the ideas of scientific racism were being discredited and apparently discarded, the role these ideas had played during the development of America's ethnic stratification system may have been replaced by ideas that served as "fronts" for a more carefully veiled racism (Pettigrew and Martin 1987:46). In this transition, the contemporary meaning of **racism** grew to include much more than the term *scientific racism.*

We use the term *racism* to represent this enlarged meaning. Racism refers to an unfavorable attitude (prejudice), and perhaps an unfavorable action (discrimination), toward people who are members of particular racial or ethnic groups; it may or may not specify the type of relationship that exists between unfavorable attitudes and actions; and the idea of group ranking may be more or less salient. Clearly, this meaning of racism is more complicated and flexible than are the meanings we have given to scientific racism or to prejudice or to discrimination,[25] and, as Hacker (1992:19) stated, it "goes beyond prejudice and discrimination."

In many discussions of contemporary racism it is necessary to infer from the context how the term is being used. In this form, it has the rhetorical advantage of drawing attention to the complex web of interconnections among the beliefs, attitudes, and actions of individuals, on the one hand, and the social and historical contexts within which these elements emerged and operate, on the other. It reminds us that the reality of ethnic stratification is located in social systems, as well as in the attitudes and actions of individuals. Nevertheless, for many analytical purposes it is still useful to focus more specifically on prejudice and discrimination, on their relationship to one another, and on their many sources.

Prejudice and Discrimination

People generally consider the relationship of attitudes to actions—and more specifically of prejudice to discrimination—to be quite straightforward: attitudes (e.g., prejudices) are thought to be the causes of actions (e.g., various forms of discriminatory behavior). This idea seems to be confirmed by much of our everyday experience. *First* a person has an attitude about something, and *then* he or she acts as a result of that attitude; therefore, if a person harbors a prejudice we may assume that he or she may engage in discrimination. Conversely, if we are aware that a person has performed an act of discrimination, we may infer that she or he is prejudiced. We may describe either of these situations as examples of racism.

There are many reasons to suppose, however, that the relationship of prejudice to discrimination is more complicated than we ordinarily assume. For example, may not people who hold prejudices refrain from discriminating? And may not people who discriminate actually, as they often claim, harbor little prejudice? Are varying social circumstances likely to encourage or restrain individuals from exhibiting discriminatory behavior? These and many other important questions have arisen as researchers have constructed theories to aid our understanding of prejudice and discrimination.

Theories of Prejudice

The causes of prejudice may be grouped conveniently into three broad categories that focus on (1) the way prejudice is transmitted through culture from generation to generation, (2) the way prejudices are bound-up with an individual's racial and ethnic group membership, and (3) the way an individual's personality is structured. We present only a few examples of these types.

Cultural-Transmission Theories of Prejudice.   Theories of this type hold that children learn prejudice in much the same way they learn to speak a particular language, dress in a given manner, or use certain eating utensils. From this viewpoint, the building blocks of prejudice are contained within the society's culture and are transmitted to children in a natural way through the culture in the home and community.[26]

Two aspects of a culture are particularly closely related to the extent and kind of prejudice found in a given society. The first aspect has to do with the shared beliefs that the members of one group have about the members of other groups in the society. Children are likely to learn—by instruction and by accident—that the members of different groups are believed to possess a cluster of distinctive traits. These presumed group trait clusters are called **stereotypes**. The second aspect has to do with a culture's prescriptions concerning the degrees of **social distance** that one group's members should permit or desire from any other group's members.

For our purposes stereotypes are shared, but not necessarily correct, beliefs concerning the characteristics of the members of different racial or ethnic groups as compared with some reference group.[27] This definition recognizes as stereotypes the favorable images that in-groups ordinarily cherish about themselves; however, our main interest centers on the derogatory images that the members of in-groups frequently share about out-groups as compared to themselves. The presence of derogatory stereotypes within a culture suggests that those who subscribe to them harbor prejudices concerning the members of given groups.[28] The term *social distance* refers to the grades and degrees of intimacy that characterize personal and social relations generally. The less favorable the stereotypes attributed to a group, the more social distance the holders of the stereotypes will try to establish.

One method of studying stereotypes is to present a list of adjectives that may be used to describe the traits of members of a given racial or ethnic group and ask various individuals to select words from the list that they think are the most typical of each group. In the earliest study of this type, Katz and Braly (1933) found that more than one-third of the college students they studied believed Germans were stolid, Italians were passionate, English were intelligent, Jews were mercenary, Americans were industrious, Blacks were lazy, Irish were pugnacious, Chinese were superstitious, Japanese were intelligent, and Turks were cruel. The researchers contended that these levels of agreement could not be understood as a reflection of the actual experiences of the study participants and, therefore, must represent the influence of shared beliefs that exist within the culture.

Stereotypes may change over time.[29] For example, public opinion polls in 1942 and 1966 showed that the proportion of respondents who described Germans as warlike and Japanese as sly fell from 67 percent and 63 percent in 1942, respectively, to 16 percent and 19 percent in 1966 (Ehrlich 1973:30). Negative stereotypes of Blacks held by Whites also appear to have declined markedly since 1933; but Whites, Hispanics, and Asians are still rated more favorably (Bobo and Zubrinsky 1996; Bobo and Kluegel 1997; Wood and Chesser 1994:20).[30]

The main research technique for studying social distance was introduced by Bogardus (1933), who asked people to select different kinds of social contacts they would be willing to permit with the members of various racial and ethnic groups. The types of social contacts shown in the list represent various points running from a high willingness to permit social contact (e.g., "Would admit to close kinship by marriage") to, at the other extreme, a low willingness to permit social contact (e.g., "Would exclude from my country").[31]

In general, people from the British Isles and from northern and western Europe (who were highly represented in the colonial and first immigrant streams) were ranked near the top of the list, indicating favorable attitudes toward these groups. People from southern and eastern Europe were next in order, and people of the racial minorities were ranked near the bottom. In short, the general pattern of social distance that is transmitted from generation to generation in the United States resembles the pattern that was created through the historical sequences of intergroup contact that we have already observed.

Group-Identification Theories of Prejudice.   We turn now to the second of the three main types of causes of prejudice we have listed—group identification. The importance of a person's group memberships as a molding force has been stated powerfully by Sumner ([1906]1960) in *Folkways*. In Sumner's ([1906]1960:27) view, as discussed in Chapters 1 and 3, a fundamental fact concerning human groups is that as their members are drawn together by a common interest and come to see themselves as an in-group, outsiders are likely to be described in terms that are scornful and derogatory, reflecting negative stereotypes. In the United States, for example, terms such as "dago," "nigger," "kike," "honkey," "spic," "mick," "limey," "chink," "gringo," and so on have been applied to out-groups as terms of extreme disrespect.

The tendency to rate all out-groups as lower than the in-group—ethnocentrism— is a pervasive sentiment. Children normally learn very early to distinguish the group to which they belong from all others; and they usually have a strong attachment to, and preference for, their own group and its ways. The group's preferences become their preferences, its beliefs, their beliefs, and its enemies, their enemies. To grow up as a member of a given group is automatically to place that group at the center of things and to adopt its evaluations as the best. Prejudice and hostility toward members of out-groups and favoritism toward members of the in-group are seen as predictable consequences of this natural ethnocentrism.[32]

The idea that this universal phenomenon is a potent cause of prejudice is quite plausible and easily fits many of the facts of everyday experience; but it has some shortcomings. For example, loyalty to one's ethnic in-group is sometimes accompanied by an admiration for some specific accomplishments of the members of out-groups (Williams 1964:22). Even in the midst of war, hated enemies may be granted a grudging respect for their skill or daring. Such departures from perfect ethnocentrism, however, do not necessarily mean that an enemy out-group that is respected in some particular way is generally rated above the in-group.

Why is ethnocentrism so prevalent? An interesting answer to this question grows out of **social self theory** (Mead 1934) and **social identity theory** (Tajfel and Turner 1979).[33] According to social self theory, human infants initially view the world only from their own perspective; however, as children learn to communicate symbolically with family members (primarily through language), they become aware of themselves as distinct individuals who are members of particular groups. Social identity theorists argue that an individual's developing self-concept consists of his or her personal identity and also of various social identities that correspond to the groups of which the person is a member;[34] consequently, according to social identity theory, as people strive to maintain their self-esteem, they may draw strength and pride both from their own accomplishments and through being affiliated with groups having relatively high prestige. In this way, a person's sense of self-worth may be raised either by accepting an exaggerated view of the value and importance of his or her group or by downgrading the value and importance of the groups of others (Baldwin 1998:42). Pride in one's group may become excessive and give rise to prejudice.

But what happens to the self-esteem of children who grow up as members of an ethnic group that occupies a position of low prestige in the social hierarchy? In-groups usually react to out-group hostility by becoming prouder and more determined to maintain their social identities; but domination by an out-group may set into motion an often vicious circle, called a **self-fulfilling prophecy** (Merton 1957:423). For example, if subordinate group children learn that others do not expect them to do well in school, they may become anxious; their anxiety may impair their efforts and lead to below-par results; these results may then be taken as "proof" that the initial low expectations were justified.[35] And this process may become a vicious descending spiral.[36]

Personality Theories of Prejudice.

Cultural-transmission and group-identification theories of prejudice have received a substantial amount of support, but they afford an incomplete view of what a person learns during the process of growing up. Why, for example, do some people accept the racial and ethnic prejudices that are common in their home community more uncritically than do others? Many everyday comments concerning prejudice reflect the idea that some kind of personality "need" or problem lies behind racial and ethnic prejudice.

One popular personality theory of prejudice is related to the widespread observation that a person who is frustrated is likely to direct his or her anger toward some external object, sometimes in an aggressive way. The scholarly version of this idea, called the **frustration–aggression hypothesis,** stated that (1) frustration always leads to aggression and (2) aggression is always the result of frustration (Dollard et al. 1939). This formulation of the hypothesis was too sweeping (Berkowitz 1969:2; Baron 1977:22) and was revised later to recognize that aggression could be caused by things other than frustration (Miller 1941:30).[37] For instance, a person who causes frustration may be too powerful to attack directly or openly (e.g., one's boss). In such cases, the frustration experienced by the individual may have no feasible outlet but may, instead, await a safe or convenient substitute target. Such a safe substitute target is called a **scapegoat** (Allport 1958:236). Since the anger that lies behind scapegoating may be released against a wide variety of targets it is **free-floating hostility** (Allport 1958:337).

Proponents of the frustration–aggression hypothesis believe that ethnic prejudices develop in response to people's need to cope with the frustrations in their daily lives. Ethnic groups in the United States, especially the newest arrivals and those in racial minorities, frequently provide scapegoats for the free-floating hostility of the majority.

This intriguing theory seems consistent with many observations from daily experience, but it leaves some questions unanswered. Why, for instance, do some frustrated people use the members of minority groups as scapegoats and other, perhaps even more frustrated, people do not (Allport 1958:210, 332)? And how does the idea of scapegoating—which makes sense in the case of majority-group prejudices—apply to the frustrations experienced by members of ethnic minorities? When minority group members strike out in apparent frustration against members of the majority, they can hardly be said to have selected a safe substitute target (Simpson and Yinger 1972:218–219).

Another prominent theory concerning the causes of extreme ethnic prejudice was presented by a group of scholars who studied the rise of fascism in Europe during the 1930s (Adorno, Frenkel-Brunswick, Levinson, and Sanford 1950). On the basis of intensive case studies, the researchers concluded that people who scored high on a questionnaire called the F-Scale (for Fascism) possessed a distinctive cluster of personality traits that predisposed them to be ethnocentric and prejudiced toward out-groups. They were found to be rigidly conventional, submissive, uncritical of in-group authority, preoccupied with power and "toughness," sexually inhibited, and intolerant of people who are members of out-groups. The authors argued that people with this type of **authoritarian personality** had been raised by domineering adults who relied on harsh discipline to enforce rigid obedience. Children who are raised in this way, the theory holds, grow up to have a highly antidemocratic and ethnocentric view of the world that leads to a high level of intolerance toward all out-groups.

Hundreds of studies have been conducted to test various aspects of the authoritarian personality theory, and the F-Scale has been used in countless other studies devoted to different purposes. High levels of authoritarianism appear to be especially prominent among people who show a generalized hatred of one or more out-groups and are attracted to organizations founded on out-group hatred. Overall, the findings of the many studies of authoritarianism support the view that an authoritarian personality structure, like frustration, is one among many sources of ethnic prejudice.[38]

Theories of Discrimination

So far we have proceeded on the assumption that prejudice is the cause of discrimination; and, in an effort to probe more deeply into that relationship, we have examined some possible causes of prejudice. But most social theorists do not believe that prejudice is the only, or necessarily the most important, cause of discrimination. The theories of discrimination we discuss also can be grouped conveniently into three broad categories: (1) situational pressures theories, (2) group conflict theories, and (3) institutional discrimination theories. As before, we present only a few examples.

Situational Pressures Theories of Discrimination.   Theories of this type are based on the well-known fact that what people "preach" (their creeds) may not always correspond to what they "practice" (their deeds). In other words, there frequently is a gap between a "creed" and a "deed." A familiar example of a **creed–deed discrepancy** involves dominant-group members who feel it is necessary for social reasons to avoid open association with members of minority groups. Such people may confide, "I am not prejudiced, you understand; some of my best friends are _____; but what would my neighbors or business associates think?" This example illustrates a simple, but fundamental, sociological idea: *The social pressures exerted on individuals in different social situations may cause them to vary their behavior in ways that do not correspond to their inner beliefs and preferences.* This idea implies that it may be a mistake either to infer prejudice from a given act of discrimination or to infer tolerance from a failure to discriminate.

A seminal exploration of the creed–deed discrepancy was conducted by LaPiere (1934). He and a Chinese couple traveled some ten thousand miles together in the United States, stopping at 251 hotels, motels, and restaurants. Despite the high levels of prejudice and discrimination against the Chinese in the United States at that time, they were refused service only once. Later, LaPiere mailed questionnaires to all of the proprietors involved asking whether they would accept "members of the Chinese race" as customers. Among those who answered the questionnaire (51 percent), about 92 percent stated they *would not* accept Chinese as guests even though they (or their employees) already had demonstrated they would sometimes accept Chinese guests.

In a society in which the standards of fairness hold that people should be judged on merit, one would expect frequent occurrences of creed–deed discrepancies in which people claim to be less prejudiced than they are; and, for that reason, many claims of tolerance in America are considered to be hypocritical. But why would the Americans in LaPiere's study have wished to be thought less tolerant than they actually were? Perhaps the answer goes something like this: In the actual situations, many social elements came into play. The Chinese couple did not fit the prevailing negative stereotype, and they were accompanied by a distinguished-looking White man. Under these conditions, the travelers met almost no discrimination; but in the hypothetical situation described in the questionnaire, the proprietors' stereotypes and fears of in-group disapproval were not restrained by concrete circumstances. The discrepancies between the proprietors' (or their employees') fair treatment of the Chinese guests and their statements that they in fact would discriminate probably were due much more to differences between the characteristics of the actual and hypothetical situations than to the individuals' levels of prejudice.

A number of other investigators pursued the question raised by LaPiere's study: Why do people's attitudes and actions frequently fail to correspond? Lohman and Reitzes (1952:242) argued that in modern industrial society "attitudes toward minority groups may be of little consequence in explaining an individual's behavior." To test this idea, they compared the attitudes and behavior of White workers who were members of a union that admitted Blacks without reservation but who lived in a neighborhood where Black residents were unwelcome. The study showed that people's behavior depended more on group membership than on their attitudes. In the job situation, the White workers united with Black workers for their common economic advantage; at home, however, the White workers accepted the view of their neighborhood-improvement association and rejected Blacks as neighbors.

These and other studies demonstrated that prejudice and discrimination do not necessarily go together, raising a serious objection to the presumption that prejudice is "the" cause of discrimination. Several investigators have studied this problem under more controlled conditions. In one study, DeFleur and Westie (1958) asked 46 White students to participate in a nationwide campaign for racial integration. Twenty-three of the students had very unfavorable attitudes toward Blacks, and the remaining 23 students had very favorable attitudes. To test the extent of a person's willingness to act in a manner consistent with his or her level of prejudice, the researchers asked the students to be photographed with a Black person of the opposite sex and to sign release agreements to permit the pictures to be used in various phases of the campaign. The study showed that prejudice was positively related to discrimination (i.e., unwillingness to sign the releases); however, it also revealed that nine of the presumably unprejudiced students were less willing than the average to have their photographs used, and that five of the presumably prejudiced students were more willing than the average to release their photographs. DeFleur and Westie interpreted these discrepancies in terms of differing peer-group pressures.[39]

These studies show that under some conditions, people who appear not to be prejudiced may discriminate and people who appear to be prejudiced may not discriminate. The specific social pressures arising in particular social situations seem, in many instances, to outweigh personal prejudice as a cause of discrimination. Indeed, most of us have a strong tendency to believe that people's actions are caused mainly by the attitudes within them and, when we do that, we often underestimate the importance of the external factors that exert pressure on people in various social situations. This tendency, called the **fundamental attribution error,** has been demonstrated in many studies (Brown 1986:169, 176).

The kinds of social pressures we have considered so far occurred in groups involving face-to-face interactions in which individuals were responding mainly to the probability of social approval or disapproval. But each of us also belongs to large groups that have histories of competition and conflict with other groups for the possession of socially desired ends such as property, prestige, and power. These intergroup conflicts may involve discrimination.

Group Conflict Theories of Discrimination.

In Chapters 2 and 3 we noted that the American Indians and Europeans struggled for possession of the land; and the present chapter has shown how the fear that immigrants would take jobs away from Americans led to nativist movements and campaigns to restrict immigration. These conflicts between groups for the control of land and jobs, to name only two important resources, led to relatively fixed social arrangements in which the members of the more powerful groups enjoyed greater privileges and higher social standing than those in the less powerful groups. A system of ethnic domination–subordination (or stratification) had been born.

Noel (1968) argued that the combination of differences in group power, competition for scarce resources, and ethnocentrism invariably leads to this result. Presumably, moreover, such a system of stratification not only comes into existence but also endures because the dominant groups gain by it. If minority-group workers are forced into the hardest, dirtiest, lowest-paying jobs, then majority-group workers may occupy the "better" jobs and thereby realize an economic gain (Glenn 1966:161). Quite aside from any prejudices that majority-group workers may harbor, they may discriminate because they believe they profit by such actions. Indeed, the prejudices themselves may be "secondary to the conflict for society's goodies" (Lieberson 1980:382).

Two issues are of special interest in regard to gaining economic advantages. First, although the historical record we have reviewed leaves little room for doubt that in the past members of certain minority groups (e.g., Blacks and Native Americans) have received lower economic rewards than they would have in the absence of discrimination, the following question still remains: Do some Americans still "pay a price" today for being members of minorities?

Offhand, the answer to this question seems to be "yes, minority-group workers still pay a price in the job market." For instance, in 1999 the median[40] income of Black families in the United States was \$31,778, of Hispanic families was \$31,663, and of White families was \$51,224 (U.S. Bureau of the Census 2001:40). In other words, Black and Hispanic families received about 62 cents for every dollar received by White families. These income differences by themselves, however, do not demonstrate the presence of discrimination by Whites. There may be other pertinent differences between the groups, such as education and experience, that help explain the overall differences in family incomes. In later chapters we consider the results of several studies that focus on these differences. For now, though, we consider this question: If, on average, the members of the majority gain economically through discrimination, would they gain even more by refusing to discriminate?

Karl Marx asserted that discrimination by dominant-group workers increases the profits of the employers (the ruling or capitalist class) at the expense of all workers, majority and minority alike. In our system White workers on the whole receive higher pay than minority workers; but, the Marxian view maintains, it is a mistake for the White workers to believe they gain more from this system than they would by refusing to discriminate. White employers may encourage the prejudices of the White workers toward minority workers because that helps keep minority workers in a large low-wage labor pool. This labor pool, in turn, can be used by employers as strike breakers and as replacement workers. The net result for the White workers is that their share of the economic pie is actually smaller in the long run than it would have been had they united with the minority workers against the employers. From this point of view, the behavior of the dominant-group workers is mistaken and "irrational." Beck (1980:148) summarized this position as follows: "Racism in a capitalist society is an ideology fostered and maintained by employers to ensure the fractionalization of the working class."

Many writers reject the Marxian analysis and argue, instead, that discrimination by White workers actually does serve to increase their economic rewards, just as they suppose (Myrdal [1944]1964:68).[41] This theme was pursued by Bonacich (1972, 1973, 1975, 1976). She agreed with the Marxian writers that economic competition is at the root of ethnic antagonisms but did not agree that the conflict between White and Black workers is economically "irrational." She attacked the Marxian notion that capitalists deliberately create a division between different groups of workers in order to subordinate them both.

Her alternative, **split labor market theory,** stated that the antagonism of White workers toward minority workers stems from the fact that the White workers received higher pay for performing the same jobs from the beginning. From this perspective, the capitalist class does not *create* but is *faced with* a split labor market (Bonacich 1972:549), which is characterized by conflict among business people (capitalists), higher-paid labor (e.g., Whites), and cheaper labor (e.g., Chinese, Latinos) (Bonacich 1972:553). In these terms, the main economic interests of the two laboring groups are not essentially alike (as in the Marxian analysis). Higher-paid labor is genuinely threatened by the presence of cheaper labor.[42] Because it is in the interest of the capitalist class to cut costs by hiring the least expensive workers, the capitalists may attempt to substitute the cheaper workers for the higher-paid ones.

How can the higher-paid laborers control the real threat against them that is posed by the cheaper laborers? Two main methods are available. The first is simply to exclude the cheaper laborers from the territory in which the higher-paid laborers work. This method frequently has been employed by workers all over the world. We saw earlier that the United States excluded Chinese laborers beginning in 1882. The same strategy was used later against the Japanese. In both cases, the hostility of the White workers, rather than of the employers, provided the force behind the exclusionist efforts. The second method used by higher-paid labor to combat cheaper labor is to organize unions that are committed to preserving the wage distinctions among ethnic groups. If the higher-paid group is sufficiently well organized and powerful, it may be able to force the employers either to continue paying different wages for the same work or to "reserve" the higher-paying jobs for dominant-group workers.

These exclusionary methods increase the probability that violent conflict between the groups will erupt. The **collective violence theory** of Olzak and Shanahan (1996) maintains that the likelihood of racial and ethnic conflict is low when ethnic and racial groups occupy segregated areas and there is little competition for jobs and resources. When two or more groups compete for the same jobs, however, and the dominant group attempts to exclude or subordinate competitors, then the subordinate groups resist and violence may occur. Since intergroup competition increases during economic recessions and depressions and during periods in which there is an increasing supply of workers from migration, these conditions favor higher levels of collective violence.[43]

Taken together, the results of the many studies concerning the total effects of the system of White supremacy in the United States afford a basis for the claim that the members of the dominant group have discriminated systematically against the members of subordinate racial and ethnic groups because they gained by it. The racism generated by this intergroup conflict was then used to help explain and justify the existing social arrangements.

From the perspectives of situational pressures theory and group conflict theory, the forms of discrimination are fairly overt. There are specific individuals within the dominant group who refuse to hire or promote minority workers, who pay minority workers less than dominant workers for performing the same job, who demand sexual favors in return for employment, and so on. However, some scholars have argued that even if, miraculously, individual prejudice and overt discrimination were eliminated completely, the normal operation of American society—our traditional institutional arrangements—would still guarantee a high level of discrimination against subordinate racial and ethnic groups.

Institutional Discrimination Theories.

American racial and ethnic relations entered a critical period during the 1960s and were still unsettled at the end of the twentieth century. The unrest of this period may have been generated to a considerable extent by the decline of scientific racism and the rise of contemporary racism. As noted earlier, the declines in prejudice among Whites that were revealed by public opinion polls were not accompanied by a commensurate willingness on the part of Whites to support public policies that would bring about desegregation in schools, neighborhoods, and jobs. During this entire period of apparently decreasing prejudice and increasing opportunity, some members of minority groups (and in particular many Black Americans, Hispanics, and American Indians) noticed that significant improvements were not taking place in their own lives. At best, the rate of improvement seemed painfully slow.[44] For example, a *Newsweek* poll published in 1992 (Morganthau et al. 1992:21) found that 51 percent of Black Americans felt that the quality of life for Blacks had gotten worse during the preceding 10 years. This finding was supported in a study by Tuch, Sigelman, and MacDonald (1999) of the opinions "of a nationally-representative survey of high school seniors." The survey, part of a long-term study by the University of Michigan's Institute for Survey Research, showed that the percentage of Black and White youths who believed that relations between the races were improving ". . . plummeted after the mid-1980s" (Tuch, Sigelman, and MacDonald 1999:124). An important question is suggested by these findings, as well as by the continuation of high rates of infant mortality, homicide, and imprisonment among Blacks: "Why are the many changes that have taken place in the laws of the land and the attitudes of Whites not more fully reflected in the actual living conditions of some of the members of minority groups?"

An intriguing answer to this question was presented by Carmichael and Hamilton (1967) in their book *Black Power*. The answer these authors suggested was that the *ordinary operations* of American institutions ensure discrimination against subordinate groups. Schools, hospitals, factories, banks, and so on do not need to be staffed by prejudiced people in order to achieve discriminatory results. For example, most employers have certain formal educational requirements for hiring, such as a high school or college diploma. When these requirements are applied uniformly to all those who apply, the *automatic* result is to exclude those who have been deprived of an equal opportunity to gain the necessary credentials. If people have been subject to discrimination in the schools, then they are less likely to have graduated and, therefore, to be qualified for a job requiring a diploma. Even if the people who conduct the hiring procedure are completely tolerant as individuals, the rules of the organization they represent require them to accept only those who have proper diplomas, test scores, certificates, and licenses. To illustrate further, a father's difficulties in finding employment may lead his son to drop out of school to go to work. The son, too, may later encounter the same employment problems as the father. Here we see how unintentional discrimination may place a self-fulfilling prophecy into operation both within and between generations.

Similarly, if an employer requires that a person must have worked in one job for 10 years in order to be qualified for another job, anyone who was deliberately excluded from the first job cannot be qualified for the second (Feagin 1977:189). For instance, during periods of economic expansion, employers frequently have not hired Black workers until no other workers were available. Then, during slack periods, the Black workers frequently were the first to lose their jobs. Under those circumstances, it was very difficult for Black workers to accumulate the years of seniority needed to qualify for many jobs. Therefore, wherever seniority rules were used in hiring and firing, and were applied uniformly, the Black workers were at a disadvantage.

Note that the main claim of institutional discrimination theorists is that prejudice *presently* is not required to keep the system of discrimination intact. They acknowledge that prejudice initially may have played a role in producing the existing system and do not deny that prejudice still produces some discrimination. The central idea was expressed by Baron (1969:144) as follows: "There is a carefully articulated interrelation of the barriers created by each institution. Whereas the single institutional strand standing alone might not be so strong, the many strands together form a powerful web."[45]

Both group conflict theories and institutional discrimination theories emphasize that discrimination has important sources other than individual prejudice. This idea is exceptionally important in the present period. Many White Americans now recognize that their forebearers profited from discrimination against minority groups; some also acknowledge that the effects of past discrimination have not been entirely erased. It is not always easy to see, however, that as levels of prejudice decline, intergroup competition and traditional institutional arrangements may continue as before and may benefit disproportionately most members of the dominant group; but from the perspectives of group conflict and institutional discrimination theories White Americans still receive an unearned "bonus" for being White whether they are aware of it or not. Stated differently, the argument here is that the rules of the economic games are rigged to favor White people (Fischer et al. 1996:130).

We reviewed in Chapter 2 through the present chapter how American society developed a system of ethnic stratification. Our strategy of presentation was organized largely in terms of the historical sequence that unfolded from the Atlantic coast following the establishment of Jamestown in 1607. We saw that this development fostered the preeminence of the ideology of Anglo conformity and strongly shaped the convictions of White Americans concerning what outsiders should be or do before they could become insiders in American society.

In Chapters 6 through 13 we turn to a more detailed examination of how America's ethnic stratification system has operated in relation to groups that have faced very high levels of discrimination. Although we continue to rely on an historical framework as it applies to each group being discussed, our primary purpose in these chapters is to analyze each group's experiences in terms of the many concepts and ideas we have introduced so far and, also, to introduce a few additional concepts that we think are essential to an effort to understand contemporary American racial and ethnic relations. We begin with a discussion of African Americans.

 Reality Check

INTERVIEW WITH JANA

Jana was born in Canada and lived in Pennsylvania, Arizona, and Texas. Her parents were both immigrants and her father has returned to Hong Kong where she visits regularly. She attended a racially mixed high school. Both parents have college degrees.

How do you refer to yourself?
Chinese, because technically I am Chinese. I guess I would add American to it but that would be second to Chinese. My parents are Chinese, and so I'm Chinese. Be-

cause I grew up in America, that doesn't mean I'm an American. I was born in Canada but I've been raised in the United States most of my life. I would definitely consider myself more American even though I technically hold Canadian citizenship.

What do you see as most important about your racial or ethnic background?
Keeping the culture is most important because I don't have very good Chinese. When I go to Hong Kong I feel very bad. I can't really pass the language on to my children but I definitely want them to learn Chinese and I definitely want my children to go to Hong Kong and visit their relatives. For me and for a lot of Chinese kids our parents expect a lot out of us. I expect A's and that's just how my parents brought me up, to expect more A's, to get more good grades, being really successful. You know the great thing about Chinese parents is when they get together they always compare their children. And they're like, "Well my daughter does this and my daughter does this." So I have to give my mom something to brag about.

When did you first become aware of your racial background?
When I was growing up, I lived in different places in America and I was basically the only Chinese kid there. I didn't realize it then. I think in middle school to high school I definitely realized I'm Chinese, because the people I hung around with weren't Asian. I'd keep hanging around them and they ended up being my group of friends and then I realized that I was more Chinese than anything else, that's when I realized my ethnicity.

Have you ever experienced an uncomfortable situation because of your race?
The high school I went to was very large and it had about 4,500 students and it was very mixed. And there were some people that could be incredibly rude or just start making fun and I'd just start cussing at them. So yeah I've had confrontations. But that's expected in a place that big. It was basically Blacks, Hispanics, Asian, and Whites. It was a very mixed group. But we were still pretty segregated within our own groups. Like the Asians hang around Asians, the Blacks hang around Blacks. We all stuck with our own racial groups. It wasn't something intentional but it just ended up being that way.

Tell me about your family.
My mom and my dad are divorced now, but during the time that I grew up it was like just a typical Asian family—you don't really show a lot of love to each other and you don't really do much with each other. A lot of Asian families believe that you are in it for the children. It doesn't matter if you love each other or not. Since we were in America and we're in the 90s, my mom decided to get a divorce because she just wanted something better. I think that would not have happened back in another time. I think it's socially acceptable now, at least to American people. I am the only child and it's an okay family. My dad's pretty intelligent because he worked really hard to get where he was at and now I'm

(continued)

reaping the benefits. My parents are definitely Chinese. They still have the Chinese ideals. My father was like, "You better graduate from the university with honors." My parents both speak four languages—their hometown language, Cantonese, Mandarin, and English.

Does your family talk about racial or ethnic issues?
They don't really talk about it. My parents, I don't know if this sounds really bad but my mom, I asked her one time when I was younger, "Do you mind if I marry a White person?" And she said, "No, I don't mind as long as you don't marry a Black person." So my parents have some racial views but a lot of Chinese have that and it's just when they come here they see it and they believe it and so that's the way they think. I guess I got a little bit of that but then it is only an add-on to what I felt in my school. I try to believe that I can see no color and no skin and I try to believe that everybody's equal, but sometimes it's very hard to believe that when people start acting their stereotype. It's hard to not be racist.

Tell me about your friends.
The main people I hang out with are from Taiwan, so I'm exposed to Mandarin. I went to Mandarin Chinese school. My group of friends right now are all Taiwanese. My ex-boyfriend was from mainland China but besides that it's mostly Taiwanese. It's not something I chose, it just ended up being that way.

I've had friends in the past who were White and Black and Hispanic, but now its just more like they're acquaintances than friends. I just basically talk to whoever is close to me and that ends up just being Taiwanese people. We can relate to each other a lot better. Chinese people and American people have different ideas. In that sense, it's a lot easier to relate to Chinese people because they know what you've been through, their parents are exactly like your parents. We don't do like, "Let's go and do some Chinese dancing together or something," we don't do that, we're not that weird! We just do college kids stuff together. We just hang out with each other. We don't do anything specifically Chinese.

Is marriage or a romantic relationship with another group acceptable?
It used to be acceptable but as I've grown up, I really believe I could only marry Chinese people because, it's actually being able to relate with them and you come from the same background and their parents are like you and your parents are like them. It's a lot easier than going with a White person and marrying them and their parents would be like, "Hmm," and your parents would be like, "Hmm." I mean my parents are pretty Americanized in that sense, but for me I wouldn't like it that much. I just don't find myself attracted to anybody else but Chinese. It just ends up being that way. Before when I was younger I went out with a Hispanic, a White, and Chinese and now it's like I don't want to. It's not something that I could be comfortable with.

Did you speak a language other than English when you entered school?
I was growing up at a time when my parents didn't realize that they should've taught me Chinese when I was young. They were afraid that I wouldn't be able to fit into the schools so they taught me only English. So that's why I never really learned Chinese. The only time I ever learned Chinese was when I was listening to my parents talk. I can understand my parents pretty well but I can't understand anybody else. It's pretty sad. I try saying something and it always ends up wrong, so I just stopped trying.

Tell me about the community in which you grew up.
It was more segregated than integrated. There were 4,500 students and they came from various areas within the district. There is the richer area that is mainly White and Chinese. And I hung out with Asian and White because those were the only people that were in my honor classes. There was maybe one Black person in my honors class. I was very surprised about that. Like maybe five White people and the rest were Asian and maybe a couple of Hispanic people. There were a lot of Chinese people in my school, a lot of Black people, a lot of Hispanic people. Sometimes we would just make jokes and be like, "Hey, where's the White people?" I still only hang out with Chinese people. When you are in college you cling to each other and try to find someone who can relate to you.

Discussion Questions

To what degree has Jana assimilated?

Why does she prefer to "hang out" with other Chinese students?

What factors affected Jana's inability to maintain her Chinese language?

How have stereotypes affected Jana's perceptions of her own ethnic group? Of other groups? How did Jana learn the stereotypes and prejudices she mentions?

In what ways did Jana's high school structure limit her primary social interactions with other groups?

We make generalizations about people all the time in our daily lives. At what point do generalizations become stereotypes?

What do you think is the most important cause of prejudice? Of discrimination?

What was significant about the Chinese Exclusion Act of 1882?

How has nativism affected the policies of the United States toward immigration?

How would you respond to the claim that there are inherent intellectual differences among races?

 Key Ideas

1. Each of the three great immigrant streams has aroused the fears of Americans concerning issues such as competition for jobs, possible disloyalty, and the effects of foreign radicalism. Increasing fear has been accompanied by increases in hostile actions directed toward immigrants, including demands that immigration be restricted.

2. The shift from the first to the second great immigrant stream brought with it a new concern about the physical differences between natives and foreigners. This concern was heightened during the latter decades of the nineteenth century by developments in several fields of scholarly research that resulted in scientific racism.

3. In addition to the rise of scientific racism, the conviction grew that the characteristic called "intelligence" basically determines the superiority of one race to another.

4. The studies of Francis Galton initiated a movement to develop tests to measure innate intellectual ability. The most successful tests created for this purpose were paper-and-pencil tests. They enabled testers to calculate a single score called the intelligence quotient (IQ) for each individual and to compare the scores of different individuals with the average scores of groups.

5. The U.S. Army conducted a massive study of intelligence test scores among its recruits during World War I. When the average IQ scores of the members of different ethnic groups were calculated, White Americans of colonial and first-stream immigrant ancestry ranked higher on average than the groups comprising the second immigrant stream; and the average of Whites was higher than for non-Whites. These findings seemed to confirm the ideas of scientific racism.

6. The efforts to define and measure human intelligence have raised many questions. Many scholars vigorously deny that a single mental quality that may be called general intelligence exists or that intelligence can be arrayed hierarchically in terms of single scores. Even when IQ scores are accepted as having some well-defined meaning, there are many objections to the idea that the scores represent an inborn quality. Environmental as well as biological factors are known to affect people's performances on tests, and there has been no conclusive demonstration of the role played by biological factors. Moreover, even if accurate estimates of the heritability of intelligence *within* populations were available, they would afford no evidence concerning the roles of hereditary or environmental factors in creating average intellectual differences *between* populations.

7. The work of Jensen in 1969 and of Herrnstein and Murray in 1994 seemed to be based on new genetic and statistical knowledge; however, the underlying ideas put forward by hereditarians during these two phases of the IQ debate were still those introduced by Galton in the nineteenth century and Spearman in the first decade of the twentieth century. The debate produced no compelling evidence that human beings possess something that may be called general intelligence, that such a factor is determined primarily by biological inheritance, or that intelligence is immutable.

8. The United States began to move away from the open-door policy in 1882. Certain individuals were ruled to be undesirable, and, through the passage of the Chinese Exclusion Act, American policy endorsed for the first time the principle that an entire group of people might be unfit for admission or citizenship because of their race or ethnicity.

9. The IQ studies conducted during the period from 1904 to 1924 provided an important basis for the quota laws to restrict immigration that were enacted in 1921 and 1924. These immigration acts were designed to restrict admissions in a way that favored the countries that were most heavily represented in the colonial and first immigrant streams. The application of quotas, based first on the number of foreign-born residents in the United States and then on the national-origins principle, achieved the desired results.

10. The scholarly attacks on the ideas of scientific racism gradually increased the influence of the environmentalist perspective, and in 1954 the U.S. Supreme Court declared public school desegregation to be unconstitutional. A decade later a new federal Civil Rights Act was passed. These great changes in the status of scientific racism and in federal law were accompanied by a decline in overt expressions of prejudice and discrimination by Americans, but the covert and subtle forms of contemporary racism may have slowed the rate at which changes occurred in the social conditions of minority group citizens.

11. Prejudice and discrimination are central elements of racism and have been the subject of numerous theories. These theories argue that prejudice and discrimination arise from a number of different sources.

12. The following are among the most important sources of prejudice:
    a. The transmission of specific attitudes and beliefs from one generation to the next.
    b. The sense of group identity, belongingness, and loyalty that people ordinarily develop toward their own group's members and culture.
    c. The effort to manage personal frustrations and personal problems.

13. The following are among the most important sources of discrimination:
    a. The social pressures that are exerted to ensure people's conformity to the norms of their group.
    b. The conflicts that occur between groups as they struggle over power, wealth, and prestige.
    c. The normal operations of the society's institutions.

Key Terms

authoritarian personality   A personality syndrome in which the individual is rigidly conventional, submissive, uncritical of in-group authority, preoccupied with power and "toughness," sexually inhibited, and intolerant of people who are members of out-groups.

collective violence theory   Maintains that there is little likelihood of racial and ethnic conflict when ethnic and racial groups occupy segregated areas and there is little competition for jobs and resources. This theory proposes that riots occur when racial or ethnic groups must compete for scarce jobs. Collective violence is even more likely when migration increases the numbers of workers competing for those scarce jobs.

creed–deed discrepancy   A gap between what people say they believe and their actions.

environmentalism   The belief that social differences arise mainly because of different environmental circumstances.

estimates of heritability   Estimates of the extent to which various individual traits are biologically inherited.

free-floating hostility   Hostility that may be released aggressively against a wide variety of targets.

frustration–aggression hypothesis   States that (1) frustration always leads to aggression and (2) aggression is always the result of frustration.

fundamental attribution error   A strong tendency to overestimate the importance of attitudes and to underestimate the importance of situational factors as causes of behavior.

hereditarianism   The belief that the social differences among groups arise mainly because of genetically inherited differences.

nativism   Actions and policies based on the hostility of natives toward foreigners.

racism   Usually refers to an unfavorable attitude, and perhaps an unfavorable action, toward people who are members of particular racial or ethnic groups; it may or may not specify the type of relationship that exists between unfavorable attitudes and actions; and the idea of group ranking may be more or less salient.

scapegoat   A safe, convenient substitute target of aggression.

scientific racism   A set of beliefs that includes (1) the belief that racial and ethnic groups form a natural hierarchy of superiors and inferiors, (2) the belief that the White race is superior to the non-White races, and (3) the belief that within the White race the "Nordic" segment is superior to other segments.

self-fulfilling prophecy   A cycle, often vicious, that begins with a false definition of the situation that evokes a new behavior that makes the originally false conception come true.

social Darwinism   The view that groups become socially dominant because they have been more successful than their competitors in the struggle to survive and, therefore, are biologically the "fittest."

social desirability bias   The distortion that occurs when people give answers they believe they are expected to give rather than their true opinions.

social distance   Refers to the grades and degrees of understanding and intimacy that characterize personal and social relations generally.

social identity theory   States that as people strive to maintain their self-esteem, they may draw strength and pride both from their own accomplishments and through being affiliated with groups having high prestige.

social self theory   States that as children mature and learn to communicate symbolically, primarily through language, they develop an awareness of themselves as distinct individuals who are members of particular groups.

split labor market theory   States that the antagonism of dominant group workers toward subordinate group workers arises because the price of the workers' labor in the two groups differs initially.

stereotypes   Shared, but not necessarily correct, beliefs concerning the characteristics of the members of different racial or ethnic groups as compared with some reference group.

stratification system   A hierarchy of social strata reflecting the distribution of society's rewards (e.g., power, wealth, property) to various groups.

vertical social class mobility   The upward and downward movement of individuals from one social class to another.

xenophobia   A fear of foreigners.

Notes

1. Alarm was expressed over the "Irish Papists" in 1728 (Adamic 1944:36).

2. Galton advocated various measures that were intended to promote genetic improvement, which he called eugenics. The eugenics movement in England sought to lower the reproductive rates of the Irish, who were thought to be of low intelligence (Miller 1995:163–164).

3. The idea behind the Binet–Simon scale is that a child has normal intelligence or an appropriate mental age if he or she can answer questions that most children of the same chronological age can answer.

4. In 1912, William Stern compared children's performances by dividing their mental age (MA) by their chronological age (CA) to obtain an "intelligence quotient" (IQ) (Klineberg 1937:323).

5. The results of the program were based on the findings of an *alpha* test (designed for those who were literate in English) and a *beta* test (designed for those who were illiterate or did not understand English). The alpha test was intended to measure things such as the *ability* to take oral directions and solve arithmetical problems, but included questions that depended on a person's knowledge (e.g., "The author of the Raven is: Stevenson, Kipling, Hawthorne, Poe").

6. "The more recent test findings . . . show that comparative studies of various national

and racial groups may not be made with existing tests, and . . . that one of the most pretentious of these comparative racial studies—the writer's own—was without foundation" (Brigham 1930:165).

7. This list has continued to be refined and extended. Fischer et al. (1996:195) report that Crane (1995) found "the black-white gap in math and reading scores could be totally accounted for by . . . family income, size of household, proportion of students in the school the mother had attended who were poor, the age the child was weaned, whether the child was read to, and, most important, how much the home was emotionally supportive and cognitively stimulating." The effects of test experience also continues to be an important focus of debate. For a discussion of whether SAT scores can be raised by training see Schwartz (1999).

8. This interpretation was strengthened by the results of a worldwide study of population genetics (Cavalli-Sforza, Menozzi, and Piazza 1994). The study confirmed the environmentalist assumption that at the genetic level, and despite the many visible differences in physical traits, all socially recognized human races are remarkably alike.

9. Spearman's method was called *factor analysis*. He referred to general intelligence as *g*. Our simplified account rests on excellent discussions of these issues by Gould (1981, 1994).

10. Suppose we had the test scores from four highly correlated tests, two of which tested people's verbal skills and two of which tested their mathematical skills. Spearman's method of analyzing the scores would yield a single measure of general intelligence based on all four tests. Thurstone's method would provide a measure of verbal intelligence and also a measure of mathematical intelligence (Gould 1981:254–255, 300).

11. See, e.g., Eckberg (1979:101); Ehrlich and Feldman (1977:138); and Taylor (1980: 10–74).

12. Nearly all of the estimates were based on samples from Whites.

13. See Nisbett (1998:87–93) for a discussion of the heritability of IQ.

14. The book's title refers to the bell-shaped curve that is produced when a particular mathematical equation, called a normal distribution, is displayed graphically. IQ tests are designed to produce test score results that approximate a normal distribution.

15. See Tittle and Rotolo (2000) for an empirical test of this thesis.

16. See Jencks and Phillips (1998) for a discussion of test biases.

17. Kamin (1995:90) observed that "The confusion between correlation and causation permeates the largest section" of the book.

18. In a comparison of fourteen countries, Flynn (1987) found that between 1950 and 1980 there had been an average increase in IQ of around fifteen points. He argued that since there seemed to have been no increase "in real-world problem-solving ability" during those years "psychologists should stop saying that IQ tests measure intelligence" (Flynn 1987:185–188). Thernstrom (1992:134), as well as many others, states that psychologists should stop trying to measure mental abilities because the results frequently are used to "track" minority children into special school classes.

19. They might also have given greater weight to the studies of geneticists and neurologists that cast doubt on the possibility of understanding group differences in intelligence without a much more advanced knowledge of the structure and development of the human brain and nervous system (Holt 1995). Several critics noted that "The people who say intelligence is genetic are the ones with no training in genetics" (Balaban, quoted by Easterbrook 1995:37).

20. "Coolies" were workers who were paid a subsistence wage and frequently were virtually slaves.

21. Merchants and students were still permitted to enter.

22. This law also defined an "Asiatic barred zone" that included not only Chinese and Japanese, but also people from all other Asian countries except the Philippines. Filipinos were exempted because the Philippine Islands were an American colony, and Filipinos were legally American nationals (Hing 1993:32–33).

23. Despite its general focus on national groups, the new law established a preference system that permitted certain people to enter the United States on a nonquota basis (e.g., artists, lecturers, singers, nurses, ministers, and professors) (U.S. Immigration and Naturalization Service 1996:A.1–6).

24. The exact levels of a given attitude may vary with the wording of the questions (see, e.g., Schuman, Steeh, and Bobo 1985:60).

25. van Oudenhoven and Willemsen (1989: 15) stated that "Racism always implies prejudice and may encompass discrimination as well. The relations between these different concepts . . . are generally not straightforward and simple."

26. The media of communication also may transmit stereotypes (Ehrlich 1973:32). Studies of characters in short stories, movies, magazines, television, and school textbooks have shown that minority group members are often presented in stereotyped ways (see, e.g., Berelson and Salter 1946; Elson 1964).

27. Stereotypes have been referred to variously as "pictures in our heads" (Lippmann 1922:16); exaggerated beliefs "associated with a category" (Allport 1958:187); "character profiles attributed to in-groups and out-groups" (Brown 1986:534); and "cognitive categories people use when thinking about groups" (Jussim, Nelson, Manis, and Soffin 1995:228).

28. Those who accept stereotypes appear to have a tendency to attribute any nonstereotypical behavior of out-groups to luck or favorable circumstances (and thus to "explain away" disconfirming evidence); hence, stereotypes assist to sustain prejudices (Hewstone 1989:37).

29. For reviews see Bobo and Kluegel (1997); Dovidio and Gaertner (1993); Ehrlich (1973: 20–60); Hamilton and Trolier (1986); Karlins, Coffman, and Walters (1969); Stephan and Stephan (1993); and Wood and Chesser (1994).

30. Most studies of the ethnic attitudes of Whites ignore gender differences. According to Hughes and Tuch (1999) the studies that have addressed this topic generally, but not consistently, have found that women are more tolerant. Hughes and Tuch conclude, though, that "there is little evidence of systematic gender differences in racial outlook among whites."

31. The number of the item (usually one through seven) representing the greatest degree of closeness each person in a study is willing to accept with the members of a particular ethnic group is used to calculate the group's average social-distance score.

32. Stephan (1985:613) noted that "discrimination . . . against out-group members" may occur even among groups whose members have been chosen randomly (called minimal groups).

33. Some theorists also believe that something in the genetic structure of human beings predisposes, but does not force, them in the direction of in-group preference (Lopreato 1984; van den Berghe 1978).

34. See, e.g., Deaux, Reid, Mizrahi, and Ethier (1995).

35. A large number of research studies have been conducted to test this idea. Clark and Clark (1939, 1958) introduced a technique called the "dolls test" in which children are asked about two dolls that are identical except for their skin and hair color. The Clarks' found, for instance, that the majority of Black children preferred to play with the White doll and said that the brown doll "looks bad." Much subsequent research on the self-esteem of Black children supported the Clarks' finding that, as stated by the U.S. Supreme Court, to segregate children "from others of similar age and qualifications solely because of their race generates a feeling of inferiority as to their status in the community that may affect their hearts and minds in a way unlikely ever to be undone" (*Brown v. Topeka Board of Education*, 1954, cited in Osofsky 1968:477). But this view has been challenged by a large body of research (see, e.g., Drury 1980; Heiss and Owens 1972; Lerner and Buehrig 1975; McCarthy and Yancey 1971; Rosenberg and Simmons 1972; Simmons 1978). Rosenberg et al. (1995) found that children's performance in school was more closely tied to their specific (academic) self-esteem than to their overall self-esteem. Stephan (1988:13) concluded that

"four decades of research on self-esteem indicate that blacks do not have lower self-esteem than whites."

36. The subordinate-group children may now have doubts about their ability, lower their sights, and perform even less well.

37. Some studies have shown that frustration will be translated into aggression only if certain triggering "cues" are present in the situation (see, e.g., Berkowitz 1989).

38. For an approach that emphasizes the multiplicity of sources, see Hecht and Baldwin (1998).

39. For a review of studies of the attitude–behavior relationship, see Schuman and Johnson (1976).

40. The median is the number that divides any set of numbers exactly in half.

41. Dollard (1957) argued that in the past White men also realized a "sexual gain" because they had access to Black women, whereas sexual relations between Black men and White women were taboo. Whites also enjoyed a "prestige gain," conferred by the southern "etiquette of race relations" that required Black people to be completely submissive in the presence of Whites (Dollard 1957:173–187; Doyle 1937).

42. Bobo (1988) and Glenn (1966) also have presented evidence showing that the antagonism between majority-group and minority-group workers in the United States arises in part because there is a genuine conflict between them over economic and other rewards.

43. Burr, Galle, and Fossett (1991:844) found that as the relative size of the minority population increases (and becomes more visible) in a given location, dominant-group discrimination and the levels of inequality between the groups increase and the probability of collective violence between the competing groups also increases.

44. See also Lieberson and Fuguitt (1967: 188–200).

45. For a critique of institutional-discrimination theory, see Butler (1978).

African Americans

From Slavery to Segregation

"Jim Crow" refers to the laws passed by southern legislatures that established a system of racial segregation that encompassed every type of public facility ranging from water fountains to schools and cemeteries.

To those of my race who depend on bettering their condition in a foreign land . . . I would say "Cast down your bucket where you are."
—Booker T. Washington

The equality . . . which modern men must have in order to live is not to be confounded with sameness. On the contrary, in our case, it is rather insistence upon the right of diversity.
—W. E. B. Du Bois

The Negro must have a country and a nation of his own.
—Marcus Garvey

We seek . . . the inclusion of Negro Americans in the nation's life, not their exclusion. This is our land, as much as any American's.
—Roy Wilkins

We turn now to a consideration of the experiences of Black or African Americans. Unlike the European minorities, African Americans did not migrate voluntarily, and unlike American Indians and Mexican Americans, they were not present on American soil when the English and Anglo Americans arrived. Therefore, the Black experience does not fit neatly into either the colonial or immigrant perspectives. As a result, both viewpoints have been prominent in the arguments concerning the place and future of African Americans in American life. As we shall see later, both viewpoints also have been prominent in the analyses of Mexican Americans and Puerto Ricans.

 ## The Period of Slavery

In earlier chapters, we learned that the first Africans to arrive in Jamestown in 1619 were purchased as bonded or indentured servants and, as such, were not in a significantly different status from that of the many White servants in the colony. Gradually the English, who were struggling to survive and to learn how to turn a profit for the colony's investors, shifted from Whites to Blacks as their main source of cheap labor.

During the 1650–1700 period, however, changes in the laws and the methods of tobacco cultivation in the colonies led to the acceptance of Black slavery as the solution to the labor problem. The numbers of Black slaves then mounted rapidly as the practice of indenturing Whites declined. Being Black became, in Bennett's (1964:38) phrase, "a badge of servitude." Black slaves had few legal rights and little hope of freedom. Slave women suffered a double burden of racial and sexual oppression. As Black workers, they were valued for their skills and physical strength; as women, they were expected to produce slave babies for sale or labor (Winegarten 1995:27). It is no wonder that individual flight and organized rebellion among the slaves increased during this time, as did the level of vigilance among the masters.

As discussed in Chapter 3, many Africans vigorously resisted enslavement. As they were transported through the terrifying and deadly Middle Passage to the New World, slaves sometimes overcame the crews and captured the ships on which they were imprisoned; and when no other forms of escape seemed possible, they committed suicide. Resistance to slavery involved the use of every method imaginable and continued throughout the long period of American slavery. After the Underground Railroad was organized, the chances of escape greatly improved.[1] In addition, many challenged the institution of slavery with covert acts of resistance. Slaves worked more slowly, feigned illness or pregnancy, secretly learned to read, broke tools or destroyed property, injured themselves, or aborted their pregnancies to prevent their children from being born slaves (Winegarten 1995).

Despite efforts to force the return of runaway slaves, and the often cruel punishment of those who attempted to rebel, at least 200 insurrections, and possibly as many as 1,200, were planned between 1664 and 1860 (Jacobs and Landau 1971:100); and at least 15 were actually carried out (Davie 1949:44). Three uprisings during the nineteenth century attracted widespread attention. Gabriel Prosser, a slave blacksmith, used the Bible to persuade other slaves that their situation was similar to that of the Israelites under the pharaohs and that God would help them to gain their freedom (Bardolph 1961:35). After a betrayal of the conspiracy brought the effort to a quick end, Prosser was captured and hanged. A second notable slave insurrection was organized in 1822 by Denmark Vesey. Vesey purchased his freedom in 1800 and used information he learned about the successful slave revolt in Haiti to inspire slaves in South Carolina to organize and rebel. Vesey and 34 slaves were hanged; others suspected as conspirators were deported from the United States (Ducas 1970:108). The most famous uprising was led by Nat Turner in 1831 in Virginia. Turner claimed to hear voices from heaven and to be "called" to free his people. A revolt began when Turner and a handful of followers killed all the Whites in his master's household. Altogether, they killed 55 White men, women, and children. After a 6-week search for the rebels, Turner was captured and later hanged.[2]

The willingness of slaves to protest their treatment increased with the onset of the Civil War. As White Southerners became ever more fearful that the slaves would rebel, patrol laws were strengthened, slave rations and supplies were increased, and picket lines were doubled to discourage escape attempts. When the Union army invaded various portions of the Confederacy, slaves were encouraged to raise objections to the way they were treated. Consequently, many slaves refused to accept punishment, were insolent to their masters, informed for the Union armies, or joined the Union armies as recruits (Davie 1949:45). The legal system of slavery became more rigid than ever before. Still, there was no large-scale insurrection; the majority of the slaves remained faithful with some even fighting loyally beside their masters in the Confederate army.

The Impact of Slavery on Its Victims

Elkins (1968) and other scholars argued that there was not still greater resistance on the part of the Black slaves because (1) the U.S. slave system was exceedingly oppressive, (2) this brutal system reduced human beings to a subhuman condition, and (3) these conditions generated extreme subservience and passivity among the slaves. Other scholars argued that Elkins's theory missed an important story of endurance and achievement (Billingsley 1968; Blassingame 1972). Using oral histories, slave diaries and letters, and other sources, these scholars emphasized the self-generative character of Black society under slavery and stressed the theme of a resilient slave culture. In contrast to the views that portrayed slaves as passive, Gutman (1975) stressed that the slaves actively charted their own course despite heavy restrictions placed on them. Members of the slave community helped and protected one another, which in turn created a sense of cohesion and pride. They maintained words from the various African languages, established family networks that persisted despite slave codes that did not recognize slave families, created a slaves' religion that was a mixture of African and Christian beliefs, and passed on to their children variations of African folktales, music, and dance. Gutman (1976) found that large numbers of slaves and ex-slaves lived in long marriages and two-parent households. He argued that a common slave culture spread over the South derived from the cumulative slave experience and was maintained by extended kin groups and reciprocal social obligations.

The Profitability of Slavery.   Probably the most controversial attack on Elkins's thesis of the extreme subservience of the slaves was presented by Fogel and Engerman (1974) in the book *Time on the Cross.* Fogel and Engerman assembled evidence to show that slaves were effective workers who developed a much stronger family life, a more varied set of occupational skills, and a richer, more distinct culture than was previously recognized. The authors demonstrated that slave owners made many efforts to reward the slaves who worked diligently, and that, as a result, the typical slave was a vigorous and productive worker. In fact, because the masters gave careful attention to such matters as slave management, diet, family stability, bonuses, and promotions, the slaves were more efficient workers than either northern farm workers or free southern laborers (Fogel and Engerman 1974:192–209).

Fogel and Engerman's thesis touched off an intellectual firestorm because the work did not include a strong moral condemnation of slavery. For this reason, Fogel wrote a second book, *Without Consent or Contract* (1989),[3] to clarify his position. The second work included an afterword that addressed the problems of slavery. He argued that the system of slavery in the United States did not produce extreme subservience, as Elkins claimed, but did have a devastating effect on the lives of the slaves because of (1) the extreme degree of dominance required by the system, (2) the denial of economic and political opportunities, (3) the denial of citizenship, and (4) the denial of cultural self-identification. Fogel argued that although slaves were able to retain certain African customs, to modify the European religions they practiced, and to produce songs and folklore, the U.S. slave system resulted in virtually unrestrained domination of the slaves' personal lives.

The debates over slavery range over a very broad spectrum of issues as the controversies continue to catch the attention of historians and others. Most agree, however, that as slavery evolved, it became the principal factor controlling relations between Whites and Blacks in the United States. Of particular interest have been the effects of slavery on the contemporary African American family and on the course of upward mobility and assimilation of African Americans.

 ## Immigrant or Colonized Minority?

The experience of Black people in America up to the time of the Civil War resembled, in some respects, that of both an immigrant and a colonized minority. African Americans were an "immigrant" minority in the sense that they had traveled from their native lands and entered the host American society as members of a subordinate group; unlike European immigrants, however, their subordinate position was not regarded as something temporary. African Americans also resembled a "colonized" minority in the sense that they had been physically "conquered" and, subsequently, had not been accepted as suitable candidates for full membership in the society of the conquerors; but they were not in their own land. The very structure of the relations between the native Whites and the "immigrant" but enslaved Africans was such that neither the immigrant nor the colonial perspective seems completely applicable.

Although some African Americans became highly assimilated culturally during the slave period, these cases were very unusual. Most Blacks were deliberately kept from learning any more of the White man's ways than was absolutely necessary and, as a result, little structural assimilation occurred during the long ordeal of slavery. Even the free Blacks were subject to a high degree of discrimination and were not readily accepted into the mainstream of American institutional life.[4] The classical solution of the colonized minority's dilemma—throwing the invaders out—was hardly possible; however, the goal of ending the domination of the Whites by leaving the United States and, perhaps, returning to Africa was the subject of serious discussion and concrete actions. The most notable example of a secessionist solution during this period began when an organization called the American Colonization Society (founded in 1816) established the colony of Liberia for free Blacks on the west coast of Africa. The colony and its main settlement, Monrovia, grew slowly and, in 1847, was declared a republic.

Although Liberia still exists today as the second oldest Black republic in the world (after Haiti), the return of African Americans to this African state was not a solution to American racial problems. Fewer than 3,000 colonists from America were present in the colony at the time it became a republic, and even some influential Black leaders in America who favored some kind of separatist solution—like Martin Delany—did not support the Liberian experiment.

 ## Emancipation and Reconstruction

As the Civil War approached, the popularity of abolishing slavery waned. Lincoln himself favored deportation as a solution to the "Negro problem," and even after the war was underway, he stated clearly that his main purpose in fighting it was to save the Union rather than to affect the status of slavery. Moreover, many people in the North shared the opinion of White Southerners that Black people were naturally suited to servitude and should not be encouraged to seek equality. This opinion was sufficiently common during the early years of the war that Northern officers were generally unwilling to accept Blacks as soldiers. There were even reports of Northern officers who returned runaway slaves to their masters! This situation was altered, however, when Lincoln issued the **Emancipation Proclamation** on January 1, 1863. Among other things, the order proclaimed the slaves to be free and authorized the armed forces of the United States to enlist freedmen. Black regiments from Massachusetts, New York, and Pennsylvania were soon organized, and when the North began to draft military recruits, Blacks were included. Altogether, around 180,000 African Americans fought against the Confederacy, winning fourteen congressional medals of honor (Moskos and Butler 1996:23). But, as usual, the inclusion of the Blacks did not mean they were treated equally. They did not at first receive the same pay as the White troops and Black regiments did a disproportionate share of the heavy labor (Litwack 1979).

Freed African Americans

Throwing off a lifetime of restraint and dependency and beginning to live like free men or free women was not an easy task. According to a former Confederate general, recently **freed Blacks** had "nothing but freedom" (Tindall 1984:671). By the end of the war, a **Freedmen's Bureau** had been established to assist all former slaves to assume their new status (Franklin and Moss 1988:208–210). There were between 3.5 and 4 million freedmen, and most of them had no way to earn a living (Davie 1949:21). Although the bureau labored under constant criticism until it expired in 1872, it made a substantial contribution to the welfare of the former slaves and of many White people as well.

The task of providing for the freedmen, however, was only a part of the broader task of rebuilding or reconstructing the economic and political systems of the South. In President Lincoln's view, the Southern states had never really left the Union; therefore, the job of reintegrating them did not require a massive reorganization. His Proclamation of Amnesty and Reconstruction in 1863 offered a pardon to nearly all Southerners who would pledge allegiance to the United States and agree to support the abolition of slavery. Lincoln's ideas concerning Reconstruction were bitterly opposed by the Radical Republican leaders in Congress. They argued that the Southern states should have the status of a conquered province and be forced to meet stiff requirements before being readmitted to the Union.

After the assassination of Lincoln in 1865, President Andrew Johnson adopted a Reconstruction plan similar to Lincoln's. By the end of 1865, the Thirteenth Amendment, which abolished the legal institution of slavery, had been ratified. All of the Confederate states had been recognized by the president, and all except Texas had held conventions and elected representatives and senators to Congress. But the end of slavery as a legal system did not end the subordination of African Americans. New Southern laws, called "Black Codes," severely restricted the rights of Blacks; and these laws gave the Radical Republicans the political leverage they needed to fight the president's program (Franklin and Moss 1988:206).[5] In response to the Black Codes, Congress passed the Civil Rights Act of 1866.

This law, based on the Thirteenth Amendment and passed over Johnson's veto, declared Blacks to be citizens of the United States, gave them equal civil rights, and gave the federal courts jurisdiction over cases arising under the act (Faulkner 1948:401). Soon after this, Congress approved the Fourteenth Amendment, which reaffirmed state and federal citizenship for persons born or naturalized in the United States and forbade any state to abridge the "privileges and immunities" of citizens. The amendment contained other provisions that have had far-reaching effects. It declared that states could not deprive any person of life, liberty, or property without "due process of law" or deny any person "the equal protection of the laws." These clauses of the Fourteenth Amendment have been applied in several civil rights cases involving minority group citizens (Tindall 1984:682–683).

Congress also passed four sweeping Reconstruction bills that divided the Southern states into five military districts, provided for elections in which the freedmen could participate equally, and required new constitutions that ensured all citizens the right to vote. An acceptable constitution and the approval of the Fourteenth Amendment were required for the readmission of a state to the Union. By 1870, all 11 former Confederate states were again represented in Congress.

Congressional Reconstruction infuriated the members of the old planter class and nurtured a hatred that was slow to die. In the elections creating the Reconstruction legislatures, 703,400 Black and 660,000 White voters were registered (Franklin 1961:80); for the first time, Black legislators were elected to public office. Among the Whites, many who were elected were "carpetbaggers" from the North and "scalawags" (Union loyalists) from the South. The composition of these conventions and the widespread bribery, fraud, and theft that became common in the governments established by them led quickly to charges that "Negro-carpetbag-scalawag" rule was the result of a "conspiracy to degrade and destroy the Southern way of life" (Franklin 1961:103). Such charges ignored certain pertinent facts. In regard to composition, only in South Carolina did Black legislators outnumber Whites, and only in Mississippi and Virginia did Northern Whites outnumber Southern Whites (Franklin 1961:102). In regard to honesty, the graft and corruption emerging within the Southern Reconstruction governments was often small by comparison with that occurring in the North during this same period. In Franklin's (1961:151) opinion, "the tragedy of public immorality in the Southern states was only part of a national tragedy." It should be said also that despite the unfavorable conditions under which they labored, the Reconstruction governments succeeded to some extent in placing political power in the hands of the common people. For the first time, many poor citizens, both Black and White, were able to vote and to participate directly in the affairs of government.

White Hostility

Many Blacks soon began to exercise the new freedoms granted by the Emancipation Proclamation, the Civil Rights Act, and the Reconstruction acts. The assertion of their rights violated the traditional "etiquette of race relations" that symbolized and helped to maintain the Whites' position of dominance.

The Whites developed direct, organized, secret methods to intimidate and punish Blacks who attempted to exercise their new rights or compete directly with them for jobs. The most notorious was the **Ku Klux Klan,** formed in 1866.[6] The Klan's purpose soon became the destruction of the Reconstruction governments and the return of Black people to their subordinate status. The main tactics of the Klan involved mysterious incantations, cross burnings, and somber warnings delivered in full costume at night. When these methods seemed insufficient, house burnings, floggings, and murder were added. Women, as well as men, were Klan members. By the 1920s, perhaps half a million or more White Protestant women had joined the Women of the Ku Klux Klan (WKKK) and in some areas constituted a significant minority of Klan members (Blee 1991:2). Women of the Klan used traditions of community gatherings, kin networks, private relationships, children's auxiliaries, and social celebrations to circulate the Klan's message of racial, religious, and national bigotry. Blee argued that it was the integration of Klan beliefs and hatreds into the normal everyday life of White Protestants that made the Klan's power so devastating. The Klan quickly created a culture that promoted White racial privilege and a convenient "cover" for anyone (whether members or not) who wished to punish or intimidate Black people. Such tactics were so effective that Black people soon found it was safer to proclaim that politics was "White men's business." This protective reaction, adopted during the Reconstruction period, lasted for many decades.

As the Klan's campaign against Blacks became increasingly terrorist, some states and the federal government passed anti-Klan laws. Even some Klan members deplored the violence and felt that things had gotten out of hand. But the efforts to control the violence against Blacks and to prevent intimidation were not successful. The disputed presidential election of 1876 led in 1877 to the complete withdrawal of federal troops and the end of Reconstruction.

The Restoration of White Supremacy

Race relations in the South were changed dramatically and irrevocably altered by the Civil War, emancipation, defeat, and Reconstruction. The successful campaign of the old planter class, with the aid of poor Whites and many business people, to end Radical Republican Reconstruction and recapture political control of the South did not put everything back into its prewar place. Having succeeded in recapturing the state governments and bringing about the withdrawal of federal troops, the Whites wished to reestablish their dominance over the Blacks; as a part of this effort, they insisted the racial problem was a Southern problem that should be resolved by Southerners without "interference." The Northerners, in turn, had been left in a state of exhaustion by all the efforts that had gone into ensuring the freedom and civil rights of Blacks. Their general response to the White Southerner's demands to be given a free hand, therefore, was to offer only token resistance.

Economic Slavery

The economic and legal weapons used by the Whites to return the Blacks as nearly as possible to a condition of slavery are of considerable interest. On the economic side, "sharecropping" developed. This new system of agricultural production reduced many Whites as well as Blacks to a state resembling slavery. The planters retained most of the productive land, but they generally were bankrupt. They had lost their slaves and were unable to pay wages for labor. Sharecropping worked in the following way: Banks and other lenders advanced money to the planters for a certain (usually large) share of the planter's next crop. The planters, in turn, advanced money and supplies to tenants for a certain share (also usually large) of their portion of the next crop. Although this system did permit the South's agricultural economy to resume production, it created a vicious cycle of borrowing and indebtedness. Because cotton was the cash crop in greatest demand, this method of financing also led to the overproduction of cotton and the rapid depletion of the soil's nutrients. Each of these elements helped to drive large numbers of landowners out of business.

The tenancy and sharecropping system worked to the disadvantage of practically everyone but the lenders. But it worked to the greatest disadvantage of the Black tenants. Many White landowners did not make public the exact records of the amounts they received for their crops or the amounts of credit they had extended to their tenants for food, clothing, and supplies during a given year. Since many tenants could neither read nor write, they had no effective way to challenge the owner's statement of what they were entitled to from the sale of the crop or what they owed the owner for supplies. Moreover, Black tenants soon learned they were in no position to insist that they be given an accurate statement of their earnings and debts. For a Black person even to hint that he or she was being cheated by a White was regarded by the Whites as the height of insolence and was sure to be punished; consequently, the tenants could do little or nothing when they learned, after the sale of the crops, that their backbreaking labor was to be rewarded by an increase in their debt. The tenants, especially the Black tenants, were kept by these devices in a condition hardly better than the slavery from which they presumably had recently escaped. The whole family, including women, children, and extended kin, worked to harvest enough crops to meet their obligations (Winegarten 1995:44, 47). When large numbers of tenants and owners could no longer earn a living in agriculture, they migrated to the cities.

Jim Crow Laws

The process of lowering the social standing of the Blacks from the pinnacle reached during Reconstruction involved legal as well as economic weapons. The primary areas of conflict for many years were the right to vote and segregation in public transportation. Following the Civil War, many railroad and steamship lines refused to permit Blacks to purchase first-class accommodations. And as a part of the Black Codes regulating the movements and privileges of the freedmen, Mississippi, Florida, and Texas each passed laws restricting the use of first-class railroad cars by Blacks (Woodward 1957:xiv–xv). The laws were the first of many **"Jim Crow"**[7] laws passed by southern legislatures to segregate Blacks from Whites. Later the term *Jim Crow* came to refer to the pattern of racial discrimination that resulted from state and local laws that required segregation in every type of public facility from schools to cemeteries. At first, only the rights to vote and to use public transportation were affected. In time, however, every aspect of life—schooling, housing, religion, jobs, the courts, recreation, health care, and so on—was included.

Even before the end of the Reconstruction period, in fact, both the churches and the schools had become almost completely segregated without any legislation whatever. Interracial violence was extremely common as Whites increasingly sought to prevent Blacks from exercising their rights as citizens. Also, during this period, the rate at which Blacks were being lynched by Whites rose dramatically (Frazier 1957:160).

Voting Restrictions

Gradually, the pressure mounted to separate the races in every way, to disfranchise the Blacks, and to place them in a position of complete subordination. To prevent Blacks from voting, Whites devised schemes to circumvent the Fifteenth Amendment, which prohibited states from denying any person the vote on grounds of race, color, or previous conditions of servitude. In 1890, Mississippi changed the voting requirements in its constitution to reduce the number of Black voters; and during the next 25 years, all of the old Confederate states followed Mississippi's lead.

The methods employed relied on three main ideas, usually used in combination. In some states, voters were required to be able to pass "literacy" tests or to be property holders. In some states, the voters were required to pay a poll tax, usually months in advance of an election. And, in some states, the procedure for nominating people to office was restricted to Whites (the White primary) on the ground that the nominations were not elections and were, therefore, a "private" matter. These qualifications also had a deterrent effect on many White voters; however, several loopholes in the laws were created to decrease their effects on Whites. For instance, to meet the literacy test, a person might be required to show an "understanding" of some portion of the federal or state constitution. Since White officials were in charge of these "tests" and decided who had passed, only the people considered to be non-White were ever found to be "illiterate" and unqualified to vote.

Another technique to permit Whites only to evade the other voter qualifications was the infamous "grandfather clause." Under one type of grandfather clause, people could qualify as voters only if their ancestors had been eligible to vote in 1860 (Frazier 1957:157). Since few southern Blacks could meet this type of test, and many Whites could, a grandfather clause disqualified many more Blacks than Whites. Some idea of the efficiency of these methods may be seen from the records in Louisiana. In 1896, there were more than 130,000 Black voters; in 1904, there were less than 1,400 (Lawson 1976:14–15).

Despite economic, political, and social oppression, Black men and women resisted in a number of ways. They took their grievances to the Freedmen's Bureau. When attacked, some responded. They defied segregation and disfranchisement with lawsuits and civil disobedience. Black women joined organizations, such as the Woman's Christian Temperance Union and farmers' alliances, and they spoke publicly, attended meetings, and convinced the men in their families both to vote and how to vote (Winegarten 1995:81).

Separate but Equal

The other main focus of the segregationists' efforts—public transportation—led to a momentous decision by the U.S. Supreme Court affecting the civil rights of all Americans. In 1890, Louisiana passed a law requiring separate rail-car facilities for Whites and Blacks. The law stated that "all railway companies carrying passengers . . . in this state shall provide equal but separate accommodations for the white and colored races" (Tussman 1963:65). Under the law, Whites and Blacks were not permitted to sit together in a coach or a section of a coach. Criminal charges could be filed for a violation of the law.

In 1896, this law was challenged in the Supreme Court in the famous "separate but equal" case *Plessy v. Ferguson*. Plessy, who was stated to be "seven-eighths caucasian," had been ordered to leave a coach assigned to members of the White race and had refused to comply. He had been arrested and jailed for violating the law. The main legal point in Plessy's case was that he had been deprived of his rights under the Fourteenth Amendment to the Constitution. The majority of the Court argued that even though the amendment was intended to achieve the absolute equality of the races, no law could abolish social distinctions based on color.

The majority opinion was eloquently challenged by Justice Harlan, who argued that the Louisiana law was unconstitutional because it violated the personal freedoms of all of the people of Louisiana. It was the purpose of the Thirteenth, Fourteenth, and Fifteenth amendments to make the Constitution colorblind and to remove the race line from our system of government. But if a state could prescribe separate railway coaches, then it could also insist that Whites and Blacks must walk on opposite sides of the street or sit on opposite sides of the courtroom or be segregated in public meetings. By this reasoning, the state could require the separation in railway coaches of Protestant and Catholic passengers or of native and naturalized citizens.

Justice Harlan also believed that in the long run, the decision would stimulate racial resentment and hatred. The real meaning of the Louisiana law, he argued, is that Whites consider Blacks to be so inferior that it is degrading to mingle with them in any way. The statute was not intended to guarantee that Blacks would not be forced to associate with Whites but that Whites would not be forced to associate with Blacks. Such an approach to race relations was a serious mistake, Harlan believed. "The destinies of the two races in this country," he wrote, "are indissolubly linked together, and the interests of both require that the common government of all shall not permit the seeds of race hate to be planted under the sanction of law" (Tussman 1963:81).

Harlan's fear that the result of *Plessy* would be the extension of racial segregation not only in railroad coaches but in many other spheres of life was clearly justified. Within 3 years, every southern state had adopted a law segregating the races aboard trains. By 1910, most of these same states had extended segregation to include the waiting rooms in railway stations; by 1920, racial segregation in the South (and a few adjoining states) had become the normal practice in almost every public matter. In time, signs proclaiming "Whites only" or "Colored" were displayed at drinking fountains, rest rooms, theaters, swimming pools, libraries, public telephones, bathing beaches, hospital entrances, restaurants, and so on. In many instances, the laws regulating the permissible behavior of the members of the two races stated exactly, in feet and inches, how far apart their separate entrances into public buildings or places of amusement must be and how close together they were allowed to sit or stand. Of course, in all of these situations, the separate facilities for Blacks were supposed to be equal to those for Whites. In fact, this was almost never the case. In only a few short years, the White southerners had succeeded by law in creating a rigid caste system. Once again, as in the period of slavery, Black people had no rights that White people were bound to respect.

In some ways, the Jim Crow system that emerged after 1890 was an even more efficient instrument of subordination than slavery had been. It is true that the Blacks under Jim Crow were no longer legally the property of the Whites, but then it is also true that the Whites no longer had as strong an incentive to be concerned about the welfare of the Blacks. Under slavery, at least some Blacks were in close daily contact with some Whites, and those contacts were often friendly and compassionate (though it is easy to exaggerate this). The Jim Crow system made many forms of friendly and understanding contacts between the races practically impossible. Residential segregation *increased* as the Jim Crow system became more pervasive. Blacks increasingly were pressured into slum areas that were occupied solely by Blacks.

The system of enforced racial segregation also may have been as difficult to bear psychologically as slavery had been. During the period of slavery, a major source of emotional sustenance for Blacks was the hope, however faint, that someday they might be released from bondage. Emancipation, the Thirteenth, Fourteenth, and Fifteenth Amendments, and Reconstruction all seemed to fulfill this dim and ancient hope. Black people voted, were elected to office, moved about fairly freely, mingled with Whites in public places, and owned property. But the Supreme Court's decision in *Plessy* cleared the way for the rise of Jim Crowism and the virtual reenslavement of Black people in many southern and adjoining states. Although under the Jim Crow system Black people still retained significant freedoms, such as the right to attend schools (albeit inferior ones) and to own property, the laws permitted under *Plessy* practically neutralized the *intent* of the post–Civil War amendments to the Constitution.

Although legal segregation, with only a few exceptions, was established primarily in the South and in some border states, many forms of racial discrimination, including segregation, occurred in other parts of the country. Even in states that had enacted special civil rights laws attempting to guarantee the rights contained in the federal constitution, many discriminatory practices existed. For example, hotels were suddenly "filled" when Black guests tried to register, or theaters were "sold out" when Black patrons arrived. Moreover, socially enforced residential segregation soon became the rule throughout the United States. The Jim Crow laws of the southern states helped create and strengthen a system of racial discrimination that went far beyond the extralegal discrimination that has been prevalent in many parts of the United States.

Migration and Urbanization

Immediately after the Civil War, some African Americans began to exercise their new freedom to move about. At first, this movement took place almost entirely within the

South and consisted primarily of migration from the Atlantic seaboard to the more westerly states of the South and from rural areas into the cities. Increasingly, however, social and economic forces favored migration out of the South.

Conditions in the North changed sharply with the outbreak of World War I. The war suddenly halted the supply of cheap labor that had been provided by European immigration, just at a time when the demand for labor to produce war materials was rising. Northern employers looked to the South for a new supply of cheap labor. During the 1910–1920 period, more than a half million Black people headed north (Farley and Allen 1987:113).[8] This movement is of special interest not only because it was the largest mass migration of Blacks from the South up to that time, but also because it originated mainly in the Deep South rather than in the border states. Most of the migrants sought jobs in New York, Chicago, Philadelphia, and Detroit. The Black population of these cities increased during the decade by nearly 750,000 (Frazier 1957:191). The newcomers found jobs in iron and steel mills, automobile construction, chemical plants, and other industrial settings. They received much higher wages than they were accustomed to in the South, and northern employers, for the most part, found them to be competent and easier to work with than immigrant laborers from foreign countries.

The urbanization of Blacks in the cities of the North, though greatly aided by industrial jobs and high wages, was hindered by the prejudice and discrimination of Whites. In the workplace, Whites struggled to prevent Blacks from gaining union membership and the better training and jobs that accompanied such membership. In the broader community, Whites fought to force Blacks into segregated neighborhoods. Prior to this time, Blacks, along with other poor people, had been concentrated in areas of low-rent housing; but if they wished to and could afford it, Blacks were able to live in various parts of the cities. Now, however, real estate agents catered to the preferences of Whites and "steered" Black customers into all-Black neighborhoods and placed clauses in real estate contracts that excluded Blacks and other non-White groups.

Many observers believe, even though African Americans undeniably were involuntary immigrants to America, that their great migration to the North may be compared in some ways to the European immigrations. From this perspective, although Black Americans have been physically present within the United States for centuries, their entry into the American industrial economy as "immigrants" actually has been underway for little more than three generations; hence, even though their experience up to the time of World War I may properly be characterized as colonial, their experience since that time increasingly has resembled that of recent immigrants (Kristol 1972).

The end of World War I, an economic depression in the early 1920s, and the Great Depression of the entire decade of the 1930s greatly reduced the migration of southern Blacks to the North and West; but the movement was by no means stopped. The Black population of these regions continued to rise throughout the period and at a much faster rate than in the South.

The next great surge of Black migration accompanied World War II. As in the case of World War I, many Blacks moved to the war plants in the cities of the North and West. Again, Chicago, Detroit, New York, and Philadelphia received large numbers of these migrants. By this time, however, the South also had become far more industrialized than previously; so many migrating Blacks moved to southern cities, such as Birmingham,

Houston, Norfolk, and New Orleans. And for the first time, western cities such as Los Angeles, Portland, and San Diego drew sizable numbers of Blacks out of the South. The favorite single destination for Black migrants was Harlem in New York City. This Black community grew during the period under discussion into the largest urban Black population in the world (Davie 1949:100).

Although Jim Crow laws continued to dominate the lives of Black southerners, many had escaped to other regions of the country, had adjusted to life in urban areas, and were working in industrial occupations. These migrants were still subjected to many types of extralegal discrimination. Nevertheless, northern Blacks enjoyed a greater degree of formal and legal equality; and this legal advantage afforded a basis from which to launch an energetic, if excruciatingly slow, judicial and legislative offensive against all forms of discrimination affecting Blacks and—by extension—all other minority groups in America. This offensive, generally referred to as the civil rights movement, may be dated from the period in which Jim Crowism was becoming established in America.

 The Civil Rights Movement

The Supreme Court's decision in *Plessy v. Ferguson* marks the point at which Black people in the South officially lost the battle to retain the advantages won in the Civil War. The *Plessy* decision not only signaled to the South that it might go ahead on a state-by-state basis to reduce Blacks to second-class citizens, but it also ratified many changes underway in the relations between the races. The level of White violence against Blacks rose sharply, the doctrine of innate Black inferiority gained strength, and many Blacks feared that open resistance to White supremacy was foolhardy. Some African American leaders concluded that the wisest course of action was to accept the fact that Whites were not going to permit Black equality, at least not in the short run. The most influential statement of this view that Blacks should accept a new accommodation with Whites on the Whites' terms was voiced by the Black leader Booker T. Washington.

Separate and Subordinate

Born in Virginia of a slave mother and a White father, Washington had overcome extreme adversity to get an education at Hampton Institute, a post–Civil War missionary school. Washington used his education to establish Tuskegee Institute, one of the leading Black colleges. At the Atlanta exposition of 1895, Washington expressed the view in a speech called the **"Atlanta Compromise"** that Blacks should focus "upon the everyday practical things of life, upon something that is needed to be done, and something which they will be permitted to do in the community in which they reside." Washington's famous speech was carefully designed to assure White people that Blacks were ready to accept their inferior status in the political arena. He stated: "In all things that are purely social, we can be as separate as the fingers yet one as the hand in all things essential to mutual progress" (Washington [1895]1959:156). He argued further that Blacks were still too recently removed from slavery to take their place as equals among the Whites. He emphasized that Blacks must adopt an economic program of manual labor and self-help as the best means to win their full rights as citizens rather than engaging in political action. Needless to say, Washington's views were very flattering to Whites and were immediately praised by them. It has been reported that many of the White people who heard Washington's speech leaped to their feet in a standing ovation, while many Blacks in the audience sat silently weeping.

Washington became a celebrity almost overnight. Until his death 20 years later, he was the most influential and powerful spokesman for Black America. His views on race relations were central to the so-called Tuskegee point of view, which stressed appeasement of the Whites, segregation, and the importance of self-help. He presented both a program (the "gospel of wealth") and an organization (The National Negro Business League) to help attain it. At the center of his strategy was the development of Black business enterprise and economic solidarity among Blacks (Butler and Wilson 1988:136–137).

The Niagara Movement

Washington's position on racial relations was widely accepted among Blacks as well as Whites, but some Black leaders bitterly criticized him for sacrificing education and civil rights for the acceptance of White conservatives. In 1902, Monroe Trotter (1971:35) attacked Washington as a "Benedict Arnold of the Negro race." W. E. B. DuBois became Washington's leading critic. Du Bois, the holder of a Ph.D. degree from Harvard University, called Washington's teachings propaganda that was helping to speed the construction of a racial caste system. In 1905, a small group of Black "radicals" under the leadership of Du Bois formed the **Niagara Movement** to express opposition to Washington's program. They disagreed with him emphatically on many major issues. Their "Declaration of Principles" stated that Black people should protest the curtailment of their political and civil rights. They pointed out that the denial of opportunities to Blacks in the South amounted to "virtual slavery." And they proclaimed their refusal to accept the impression left by Washington and his followers "that the Negro American assents to inferiority, is submissive under oppression, and apologetic before insults." In contrast to Washington's strategy of political submission coupled with economic development, the members of the Niagara Movement insisted that agitation and complaint was the best way for Blacks to escape the "barbarian" practices of discrimination based on race (Meier, Rudwick, and Broderick 1971:58–62).

Given the time at which it was made, the Niagara Declaration seemed very radical. Jim Crowism was reaching fruition. In the minds of most people, Blacks as well as Whites, segregation would remain the "solution" to problems in race relations. We should observe, though, that for all their differences the Washington "conservatives" and the Du Bois "radicals" agreed that Blacks should strive to establish economic independence, that they should join together to attempt to solve their problems, and that the ultimate goal of any strategy should be the full acceptance of African Americans as first-class citizens of the United States (Meier, Rudwick, and Broderick 1971:xxvi). They disagreed sharply on whether the proper means to the attainment of their ends should be humility, subservience, and patience or an aggressive, indignant demand for the immediate recognition of their rights.

The NAACP.   The Niagara group was not large or immediately very influential, but its declaration revealed dramatically that not all Blacks accepted Washington's policies. More important, however, is that, in 1909, most of the Niagara group's members merged with a group of White liberals to form the National Association for the Advancement of Colored People (NAACP). The leaders of the NAACP opposed "the ever-growing oppression," "the systematic persecution," and the disfranchisement of Black people. They demanded that everyone, including Blacks, be given free public schooling that would focus on professional education for the most gifted—what Du Bois had earlier called "the talented tenth"—as well as industrial training for all who wished it; however, this goal could not be achieved unless Blacks received equal treatment under the law. The NAACP adopted a legal and legislative strategy. It called on Congress and the president to enforce strictly the Constitution's provisions on civil rights and the right to vote, and it urged that educational expenditures for Black children be made equal to those for Whites (Meier, Rudwick, and Broderick 1971:65–66).[9]

The NAACP soon began to make its presence felt. As editor of the organization's official magazine, *The Crisis,* Du Bois was able to place his ideas before a large audience; in 1915, the organization's legal efforts helped to bring about a Supreme Court decision declaring the "grandfather clause" unconstitutional. After Booker T. Washington died later in that same year, the NAACP became the leading organization devoted to the civil rights of Black Americans.

At the very time of the inception of the NAACP, however, certain events were forcing many Blacks to conclude that no amount of legal action could guarantee them first-class citizenship. Many cities became powder kegs of racial resentment and unrest.

Continued Racial Violence

Three types of interracial violence were prominent during this period. Lynchings, especially of Blacks by Whites, had been an important form of violence for several decades and were still a source of great concern. Although the Klan went through a dormant period in the early 1900s, the massive immigration from Europe, coupled with the nation's employment ills, revived it. In 1915, the Klan's leader, Imperial Wizard William Simmons, initiated a new era of hatred and intolerance. At the same time a widely shown film, *Birth of A Nation,* glorified the Klan as a group that had preserved the American South from uncivilized Blacks (Salzman 1992). Although the actual number of lynchings that were recorded was somewhat lower between 1910 and 1920 than in the two previous decades, many lynchings were conducted in an especially sadistic way and in a carnival atmosphere. Some victims were tortured and burned at the stake, and some newspapers issued invitations to Whites to come to witness a lynching or a burning. Between the period from the emancipation to the Great Depression, about 3,000 Blacks were lynched in the American South (Beck and Tolnay 1990:526). Unsurprisingly, some militant Black leaders advocated armed resistance as a solution to these problems (Franklin and Moss 1988:318–321).

Another main form of violence during these years consisted of mob attacks by Whites on Blacks and their property. This type of violence was most common in the cities of the South. For the most part, in these outbreaks, Blacks were unorganized and defenseless, but in some cases they fought back. For example, in 1921 between 50 and 75 armed Blacks confronted a White mob of 1,500 to 2,000 people in Tulsa, Oklahoma. In the conflict that followed, over 50 people died and "the entire section known as Black Wall Street—more than one thousand homes and businesses—lay in ruins" (Butler and Wilson 1988:147). In several outbreaks in cities of the North, Blacks also organized and retaliated against Whites. The summer following the end of World War I was filled with such a large number of mob attacks by Whites, and so much blood was shed in the summer of 1919 that James Weldon Johnson (1968:304), head of the NAACP, referred to it as "the Red Summer." Approximately two dozen outbreaks occurred in American cities, and 14 Blacks were publicly burned, 11 of them alive (Lincoln 1961:56). These conflicts were of the type usually described as race "riots."

The rise of White nativist sentiment expressed in the revival of the Ku Klux Klan and the lynchings, burnings, mob attacks, and race riots occurred during or immediately following World War I, a war that had been fought "to make the world safe for democracy." Since between 350,000 and 400,000 Black Americans had served during the Great War, the gap between the nation's lofty ideals and the actual conditions at home was not lost on many Blacks.

All of these elements combined following the war to give a large number of Blacks a new sense of racial identity. This **"Black Renaissance"** was visibly furthered by a group of writers and artists located in Harlem, among them Langston Hughes, Zora Neale Hurston, and Claude McKay. These writers generated poetry, novels, and newspaper columns that exalted Black pride, Black cultural expression, and Black exclusiveness. This renaissance, with its bristling spirit of protest, also generated an extreme form of nationalism that promoted separatism.

Separatism

Many Blacks were more convinced than ever before that the prospects of Black people in America were very poor. Under these conditions, the legalistic approach of the NAACP did not seem sufficiently direct or vigorous to many Blacks. In the minds of hundreds of thousands of Black Americans, the program offered by a new leader, Marcus Garvey, seemed the answer to a prayer.

Back to Africa.   Garvey, a dark-skinned man, was born in Jamaica in 1887. He came to the United States during World War I and organized the Universal Negro Improvement Association (UNIA). The UNIA's major long-range goal was to enable African Americans to leave the United States and settle in an independent nation in Africa. The philosophy of independence preached by Garvey appealed mainly to the lower-income, urban masses. Middle-class or professional and business people were offended by his attacks on them and their acceptance of White standards and by his contempt for those who had light-colored skin.

Garvey's heroes were men like Denmark Vesey, Gabriel Prosser, and Nat Turner who had promoted violent resistance to slavery. Somewhat ironically, his colonization program was inspired by "conservative" Booker T. Washington's autobiography *Up From Slavery*. Garvey admired Washington's emphasis on racial separation and self-help. Garvey's ideas concerning the eventual solution of America's racial relations, though, were radically different from Washington's. Whereas Washington saw separation as a tool to be used to gain eventual acceptance by White Americans, Garvey visualized the renunciation of American citizenship and the permanent separation of the two races. As Baker (1970:8) said, "Garvey's UNIA was an effort to have Black Americans vote with their feet."

The idea of recolonization, of course, was not at all new, but Garvey's "back to Africa" movement represented the first time a Black person had attempted to organize such a venture. Moreover, the effort came at a time when large masses of Black Americans were concentrated in urban ghettos and were ready to listen. Garvey (1970:25) lashed out at most Black leaders for "aping white people" and for exhibiting "the slave spirit of dependence." These so-called leaders, he said, were "Uncle Toms" who could not be trusted. He argued that the time had come for Blacks to be self-reliant, to have a country of their own in Africa. The purpose of the UNIA was to inspire "an unfortunate race with pride in self and with the determination" to take its place as an equal among races (Garvey 1968a:295).

Under Garvey's leadership, the UNIA established a number of Black-run business enterprises, including the Black Star Steamship Line. This line was intended to link Black people throughout the world and to provide the transportation they would need to return "home." The UNIA also established the Universal African Legion, the Black Eagle Flying Corps, the Universal Black Cross Nurses, and some other organizations designed to promote self-reliance and Black pride. These organizations—with their members dressed in smart uniforms—dramatized Garvey's ideas and attracted widespread attention and admiration. These tactics also earned him the enmity of most other influential Black leaders and the federal government.

Garvey's numerous enemies slowly closed in on him. Both the NAACP, which by comparison seemed "conservative," and the socialists under A. Philip Randolph agreed that Garvey must be stopped. They were assisted in their efforts by Garvey's own shortcomings as an administrator. In 1922, Garvey was indicted for mail fraud; in 1923 he was convicted and imprisoned in the federal penitentiary in Atlanta. One news magazine proclaimed "Garvey defeated Garvey." Although the bulk of the Negro press approved of this end to Garvey's career, a White newspaper, the *Buffalo Evening Times*, noted that many White men who were greater offenders had received lighter sentences or no punishment for similar crimes (Cronon 1969:135). Although his sentence was commuted in 1927, Garvey was deported to Jamaica as an undesirable alien. After his deportation, the UNIA no longer had an inspiring leader; therefore, the influence of the largest mass movement among Black Americans to that date waned. The scandal and suspicion created by the trial, imprisonment, and deportation of Garvey led to a rapid decline of the UNIA. The organization's nationalistic message, though, has had an enduring influence among African Americans. It appealed to the masses, profoundly stirred the race consciousness of Blacks around the world, and served as a focal point for pride in African culture.

Two direct descendants of the UNIA have been very prominent. The first of these, the Lost Nation of Islam, came into existence less than five years after Garvey's deportation. The second, to which we turn later, did not arise until the mid-1960s.

Black Muslims.
W. D. Fard established the Lost Nation of Islam (or Black Muslims) in the early 1930s. Fard's primary doctrine was that the White race was the devil on earth, that African Americans were the lost tribe of Shebazz, and that the salvation of Blacks lay not in the White man's religion, Christianity, but in the Black's true religion, Mohammedanism (Lincoln 1961:72–80). Fard founded the Temple of Islam and assembled a devoted following. Chief among his disciples was Elijah Poole, who became known as Elijah Muhammad. After Fard's sudden disappearance in 1934, Elijah Muhammad assumed the leadership of the movement and took the title "Messenger of Allah" (Lincoln 1961:15–16).

The teachings of Elijah Muhammad, like those of Marcus Garvey, advocated race pride, self-help, and the separation of the races; however, his views differed from Garvey's in at least two important respects. First, although Garvey stated that Jesus had been Black and that Black people should renounce Christianity and its White symbolism, religion had been secondary to politics in the UNIA. Among the Black Muslims, however, religion has been the dominant element. They developed an extremely demanding moral code that forbade the use of tobacco or drugs, extramarital sexual relations, racial intermarriage, dancing, attendance at movies, participation in sports, laziness, lying, and a host of other things. Second, the political goals of the Black Muslim movement also differed from those of the UNIA. Garvey's main goals were to return Black people to Africa and Africa to Black people. The Muslims have called at various times for a separate nation right here in the United States and have suggested that several states should be set aside for this purpose.

The most important difference between the Garvey movement and the Black Muslim movement, however, is that the Muslims gradually gained in strength and influence over the years. The number of people who are officially members of the Black Muslim organization is unknown, but the effect of the movement extends far beyond its membership. Certainly, the teachings of Elijah Muhammad and his famous convert Malcolm X have been widely circulated within the United States and overseas. Many people who do not belong to the Muslim church or subscribe to all of its teachings nevertheless have developed respect for the Muslims' high standards and strict discipline. The Muslims have been notably successful in the rehabilitation of ex-convicts and drug addicts, and they have been successful in their efforts to build a strong economic base. The strict moral code and philosophy of economic independence have had an especially powerful appeal to the many Black people who reside in the urban ghettos of America. It has played a significant role in "revitalizing" the lives of many people who previously had given up in the face of seemingly overwhelming difficulties.

The importance of the Black Muslim movement cannot be measured solely in terms of its official size. After the collapse of the Garvey movement, it served as a valuable repository of Black separatist philosophy and as a continuing reminder to Black Americans that there was an alternative to the goal of "integration." In the 1990s, the Nation of Islam's leader, Louis Farrakhan, revived many aspects of the Garvey movement's Black pride and separatist ideology.

Strategy, Tactics, and Conflict

The NAACP had maintained its legal warfare against discrimination throughout the period under discussion. But with the onset of the Great Depression in 1929, the association was increasingly criticized for its relative inactivity in economic matters. The Depression struck hard at all American workers, but its effects on Black workers were particularly devastating. Blacks were systematically excluded from most units of the leading labor organization, the American Federation of Labor (AFL), and they were "the last hired and the first fired."

These circumstances led to the organization of a number of new protest groups whose main objective was more and better jobs for Black people. These organizations urged African Americans to use their substantial economic power as a lever to improve conditions. The common slogan of these organizations, "Don't Buy Where You Can't Work," emphasized that their main weapons were the economic boycott and the picket line.

One of the new organizations to employ these direct-action tactics was the New Negro Alliance, Inc. The alliance grew out of a spontaneous protest occurring at a hamburger grill in Washington, D.C. (Bunche [1940]1971:122). This grill was located in a Black residential area and depended entirely on Black customers. In 1933, the Black workers at the grill were fired, and White workers were hired to replace them. Several onlookers were outraged by this act of blatant discrimination and formed a picket line at the grill. This tactic quickly led to the reinstatement of the Black workers. This form of protest was so successful that many other groups, including the NAACP, adopted it. The NAACP's new willingness to address the economic problems of Black people, however, continued to be secondary to its main focus on the issue of school segregation.

The beginning of World War II signaled the close of the Great Depression. The demand for labor rapidly increased as armaments production rose. The boom spread to construction, service industries, transportation, and other sectors of the economy; but the sudden increase in the demand for labor served mainly to put the huge force of unemployed Whites back to work. The main jobs that opened up for Blacks were as service workers and farm laborers (Myrdal [1944]1964:409–412).

The continuation of conspicuous discrimination in the midst of still another global war "to make the world safe for democracy" enraged many African Americans. Two forms of discrimination were particularly galling: discrimination in war production and in the armed forces. Both of these areas involved federal dollars and, therefore, seemed to represent national policy. One leader, A. Philip Randolph, established in 1942 the March on Washington movement, which sought to organize millions of Black people. He argued that "mass power" used in an orderly and lawful way was "the most effective weapon a minority people can wield" (Randolph 1971a:230). Although the United States still had not entered the war at the time Randolph issued his first call to march,

President Franklin D. Roosevelt was eager to prevent any large demonstration of unrest. In June 1941, the president issued an executive order (No. 8802) prohibiting racial discrimination in defense industries, in government, and in defense training programs. The order also established a Fair Employment Practices Committee (FEPC) to investigate possible violations of the order.

CORE: The Expansion of Nonviolent Protest. The principle of nonviolent direct action had a broad appeal. A new protest organization, the Congress of Racial Equality (CORE), was formed in 1942. CORE attempted to apply the methods of Jesus and Gandhi to the race situation in America. It rested on the conviction that social conflicts cannot be solved by violent methods, that violence simply breeds more violence, and that "turning the other cheek" has the power to shame the evildoer. This approach was later adopted and refined by Martin Luther King, Jr. The practical expression of these beliefs involved a carefully graduated set of steps. In a conflict situation, the first step was patient negotiation. If this effort failed, the next step was to attempt to arouse public opinion against the opponent's discriminatory actions. Only after these remedies were exhausted did CORE advocate the use of boycotts, picket lines, and strikes.

In addition to patient negotiations, agitation, and the use of labor's protest methods, however, CORE developed a new technique of nonviolent direct action. The technique's first use appears to have occurred in 1942 following an incident of discrimination in a cafe against two CORE leaders, James R. Robinson and James Farmer. After nearly a month of attempts to negotiate, the CORE leaders stated that unless the management agreed to talk with them, they would be forced to take some other course of action. About a week later, an interracial group of 25 people entered the restaurant and took seats. The White people among the group were served promptly, but the Black people were not served at all; however, the White people did not eat. Instead, they told the manager that they did not wish to eat until their Black friends had also been served. The manager angrily refused; so the group simply continued to occupy a large number of the restaurant's seats. When customers who were waiting to be served saw they would be unable to be seated, they left. After a period of fuming, the manager had all of the protesters served. Thus ended successfully the first "sit-in," a technique of protest that became increasingly popular during the next two decades (Farmer 1971:243–246).

The protest tactics of organizations such as the March on Washington movement and CORE were only a part of the complicated interracial situation that existed in the United States during World War II. We saw previously that the tense early years of the war were marked by numerous open confrontations and violence between ethnic groups. During this period, various forms of violence involving Blacks and Whites also erupted. Confrontations reminiscent of the "Red Summer" of 1919 occurred in Mobile, Alabama, in Beaumont and El Paso, Texas, in Philadelphia, Pennsylvania, and in Newark, New Jersey. The largest outburst took place in June 1943 in Detroit, Michigan. Racial tensions in Detroit had been building over a long period of time as both White and Black southerners moved there to work in the automobile industry. According to one account, 25 Blacks and 9 Whites were killed, and more than 700 other people were injured (Osofsky 1968:420).

The Decline of Colonialism.   The Allies in World War II had fought not only against fascism but also, officially, against the doctrine of White supremacy. During the course of the war, large numbers of non-White peoples in the United States became aware that many people like themselves were fighting and dying to save the very nations that had been historically the main representatives of the White-supremacy theory. Certainly, the experiences of many men and women in uniform emphasized the disparity between the official principles of the United States and the actual practices within it. Throughout the military services, Jim Crow practices were common. And since many military training camps were in the South, Black servicemen faced segregation when they left the camps. They were frequently in danger of physical assault not only by local citizens but by officers of the law as well. For instance, a Black soldier was shot in Little Rock, Arkansas, because he would not tip his hat and say "sir" to a policeman. Another Black soldier was shot by two police officers because he had taken a bus seat reserved for a White in Beaumont, Texas (Rustin 1971:235).

As the old colonial empires were dissolved following the war, and as new independent nations arose in their place, incidents such as those described became increasingly embarrassing to American leaders. How could the United States explain to the peoples of other nations the discrepancy between its ringing declarations of human rights and the treatment of its own minority groups at home?

Increased external pressures on the American government to attend to these conditions resulted in a series of important changes in official domestic policies. The legal work of the NAACP and the direct-action methods of the March on Washington movement and CORE began to show dramatic results. In 1948, as President Harry Truman and Congress considered the advisability of instituting a peacetime military draft, the leader of the March on Washington movement, A. Philip Randolph, took a strong stand against segregation in the armed forces. Randolph stated that unless the military services were desegregated, he would lead a nationwide campaign to encourage young people to refuse to enlist. He stated further, "I personally will advise Negroes to refuse to fight as slaves for a democracy they cannot possess and cannot enjoy" (Randolph 1971b:278). Later that year, President Truman acted to end all segregation in the armed forces of the United States (Osofsky 1968:465).

Victories in the Courts

The NAACP's battle to end segregation in public education had gradually gained strength through an impressive series of court victories. As early as 1938, the Supreme Court ruled that the State University of Missouri must admit a Black applicant to its law school. Similar rulings were made in cases affecting the law school of the University of Oklahoma (1948), the law school of the University of Texas (1950), and the graduate school of the University of Oklahoma (1950). These rulings led to an all-out effort by the officials of segregated school systems to improve the facilities for Black students and, if possible, to make them physically equal to those for Whites. These victories also laid the groundwork in 1954 for one of the most important court cases in the history of the United States.

Brown v. Topeka Board of Education.   The *Brown* case differed from the other cases just mentioned in a very important respect. The earlier cases had not called into question the "separate but equal doctrine" approved in the Supreme Court's *Plessy* decision in 1896. Now, however, the Court brought this doctrine directly under review. The question of central importance was this: Even if the separate educational facilities for the minority group are equal in buildings, libraries, teacher qualifications, and the like, do these "equal" facilities provide educationally equal opportunities? The Court ruled that they do not. Chief Justice Warren, speaking for the Court, argued that to separate children "from others of similar age and qualifications solely because of their race generates a feeling of inferiority as to their status in the community that may affect their hearts and minds in a way unlikely ever to be undone. . . . We conclude that in the field of public education the doctrine of 'separate but equal' has no place. Separate educational facilities are inherently unequal" (Clark 1963:159). Segregation in public schools was unanimously held to violate the "equal protection" clause of the Fourteenth Amendment and was declared unconstitutional. In a separate ruling on the same day, the Court also declared segregated schools to be a violation of the "due process" clause of the Fifth Amendment.

In its *Brown* ruling in May 1954 (*Brown I*), the Supreme Court recognized the difficulties that would be encountered in the effort to desegregate public schools; consequently, the Court issued another decision in 1955 (*Brown II*) on the question of *how* the transition from segregation to desegregation was to be achieved. The Court emphasized that variations in local conditions had to be taken into account in planning for the change and that the primary responsibility for the implementation of the 1954 ruling rested with local authorities and the lower courts. The Court insisted, however, that local school systems must "make a prompt and reasonable start toward full compliance" with its decision and racial discrimination in school admissions must be halted "with all deliberate speed" (Tussman 1963:45–46).

The *Brown* rulings ushered in a new era of hope among Blacks and of heightened resistance to "integration" among Whites. White citizens councils, described by some Blacks as "the Klan in gray flannel suits" (Osofsky 1968:479), were formed throughout the South to find ways to prevent school desegregation. The KKK itself underwent another revival. The old charges of the White supremacists were again brought forward. And many southern politicians searched frantically for the legal grounds needed to overturn the Court's school desegregation decisions. Although school desegregation was initiated promptly and successfully in many southern communities, the general intensity of White reactions to desegregation efforts began to make clear to Black Americans that change "with all deliberate speed" might, in fact, be very slow. The growing pessimism among Blacks was fueled by numerous incidents of intimidation and violence throughout the South.

An important episode in the struggle to desegregate the schools occurred in Little Rock, Arkansas, during the 1957–1958 school year. The Little Rock school board had gone to work on a school desegregation plan in 1954, almost immediately after the first *Brown* decision. While the board was developing its plan, the state officials of Arkansas were attempting to "nullify" the *Brown* decisions. The central feature of the Arkansas nullification plan was an amendment to the state constitution declaring the *Brown* decisions to be unconstitutional. Despite the stand by the officials of the state, the school officials of Little

Rock moved ahead to desegregate. Nine Black school children were selected to attend Central High School beginning in September 1957. On the day before school opened, the governor of Arkansas, without notifying the school officials, assigned units of the Arkansas National Guard to Central High School and declared the school "off limits" to Black children. When the nine Black students attempted to enter school the next day, the national guardsmen, on the governor's orders, prevented them from entering. Each day for the next 3 weeks, this performance was repeated. At the end of this time, President Eisenhower sent regular federal troops to Central High, and the students at last were admitted. Federal troops remained at the school for the rest of the school year, a year filled with tension and disturbances. The threat to law and order was so serious that by the end of the year the school board begged the courts to permit them to discontinue their plan.

These events raised some very serious questions. Could a state nullify a Supreme Court decision? Who was responsible for the chaos surrounding the effort to desegregate Central High? Should a desegregation effort be discontinued or delayed if it threatens to lead to racial conflict? The Court's rulings on these questions were unanimous. No state can nullify a decision of the Court. The state of Arkansas, therefore, acted unconstitutionally in preventing Black children from attending Central High. Moreover, the actions of the governor and other officials of the state of Arkansas had been, in the Court's view, largely responsible for all of the turmoil surrounding the desegregation effort. The governor's actions had increased opposition to the desegregation plan and encouraged people to oppose it. Finally, the Court refused to accept the idea that desegregation attempts should be carried out only if no violence or disorder were threatened. The importance of Black children's rights to an equal education were not to be sacrificed in the name of law and order.

Despite the Court's unwavering stand on the correctness of its *Brown* decisions, it could not convince many Black people that the law's unaided power could bring about a swift end to the many forms of racial discrimination they faced (of which school segregation was only one). The conviction grew that some further action was needed, something bolder and more direct. The "something bolder" produced a dramatic shift in the direction of the civil rights movement.

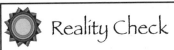 Reality Check

INTERVIEW WITH CARLA

Carla's grandparents attended historically Black colleges and were educators. Her greatgreatgrandmother was a slave. Carla's mother is a pharmacist. Her father's family is Cajun or Creole from Louisiana. She grew up with her mother in a single-parent home in Houston, Texas, where she attended a predominantly White, highly ranked academic high school. Her neighborhood was mixed when her mother first moved there, but is now predominantly Black. Carla is the first in her family to attend a predominantly White university as an undergraduate. She is a freshman planning to major in communications.

How do you refer to yourself in terms of race or ethnicity?
Either Black or African American. My family usually calls themselves Black. I think African American is a word that came about recently to link Black people with their history, which is Africa, but I don't know anybody in my family who is directly from Africa and I don't feel a part of that. I usually refer to myself as Black.

What is most important to you about your racial or ethnic group?
The struggles that Black people have gone through in the past to get to where they are now stand out as very important about my heritage. You had to work a little harder than other people, like Whites or other minorities, to accomplish the things you wanted to accomplish.

How does being Black affect you in your daily life?
It affects me by the way I identify myself. It motivates me to work harder and to be outstanding, whether it be work, school, or social activities. It's a factor that motivates me to strive for perfection.

When did you become aware of your racial/ethnic identity?
In elementary school you are exposed to other children. I guess because I was light skinned, other kids were saying, "Are you White?" and I would go home to my mom and I would ask her. When I confronted that, having to identify myself with a particular race, I became aware that I was Black or African American. They told me I was Black. I didn't understand at that early age, but as I grew older the society made me aware of it.

Have you ever experienced any uncomfortable situations because of your racial or ethnic identity?
It makes me uncomfortable when White people think I am a spokesperson for Black people. They think I am the one who can answer all the questions about their curiosities about Black people, especially Black hair; they don't know about Black hair. A lot of White people are curious about African American culture, but I am just one person. I am not representative of the whole African American people. African American people are as diverse as any other group. They are each unique human beings. What we all have in common is that we are African American.

Tell me about the schools you went to.
Growing up I went to a Black elementary school. In middle school I went to a more integrated school. It was a better quality of education and from then on I went on to a high school that was a similar type. It was predominantly White, but we did have lots of minorities there as well. Growing up in that environment and being exposed to different people, I felt that I wanted to do that in higher

(continued)

education. My mom felt that I would be competing among these people and the more interaction I got, the better my chances. That opportunity was not available to my mother and others before her and it is available now to us and I think it is important to seize that and not deny yourself that opportunity. And there is no shame in doing that.

Tell me about your high school.
It was a rich school in an upper class area of Houston and a good school academically. It was predominantly White, but minority enrollment was increasing. The greatest minority group in terms of population was Hispanic, followed by Asians, and then Blacks. Most of the minority groups stuck together. The White people stuck together and had different groups of White people; the kickers, preps, different types. The Asians would stick together and the Hispanics would stick together. Everything seemed to be divided, not officially, but it was pretty much divided racially. I was in a volunteer group, the Key Club, and I could have interaction with other people outside of my group in that. I was in the magnet program at my school, and in the honors program, and there weren't very many Black people involved, so within the classroom I was pretty much surrounded by mostly White people or Asian people. Not many Black or Hispanic people were in the program.

Tell me about your friends.
Most of my close friends are African American. I do have some associates and acquaintances from different races. I've been involved in school organizations where I was a minority and the majority were White. I formed close relations with them, but as far as personal relationships go, my close girlfriends are African American. But then I do have a White boyfriend. I think I am a pretty well-rounded person as far as my contacts with people from different backgrounds goes.

Is marriage or a relationship with someone outside of your racial/ethnic group acceptable to you?
It is acceptable to me. Maybe not to all people, but it is acceptable to me. We've had to deal with that because I'm in an interracial relationship. I have a White boyfriend and so it does come up in our family. My boyfriend's father is Christian and his mother is Jewish, so we've had to deal with that from my household and his household as well. I don't think relationships should be based on color. If it happens that you are more comfortable with people of your own race then I guess that is appropriate. I don't think you should limit yourself at all, or deny yourself. You never know, you may be attracted to somebody outside your race. A lot of African American people will question me about why I have a White boyfriend, why I'm dating somebody White. It's because I'm attracted to that person and because I wanted to and because I could. It's not as taboo as it used to be in the past, particularly Black and White couples. It's a small group, but it's acceptable in my family, and it's acceptable in my boyfriend's family as well. It's easier to do so these days.

Discussion Questions

Does the three-generations model of assimilation apply to Carla? Explain.

What helped Carla cross ethnic/racial boundaries in her friendships and personal relationships?

Explain what Carla meant about being uncomfortable as a "spokesperson for the Black community."

When did the civil rights movement begin? Is it over? What has been accomplished by this movement?

Is violence ever justified as a way of reducing inequalities? If so, when? If not, why?

Key Ideas

1. Elkins argued that the slave system of the United States dehumanized the slaves, creating in them extreme subservience. Fogel and Engerman state that in a plantation economy slaves were valuable property and, as such, were well treated and rewarded for productive work. The debate over the nature of the system of slavery and its impact continues. Scholars agree, however, that slavery had a profound effect on both slaves and owners and on the relations between Blacks and Whites throughout the United States.

2. Blacks resisted slavery in many ways, including escape, suicide, armed rebellion, legal challenges, and covert acts. Their resistance was met with harsh repression and even greater restrictions. Slaves often coped with slavery by submitting to its authority and finding other ways to preserve their families, culture, and identity.

3. After the Civil War, Whites developed a number of techniques to intimidate Blacks and to restore control of the southern governments to the Whites, including the organization of the Ku Klux Klan, a system of tenant farming, and voter restrictions. The Jim Crow system of legal segregation developed mainly between 1890 and 1920, during the period of the second immigrant stream. Jim Crow was strongly encouraged by the Supreme Court's "separate but equal" decision in *Plessy v. Ferguson.*

4. As the Jim Crow system developed, African Americans organized to resist it and to claim their full rights as American citizens. The NAACP, the leading protest organization for decades to come, demanded full equality for Blacks and launched a legal battle to attain it.

5. Like Mexican Americans and Puerto Ricans, African Americans appear to be, in some ways, a colonized and, in some ways, an immigrant minority. Up to the time of World War I, the Black experience was so marked by oppression that the colonial model

seems quite apt. The great northward "immigration" of World War I, however, laid a foundation for arguing that African Americans resemble a recent immigrant group.

6. Numerous episodes of Black–White conflict followed World War I. A mass secessionist movement was formed by Marcus Garvey. Garvey emphasized race pride, self-help, the unity of Black people everywhere, and a return to Africa.

7. During the Great Depression, African Americans began to adopt the boycott and other weapons of the labor movement as tactics to force equal treatment. The NAACP began to focus on the issue of school segregation.

8. The years during and immediately after World War II produced changes in federal policies aimed at reducing discrimination in employment, in schools, and in the armed forces. In 1948, President Truman ended all segregation in the military.

9. In 1954, the Supreme Court ruled in *Brown v. Topeka Board of Education* (*Brown I*) that public school segregation was unconstitutional and was psychologically damaging to the segregated children. In a second *Brown* decision (*Brown II*), the Court declared that desegregation should occur with "all deliberate speed." Despite the Supreme Court's rulings, many state and local governments continued to resist desegregation.

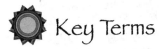 # Key Terms

Atlanta Compromise   A term referring to a speech given by Booker T. Washington designed to assure White people that Blacks were ready to accept their inferior status in the political arena. Washington, a former slave, believed that Blacks should concentrate on agricultural and vocational training, areas in which they could earn livings separate from Whites.

Black Renaissance   The emergence in the 1920s of Black writers, artists, and intellectuals in Harlem that resulted in an upsurge of Black pride and cultural expression.

Emancipation Proclamation   President Lincoln signed a proclamation on January 1, 1863 that freed slaves in the "states in rebellion against the United States."

freed Blacks   Blacks gained freedom as a result of the Emancipation Proclamation, by purchasing it, or through service in American wars. Many freed Blacks were skilled artisans, farmers, or laborers. About half of the freed Blacks lived in slave states.

Freedmen's Bureau   A government agency set up in the War Department after the Civil War to issue provisions, clothing, and fuel to "refugees and freedmen and their wives and children." The bureau was also authorized to rent land, negotiate labor contracts, provide medical care, and set up schools for the freed slaves.

Jim Crow   A term used to refer to laws that were passed, but then repealed, in the 1860s that segregated Whites and Blacks in public transportation, housing, work sites, restaurants, theaters, hospitals, playgrounds, public parks, swimming pools, organized sports, churches, cemeteries, and schools, to mention a few examples. In the 1890s these laws were revived and became even more extensive, supported by the

Plessy v. Ferguson decision that laid down the "separate but equal" rule for the justification of segregation.

Ku Klux Klan   A secret organization of Whites formed in 1866. The KKK used intimidation, lynchings, and other terrorist tactics to keep Blacks in a subordinate position to Whites.

Niagara Movement   The "radical" position led by W. E. B. DuBois that criticized Booker T. Washington's position of submission and economic development. Du Bois emphasized agitation and complaint to gain the full acceptance of African Americans as first-class citizens. The Black leaders of the Niagara Movement joined with White liberals to form the NAACP.

 Notes

1. Many freed Blacks participated actively in the abolitionist movement and in the Underground Railroad. David Walker, Martin Delany, and Frederick Douglass issued ringing denunciations of slavery. Sojourner Truth and Harriet Tubman also became famous as abolitionists. Tubman, "The Moses of Her People," is reported to have assisted 200 to 300 slaves to escape (Burner, Fox-Genovese, and Bernhard 1991:402). Perhaps as many as 100,000 slaves fled the South through the Underground Railroad (Franklin and Moss 1988:172).

2. The largest slave insurrection to take place in the United States occurred in Louisiana during 1811 and involved between 300 and 500 slaves. The rebels were engaged by a force of militia and regular troops and were rapidly defeated (Genovese 1974:592).

3. In 1993 Fogel was awarded a Nobel Prize in Economic Science for his application of economic theory and quantitative methods to the history of slavery.

4. Martin Delany described the situation in these words: "The slave is more secure than we; he knows who holds the heel upon his bosom—we know not the wretch who may

grasp us by the throat" (quoted by Jacobs and Landau 1971:149).

5. The Black Codes resembled the antebellum "Slave Codes," but in some states Blacks now could acquire, own, and sell property; enter into contracts; and be legally married (Jordan and Litwack 1987:378).

6. The name is based on the Greek word for circle, *kyklos* (Franklin and Moss 1988:226).

7. During the 1830s, Thomas D. Rice, a White performer in blackface, presented a song that referred to Jim Crow. The term became a popular code word for the segregation of Black people (Jordan and Litwack 1987:397).

8. Jobs and higher wages "pulled" from the North; but the boll weevil's destruction of the cotton industry and increased violence against Blacks also "pushed" from the South (Tolnay and Beck 1992:104).

9. Another important organization, the National Urban League (1911), was an interracial effort to help Blacks who were migrating to the cities to find jobs and get established. The Urban League always has been considered more conservative than "protest" organizations such as the NAACP.

African Americans

Protest and Social Change

African American women, such as this university law professor, have taken leadership roles in confronting civil rights issues affecting the African American community. As large numbers of African Americans move into middle-class economic and professional positions in the United States, they continue to take pride in their African American identity and heritage.

 # The Rise of Direct Action

On December 1, 1955, in Montgomery, Alabama, Mrs. Rosa Parks refused to yield her bus seat to a White person and was arrested. As the news of Mrs. Parks arrest spread, Black people in the city, at the urging of NAACP leader E. D. Nixon, began a boycott of the local buses. In less than a week, nearly all of the more than 40,000 Black citizens of Montgomery had rallied around the dynamic young pastor of the Dexter Avenue Baptist Church, Martin Luther King, Jr., in a massive boycott of the buses. At first, the boycott was intended to last only one day, but various incidents of harassment and intimidation by Whites led to a decision to continue the boycott indefinitely. This decision was followed by further acts of intimidation. For instance, on January 30, 1956, Martin Luther King's home was bombed; two days later, the home of E. D. Nixon also was bombed. On February 22, 24 Black ministers and 55 others were arrested for nonviolent protesting (King 1971a:297).

The confrontation between Blacks and Whites over segregation in Montgomery ended in the desegregation of the buses more than a year later. During that time, the bus boycott became a symbol of nonviolent protest throughout the world. Martin Luther King, Jr., became the leading spokesman for the philosophy of nonviolence and the most prominent figure in what rapidly became a new phase of the relations between Whites and Blacks in America. The events in Montgomery contributed to a growing conviction among Black Americans that, in King's (1964:80) words, "privileged groups seldom give up their privileges voluntarily." To promote the philosophy and practices of nonviolent protest, King founded the Southern Christian Leadership Conference (SCLC) in January 1957.

Increasing Militancy

In the decade following the Montgomery bus boycott, various forms of direct action became far more popular, especially among young people. A sit-in by college students at a Woolworth's store lunch counter in Greensboro, North Carolina, in 1960 set off a veritable chain reaction of student sit-ins throughout the South. These events led rapidly to

179

the formation of yet another organization devoted to nonviolent direct action, the Student Nonviolent Coordinating Committee (SNCC). Although the members of the new organization accepted the philosophy of nonviolence espoused by CORE and SCLC and were clearly inspired by Martin Luther King, Jr., they believed their goals could not be pursued vigorously enough within any of the existing organizations. The many lines of cleavage within the Black community became prominent once again. The older organizations, such as the once "radical" NAACP, were now regarded by many as "too conservative." Simultaneously, however, the older organizations were being changed by the "radical" tactics of direct action.[1]

Amid charges of excessive "conservatism" and "radicalism," nearly all of the main Black protest groups adopted some combination of legal and direct-action methods, though the new organizations were in the vanguard (McAdam 1982; Morris 1984). In this process, the entire civil rights movement became more militant. The battle cry "Freedom Now!" gradually gained acceptance even among many Black "conservatives." The NAACP, for example, sponsored many demonstrations during this period; and CORE pioneered still another new protest tactic by conducting an interracial "Freedom Ride" on a bus headed for New Orleans. Here, for the first time, White people joined in the protest. This ride ended when the bus was fire-bombed in Alabama, but many others were to follow (Burns 1963:55). The representatives of the different protest organizations found that whatever their legal rights were supposed to be, sit-ins, kneel-ins, lie-ins, boycotts, picket lines, and freedom rides might each be met by mob violence, tear gas, police dogs, arrests, jail terms, and, in some cases, by death.

The tempo of direct action increased during the spring of 1963. As the number of demonstrations in the South reached a new high, the nonviolent technique was frequently used in the North as well. Two protests in 1963 stand out. The first of these took place in Birmingham, Alabama, which was a symbol of southern White resistance to desegregation. A coalition of Black leaders under the direction of Martin Luther King, Jr., joined an ongoing nonviolent protest campaign in Birmingham. The protests began with well-organized demonstrators going to jail for conducting sit-ins at lunch counters (King 1964:60). Within a month, thousands of demonstrators, including King, had been jailed and many others had been physically assaulted by police. Later, protesters were met by police with clubs, high-pressure water hoses, cattle prods, and dogs. This attack on unarmed, unresisting men, women, and children aroused enormous national and international support, leading to a truce with Birmingham's business leaders. It was agreed that lunch counters, rest rooms, and other public places would be desegregated. The Birmingham protests had demonstrated dramatically that "the theory of nonviolent direct action was a fact" (King 1964:46).

A second outstanding protest of 1963 was a huge (approximately 250,000 people) March on Washington. Reviving the technique he had pioneered during the early years of World War II, A. Philip Randolph called for a massive protest march on the nation's capital to dramatize the problem of unemployment. The march captured the attention of the entire country. For millions of people, Martin Luther King, Jr.'s famous "I Have a Dream" speech encapsulated the aspirations of the civil rights movement. The march showed that the movement was beginning to look beyond direct-action protest toward a new focus on political action, beyond civil rights to a heightened concern for economic opportunity, and beyond appeals to the conscience of White people to a demand for equality.

The effects of the direct-action protests between 1956 and 1964 were mixed. In most states of the South, the protests had achieved rapid changes in desegregating restaurants, theaters, buses, hotels, and so on. Black men and women increasingly could expect to be served courteously; however, the protests had been less than successful in some states and had done little to bring about changes in segregated schooling, poor housing, and discrimination in law enforcement. Moreover, throughout 1964, instances of White violence increased. For example, three voter-registration workers (James Chaney, Andrew Goodman, and Michael Schwerner) were killed in Mississippi. Members of the KKK were suspected; and in 1967, seven of the suspects were convicted on civil rights charges (Bullard 1991:21–22).

Civil Rights Legislation

The escalation of violence by Whites weakened the allegiance of many Blacks to the philosophy of nonviolent resistance. The political pressure mounted by the March on Washington was increased through voter registration and "get out the vote" drives. With the strong support of President Johnson, President Kennedy's civil rights program was passed as the Civil Rights Act of 1964. This legislation prohibited discrimination in voting, public accommodations and facilities, schools, courts, and employment; however, official violations of the voting rights section of the law (Title I) continued in the South after the law was passed. In response to these violations, Martin Luther King, Jr. led a nonviolent demonstration in Selma, Alabama; and, shortly thereafter, Congress passed the Voting Rights Act of 1965. This law suspended all literacy tests for voters and permitted the federal government to station poll watchers in all of the states of the South (Osofsky 1968:570–581).

The legislation of 1964 and 1965 marked the end of official segregation in America. Yet something was clearly wrong. The laws had not, in fact, ended discrimination; and, like the direct-action demonstrations that preceded them, they had had little visible effect on conditions in the Black ghettos of the cities. After a decade of notable victories, there still was pervasive unemployment, underemployment, and poverty. Many Black neighborhoods were characterized by high "street" crime, poor health and sanitation, poor housing, inferior schools, poor city services, high divorce and separation rates, low access to "city hall," demeaning and inadequate welfare services, high prices for inferior goods and services, and poor relations with the police. What now was to be done? An answer from the past attained renewed popularity.

Black Power

The *Brown* decisions encouraged most Black Americans to believe that school segregation and other forms of inequality were nearing an end. These hopes, however, were soon dampened by the strong evidence—as in Montgomery and Birmingham—that many

Whites intended to resist the Court's rulings in every way possible, including the use of violence. The primary reaction among Blacks to the massive resistance of the Whites, as noted earlier, was nonviolent protest. This was not the only reaction, however. Not since the days of Marcus Garvey had so many Black Americans been ready to listen to those who doubted the possibility or desirability of "integration" and who urged, instead, some form of separation. The organization that was best able to capitalize on this renewed interest in a separatist solution was the Lost Nation of Islam (the Black Muslims).

The Black Muslims had been led since the mid-1930s by Elijah Muhammad but had not attracted many converts. During the late 1950s and early 1960s, however, they attracted many new converts and a great deal of attention from the mass media when a dynamic new Muslim leader, Malcolm X, advocated the Black nationalist philosophy.

Renewed Black Nationalism. Malcolm X, who substituted an "X" for the surname his grandparents had received from their slave master (Little), became the minister of the large Muslim temple in Harlem. Like his teacher, Elijah Muhammad, Malcolm X emphasized that Black people must organize to regain their self-respect and to assert their collective power. Consequently, he and his followers sought some form of separation from White America. If the U.S. government would not pay the costs of sending Blacks to Africa, then, Malcolm X argued, the United States should set aside some territory within its borders so African Americans could move away from the Whites. Malcolm believed that such a separate territory should be given as payment for the long period during which Black slaves worked without pay to help build America (Malcolm X and Farmer 1971:390).

Malcolm X was very interested in Africa and believed strongly that Black people throughout the world shared a similar destiny. In time, Malcolm and Elijah Muhammad came into conflict over various matters; and in 1964, Malcolm left Elijah's organization to found a rival Muslim group, the Organization of Afro-American Unity. The organization's charter emphasized the right of African Americans to defend themselves against violence in any way necessary (Malcolm X 1971). In addition to this "defensive" use of violence, however, some African Americans began to think in terms of attack. The most militant members of the group began to use the word "revolution" as more than a metaphor.

Violent Protests. The clearest evidence of a shift among some Black Americans toward the acceptance of "offensive" violence began to appear in 1964. For example, in July an off-duty New York City police lieutenant intervened in a dispute between some Black youths and a White man. When one of the youths attacked with a knife, the officer shot and killed him. Two days later, a rally called by CORE to protest the lynchings of civil rights workers in Mississippi led to a clash with police in which one person was killed. In the following days, a crowd attacked the police with Molotov cocktails, bricks, and bottles in the Harlem and Bedford–Stuyvesant areas of New York; the police responded with gunfire (National Advisory Commission 1968:36). Then, on a hot evening in August 1965, a California motorcycle patrol officer stopped a young Black man for speeding near the Watts area of Los Angeles. After the driver failed a sobriety test, he was arrested. The officer radioed for assistance while a large crowd of people gathered. When the prisoner's brother and mother arrived and began to struggle with the police, they too were arrested. As the police departed, the angry crowd threw stones at the police car (McCone 1968:608).

Rumors that the police had beaten the intoxicated driver, his family, and a pregnant woman spread throughout the area. Later, groups of Black people stoned and overturned some passing automobiles, beat up some White motorists, and harassed the police (National Advisory Commission 1968:37). The next evening, three cars were set on fire, snipers opened fire on the firefighters, and people began burning and looting stores and buildings owned by Whites. The burning, looting, and sniping then spread into the Watts area; and two city blocks on 103rd Street were burned out while firemen were held off by sniper fire (McCone 1968:615). Late in the day, the governor of California ordered nearly 14,000 national guardsmen into the area to restore peace. Burning and looting spread into other parts of southeast Los Angeles, and the fighting between rioters, police, and guardsmen continued for two more days.

The Watts area rioting was the worst in America since the 1943 outbreak in Detroit. Thirty-four people were killed, over 1,000 were injured, and more than 600 buildings were damaged or totally destroyed. The pattern of burning and looting strongly suggested that the Black rioters had intentionally focused their attacks on food, liquor, furniture, clothing, and department stores owned by White people.

The level of Black protest increased during 1966. According to the National Advisory Commission (1968:40), 43 major and "minor disorders and riots" occurred during that year, including a new outburst in Watts. Two of the major disorders in Chicago and Cleveland involved extensive looting, rock throwing, fire bombing, and shooting at the police. In each case, the disorders and riots were preceded by a history of dissatisfaction among Blacks in regard to police practices, unemployment, inadequate housing, inadequate education, and many other things (National Advisory Commission 1968:143–144); and they were usually precipitated by some seemingly minor incident, frequently involving the police. For example, in Chicago, the rioting commenced after police arrested a Black youth who had illegally opened a fire hydrant in order to cool off with water.

A speech by Stokely Carmichael dramatized the heightened militancy of many African Americans and, also, their impatience with the rate of social change (Osofsky 1968:629–636). Like many Black leaders before him, Carmichael, the chairman of SNCC, urged Black people to "get together" in their own behalf. He rejected the idea that Black Americans could "get ahead" through individual ambition and hard work. What was needed, he said, was "Black Power." The slogan "Black Power" was not completely new; neither were the ideas of race pride and self-help suggested by it; however, this phrase now took on special significance. It symbolized the frustration of many integrationists as well as Black nationalists. In the minds of many White people, though, the slogan was identified primarily with Black revolutionaries and separatist organizations.

The increasing willingness of African Americans, especially the young adults, to demand an immediate end to racial inequalities and to back their demands with violence, if necessary, ushered in still another phase in Black–White relations. Just as the legal approach had been made secondary by the advent of widespread nonviolent protests, the use of violent methods now moved to the fore. As in the earlier shift, organizations, leaders, and methods that had at first seemed "radical" now seemed "conservative" by comparison.

The level of violence was escalated again during 1967, with most of the disorders occurring in July.[2]

The violent protests declined after 1968.[3] The most influential Black leaders had never accepted the principles of separation or violent protest. For example, shortly before his assassination on April 4, 1968, Martin Luther King, Jr. (1971b:586) argued that "the time has come for a return to mass nonviolent protest." In his view, nonviolence was more relevant as an effective device than ever before: "Violence is not only morally repugnant, it is pragmatically barren" (King 1968:585). Apparently, most African Americans soon accepted this assessment. By 1973, legal and political approaches to the solution of the problem of racial inequality had once again become the primary weapons of African Americans.

Declining Momentum.   Civil rights activities by African Americans during the 1970s and 1980s were, in Brisbane's (1976:575) words, "calmer, more sober, more conservative." Global economic and political problems during the 1970s thrust such issues as inflation and military spending to the forefront. These changes were joined in the 1980s by a shift to the political right during the administrations of Presidents Ronald Reagan and George H. Bush. These social and political trends were reflected in a decreased willingness by the dominant group to support the social spending that was needed to maintain the levels reached during the 1960s. Even though many other groups—including women, homosexuals, the elderly, and the physically handicapped—also organized to combat discrimination and gain equal rights, the 1970s and 1980s witnessed a "dramatic loss of momentum" (Tabb 1979:349). The U.S. Commission on Civil Rights (1981a:35) expressed concern that in such matters as school and job desegregation, police protection, voting rights, housing, and affirmative action, the federal government's civil rights enforcement effort was not adequately funded and coordinated. In some cases, according to the Commission (U.S. Commission on Civil Rights 1979a), changes in the laws have "aided and abetted the obstructionists." Numerous court rulings during the 1980s served to restrict the scope of effective minority action against civil rights violations. Even though the Civil Rights Act of 1991 reversed the effects of some rulings of the U.S. Supreme Court concerning discrimination in employment, the fact that the rulings had been made still increased the concern of many African Americans that their civil rights were in jeopardy.

Renewed Visibility of Black–White Conflict

There were numerous other signs in the 1980s that the gains of the 1960s and 1970s were under attack. Various incidents, often involving conflict with police officers, exploded into major urban riots. For instance, in Miami, Florida, three large disturbances took place during the 1980s. In 1980, 18 people were killed and more than 400 were injured in the Liberty City section; in 1982, two people were killed and more than 25 were injured in the Overtown section; and in 1989, six people were injured and 30 buildings were burned, again in Overtown, after a policeman killed an African American motorcyclist (Reinhold 1992:A12). These and many other events were reminders that America's racial problems had not been solved.

The Beating of Rodney King

These problems returned to national prominence and a higher place on the political agenda in 1991, after an African American man named Rodney King was arrested for traffic violations by four White Los Angeles police officers (one of the four was Hispanic). The arrest was videotaped covertly by a nearby citizen. The videotape, run repeatedly on national television, showed Mr. King writhing on the ground while being kicked and beaten with batons by the officers. According to press and television accounts, most viewers, White as well as Black, thought that the arrest and beating of Mr. King constituted a clear case of police brutality; consequently, when the officers were tried more than a year later, the nation was "stunned" (as many newspapers reported) by the acquittal of all four officers on the charge of "assault with a deadly weapon" and of three officers on the charge of an "excessive use of force as a police officer."

Major urban disorders erupted in several American cities, with the largest and most severe rioting of the twentieth century occurring in Los Angeles itself. The violence started in the Florence–Normandie area of South Central Los Angeles and spread southeast into Watts and north into Koreatown. As in the case of the Watts riots in the 1960s, Blacks were prominent among the rioters and non-Blacks were the main targets; but in this case, Hispanics also were prominent among the rioters, and Asians, principally Koreans (but also some Cambodians), were among the targets. City, state, and federal officials called for the rioting to end. Mr. King, in a halting yet eloquent appeal for peace, asked the crucial question: "Can we all get along?" Again, as in the 1960s, thousands of troops were rushed to the scene; and by the end of the first week in May, the explosion was over. Estimates of the deaths and damage vary; but at least 51 people were murdered (*New York Times*, May 17 and August 13, 1992), hundreds more were injured, and burning and looting were responsible for millions of dollars in damage. Twenty-seven of the victims of the rioting were Black. Whites were almost as upset about the videotaped beating as Blacks. Almost 86 percent of White Americans disagreed with the jury's decision, were angered by the absence of Blacks from the jury, and did not believe the trial should have been held in the lily-white suburban venue of Simi Valley (Blauner 1996:168).

Whites were much less likely than Blacks, however, to see the arrest of King and the release of the officers as evidence of a larger pattern of racism in the United States. A TIME/CNN poll taken during this period made clear some of the differences between the views of Black and White Americans concerning the state of race relations in the United States. Consider the answers to the following questions: "Have prejudice and discrimination against Blacks become more prevalent in recent years?"—54 percent of the Blacks and 31 percent of the Whites answered "yes" (Kramer 1992:41); "Would the verdict [in the King trial] have been different if the police and the man they had beaten had all been White?"—82 percent of the Blacks and 44 percent of the Whites answered "yes" (Lacayo 1992:32); "Which makes you angrier, the verdict or the violence that followed?"—twice as many Blacks as Whites said the verdict made them angrier, whereas almost three times as many Whites as Blacks said the violence made them angrier (Ellis 1992:28); and when asked to give "the reason for the jury's not-guilty verdict," 45 percent of the Blacks and 12 percent of the Whites said "racism" (Church 1992:25). Blauner (1996:169) emphasized that White Americans tend to view racial incidents as aberrations in American life, whereas Blacks believe that racism is a central part of American society.

The O. J. Simpson Trial

Four years after the trial of Rodney King's assailants, another spectacular trial divided the nation largely along racial lines and once again focused attention on racial relations. A popular and wealthy African American former professional football player and movie star, O. J. Simpson, was accused of murdering his former wife, Nicole Brown Simpson, and her friend Ron Goldman. Both Ms. Simpson and Mr. Goldman were White. The trial lasted 9 months and was followed on television by millions of viewers throughout the United States and in other countries. Reactions to the trial seemed to be especially shaped by race, and sometimes by gender. Almost every opinion poll taken during the trial showed a gap of about 40 percentage points between the views of Blacks and Whites. Most Whites held fast to the belief that Mr. Simpson was guilty; most Blacks maintained that he was innocent. The polls suggested that Blacks held a deep suspicion of the police and the criminal justice system. A verdict of "not guilty" was decided by a jury panel of nine Blacks, two Whites, and one Hispanic. Ten jury members were women and two were men.

The testimony and racial attitudes of a witness for the state, police detective Mark Fuhrman, were key elements in the trial that fanned racial tensions. In the tapes, which were played in court as evidence, the former detective used the word "nigger" more than three dozen times and talked about police officers who routinely perjured themselves, destroyed evidence, arrested people without probable cause, and beat confessions out of those they arrested. Many Black police officers did not see the attitudes expressed on the tapes as surprising or exceptional. Many White officers were upset by the tapes and said they did not reflect the views of most people in Los Angeles or in the police department.

The racial conflicts seen in these incidents (and dramatized in the riots) certainly shows that the long road of change traveled by Black and White Americans since 1619 has not yet produced the levels of merger called for by the various ideologies of assimilation. Many Black Americans are disappointed, angry, and bitter and do not believe that they yet have achieved equality as citizens. Even the new Black middle class has not overcome fully the barrier of racism. Hochschild (1995:115) attributed the continued elusive racial bias that African Americans face in the United States to "the permanence of racism." In her interviews with Blacks she found that despite the gains made in many areas, successful Blacks still contend with "inhospitable personnel officers, informal social ostracism, excessive penalties for mistakes, exclusion from communication networks, resistance from subordinates, assumptions about cultural and personal inferiority, lower ratings from bosses, and 'ghettoized' assignments."

Racial Profiling

The O. J. Simpson trial and the Rodney King incident involved acts of perceived racial injustice in the administration of criminal law. Other examples include the California Watts riot of 1965; the Liberty City, Florida riot of 1980; and the Los Angeles riot of 1992; all of which were ignited by incidents perceived as involving racial unfairness in law enforcement (Kennedy 2001).

Randall Kennedy, a Professor at Harvard Law School, has written numerous articles about the regulation of race relations. His book *Race, Crime and the Law* (1998) won the Robert F. Kennedy Book Prize in 1998. A major area of racial discrimination that Kennedy has studied, and one that directly touches many people who are not involved in breaking the law, is racial profiling. Although no persons in positions of authority defend discriminatory actions in any form of law enforcement, many people, including people in government and policy, do defend some forms of racial profiling, especially in policing citizens. Racial profiling occurs when police, or other authorities, use a person's race in calculating whether, or to what extent, to subject that person to surveillance, questioning, searching, or perhaps some greater level of investigation (Kennedy 2001:3).

Using this approach, police or other inspectors, such as those who search luggage at airports, often stop, question, or search persons, perhaps solely on the basis of their race. The racial appearance of an individual is seen as a negative trait that marks the person as one more likely to cause a criminal problem than people in a similar situation without that trait. For example, police often view and treat Blacks, especially young Black men, differently than they treat young White men in similar situations. Such differential treatment on a racial basis is, according to Kennedy (2001:3), racial discrimination, even though those using the practice often decline to use the term *discrimination* when defending it. Studies of patterns of arrests, tickets, and other police actions have shown that police routinely use racial proxies in making determinations of suspiciousness and in acting on those suspicions. Kennedy noted that judicial discouragement of governmental use of racial discrimination has been vigorously pursued against affirmative action programs, but such discouragement of the use of race has been absent or much less intense in the context of police actions.

Kennedy (2001:5) points out that the use of racial profiling generates anger, humiliation, distrust, and resentment that is deeply felt by large sectors of the Black community. Henry Louis Gates, Jr. wrote an article about the O. J. Simpson acquittal and described how Black males exchange stories of their experiences with the police like war stories. He remarked that there is a "moving violation that many African Americans know as D.W.B.: Driving While Black" (quoted in Kennedy 2001:6). Racial profiling is a serious form of racial discrimination because it is often implemented in subtle ways without clear confrontations and many people are unaware of or unwilling to acknowledge the damage it can cause.

Some Corporate Cases of Discrimination

In 1994, in the largest court case in the history of the public accommodations section of the 1964 Civil Rights Act, Denny's restaurant chain was ordered to pay millions of dollars to Black customers who were discriminated against in its restaurants. Employees testified that they were told to follow what were called "Blackout" policies to keep African American customers to a minimum, including actions taken against military officers, police officers, teachers, and government officials.[4] These policies resulted in service so disrespectful to African Americans that it would be hard to deny racist intent (Kohn 1994).

Just a year earlier, a federal court approved one of the largest financial settlements in a class action race discrimination suit against another restaurant chain, Shoney's. Employees of Shoney's charged that the chain deliberately shunted Blacks into low-paying, low-visibility kitchen jobs, when it hired them at all, and clearly showed a preference for Whites (Smothers 1993:12). In 1994, the U.S. Department of Labor, the federal agency responsible for protecting workers' rights, also settled the largest race discrimination suit ever brought by government workers. African American employees claimed that they had been unfairly dismissed, demoted, or denied promotion in 1981, 1983, and 1984. The Justice Department also reached out-of-court settlements in 1995 with a number of banks accused of showing bias in lending to Blacks. The suit contended, among other things, that banks refused to allow African Americans to clear poor credit histories, an opportunity normally given to Whites. It also maintained that banks required Blacks to meet unnecessarily high standards to qualify for loans and denied Black applicants mortgages at a rate about five times the denial rate of White applicants (Holmes 1995:C1).

Another major discrimination case focused nationwide attention on Texaco, Inc., the fourteenth largest corporation in the United States (Eichenwald 1996). In November 1996, a Texaco executive released secretly recorded tapes of a meeting in which senior Texaco executives planned the destruction of documents requested in a Federal discrimination lawsuit. The tape recordings also showed the executives berating minority employees by using racially insulting language. Although Texaco had antidiscrimination policies, equal opportunity programs, and appropriate channels for filing discrimination complaints, the White managers and executives operated by their own, often discriminatory, rules with little corporate oversight. Faced with threats of a national boycott of Texaco products, the corporation settled the discrimination suit by agreeing to pay damages to employees who claimed discrimination, raise salaries for Black employees, provide diversity training programs, and create an independent task force to oversee the changes. Farley (1996) pointed out that these continuing successful law suits about employment discrimination are indications of persistently unequal opportunities for African Americans in the job market, which result in a growing gap in earnings between Blacks and Whites.

African Americans have moved slowly and painfully out of slavery to citizenship and out of rigid segregation and the denial of equal rights to a legal and official form of equality. But the many evidences that "old-fashioned racism" has been replaced to some extent by "modern racism," and the widespread belief among African Americans that the gains of the 1960s have been eroded, make the careful analysis of social and economic changes and trends all the more important. We turn, therefore, to the question of the extent to which assimilation has occurred among African Americans.

 African American Assimilation

Cultural Assimilation

Each ethnic group we have considered so far has faced the question, "As we adopt American culture, what shall become of our own culture?" We saw that, although there are important group differences in this respect, each group has made an effort to retain, transmit, and elaborate its heritage. The tendency of an ethnic group to attempt to adopt these strategies has been shown to be intimately related, among other things, to whether a group has entered the country voluntarily. As a rule, groups that have come into the United States voluntarily have been more willing to undertake cultural assimilation than have groups that entered the United States in an involuntary manner. From this perspective, since separation from their African homelands did not arise in any way from the desire to start anew in another land, the slaves resisted cultural assimilation. They had little choice, however. Those who survived the horrors of being transported to America as slaves were in an extremely poor position to retain, transmit, or elaborate their heritage. The entire system of American slavery was constructed, as noted in Chapters 3 and 6, to strip the slaves of their cultures, to destroy the link between Africans and their past, and to replace their cultures with ways of thinking and acting that were deemed appropriate for slaves.

It has become increasingly accepted that Black Americans succeeded, nevertheless, in constructing a distinctive culture based on their African roots. To illustrate, Levine (1977:6) found that a number of the characteristics of African cultures, such as the high praise given to verbal improvisation, have remained central features of Black American culture. Levine argued that it is a mistake to assume, however, that cultural elements must be unchanged in order to be derived from African traditions. In his view, "Culture is not a fixed condition but a process. . . . The question is not one of survivals but of transformations" (Levine 1977:5). Gutman (1976:212) also believed that some important continuities existed between the lives of the plantation slaves of the early nineteenth century and those of rural Mississippi Blacks in the third decade of the twentieth century.

The Moynihan Report.   Sociologist Daniel P. Moynihan (1965) helped to shape the federal government's War on Poverty in a document commonly called the Moynihan Report. The document stated that the "fabric of Negro society" and "the Negro family" were deteriorating (Moynihan 1965:5). He argued that these problems were the lasting result of the indescribable oppression experienced during slavery. He then called for government action to enhance "the stability and resources of the Negro American family" (1965:48).

Many critics have noted that Moynihan's analysis emphasized the effects of past racism but ignored or minimized the effects of present racism. In this way, the modern social problems of African Americans appeared to result from *their* inability to take advantage of opportunities rather than the *society's* failure to expand opportunities. Many believe this view "blames the victim."

An Ethnic-Resource Model.   Many scholars reacted angrily to Moynihan's analysis. Critics attacked the idea that the problems of Black Americans stemmed from the presumed weaknesses and failures of the Black family. They emphasized, instead, the many strengths, resources, and achievements of the Black family (e.g., Billingsley 1968; Jackson 1991; Rainwater and Yancey 1967; Wilkinson 1978). The work of these scholars supported an **ethnic-resource model** that suggested that cultural strengths have protected the Black family through the devastating effects of slavery and through more recent patterns of Black male unemployment. Cultural resources also have fostered adaptive marriage and family patterns that help families keep functioning through extreme hardships. Hill (1971), for instance, argued that Black families emphasize strong kinship bonds, hard work, and ambition. These elements buffered the deleterious effects of male unemployment and White discrimination. Moreover, accumulating evidence supports the idea that the extended family, rather than the nuclear family, is the proper unit of analysis for studies of the strengths and weaknesses of the Black family (Hatchett, Cochran, and Jackson 1991:49).

Gutman (1976:95–100) provided additional support for the ethnic-resource model. His analysis of slave marriages and families showed that despite the undeniable hardships and restrictions of slavery, Black slaves placed a high value on family stability and responsibility. A subsequent study comparing Black and White family structure in Philadelphia in 1850 and 1880 found that roughly three-quarters of the families in both groups consisted of two parents and their dependent children. The study found also that the households of former slaves were more likely than other Black households to be headed by couples (Furstenberg, Hershberg, and Modell 1985).

Slavery surely narrowed the choices available to the slaves; but, according to ethnic resource theorists, these downtrodden people were able, nevertheless, to create both an effective culture and a distinctive social identity that were rooted in, and transmitted by, families. From this perspective, contemporary family problems are not a continuing legacy of slavery but, rather, are the result of contemporary structural problems rooted in continuing racism.

We see in these opposing interpretations of Black family problems—the legacy of slavery versus the ethnic-resource model—a clash of cultural and structural explanations of social events.

Contemporary Families.   The proportion of families headed by husbands and wives has declined in recent decades among both Blacks and Whites, although the decline among Blacks has received more notice (Eggebeen and Lichter 1991:803; Farley 1988: 24–25). In 2000, families headed by husbands and wives comprised about 81 percent of White families and 48 percent of Black families. As the number of families headed by husbands and wives has declined, the number of children living in one-parent homes has risen. In 2000, 22 percent of White children and 56 percent of Black children who lived in family households were in one-parent homes (U.S. Bureau of the Census 2001:41, 51, 52).

The causes of these changes in family organization are still the subject of intense debate among scholars of family life. The prevailing view appears to be that Black Americans have responded in adaptive ways to economic and social changes beyond their control and, in so doing, have constructed a resilient new culture.[5] From this perspective, the higher frequency of family problems such as father-absent households and unwed teenage mothers is created by contemporary discrimination (in all its forms) against African Americans and cannot be explained in terms of cultural changes during slavery. Patterson (1998:25), on the other hand, has argued that the slave system's "ethnocidal assault on gender roles, especially those of the father and husband," must still be counted as a major (though not an exclusive) factor in an understanding of the contemporary problems of African American families.

These competing positions make it clear that much remains to be done before we will have an adequate understanding of the lengthy and complicated processes involved in the cultural assimilation of African Americans. It seems clear that the African Americans have "helped to create themselves out of what they found around them" (Ellison 1964:316); but it also may be the case that we still do not recognize fully the protracted and destructive effects of the American system of slavery on the African American family.

The "Million Man March."   In 1995, African Americans used a public march with the theme of unity and the responsibility of Black men to their communities to call attention to the needs of the Black family and to focus attention on Black pride and culture. The march was seen by many as a way to counter the overwhelmingly negative images of Blacks, particularly Black males, that dominate the media. Attracting between 400,000 and 1 million Black males to Washington, D.C., and exceeding the turnout at the March on Washington in 1963, the Million Man March was said to celebrate the majority of Black men who work hard, support their families, and contribute to their communities. Glenn Loury, a conservative Black economist, claimed that the majority of Blacks are part of the middle and working classes, but that the 10 percent who are poor and have multiple problems have come to represent the entire Black community.

The march was an acknowledgment of the reality of Black culture and the view that its development is a positive thing. The participants also clearly wished, however, to be an integral part of mainstream America—to have good jobs, better incomes, and strong families. As is true for many African Americans, the marchers were committed to both Black culture and mainstream culture—an option we have referred to as cultural assimilation by addition. Indeed, many scholars have suggested that Blacks and Whites of the same social class levels are more alike than different in their values, behavior, and family organization (e.g., Gordon 1964:173; Wilson 1980:140). We conclude, therefore, that although African Americans are not identical to middle-class Anglo Americans in culture, their level of cultural assimilation is high.

Secondary Structural Assimilation

There can be no doubt that since emancipation African Americans have moved in many important ways toward the goal of full secondary assimilation; however, it is equally clear that a number of gaps still exist between the levels of Whites and Blacks in signifi-cant matters such as jobs, income, education, and housing. Moreover, as we shall see, if contemporary trends continue, the differences in these areas will not disappear soon.

Occupations.   Whites, of course, always have been more heavily concentrated than Blacks in the higher-prestige, better-paying jobs, and they still are. For example, although the proportion of Black males in professional and managerial jobs increased almost sixfold between 1940 and 1980 (Farley and Allen 1987:264), their proportion in those top jobs was still lower than among White males in 1994.[6] In 2000, 33 percent of White males and 21 percent of Black males were in professional jobs (U.S. Bureau of the Census 2001:384). The pattern among Black and White females was similar. Despite a more than threefold increase in professional jobs and a more than fivefold increase in jobs as proprietors, managers, and officials, Black women in 1980 were less likely than White women to be employed as professionals (U.S. Bureau of the Census 1994). By 1994, the percentage of Black women in professional and managerial jobs had risen fur-ther but was still below that of White women (20.1 versus 31.1 percent). In 2000, the proportion of Black female professionals was 27.7 percent and the proportion of White female professionals was 37.7 percent (U.S. Bureau of the Census 2001:384).

During the last six decades, the overall occupational distributions of Blacks and Whites have become more similar, though unemployment rates have remained higher among Blacks. For example, in 1970, compared to Whites, the labor-force participation rate among Blacks was roughly 3 percentage points lower than among Whites, but their unemployment rate was roughly 3 percentage points higher. Moreover, the labor-force activity of Black men deteriorated substantially during the 1970s and 1980s relative to Whites. Part of this can be attributed to increases in school enrollment rates among young Black men, but the trend can be found even among those not enrolled in schools. Of course, employment and unemployment rates for both Whites and Blacks follow a strong cyclical pattern; but overall unemployment rates in 1994 were more than twice as high among Black men as among White men. Unemployment rates were dramatically higher among teenagers than among prime-age (25 to 64 years old) workers. The num-bers for Blacks were particularly striking, as almost 40 percent of Black teenagers in the labor force in 1994 were unemployed (Holzer 2001:101).

Five additional considerations concerning occupations are in order. First, since Blacks are more likely than Whites to occupy the lower positions of pay and prestige within each occupational category, occupational assimilation probably would still be in-complete even if the index of occupational dissimilarity were zero. Second, on the basis of detailed analyses of occupational data, Farley and Allen (1987:270–274) found that the rate at which Blacks were moving into high-prestige jobs during the 1970s slowed during the 1980s. Third, rapid technological and economic changes, such as increasing automation and the transfer of unskilled jobs to other countries, are permanently dis-placing Black workers who are concentrated in the secondary labor market (Bowman 1991:159; Wilhelm 1983). Fourth, the basic reading and math skills of young Black male workers in the 1990s were not, on average, as well matched to changing patterns in the demand for labor as were the basic skills of young Whites who had the same years of schooling and lived in the same regions (Ferguson 1996:77). Finally, the apparent reductions in occupational inequality cited before are based on figures for Blacks who are a part of the employed labor force; but large numbers of Blacks are unemployed, under-employed, or are employed at substandard wages.

For most of the years between 1955 and 1975, the unemployment rate for Black males was roughly twice as high as for Whites; and after 1975, the gap widened. In 1994, approximately 13 percent of the Black population 16 years and older was unemployed compared to 5.7 percent of the White population of the same age. In 2000, the unemployment level among Blacks (5.4 percent) remained substantially above the level among Whites (3.0 percent) (U.S. Bureau of the Census 2001:389), especially among teenagers (Farley and Allen 1987:214, 238). Research suggests that since 1940 the economic status of older Black workers stabilized relative to Whites but that of younger workers deteriorated in the late 1980s and the 1990s (Cancio, Evans, and Maume 1996:551–554; Ferguson 1996:78). Thus, although Black males are now more likely to get jobs that previously were "reserved" for Whites, they still are much less likely to get a job at all.

Social and spatial factors help to maintain these racial differences in employment. As jobs move away from inner cities where many Black residents are concentrated, access to employment opportunities decrease. Data presented by Holzer (2001) suggest that the skills and employment credentials that young Black men bring to the labor market must be a top priority if we are to achieve structural assimilation in the economic arena.

Incomes.   Holzer (2001) provides a historical review of the evidence of differences between Black and White men in labor-market outcomes, such as wages, employment, and labor-force participation. Improvements in the relative earnings of Blacks during the pre–Civil Rights period seem to be explained primarily by their immigration from the rural South to the industrial North and Midwest, and by improvements in the quality and quantity of their education. These educational improvements seem, at least partly, to reflect political and legal developments, such as the U.S. Supreme Court decision in *Brown v. Board of Education of Topeka* in 1954. Holzer (2001) noted that improvements during the 1940s seem to reflect advances made by Black men during World War II as they moved into more skilled positions vacated by White men who went to war. Additionally, African Americans who went into military service gained leadership and mechanical skills and, after the war, used the GI Bill's educational benefits to pursue higher education.

The dramatic progress made by Black men in income during the 1960s and the early 1970s reflects rapid improvements in education and occupational status as well as gains in relative earnings within education and occupation groups. Much of this improvement is linked to social and economic changes induced by the Civil Rights Acts of 1964 and 1967. The implementation of **affirmative action** requirements for government contractors and various discrimination cases challenging the **disparate impact** of certain policies probably contributed as well.

There has been a disappointing stagnation, and even deterioration, in relative earnings and employment of Black men since 1975 (Holzer 2001:104–105). A number of supply-and-demand developments seem to be responsible for these reversals. For example, employers have demanded higher-level skills. There also has been a decline in industrialization and unionism, with many high-wage industrial jobs leaving the United States for countries that offer lower wages; and labor unions have lost much of their ability to demand higher wages. Labor-market discrimination has not necessarily worsened over time, but the continuing incidents of discrimination in prominent companies suggest that subtle discriminatory practices in hiring, promotion, and firing no doubt contribute to the persistence of racial gaps in employment and earnings.

In regard to family incomes, little change took place during the last decade of the twentieth century. In 1989, Black families received an average of 62 cents for each dollar received by White families. By 1999, there had been no change (U.S. Bureau of the Census 2001:37). In short, although the median family incomes of both groups had risen during the decade, there was no movement toward increased equality. Cotter, Hermsen, Ovadia, and Vanneman (2001) studied racial and gender differences in earnings at lower and higher levels of the earnings scale to learn whether there was a **glass ceiling effect.** As a basis for comparison, the researchers used the amounts of money that divided the earnings of White men into four equal groups, i.e., the amounts up to the 25th, the 50th, the 75th, and the 100th percentiles. Their findings showed that women and African American men have lower chances of receiving pay that exceeds each percentile level than do White men, and that for women, but not African American men, this disadvantage increases at the higher earnings and authority levels. These findings indicate that both women and African American men face earnings disadvantages at all levels of pay but that only for women does the inequality increase with higher levels of experience.

The general figures presented here conceal many specific differences of importance. For instance, since women typically have lower incomes than men, and since a higher percentage of Black families are headed by women, a higher percentage of Black families are poor. Nevertheless, when Black and White women only are compared, the average earnings of Black women have been found to be *above* those of White women of similar education and experience; however, as Hacker (1992:96) observed, women of both races are underpaid. For African Americans of both sexes, however, educational gains (especially at the college level) appear to make a substantial difference in the incomes they receive (Smith and Welch 1978, 1986; Farley and Allen 1987:347).

Growing African American Affluence.   Even though the employment and income gaps between Blacks and Whites appear not to be narrowing, the number of affluent Blacks—those with yearly incomes of $50,000 or more—has grown substantially since the 1960s. In 1989, nearly one in seven Black families was affluent, compared with one out of every seventeen in 1967. These affluent Americans are the first generation of African Americans to benefit from desegregation and expanded opportunities. By the 1990s, they had reached the age when increased educational attainment begins to pay off financially.

A report by O'Hare, Pollard, Mann, and Kent (1991) showed that affluent Blacks are well educated (32 percent college graduates), own their own homes (77 percent), are in their prime earning ages (66 percent are age 35–55), are married (79 percent), and live in the suburbs. Like affluent White families, most Black families reach the $50,000-a-year income level by combining earnings from two or more family members. Less than 2 percent of Black single adults have personal incomes that could be considered affluent. Although these figures suggest that economic assimilation is occurring among this group of Black families, we have seen also that, overall, Blacks have lower participation in the labor force, higher unemployment rates, and greater percentages of single-parent households than Whites. Because of the close relationship of education and income, estimates of Black progress in the area of income usually focus on changes in the level of education and on changes in patterns of schooling (e.g., desegregation). The following section looks at educational attainments of African Americans.

Education.   In *An American Dilemma*, Myrdal (1964) saw education as a solution to America's race problem. Education represented a vehicle for combating racist beliefs as well as a means of improving the material conditions of Blacks. Prior to emancipation, few Blacks received any type of formal schooling; hence, in 1870, 80 percent of African Americans were illiterate. In the same year, illiteracy among Whites stood at 12 percent. By 1970, these levels had fallen to approximately 4 percent of all Blacks over 14 years old and to less than 1 percent for Whites of the same age group (Goff 1976:422). Race differences in illiteracy rates in the 1980s and 1990s were negligible, even though the definition of literacy involved more complex functional literacy skills compared to the earlier measures, which were usually determined by the ability to sign one's name (Allen and Jewell 1996:174).

The absolute gains in years of school completed since the 1940s have been much greater for Blacks than for Whites. By the 1960s, racial differences in school enrollment were basically nonexistent (Allen and Jewell 1996:174); and, by 1990, 88 percent of Blacks between 5 and 20 years of age were enrolled in school, compared to 89 percent of Whites in this age group. In 1992, there was no substantial difference between Blacks and Whites in the median number of years of school completed. Within low-, middle-, and high-income groups, there were few differences between the high school dropout rates of Whites and Blacks during the 1980s and early 1990s (McMillen, Kaufman, Whitener 1994:31).

This review of educational progress demonstrates that in terms of illiteracy, school enrollment, and dropping out of school, Blacks have achieved near parity with Whites. The findings show that the educational patterns of African and White Americans are moving in the direction of complete educational assimilation. These findings do not show, however, that the overall educational gap between Blacks and Whites has closed or will soon close. For instance, even though in 1994 the percentage of those who had completed only high school was slightly higher among Blacks than Whites (36.2 versus 34.5), and students from the two groups went on to college in equal proportions (17.5 percent), a substantially higher percentage of the White students graduated from college (15.1 versus 9.5); and, proportionally, more than twice as many Whites as Blacks obtained an advanced degree (7.9 versus 3.4) (U.S. Bureau of the Census 1996:158). Overall, the gap between the two groups in the percentage of those completing college doubled from 5 percent in 1960 to 10 percent in 1994.[7]

The educational test scores of Blacks improved rapidly until the mid-1980s, but leveled off thereafter (Holzer 2001:105); hence, according to Smith (2001) educational differences between Blacks and Whites still persist. The remaining difference, nevertheless, is less than at any other time in American history. Between 1940 and 1990 almost three-quarters of the educational gap between Blacks and Whites was eliminated. By 2000, over 84 percent of Whites and 78 percent of Blacks had completed high school, although the difference between the two groups was larger at the college level (U.S. Bureau of the Census 2001:40). Over 26 percent of Whites and 16 percent of Blacks had, by 2000, completed four years of college. Black females continued to complete college at a higher rate than Black males, which contributed to the narrowing of the overall gender gap.

As in the case of income gains, Black progress in education, though real, is a part of a general increase within American society. As we have seen, even when a group's level is rising, the absolute differences between groups may actually widen. Also, the educational increases for African Americans do not necessarily pay off in comparable salaries. According to a 1993 Census Bureau report (Ross 1993), higher education translated into greater earning power for both Blacks and Whites; but Whites gained more.

Educational levels, of course, reveal little concerning educational quality. If, as the *Brown* decisions state, segregated schooling is damaging to those who are set apart, then the continuation of segregated schools reduces the quality of education for Blacks. From this standpoint, educational assimilation is incomplete as long as the schools are segregated or classrooms within desegregated schools remain segregated. Although a substantial amount of school desegregation occurred between 1968 and 1973, primarily because of court-ordered busing, many urban schools remained segregated despite court-mandated desegregation plans or voluntary actions. We return to the issue of inequalities in education, income, and employment in Flashpoint 3 after the discussion of assimilation.

Residential Assimilation.   Another important indication of the extent to which secondary assimilation is occurring for a given ethnic minority is the degree to which the group lives in desegregated residential areas. We emphasized previously that American ethnic groups have always tended to congregate in certain areas, as well as to be segregated, and that these areas frequently have become known as "their" parts of town; however, to the extent that an ethnic group's members accept either the Anglo conformity or pluralist models of adaptation, we would expect that as assimilation occurred they would leave their old neighborhoods and move into less separated neighborhoods, even if the initial separation was largely voluntary (Zhou and Logan 1991:388). This expectation is called the **theory of spatial assimilation** (Gross and Massey 1991:350).

Sociologists frequently have studied the extent of residential segregation of different groups by calculating and comparing what are called **indexes of dissimilarity** (Taeuber and Taeuber 1964:29). These indexes may range from a low of 0 (no segregation) to a high of 100 (complete segregation). Index values above 60 are considered high, those below 30 are considered low, and those between 30 and 59 are considered moderate (Kantrowitz, cited by Denton and Massey 1988:804). Although this way of estimating residential segregation has faults, it is easy to understand and extremely useful. Both the historical development of metropolitan areas and the local conditions within these areas affect residential segregation. In the antebellum South, the slaves and their families commonly lived in the backyards of the White masters (Taeuber and Taeuber 1969:48). Although Whites typically enjoyed superior dwellings, Blacks and Whites were found side by side in various parts of the cities (Farley and Allen 1987:136–137); consequently, the level of residential segregation at that time was typically less than it is in most parts of the United States today. Even when the Jim Crow system of deliberate, legal segregation came into being between 1890 and 1920, the southern pattern of interracial housing was not much affected. Tradition and the Jim Crow system created such a vast social distance between the races that residential closeness did not threaten the respective social "places" of the two races. As African Americans began to stream out of the South during World War I, however, they entered northern states in which they were, in most respects, legally equal to Whites. Certain facts of northern life, nevertheless, prevented Blacks from dispersing throughout all parts of the cities.

There was, first of all, an economic barrier. Like the European immigrants before them, most Blacks could afford to live only in the least expensive areas of the cities. But also of great importance, as noted in Chapter 6, was that Black people faced an enormous amount of legal and extralegal housing discrimination. Even when African Americans had the money to afford housing outside of the ghettos, they usually were unable to purchase it (Jaynes and Williams 1989:145).

Comprehensive, detailed studies of trends in housing segregation in the United States prior to 1940 are unavailable. Some studies of selected cities, however, suggest that residential segregation increased gradually from emancipation to World War I and then accelerated sharply until 1930 (Taeuber and Taeuber 1969:43–55). Using housing information published by the U.S. Bureau of the Census, Taeuber and Taeuber (1969:32–41) calculated residential segregation indexes (indexes of dissimilarity) for 109 American cities during 1947–1960 and for 207 cities in 1960. Their analysis established two important points. First, the average level of residential segregation of Blacks and Whites in American cities by 1940 was very high in every region of the country. Second, although there was a slight decline in residential segregation between 1940 and 1960 in most of the 109 cities that were studied, the declines were usually small, and the patterns within the cities varied. For instance, some cities had an increase in residential segregation during one or both of the two decades studied.

What has happened to residential segregation in U.S. cities since 1960? Although some studies have found that during some periods the level of African American residential segregation has declined little or has remained about the same (Massey and Denton 1993:83; Van Valey, Roof, and Wilcox 1977:842), a number of other studies have shown that the efforts to reduce segregation in some American cities and metropolitan areas with large Black populations have been effective (Farley and Allen 1987:140–146; Farley and Frey 1994; Harrison and Weinberg 1992). Farley and Allen, for instance, have shown that among the 25 central cities with the largest Black populations, all but two (Philadelphia and Cleveland) experienced some decline in Black–White residential segregation between 1970 and 1980. Overall, declines occurred during the decade in 20 of the 25 cities. In a similar study of all metropolitan areas in the United States using 1990 data, Harrison and Weinberg (1992) found decreases in the residential segregation of Blacks in most of the metropolitan areas.[8] The declines were substantial in 18 large areas, most of which were in Florida and Texas. During the entire period from 1960 to 1990, the average level of residential segregation of Blacks in American cities declined from a segregation index of about 86 to an index between 64 and 69, depending on the study.[9]

Farley and Frey (1994:32–33) found that, although segregation varied widely among cities, the segregation of Blacks remained much greater than that of Hispanics and Asians. The average segregation score in 1990 for Blacks was 20 points above the average score for Hispanics or Asians. Farley and Frey (1994) also identified four practices that exacerbated segregation: (1) mortgage lending policies were discriminatory, (2) Blacks who sought housing in White areas faced intimidation and violence, (3) suburbs developed strategies for keeping Blacks out, such as zoning laws, real estate agents who dealt only with Whites, and intimidation by the local police, and (4) federally sponsored public housing encouraged segregation.

The persistence of residential segregation has led to legal battles similar to those that have occurred in the effort to desegregate schools, jobs, voting, public accommodations, and other social arenas. For example, agreements among homeowners to sell their homes only to members of certain groups have been declared illegal,[10] rules requiring segregation in federally funded housing have been removed, and open-housing laws have been passed. And, in 1968, Congress passed the Fair Housing Act barring "racial discrimination on the part of any parties involved in the sale, rental, or financing of most housing units" (Farley and Allen 1987:139).[11]

Some observers have suggested that residential segregation may persist, however, not so much because of discrimination but, rather, because African Americans prefer to live in racially homogeneous, isolated neighborhoods. Krysan and Farley (2002) explored this idea and found that African Americans prefer to live in areas that are about equally shared by White and Black residents, a density that is uncomfortable for most whites. The researchers found that Blacks' residential preferences were not driven by racial solidarity or ethnocentrism. They live mainly among other African Americans because they fear that Whites will be hostile, blame them for troubles that arise, and treat them like unwelcome intruders. It is clear that in the 1980s and 1990s, income and educational gains made by African Americans since World War II have not been translated commensurately into residential assimilation (Hwang, Murdock, Parpia, and Hamm 1985). High-status Blacks are much more likely than high-status Whites to live in "poorer, more dilapidated areas" that are "characterized by higher rates of poverty, dependency, crime, and mortality" (Massey, Condran, and Denton 1987:29). Many affluent Black families also choose to live in expensive all-Black suburbs (Dent 1992; O'Hare, Pollard, Mann, and Kent 1991:31). Massey and Hajnal (1995:539) proposed that segregation patterns in the United States have consistently evolved to minimize White–Black contacts, with only the level of segregation changing over time. They concluded that racial segregation in the United States resembles the apartheid system that previously existed in the Union of South Africa. In the United States, Blacks have been forced into segregated suburbs and channeled into segregated cities through institutionalized discrimination in the real estate and banking industries, racially biased public policies, and persistent White prejudice (Massey and Denton 1993). Farley and Frey (1994:33) noted that while racial attitudes have changed, with most Whites endorsing the *principle* of equal opportunities for Blacks in the housing market, Whites, nevertheless, were uncomfortable when numerous Blacks moved into their neighborhoods; and they were reluctant to move into predominantly Black neighborhoods.

In a study of Los Angeles, California, Bobo and Zubrinsky (1996) found, in a survey of the attitudes of Whites, Asians, Blacks, and Hispanics, that for Whites, sharing residential areas with any subordinate group, but especially with Blacks, brought the threat of a loss of advantages in relative status. The researchers concluded that Black–White separation was likely to continue, even in a diverse city such as Los Angeles, because Whites viewed desegregation as undermining their superior status.

Our consideration of changes in occupations, incomes, educational levels, and housing patterns suggests that, on average, African Americans have been moving slowly during recent decades toward the patterns found among Whites, though there are significant differences in the experiences of males and females in these respects, and the movement toward assimilation was halted or slowed during the 1970s and 1980s. When compared to an ideal of complete secondary assimilation, all of the changes we have discussed are small. For this reason, most observers appear to agree with Farley (1988:24) that although gains among Blacks "are widespread," Blacks "will not soon attain parity with whites."

Primary Structural Assimilation

The gains previously discussed show that Black–White relations in the United States are changing as the social and historical contexts of racial relations change, individuals' attitudes change, and younger people replace the older generation who experienced legal segregation. Many interactions between Blacks and Whites that were once infrequent, and often illegal, now occur with little notice (e.g., swimming, dancing, eating together, dating, mixed schools, churches, public transportation, and sports teams). Between 1964 and 1974, researchers at the University of Michigan (Institute for Social Research 1975:4) found an increase in contacts between Blacks and Whites in neighborhoods and on the job as well as in schools. According to research compiled by the Committee on the Status of African Americans (Jaynes and Williams 1989), Blacks and Whites share a substantial consensus, in the abstract, on the broad goal of a desegregated and equalitarian society. Nearly 100 percent of Blacks surveyed in studies of racial attitudes endorsed the principles of school desegregation and free residential choice; they also reported that race would not be a deciding factor in their voting patterns. However, for Whites, these principles of equality are endorsed less when social contact is close, of long duration, frequent, and involves significant numbers of African Americans (Jaynes and Williams 1989: 129–130). The committee concluded that race still matters greatly in attitudes and behaviors in the United States. There remains a reluctance on the part of Whites to live in racially mixed neighborhoods. There continues to be an awkwardness in interracial, interpersonal relationships. In the midst of closer ties in terms of culture, employment, and incomes, resistance to high levels of primary structural assimilation continues to be high.

For example, Schofield (1995) reported that evidence from a wide variety of situations, ranging from conflicts between youth gangs of different ethnic and racial backgrounds to racial incidents on college campuses, showed that serious problems still exist in intergroup relations. Because of pervasive residential segregation, children often have their first close and extended contacts with those from different racial and ethnic groups in school. Many of those relationships are no longer just between Blacks and Whites. With minority group members becoming an increasingly large proportion of the U.S.

population, children in the schools are likely to encounter multifaceted, multiethnic situations. Schofield also emphasized the difference between mere desegregation, which results in a racially mixed environment, and true integration, which refers to positive relations among members of different groups. Schofield (1995:637) noted that because of anxiety and uncertainty about dealing with out-group members, resegregation or clustering in racially homogeneous groups results. In a study by Hallinan and Williams (1989) of over a million high school friendship pairs, only a few hundred cross-race friendships developed. In colleges and universities as well, it is common for Black students to form their own sororities, fraternities, and political organizations. The reasons usually given by Black students for the latter phenomenon is that "such activities make predominantly White campuses more hospitable" (Collison 1988:A35).

In a report on diversity at the University of California at Berkeley (Institute for the Study of Social Change 1991), group interviews with students were used to explore primary structural relationships. Black students reported that the environment they encountered on the campus was one in which racial and ethnic segregation was "everywhere" and they perceived subtle and pervasive racism. They felt that students were "categorized," "labeled," and "stereotyped" according to their perceived group identity. They joined clubs and organizations that celebrated and affirmed their African American identity and culture. However, Black students also experienced new pressure from African Americans to make decisions about friends, social networks, and even who they would sit with at lunch, on the basis of race. Some felt ill at ease in the White community and not really accepted by their own group.

Black students from desegregated urban high schools or from predominantly Black schools had an easier adjustment to racially mixed social groupings. Many Black students were sensitive to their high visibility in mostly White classes at Berkeley and felt that they were the subjects of subtle discrimination by professors, teaching assistants, and other students. Many felt that ethnic and racial politics on the campus forced them to choose "what kind of Black" they were going to be—one who was committed to Anglo conformity, pluralism, or separatism. Many Black students said they associated mostly with other Black students where they were less likely to be rejected or stereotyped (Institute for the Study of Social Change 1991:30).

Increasing diversity in the United States has meant a decline in the percentage of White students in many schools and an increase in the number of schools with multiracial populations, especially increasing numbers of Hispanics and Asians. Quillian and Campbell (2003) used data on 70,000 students from the National Longitudinal Study of Adolescent Health to explore multiracial friendships in these multiracial schools. They were interested in the influence of the new immigrant groups on the patterns of assimilation. The researchers found that the share of cross-race friends depends strongly on the share of potential friends in the school context who are of another race.

Quillian and Campbell suggested that the strong own-race preference of all groups in their friendship choices indicated that most students may continue to have an overrepresentation of social networks consisting of friends of the same racial or ethnic group. Students in schools where they were members of a small racial minority had stronger odds of having own-race friends. The authors speculated that students desire several friends of their own racial group for social support because adolescents are at a stage of life in which racial identity and racial awareness crystallize. The study also showed especially high levels of segregation of Blacks, including Black Hispanics (e.g., Puerto Rican, Cuban, Dominican, Panamanian) from all other racial groups.

The authors concluded that Black–Non-Black continues to be an important dividing line in multiracial schools and they speculated that this division will be more pronounced as the share of school populations neither White nor Black increases. The authors posited that small groups of different racial and ethnic minorities do not maximize cross-race friendships but that a more balanced racial proportion might lead to more cross-race friendships.

Presumably the changes in legal and social segregation that have occurred since the 1950s should have helped turn many of the increased personal contacts into friendships. In fact, this has happened; but, as shown by the studies cited, as important as these reported changes are, they are modest in relation to the Anglo conformity ideal of complete primary assimilation.

Marital Assimilation

Interracial marriage—especially of Blacks with Whites—has long been a subject of interest. An understanding of this process, though, has been complicated by laws in many states prohibiting Black–White intermarriage, by differences in recordkeeping procedures, and by a trend toward removing racial identifications from marriage records. In 1967, when the Supreme Court ruled that laws prohibiting interracial marriages were unconstitutional, 16 states still had them. At that time, too, only three states (Hawaii, Michigan, and Nebraska) published official records on interracial marriages (Heer 1966:263). By 1976, the effort to remove racial identifications from marriage records had been successful in seven states and the District of Columbia (Monahan 1976:224). Also, the social practice of designating those with any Black ancestry as Black has meant that the children of interracial marriages are identified only as African American. When those children marry, efforts to determine the number of racial intermarriages are complicated further (McDaniel 1996).

Despite the technical problems created by these conditions, some excellent studies have been conducted.[12] Some of the main findings of these studies are that (1) out-marriages among Blacks have been much less common than out-marriages among other racial and ethnic groups; (2) the rate of Black–White intermarriage went up rapidly during the 1960s and nearly doubled in the 1980s and 1990s; and (3) the declining pool of Black males who are eligible as marriage partners has resulted in more Black families that are headed by women who have never married and has encouraged those who do marry to marry outside their racial group.

In a study of interracial marriages in Los Angeles during the years 1948–1959, Burma (1963:160) found that Black males were much less likely to marry out than were Japanese, Chinese, Filipino, or Native American males and that Black females were even less likely to marry out than were Black males. Even after all the turmoil and change of the 1960s, Blacks were still found to be the least likely of 35 different American racial and ethnic groups to marry out (Gurak and Kritz 1978:38). Lieberson and Waters (1988:173,

176) showed that although Black women seemed less likely to marry within their group than in the past, the probability of in-group marriages is still *very much* higher than among any of the 21 other groups included in their analysis. To be more specific, almost 99 percent of Black women in their first marriages had married Black men.

Even though the level of Black out-marriage is still extremely low when compared to other racial and ethnic groups, the rate of change has jumped noticeably since 1960. Monahan (1976) conducted a nationwide survey of Black–White intermarriage and found that the total proportion of mixed marriages rose from 1.4 per one thousand marriages in 1963 to 2.6 in 1970. By 1990, the rate was nearly 4 per one thousand marriages (Wilkerson 1991:A1). Throughout this period, the proportion of Black–White intermarriages was three to four times higher in the North than in the South, though the rate of increase was much faster in the South than in the North, and highest in the West. Altogether, the rates of intermarriage of African Americans and Whites nearly doubled over the years 1980–1996, but such behavior was still relatively rare. Only about 1 percent of African American women and 3 percent of African American men were interracially married (McDaniel 1996).[13]

In their analysis of data from the 1980 census, Lieberson and Waters (1988:176) found that although the first marriages of Black women under the age of 25 were still very likely to have been with Black men, the younger women were much more likely to have interracial marriages than older Black women. According to 1980 census data on interracial married couples, of Black–White interracial couples about 3 percent were marriages of White husbands and Black wives, 10 percent were Black husbands and White wives, and 5 percent were Black spouses with spouses of backgrounds other than Black or White, such as American Indian, Japanese, or Chinese. Older Blacks were more likely than younger Blacks to wish to maintain their group boundaries and culture and, therefore, to oppose interracial dating. Better-educated Blacks and those with higher family incomes were less likely than other Blacks to oppose interracial dating and interracial marriages (Jaynes and Williams 1989:130).

In 1954, the National Opinion Research Center began asking those who participated in the General Social Survey how they felt about intermarriage.[14] At first only 4 percent of the White population approved of such a possibility. Since that time, responses to the intermarriage question have shown a steady movement up, but there has been less approval for intermarriage than for equity in jobs and for school desegregation. For example, in 1972 two in five Whites interviewed believed that intermarriages between Blacks and Whites should be illegal; this proportion fell to one White in five nearly two decades later (Wilkerson 1991:A1). In 1991, some 66 percent of the Whites polled in the General Social Survey still disapproved of racial intermarriage. A Gallup Poll in 1983 also found that 22 percent of Blacks expressed disapproval of interracial marriages (Schuman, Steeh, and Bobo 1985:75, 145). These considerations all suggest that the color line will be slow to shift (Spickard 1989:341).

Other Forms of Assimilation

Black Americans appear to be simultaneously adapting to many aspects of Anglo American culture while preserving and elaborating a distinctive African American culture, and their level of secondary assimilation is generally rising. But although Blacks and Whites seem to be coming together in cultural and secondary structural ways, they appear to be remaining largely apart in their private relations and identificational commitments. W. E. B. DuBois ([1903] 1965) emphasized an African American duality or "double consciousness" when he wrote that "One ever feels his twoness,—an American, a Negro; two souls, two thoughts, two unreconciled strivings. . . . He simply wishes to make it possible for a man to be both a Negro and an American, without being cursed and spit upon."

Despite all of the legislation designed to prevent discrimination, even middle-class African Americans still face discrimination in jobs, incomes, education, housing, and public places (Feagin and Sikes 1994) and "speak again and again of 'living in two worlds' " (McCarroll, McDowell, and Winbush, cited in Lacayo 1989:58). Such circumstances show that identificational, attitudinal, and behavioral assimilation are far from complete; and our findings concerning the differences in the opinions of Blacks and Whites following the riots in Los Angeles in 1992 and the trial of O. J. Simpson show that value and power conflicts between the groups are very much alive.

The contemporary pattern of Black–White relations suggests that African Americans may be moving toward the goal of ideal pluralism described in Chapter 2; but for those who advocate pluralism, there is no assurance that Black culture will survive either the centripetal pressures of Anglo conformity, on the one hand, or the centrifugal pressures of separation, on the other.

Flashpoint 3: The Affirmative Action Debate

Affirmative action is a policy designed to ameliorate racial and ethnic disadvantage. The formal end of Jim Crow laws and the enactment of the civil rights legislation of the 1960s did not create true equality between the dominant group and subordinate groups because the achievement of true equality requires more than the absence of discrimination. President Lyndon B. Johnson stated that "You do not take a person who for years has been hobbled by chains, and liberate him, bring him up to the starting line, and then say, 'You are free to compete with all the others' " (Hacker 1992:119). Instead, "a positive policy of nondiscrimination" is needed (Richard Nixon, cited by Robinson and Spitz 1986–87:86).

President John F. Kennedy established such a policy in 1961 in Executive Order 10925. This order stated that the government would encourage "equal opportunity for all qualified persons" through "positive measures" (Robinson and Spitz 1986–87:86). This order played a pivotal role in shifting governmental policy away from the assumption that the cumulative effects of past discrimination may be removed simply by adopting neutral policies and toward the assumption that some **preferential** or **compensatory treatment** of the victims of discrimination is required.

Affirmative action grew in the years after 1961 through various actions by presidents, Congress, and the courts. It was extended to include women and the members of some minority groups other than Black Americans who had experienced legal discrimination, such as Mexican Americans and Native Americans.

During the 1960s and 1970s, affirmative action programs expanded the pool of applicants for jobs and federal contracts and changed the treatment toward women and minority applicants as practiced by employers, university admissions officers, and government institutions and agencies. By the 1980s and 1990s affirmative action programs had come under fierce attack. To illustrate, in the mid-1990s, Ward Connerly, a successful African American businessman and a member of the University of California Board of Regents, led a fight to end affirmative action in university admissions. He also played an active part in forcing a statewide referendum on affirmative action (Ayres 1996:A1). Connerly was hardly alone in his dissatisfaction. California voters passed Proposition 209, which did away with racial, ethnic, and sex preferences in public education, employment, and contracting. The state of Washington passed a similar ordinance. White students challenged the race-based admissions policies of public schools and universities in several states. Although a brief treatment cannot grasp the complexities of this debate, we will refer to a few key events in its development and to some of the basic issues affirmative action has raised.

A long series of earlier presidential actions laid the legal foundation for Executive Order 10925. As the United States prepared for entry into World War II, the Black civil rights leader A. Philip Randolph threatened to lead "an 'all-out' thundering march on Washington" unless the government's hiring policies were changed. In response, President Franklin D. Roosevelt responded to the threat by announcing that the policy of the federal government was the "full participation in the defense program by all persons, regardless of race, creed, color, or national origin" (Roosevelt [1941] 1967:400). President Harry S. Truman expanded Roosevelt's program to ensure fair employment practices, and President Dwight D. Eisenhower issued an order requiring contractors to avoid discrimination in all business matters (Benokraitis and Feagin 1978:9). Although overt discrimination declined, Black workers still were underrepresented in federally funded jobs and were among "the last hired and the first fired."

Early Legal Challenges.   Throughout this period various lawsuits concerning discrimination in education and employment came before the courts. A particularly important case was *Griggs v. Duke Power Co* (1971). Duke Power Company required applicants for a job or promotion, who did not have a high-school diploma, to pass a written test—one that Whites passed more frequently than Blacks. The plaintiffs argued that the test was unfair because it did not test the specific abilities that were required to perform the job in question. The defendants argued that the test was fair because the same test was given to all job applicants. The U.S. Supreme Court sided with the plaintiffs and ruled that employers must give tests that measure the abilities pertinent to the job for which an application is being made. Tests that routinely lead to higher failure rates among members of minority groups—that is, that have a **disparate impact**—are suspect. This decision placed the burden of proof on employers to demonstrate that their procedures were fair; and it strengthened the argument that apparently "neutral" and "fair" procedures might be deemed to be discriminatory if they consistently produced unequal results.

The* Bakke *Decision.   The U.S. Supreme Court case *Regents of the University of California v. Bakke* (1978) is famous and far-reaching. A White applicant to the medical school at the University of California at Davis, Allan Bakke, argued that the university's medical school had discriminated against him because it had established a quota for minority applicants. Although Bakke's grades were higher than those of some of the minority applicants admitted to the school, he was denied admission twice.

The Court ruled, in a complicated, closely contested decision, that the medical school could give some consideration to the race of an applicant and could set a "goal" for the number of minority admissions, but it could not establish a rigid numerical quota. The difference between a goal and a quota, in principle, is that a goal may be reached by showing "evidence of good faith and positive effort" and involves no lowering of standards of merit and ability (Pottinger 1977:44). Quotas may be reached only by selecting a certain number of people in each target group even if the usual standards of merit and ability suffer.

Salient Issues. The *Brown* decisions and the passage of the civil rights laws of 1964 and 1965 fulfilled a formal political commitment to the civil equality of all persons without regard to "race, color, religion, sex, or national origin"; but these actions had not removed the effects of past discrimination. The continuance of the effects of past discrimination, and of present discrimination as well, fostered the belief that something beyond simple neutrality, something "affirmative," was required to compensate the victims of discrimination so that they would be in a position to achieve economic equality.

Some critics of affirmative action contend that preferential hiring and admissions are always wrong in principle no matter how attractive the consequences. They often cite the language of the Civil Rights Act of 1964 to show that affirmative action is unlawful and is **reverse discrimination.** The Civil Rights Act of 1964 stated that the law shall not "grant preferential treatment to any individual or to any group because of race, color, religion, sex or national origin because of an imbalance" in percentages or the total number of employees (Todorovich 1977:13). Some reject the use of the term *reverse discrimination* on the grounds that it would require that the previous Black victims have to become the dominant group and enforce institutionalized discrimination against the newly subordinate White group.

Those who defend affirmative action programs reply that the courts have stated repeatedly that affirmative action is not reverse discrimination. They point out that preferential treatment may not be used unless it has been shown that there has been discrimination in the past, either against a particular individual or a group, that has not been overcome (U.S. Commission on Civil Rights 1981a:15–37). For example, the continuation of Jim Crow segregation into the 1960s established the grounds for many later claims. One ruling stated that unless "affirmative relief against continuation of the effects of past discrimination" is permitted, the purposes of the Civil Rights Act of 1964 would be completely nullified (Glickstein 1977:15). In rebuttal, Steele (1990:114) said that in practice, past discrimination frequently is assumed rather than proven.

The* Hopwood *Decision. In upholding affirmative action in the *Bakke* decision, Justice Blackmun expressed the hope that such a policy would be unnecessary "within a decade at the most" (Graham 1992:51). Many believed that *Hopwood v. Texas* would be a test of the *Bakke* ruling. Four White students who were denied admission to The University of Texas's Law School in 1992 sued the university. The plaintiffs alleged that their grades and test scores were above those of some Hispanic and Black students admitted to the school, that they had been denied their right to equal protection of the law, and that they therefore were victims of reverse discrimination.

When the case came to trial, U.S. District Judge Sam Sparks noted that the problem of segregated schools in Texas "is not a relic of the past" and that Texas schools at all levels have "a history of state-sanctioned discrimination" (Sparks 1994:4, 5). The University of Texas Law School, for example, denied admission to Black students prior to an order by the U.S. Supreme Court in 1950 (*Sweatt v. Painter*) to admit the plaintiff, Mr. Heman M. Sweatt, an African American, and to open its admissions procedures to other minority students. Judge Sparks ruled in *Hopwood* that the plaintiffs, as they claimed, had been denied the equal protection of the law because the law school used two separate and different admission processes for White and minority students. He ruled that the plaintiffs were entitled to reapply for admission, but that the Law School was not required to admit them (Sparks 1994). The plaintiffs took their case to the Fifth Circuit Court of Appeals in New Orleans.

In a ruling directly affecting Texas, Louisiana, and Mississippi but having national implications, a three-judge panel of the Fifth Circuit ruled against the University of Texas, saying, contrary to *Bakke*, that the university's use of race as a factor in admissions was not constitutional (Smith 1996:29). The panel said that the university had given preferential treatment to "blacks and Mexican Americans . . . to the detriment of whites and non-preferred minorities" (Smith 1996:2). The Circuit Court stated, however, that although the use of race as a factor in admission was prohibited, it was constitutional to consider such factors as an applicant's "ability to play the cello, make a downfield tackle, or relationship to school alumni" (Smith 1996:29). The university then appealed to the U.S. Supreme Court to overturn the Fifth Circuit's decision, but the Supreme Court refused to hear the case because, by then, the Texas Law School had changed its admissions procedures.

The opposing conclusions of the *Bakke* and *Hopwood* cases about whether race could be used as a "plus" factor in admissions left college and university administrators throughout the country uncertain about whether or how to conduct affirmative action programs. The Texas Attorney General at the time, Dan Morales, ruled that the *Hopwood* decision extended to scholarships and fellowships as well as to admissions. Public and private colleges and universities throughout the state struggled to devise ways to make sure their student body included members of underrepresented groups without considering race or ethnic background in admissions or financial aid.

Percent Plans.   In response to antiaffirmative action initiatives, several states adopted race-neutral means of college admissions as an alternative to race-conscious admissions. The Texas legislature passed a "Top 10 Percent Plan" that allowed the top 10 percent of the students in any high school in the state to be admitted to a state university of their choice. California adopted a 4 percent plan that guaranteed high school graduates in the top 4 percent of their high school class that they would be admitted to at least one institution in the University of California's eight-campus system. The program did not guarantee admission to the student's first choice among the campuses. Florida's Governor Jeb Bush signed an executive order eliminating affirmative action in admissions decisions and instituted the Talented 20 Program. This program guaranteed admission to one of Florida's eleven public institutions to the top 20 percent of public high school gradu-ates. These plans did not affect professional or graduate schools.

Reports by the U.S. Commission on Civil Rights and the Harvard Civil Rights Pro-ject concluded that percent plans are largely unsuccessful and do not yield diverse student bodies comparable to the diversity achieved using race-conscious admissions. At the Uni-versity of Texas, for example, the number of undergraduate minority students applying to their Austin branch has continued to increase since *Hopwood,* but the percentage of those admissions declined, as did the number of those who actually enrolled. At Texas A&M University, enrollment of African American and Hispanic students has not yet reached the pre-*Hopwood* levels, despite the fact that the population of college-age students from those groups has continued to increase. White students without top test scores who at-tended primarily White high schools benefited the most from the Texas 10 Percent Plan.

By the fall of 2003, almost 70 percent of the freshman class at the University of Texas at Austin was comprised of students who had been in the top 10 percent of their high school classes. Students with high grades and test scores at the most competitive high schools often did not gain admission because they were not in the top 10 percent at their high-achieving schools. Two unintended consequences of the top 10 percent plan at the University of Texas at Austin, therefore, were, first, to leave the student body pre-dominantly White and, second, to reduce the average test scores and grades of the fresh-man class. It may also have lowered the quality of their high school course preparation because, with the new plan, students' priorities also changed. Instead of focusing on the SAT exam and extracurricular activities, they competed for top 10 percent class rank. In California fewer African American, Hispanic, and Native American applicants have been admitted to the most selective campuses and proportionally fewer minorities even both-ered to apply as compared to 1995 when the ban on affirmative action took effect.

The Michigan Law School and Undergraduate Admissions Decisions.   The Center for Individual Rights—the Washington law firm that won the Federal appeals court case that overturned the admissions policy of the University of Texas in the *Hop-wood* case—represented plaintiffs who filed suits against the University of Michigan Law School and the undergraduate college. The plaintiffs charged that the Michigan admis-sion policies granted illegal advantages to Black and Hispanic applicants (Holms 1995). The U.S. Supreme Court heard the Michigan case. The split-court decisions handed down in the two Michigan cases in June 2003, 25 years after the *Bakke* decision, reflect the ongoing debates about affirmative action. The following issues are drawn from the briefs written by the U.S. Supreme Court Justices who ruled on the Michigan cases and a summary of the effects of the ruling prepared by Douglas Laycock (2003), a faculty member at the University of Texas Law School.

In the two Michigan cases, the U.S. Supreme Court reached opposing conclu-sions. In the Michigan Law School case, *Grutter v. Bollinger,* the Court ruled 5 to 4 to uphold the right of the law school to use race, in either a holistic or individualistic way, as a factor in affirmative action admissions. In the case on undergraduate admissions to Michigan's College of Letters, Sciences, and Arts, *Gratz v. Bollinger,* the Court ruled

6 to 3 against affirmative action because the process was too mechanical. Amidst its apparent ambivalence, the Court confirmed that the government has a compelling interest in promoting diversity in its institutions. It approved the pursuit of racial diversity only as part of a broader conception that values many forms of diversity. Examples of nonracial diversity offered by the Court included experience abroad, foreign language skills, hardships and adversities overcome, community service, and previous career experience. The Court offered a broad account of the benefits of diversity, emphasizing that diversity is important because it "breaks down stereotypes," "promotes cross-racial understanding," and "better prepares students for an increasingly diverse workforce and society."

In the Michigan Law School case, the Court reaffirmed the *Bakke* decision that race can be used as a "plus" factor if it is used in a "flexible, nonmechanical way." Justice Sandra Day O'Connor wrote the majority opinion in *Grutter v. Bollinger* and argued that "universities occupy a special niche in our constitutional tradition" and that the benefits of diversity are substantial.

In addition to the importance of a diverse environment in the education of students, the Court emphasized the importance of diversity throughout our society. Justice O'Connor referred to the briefs submitted by high-ranking retired military officers and other leaders who argued that a highly qualified, racially diverse officer corps is essential to the military's ability to provide national security. She also cited a number of briefs from CEOs of prominent companies, such as Microsoft, Coca Cola, and General Motors, supporting affirmative action. She affirmed that the country's most selective institutions must remain both diverse and selective. Justice O'Connor argued that in order "to cultivate a set of leaders with legitimacy in the eyes of the citizenry, it is necessary that the path to leadership be visibly open to talented and qualified individuals of every race and ethnicity." The Court warned, however, that race-conscious admissions policies must not "unduly burden individual members who are not members of the favored racial and ethnic groups."

Chief Justice Rehnquist criticized the concept of "critical mass" which the Michigan Law School defined as "meaningful representation." Michigan argued that they must admit enough minority students to encourage minority participation in classroom discussion, to represent different minority viewpoints, and to avoid feelings of racial isolation. Justice Rehnquist made much of the fact that the Michigan law school admitted about twice as many Blacks as Hispanics and only a few Native Americans. He noted that the Law School could not offer any race-specific arguments to explain why significantly more individuals from one underrepresented minority group might be admitted compared to another underrepresented group. He proposed that practices extending admission to members of selected minority groups in proportion to their statistical representation in the applicant pool resulted in quotas in which a certain proportion of opportunities are reserved exclusively for certain minority groups. He argued that this appeared to be "racial balancing," which the Court has ruled unconstitutional.

Justice Clarence Thomas, the only African American on the Supreme Court and a beneficiary of affirmative action himself, wrote a dissenting opinion in the Michigan Law School case. He argued that the use of race as a factor in admissions violates the Equal Protection Clause of the Constitution. Justice Thomas claimed, from his own experiences, that affirmative action casts a stigma on all minorities as being less qualified than their peers, even if they gain their positions with the highest qualifications.

In the Michigan undergraduate admissions case, the Court affirmed that universities may not set aside a fixed number of seats for minority applicants; they may not award a fixed number of points to minority applicants; and they may not put minority applications on separate admissions tracks. The justices argued that the Michigan admissions policy of distributing 20 points out of a total of 150 points automatically to members of underrepresented minority groups was too mechanical and not sufficiently "narrowly tailored."

Justice Ginsburg also wrote a dissenting opinion in the undergraduate case. She supported affirmative action, arguing that "we are not far distant from an overtly discriminatory past and the effects of centuries of law-sanctioned inequality remain painfully evident in our communities and schools." She emphasized the persistence of "irrational prejudice" and "conscious and unconscious bias." She argued, "The Constitution is both color blind and color conscious. . . . It is color conscious to prevent discrimination being perpetuated and to undo the effects of past discrimination."

Universities with large numbers of applications face a serious challenge to ensure that each applicant receives individualized consideration. The University of Michigan planned to hire additional staff to review the approximately 25,000 applications it receives for the 5,000 available places in its fall freshman undergraduate class and to make decisions in "flexible, nonmechanical ways."

In a concluding statement, Justice O'Connor suggested that affirmative action should no longer be needed 25 years from now, although the Court did not give specific suggestions about how to devise equitable admissions systems. Institutions must devise systems that are fair and ensure a diverse student body and must periodically review their policies to determine whether racial preferences are still necessary to achieve diversity. In the meantime, the Center for Individual Rights has vowed to monitor university responses to the Michigan decision and promised further lawsuits against institutions that overstep the rulings' limits on the consideration of race in university admissions.

The Effectiveness of Affirmative Action.

An important consideration in attempting to assess affirmative action programs is "Do they work?" Robinson and Spitz (1986–87:88) cited several large-scale studies showing that affirmative action has "proven its effectiveness in increasing the employment of minorities and women while producing positive business results." A review of studies conducted by the Committee on the Status of Black Americans (Jaynes and Williams 1989:319) concluded that "while we cannot determine with the available data the precise numerical effect of antidiscrimination programs, the evidence does show positive effects."

Officials at the Mellon Foundation recognized that both the race-sensitive admissions policies at universities and the arguments against them rest on assumptions that had not been tested empirically. They, therefore, funded an analysis by a former president of Princeton University, William G. Bowen, and a former president of Harvard University, Derek Bok, of the undergraduate admissions process and the college experiences of 45,000 students of all races who entered selective colleges and universities. The study focused on African Americans because of greater availability of data for this group, but the basic policy issues are important for Hispanics and Native Americans as well. Extensive findings were published in the book *The Shape of the River* (Bowen and Bok 1998). The authors' main conclusions regarding affirmative action were the following: (1) the presence of a diverse student body enabled students of all races to have a more valuable educational experience; (2) alternative class-based admissions policies or admissions tied to high school rank in class are much less likely to enroll a well-prepared and racially diverse student body; and (3) minority students, because of poor preparation in high school, peer pressures, and stereotypes, may not make grades as high as White students at these selective colleges. Nevertheless, a large percentage of the minority students admitted do graduate, go on to enter professions, and assume positions of civic and community leadership. The scholars also concluded that U.S. universities have a high reputation for academic excellence and should be allowed to make their own determinations about admissions processes based on careful consideration of the qualifications of individual candidates.

Opponents of affirmative action, including some prominent African Americans, have argued that the policy has not been effective. Sowell (1977:130) maintained that even if affirmative action programs do "here and there" help someone get a job or be admitted to college, the general effect of such programs has been to hamper the progress of Black Americans. Randall Kennedy, a professor at Harvard Law School, explained that a literal interpretation of the word *discrimination* can obscure the disadvantage brought about by historic inequality in access to jobs and the experiences of poverty (Clemetson and Holmes 2003).

In Lacayo's (1995:40) opinion, affirmative action programs have become vulnerable, in part, because of their success. Without such programs "it's unlikely that African Americans—or women—would have been able to open up such White male bastions as big-city police and fire departments." Without such programs, White males would have many fewer competitors to threaten their dominance in the workplace. In fact, the economic stagnation of the 1970s and 1980s and the economic recession of 2001 and 2002 made middle- and working-class Whites less supportive of programs to help poor Blacks and resentful of efforts like affirmative action that primarily helped middle-class Blacks. Many Whites also believe that the goals of affirmative action have been reached. In a Gallup Poll taken in June 2003, 17 percent of Black respondents said they believed that Blacks have job opportunities equal to Whites. In contrast, among White respondents, 55 percent said they thought Blacks and Whites had equal chances for employment (Clemetson and Holmes 2003).

A Final Consideration.   As we have seen, Blacks, women, and the members of some other groups today do occupy many more positions in our society that command high prestige and income than they did before affirmative action was put into place. As the U.S. Supreme Court in the Michigan cases concluded, if affirmative action were dismantled today, there is no back-up policy that promises to continue to help level the playing field. Many legal scholars expect the debate over affirmative action to continue. In the meantime, the antiaffirmative action challenges have caused universities to rethink their admissions policies. Many have decided to place less emphasis on test scores and other rigid criteria. Other universities have focused on recruiting top minority students and making the K–12 educational programs stronger so that a greater diversity of students is prepared for university admission.

We conclude our discussion of affirmative action by noting that this approach is consistent with the thinking of those who emphasize the possibility and importance of direct methods of controlling discrimination, even though there are some important differences in the methods preferred. The rules governing hiring and firing, admission into prestigious graduate and professional programs, and eligibility for various licenses and certificates play an enormously important role in the day-to-day lives of everyone in our society. Strong educational programs, opportunities to meet and interact with others who express challenging and creative ideas, and access to good jobs are important gateways to social and economic upward mobility in the United States. Additionally, the countless laws of the large bureaucracies of modern society must change before any attitudinal changes about equality that may have occurred over the history of the United States can be made effective.

 # African American "Success"

Our discussions of immigration to America, nativism, and racism showed that the less the members of a group resembled the Anglo American ideal of an "American," the less acceptable they were to the dominant group and the more prejudice and discrimination they suffered. Groups that are socially, culturally, and physically most "distant" from the dominant group's notion of the ideal American were considered to be the lowest in "assimilative potential." Of all the factors that affect a minority group's prospects of "getting ahead" economically and socially in America, the most troublesome is whether the dominant group classifies them as "non-White."

During the colonial period, Africans and American Indians were defined as non-White and, therefore, as standing outside of the developing Anglo American society. From the earliest days of our country's history, non-White people in America have faced higher levels of prejudice and discrimination and have had fewer opportunities to achieve material or worldly success than have White people. The opportunity for these groups "to climb the ladder of success" (i.e., to undergo secondary assimilation in the public sphere) has been lower from the beginning and, as our discussions have emphasized, is still lower.

Many Americans agree that non-Whites have faced higher levels of prejudice and discrimination than Whites but, at the same time, they do not agree that these barriers have continued to be large enough to explain why African, Mexican, and Native Americans have remained outside the mainstream of American life. Most White Americans appear to believe that hard work, education, perseverance, and faith in the American dream are still the main ingredients of "success" in American society (Kluegel 1990:513). They appear to believe, further, that even those who suffer high levels of prejudice and discrimination should be able to succeed if they will only try hard enough. Their task may be more difficult, this argument concedes; but if they work hard opportunities will appear, and they will gradually earn their place in American society.

The preceding explanations draw a contrast between differences in (1) *the levels of discrimination* various groups have faced and (2) *the levels of effort* put forth by the members of various groups. This contrast ignores the many other factors we have mentioned that affect the rate of assimilation of minorities and is, therefore, too sharply drawn. The contrast nonetheless reflects real political differences in contemporary debate. It therefore serves as a useful reference point for our further consideration of the experiences of all non-White groups in America.

Speaking quite broadly, theories that focus primarily on the role of cultural factors represent the view that differences in the levels of worldly success among ethnic groups may be explained mainly by differences in how much effort the groups' members put into the task. Theories that focus primarily on the role of structural factors represent the view that differences in success are caused mainly by the different levels of discrimination that various groups face.[15]

The Cultural View

Advocates of the cultural view emphasize the role of family and community in the transmission of values, such as the relationship of hard work and dependability to the achievement of worldly "success." Transmitted also are "culturally codified notions of appropriate behavior that, when learned, serve as cues to others as to an individual's level of cultural and social competence" (Alba & Nee, 2003:42). Our discussion of race and ethnicity in Chapter 1 suggested that culture shapes people's attitudes and behaviors concerning racial relations and that culture is also used as a way to ascribe various social characteristics, including the idea of a shared essence, to a group of people.

As a result of cultural classifications, we often expect the people of a certain group to behave in given ways because they share certain aspects of that group's culture. The set of social characteristics that may be ascribed to a group of people because they share a culture, however, may not characterize all of the members of the group and may, in fact, not describe a single person in it. Appiah and Gutman (1996:76) argue that we use labels, such as *African American* or *Black,* to apply to a group of people who are assumed to have more in common socially, intellectually, and religiously than they actually do. Despite the error of these assumptions, the labeling has its effects. For example, as slavery became "racialized" during the colonial period, being identified as an African, or later, as Black, had predictable negative consequences. Du Bois captured these consequences in the phrase "the social heritage of slavery; the discrimination and insult" (quoted in Appiah and Guttman, 1999:76).

Culture is dynamic, and the particulars of thinking, feeling, and acting are changed by the experiences of each generation. Ideas, values, and intergroup relations evolve over time and, in this way, are transformed into something both familiar and new. For that reason our consideration of the history of various ethnic groups aims to show that the relations that existed among dominant and subordinate groups at earlier times in American history are pertinent to our thinking and actions about issues affecting these groups today (Jones 1999).

Consider in this context, for instance, the difficult problem of understanding poverty in America. Early observers of the poverty in the tenement house districts inhabited by European immigrants commented on the cultural differences of those groups and often equated these differences with inferiority. Discussions of poverty were often framed in racial terms and applied to nationality groups, as may be seen in the stereotyping and discrimination the Irish, Italian, and Jewish immigrants experienced (Lamont 1999:x). Later on, Moynihan's (1965) report about the Black family influenced political and academic analyses of the War on Poverty. Moynihan and other scholars explored differences in values to explain inequities in economic attainment, thus contributing to the "culture of poverty" thesis which evoked cries of racism from the Black community. Lamont (1999:x) pointed out that "this thesis identified pathological and self-perpetuating subcultures as the main cause of racial inequality and was sharply criticized for 'blaming the victim' and for being unable to look at alternative cultures on their own terms." Many studies have disputed the culture of poverty argument, and many critics have seen it (along with the Moynihan report) as an elaborate way to shift the responsibility for social change away from the White majority and onto the shoulders of poor people and racial and ethnic groups (Ryan 1971). The implications of the argument are that something must be wrong with them and, therefore, if they wish to succeed in life, they must relinquish elements of their own culture and become more like White Americans.

Other cultural interpretations of racial and ethnic group behaviors also have been criticized for downplaying the structural determinants of racial inequality. Critics of cultural interpretations of racism and discrimination have argued that institutional racism and other structural factors are more adequate explanations of continued racial inequality in the United States. Indeed, assimilation theory in general, as noted previously, has been criticized for emphasizing cultural interpretations of inequality and for downplaying the contributions of ethnic and racial groups to the development of American society. Still, many observers have recognized the role of cultural elements in maintaining segregation, ethnic identity, patterns of migration, and racial discrimination (e.g., Kandel and Massey 2002; Waters 1999; Wilson 1996).

In this and later chapters, as we consider the worldly "success" of the efforts of various groups to move into the social and economic life of the United States, we will see that some groups are viewed as being more "successful" than others. Often explanations for the achievements of one group as compared to another tend to stress either cultural explanations or structural explanations. We incorporate both perspectives into our analyses. We include structural factors such as the way group differences in labor force participation rates and social circumstances lead to different opportunities. We also argue that these structural differences are often given stereotypical cultural explanations that can be damaging to the groups and to our understanding of the complexity of racial and ethnic relations. In the process, we consider the culture that the new immigrants bring with them and, also, the cultural values and behaviors they encounter among the members of their own and other groups who already are settled in this country. These discussions of value differences among groups are placed throughout within a context of structural differences and are viewed only as elements within a broader interpretation of group differences.

The Structural View

Advocates of the structural view focus attention on the relationship of worldly success to noncultural factors. Such factors include the level of discrimination a group has faced or now faces, the timing of their entry into the United States, their location within the U.S. economy, and the extent to which entrepreneurial skills are prevalent in the social networks in which they participate. An influential example of the structural view focuses on **middleman minorities**.

Middleman Minorities.   Minority groups of this type are referred to as "middlemen" because "they occupy an intermediate rather than low-status position" (Bonacich 1973:583). The **middleman minority theory** is based on the idea that sojourning is a necessary ingredient in the development of an intermediate economic position. Because sojourning groups are strangers in a new land and may face strong hostility from natives if they compete with natives for jobs, they typically concentrate in commerce and trade. To increase their chances of success in these pursuits, they cultivate social ties with other members of their own group, and avoid noneconomic ties with members of the host group.

The extent to which the middleman minority theory may assist us to understand the worldly success of African Americans is an open question. Although African Americans have been in many respects estranged from American society, they have not been sojourners. And although they have faced strong discrimination in the economic arena, the entrepreneurial mode of adaptation to out-group threat has been lower among African Americans than among a number of other groups. For example, even though the number of Black-owned businesses has grown in recent years, several other minority groups—including Korean, Asian Indian, and Cuban Americans—have relied much more heavily on self-employment (O'Hare 1992).[16] These facts have led some to express the belief that African Americans do not have a strong tradition of business activity and self-help.

Butler (1991, 1996) has challenged this belief. He argued (1) that beginning during the colonial period, a noticeable segment of the African American population followed an entrepreneurial path similar to that of the middleman minorities; (2) that a substantial Black middleman economy was constructed before 1900; but that (3) with the development of the Jim Crow system, segregation forced Black business development to detour from the usual path of middleman groups and to develop, instead, as a **truncated middleman minority** (Butler 1991:143, 228). As the Black entrepreneurs were separated from White consumers, they became dependent on "Protected markets in personal services catering to other Blacks" (Boyd 1991:411). Butler found that African American individuals became entrepreneurs and professionals within the Black community because they were cut off, or truncated, from the main business districts of America as a result of segregation. Racism forced them to do business exclusively within their own group. He argued that the modern-day descendants of Black Americans who engaged in business have inherited a philosophy of life and a way of adapting to extreme hostility resembling that of the descendants of other middleman minorities, and with similar socioeconomic consequences (Butler 1991:258, 314). Yet despite the racism that prevented them from continuing as middlemen, Butler (1996:145) found that there was "really no difference between the offspring of African Americans today whose parents, grandparents, and great-grandparents adjusted to America by self-help and the offspring of other self-help ethnic groups."

An important consequence of this historical pattern, Butler argued, is that African Americans have followed two routes to worldly success in American society, the immigrant model of assimilating into the mainstream and the entrepreneurial route as a truncated middleman minority. The first route to success, described in our discussion of the secondary assimilation of the new Black middle class, resembles what one would expect on the basis of the immigrant model (Butler 1991:242–244). Despite the extremely high levels of discrimination against them, the new arrivals in the northern and southern cities, like many immigrants before them, worked hard to establish themselves in the society's mainstream and to make a place in the world for their children. Many third- and fourth-generation descendants of this group are now "making it in America." The second route to success, in Butler's view, stems from a strong, misunderstood, and underestimated tradition of business enterprise among African Americans. He stated that, with appropriate adjustments for new conditions, the example of the truncated middleman minority may afford a blueprint for adjustment for many of those African Americans who do not wish to follow, or are unable to follow, the immigrant model (Butler 1991:322).[17]

All of the arguments presented concerning the worldly success of African Americans are hotly contested and are of great public importance. As emphasized previously, positions taken in the public debate over what should be done to promote the assimilation of minority groups are closely connected to competing social policy views. Liberals, generally, stress the role of past and present discrimination and other structural factors in creating and maintaining group differences. Conservatives, on the other hand, focus strongly on the role of cultural differences as important causes of group differences in success. Wilson (1991:1) argued that his approach transcends the "simplistic either/or notions of culture versus social structure" by showing some of the links between these notions. Butler (1991:324), too, argued that his approach "is neither conservative nor liberal" but rather one that encourages African Americans to consider "a path which has been followed for centuries by oppressed and outcast groups."

Many observers have expressed the fear that the most disadvantaged of the inner-city dwellers, the "hard-core" poor, are becoming so separated from the rest of the society that there is a danger they will become a permanent "underclass." Hochschild (1995: 250–260) presents strong evidence that, for perhaps the first time in American history, a group of poor Blacks have become so alienated that they threaten the existence of stable communities. She contended that most poor Blacks have continued to pursue the American dream of "success" through legitimate hard work and have rejected succeeding financially through drug sales, gaining concessions through protest and violence, or withdrawing from all effort. But, she warned, there is no reason to expect society's "luck" in these respects to last if the discrepancy between their hopes for success and the realities they face each day continues to grow.

A Social Class Analysis.   In 1978, sociologist William J. Wilson wrote a controversial book, *The Declining Significance of Race,* based on the thesis that race as a factor affecting socioeconomic status was diminishing.[18] Stated briefly, the reasoning behind this thesis is as follows: Throughout the long years between the beginnings of African American slavery and the end of World War II, practically all Blacks, professionals as well as the poor, were members of an oppressed lower caste. Under these conditions, Black people's racial affiliation rather than their economic circumstances determined their chances for occupational advancement; therefore, the inequalities between Blacks and Whites were, strictly speaking, *racial* in nature. Since World War II, however, the United States has seen the creation of a significant Black middle class, as discussed earlier, among whom occupational advancement depends more on *class* location than on racial membership. The result is a growing cleavage *within* the Black community in which socioeconomic classes have become more visible (Featherman and Hauser 1978:381–382). In short, well-educated Blacks increasingly have opportunities for occupational advancement that are similar to those of Whites, whereas the uneducated members of all groups, including Whites, increasingly descend into a growing population of multiracial poor.

Wilson's conclusion that the life chances of Blacks had more to do with their economic class position than with their day-to-day encounters with Whites angered many scholars and stirred a debate that has not yet been settled.[19] At the time of the publication of *The Declining Significance of Race,* the Association of Black Sociologists (ABS) published a denunciation (*Footnotes,* December 1978:4) of the book and accused Wilson of omitting significant facts "regarding the continuing discrimination against Blacks at all class levels," of misinterpreting some of the facts presented, and of drawing unwarranted conclusions. The ABS members were "outraged over the misinterpretation of the Black experience" and "extremely disturbed over the policy implications" of the book. Wilson, of course, was aware that in matters such as public school education, residential segregation, and full political participation, racial antagonism was still very much alive. He also recognized that older Black workers, due to the historic effects of discrimination, did not earn the same incomes as Whites. His argument, however, was that as younger talented and educated Blacks entered the labor market in competition with Whites, the racial barriers to advancement would be largely eliminated (Wilson 1980:177).

Wilson (1987) expanded his analysis of the ghetto poor[20] in another controversial book, *The Truly Disadvantaged.* He acknowledged that despite the Great Society programs of the 1960s, the proportion of Black births occurring outside of marriage and the proportion of Black families headed by women had both risen. He also acknowledged that welfare dependency, violent crime, and increased joblessness among Blacks had reached "catastrophic proportions" (Wilson 1987:21). In Wilson's view, problems such as poverty, unemployment, street crime, and teenage pregnancy cannot be explained fully as simple consequences of either culture or discrimination. He stated that explanations must include "societal, demographic, and neighborhood variables," and argued that "the sharp rise of Black female-headed families is directly related to increasing Black male joblessness" (Wilson 1987:30, 105). In a third important book, *When Work Disappears,* Wilson (1996) proposed that many of the problems in the inner-city neighborhoods are fundamentally a consequence of the disappearance of work. Wilson acknowledged that cultural factors do play a role, but he argued that the loss of blue-collar jobs, the relocation of other jobs to the suburbs, the lack of locally available training and education, and the dissolution of government and private organizations that once supplied job information and employment opportunities have had devastating effects on the Black urban poor and their families.

We have seen in this brief summary that many questions concerning the "success" of African Americans are still unanswered. How one interprets these persistent differences in levels of achievement—as a consequence of lesser abilities, biases, an oppositional culture, differences in family income or education, barriers of social class, regional economic changes, or differences in cultural capital—has implications for policies that facilitate assimilation. Some of the evidence reviewed so far shows that in the important areas of occupations, income, and education, racial differences have declined substantially. These findings show that as a group African Americans *are* succeeding in some ways and that the gains *are* significant. But we also saw that in some ways the gaps between the achievements of Blacks and the rest of the population are growing. It is possible, as Wilson contended, that better-educated Blacks have taken advantage of the opportunities created by the civil rights movement and have moved out of the inner cities, leaving behind an increasingly visible group of poor Blacks.

Black Immigration

The growth of non-White voluntary immigrants to the United States since 1965 challenges some of the assumptions of the traditional three-generations model of assimilation. Black immigrants have come from the Caribbean, particularly Haiti where the people speak French and the West Indies where the people speak English. New immigrants have also come from various countries in Africa, such as Ethiopia and Nigeria. These immigrants are still categorized racially in the United States but, unlike the African Americans who came involuntarily to the United States as slaves, these Blacks are voluntary immigrants. Moreover, these immigrants often enter the country under an immigrant preference system that selects people with jobs and education well above the average of residents who remain in their country of origin and, also, above the levels of the majority of U.S.-born African Americans.

Mary Waters (1999a, b, 2004), a sociologist at Harvard University who has studied the experiences of first- and second-generation West Indians and Haitians in New York City, found that first-generation Black immigrants "tended to distance themselves from American Blacks." West Indians found that their immigrant ethnic identities enabled them to get better jobs than American Blacks. White employers stated that they found American Blacks to be more confrontational and quick to identify acts of discrimination than were the immigrants. As a result, the employers preferred to hire West Indian or Jamaican workers over native Black Americans.

Kasinitz (1992) found that job competition led to a great deal of tension between foreign-born and American-born Blacks in both working- and middle-class work sites, as well as to mutual stereotyping. The immigrants saw themselves as hardworking, ambitious, not overly sensitive about race, and committed to education and family. They saw American Blacks as lazy, obsessed with racial slights and barriers, and with a more casual attitude toward family life and child raising. American Blacks described the immigrants as arrogant, exploited in the workplace, oblivious to racial tensions and political issues affecting Blacks, and unfriendly toward Black Americans. McDermott (2003) also found that the encounters of African immigrants and native-born Blacks often led to conflict and that native-born Whites frequently viewed African immigrants simply as "Black." Because of differences in language and culture, however, Whites in Boston saw Haitians as immigrants rather than as "Blacks."

Waters (2004:494) found that West Indian Black immigrants tended to maintain their parents' accents and other identifying characteristics as a way of distinguishing themselves from American Blacks. They realized that if they did not distance themselves from American Blacks and reject their cultural values, Whites would group them with American Blacks on the basis of skin color. McDermott (2003) also suggested that the increasing presence of Black immigrants in U.S. cities is a source of ethnic conflicts within the Black community. She noted that differences in the identities of Black immigrants and American Blacks highlight the ways White Americans respond to these groups, draw racial boundaries, and maintain the racial basis of Black–White interactions.

A number of factors influenced the type of identity the children of Black immigrants developed. The class background of the parents, the parents' social networks, the type of school the child attended, and the family structure in which they lived each caused some second-generation Blacks to accept negative portrayals of poor American Blacks. These factors caused others to stress that they were American citizens and had been born in the United States. Waters (2004:507) found that some Black immigrant teens who lived in all-Black neighborhoods and attended all-Black schools identified with the peer culture at their schools. They began to speak Black English, listen to rap music, and to adopt the "stylish," and sometimes confrontational, behaviors of their American peers. Unlike the middle-class youths, they did not automatically associate their parents' values of hard work, scholastic achievement, and lack of dating and socializing outside the family with upward mobility. Research in New York City, Los Angeles, Miami, Boston, and other major immigrant destinations suggests that Black immigrants face issues and conflicts that raise questions concerning modes of adaptation to American life they will adopt and how many generations may be needed to complete the process.

It is probable that the issue of the worldly success of African Americans and of Black immigrants will continue to animate political debate for some time to come. An important part of the debate concerns the relative weight one should give to various cultural and structural factors that may be related to worldly achievement. In Steinberg's (1989:87) opinion, a proper balance may be achieved only when ". . . a theoretical approach that explores the interaction between cultural and [structural] factors . . ." is used. An exclusive focus on the role of values in ethnic mobility imputes ". . . a cultural superiority to groups that have enjoyed disproportionate success." *This important point must be kept in mind each time the subject of group differences in worldly success arises in later chapters.* This should also remind us that the various ideologies of group adjustment we have outlined lie just beneath the surface of controversies concerning various proposals about the social policies that should be adopted in regard to the assimilation of minority groups.

 Reality Check

INTERVIEW WITH JEFFREY

Jeffery is a graduate student in educational psychology. He is married and has 2-year-old twin daughters. His grandfather left school in fifth grade to work in the cotton fields. His mother completed high school. Jeffery grew up with aunts, uncles, and cousins living nearby.

How do you define yourself in terms of racial, ethnic identity?
I refer to myself as Black, plain and simple. In my family there are no active ties to African culture or even African American culture, so I don't think it is representative to call myself an African American. I never heard the term *African American* in my family. "Black" represents a color difference for sure, recognizing the difference between Black and White and Brown. But it also represents a cultural difference. When I say Black, or African American, I'm actually saying something that begins to identify a cultural difference.

What is most important to you about being Black?
The Blacks I know have a lot of internal self-power that impresses me. It's how Blacks tend to—I hate to use the word persevere—but Blacks seem to, no matter what comes up, find a way to keep going.

How does your racial background affect your daily life?
I'm a pretty lucky person. I'm in a position where a lot of the people on a daily basis give me a lot of respect for being Black and succeeding academically. I don't think that's necessarily the case for all Blacks, especially in school.

Have you experienced uncomfortable situations because of your racial or ethnic background?
A number of times. I don't go out on New Years anymore, because for 3 years somebody, somewhere looked me in the eyes and said: "Nigger, I'm gonna kick your ass." I don't know what I was doing wrong.

Does your family talk about racial and ethnic relations?
Not in terms of working toward a solution, but they talk about recognizing differences, and the stress of being Black in central Texas and being Black in America. They talk about some of the frustrations.

Tell me about your friends.
Currently all the people that I hang out with on a regular basis are different from my background. It is a rare occasion that I hang out with Blacks anymore. Some of it has to do with educational status. Right now I'm immersed in academics and I don't have any Black friends who have pursued school the way I have. So I

(continued)

self-selected out of some of my relationships based on the time that I have to give. It's inconvenient to go out and pursue Black friends right now.

When I hang out with Black people, it's mostly eating and talking, and that's fun. It just seems that there is something easier about hanging out with Blacks. There is an expectation when I say something, when I am with my group of Black friends, that they will automatically know not only what I'm talking about, but the context from which I talk about it. And they will have a similar connection. When I hang out with my White friends, that's not the case. Frequently there are conversations about race and ethnic relations, but before we have any conversation we have to catch one another up to speed on where we are coming from. That first piece of dialogue doesn't have to happen with my Black friends. I make a comment and it is automatically "Oh yeah, absolutely." Last night I was with a friend in the graduate program who is White and he asked me: "Are you going to the retreat tomorrow?" And I said: "You know, I don't think I want to be into White people on my time off." And it's a racist thing to say, but at the same time it's an effort I have to make to help myself be more comfortable. And we talked about what it means to not want to have to deal with White people because you have to deal with White people every day.

How did it happen that you married outside of your racial group?
My wife is a generic White lady from the Midwest. In high school, there was tension with my mother about who we dated. My father thought, "people are going make their own decisions." My mother made efforts to set us up with eligible Black ladies. She was very clear that dating Whites wasn't cool. I assume that one reason is social upbringing or religious background or just the idea a lot of people in America have that Blacks ought to be with Blacks, Whites with Whites, and Hispanics with Hispanics. And some of it is a lot of Black women feel disrespected and fearful about the fact that a lot of Black men are going outside of their race to find partners. I think Mom may have thought this was disrespectful, that there are eligible Black women out there, "why can't you be with one of them?" Fair enough.

What was your school experience like?
In the sixth grade, the last weeks of class, we had a dance and the only Blacks at the school were my cousins. At that dance, one of my best friends said: "Who are you going to dance with? You could dance with your cousins, but there is nobody else you could dance with." And it started to become clear to me. There had been other things that had happened before that but I don't think I clued into what was going on as well as that night. It was clear, and it came to be clearer all the time.

In high school, it was very segregated. I was definitely a Black person on a mostly White campus with a few Blacks and a few Hispanics. I was reminded of that periodically. Certain members of my family crossed over racial boundaries in academics, extracurricular activities, and athletics and were well accepted across all the ethnic groups, Hispanic and Blacks. We were class presidents and vice presidents. You couldn't get elected without help from cross-cultural people. Other cousins were not well accepted. I was definitely a Black person. At the same time, I had many White friends, and friends with diverse backgrounds, and I was accepted into many different groups. In that way I was part of the majority. I was exempted from minority status by some people.

In college—some Blacks feel total isolation—I don't feel that. I see different ethnic groups trying to be part of a large White institution and be connected to one another, and it's a struggle. I'm involved with a support network of Black graduate students who are trying to help one another.

Discussion Questions

What social factors contributed to rise of direct action by African Americans in the 1960s?

What is your opinion of affirmative action? Explain your view. If current affirmative action measures are abandoned, what types of policies to promote equality of opportunity should take their place?

Which one of the theories that seek to understand the "worldly success" of American minorities do you think is most persuasive? Why?

If you were asked to suggest social measures or interventions to increase or decrease the speed of African American assimilation, what would you suggest? Why? Examine your suggestions in relation to the models of assimilation discussed.

Which cultural or structural factors, or combination of factors, do you find to be most useful in understanding the "worldly success" of African Americans?

How has academic success influenced Jeffrey's experiences?

Jeffrey gets along well with various members of all groups, and he is highly educated. Nevertheless, he continues to have racist experiences. Why? How should he respond?

Key Ideas

1. Massive resistance by Whites to the *Brown* decisions was met by a sharp increase in the use of nonviolent protest tactics by Black Americans. Racial confrontations in southern cities such as Little Rock, Montgomery, Greensboro, and Birmingham crumbled the structure of Jim Crow segregation in public places and

accommodations and paved the way for the passage of the Civil Rights Act of 1964 and the Voting Rights Act of 1965.

2. The slow pace of social change led many African Americans to shift their protest strategies from nonviolence to "offensive" violence. The years 1967 and 1968 were the peak years of violent protests; but violent outbursts, as well as large peaceful demonstrations, occurred in the 1970s, 1980s, and 1990s as a consequence of continued experiences of racial injustice.

3. Black Americans, especially females, appear to be moving toward secondary assimilation in jobs. There also has been secondary assimilation in incomes, again especially among females; but the trend among males slowed during the 1970s. The evidence on the education gap also is mixed, with the overall trend pointing toward educational assimilation (especially through high school); but there is increased re-segregation of schools because of continued residential segregation.

4. While the rate of primary and marital assimilation has increased and many African Americans identify themselves as multicultural, the total amount of these forms of assimilation is still very low. Therefore the separation of Blacks and Whites (at present rates of change) will remain for a long time to come. The continued primary and marital separation of Whites and Blacks, along with the visible changes in cultural and secondary assimilation, suggests that Blacks are moving toward the goal of cultural pluralism.

5. Affirmative action is one of the most important and controversial methods of attacking discrimination. At the heart of a heated national controversy is the issue of whether employment or admissions to educational and training programs may take race and ethnicity into account without also compromising the nation's commitment to the ideal of equal treatment. Opponents of affirmative action maintain that departures from policies of neutrality that grant preferential treatment to minority-group members amount to reverse discrimination. Supporters of affirmative action deny that it is reverse discrimination and maintain that it is the most effective policy yet developed for bringing minority-group members into the American mainstream.

6. The continuation of educational, income, occupational, and wealth gaps between African and White Americans have been interpreted by some as being a consequence of the presence of certain values in Black culture and the absence of other values. Research focusing on cultural resources, rather than values, has shown that African American culture has adapted to cope with the devastating effects of slavery and has been a resilient source of support. Other research has pointed to structural changes in job opportunities, mobility patterns, and majority-group discrimination as continuing, important barriers to minority-group achievement.

7. Business enterprise has been a source of economic advancement for African Americans since before they gained their freedom from slavery. Entrepreneurship is increasing rapidly among African Americans, though this mode of adaptation to

out-group threat is still comparatively low. The role of self-help and Black institutions in the lives of African Americans has received renewed scrutiny.

8. Increasing immigration from Haiti, the West Indies, Africa, and other areas of the world has raised new questions concerning the distinction between, and the prospects of, colonized and immigrant minorities in the United States.

9. An adequate explanation of any group's worldly success requires a consideration of both cultural and structural factors.

 # Key Terms

affirmative action   Policies and programs that go beyond neutrality by seeking out and encouraging *qualified* minority-group members and women to become a part of the pool of applicants for openings and opportunities in schools, training programs, employment, contracting, and various other competitive settings.

disparate impact   Consistently unequal outcomes among groups that are produced by various selection procedures used in admission to educational and training programs, in hiring and promotion, or in ensuring equal access to social and economic opportunities. Disparate results may arise either from treating equal groups unequally or from treating unequal groups as if they were equal.

ethnic-resource model   A theoretical perspective that emphasizes the strengths, resources, and achievements fostered by ethnic cultures rather than deficits.

glass ceiling effect   Increases in racial or gender inequalities at the higher levels of earnings, experience, and authority.

index of dissimilarity   A measure of the extent to which groups differ from one another.

middleman minority   A minority that occupies an intermediate economic position in a society.

middleman minority theory   States that groups occupying intermediate economic positions are strongly motivated to work hard, to be thrifty, to take economic risks, and to concentrate funds in businesses that may easily be converted into money.

preferential (compensatory) treatment   Awarding preferred standing and/or additional opportunities for contemporary social and economic advancement to the designated members of various racial, ethnic, and gender groups that have experienced past discrimination.

reverse discrimination   The belief that all or some members of the dominant group unjustly pay the direct and indirect costs of compensatory treatment.

theory of spatial assimilation   States that the members of minority groups move into neighborhoods with better schools, more expensive homes, and higher prestige as their socioeconomic status rises.

truncated middleman minority   The disruption (or cutting off) of the middleman minority tradition among African Americans by the rise of Jim Crow segregation.

Notes

1. During this period, many new organizations came into being. Jaynes and Williams (1989:186) reported that more than 1,100 organizations were founded between 1965 and 1987.

2. The major disorders involved a combination of four factors: (1) many fires, looting, and reports of sniping; (2) more than 2 days of violence; (3) large crowds; and (4) the use of National Guard and federal forces along with local law enforcement agencies.

3. Some observers believe the peak was reached later (see, e.g., Feagin and Hahn 1973: 105–106).

4. Whites were seated ahead of Blacks; Blacks were seated in the rear of the restaurant and service to them was slow; Blacks were asked to pay before eating, were required to make minimum purchases, and were even sometimes "locked out" of the restaurants.

5. An excellent illustration of ethnogenesis is the establishment of the Kwanzaa holiday period by Mavlana Ron Karenga. The 7-day holiday is celebrated each year, beginning on December 26. Each day is devoted to one of the seven cardinal principles of the Black Value System (Monsho 1988).

6. In 2000, 21 percent of Black males and 27.7 percent of Black females were in professional jobs (U.S. Bureau of the Census 2001: 384).

7. To illustrate, in 1960, 3.1 percent of the Black population and 8.1 percent of the White population had completed college. At that time, therefore, 5 percent more Whites than Blacks had completed college. By 1994, even though the percentage of Blacks who completed college had risen to 12.9, the gap between the groups had increased to 10 percent. The percentage of Whites completing college had by then reached 22.9 percent (U.S. Bureau of the Census 1996:157).

8. We thank the authors for sending us a copy of their report. We also thank Teresa A. Sullivan for calling the study to our attention.

9. Harrison and Weinberg (1992) reported the higher figure; Farley and Frey (1994) reported the lower figure. The segregation scores for Black Americans among 25 of America's largest metropolitan areas in 1990 ranged from a low of 44 in Anaheim–Santa Ana to a high of 89 in Detroit (O'Hare and Usdansky 1992:7).

10. Such agreements are called restrictive covenants.

11. Schuman and Bobo (1988:295) found that some of the opposition to open-housing laws may reflect a general opposition to federal coercion, but they found also that "personal prejudice against blacks" is an important element. Bobo and Zubrinsky (1996) found a general openness to integration among Whites, but concluded that ongoing patterns of individual and institutional discrimination in the housing market still contribute to high levels of residential segregation.

12. For references to this literature, see Monahan (1976:223–231) and Tucker and Mitchell-Kernan (1995).

13. The female out-marriage rate is higher for every other racial and ethnic group (McDaniel 1996). White Americans have very high rates of ethnic intermarriage, but there is a strong tendency to select out-group spouses who are also White.

14. The National Opinion Research Center and the Gallup Poll both use a series of questions posing hypothetical social settings that vary in racial composition. Respondents are asked to indicate whether they would take part in such settings.

15. There is general agreement that *cultural* describes one side of this dichotomy; but, several different terms are used to designate all the many factors we call *structural,* including *situational, contextual,* and *material* (Bonacich and Modell 1980:29–30).

16. An alternative to middleman minority theory, ethnic-enclave theory, is based on the idea that immigrant workers may be part of a

special type of economy that provides unusual routes of upward mobility (Portes 1981; Wilson and Martin 1982; Butler and Wilson 1988). The immigrants in an ethnic enclave work together to organize a variety of business enterprises but, despite some resemblances, do not constitute a middleman economy (Portes and Bach 1985:203, 340).

17. Butler (1996:156) found that many of the top 100 Black enterprises are quite new; 47 percent were founded in the 1970s and 21 percent in the 1980s. A sizable number of those enterprises serve the entire business community, not just the Black community. Butler also pointed out that as these middlemen gain economic stability, they send their children to college to become professionals and managers.

18. This argument has appeared in several different analyses during the past century. For incisive comments concerning a number of these, see Wilhelm (1983:117–119) and Boston (1988:1–21).

19. See, for example, the debate in *American Sociological Review* (August 1996). Cancio, Evans, and Maume (1996) analyzed the effect of race on earnings among young workers who, in Wilson's view, should experience little discrimination. The study showed that the proportion of the racial gap in hourly wages due to discrimination increased between 1976 and 1985; however, a later study by Sakamoto and Tzeng (1999), based on findings for a 50-year period, found that by 1990 social class had become more important than race as a factor affecting occupational success, which supported Wilson's thesis. See also Sakamoto, Wu, and Tzeng (2000).

20. Wilson (1991:6) adopted the term *ghetto poor* in an effort to shift attention away from the debate over the term *underclass* and toward a focus on research issues.

Mexican Americans

From Colonized Minority to Political Activists

Community-based organizations have promoted opportunities for immigrants and second and third generation Hispanics to learn about their legal rights in the United States. Mexican Americans have increasingly voted in elections, run for public office, and participated in public affairs at the local, state, and federal level.

*In spite of what many Anglo pioneers may have thought generally
of Mexicans, most were careful to make the proper distinctions between
different "types" of Mexicans. Mexican landowners were "Spanish"
or Castilian, whereas Mexican workers were "half-breeds" or
"Mexican Indians." The well-known aphorism explains
the situation—"money whitens."*

—David Montejano

*. . . the Borderlands are physically present wherever two or more cultures
edge each other, where people of different races occupy the same territory,
where under, lower, middle and upper classes touch, where the space
between two individuals shrinks with intimacy. I am a border woman.
I grew up between two cultures, the Mexican (with a heavy Indian
influence), and the Anglo (as a member of a colonized people
in our own territory).*

—Gloria Anzaldua

The preceding chapters highlighted the point that the population of the United States
has been built up mainly by successive waves of immigrants from various parts of the
world and that these immigrants, broadly speaking, entered this society voluntarily. In
the case of the Mexican Americans,[1] however, we confront a second kind of situation.

Unlike nearly all other groups we have discussed, the Mexican Americans did not
initially become "newcomers" to American society by leaving the old country and crossing oceans. Instead, like African Americans and American Indians, they originally became
a part of American society through conflict and coercion. The southwestern or **borderlands** region of what is now the United States, in which the Mexican American population still is concentrated, was settled by people of Spanish–Mexican–Indian ancestry long
before it was settled by Anglo Americans; and, along with the American Indians, the Mexican Americans entered the society through the direct conquest of their homelands.

Some observers believe this is a fact of overriding importance, a fact that makes totally inapplicable to the Mexican Americans the assimilationist ideas we have explored
thus far. As Sanchez stated, "the Spanish Mexicans of the Southwest are not truly an immigrant group, for they are in their traditional home."[2] From this standpoint, the expectation that the experience of the Mexican Americans can be analyzed properly in terms
of any or all of the three main ideologies of assimilation discussed previously is considered to be a serious mistake. It is rather argued that to understand the Mexican American
experience we must employ an antiassimilationist ideology and framework.

Early Indian–Spanish Relations

To assess the competing claims of the assimilationist (immigrant model) and antiassimilationist (colonial model) interpretations of the Mexican American experience, we

begin with the landings of the Spaniards in Mexico during the second decade of the sixteenth century. Here, as in the case of the landings of the English in Virginia and Massachusetts approximately 100 years later, a conquering European, Christian group established itself on lands previously occupied by indigenous American groups. In both instances, the dominant migrant group gradually expanded its frontiers to create an increasingly large colonial territory. The expansion of the English toward the west and of the Spanish toward the north were the processes that would one day bring these two enormous colonial developments together.

The specific course of colonial development in the English and Spanish territories differed in a number of significant respects. For one thing, the two powers' entire approaches to colonization were different. The exploration and colonization of the Spanish territories relied more strongly on the initiatives of the crown and the church. The Spanish monarchs were interested primarily in acquiring lands and precious metals, whereas the Roman Catholic Church wished to save the souls of the "heathens." The English, too, were interested at first in these very same things; but after a while it became clear that there was no gold and silver treasure on the Atlantic coast. So the efforts to Christianize the Indians proved to be largely futile.

These differences in colonization methods and experiences had one consequence of special importance for us: The relations between the conquering Europeans and the conquered Indians developed along significantly different paths in the two cases. As noted in Chapter 3, the relations between the English and the Indians became predominantly hostile and were interspersed with warfare. The policy of the Anglo Americans toward the Indians became one of exclusion and extermination. By and large, the Indians were forced to move west as the Anglo American frontier advanced.

The relations between the Spaniards and the Indians in Mexico also were frequently hostile, but the Spaniards were much more successful than the Anglo Americans in the matter of converting the Indians to Christianity, at least to many of its outward forms. Consequently, even though the Spaniards also took an enormous toll in human lives and misery, the cross as well as the sword marked the advance of the northern frontier of Mexico.[3] The place of the Indians in Mexican society, to be sure, was at the very bottom. They provided most of the manual labor that was needed to construct and maintain the *haciendas* and to exploit the riches of the earth. They were the *peons*, who were bound to the Spanish masters and the land in a form of human slavery; but they also were human beings and Christians, and they were accepted as an integral, if lowly, part of Mexican society.[4]

The Spaniards' policy of counting the Indians "in" rather than "out" led, during a period of three centuries, to a much higher degree of marital assimilation of the Indians with the dominant Europeans. Two related points should be noted. First, just as the English subscribed generally to the Anglo-conformity ideology of assimilation, the Spaniards adhered generally to an Hispano-conformity ideology. The Indians were expected to do their very best to move toward a mastery of Spanish culture and ways of acting. Second, by the time Mexico achieved independence in 1821, the culture and population of Mexico had become very much more "Indianized" than had the culture and population of the United States. Whatever may have been the intentions of the dominant Spaniards, the melting-pot process of assimilation was more significant in Mexico than in the United States.

The Hispano–Indian society of Mexico and the Anglo American society of the United States came into direct and continuous contact after the Louisiana Purchase in 1803. The line of contact between these groups was exceptionally long and blurred. The treaty through which the United States secured Louisiana from France did not give a detailed description of the boundaries of the territory. This fact helped to create and maintain an almost constant state of tension along the frontier, first between Spain and the United States and then, later, between Mexico and the United States. Many Americans seemed to believe that Texas definitely had been included in the purchase; but the Spanish and Mexican governments disagreed. Many other Americans believed that it was the "Manifest Destiny" of their country to span the continent. In this way, a struggle began that led, by 1848, to the transfer of what we now know as the American Southwest from Mexico to the United States and to the creation of the Mexican American minority group. The incorporation of Texas into the United States was an important part of that story.

 # The Texas Frontier

The process through which the Mexican American group has emerged may be visualized more clearly by a consideration of some of the events that occurred in Texas after 1803. The United States recently had been flexing its muscles in international affairs (e.g., the Monroe Doctrine) and was clearly in a stronger military position than the young Mexican nation. Also, the Americans generally did not hide the fact that they regarded themselves to be racially superior to the heterogeneous population of Mexico. The majority of Mexico's citizens were either Indians or Spanish Indians (*mestizos*). Basically, the heritage of the "pure" Spaniards was itself suspect in the Americans' minds because of the centuries of interaction between the Spaniards and various African populations (e.g., the Moors). Hence, racism played an important role in Mexican and American relations.

Less than 15 years after Mexico gained her independence from Spain, Texas broke away from Mexico to establish still another independent republic. Nevertheless, a basis for *Tejano* and Anglo American immigrant cooperation was created and maintained by able leaders from both sides. Stephen F. Austin, the leader of the first group of Anglo American immigrants to Texas, was enthusiastic about the prospect of an independent Mexico and the development of Texas within it. He sincerely accepted Mexican citizenship and was a respected link between the native and immigrant groups. From the native Mexican side, such men as Ramón Músquiz and José Antonio Navarro worked energetically to assist the assimilation of the Anglo Americans into Mexican society. But the goodwill and substantially similar interests of the native and immigrant leadership in Texas did not extend to Mexico City. In a way, the central authorities fell victims to their own plan. The colonization program was so successful that by 1835 the Anglo American immigrants outnumbered the *Tejanos* by about five to one; hence, as the talk of revolution spread, most of those who favored it were, simply as a matter of numbers, Anglo Americans. When the revolution erupted, the Texan armies were comprised mainly of Anglo Americans; nevertheless, a large proportion of the native Mexicans in Texas believed that various actions of the central government had been unjustified. Kibbe (1946:33) estimated that as many as one-third of those who opposed the government of Santa Anna were *Tejanos,* and several *Tejano* units participated in the actual fighting during the Texas revolution (Barker 1943:333).[5]

Although the *Tejanos* were a numerical minority, they were not yet treated systematically as an ethnic minority. An ethnic line of distinction did exist, but it was a blurred rather than a sharp line. Taylor (1934:21) described the situation as follows: "During the period of confusion some Texans were fighting with Mexicans . . . other Texans were committing depredations against both Texans and Mexicans, while Mexicans could be found on both sides." Gradually, however, friendships between the *Tejanos* and the Anglo American Texans became more difficult to maintain, and the relations between the groups became more strained. Anglo American Texans, in particular, increasingly failed to distinguish the *Tejanos* from Mexican nationals and came to regard the conflict in Texas as one of "Mexicans" versus "Americans" (Montejano 1987:26–30).

Many of the Anglo American Texans did, in fact, still regard themselves as Americans and were eager to have Texas join the United States. This goal was shared by many people within the United States. It is hardly surprising, therefore, that after only some ten years of independence, Texas agreed to become a part of the United States.

☼ Conflict in the Borderlands

The annexation of Texas aggravated rather than ended the hostilities in the borderlands. President Santa Anna had warned in 1843 that "the Mexican government will consider equivalent to a declaration of war against the Mexican Republic the passage of an act for the incorporation of Texas with the territory of the United States" (Faulkner 1948:324). In May 1846, President Polk claimed that Mexico "has invaded our territory and shed American blood on American soil" (Faulkner 1948:325), and he asked Congress for a declaration of war against Mexico. Abraham Lincoln disagreed with Polk and stated that the war was "unnecessarily and unconstitutionally commenced by the President" (Faulkner 1948:325).

Constitutional or not, "one of the most obviously aggressive wars in American history" was under way (Jordan and Litwack 1987:315). The conflict involved not only the disputed territory between Texas and Mexico but all of Mexico. In February 1848, Mexico surrendered under the terms of the **Treaty of Guadalupe Hidalgo.** The treaty ceded to the United States nearly one-half of the territory of Mexico. The Rio Grande was established as the boundary of Texas. So the great bulk of the land that now comprises the southwestern region of the United States was acquired.[6] The "Manifest Destiny" of the United States to stretch from the Atlantic to the Pacific had now been achieved. The Spanish–Mexican–Indian group that was left behind as Mexico's northern frontier receded (75,000 to 100,000 people)[7] was now a conquered group. As individuals, they had the right either to "retain the title and rights of Mexican citizens, or acquire those of citizens of the United States" (Moquín and Van Doren 1971:246). Those who did not declare their intention to remain Mexicans automatically became citizens of the United States after 1 year. At this point, although they were U.S. citizens, they generally were viewed as a defeated and inferior people whose rights need not be taken too seriously (Griswold del Castillo 1990). They "gradually saw their property and influence dwindle as they faced . . . the flood of Anglo Americans" (Burner, Fox-Genovese, and Bernhard 1991:387).

In this way, the Mexican Americans became a minority within the United States. Their entry into the society was by conquest and, to repeat, was quite different from that of the Irish and Germans who were arriving in large numbers in the East during this very same period. The **Creation Generation** of Mexican Americans had not decided to leave their native land and go to the United States. They simply discovered one day that by a mutual agreement of the United States and Mexico (at gunpoint), the places where they lived were no longer in Mexico. In fact, to continue being Mexicans, they either had to leave their homes and move south of the new border established by the treaty or declare officially their intention to remain Mexican nationals within the United States. Acuña (1981:19) states that "About 2,000 elected to leave; most remained in what they considered *their* land."

The Treaty of Guadalupe Hidalgo did not end the violence in the borderlands, but it did mark the point beyond which those of Mexican descent were subordinated to the Anglo Americans. A system of ethnic domination had been born. The Americans had ample incentives to compete with the Mexicans for Texas; they had the power to seize it if necessary, and they typically had a low regard for the Mexican people. Most Mexican Americans found themselves in a position in society not much better than that occupied by Indians and African Americans elsewhere in the United States. The combination of these ingredients created a highly unstable situation along Mexico's northern frontier, especially in the area of Texas.

The strip of land between the Nueces River and the Rio Grande was the staging area for many violent conflicts. Numerous "filibustering expeditions" were launched into this area by Anglo Americans in an attempt to extend U.S. territory even more deeply into Mexico. The traffic was not entirely one way, however. Between 1859 and 1873, the flamboyant Mexican leader Juan N. "Cheno" Cortina initiated a series of raids along the Texas border (Acuña 1981:33–37; Rosenbaum 1981:41–45; Webb [1935] 1987:173–193). Cortina, who was born near Brownsville, Texas, came prominently to attention in July 1859 in the first of a series of **"Cortina Wars."** Cortina's daring exploits won him labels ranging from "cattle thief" to "champion of his race" (Lea 1957:159). Among the Mexican people, Cortina was immortalized as a border hero in several *corridos*, or ballads, about the border raids (Paredes 1958). These border conflicts provoked continuous, bitter confrontations with military and law enforcement authorities on both sides of the Rio Grande.

The interethnic violence in Texas reached a peak during the early 1870s, but the disorders subsided by 1875. The combined actions of the authorities on both sides of the Rio Grande led to a reduction of border raiding. Cortina was commissioned as a general in the Mexican army and was stationed far from the border in Mexico City. By 1878, after more than 40 years of almost continuous friction and warfare, the Anglo Americans had established an uneasy control over the land between the Nueces River and the Rio Grande and over the Mexican American people who lived there.

The next three decades were relatively quiet along the Rio Grande. But if this period seemed to be one of accommodation, the hatreds and antagonisms smoldered at its very surface. Violent group conflict was always a possibility and was frequently a reality. Various incidents—shootings, lynchings, beatings, and so on—continued. Each incident usually led to some form of retaliation from the injured side, which only aggravated the matter further. Relations between the Mexican Americans and the Texas Rangers, in particular, were very poor (Acuña 1981:25–29). In the years to come, the Rangers increasingly were viewed by Mexican Americans as an official expression of hatred against them. The period of relative quiet was brought to an end by political and economic troubles. There was mounting opposition to the repressive regime of the dictator Porfírio Díaz, until he was overthrown by liberal revolutionaries in 1911. The new government was short lived, however; and the following period of conflict kept the border in a state of agitation.

Angered by the diplomatic recognition of the new revolutionary Mexican government by the United States, Francisco "Pancho" Villa began attacking Americans. When Villa crossed the border, raided Columbus, New Mexico, and killed a number of Americans, President Woodrow Wilson sent General John J. "Blackjack" Pershing into Mexico to capture Villa. Pershing searched for Villa for 9 months but returned home empty handed. The years of revolution in Mexico and the border crossings by Villa and Pershing severely damaged the relations between Mexico and the United States. They also fanned the flames of distrust, hatred, and violence that had existed for so long between the Mexican Americans and Anglos. Quite clearly, the period of apparent accommodation between Mexican Americans and Anglos had ended.

The "reversion" to an earlier stage in Park's race cycle, that of intergroup conflict, is a dramatic illustration of the point that the experience of the Mexican Americans has differed fundamentally from that of the European minorities. The periodic eruption of organized conflict between Mexican Americans and Anglos poses a serious challenge to the central ideas of the assimilationist perspective and suggests that a perspective that includes the colonialist view may be more appropriate for analyzing the incorporation experiences of this group.

A defense of the assimilationist view of the Mexican American experience, however, concerns the question of *when* the analysis actually should begin. Although it is undeniable that the Mexican Americans were in the borderlands for more than three centuries before this territory was annexed by the United States, the critics of colonial theory are more impressed by a series of events that coincided with the peak of the second immigrant stream from Europe. These events laid the groundwork for arguing that the Mexican Americans, though initially Americans through conquest, are nevertheless similar in most essential respects to the Europeans of the second stream. We turn now to the basic ideas of this contention.

The Immigrant Model

How can a comparison of the Mexican Americans to the immigrants of the second stream be valid? The basic argument is this: Although the Mexican Americans occupied the Southwest long before the Anglos, comparatively few of them resided on the American side of the border prior to 1900. For nearly 50 years after the signing of the Treaty of Guadalupe Hidalgo, relatively few Mexican nationals moved to the United States with the intention of becoming permanent residents. An unknown but probably large number of people did move back and forth across the border in search of work. At this time, however, such movements were mainly informal; few records were kept. For one period, in fact, between 1886 and 1893, there are no official records of immigration from Mexico into the United States.

In a way, this is not so strange. The first major federal law restricting immigration was not enacted until 1882. America's policy had been to have an "open door" to the world, to encourage people to move to the United States and share the labors (and rewards) of developing the continent. Even when the attention of the nation did turn to immigration, the main focus of debate was the second immigrant stream and the "yellow peril" from Asia, not people from Mexico. After the Chinese Exclusion Act was passed and later was made permanent, there still was little concern about the immigration of Mexicans. United States policy toward Mexico remained unrestrictive. The border patrol did not begin operations until 1924, and its first efforts to control immigration from Mexico, paradoxically, seem to have been directed primarily against the Chinese (Grebler, Moore, and Guzman 1970:519). Mexicans continued to cross into the United States legally and with ease. For most practical purposes, a Mexican national could enter the United States (at a small fee) simply by obtaining permission at a border station. Still, as had been true since the end of the Mexican–American War, the flow of legal immigrants was only a trickle. Less than 14,000 entrants were counted during the entire last half of the nineteenth century.

Beginning with 1904, however, the number of entrants from Mexico began to rise substantially (see Table 8.1). The rapid expansion and growing scale of the agricultural, mining, transportation, and construction sectors of the southwestern economy required a massive infusion of labor. The official count during this period appears greatly to understate the actual rate at which Mexicans were entering and remaining in the United States. One official report estimated that "at least 50,000 'nonstatistical' aliens" arrived in "normal" years (Gómez-Quiñones 1974:84). Another estimate suggested the figure may have reached 100,000 (Bryan 1972:334). No one can be sure, of course, how many of those who entered in a nonimmigrant status then became permanent residents of the United States; but it seems certain that a great many did.

The sudden sizable flow of immigrants from Mexico during the first decade of the twentieth century was greatly exceeded during the second decade, but a still greater wave of Mexican immigrants came during the 1921–1930 period. During this period, the composition of the Mexican American population was transformed. Before 1900, most Mexican Americans either had been among those conquered in the Mexican–American War or were their descendants. From this standpoint, the Mexican immigrants of the period after 1900 were in many respects the first generation—entering more or less voluntarily—of what has become our nation's largest minority. From this standpoint also, just barely enough time has passed to test the three-generations hypothesis in regard to those who arrived after 1900. The modern Mexican Americans are predominantly either Mexican nationals, who have entered the United States since 1900, or their descendants. From an assimilationist perspective, therefore, the reason they have seemed

TABLE 8.1   Mexican Immigration to the United States, 1820–2000

Years	Number
1820–1830	4,818
1831–1840	6.599
1841–1850	3,271
1851–1860	3,078
1861–1870	2,191
1871–1880	5,162
1881–1890	1,913
1891–1900	971
1901–1910	49,642
1911–1920	219,004
1921–1930	459,287
1931–1940	22,319
1941–1950	60,589
1951–1960	299,811
1961–1970	453,937
1971–1980	640,294
1981–1990	1,655,843
1991–2000	2,249,421
Total	6,138,150

Source: U.S. Immigration and Naturalization Service, *Statistical Yearbook of the Immigration and Naturalization Service, 1998,* 2001:20–22; U.S. Immigration and Naturalization Service, *Statistical Yearbook of the Immigration and Naturalization Service, 2000,* 2002:19–22.

slow to assimilate is that Mexicans are comparatively recent immigrants. They are not, strictly speaking, people who "got here first"; and they have not had as long to adopt the "American way" as those who arrived in the United States before 1900. In short, the immigrant model downgrades the significance for the process of assimilation of the "historical primacy" of the Mexican Americans.

Alvarez (1985) argued that this application of the immigrant model is not valid. Even though, technically, those who have moved from Mexico to the United States since 1900 are "immigrants," is it reasonable to say that people have emigrated when they move from one side of a politically arbitrary (and mostly imaginary) border into a territory that previously had been a part of their homeland, with which they have maintained continuous contact, and in which their native culture still flourishes? In addition to the similarities between their homes and the U.S. portion of the borderlands, the hardships of immigration were buffered for many Mexicans because they were able to live transnational lives. Many people lived and worked in the United States part of the year and returned to Mexico the rest of the year. Others crossed the border regularly to work.

Alvarez (1985) presented two main reasons to consider that it is more accurate to say the people in this movement were migrants rather than immigrants. First, it is hard to believe, he maintained, that the psychological impact of moving across the U.S.–Mexican border would be similar to that of leaving Europe for America. In most instances, the European immigrants realized that they were leaving the Old Country for a long time, possibly for good, that they would arrive in a very different and strange land, and that their children would grow up under quite new social conditions. Can the same things be said of the Mexican "immigrants"? Alvarez argued that there is little reason to suppose that most of those who participated in the "immigration" from Mexico during the early part of the twentieth century thought of themselves as moving irrevocably from an old, familiar environment into a new and alien one. Mexico and the United States are physically continuous and culturally overlapping countries. Urbanization and industrialization brought many Mexicans into Southwestern cities, such as San Antonio, Houston, El Paso, and Los Angeles, where the migrants established large ethnic *barrios*. Even at considerable distances from the border, Spanish has continued to be the primary language spoken by many Mexican Americans and numerous Spanish words and terms have found their way into the vocabularies of the Anglo Americans. In short, the presence of these familiar cultural elements almost surely has served further to modify the Mexican's "immigration" experience. It seems unlikely that they have felt unalterably separated from their native land, as have so many other immigrants. Rather it seems more likely that Mexicans have felt right at home in the Southwest and have not felt, or could more easily resist, the usual pressure that is placed on immigrants to become "Americans."[8]

A second reason offered by Alvarez for regarding those who moved from Mexico to the United States after 1900 to be simply migrants rather than immigrants stems directly from the colonial model itself. Whatever may be concluded concerning the attitudes and reactions of the post-1900 Mexican newcomers, the relationship of this group to the host society was still strongly influenced by the fact that the Creation Generation were a conquered people in their own land. Even if we assume that the Mexicans who came to the United States after 1900 did regard the change as large and permanent, and even if they did feel that they were foreigners in the United States, they still could not assume the "normal" status of immigrants. The host society did not distinguish between the "colonized" Mexicans and the "immigrant" Mexicans. The latter group could not function as immigrants because they were forced into the same kinds of jobs, housing, and subservience as the former. As Alvarez (1985:43) stated, "Socio-psychologically, the migrants, too, were a conquered people." From this perspective, Mexicans who came to the United States as part of the **"Migrant Generation"**—and even those who have come since 1930—merely joined the ranks of the existing colonized Mexican American minority (Alvarez 1985:39). From this standpoint, the similarities between Mexican "immigration" and European immigration are superficial.

Our comparison of the colonial and immigrant models shows that each emphasizes different aspects of the history of Anglo and Mexican American relations. Many of the most important facts are not in question. It is true, as is stressed in the colonial account, that (1) the Mexicans occupied the borderlands hundreds of years before the

Anglo Americans arrived and, thus, may claim historical primacy; (2) the Anglo Americans, through the annexation of Texas and the Mexican–American War, forced Mexico to cede the Spanish Southwest; (3) the relations between the Mexican Americans and Anglos in the borderlands have been filled with more tension and conflict than usually has been the case for immigrant minorities; and (4) the processes of assimilation have not produced as much change among the Mexican Americans as one would expect to occur in an immigrant population during a period of over 150 years. But it also is true that the great majority of the Mexican American population is comprised of people who have entered the United States from Mexico since 1900 and their descendants. It may be possible, therefore, if one starts the analysis with the Migrant Generation of the early 1900s rather than with the Creation Generation of 1848, that the processes of assimilation may be operating among the Mexican Americans in a fairly "normal" way. To help evaluate these clashing interpretations, let us review some of the main features of the Mexican American experience since 1900.

Mexican Immigration and Native Reaction

We have seen that a combination of social turmoil in Mexico and economic opportunities in the United States led to a sharp rise in Mexican immigration during the first decade of the twentieth century.[9] The Mexicans' opportunities for work, as already stated, were mainly in the hard, dirty, and poorly paid jobs in railroading, mining, and agriculture. The work conditions experienced by large numbers of Mexicans and Mexican Americans in these three industries during the early portions of the twentieth century had a lasting effect on the Mexican American community. Railroad work, which was the main kind at first, helped to take significant numbers of Mexicans out of the Southwest into other parts of the United States. In many instances, railroad crews completed their jobs far from the border area and were forced to accept other jobs wherever they happened to be. Many Mexican American communities outside the Southwest started in this way (Gómez-Quiñones 1974:88; Kerr 1977:294).

The movement of Mexican labor into agricultural work was stimulated by America's entry into World War I. In California, the demand for workers in the citrus, melon, tomato, and other industries increased sharply, encouraging Mexicans to come across the border to perform these necessary tasks. The other southwestern states were similarly affected. Workers were needed in Texas to tend the cotton, spinach, and onion crops and in Arizona, New Mexico, and Colorado to raise vegetables, forage crops, and sugar beets (Reisler 1976:77–100). From the beginning, these forms of labor were "seasonal, migratory, and on a contract basis" (Gómez-Quiñones 1974:89). To meet this increased demand for "stoop" labor, the Commissioner of Immigration and Naturalization approved, in 1917, some special regulations to permit Mexican farm workers to enter the United States in large numbers. Although the regulations soon were modified to permit temporary workers from Mexico also to fill jobs in railroad maintenance and mining, the "invasion" of agricultural work by both temporary and permanent immigrants from Mexico was the most prominent result.[10] The events of this period stamped into the public's mind a stereotype of the Mexicans and Mexican Americans as agricultural workers.

As noted previously, the increasingly large migration of Mexicans to the United States during this time was not a topic of general concern or debate. Even though the Mexican migration reached its peak in 1924—the same year in which the Immigration Act established the quota restrictions on European immigration and excluded the Japanese—the open-door policy remained in effect for Mexicans. The new law, in fact, contained provisions that made it possible for a Mexican immigrant to work on the American side of the border during the day but to stay at his or her residence in Mexico during the night (Moore 1976:48). Moreover, as the open door began to close on people of many other nationalities, cheap labor from Mexico became even more attractive to employers in the United States; consequently, Mexican immigration jumped sharply during the 1920s both in absolute numbers and as a proportion of the total of all immigration to this country (Grebler, Moore, and Guzman 1970:64).

The mutual attraction of Mexican labor and American employers, however, began to subside shortly after the immigration restrictions on other nationalities went into effect. Both because the Mexican immigration became so large and the agricultural sector of the American economy went into a downturn, Mexican immigration now became a subject of national controversy. Predictably, the demand arose to extend the quota system established in 1924 to cover Mexicans. To support this demand, some of the restrictionists used racist stereotypes to support their claims that the Mexicans were socially undesirable. A Texas congressman referred to them as "illiterate, unclean, peonized masses" who are a "mixture of Mediterranean-blooded Spanish peasants with low grade Indians" (Moore and Pachon 1985:136). As things developed, however, no extension of the restrictive legislation was needed.

The flow of Mexican immigration was dampened in the late 1920s when the United States discontinued the practice of issuing permanent visas at the border stations and instead now required applicants to file at an American consulate.[11] Under these circumstances, many people preferred to cross the border illegally to avoid the cost of waiting at the border, as well as the possibility that they would not be admitted. Of course, once these undocumented people reached the United States, they were fugitives and were in no position to insist on ethical treatment or to stand upon legal rights. As a result, they frequently fell prey to the unscrupulous and discriminatory acts of labor contractors, employers, and underworld businesses. The life of the migratory or contract laborers also became harsher because they often were regarded with special hostility and suspicion by Mexican Americans as well as Anglo Americans, who feared that the uncontrolled entrance of Mexican laborers to the United States would depress working conditions.

The Great Depression

Although Mexican immigration appeared to be tapering off in the face of these control measures, a dramatic reduction in the flow followed the great financial crisis of 1929. The immediate and primary cause of this decline, of course, was the sharp reduction in employment opportunities. The prospects were so unattractive, indeed, that the Mexican immigration of 1931 fell below 4,000 for the first time since 1907. The annual number of new arrivals fell even further in the subsequent years of the 1930s and did not begin to recover noticeably until the beginning of World War II.

In addition to the fact that the Great Depression made the United States a less attractive destination for migrants, there was another development of special importance. Many groups and officials within the United States sought to decrease unemployment and the costs of government welfare by deporting Mexican aliens (Hoffman 1974). Some aliens, as in the previous periods, had returned voluntarily to Mexico when their jobs dried up, but many had not; and the border patrol increased its efforts to locate and deport people who had become public charges or were in the United States illegally. At the same time, the authorities in many American cities found that it was much less expensive to pay the transportation and other costs of sending people to Mexico than it was to maintain them on welfare rolls.[12] These combined national and local efforts to save money by "sending the Mexicans home" were in some ways a preview of the evacuation of the Japanese and Japanese Americans. As in the case of the later "roundup" of the Japanese, little attention was paid either to the preferences of the evacuees or to their legal status (Moore and Pachon 1985:137). Mexicans who were naturalized citizens frequently were deported along with Mexican nationals. Many native Americans of Mexican ancestry were scrutinized closely and were intimidated by the prospect of "**repatriation.**" In some cases, families were broken apart when the Mexican father was sent "home," while his American-born children remained behind.

The entire repatriation program emphasized to the Mexican American community just how vulnerable they were to the actions, sometimes whimsical, of government officials. In some instances, the deportations spread panic within the *barrios*. People became afraid that if they applied for relief they would be sent to Mexico. As a result, it is quite possible that many people who were eligible for relief did not apply. McWilliams (1972:386) indicated that more than 200,000 Mexicans left the United States during a 12-month period of 1931–1932 alone, while Grebler, Moore, and Guzman (1970:526) stated that the Mexican-born population of the United States declined during the 1930s from 639,000 to around 377,000. More important, though, than the sheer number of deportations is that American citizens of Mexican heritage were shown dramatically that they were not necessarily considered to be full-fledged citizens. As long as there was a shortage of cheap labor, the "Mexicans" were welcomed and praised as cooperative, uncomplaining workers; but when economic times were bad, American officials wanted the "Mexicans" to go "home."

The *Bracero Program*

World War II created a manpower emergency in the United States, leading the American and Mexican governments to negotiate a "guest worker" program for farm laborers to enter the United States. Despite Mexico's insistence on stringent protections for the workers—such as free transportation and food; guarantees concerning wages, working conditions, and housing; and the right of Mexican officials to make inspections and to investigate workers' complaints—many problems arose. For instance, U.S. growers and ranchers found they could save time and money by hiring undocumented workers rather than *braceros,* and many Mexican workers also found it to be more convenient to be undocumented workers. As a result, the undocumented workers and *braceros* were often receiving different wages and benefits while working together in the same fields (Grebler, Moore, and Guzman 1970:67). This situation led the border patrol to increase its efforts to locate, arrest, and deport undocumented workers, culminating during 1954–1955 in a highly publicized roundup called "Operation Wetback" (Reimers 1985:56). Such actions by officers in the United States created frictions between the Mexican and U.S. governments.

Another important feature of the **Bracero Program** was that it gave the Mexican government a firm basis on which to protest acts of discrimination against Mexican Americans as well as against *braceros*. For example, because the practice of establishing segregated "Mexican" schools existed throughout the state of Texas, the Mexican government issued a formal protest against this practice. Other incidents of discrimination also aroused the anger of Mexican officials. One of these occurred when Sergeant Macario Garcia, a winner of the Congressional Medal of Honor, ordered a cup of coffee in a cafe in Sugar Land, Texas, and was refused service. A fight developed, and Sergeant Garcia was arrested on a charge of aggravated assault (McWilliams 1973:261). In another incident, a Mexican American PTA group in Melvin, Texas, was refused a permit to use a community center building. These and many other cases of overt or probable discrimination against Mexican Americans, as well as Mexicans, led the Mexican government in 1943 to halt the *Bracero Program* in Texas. This action led Governor Coke Stevenson of Texas to make a goodwill tour of Mexico, to proclaim a good neighbor policy for Texas, and to appoint a Good Neighbor Commission (McWilliams 1973:270). But these efforts, as well as some others on the local level, failed to satisfy the Mexican government, and the *Bracero Program* was not resumed in Texas during World War II.

The Zoot-Suit Riots

The problem of discrimination against Mexican Americans during World War II was by no means restricted to Texas. Certain events that took place in the Los Angeles, California, area during this period were at least equally alarming and may have had a more lasting effect on the relations of Anglos and Mexican Americans. At about the same time the Japanese were being evacuated and interned, the **Zoot-Suit Riots** were given wide publicity in the Los Angeles newspapers. According to Mazon (1984:1), the Zoot-Suit Riots, which occurred June 3–13, 1943, "were not about zoot-suiters rioting, and they were not, in any conventional sense of the word, 'riots.' No one was killed. No one sustained massive injuries. Property damage was slight." These disorders may be described as a series of mob attacks by off-duty policemen, U.S. sailors, and other servicemen directed mainly at Mexican Americans who called themselves *pachucos* and wore zoot suits. The zoot-suit look included pants with full trousers and a waist extended high to the chest, a broad-shouldered jacket, long ducktail haircuts, and pointed shoes. Probably of greater importance though, the zoot suits flaunted the distinctiveness of being Mexican American, pride in the Mexican heritage, and resentment of the racism of the dominant group (Romo 1983:166). The zoot suit was an international phenomenon worn by street traders in London and associated with American gangsters. This dress style gained notoriety among fad-conscious adolescents and was popularized in Harlem among Blacks. The Mexican American zoot-suiters, alien to both Mexican and American cultures and fluent in neither Spanish nor English, were the antithesis of the servicemen and were met with anger and shock by the dominant society.

The summers of 1942 and 1943 witnessed two particularly notable events involving zoot-suiters. The first of these centered on the mysterious death of a young Mexican American, José Díaz, following a fight between two rival gangs near an East Los Angeles swimming hole. The press coverage of this event was described by McWilliams (1973:229) as "an enormous web of melodramatic fancy." The gravel pit near which the gang fight occurred was referred to as "The Sleepy Lagoon," and the newspapers emphasized that the case involved Mexican Americans. Twenty-two young men of a 38th-Street gang were arrested and charged with conspiracy to commit murder. Following a trial, called the **Sleepy Lagoon Trial,** that lasted several months, three of these young men were convicted of first-degree murder, nine were convicted of second-degree murder, five were convicted of lesser offenses, and five were acquitted (Romo 1983:166). The convictions were appealed by an organization of East Los Angeles citizens on the grounds that the trial had been conducted in a biased and improper way, in an atmosphere of sensationalism. The prosecution had played on the fact that the defendants were of Mexican heritage, had ducktail haircuts, and wore zoot suits. These improper tactics were criticized by the appeals court, which overturned the lower court's decision. After nearly 2 years of imprisonment, the defendents were released "for lack of evidence" (McWilliams 1973:231). Although this outcome was viewed as a great victory for justice and the Mexican American community, the fact still remains that 17 young men served prison sentences for a crime they were not proven to have committed. Their crime, it seems, was that they were Mexican Americans.

The Sleepy Lagoon Trial, conducted as it was during the period of the Japanese internment and with generous press coverage, strengthened the impression held by many people that the Mexican Americans were "just naturally" criminals. The supposed natural link between Mexicanness and criminality seemed to receive official support shortly after the arrest of the Sleepy Lagoon defendants. Captain E. D. Ayres of the Los Angeles Sheriff's Office presented to the grand jury a report of the results of his investigation of what was considered to be the "problem of Mexican delinquency." Captain Ayres's suppositions, conclusions, and chain of reasoning sounded much like those presented by General DeWitt to justify the wartime treatment of the Japanese. In Captain Ayres's view, those of Mexican ancestry are more likely to engage in violent crimes than Anglos because such behavior is an "inborn characteristic." Anglo youths, said Captain Ayres, may use their fists or kick when they fight, but the "Mexican element" feels "a desire to use a knife or some lethal weapon . . . his desire is to kill, or at least let blood" (McWilliams 1973:234). Such opinions, presented by a police official during these tense days, could hardly have increased the dominant group's understanding of the underlying causes of the behavior of the *pachucos.* The answer lay in an entirely different direction. As noted by Sanchez (1972:410), the *pachuco* movement grew not out of the violent nature of the

Spanish-speaking people but from the discriminatory social and economic situation in which the Mexican Americans lived. Nevertheless, the stereotype of the naturally violent *pachuco* gangster was apparently widely believed.

The publicity surrounding the Sleepy Lagoon Trial, the presentation of the Ayres Report, and numerous contacts between the police and *pachuco* fighting gangs prepared the way for the Zoot-Suit Riots (Mazon 1984). Mexican youths wearing zoot suits had gradually come to represent for many members of the dominant group an open defiance of constituted authority, and the zoot suit itself became a symbol of moral degradation; consequently, those who wore them appeared to many to be enemies of the state who needed to be "taught a lesson."

There had been some intermittent fighting during this time between the "zooters" and sailors and marines who were stationed near the East Los Angeles *barrio*. The servicemen considered the *pachucos* to be draft dodgers, and the Mexican Americans resented the servicemen's frequent visits to their neighborhood (Romo 1983:167). Widespread violence between the servicemen and the "zooters" began when a group of sailors was beaten up, allegedly by a gang of Mexican Americans, while they were walking through the *barrio* area. On the following night, about 200 sailors "invaded" East Los Angeles in a caravan of some 20 taxicabs. On their way, they stopped several times to beat severely at least four Mexican American youths wearing zoot suits. In the following days, the local newspapers featured reports concerning violence (and threats of violence) between servicemen and "zooters." By June 7, the numbers of people engaged in the disorders had swelled into the thousands. Throughout all of this, the Los Angeles Police Department reportedly took few steps to curb the activities of the servicemen and, for the most part, seemed to avoid the areas in which violence was occurring until after the conflict was over. In some cases, the police simply followed along behind the servicemen to arrest the Mexican Americans who had been attacked! The disorders were not brought under control until the military authorities intervened. Servicemen were ordered to stay out of downtown Los Angeles and the *barrio,* and the order was enforced by the shore patrol and military police.[13]

There can be little doubt that many members of the Anglo American group subscribed to the theory of innate criminality among Mexican Americans and more or less openly approved of the efforts of the servicemen to "clean out" the "zooters." It seems clear, too, that the zoot suit itself became a hated symbol of Mexican American solidarity and defiance. In a large number of instances, the servicemen stripped the suits from their victims and ripped them apart. An official view of all this was illustrated dramatically when the Los Angeles City Council declared that it was a misdemeanor to wear a zoot suit (McWilliams 1973:245–250).

The repercussions of the Sleepy Lagoon Trial and the Zoot-Suit Riots were felt throughout the United States as well as abroad. The disorders were headline news in newspapers all over the United States. Zoot-suit and other race-related conflicts broke out in several other cities across the United States following the Los Angeles disorders. And just as the incidents of discrimination against Mexican Americans in Texas had led the government of Mexico to end the *Bracero Program,* the ambassador from Mexico asked for an official explanation of the Zoot-Suit Riots. The explanation—that there was no prejudice or discrimination against people of Mexican ancestry—was hardly convincing. The war effort of the United States had been damaged; the allies of the United States had been given yet another reason to wonder about the strength of this country's commitment to racial and ethnic equality; and the enemies of the United States had been given a powerful weapon of propaganda that they did not hesitate to employ.

The Mexican American Civil Rights Movement

During all this time, Mexican American youths (and even some noncitizen aliens) were subject to the wartime military draft in the United States (Scott 1974:134). Considering the level of discrimination against these young men at the time, they seemed more eager to serve and fight for the United States than might have been expected. As in the case of The Nisei, the displacements and humiliations experienced by the Mexican Americans during the early war years appeared generally to heighten their desire to prove their loyalty and worth rather than the reverse. As a result, a disproportionately high number of Mexican Americans served in the armed forces. They also comprised a disproportionately high share of the casualty lists and were frequently cited for their outstanding fighting qualities and contributions to the war effort. The first Congressional Medal of Honor awarded to a drafted enlisted man during World War II went to José P. Martinez of Los Angeles. Altogether, 39 Mexican Americans received the Congressional Medal of Honor (Scott 1974:140). Although in the early days of the war Mexican American servicemen frequently had been shunned or harassed by other servicemen as disloyal, undisciplined *pachucos,* their valor earned them acceptance on equal terms.

On this basis, Mexican Americans fully expected their position in civilian life after the war to be far better than it had been before the war. Their return to civilian life, however, was marked by bitter disappointment. They found mainly that the prejudices and the various forms of discrimination they had encountered before the war remained. They still might be refused service in a restaurant, they still had difficulty obtaining work outside of the occupations that traditionally had been assigned to them, and they still saw that the young people of **La Raza** typically attended segregated schools (Scott 1974:141). The reality of the continuation of prejudice and discrimination against them came as a severe shock to many returning veterans. Despite their loyal and costly services to the country, they remained second-class citizens. This discovery jolted not only the Mexican American veterans but their friends and families as well. Since the entire Mexican American community was affected, an increased awareness of their collective problem as a minority group was stimulated. Hence, in the period since World War II—and especially the 1960s—Mexican Americans launched a distinct phase of the civil rights movement. This movement was marked by a sharp increase in organized political and protest activities by Mexican Americans in all of the main sectors of American life.

For roughly 75 years after the end of the war between Mexico and the United States, Mexican Americans in the Southwest contended with segregation in the public schools; segregation and discrimination in public facilities such as restaurants, movie theaters, swimming pools, and barbershops; primary election procedures that prevented them from exercising their right to vote; and discrimination in housing. They also suffered discrimination in the administration of justice that prevented them from serving on juries and treated violence against them as so common as to pass almost unnoticed (Garcia 1989:27). Mexicans had long protested discrimination in the United States through mutual-aid societies and the Mexican consulates, but a growing middle class of Mexican Americans began to think about integration into the American political system. The most famous and successful organization of Mexican Americans—the League of United Latin-American Citizens (LULAC)—was formed in 1929. LULAC emphasized both assimilation and the elimination of discrimination. Its leaders felt it was the duty of Mexican Americans to develop "true and loyal" citizens of the United States (Cuéllar 1970:143; Garcia 1989:30; Marquez 1987). LULAC members reaffirmed the need to maintain bilingualism, but voted English as the organization's official language and to exclude Mexican nationals. We should not be surprised to learn, however, that even with these principles and the presumably uncontroversial goal of developing "the best, purest and most perfect type of a true and loyal citizen of the United States of America" (Garcia 1989:31), LULAC aroused the fear in some Anglo Americans that the "Mexicans" were forgetting "their place."

The years of World War II brought significant changes in the Mexican American community. In the first place, as noted earlier, a large number of Mexican Americans served in the armed forces. This experience permitted them to work side by side with Americans from different regions of the country and from different socioeconomic origins. In the process, they learned a great deal about the opportunities and privileges that most American citizens took for granted. These veterans felt "completely American." As such, they were unwilling to think of themselves as "Mexican" or to accept the inferior status generally accorded Mexicans. As expressed by Alvarez (1985:44), they were more likely to argue, "I am an 'American' who happens to be of Mexican descent. I am going to participate fully in this society because, like descendants of people from so many other lands, I was born here." In short, they accepted the immigrant model.

The war years did more than solidify the servicemen's acceptance of American identity, however. The events of the war accelerated the movement of Mexican Americans into the cities. As a result, this traditionally rural population was brought into a more extensive and intimate contact with the Anglo Americans. Large numbers of these migrants were exposed to even more overt forms of discrimination than they had learned was customary—for example, the Zoot-Suit Riots. They learned in this way that the opportunities of the city, attractive though they were in many cases, were nonetheless severely limited for "Mexicans."

The combination of continued, and even increased, discrimination against Mexican Americans on the home front and the new expectations of the returning servicemen set the stage for the emergence of some new, more aggressive, political and social organizations following the war. In the immediate postwar years, one such organization, the Community Service Organization (CSO), was formed in California; another, the G.I. Forum, was formed in Texas. Both of these groups have sought to represent the interests of Mexican Americans on a wide social, economic, and political front (Allsup 1982). As the decade of the 1950s drew to a close, however, some Mexican Americans came to feel that organizations like LULAC, CSO, and the G.I. Forum were not pressing vigorously enough for equal rights. They thought, too, that the established organizations were not pursuing the correct strategy in the political arena. For these reasons, the Mexican American Political Association (MAPA), the Mexican American Youth Organization (MAYO), and the Political Association of Spanish-Speaking Organizations (PASO) were formed with the intention of putting direct pressure on the major political parties, including the nomination or appointment of their members to public office. A spectacular example of the success of this approach may be seen in the election of Mexican Americans to various offices in Crystal City, Texas.[14] These separate efforts were thought of as part of a larger movement, *La Causa* (Valdez 1982:271).

Another organization, The United Farm Workers Union (UFW), organized in California in 1962 by César Chavez and Dolores Huerta, was instrumental in publicizing the plight of Mexican Americans to a national public. Originally begun as an effort to gain collective bargaining rights and union recognition for Mexican American and Filipino farmworkers in California, the movement used nonviolent tactics and "emotionally charged ethnic symbols" such as a stylized black Aztec eagle flag and images of the Mexican Virgin of Guadalupe to attract members and publicity (Gutiérrez 1995:196). The UFW protested the use of undocumented Mexican workers to break strikes by American citizens and urged the repeal of the *Bracero Program*. This stand against immigration was criticized by other Chicano and Mexican American groups, and by the mid-1970s the UFW and other Mexican American organizations expressed solidarity on the immigration controversy arguing that many Mexican Americans would not be in the United States "if their fathers had not been illegal aliens" (Gutiérrez 1995:199). Many of the more conservative Mexican American organizations and the Chicano advocates became more united in the late 1970s as they focused on policies to regulate immigration. The groups feared that the negative feelings toward Mexican immigration would once again "open the door to discrimination against anyone who looked Latino" (Gutiérrez 1995:195).

In the late 1960s, Mexican American organizations turned to litigation as an instrument for political mobilization and incorporation. The Mexican American Legal Defense and Education Fund (MALDEF), established in 1967 by two attorneys, Pete Tijerina and Gregory Luna, with the help of the African American civil rights organizations and funding from the Ford Foundation, initiated an organized legal attack against the continued segregation of Mexican American students in schools. A series of cases were filed in the late 1960s and the 1970s demanding the desegregation of schools in the Texas cities of Houston, Dallas, El Paso, Del Rio, and New Braunfels, and in Portales, New Mexico, and Denver, Colorado. MALDEF also extended provisions of the Voting Rights Acts of 1965 and 1970 to the Mexican American community by challenging the political practice of using multimember voting districts that denied Mexican Americans representation in city and county elections in Texas and California. The *United States v. Texas Bilingual* case initiated by MALDEF in 1981 made Texas school districts implement bilingual programs and required the state to enforce the decision and evaluate the programs. In 1982 MALDEF won the *Plyler v. Doe* case in the U.S. Supreme Court, a decision that determined it was unconstitutional for school districts to deny a free public education to undocumented immigrant children. Extending the struggle for improved educational opportunities, MALDEF filed the *Edgewood v. Kirby* case in 1984 that, when it was finally won in 1991, reformed the Texas school finance system by making the distribution of money for schools more equitable. The *Edgewood* case moved more money toward school districts with a poor tax base and high concentrations of Mexican American youth. In 1992, MALDEF won the *LULAC v. Richards* case that declared the system of financing higher education in Texas unconstitutional. Although the decision was reversed by the Texas Supreme Court in 1993, the case resulted in changes in the ways all universities and professional schools were funded in Texas and doubled the budgets for universities serving geographic areas with high concentrations of Mexican American students. The efforts of MALDEF and other community-based organizations to serve as advocates for Mexican American interests, train leaders, and register voters helped reduce structural barriers to assimilation. At the same time, these struggles heightened the consciousness of Mexican Americans regarding their ethnic identity and sense of community.

The Post-Chicano Era

As many of the Chicano activists have moved into the middle class, the push for cultural nationalism has largely subsided, although there continues to be strong advocacy for structural assimilation (Richardson 1999). Richardson conducted a large study of the border area in Texas and found strong evidence of both pluralism and cultural assimilation among Mexican Americans in South Texas. In the "post-Chicano era" social behavior and attitudes were closely related to social class. For example, wealthy Mexican immigrants were much less likely to report prejudice and discrimination from Anglos than were lower-income Mexicans. Although many Mexican immigrants reported some difficulties with Mexican Americans, they felt more acceptance and less prejudice from them than from Anglos. Young people found the lifestyle of the United States appealing, but proximity to Mexico and the constant contact with Mexico, Mexican immigrants, and Mexican shoppers were counterpressures to maintain elements of Mexican culture. Many Anglos and Mexican Americans in South Texas had no problems with a mixed identity; Mexican Americans especially felt a strong cultural loyalty to the United States but maintained a cultural identity that was neither Mexican nor Anglo. Richardson called South Texas a "stirring pot" (Richardson 1999:244), an area in which many diverse groups give, take, and create new culture; they participate in a central culture, but retain basic elements of their own. Anglos, Blacks, Mexican Americans, and Mexicans recognized the importance of learning both English and Spanish. Richardson concluded that the Anglo culture was enriched, not destroyed by this pluralism. The younger generations knew little about the historical border conflicts and segregation, looked past the discrimination, and participated in the many cultures present in the area.

We may summarize by saying that the prominent early Mexican American organizations moved gingerly into the political arena. They took great pains to reassure Anglo Americans that they only wanted to make Mexican Americans into "better" (i.e., more Anglicized) citizens. As time passed, different organizations formed for the purpose of placing greater pressure on the dominant society to gain more equal treatment. In this way, a renewed emphasis on cultural nationalism emerged as a central feature of the Mexican

American movement beginning in the 1960s. The increased immigration from Mexico in the 1980s and 1990s, which has resulted in intergenerational experiences among recent Mexican immigrants and Mexican Americans, and the cultural and structural assimilation that has occurred for many Mexican Americans have brought into sharp relief many of the issues that are of greatest interest to us here. We will consider the usefulness of the colonial and immigrant models as we continue to explore the issues of assimilation as applied to the experiences of Mexican Americans and Puerto Ricans in Chapter 9.

 Reality Check

INTERVIEW WITH EDDIE

Eddie was born in El Paso, Texas, and grew up in the small town of Canyon, Texas. His grandparents did not complete elementary school. Both parents dropped out of high school. His grandfather participated in the *Bracero Program*. Eddie is a college freshman considering a social work major.

How do you refer to yourself in terms of racial or ethnic identity?
It depends on the situation. Most times I'll say "Hispanic," "Latino," "Mexican American," or "Mexican." When I first meet somebody, I don't want to go into a huge explanation about how I identify myself because that would probably just turn people off. I don't have a problem with any of those terms but it's hard to find one. With "Mexican American" or "Mexican" I feel like I'm in-between. In terms of recognizing my Mexican background it's hard to find a term that fits me. "Latino" really acknowledges the Latin American influence but there are so many Latin American backgrounds. Some say, "Well, how about Hispanic"? But "Hispanic" seems more Americanized. I'm a first-generation American citizen. My mother comes from Mexico and Spanish is my first language, but I grew up here, so my experiences are different from Mexican Americans who lived here for generations. Some things I can relate with the Mexican culture more, other things it's the Mexican American culture. Some people try to be more politically correct so they don't say "Mexican."

What stands out as most important to you about your racial/ethnic group?
The thing that stands out is the struggle we went through to get to where I am. I feel that getting where I am now is my greatest accomplishment. I look at all the things my mother has been through. They couldn't put food on the table, that's why they came over here. That instinct to survive and to be successful is the main thing I get from my background because there are a lot of people, Mexicans and Mexican American, who are really just trying to make it. That's the thing that makes me the proudest of my background.

When did you first become aware of racial and ethnic differences?
The first time I became aware on a surface level was when I was in elementary school. It was a predominantly White school, and some of the kids were calling me "Mexican, Mexican" and I didn't even know what they meant. I went crying to my mom. I guess that would be the first time I became aware of it. I was just like, "Oh, okay, I guess I'm Mexican" and that was it.

Have you ever experienced any uncomfortable situations dealing with racial/ethnic relations?
When I got older, in high school, I commented to my mom about things I saw. Mostly just sharing bad experiences. In college, there was a guy who lived in my dorm who had a confederate flag, a KKK mask, and a rope hanging on his wall. This past year, I went out with people from my dorm, and we passed a police officer. A girl commented that because I was in the car, we were going to get pulled over and stopped by cops. And there are uncomfortable situations when people try to be funny. When it comes to racial or societal jokes based on socioeconomic status, I don't think they're funny.

Tell me about your friends.
The majority of my friends are not from my background. I have African American, Indian, and Asian friends, just a variety from different backgrounds. It's beneficial because I've learned about different cultures and groups. I've noticed things I can relate to in different cultures.

Is it acceptable to marry someone outside of your ethnic racial group?
It is definitely acceptable, but I don't know if that is what I want. I would prefer to marry someone of my background, not necessarily someone who is Mexican but someone from a similar background. I experienced the Mexican culture growing up so I want my kids to have the same thing. I don't want to ignore any race, I just want my children to be able to have the same culture I had. I want them to speak Spanish. I want them to go to Mexico. I want them to identify with my grandparents.

Did you begin school speaking a language other than English?
I spoke Spanish as my first language because my mother didn't speak English. When I started school, I learned English. I wanted to have blond hair and blue eyes. During that time my mom remarried and her husband was Caucasian and it made it difficult to speak Spanish around the house. I started speaking Spanish again in high school and didn't learn to read or write Spanish until then. That's basically all I speak with my mom. I have family who don't speak English so I speak Spanish to them. Some Latinos don't know Spanish that well and some don't speak it at all, so I don't speak Spanish much on campus. I speak Spanish with the food service and gardening staff.

(continued)

Tell me about your high school.
There were about 800 people in my high school. The graduating class was 90 percent White. There were maybe two Latinos in my class, so it was really hard to segregate. There were just so many White students, you just got used to it. In high school I was definitely in the minority. I had a hard time identifying. I isolated myself in a way, like going into a shell inside of me. I withdrew from everyone else.

What experiences have you had with racial and ethnic relations on campus?
The majority of the bad experiences have had to do with socioeconomic background. The majority of the people in college are from a higher socioeconomic background than I am. Often I hear something and it bothers me. Sometimes I interject. It often has to do with socioeconomics rather than race. For example, people refer to things as being "ghetto." If something isn't done right they will say, "That's ghetto." If a car doesn't look nice, they'll say, "That's ghetto." They look down on anything that is associated with low socioeconomic status. I don't feel that it should be that way. The other night we were with a group. They left a six-dollar tip minimum and I don't just have money to give out. They'll look at me like "You're so cheap." To me it's being economical. In that group it's like you're a cheapskate and it carries a bad connotation.

Discussion Questions

Why does Eddie consider himself "in-between" Mexican and Mexican American?

In what ways has Eddie maintained his ethnic cultural identity?

How has social class affected Eddie's experiences?

Is the prejudice/discrimination Eddie has experienced a result of his ethnicity or his poverty?

Is Eddie being too sensitive about his college classmates' joking and behavior? Why or why not?

Is Eddie likely to marry someone outside of his ethnic group?

How important is it to Eddie and other Mexican Americans that their culture be strengthened and developed?

To what extent are the processes of assimilation affecting the distinctiveness and solidarity of the Mexicans and Mexican Americans?

Key Ideas

1. The relations between Mexican Americans and Anglos represent a second kind of intergroup contact. Like American Indians and African Americans, Mexican Americans originally became part of the United States through force rather than through voluntary immigration.

2. The Spanish approach to colonization differed from that of the English. A key difference was that the Spanish included the Indians in the developing colonial society, whereas the English excluded them. As a result, the Indians of Mexico have moved much further toward full assimilation than have the Indians of the United States.

3. The Mexican American group emerged out of a long series of conflicts between the United States and Spain and between the United States and Mexico. Although the Texas revolution was not based on ethnic differences, the ethnic cleavage gradually deepened following Texas's independence. The Mexican American group emerged as a distinct minority group at the end of the Mexican-American War.

4. The Treaty of Guadalupe Hidalgo did not end hostilities between the Mexican Americans and Anglos in the borderlands. Continuous struggle, marked by intermittent open conflict, was a conspicuous element of border life well into the twentieth century.

5. Although the Mexican American group was created when the United States forcibly occupied the southwestern and western lands previously owned by Mexico, most of the present members of the group are not the descendants of that "Creation Generation." The Mexican American population of the United States has grown overwhelmingly through immigration from Mexico since the beginning of the twentieth century.

6. Since Mexican immigration reached its peak later than the peak of the second immigrant stream, many social analysts think of the Mexican Americans as having begun their stay in America near the end of that stream. The apparent slowness of the group to assimilate, therefore, may be due to the comparatively recent arrival of large numbers of immigrants in the United States.

7. Opponents of the immigrant model propose that Mexicans who move to the United States are better thought of as migrants rather than immigrants. From this viewpoint, the movement of Mexicans across an arbitrary political boundary into an area that is both geographically and culturally similar to their homeland is not to be compared to movements of Europeans across oceans into a country with a much different culture. Moreover, when Mexican nationals have reached the United States, the members of the dominant group typically have greeted them with even higher levels of prejudice and discrimination than usually have been directed toward European immigrants.

8. Three widely publicized examples of dominant-group discrimination against Mexican Americans are the repatriations of the 1930s, the "Zoot-Suit Race Riots" in the

1940s, and "Operation Wetback" in the 1950s. In each of these cases, some officials of the dominant group demonstrated that they made no real distinction between Mexican American citizens and Mexican nationals. They also revealed their belief that all people of Mexican ancestry were innately inferior. Many Mexican American citizens were illegally punished through deportation, intimidation, and physical assault.

9. The *Bracero Program* illustrates how the relations of the dominant group in America to its minorities may be altered by international events.

10. World War II and the Mexican Americans' active participation in it increased the group's commitment to full rights as American citizens and led many of its members to expect a sharp decline in prejudice and discrimination following the war. When the expected changes did not occur, the Mexican Americans demanded their civil rights. Those demands have been expressed in a higher degree of formal social and political organization, legal actions, and a sharp increase in interest in the goals of cultural pluralism.

 # Key Terms

barrios   Ethnic communities with large concentrations of Spanish-speaking residents. In the southwest region of the United States these residents are usually Mexican Americans and Mexican immigrants.

borderlands   The region, originally a part of Mexico, that stretches inland from the U.S.–Mexico border to include the southwestern United States.

Bracero Program   An agreement between the U.S. government and the Mexican government to allow Mexican agricultural laborers to work in the United States.

braceros   Mexican agricultural workers who came to the United States as part of the *Bracero Program*.

Cortina Wars   A series of border raids led by Juan Cortina, a Mexican leader. These raids heightened antagonisms between the United States and Mexico.

Creation Generation   The original Mexican population who became U.S. citizens as a result of the Treaty of Guadalupe Hidalgo.

La Raza   A term used to refer to the Mexican American ethnic group.

mestizos   The mixture resulting from intermarriage of indigenous Mexican Indians and the Spanish.

Migrant Generation   The group of Mexicans who came to the United States between 1900 and 1930.

pachucos   Another term used to refer to the zoot-suiters, often associated with gang-related youth and youth rebellion against both Mexican and American cultures.

repatriation   The practice of rounding up and deporting Mexican-origin residents to Mexico. Both Mexican American citizens and immigrants were affected by the deportations.

Sleepy Lagoon Trial   A well-publicized trial of young Mexican Americans convicted of murder in Los Angeles. The case was eventually dismissed for lack of evidence and biased procedures.

Tejanos   The native Mexicans living in Texas when it broke away from Mexico to become an independent republic; also applied to all contemporary Mexican American Texans.

Treaty of Guadalupe Hidalgo   The treaty signed in 1848 between the United States and Mexico that ceded nearly one-half of the territory of Mexico to the United States. The Rio Grande was established as the boundary of Texas. Mexican citizens who resided in the territory were given the right to retain Mexican citizenship or acquire U.S. citizenship.

Zoot-Suit Riots   Confrontations between Anglo servicemen and Mexican American youths who wore distinctive outfits called zoot suits.

 Notes

1. Probably no other American ethnic group has been more absorbed by the question "What shall we call ourselves?" The members of this group vary widely in their specific histories, geographic locations, and social characteristics; a term of identification adopted by one segment of the group may be considered inaccurate or offensive by others. In addition to *Mexican American*, the terms *Chicano, Latino, Latin American, Spanish American, Spanish speaking, Hispano, Spanish surname, Mexican origin,* and *Mexicano* have been prominent as identifiers. Each has a specific connotation that distinguishes it. Government documents often use the term *Hispanic;* but it refers not only to Mexican Americans but also to Puerto Ricans, Cubans, and others of Spanish ancestry. The term *Mexican American* appears to be the most widely accepted and is used in this text to refer to all those who trace their ancestry to Mexico. For discussions of terms of self-reference see Garcia (1981), Nostrand (1973), and H. Romo and R. Romo (1985: 318–321).

2. George I. Sanchez, quoted by Grebler, Moore, and Guzman (1970:545).

3. Diseases played a very important role in the conquest. Crosby (1972:52) stated in this regard that "we have so long been hypno-tized by the daring of the conquistador that we have overlooked the importance of his biological allies."

4. Had the official policy of Spain been followed in general practice, the status of the Indians would have been higher. The Laws of the Indies, promulgated in 1542, stated that "Indians are free persons and vassals of the crown. . . . Nothing is to be taken from the Indians except in fair trade" (quoted in McNickle 1973:28).

5. Nine of the defenders killed in the Alamo were *Tejanos*.

6. An additional 54,000 square miles along the southern border of the New Mexico Territory was bought from Mexico in 1853. Moore and Pachon (1985:19) stated that "as it happened (and no Mexican thinks it accidental), the Gadsden Purchase . . . included some of the richest copper mines in the United States."

7. Pachon and Moore (1981) stated that there were around 75,000 Mexicans in the Southwest in 1848, whereas Griswold del Castillo (1990) estimated 100,000.

8. The rate of naturalization among Mexicans has been, in Moore's opinion, "extraordinarily slow" (Moore 1976:49; see also Moore and Pachon 1985:135).

9. For an analysis of some of the specific forces lying behind these broad currents, see Acuña (1981:194–206) and Barrera (1979:67–75).

10. Portes and Rumbaut (1990:17) point out that these "invasions" occur because employers in the host society are willing to hire new workers.

11. The consular officers began to apply strict standards to determine whether an applicant for a visa was likely to become a public charge in the United States (Moore and Pachon 1985:136).

12. Although Mexican labor had been brought to the United States initially to perform mainly rural tasks, by 1930 the majority of the Mexican-origin population lived in cities (see, e.g., R. Romo 1983).

13. These orders were given after the Mexican government protested and the U.S. State Department ordered the Navy to act (R. Romo 1983:167).

14. For accounts of the Mexican American movement in Crystal City, see Camejo (1973) and Gutiérrez and Hirsch (1973).

Puerto Ricans and Mexican Americans

Identity and Incorporation

*Puerto Ricans are divided over whether Puerto Rico should become
independent, become a state, or continue to be a territory of the
United States. Many Puerto Ricans believe the island's current
relationship with the United States is a continuation of colonialism
and stage vigorous protests in support of independence.*

All Puerto Ricans, regardless of actual birthplace, have been "born in the U.S.A." because all are subject to federal laws and to an imposed U.S. citizenship that was neither sought nor particularly desired.

—Clara Rodríguez

The idea that we only need one language leads to isolation and cultural arrogance. This type of thinking can lead to laws that exclude, prohibit and punish those who don't speak English. . . . It's happened before.

—Reynaldo Macias

According to the 2000 census, Latinos, who comprise 12.5 percent of the total U.S. population, now make up a larger portion of the population than African Americans who make up 12.3 percent of the total U.S. population. Latinos, however, do not constitute one homogeneous culture. Mexican-origin residents are the largest group within the Latino population at 66.9 percent. Central and South Americans, who are of many national origins, are the second largest group, comprising 14.3 percent of the Hispanic-origin population. Puerto Ricans are the third largest group, comprising 8.6 percent; other Hispanics, such as those from the Dominican Republic and Spain, comprise 5.6 percent.

Mexican immigrants and Mexican Americans, who are concentrated in the U.S. Southwest, are culturally very different from Cubans in Miami, Dominicans in Boston, or Puerto Ricans in New York City. High birth rates and continued increases in immigration from Mexico, Central and South America, and the Caribbean combine to make the Latino population one of the fastest-growing ethnic populations in the United States. Some members of these groups are achieving impressive upward economic gains, better jobs, higher levels of education, and better homes in safer neighborhoods. Others continue to experience deepening poverty and are economically and socially isolated from opportunities in the larger society. The Mexican-origin population of New York is challenging Puerto Ricans as the largest Latino population in that city.

The historic concentration of the Latino population in the U.S. Southwest, especially California and Texas, continues into the present. Since World War II, the Latino population has been highly concentrated in urban areas, particularly in the established *barrios* of the central cities in Los Angeles, Houston, San Antonio, and El Paso. Midwestern cities, such as Chicago, Illinois, and Cleveland, Ohio, have large concentrations of Latinos living in segregated inner-city neighborhoods. Increasingly, the majority of the Latino population of New York City is of Mexican origin rather than Puerto Rican. Mexican immigrants are also moving into states that have not traditionally had large Mexican-origin populations, such as Georgia, Montana, Mississippi, Indiana, Wisconsin, North and South Carolina, and Kentucky. In fact, according to the 2000 census, growth in the Hispanic population in the cities of Atlanta, Greensboro, Charlotte, Orlando, Las Vegas, and Nashville, exceeded 500 percent (Hood 2003:2).

In 2002, 40.2 percent (or 15 million) of the Hispanic population in the United States was foreign-born. Over half of this foreign-born Hispanic population entered the United States between 1990 and 2002 and another 25.6 percent came in the 1980s (Ramirez and de la Cruz 2003). The increasing national attention on Hispanics in the United States has been largely driven by the spectacular growth of this population, especially since the 1960s (Camarillo and Bonilla 2004:510). Hispanics are of interest to us because of their diversity, their attachment to the Spanish language, their various cultures, and their marked concentration in particular regions. Their experiences with colonialism and the continuing disparities in income, education, and occupations among the Hispanic subgroups as well as between Hispanics and non-Hispanic Whites raise some disquieting questions about the operation of the assimilation processes. In fact, no other American ethnic group presents such a variegated picture of mode of entry into U.S. society, racial and cultural characteristics, and levels of assimilation. The historical experiences of the Mexican Americans presented in the previous chapter—as seen through the lenses of both the colonial and immigrant models—demonstrated how important modes of entry into the United States and intergenerational differences are in understanding the processes of intergroup relations.

The largest subgroup of Hispanics, the Mexican-origin population, includes the descendants of the original Mexican settlers as well as migrants to the United States since 1900. Nevertheless, since the Mexican immigration of the twentieth century (including undocumented immigration) has continued at a high level, a large majority of the natives of native parentage are the descendants of relatively recent migrants. The proximity of Mexico and the frequent movements back and forth across the border by some members of each of the nativity and parentage groups call into question the easy assumption that each generation should be more assimilated than the preceding one. This is one reason why those who regard Mexican Americans as a colonized minority believe that intergenerational differences within their group will remain smaller than would be true for an immigrant minority.

The second-largest Hispanic subgroup, the Puerto Ricans, also represents unique migration patterns that challenge the assimilation model. Unlike Mexican immigrants and other U.S. Latinos, Puerto Ricans are native U.S. citizens, whether born within the 50 states or on the island of Puerto Rico. As citizens, their migrations from the island to the U.S. mainland and back are unrestricted by the state, and access to Puerto Rican culture on the island plays an important role in cultural maintenance. The history of the relationship of Puerto Rico to the United States is clearly one of colonialism. Puerto Ricans today continue to be affected by the colonial experience because the island is a U.S. **commonwealth.** As a commonwealth, unequal relations are maintained between the U.S. and Puerto Rican governments in economic, political, and social and cultural relationships. A major issue among Puerto Ricans is whether to maintain the island's commonwealth status, push for admission of Puerto Rico to the United States as the fifty-first state, or reject any form of U.S. incorporation and demand independence. At the heart of each of these visions for the future is how the Puerto Rican people define and maintain a distinct cultural identity. The crucial questions for us in this regard include the following: Is the ethnic culture being renewed and invigorated among the third and subsequent generations of Mexican Americans and Puerto Ricans? Do the U.S.-born children exhibit levels of cultural assimilation that are consistent with the predictions flowing from the immigrant model? Has a new, emergent culture been formed?

 Identification and Diversity

So far, we have referred to Mexican Americans and Puerto Ricans without attempting to define exactly who the members of these groups are. Mexican-origin Hispanics are the largest Hispanic group in the United States. Because Mexican Americans are dispersed over a large geographic area, because they have come into American society both through conquest and through immigration, because their immigration has been heaviest during the twentieth century, and because legal immigration has been greatly exceeded by undocumented immigration, they are an extremely heterogeneous group. Persons of Puerto Rican origin residing in the United States form the second largest Hispanic group, even when those residing in Puerto Rico are not included. If the island is included, Puerto Ricans make up approximately 11 percent of the Hispanic population (U.S. Bureau of the Census 1998b). The difficulties of making accurate generalizations about Mexican Americans or Puerto Ricans may be illustrated by considering the efforts of the U.S. Bureau of the Census to identify the members of these groups.

Before the 1930 census, people of Mexican and Puerto Rican origin were placed in the category of "Other." Beginning in 1930, the enumerators were asked to classify people on the basis of their "racial" characteristics. This was particularly confusing for Puerto Ricans because this group is racially heterogeneous, and many Black Puerto Ricans did not think in terms of Black or White racial identity (Rodríguez 1991, 1994). In 1940, the Census Bureau attempted to count the people who listed Spanish as their mother tongue, which was also problematic. The racial categorization relied on the census takers' judgment, and the "mother-tongue" approach included people from all Spanish-speaking countries. Still, these attempts did enable investigators to distinguish among the foreign born, natives of foreign or mixed parentage, and natives of native parentage.

In 1950, 1960, and 1970, the Census Bureau approached the identification of the various Hispanic subgroups in still another way. Lists of Spanish surnames were drawn up, and Mexican Americans and Puerto Ricans were identified as "white persons of Spanish surname." This way of identifying Hispanics did not recognize the mixed racial heritage of many Puerto Ricans. In 1950 approximately 23 percent of the island's population was identified as "non-White" (Santiago-Valles 1996). Additionally, many women who marry non-Hispanic husbands lose their Spanish surname, but not necessarily their Mexican American or Puerto Rican identity. Similar miscounts affect non-Hispanics who marry persons with a Spanish surname. Adding to the problem, the names of some Mexican Americans and Puerto Ricans were not listed as Spanish surnames. In the 1980 census, a special "origin or descent" question was asked that permitted people of Hispanic origin to classify themselves as "Mexican," "Mexican American," "Chicano," "Puerto Rican," "Cuban," or "other Spanish/Hispanic" (Bean and Tienda 1987:50). These categories, too, have been criticized as failing to reflect the increasing racial and ethnic diversity of the Hispanic population. In a scientifically selected sample of the 1995 Current

Population Survey (CPS), households were asked what categories and terminology they preferred. When asked about their preferred racial-group term, about 7.5 percent of the respondents chose Hispanic rather than White, Black, American Indian, Asian, or Other. When given the opportunity to identify themselves as "multiracial" in the survey, approximately 3 percent of Mexican-origin respondents and 7 percent of Puerto Rican respondents did so. When asked about their preferred ethnic-group term, 58 percent of the respondents chose "Hispanic" rather than "Latino"[1] (12 percent), "Of Spanish origin" (12 percent), "Some other term" (8 percent), or no one term (10 percent).

Despite the imperfections in classifying and counting the Mexican American and Puerto Rican population, U.S. Census Bureau reports have made possible a number of highly informative (if not completely exact) analyses concerning these ethnic groups. Using these, we may now examine the changes that are occurring in occupations, incomes, and levels of education among Hispanic subgroups and compare these with changes occurring among non-Hispanic White Americans; we may also describe some of the ways in which the various ethnic groups are becoming more or less similar. The census tabulations also enable researchers to study generational changes. However, these comparisons do not reflect completely the diversity among Hispanic Americans. Many reports continue to group Mexican, Puerto Rican, Cuban, and other populations under the broad category Hispanic. For this reason, we also rely on a number of other sources of information.

Consider some basic points about this large, diverse group. Although substantial Mexican American groups are to be found in several states outside the Southwest—mainly Illinois, New York, and Florida—in 1980 approximately 83 percent of their members lived in the five southwestern states of Arizona, California, Colorado, New Mexico, and Texas (Bean and Tienda 1987:80); hence, the special reports of the U.S. Census Bureau focus entirely on the latter states. By 1997, the Mexican-origin population had increased to about 18.7 million people (U.S. Bureau of the Census 1998a) and has continued to increase at each census period both in absolute size and as a proportion of the total population.

A majority of the U.S. Puerto Ricans live in Northeastern states and are concentrated in large urban areas. New York City has the largest Puerto Rican community in the United States with approximately 33 percent of the total mainland Puerto Rican population living there (Torrecilha, Cantú, and Nguyen 1999). Over the past three decades, there has been an increased migration and decentralization among Mexican Americans and Puerto Ricans away from these geographic centers because of changes in social and economic opportunities. Puerto Ricans have tended to migrate to smaller cities and toward California, Colorado, Texas, Florida, and North Carolina (Torrecilha, Cantú, and Nguyen 1999). Similarly, although Mexican Americans were historically concentrated in farm and rural areas, by 1979 over 80 percent of the Mexican American population was located in urban areas (Pachon and Moore 1981:116). California reported the highest proportion of urban Mexican-origin dwellers and New Mexico the lowest. The most "Mexican" metropolitan areas in the United States were Los Angeles–Long Beach, San Antonio, Houston, and Chicago (Bean and Tienda 1987:150). In 1996, the following metropolitan areas, all in Texas, had majority Hispanic populations: San Antonio, El Paso, McAllen–Edinburg–Mission, Brownsville–Harlingen–San Benito, Corpus Christi, and Laredo. In addition, metropolitan areas such as Los Angeles, Miami, Albuquerque,

Bakersfield, Salinas, and Santa Barbara all had Hispanic populations that exceeded one-third of their total populations (U.S. Bureau of the Census 1998b).

These facts highlight again two basic characteristics of the Hispanic group: It is very heterogeneous and it is concentrated in specific geographic areas, with Mexican Americans predominant in the Southwest, Puerto Ricans in the Northeast, and Cubans in the Southeast, especially in Florida. Our generalizations about these groups, therefore, must be rather tentative. With these limitations in mind, we turn to a consideration of the two largest Hispanic groups—Mexican Americans and Puerto Ricans—and their experiences with the main subprocesses of assimilation. We begin with a brief historical overview of the relationship of Puerto Rico and the United States, since we discussed the historical circumstances of Mexican-origin populations in Chapter 8.

 # The Colonization of Puerto Rico

Christopher Columbus landed on Puerto Rico in 1493, claimed the island for Spain, and named it San Juan Bautista.[2] Juan Poncé de Leon led the colonization of the island in 1508, and the population of Tainos, the Native Americans who had been living on the island, was decimated. Spain gave little attention to Puerto Rico and the island was often attacked by Spain's rivals, who desired the wealth found in the New World Spanish Empire. By the eighteenth century Puerto Rico had become a strong agricultural colony, but Spain considered the island little more than a military outpost. The population at that time consisted of about 40 thousand free persons (White and of color) and about 5,000 slaves. Independence movements throughout Latin America and a growing creole (mixed) population in Puerto Rico fostered a nationalistic movement. In 1868 rebels declared Puerto Rico a republic and eventually the island negotiated the right to elect representatives to the Spanish Parliament. However, in 1898, when the U.S. government recognized Cuba as an independent country, the Spanish government broke off relations with the United States and the United States invaded Puerto Rico. Without firing a shot, the U.S. troops raised the U.S. flag and issued a proclamation that they were bringing freedom from Spanish rule. At the peace conference, the United States demanded the cession of Puerto Rico, and the island passed from the control of Spain to the sovereignty of the United States in 1898. After 2 years of military government, the U.S. Congress, pressured by the Puerto Rican people, established a civil government for the island. The U.S. president appointed all officials, from the governor to the judges. A Chamber of Deputies and a Commissioner to the United States were to be elected directly by the islanders. The U.S. Congress reserved the right to legislate for the island and to annul any legislation passed by the Chamber. Officials ruling the island knew little about Puerto Rican culture or values and attempted to legislate "Americanization" of the Puerto Ricans. They decreed that all education was to be conduced in English, despite the fact that the people of the island spoke Spanish. It was not until 1991 that Puerto Ricans were able to vote to reestablish Spanish as their official language. In 1917, under the Jones Act, Puerto Ricans were granted U.S. citizenship, and Puerto Rican males became eligible for the military draft.

The island did not benefit economically from U.S. administration. Puerto Rican goods were taxed entering the United States and the island's economy was dominated by large sugar plantations owned by Whites. In the 1920s and 1930s a resurgence of support for independence occurred, including a violent confrontation between Nationalist Party members and the police in which 21 people were killed and over 150 were wounded. Luis Muñoz Marín founded the Popular Democratic Party in 1938 and became the first Puerto Rican governor of the island in 1949. A referendum in 1950 gave Puerto Ricans the option of continuing the status quo or creating a commonwealth government based on the British model. The people chose the commonwealth. As a commonwealth, Puerto Rico has full autonomy in internal affairs and shares with the United States a common currency, defense, market, and citizenship.

Some Puerto Rican migration to the United States occurred before the Spanish American War, but the largest migrations from the island occurred after World War II. In 1950, only about one-fourth of the 300,000 Puerto Ricans who lived in the United States had been born there. By 1990 over half (53.8 percent) of the mainland Puerto Rican population was U.S. born (Torrecilha, Cantú, and Nguyen 1999:234). U.S.-born Puerto Ricans are less likely to have problems communicating in English, to drop out of school, or to hold low-paying jobs than Puerto Ricans born on the island; those born in the United States also have higher household incomes (U.S. Commission on Civil Rights 1976).

At this point Puerto Rico's future political status remains undecided. Three strong political parties on the island debate alternatives to the island's present relationship to the United States: Autonomists support the present commonwealth status, annexationists support integration as a state of the Union, and separatists call for political independence from the United States. Walsh (1998) argues that *a focus* on colonialism and the experience of being both U.S. citizens and colonial subjects is important in understanding the historical bases of language, culture, and migration-related issues Puerto Ricans face today.

Cultural Assimilation: English and Spanish

We have seen that ethnic groups in America, whether immigrant or colonized, typically have tried to maintain their cultural heritages. The degree to which this has happened—as well as the group's success in doing so—has varied among ethnic groups. In regard to the maintenance of heritage, Mexican Americans and Puerto Ricans have been among the most successful ethnic groups in America. Consider again, for instance, what usually has happened in the important matter of language use.[3] Despite many exceptions and local variations, the general pattern among American ethnic groups has been for the use of the ethnic language to diminish across the generations and for English to become the usual language among the third and subsequent generations.

Although it is not possible to state even roughly what proportions of the Mexican American and Puerto Rican population have, over the years, preferred to maintain their native culture, it seems likely that the proportions have been high in comparison to most other American ethnic minorities. Mexican immigrants and recent arrivals from the island of Puerto Rico have been the primary contributors to the maintenance of the Spanish language in the United States over a comparatively long period of time. For example, the number of students enrolled in U.S. schools who are English language learners is growing; there was a 70 percent increase of such students from 1984 to 1992. Most of those students were immigrants, but many were not. Forty-one percent of the children with **limited English proficiency** who are students in U.S. elementary schools were born in the United States. Almost three-fourths of these students speak Spanish as their native language, and of those Spanish speakers, 40 percent were born in Mexico.[4]

Although many of the island-born Puerto Ricans speak English better than Spanish or are bilingual, almost 49 percent of the foreign born reported they communicated better in Spanish and an additional 11 percent reported they used only Spanish (Padilla 1985). Thus, with the two largest Hispanic groups seeming to maintain Spanish fairly well, the Spanish language is more likely to survive in the United States than any other foreign language. In 1990, for example, Spanish was the home language for over 7 percent of the people in the United States and was more commonly used in the home than all other non-English languages combined (U.S. Bureau of the Census 1996:53). However, the longer Puerto Rican and Mexican immigrant children reside in the United States, the more likely they are to become monolingual English speakers.

Many factors determine when Spanish is no longer transmitted to the succeeding generations. Most important is whether the parents either speak English predominantly or teach their children English as their first language. Veltman (1988) estimated that there were some 4 million Hispanics in the United States who did not speak Spanish at all. The propensity to abandon speaking Spanish varies with age, place of birth, length of time in the United States, whether a group is too small or scattered to resist outside pressures effectively, and the immigrants' income, sex, and education (Stevens 1992; Grenier 1985). Portes and Hao (1998) examined the patterns of language adaptation by over 5,000 second-generation students in south Florida and southern California. They found that among most immigrant nationalities, knowledge of and preference for English were nearly universal. Mexican second-generation students were the most likely to maintain proficiency in a language other than English. When both parents spoke the native language at home, the children were also strongly encouraged to maintain that language. Female students had greater competence in their parents' languages than male students and were more likely to be fluent in both their native language and English, possibly because daughters spend more time at home and may be more exposed to their parents' influences. Students with friends from the same ethnic background were more likely to maintain their parents' non-English language. Also, high levels of concentration of Spanish-speaking students in particular schools promoted the maintenance of Spanish.

The majority of the monolingual Spanish speakers in the United States are recent immigrants, Spanish-speaking children not yet enrolled in school, and the elderly. Veltman (1990) estimated that less than one-fourth of the grandchildren of immigrants maintain Spanish as their first language. Portes and Hao (1998) concluded that English quickly became the strongest language among second-generation youths, and only a few became fully bilingual and were able to teach their own children Spanish.

As incomes and levels of education increase, Mexican Americans and Puerto Ricans are more likely to be fluent in English than in Spanish (Portes and Rumbaut 1990:213; Portes and Schauffler 1996).[5] The proliferation of Spanish-language media—from local newspapers to national television chains—and the presence of large Spanish-speaking populations in many cities help maintain Spanish. The high concentration of Mexican Americans at various points throughout the borderlands and of Puerto Ricans along the East coast, the closeness of Mexico and Puerto Rico, and the steady reinforcement by continuing migration also contribute to the prominence of Spanish. Still, second-generation youths learn English quickly and often prefer to use it with their peers and siblings. Even parents who value bilingualism do not have much chance of transmitting the Spanish language to their children if they do not have strong community and social supports to do so (Portes and Schauffler 1996:8–29).

A controversial method of maintaining the native language against the forces of assimilation is **bilingual education.** Although many immigrant groups have tried to promote their native language in the schools, bilingual education is often associated with Spanish-speaking groups because so many recent immigrants, as well as the Mexican Americans and Puerto Ricans who were part of the "colonized" territories of the United States, speak Spanish.

Flashpoint 4: Bilingual Education

The debate over bilingual education in U.S. public schools has provoked bitter political disputes throughout the nation's history. These debates became especially heated in the 1980s and 1990s as bilingual education emerged as a target of antiimmigration groups. For example, in 1996 eight bills were placed before Congress that proclaimed English as the only official language of the United States and outlawed bilingual education. Supporters of those bills asked, "Why should the 1 in 20 public school students in the nation who can't speak English be taught in their own language today when the immigrant children who entered school speaking only Italian or Yiddish or German a century ago managed to get along just fine?" (Celis 1995a:5). Others argued that bilingual education did not work and even inhibited the learning of English.[6]

The bilingual education debate is framed by two positions that reflect the Anglo conformity and the cultural pluralist models of assimilation. Anglo conformists argue that it is the responsibility of the schools to teach English and to promote assimilation by substitution. The pluralists counter that the schools should strive to recognize that children learn best in a language they understand and that to maintain a strong nation, bilingual programs should strive to protect the language and culture of immigrant groups.

Pluralists view bilingual education as a way to maintain the pluralistic nature of the United States and as a way to encourage all children, including Anglo American children, to be bilingual. They claim that the United States has never really supported true language-maintenance bilingual programs. Let us now look at some of the controversies that have accompanied bilingual education in the United States.

Historical Perspectives.   The English colonists believed that America and its citizens should be defined by a common language, and, of course, they believed that English should be that language. They argued that English reflected the democratic and traditional values brought from England and that immigrants became "real Americans" by speaking it. Upper- and middle-class colonists encouraged their children to learn Latin, French, or German; but bilingualism on the part of immigrants was frowned on, was considered poor social adaptation, and was believed to indicate mental confusion and low intelligence (Portes and Schauffler 1996:433).

The 1848 constitution of California and the early laws of New Mexico required that all laws and regulations be written in Spanish and English. The Treaty of Guadalupe Hidalgo also gave Mexican citizens who became Americans the right to maintain their cultural traditions. Still, although speaking some foreign languages was admired, the speaking of Spanish was considered inferior (Kloss 1977).[7]

In Texas in 1858, laws declared that English must be the principal language in the public schools, despite the fact that many Mexican-origin children came to school speaking only Spanish. In New Mexico, Spanish had always been spoken; and in 1930, children from Spanish-speaking homes constituted one-half of the school enrollment, but less than one-fifth of those who made it to the twelfth grade. Educator George I. Sánchez pointed out that "The use of standard curricula, books, and materials among these children is a ridiculous gesture" (cited in McWilliams 1945:133). Mexican migrant workers throughout the Southwest were "socially ostracized and sharply set apart from the resident white communities. All or most members of the families worked in the fields. Thus, most continued to speak Spanish, lived among their own group, and followed their own mode of living with few opportunities to become acculturated" (McWilliams 1945:119).

The debate over Spanish language versus English was crucial in Puerto Rico. When the island was ceded by Spain to the United States, the Puerto Ricans were not included in the discussions of the civil rights and political status of the native inhabitants of the territory. English was imposed as the language of instruction in the schools on the island, where few people, including teachers, knew English (U.S. Commission on Civil Rights 1976).

In the United States, Mexican American community-based organizations, such as LULAC and El Congreso, called for more Mexican teachers in American public schools and for bilingual education for children as a way to wipe out illiteracy (Sanchez 1993:247; Gutiérrez 1995:215–216). Despite these efforts, much of the segregation of Mexican students throughout the Southwest was rationalized in terms of their presumed language "deficiency." School officials argued that the segregation of Mexican children into "Mexican schools" would facilitate the learning of English and other subjects because the Mexican children would not have to compete with Anglo children. They also argued that segregation would allow special attention to the language difficulties of Mexican American children who entered school speaking only Spanish and that segregation would allow more time for Americanization (Garcia 1989:265–266). On the other side, Mexican American parents and educators argued that both the school districts that segregated Mexican children and the courts of law that allowed the segregation to continue based on language differences were "confusing education with English" (Garcia 1989:267). Mexican parents argued that learning English could be accomplished more quickly in a classroom with English-speaking peers. They also pointed out that the rest of education suffered under segregation because the Mexican schools were overcrowded, poorly staffed, and inadequately funded. They pointed out that segregated schools would not make "good Americans" out of Mexican children.

Similar struggles over the schools were occurring in Puerto Rican communities. In 1962, a well-known Puerto Rican woman activist in the United States, Antonia Pantoja, founded a Puerto Rican organization, ASPIRA. ASPIRA took on legal challenges and projects similar to those initiated by LULAC. ASPIRA also brought Puerto Rican high school and college students together to learn leadership skills, problem solving, and activism. The organization challenged the high dropout rates of Puerto Rican students and fought for educational opportunities, cultural recognition, and community development for Puerto Ricans throughout the United States.

Legal Developments.   Hispanic leaders and organizations identified school segregation as the most despicable form of discrimination practiced against Spanish-speaking children. As the debate over school segregation and language issues continued, schools neglected the academic performance of Mexican American and Puerto Rican students and, as a result, children learned neither English nor Spanish well. The compulsory school attendance laws were not enforced for Mexican children and local school officials channeled those who did attend into nonreading, pre-first grade classes or industrial and vocational education programs (San Miguel 1987:46–53). A report of the U.S. Commission on Civil Rights (1976) noted that non-English-speaking children were placed in classes for slow learners or classes for the mentally retarded without sufficient justification. These practices resulted in high numbers of Puerto Rican students being held back in school. The problem was particularly acute among transfer students from Puerto Rico (U.S. Commission on Civil Rights 1976:101).

In 1930, LULAC supported a group of Mexican parents in Lemon Grove, California when the Anglo school board built a two-room building designated as the "Mexican school" and required all Mexican students to attend classes there. The appeals court upheld the school district's right to separate children based on "their English language handicaps"; but the San Diego Superior Court overturned the case arguing that segregation "deprived Mexican children of the presence of American children so necessary for learning the English language."[8] LULAC also assisted several Mexican American families in challenging the practice of school segregation—in *Mendez v. Westminister School District*—claiming that Mexican American students in Los Angeles were being denied their constitutional rights by being forced to attend separate "Mexican schools." In 1946 the judge ruled that the practice of segregating children of Mexican descent was in violation of the equal protection clause of the Fourteenth Amendment. The court also agreed with one of the plaintiff's central arguments—that Spanish-speaking children learn English more readily in mixed than in segregated classrooms. Another point that the case affirmed was that children should not be grouped for special instructional purposes solely on the basis of racial origin or social background. The ruling was upheld by the appeals court, setting the stage for the famous desegregation case, *Brown v. Board of Education* in 1954, which challenged the "separate but equal" policy of segregating African American children.

Although these court cases eliminated separate schools for Mexican Americans, many Mexican American students continued to be placed in segregated classes solely because of their inability to speak or understand English. Moreover, negative attitudes toward Spanish continued and many Mexican and Puerto Rican children were punished or ridiculed for speaking their native language in the schools.[9] A Mexican American and Puerto Rican civil rights movement developed within the context of the broader civil rights movements of the 1960s with educational equity for children as a central organizing point (Donato 1997).

With the influx of Spanish-speaking Cuban refugees into Florida in the late 1950s and early 1960s, the Ford Foundation funded an experimental program in bilingual education in Dade County, Florida.[10] Subsequent evaluations of the program showed that both English-speaking and Spanish-speaking children improved their reading test scores and seemed to learn well in both languages (Hakuta 1986:194–198). In the wake of the Dade County program's success and the Black civil rights movement that spread to the Southwest, Mexican American and Puerto Rican organizations demanded bilingual education for the large numbers of Spanish-speaking children who were failing in English-only classrooms. The passage of the Bilingual Education Act of 1968, Title VII (an amendment to the 1965 Elementary and Secondary Education Act), provided funds to promote research and demonstration programs in bilingual education. The programs emphasized the early elementary school levels, especially kindergarten through third grade. New York State, home of the great majority of Puerto Rican students, had no law mandating bilingual education and its "English only" law had to be amended to permit bilingual programs in the public schools (U.S. Commission on Civil Rights 1976:113).

ASPIRA of New York, Inc. v. Board of Education of the City of New York.[11]

This was the first major case concerning equal educational opportunity for Puerto Rican children. The suit alleged that the school system had failed either to teach Spanish-speaking children in a language they understood or to provide them with the English language skills needed to progress effectively in school. The plaintiffs, an estimated 182,000 Spanish-speaking students in New York City public schools, charged that they were faced with unequal treatment based on language and denied equal educational opportunity as compared with English-speaking students.

Bilingual education received strong support through the 1974 Supreme Court case *Lau v. Nichols.* The *Lau* decision, based on the experiences of Chinese immigrant students in California, determined that the failure of the San Francisco school system to provide English-language instruction to Chinese students who did not speak English denied those students a meaningful opportunity to participate in the public educational program. The Court reasoned that merely providing the same facilities, textbooks, teachers, and curriculum for students who did not understand English was not equal treatment.[12] The **Lau Task Force Remedies** recommended bilingual education as the best way to provide assistance to elementary school students with limited English proficiency. Many states and school districts resisted these recommendations.[13] Organizers of a movement for making English the official language of the United States have led the opposition to bilingual education.

In December 1995, the U.S. Senate Governmental Affairs Committee heard testimony regarding a Senate bill to declare English the nation's official language and severely restrict the federal government's use of other languages. Advocates for language-minority groups protested that groups that opposed the English-only movement had been excluded from the hearings. Arguments for such legislation were that English as a national language was needed because there were some 323 languages now spoken within the borders of the United States and bilingual education had denied English-speaking children access to schooling in English. Senator Ted Stevens, representing Alaska, testified that he was concerned that "California was becoming a Spanish-speaking state."[14] On August 1, 1996, after nearly 6 hours of emotional debate, the House approved a bill that would make English the official language of the United States. The debate, which has been a familiar one in history, was over the need to codify the use of English into law and over the importance of English as defining what it means to be an American. Supporters of the English-only legislation argued that the bill would encourage immigrants to learn English, give them a common bond with other Americans, and help them assimilate. They contended that pluralism in the United States was leading to dangerously segregated linguistic ghettos that the federal government accommodated with bilingual education and ballots in languages other than English. They warned that if bilingual instruction continued it would lead to "the decay of the core parts of our civilization."

Falcoff (1996)[15] claimed that the legislation represented "an irrational fear of Spanish." He noted that the United States is one of the world's major Spanish-speaking countries—producing important Spanish-language television and radio programs[16] and supporting a vigorous Spanish-language press. He pointed out that having a large Spanish-speaking population does not mean that the country is likely to become linguistically divided. Most immigrants want to learn English because they see English as fundamental to economic and social advancement; young immigrants see English as the key to U.S. popular culture. Falcoff (1996) also noted that the persistence of Spanish in the United States reflects the uninterrupted flow of newcomers, rather than a resistance to assimilation.

The tensions displayed in these debates are similar to those that aroused the "Americanization" movement prior to the passage of the 1924 Quota Act when Anglo conformity and English language homogeneity were seen as essential for nationhood and collective identity. Immigrants were compelled to speak English as the prerequisite of social acceptance and secondary assimilation. Former President Theodore Roosevelt proclaimed shortly after World War I, "We have room for but one language here, and that is the English language; for we intend to see that the crucible turns our people out as Americans, and not as dwellers in a polyglot boardinghouse; and we have room for but one sole loyalty, and that is loyalty to the American people" (cited in Portes and Rumbaut 1990:184).

Anglo conformity is not logically inconsistent with transitional versions of bilingual–bicultural education. Some Anglo conformists are willing to support bilingual–bicultural programs in the public schools for a comparatively short period of time. The aim of such programs is to act as a "bridge" between the culture of the home and the culture of the larger society. The expectation is that minority children can be "weaned" most successfully from the parent culture if their primary instruction is conducted in the language of the home. Under the Anglo-conformity doctrine, children taught in this way are expected, after a few years, to complete the crossover to the English language and Anglo American ways and to leave their ethnic cultures permanently behind. It is here that Anglo-conformist and pluralist policies differ. Cultural pluralists agree that bilingual–bicultural education should give children a full command of English and the customs and values of the dominant society. They do not agree that the object of such an education should be to wean the children away from the parent culture. On the contrary, from the perspective of cultural pluralism, bilingual–bicultural education should ensure not only that minority children will master the dominant culture but also that they will be assisted to preserve and elaborate their heritages in a full and appreciative way. Cultural pluralists would also encourage all children to learn more than one language.

These differences in the educational policies favored by Anglo conformists and cultural pluralists should dispel any notion that the debate between them is purely academic. The public schools in America, as traditionally operated, clearly promote Anglo conformity. Furthermore, the implementation of an educational program that would genuinely meet the criteria of pluralism would require significant changes in U.S. educational institutions. Hakuta (1986) argues that bilingual–bicultural education openly acknowledges the legitimacy of non-English languages and cultures, and, as a consequence, appears to threaten the status of English and the dominance of Anglo Americans. In response to such a threat, in June 1998, by a 61 percent margin, California voters passed Proposition 227, which demanded that all children in California public school "shall be taught English by being taught in English."[17]

Long-Term Implications.   The continued political pressure against bilingual education and the low levels of educational achievement among Mexican American and Puerto Rican children afford strong evidence that cultural assimilation is not occurring for these groups in the same way as it typically has among the European minorities. It is true, of course, that the older members of these groups, those who are recent Mexican immigrants, and those from the island of Puerto Rico rely most heavily on Spanish; and it is true that this pattern has been common among other ethnic groups. Linguists have noted that many third- and fourth-generation Mexican Americans and Puerto Ricans often speak only a popular variety of Spanish or mix Spanish and English in a style called **code-switching.** These Puerto Ricans and Mexican Americans may have a limited verbal Spanish repertoire, but they still take great pride in their language as a symbol of cultural identity (Peñalosa 1989).

Puerto Rican scholars (Walsh 1998; Nieto 1998) argue that Puerto Ricans' efforts to maintain a language and ethnic identity within the U.S. context of "Americanization"— even for those who are U.S. born and whose dominant language is English—illustrate a position that is referred to as a "**postcolonial perspective.**" This perspective is illustrated by political, economic, and cultural efforts to preserve the ethnic heritage of Puerto Ricans and is a cultural pluralistic perspective as we have defined pluralism. The effort is difficult, as illustrated by a study of return migrants. Zentella (1997) explored the question of language and identity among English-speaking Puerto Rican teens who returned to the island. Many of the youths she interviewed had been called "gringo" (74 percent), "nuyorican" (58 percent), and "americano" (51 percent). The use of the terms *gringo* and *americano* suggested that the native islanders defined these youngsters as distinct from the native population and associated the returnees with national groupings formerly limited to Anglos.

Mexican Americans and Puerto Ricans, so far, may not be following the Anglo-conformity pattern of cultural assimilation by substituting English for Spanish, although some scholars believe otherwise;[18] or, even if this switch is occurring, a change in only one cultural element (albeit a very important one) may not be sufficient to produce cultural assimilation in other respects. Some evidence shows that as language loyalty declines, loyalty to the ethnic heritage nevertheless continues (Keefe and Padilla 1987:16–18; Zentella 1997).

Cultural Assimilation: Family Patterns

A vigorous, often heated, controversy has swirled around the subject of the characteristics of Hispanic families and **familism.** Most research on this topic has agreed that even the fourth generation retains aspects of familism, particularly the value of, and involvement in, large and local **extended families.** Much of the early research on Hispanic families focused on the deviant aspects of the Hispanic culture, did not examine intragroup differences, and used frameworks that failed to capture adequately the change and strengths in Hispanic families.[19] For example, Mexican-origin families have been described as patriarchal, religious, cohesive, and traditional. Men, particularly older men, have been portrayed as regulating family life in a strict and austere way (much has been made of the notion of "*machismo*"), whereas women have been portrayed as subordinate, religious, and patient sufferers. Many critics of such portrayals (Williams 1990; Zambrana 1995) have agreed that some influential scholarly works have been affected by the stereotypical definitions of Mexican Americans and Puerto Ricans held by the majority group.

Williams (1990) conducted a valuable study of continuities and changes within the Mexican American family through in-depth interviews with 75 Mexican American couples of "working" and "business/professional" backgrounds. She gathered information on the way the important life cycle events of birth, marriage, and death were handled between the 1920s and the 1950s, and then compared the findings with "current" practices. Williams interpreted the findings within a broad framework concerning the general effects of industrialization, urbanization, and bureaucratization on family life in America. She argued that during the last several decades Mexican American families (on the whole) have become more like Anglo American families, but that this trend toward convergence does not mean that Mexican Americans are assimilating by "attempting to become like Anglos." Her thesis, instead, is that the groups are becoming more similar because both sets of families "are responding to major changes on the societal and global levels" (Williams 1990:148).

In another important study of family structure and ethnicity, Keefe and Padilla (1987) examined generational differences among Mexican Americans and also compared the family structures of Mexican Americans to those of Anglo Americans. Among the many (and complicated) findings, three stand out. First, primary kin ties were the most significant for both Anglos and Mexican Americans; Anglos, however, had fewer primary kin close at hand and Mexican Americans maintained closer ties. Second, Mexican Americans were more likely than Anglos to have a local extended family and to maintain contact with relatives. These two findings lead to a third finding that is of special importance in relation to cultural assimilation: Even though Mexican Americans in the second and third generations appeared to be assimilating culturally in some important respects, the effect of these changes was to strengthen, rather than weaken, the extended family. The U.S.-born Mexican Americans have become highly urbanized and are exposed to many sources of family breakdown, but "The Chicano family," as Keefe and Padilla (1987:144) stated, "is far from being a declining institution."

A third important study of Mexican immigrant families looked at the ongoing processes of gender as they relate to migration and settlement (Hondagneu-Sotelo 1994). Her research found that many immigrants lived and worked in the United States for many years with dreams of eventually returning to Mexico. As time passed, they developed ties to jobs, financial institutions, churches, schools, friends, and neighbors that connected them to the United States. Hondagneu-Sotelo found that migration patterns—whether a husband preceded his wife and children, intact families migrated together, or men and women migrated independently and then formed a family—made a big difference in assimilation patterns. She found that the immigration process did shape family relationships. When Mexican men migrated to the United States to work, the wives and daughters who remained behind assumed traditional male responsibilities. When families immigrated to the United States intact, they arrived with a set of cultural beliefs and practices based on their lives in Mexico, but new demands and opportunities offered by life in the United States reshaped preexisting family relationships. For example, women worked outside the home for wages, men performed more domestic tasks, and children, who learned English in the schools, began to mediate between the family and U.S. institutions. These changes both fostered assimilation and produced conflict as families adapted to U.S. society.

Studies of Puerto Rican families suggest that there are both similarities and differences in the degrees of cultural assimilation of Mexican Americans and Puerto Ricans. As the needs of families change, factors that are not viewed as "cultural" also have an impact on Hispanic families. For example, among both Puerto Ricans and Mexican Americans relationships and family solidarity are emphasized. A study of caregiving arrangements for a population of elderly and disabled Puerto Ricans showed that family members provided most of the care needed for their elderly with very minimal use of formal social services or community agencies (Delgado and Tennstedt 1997). In a study of child-rearing values, Puerto Rican mothers ranked honesty, respect, and responsibility most highly, followed by loyalty to family, affection, and sharing. The Puerto Rican mothers ranked values associated with Anglo culture (assertiveness, independence, and creativity) as being less important (Gonzalez-Ramos, Zayas, and Cohen 1998). A study of Puerto Rican adolescents found that just spending time with family members on the weekends and evenings, and not anything particularly cultural, reduced opportunities for delinquency (Pabon 1998). Although the tradition on the island is one of strong extended-family networks, when young families migrated to the mainland they lost that support. Thus, family obligations and support from relatives continue to be important to Puerto Rican families, but attitudes toward familism may or may not encompass the many dimensions of family life.

We conclude that the kind of cultural assimilation we might expect on the basis of Gordon's theory—a substitution across the board of Anglo for Mexican American or Puerto Rican culture—seems not to be occurring. Movement toward assimilation in some respects has not been accompanied by changes in all of the other aspects of culture; however, if the ideas of assimilationist theories seem inadequate to explain what is occurring among the Mexican Americans and Puerto Ricans, the ideas of colonialist theory also fall short. Although Mexican Americans and Puerto Ricans reject many facets of Anglo-American culture, they may also be incorporating Anglo-American culture in some important ways; the necessity, if not the desirability, of secondary structural assimilation seems to be accepted. Let us examine some facts in this regard.

 # Secondary Structural Assimilation

Our exploration of secondary assimilation among Mexican Americans and Puerto Ricans focuses on their occupations, incomes, educational achievements, and residential location.

Occupations

Since the beginning of World War II, Mexican Americans have been moving out of the customary occupations in farming, mining, or railroad labor they occupied in the 1920s and into many different jobs that carry with them higher levels of pay and social prestige. For example, the proportion of native-born Mexican American men engaged in "professional" occupations has quadrupled since 1960 (Bean and Tienda 1987:328; U.S. Bureau of the Census 1996:404).

Mexican and Mexican American women in the U.S. Southwest have historically had lower labor force participation rates than their White and Black counterparts (Badar, Broman, Bokemeier, and Zinn 1995). In recent years, however, Mexican-origin women have been entering the labor force at an increasing rate. This pattern does not necessarily reflect increased cultural assimilation, since many of the women working outside the home maintain a high level of cultural identification, use of Spanish, and ethnic pride. Badar, Broman, Bokemeier, and Zinn suggest that lower participation in the labor force by Mexican and Mexican American women in the past was due to lower levels of education, which limited job opportunities. Additional factors, such as increased economic development in the Southwest, also resulted in greater opportunities for employment by females outside the home. The study found that some processes of cultural assimilation, such as learning English, opened up more job opportunities; but the majority of the working Mexican American women were employed in peripheral industries and secondary occupations, such as clerical service, agricultural work, health service, education, or manufacturing. Thus, although some changes have occurred in the direction of occupational assimilation, others have not.

Occupational assimilation takes place as immigrants invest in U.S.-specific human capital, such as English-language skills and education, and disperse into nontraditional occupations. Many Mexican immigrant workers are hindered in their assimilation processes because they do not have official papers to be residents of the United States. A study by Cobb-Clark and Kossoudji (2000) looked at the employment and occupational changes of Latinas after they received amnesty under the 1986 Immigration Reform and Control Act. They found that women who had taken traditional immigrant jobs in private households, such as housekeepers or childcare providers, showed little change in occupational distributions after receiving legal resident status. Even though many changed jobs, earned more, or had better working conditions over time, they did not follow the occupational notion of assimilation—leaving traditional occupations and entering the mainstream labor market. They remained in traditional occupations in households, hotels, laundries, and sweatshops. The researchers found that the social support provided by ethnic networks promoted continued employment in the initial occupations. Education and ability to speak English almost doubled the chances that a woman would move out of a traditional occupation. Also, a woman who had children at the time of migration had a much higher probability of moving out of a traditional occupation than a woman who did not.

The unemployment rate for Puerto Ricans age 16 and older in the 1980s was more than twice that of non-Hispanic Whites and greater than that of Hispanics in general. In 1993, a majority of Puerto Rican women were employed in technical, sales, and administrative jobs and a majority of the Puerto Rican men in precision production and operator jobs; approximately 20 percent of the Puerto Rican workers had professional jobs (Torrecilha, Cantú, and Nguyen 1999:240, 241). The movement of industrial plants and factories from the Northeast and Midwest, areas in which Puerto Rican populations are concentrated and an expansion of the service economy characterized by low-skill, low-wage work have seriously affected the well-being of Puerto Ricans. A 125 percent increase in growth of the Puerto Rican population in the southern urban areas of the United States suggests that Puerto Ricans have been drawn by the job growth in the "Sunbelt" (Torrecilha, Cantú, and Nguyen 1999:236).

Incomes

Even when Mexican Americans and Puerto Ricans gain access to more "desirable" occupations, they frequently are in the lower-paid positions within them. Combining this fact with the continuing differences between the occupational distributions of Anglos and Hispanics in general, it is not surprising to find a continuation of income differences between non-Hispanic Whites and Mexican Americans and Puerto Ricans. This is, indeed, the case. Although Mexican Americans showed a steady improvement in incomes during the 1960–1980 period, the personal income for Mexican Americans hovered around 67 cents for each dollar received by Anglos.[20] This means that even during a period of rising occupational standing and increased incomes, the average (mean) income for Mexican Americans remained about one-third lower than the average income for Anglos. The absolute gap between the median family incomes of Whites and of Mexican American families almost doubled between 1980 and 1993–1994. We conclude, therefore, that although the real economic situation of Mexican Americans may be improving gradually, the relative and absolute gaps between Mexican American and White families are still growing. Additionally, a much higher percent of Mexican American than White families live in poverty (26 versus 9 percent) (U.S. Bureau of the Census 1996:48, 51).

Census data show that Puerto Ricans continue to be the worst-off ethnic group in the United States, with nearly half of all Puerto Rican families living in poverty in the mid-1980s (Lemann 1999). The statistics also show that Puerto Ricans are more severely afflicted than Mexican Americans by the secondary effects of poverty, such as family breakups and not trying to find employment. Lemann (1999) reported that in 1988 about two and a half times as many Puerto Rican families compared with Mexican American families were headed by females and only a third of the Puerto Rican women were in the labor force. Lemann suggested that on the mainland, racial prejudice may play a role in shutting Puerto Ricans out of jobs. Puerto Rico never developed the rigid caste system that characterized racial relations in the U.S. southern states, and there were no legal and social lines between those having African heritage and others. Thus, intermarriage was common. Lemann suggests that dark-skinned Puerto Ricans may encounter color prejudice when they arrive in the United States. Another factor Lemann proposes is that prior to 1970, those who left the island were less well educated and less well off than those who stayed behind. More middle-class Puerto Ricans have migrated since 1970 because of a shortage of middle-class jobs on the island. The consequences of these patterns are that the Puerto Rican poor experience greater poverty and isolation than the African American or Mexican American poor.

Whether people find it possible to move out of low-prestige, poorly paid jobs into more desirable jobs may depend to a considerable extent on the educational levels of the people involved. It is of special importance, therefore, to know whether the educational levels of the Mexican American and Puerto Rican population have been increasing over time. Such increases would be expected if this ethnic group has been moving in the direction of secondary assimilation.

Education

We must be cautious in interpreting evidence of increases in schooling among Hispanic groups. Even though successive generations of Mexican Americans seem to be achieving higher levels of education,[21] one careful analysis (Bean, Chapa, Berg, and Sowards 1994) showed that within different age categories the third generation generally has not reached the educational level of the second generation. Another study found similar patterns of lower achievement among third-generation Mexican Americans. Wojtkiewicz and Donato (1995) found that members of the second generation were more likely to graduate from high school than Whites, whereas members of the third or higher generation were less likely to graduate from high school than Whites. They suggested that immigrant parents may pass on higher levels of motivation to their children than do native

U.S. parents (the second generation). These findings call into question the adequacy of the view, based on overall statistics, that each generation of Mexican Americans is attaining a higher level of education than its predecessors.

A problem that continues to be particularly prominent among both Mexican American and Puerto Rican youths is the high rate at which they drop out (or are "pushed out") of school before reaching high school graduation. Female students tend to do better in school than males; Carter and Wilson (1993) reported that almost 63 percent of the Hispanic female students in 1992 graduated from high school compared with 52 percent of the Hispanic male students. An important factor affecting these levels is the frequency with which Hispanic children, particularly males, are required to repeat grades (Fligstein and Fernandez 1985:165).

From 1989 to 1992, Romo and Falbo (1996) followed the school careers of 100 Mexican-origin youths whom their school district had designated as "at risk" of dropping out of school.[22] Only 19 of the original 100 youths graduated at the end of their senior year. Romo and Falbo focused on the success stories of those youths completing high school. The study revealed that the process of earning a high school diploma is a complex one, influenced by peer cultures, parental resources and education, the availability of effective school programs and policies, and strong parental support. They found that education was highly valued by all the students and their families; parents wanted their children to go to college and students wanted to be doctors and lawyers, but by age 20 they had earned only a fraction of the credits needed to earn a high school diploma. Many parents did not understand the school system and did not realize that their children were tracked into low-level courses. Students and parents reported experiencing frustration over the schools' unwillingness or inability to provide help and encountering hostility from teachers, counselors, or administrators. Many of the students who dropped out of school made rational decisions to leave a school system in which they had few alternatives but failure. The National Commission on Secondary Schooling for Hispanics found that 45 percent of Mexican American and Puerto Rican students who entered high school never finish (Guzmán 1997:87).

Puerto Rican youths, because of their concentration in urban areas, are being educated in school systems that are large and bureaucratic (New York City, Chicago, Los Angeles). Access to quality schools is clearly tied to graduation rates, and the schools many Mexican American and Puerto Rican youths attend are poorly funded, less likely to be able to meet the needs of students, and increasingly segregated. Moreover, tracking into low-level courses in high school leaves many Mexican American and Puerto Rican students inadequately prepared for college-level work.

Although there has been increased Hispanic representation among college undergraduates and graduates, Hispanic students complete college at a lower rate than the general student population. Of those Hispanic students who go on to postsecondary education, most enroll in two-year institutions. This does not help their upward mobility significantly, since for most Americans the educational gateway to opportunity is a four-year college degree (LeBlanc Flores 1994). A study by Jasinski (2000) found that Mexicans and Puerto Ricans were the least likely of the Hispanic groups to participate in postsecondary education. Non-Hispanic Whites and Cuban families had both a higher socioeconomic status and the most educational resources compared to Mexican and

Puerto Rican families. Economic resources available to the families seemed to be more important predictors of their children's participation in higher education than sociocultural factors, such as English ability.

The broad figures we have presented concerning the occupations, incomes, and educational levels of Mexican Americans and Puerto Ricans conceal many underlying differences of interest. For example, since Anglos, on average, have higher levels of education and hold better-paying jobs, some of the difference in median incomes is due to these factors. It is accurate to say, therefore, that some of the inequality in income between Hispanics and Anglos arises from the educational and occupational differences between the two groups.

We have mentioned that one way of assessing the extent to which the dominant group discriminates against minority groups is to calculate the pay of similar workers in different ethnic groups to discover whether it "costs" to be a member of a minority group.[23] For example, in 1959, the mean income of male Mexican American workers who had completed 4 years of college or more was $1,251 less than that of Anglo workers with the same level of education.[24] Similarly, Anglos who had completed less than 8 years of school earned slightly more, on average, than Mexican Americans who had attended high school for up to 3 years. In other words, *so far as education alone* was concerned, it appears that Mexican Americans "paid a price" in the job market because of their group membership (Poston and Alvírez 1973:708).[25] Subsequent analyses (Cotton 1985; Poston, Alvírez, and Tienda 1976) found that the economic "cost" of being a Mexican American worker increased during the decade of the 1970s despite the increasing levels of education among Mexican Americans![26]

The "cost" of being Hispanic continued into the 1980s and 1990s. An Urban Institute/ GAO hiring audit[27] completed in Chicago and San Diego provided revealing results. Pairs of one Hispanic and one Anglo, with similar resumes, applied for the same jobs. Forty-three percent of the Anglos compared to 23 percent of the Hispanics applying for the jobs got job offers. On several occasions both the Anglos and the Hispanics completed the application, got interviews, and received job offers, but the Hispanics were directed to lower status jobs. Overall the Hispanic applicants received unfavorable treatment in 31 percent of the audits (Cross et al. 1990).

Residential Assimilation

As noted previously, another important measure of the extent to which secondary assimilation is occurring for a given group is the degree to which that group lives in the same residential areas as the members of the dominant group. In most cities of the United States, Mexican Americans and Puerto Ricans long have been, and still are, noticeably segregated. The extent of this segregation varies greatly among cities and regions of the country. For example, the lowest regional index of residential segregation (dissimilarity) of Mexican Americans and Anglos in the United States in 1980 was 48.3 (the South) and the highest was 62.3 (the Northeast). Among 10 standard metropolitan statistical areas (SMSAs) having large Mexican American populations, the lowest level of residential segregation was 39.1 (Riverside, California) and the highest was 66.0

(New York City). Intermediate levels were found in cities such as Chicago (64.0), Los Angeles (61.1), San Antonio (58.9), and Houston (50.4) (Bean and Tienda 1987:174). Most of these residential-segregation indexes lie within the moderate range, although the average for the cities of the Southwest is higher than the average for the nation (Lopez 1981:53–54); hence, although there are large and important differences among cities, the typical situation is a moderate degree of Hispanic–Anglo residential segregation. Some findings for the period 1980 to 1990 suggest that this general pattern of residential segregation may have continued through that period (Harrison and Weinberg 1992).

Among Hispanics, Puerto Ricans are the only Hispanic group whose segregation indices are routinely above 70 (Massey and Denton 1993:146). Massey and Denton (1993:12) noted that this high degree of segregation was directly attributable to the fact that a large proportion of Puerto Ricans are of African origin. The researchers found that although other minority groups experienced growing poverty during the 1970s, poverty became spatially concentrated only among Blacks and Puerto Ricans, and only in certain places. Older metropolitan areas, such as New York, Chicago, Philadelphia, and Baltimore, in which Puerto Ricans are most concentrated, experienced industrial restructuring and economic reversals. These economic factors drove poverty rates sharply upward in cities in which Puerto Ricans were most segregated. Massey and Denton concluded that only Puerto Ricans share Blacks' relative inability to assimilate spatially. They noted that although White Puerto Ricans seemed to achieve rates of spatial assimilation comparable with those found among other ethnic groups, Puerto Ricans of African or racially mixed origins experienced "markedly low abilities to convert socioeconomic attainment into contact with whites" (Massey and Denton 1993:151).

To interpret these facts, it is helpful to have a standard of comparison. Although the extent of residential segregation will be discussed more fully in later chapters, we may note here that in 1980, the average Hispanic–Anglo index in the 60 SMSAs studied by Massey and Denton (1987:816) was 43.4, whereas the Black–White average was 69.4. Although Massey and Denton did not focus on Hispanics in their 1993 study of racial segregation, they noted that residential segregation of Hispanics generally begins at a relatively modest level among the poor and falls progressively as socioeconomic status rises. The researchers found that in the Los Angeles metropolitan area, the *poorest Hispanics* (with a segregation index of 64) were less segregated than the *most affluent Blacks* (whose score was 79). The evidence points strongly to persisting racial discrimination and to the conclusion that among Whites, segregation declines sharply with rising socioeconomic status, suburbanization, and the number of generations spent within the United States (Massey and Denton 1987:803, 819; 1993:113–114). However, higher status Blacks and suburban Blacks are as likely to live in a segregated neighborhood as are those who are less affluent (Clark and Mueller 1988; Massey and Denton 1993). The apparent increases in education, socioeconomic status, and suburbanization for those who are native born are consistent with the view that secondary assimilation in these respects is underway. Experts (Massey and Denton 1993; Orfield and Eaton 1996) agree, however, that for those remaining in segregated neighborhoods, spatial isolation by housing is a central reason for the cumulative and reinforcing nature of social inequality.

Primary Structural Assimilation

The evidence reviewed shows that, in general, Mexican Americans have been moving out of rural areas and into the cities, and that within the cities they are less segregated from Anglos than are Blacks. It shows that Puerto Ricans are moving out of large cities such as New York City and Chicago toward the cities in California, Colorado, Texas, Florida, and North Carolina, and that the last quarter of the twentieth century was a period of substantial growth for the U.S. Puerto Rican population (Torrecilha, Cantú, and Nguyen 1999). It shows, too, that Mexican Americans and Puerto Ricans are more likely now to be working in jobs that previously were held almost exclusively by Anglo Americans. Each of these forms of secondary assimilation favors an increase in the amount of equal-status interaction that will occur between these two Hispanic groups and Anglos, and, thereby, raises the probability that friendships will develop across ethnic lines.

Friendship Patterns

Although little is known concerning the trends in Mexican American–Anglo or Puerto Rican friendship formation, some valuable evidence was provided by the work of researchers in UCLA's Mexican American Study Project (Grebler, Moore, and Guzman 1970). This study of New Mexico, California, and Texas—the main centers of Mexican American culture—suggested that with the passage of time, Mexican Americans decreasingly have only Mexican American friends. Although this generational trend is much more pronounced among those living in desegregated neighborhoods and among those of higher income, it suggests that if the occupational, educational, and residential assimilation of Mexican Americans continues, primary assimilation will also increase. On the other hand, if the younger generation attends increasingly segregated schools, as the Howard Civil Rights Project has documented, then Mexican and Puerto Rican students will have few contacts with Anglo peers and will form few friendships with members of the dominant group.

A study by Quillian and Campbell (2003) on friendship segregation found that Hispanic-origin groups tended to maintain friendships among their own groups across immigrant generations. The researchers found that Hispanic origin was an important basis for individual friendships, especially among the White Hispanic students and those who indicated their race as "Other." The friends of White Hispanic students were generally White, White Hispanics, and other Hispanics. The friends of Black Hispanics were generally Black and other Black Hispanics. The researchers concluded that while ethnic solidarity exists within the Hispanic groups, White and Black Hispanics are assimilating in different ways, with racially White Hispanics joining White peer groups and racially Black Hispanics joining Black peer groups. The authors make the point that "the racial categorization of an immigrant group may have a lasting influence on the incorporation of the group members into the host society" (Quillian and Campbell 2003:559).

The researchers also found evidence that interracial and interethnic friendships in schools will increase as the share of students who are of Asian and Hispanic origins increases because race is a less formidable barrier to friendships among Hispanic and Asian students than between non-Hispanic White students and Black students. The authors concluded that their findings about cross-racial friendships reflect the organizational and racial environments present in the schools and racial relations in American society more generally. The researchers also noted that the increasing diversity of student populations in the United States may not translate into increasing diversity within schools because a large share of Hispanic students in the Southwest are educated in almost entirely Hispanic schools.

We emphasized previously that when a dominant and subordinate group are brought together by conquest, the groups frequently react to one another with greater mutual hatred and rejection than if the minority arose through immigration. For this reason, Mexican Americans and Puerto Ricans frequently have been described as having a low assimilative potential. Despite the forces working toward ethnic separateness, however, we have seen that Mexican Americans and Puerto Ricans are in some respects showing patterns of assimilation. Let us turn now to that "most infallible index" of assimilation—intermarriage (Kennedy 1944:331).

Marital Assimilation

The question of marital assimilation concerning Puerto Ricans presents some interesting challenges for the assimilation model. Early reports of the Puerto Rican island population listed nearly twice as many Blacks, Mullatos, and Mestizos as Whites. One report described Puerto Ricans as being of three distinct types or "races": "Spanish," "white or light mullatto," and "pure-blooded Africans" (Róman 1996). Over time, the high levels of interaction between Black and White workers and the many points at which their interests and lives converged resulted in high rates of intermarriage. As a result, although there was discrimination against darker Puerto Ricans on the island, the binary categories of "Black" or "White" that dominate in the United States did not exist in Puerto Rico. Clara Rodriguiz (1994) argued that in Puerto Rico and among Puerto Ricans in the United States, racial identification is subordinate to cultural identification. The dominance of racial categories in the United States has resulted in high levels of segregation and discrimination for Puerto Ricans and has been a limiting factor in out-marriages with Anglos.

Several studies of Mexican American intermarriage have been conducted, with the majority of them focusing on Los Angeles, Albuquerque, and San Antonio.[28] Three main findings stand out. First, the occurrence of out-marriage for Mexican Americans is much lower in some places than in others. Second, there has been a gradual long-term increase in the rate of out-marriage. And third, Mexican Americans who are natives of native parentage are more likely to marry-out than are Mexican Americans of mixed parentage, who, in turn, are more likely to marry-out than are those born in Mexico (Grebler, Moore, and Guzman 1970:409; Moore and Pachon 1985:108). In short, whether the overall out-marriage rates at different points in time or the rates for those in different generations are examined, the main conclusion appears to be the same: Mexican Americans are moving slowly toward marital assimilation (Murguía 1982:50).

Although most research on Hispanic intermarriage has focused on individual characteristics, such as generational status, age, sex, and social class as predictors of intermarriage, Anderson and Saenz (1994) found that structural conditions can influence intermarriage independently of cultural values and individual preferences. They identified five major structural determinants of intermarriage: (1) opportunities for contact or the extent of segregation, (2) social differentiation (differences in education, income, or occupational prestige between ethnic groups, and the extent of such differences within a group), (3) ethnic language maintenance (which affects the development of primary and secondary relationships), (4) group size (total population of an ethnic group in a particular area), and (5) an imbalance in the sex ratio (number of males per 100 females). Each of these factors either facilitated or represented barriers to favorable relations between Mexican Americans and Anglos, but three of these five conditions—opportunities for contact, status diversity within the ethnic group, and levels of Spanish-language maintenance—were *significant predictors* of out-marriage. Based on this research, Anderson and Saenz argued that we must consider a combination of structural- and cultural-level factors to obtain a more complete understanding of assimilation.

This is particularly true for Puerto Rican out-marriage patterns. U.S.-born Puerto Ricans display a much faster rate of cultural assimilation than island-born Puerto Ricans. According to 1970 census figures, more than 80 percent of the married migrants had Puerto Rican spouses, whereas only slightly more than 50 percent of the married U.S. born had married within their ethnic group (U.S. Commission on Civil Rights 1976:36).

Some writers believe the evidence on out-marriage supports the immigrant model. Mittlebach and Moore (1968:53) stated that in Los Angeles, at least, the rate of Mexican American out-marriage "is roughly that of the Italian and Polish ethnic populations in Buffalo, New York, a generation ago"; and in a reanalysis of these data, Schoen and Cohen (1980:365) agreed that the assimilation of Hispanics "appears to be very much in the tradition of earlier American immigration." Barrera (1988) concluded that a considerable amount of intermarriage is taking place, the rate has been increasing over time, it is strongly affected by generation and social class, and it is related to other indices of assimilation, such as language. Similarly, Peñalosa (1970:50) concluded that many contemporary changes suggest that Hispanics are coming to resemble "a European immigrant group of a generation ago."

 # Other Forms of Assimilation

One indication of declines in prejudice and discrimination is that Hispanics are joining traditionally Anglo social organizations. Belonging to the more "social" mainstream institutions and becoming more actively involved in political organizations are two other indicators of the extent of assimilation. Catholicism is the most common religious affiliation of Hispanics, but recent analyses have shown a "defection of Hispanics from Catholicism" with Protestant fundamentalist affiliation as the largest type of non-Catholic affiliation (Hunt 1999). The United States is predominantly Protestant and many Anglo values, such as individualism and success, derive from the Protestant ethic. More Puerto Ricans identified themselves as Protestant (22.3 percent) than did Mexicans (15 percent), and an increasing number reported "fundamentalist religious" experiences (Torrecilha, Cantú, and Nguyen 1999:248). Hunt cautioned, however, that this pattern might be a result of the tendency for first-generation Hispanic women to convert to fundamentalist religions. The patterns might reflect a need for the social and moral support of church-based social networks after migration to the United States, rather than assimilation into the American Protestant mainstream.

A stronger case can be made for Hispanic civic assimilation. Passage of antiimmigration initiatives in California galvanized Hispanic voters and civil rights groups to stage one of California's largest protests in history. More significantly, Hispanic organizations demonstrated political power in a legal challenge that permanently voided the provisions of Proposition 187, a 1994 California referendum passed by 60 percent of the voters, which, if implemented, would have barred illegal immigrants and their children from receiving government services such as a public education. These efforts demonstrate that Mexican Americans and Puerto Ricans are increasingly able to pursue their goals from within the political system.

Additional factors in the larger context of immigration in the United States are also affecting the assimilation processes of Mexican Americans and Puerto Ricans. One of the most dramatic changes over the last quarter of the twentieth century has been the growing diversity of the Latino presence in the United States. The terms *Hispanic* and *Latino*, which bring a sense of unity across national lines, have come into wide use, especially since the official use of "Hispanic" in the 1980 census. The terms emphasize commonalities and interactions across groups, or a **pan-ethnic identity.** Flores (1996) noted the growth of the Dominican community in New York and in Puerto Rico, the "Mexicanization" of New York as a result of the proportional arrival rates of recent migration from Mexico, and the large numbers of Colombians, Salvadorans, Ecuadorians, Panamanians, Hondurans, Brazilians, and "new" immigrants from almost every country of Latin America. New York joins Chicago, Miami, Houston, and Los Angeles as "pan-Latino" cities. Arguments abound about the differences and similarities among the groups of Latinos, but Flores documents the use of the term in media references, government reports, and the writings of Latino scholars. He notes that an increasing number of Puerto Ricans themselves recognize the validity of the pan-ethnic category. Flores (1996:176) points out that the terms *Latino* or *Hispanic* "refer to something real or in the making, whether a demographic aggregate, a voting bloc, a market, a language or cultural group, a 'community,' . . . or a 'condition.'" The underlying premise is that Latinos comprise a definable group and an ethnicity.

Mexican American and Puerto Rican "Success"

What does the evidence on the various forms of assimilation among the Mexican Americans and Puerto Ricans tell us about the success with which they have adapted to

American life? Although Mexican Americans and Puerto Ricans have been moving toward the American mainstream, they have not been as successful (from the perspective of Anglo conformity) as some other groups. In some aspects of assimilation, Mexican Americans and Puerto Ricans approximate the Anglo American ideal less than do the Japanese Americans. They have not relinquished their culture as rapidly; they have not attained equal levels of occupation, education, and income; and they appear to be more segregated in their friendship and marital patterns. Why is this true?

This question lies at the heart of the ideological issues we have discussed throughout this book. In some respects, the comparative "failure" of the Mexican Americans and Puerto Ricans in terms of Anglo conformity may, with equal force, be seen as "success" from the perspective of cultural pluralism. The Mexican Americans and Puerto Ricans have been successful in their efforts to maintain and develop their own distinctive heritage, the desirability of which seems clearly to be acknowledged by many ethnic Americans. Recall, though, that ideal cultural pluralism (as described in Chapter 2) calls for a high level of secondary assimilation, as does Anglo conformity; hence, in this regard, Mexican Americans and Puerto Ricans still have not reached the goal of ideal pluralism. The trick, of course, is to be successful in worldly ways without giving up the distinctive cultural, social, and marital spheres of group life. But what if worldly success can be purchased only through cultural assimilation by substitution or taking on key aspects of the Anglo culture? What if the maintenance of the ethnic culture is itself an obstacle to the attainment of worldly success? These explosive questions have been in the forefront of the frequently bitter debate concerning public policies.

Consider again, for example, the question of the use of Spanish in the schools. The dominant group insisted until the latter part of the 1960s that only English was the legal and proper language of instruction in the schools. Spanish-speaking children have been said to suffer from a language "barrier" that must be "surmounted." The assumption underlying this stand is that the possession of a Mexican or Puerto Rican heritage retards assimilation and is a handicap in the modern world. From the Mexican American and Puerto Rican points of view, however, this assumption is simply a part of a broader struggle among cultures. A frequent observation concerning classical colonialism is that oppressor groups not only conquer the territories of the groups they subordinate, they also attempt to destroy the native cultures as well; thus, many Mexican Americans and Puerto Ricans consider the insistence that they give up Spanish and undergo full cultural assimilation by substitution to be an example of "cultural imperialism."

Mexican American and Puerto Rican scholars have launched a scathing critique of cultural explanations for the lack of their groups' success. Concepts such as "present orientation," "fatalism," and "familism" have been used by Anglo American scholars to label Hispanics as passive recipients of whatever fate may thrust on them. Such ideas, Romano (1968:24) contended, are simply social-science stereotypes that strengthen the popular notion that Mexican Americans and Puerto Ricans are largely responsible for their own circumstances—a situation that presumably can be changed only through full cultural assimilation by substitution. In a similar vein, Vaca (1970:26) argued that an attack on the values of Mexican American or Puerto Rican culture is only a mask for the Anglo-conformity ideology. Cultural analysis, he said, presents a "vicious," "misleading," and "degrading" portrait of Hispanic culture. It is a portrait that distorts reality and implies that Mexican American and Puerto Rican culture should not continue to exist within contemporary American society.

Of greater importance, however, has been an increasing emphasis on structural explanations of the socioeconomic position of the Mexican Americans and Puerto Ricans. We noted earlier, for example, that a substantial portion of the average difference between the incomes of Hispanic and Anglo workers may be caused by discrimination. We noted, too, that documented and undocumented immigration to the United States has been intimately related to changing economic circumstances (Portes and Rumbaut 1990:14). And we emphasized that Puerto Rican migrant workers and both Mexican immigrant workers and native Mexican American workers typically have entered a "dual" labor market in the United States. One set of jobs, historically "reserved" for Anglo workers, has offered good pay, security, and the possibility of advancement. The second set of jobs, into which "cheap" labor typically has been funneled, has consisted of the back-breaking, seasonal, and "stoop" work that Anglo workers ordinarily have refused to perform (Pachon and Moore 1981:118–119; Portes and Bach 1985:69). The latter jobs have offered little hope of advancement even when the workers were educated and experienced. When minority workers are routinely allocated to dead-end jobs, according to this line of criticism, no amount of "activism" or "future orientation" will lead to significantly improved economic circumstances.

Both the critics of the cultural explanation and its defenders agree, of course, that Hispanic culture is different from Anglo American culture in certain respects (Moore and Pachon 1985:122–131). Indeed, were that not the case, all talk of cultural explanations would be pointless; and it is the determination of many Mexican Americans and Puerto Ricans to maintain a distinctive culture, even if it is a source of conflict with the dominant group. But to agree that Mexican American or Puerto Rican culture is *different* is by no means to acknowledge that it is *deficient*. As Barrera (1979:180) argued, "The cultural apparatus of any people is so complex that presumably negative traits can always be found." Unless a comparison is conducted of the "negative" and "positive" traits in both the dominant and subordinate groups, Barrera stated, no valid inferences concerning the relation of values to success are possible.

The evidence we have reviewed concerning the cultural, secondary, primary, marital, and other assimilation processes of Mexican Americans and Puerto Ricans may be interpreted as lending partial support to either the immigrant or the colonial models. Neither interpretation seems to fit all the facts. Some scholars have argued that we should replace both perspectives with models that stress the complexity and variability of the immigrant experience and individuals' own influence and control over the "pace" and direction of their "adaptations" to American life. Some Mexican immigrants and Puerto Ricans attempt to follow the Anglo-conformist prescriptions for inclusion while laying their ethnic heritage aside. Others, adhering to the pluralist model, maintain strong ties to the country of origin and persist in their own cultural practices while selectively incorporating elements of Anglo culture (Gutiérrez 1996). Mexican Americans and Puerto Ricans appear to be statistically, as they are in reality, both a conquered and an immigrant minority. We will return to this puzzle in the final chapter.

Reality Check

INTERVIEW WITH JOHNANA

Johnana is a freshman premedical college student. Her family has lived in Texas for four generations. Her mother completed college and is a special education teacher. Her father graduated from high school. He is disabled. She grew up in a small town near members of her extended family and graduated as valedictorian of her class.

How do you refer to yourself in terms of ethnicity?
I refer to myself as Hispanic. A lot of people say Mexican American or Texan. We're from Texas. People can be racist and refer to you as Mexican but I don't get offended. A lot of people when I was growing up used to say Mexican American or Mexican and I never really liked that. I talked to mom and she said, "I refer to myself as Hispanic and that's the way you should refer to yourself." Within our own family we kid around, and call names. We use *wetback* a lot. We get together for holidays, and relatives fly in from California and Minnesota and from all over Texas, so we joke around.

What stands out as most important about your ethnic identity?
It would have to be our family because family is there for you and we are always very protective of our family. Our family is mainly our culture so we try to keep our family very close and we learn from each other.

How does your ethnic background affect you in your daily life?
I'm used to it so it really doesn't affect me much. You go to class and you go to work. I'm involved with organizations that have a lot of Hispanics. In most of my classes, the other students are from very different ethnic backgrounds. It doesn't bother me as long as I get my work done.

When did you first become aware of your ethnic background?
Probably in junior high. Parents are hesitant to tell you there are different races and people who actually have feelings of hatred toward other people. When I got into junior high, my mom had already explained to me, "You are Hispanic and there are people that are Caucasian and White and Black." In junior high, we got really competitive with our grades. I always wanted to be in the top percent and I'd notice some teachers not giving me points that I deserved. My mom said, "You just keep working hard and it'll pay off," and it did. Teachers in junior high would hand out papers and look the other way. In high school, our class was very competitive and the points actually determined our ranking in class and it was very close. If you didn't think you were being graded fairly you had to speak up or nothing was gonna happen. . . . I was valedictorian of my class and about the end of school, we found out there were secret meetings between a parent and the principal and the teachers. My best friend,

(continued)

the salutatorian, wanted grades changed because she didn't think it was fair. The ranking was going back and forth between me and her. I was the valedictorian at the end but it was really hard and it makes you aware of the way some people feel about you. They put on these masks that they're good Christians and they're really good people and they are very nice to you. We were best friends and we would go stay over at each others house and for something like this to happen is disconcerting. You are like, "How could people do that?" I was Mexican American and the other two people were Anglo. I had been ranked first in my class all four years of high school. My mom said it looked very suspicious all of a sudden. That's why she got involved. We met with teachers and they swore that some people were given extra credit and some people weren't. That was what upset my parents because if you do something, you should do it for everyone. It was a small town and people talk and it comes up that maybe I'm there because I didn't take the hard classes, but we were all in the same classes. We all took the honors classes and we all took the same thing.

How did you learn about racial and ethnic differences?
When you start growing up, you see more differences. These people are Jewish and maybe these people are Indian. When you're younger, it's just Black, White, and Mexican. Only a handful of people from my town went to college. A lot of the Hispanics were very much in poverty, but my mom always made sure we had the best she could provide.

Would marriage outside your ethnic group be acceptable?
My mom has always said as long as they love you and they treat you right there is no reason not to marry someone outside of your ethnic group if they can make you happy. My sisters and I have dated from other races so it's not a big thing. I dated a Black guy, my sister dated an Anglo and Blacks. Some of them were really big jerks. My parents don't discourage against race, they just discourage people with certain attitudes, if they are cocky or macho.

Did you speak a language other than English before entering school?
No. My mom went to school speaking Spanish and she didn't really understand what was going on, so she thought she'd save us a lot of pain and never teach us Spanish so we wouldn't have to go through the same thing. She realizes now that we need Spanish.

Tell me about your high school.
Our high school class was about 60 students. People were skeptical when I said I was going to college to major in premed. They were like, "How long is that gonna last?" The community is mostly Hispanics and some Whites. What you'd call "people of power" are mostly all White. I think we got breaks here and there because people knew my mom was a good teacher. There were people who were very nice to us in public but sometimes you got the feeling we weren't good enough to hang out with their children. We had no problems with anyone, so it was not a big deal to hang out with me.

 Discussion Questions

Are the incidents Johnana described acts of racial or ethnic discrimination? Why or why not?

Do you think it is acceptable for Johnana's family to use the term *wetback* in a joking way among themselves? How would her family react if others used the term in reference to them?

Why does Johnana find the term *Mexican* objectionable in respect to her ethnic identity?

In what ways has Johnana assimilated to the Anglo core culture?

What factors encouraged Johnana to leave her home community, go to a large college, and major in premed?

Why is language an important assimilation issue for most Hispanic groups?

In what ways are Mexican Americans and Puerto Ricans similar and in what ways are they different?

 Key Ideas

1. Language is an important element of cultural identity. In the United States, acquiring English-language skills has been viewed as a key measure of cultural assimilation. Most immigrant groups try to maintain their native language; however, this is very difficult to do over several generations without strong community support. Bilingual education has created heated debates over the status of English and other languages. Most educational programs in the United States are Anglo conformist in that they try to move Spanish-speaking Hispanic children into English-only classes as quickly as possible (i.e., they advocate cultural assimilation by substitution). Mexican Americans and Puerto Ricans have been more successful than some other groups in maintaining their native Spanish language, mainly because of a continued influx of new immigrants, return migrations to their homelands, and the proximity of Mexico and Puerto Rico to the United States.

2. Today, although Mexican Americans and Puerto Ricans in general show higher levels of cultural, secondary, primary, and marital assimilation than they did in the past, it seems unlikely that the differences between these Hispanic groups and Anglos will soon disappear. Increased Mexican immigration and continued Puerto Rican migration to the mainland have heightened discrimination, segregation, Spanish-language maintenance, and cultural awareness. Assimilation in jobs and income, for example, is not occurring rapidly and, in fact, may have been halted during the 1970s and 1980s.

3. A popular explanation of the comparative lack of worldly success by Mexican Americans and Puerto Ricans has focused on the way their values differ from those of Anglos. From this perspective, Hispanics must hasten to rid themselves of their culture if they wish to get ahead in American life. The value-orientations approach has been vigorously attacked as a form of cultural imperialism that works in the service of the Anglo-conformity ideology. Many social scientists, particularly Mexican American and Puerto Rican scholars, have identified a number of conditions, such as dominant-group discrimination and the traditional allocation of Mexican Americans and Puerto Ricans to dead-end jobs, as the biggest barriers to secondary structural assimilation.

4. There are differences between recent Latino immigrants and long-term Puerto Rican and Mexican American residents who have historically structured relationships based on colonial experiences. Neither the colonial model nor the immigrant model fits all the facts of the Mexican American and Puerto Rican experience. The histories of both groups include colonization, immigration, and back-and-forth migrations. An adequate account of the present and future social realities of Mexican Americans and Puerto Ricans must reconcile these facts.

5. Even as various subgroups forge a pan-ethnic identity as Hispanic or Latino, the subgroups maintain distinctions. Marked differences for Puerto Ricans are their U.S. citizenship and their greater cultural and economic similarities to African Americans than to the other Latino groups. Mexican Americans and Puerto Ricans bear close historical ties because of their shared colonial experiences.

Key Terms

bilingual education   The use of two languages in teaching subjects other than the use of a foreign language. Transitional bilingual programs teach subject matter in the students' native language until they can learn in English; partial bilingual programs teach oral skills in both languages, but make only limited use of instruction in the child's native language; and full bilingual programs aim at maintaining and developing both the minority language and English.

code-switching   The speaking style of switching back and forth from English to Spanish and vice versa. Code-switching is common among second- and third-generation Mexican Americans and Puerto Ricans.

commonwealth   The special status of the island of Puerto Rico as a self-governing, autonomous political unit associated with the United States.

extended families   Families that include parents, children, grandparents, and other relatives or godparents. All family members usually do not live in the same household.

familism   An orientation in which the needs of the family are more important than the needs of the individual. Familism implies close reciprocal relationships among family members.

limited English proficiency   An inability to speak, read, or write English well enough to function in an English-speaking society.

Lau Task Force Remedies   Guidelines interpreting the *Lau v. Nichols* decision that recommended bilingual education at the elementary school level for children with limited English skills.

machismo   A Spanish term referring to an attitude of masculine superiority and dominance. Stereotypes have portrayed Hispanic males as being *macho* and families, particularly Mexican families, as patriarchal or dominated by a male father figure.

pan-ethnic identity   The emergence of an ethnic identity and behavior, distinct and separate from the groups' individual ethnic identities. For example, Padilla (1985) explored the conditions in Chicago in the 1970s that have enabled Mexican Americans and Puerto Ricans to transcend the boundaries of their nationally and culturally based communities and adopt a new and different collective "Latino" or "Hispanic" identity.

postcolonial perspective   From this perspective, the legacy of colonial relations is seen not just as domination by the colonizer but also as strategies of survival and resistance on the part of the colonized people. Puerto Rico is considered to be a modern colony that may have transcended the colonial system but not the policies and conditions of poverty, unemployment, and low levels of education associated with colonialism.

 Notes

1. A *CPS Supplement for Testing Methods of Collecting Racial and Ethnic Information: May 1995*, U.S. Department of Labor, Bureau of Labor Statistics (October 1995) reports more details of the census survey. Also, Murguía (1991) notes that the pan-ethnic terms *Latino* and *Hispanic* are different in connotation, with *Latino* coming from the Spanish language and suggesting cultural pluralism and cultural maintenance, and *Hispanic* coming from the English language and emphasizing assimilation.

2. Much of the discussion of the history of Puerto Rico is drawn from the *Encyclopedia of Latin American History and Culture,* Barbara A. Tenenbaum, Editor in Chief, Vol. 4, 1996. London: Charles Scribner's Sons, Macmillan Library Reference USA, pp. 493–498.

3. For a broader discussion of the measurement of cultural assimilation, see Hazuda, Stern, and Haffner (1988).

4. Additional statistics regarding non-English-speaking students can be found in the report *Descriptive Study of Services to Limited English Proficient Students* (Washington, D.C.: U.S. Department of Education, Office of the Under Secretary, 1993).

5. Research on language maintenance shows that Spanish speakers who live in segregated neighborhoods are likely to use Spanish more frequently than those who live in less segregated neighborhoods. Similarly, immigrants who work mostly or exclusively with other recent immigrants and use Spanish in the work context maintain the language longer (see Portes and Schauffler 1996).

6. The Bushwick Parents' Organization filed suit against District 32 in Brooklyn, New York in 1995 arguing that after 3 years of bilingual education, one-third of the bilingual students in that district scored lower on English-language tests than when they started (see Stern 1996).

The press did not cover the strong support for bilingual education among Puerto Rican parents. The lawsuit was dismissed after the court ruled that the assessments and placements of the districts were appropriate (see *Bushwick Parents Organization v. Mills,* 5181 Civ. 95 [Sup. Ct. New York.] Verified Petition [1995]).

7. In San Francisco, Cosmopolitan Schools were established as early as 1867 in which particular attention was given to teaching German and French; but it was not until 1913 that Spanish was added to the curriculum, some 46 years after the other European languages had been recognized.

8. The Lemon Grove case is described by Balderrama (1982).

9. Steiner (1969:209) documented incidents of children who were forced to kneel on the playground and beg forgiveness for uttering a Spanish word, to stand in the corner for using Spanish in the classroom, to go to "Spanish detention" for speaking their native language, and to endure paddling if they persisted in being "Spanish-speaking."

10. The 1963 Dade County Bilingual Program was designed to maintain the Cuban children's Spanish language skills as well as teach them English. The plan included English-speaking children who would also learn in Spanish. Talented bilingual teachers among the refugees in Miami were recruited to teach in the bilingual program.

11. *Aspira of New York, Inc. v. Board of Education of the City of New York,* 72, Civ. 4002 (S.D.N.Y., Sept. 20, 1972).

12. The interpretive guidelines for the *Lau* decision published by the Office for Civil Rights of the U.S. Department of Health, Education, and Welfare (1970) indicated that the schools were required to "open up instruction" so that students who did not speak English could benefit. In the summer of 1975, the Office for Civil Rights offered specific remedies to school districts to help them comply with the *Lau* decision.

13. Almost 8 years after the *Lau* decision, the Texas federal district court mandated the phasing-in—starting in September 1981—of a statewide kindergarten through twelfth-grade

bilingual education program. Judge William Wayne Justice wrote in his decision that "unless [these children] receive instruction in a language they can understand . . . thousands of Mexican-American children in Texas will remain educationally crippled for life."

14. A summary of this debate was reported by Crawford (1995). House Speaker Newt Gingrich supported the English-Only legislation and cited the perils of linguistic pluralism.

15. Falcoff (1996:A11) argued that there are many divisive forces in American society, but language is not one of them. He claimed that the English-only legislation was led by hysterical "populist xenophobes."

16. Grebler, Moore, and Guzman (1970:429) noted that U.S. Spanish-language radio stations play an important role in assisting people to maintain both their language and their ethnic identity. Over one-half of all foreign-language radio broadcasting in the United States is conducted in Spanish, and Spanish is the only foreign language that is used exclusively by any U.S. station.

17. Cornejo, Ricardo J. "Bilingual Education: Some Reflections on Proposition 227." *Hispanic Outlook* (October 1998):27–30.

18. See, for example, Fishman, "Language, Ethnic Identity, and Political Loyalty," cited by Moore and Pachon (1985:120).

19. For critiques see Williams (1990) and Zambrana (1995).

20. Calculated from Table 10.6 in Bean and Tienda (1987:368–369). In addition, despite the higher rate of increase in professional employment among Mexican American males compared to Anglo males, the level of professional employment among Mexican Americans in 1980 still had not reached the Anglo level for 1960 (Bean and Tienda 1987:334–335). Although Mexican American men, as compared to Anglo men, experienced a relative gain in professional work between 1960 and 1980, the actual gap between the two groups increased slightly from 6.0 percent in 1960 (3.3 versus 9.3) to 6.4 percent in 1980 (5.7 versus 12.1) (Bean and Tienda 1987:329). This seemingly paradoxical result arises because a low rate of increase when applied to a large number may

yield a larger absolute increase than a higher rate of increase applied to a small number.

21. Differences in educational levels between Hispanic and non-Hispanic groups have persisted over many years. Past research has emphasized that Mexican American and Puerto Rican children have faced severe discrimination in the schools and, as a consequence, have had lower achievement levels than Anglos (Fligstein and Fernandez 1985:164; Valdivieso and Davis 1988:6). Although Mexican Americans and Puerto Ricans still lag behind the Anglo population, the available evidence suggests strongly that they are, as a group, becoming more assimilated in regard to education (see various articles in Darder, Torres, and Gutiérrez 1997).

22. Data included school records, questionnaires administered to each parent and teenager in their homes, and tape-recorded, transcribed interviews and participant observations with a subsample of 26 of the families.

23. See, for example, Farley and Allen (1987: 335–342), Poston and Alvírez (1973), Poston, Alvírez, and Tienda (1976), Siegel (1965), and Williams, Beeson, and Johnson (1973).

24. Calculated from Poston and Alvírez (Table 1, 1973:707).

25. Before this conclusion is accepted, however, other factors affecting income must be considered. Since older, more experienced people generally have higher incomes, some of the differences in income we have noted may be due to the differences in experience between older Anglo and younger Mexican American workers. Our comparison, consequently, should be restricted at least to Anglos and Mexican Americans who have similar levels of education and are of similar ages. When the groups have been "matched" in several important respects, it is reasonable to suppose that any remaining difference in income is due largely to discrimination. Using a similar method, Poston and Alvírez (1973:708) showed that in 1959, approximately $900 of the $1,251 difference between Mexican American and Anglo workers may have been a result of discrimination.

26. There is also evidence that among Mexican Americans, the "costs" are greater for those whose appearance is darker and more Indian that for those who are lighter and more "European-looking." For analyses and discussion see Telles and Murguía (1990, 1992), and Massey and Denton (1993:113).

27. The audit was conducted as follows: Latino men between 19 and 24 years of age were paired with Anglo men of the same age. Resumes were prepared and standardized so as not to reflect any significant differences in prior training or experience. A sample of entry level jobs was selected from newspapers and the pairs of job candidates each applied for the same job. There were 360 audits completed and 302 went all the way to the job offer stage.

28. In a study comparing rates of out-marriage in San Antonio, Bradshaw and Bean (1970:393) demonstrated that the rate for marriages in 1850 was about 10 percent. One hundred years later, the rate had approximately doubled. This general trend may be seen even in some small, comparatively isolated communities that have a tradition of high levels of social distance. In the early 1960s, the rate of out-marriage (for marriages) was 20 percent in San Antonio (Alvírez and Bean 1976:285), 33 percent in Albuquerque, and 5 percent in Edinburg, Texas (Murguía and Frisbie 1977:384). Some studies show that the rise in out-marriages is not rapid or that a rise may be followed by a decline. In Corpus Christi, for instance, the rate hardly changed between the early 1960s and 1970s, rising from 15 to 16 percent (Alvírez and Bean 1976:383). By 1988, the rate had reached 18 percent (Sherwood 1988:D14). In Albuquerque, a rapid rise from 33 percent in 1964 to 48 percent in 1967 was followed by a sharp decline to 39 percent in 1971 (Murguía and Frisbie 1977:384), and in California, there was a gradual decline from 55 percent in 1962 to 51 percent in 1974 (Schoen, Nelson, and Collins 1978).

Native Americans

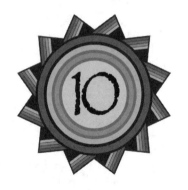

Many Native American leaders have contested the loss of native lands and have worked to maintain and promote the sovereignty of Indian tribes. The extent to which these goals illustrate or are compatible with pluralist ideology is a subject of intense controversy.

The Indian people are going to remain Indians for a long time to come.

—Melvin Thom

In a struggle to maintain political and cultural pluralism American Indians changed when it was necessary for their survival, but they have adjusted in ways that have allowed them to preserve their most valued traditions and lifestyles.

—C. Matthew Snipp

All cultures must depend on their younger generations to keep perpetuating age-old traditions. . . . They are the future leaders of our tribal people and in many ways are helping to keep our traditions alive. The work we are doing in the court room and in the state and federal legislatures is not just for our clients—the Native peoples of this country— but it is also for ourselves, our children, and our children's children.

—Native American Rights Fund

They were called "the vanishing Americans." After three centuries of contact with Europeans, diseases, bullets, alcoholic beverages, and industrial civilization had taken their appalling toll. The Indians declined in number from at least 2 million to less than one-eighth of that (Snipp 1989:10, 63). Whole tribes, bands, or nations—perhaps 50 altogether— disappeared (Spicer 1980a:58). McNeill (1976:190) estimated that, overall, more than 90 percent of the Indian population was decimated by epidemic diseases.[1] Deneven concluded that "the discovery of America was followed by possibly the greatest demographic disaster in the history of the world" (quoted in Snipp 1989:15).

At the time of the American Revolution, a swelling population in Europe created an enormous emigration to America. The developments in machine technology radically altered the competition between the Americans and the Indians and set the stage for the military conquest of the West during the last half of the nineteenth century. This conquest seemed to spell the end for the Indians as bearers of distinctive cultures. In fact, many tribes *have* vanished (Deloria 1969:20). But by 1996, the U.S. government still recognized 318 tribes in the 48 contiguous states (Nagel 1996:14) and 226 Alaskan tribes (*NARF Legal Review* 1994), and additional Indian groups sought official recognition.

According to data on those who identified themselves as American Indian and no other race, the Indian population reached a low of 237,196 in 1900 and then grew to 1.88 million by 1990 (Nagel 1996:5). Between 1990 and 2000, the number of those who identified themselves as American Indian and Alaska Native had increased by an additional 26 percent to 4.1 million persons (Ogunwole 2002). Hence, the American Indians have not "vanished" as anticipated. Instead, their population has *increased* so rapidly that today the Indians are one of the fastest growing groups in the United States. Their

289

amazing increase during the twentieth century has produced a population that may be approaching in size of the one existing in 1600.

During the twentieth century traditional Native American culture, along with Indian popular culture, has thrived. Indian newspapers and newsletters are published by tribal organizations; and tribal leaders strive to restore lost languages by encouraging their use (Nagel 1996:15, 47). Although many languages have completely disappeared, more than 150 Indian languages are still used, not counting dialects (Stewart 1977a:501). Moreover, American Indians "were not and have not become a single . . . people justifying a single label . . . as most Americans believe" (Spicer 1980a:59). The tribes represent a great many people with different cultural backgrounds, different historical experiences, and different identities. The tribes have, however, made numerous accommodations over time, which we discuss in this chapter.

In earlier chapters we noted the relations between some of the coastal tribes and the English during the seventeenth century to help explain the origin of the Anglo-conformity ideology and to illustrate its application. Now we enlarge our inquiry to trace some of the key events, people, and social processes that help to explain the present circumstances of the diverse people called "Indians."

The English Penetration of the Continent

The French and Indian War

Decades before the English founded Jamestown and Plymouth, French fur trappers, explorers, and priests rapidly expanded alliances with various Indian tribes and extended French claims to the entire Mississippi River Valley and portions of the Gulf Coast. The English at this time were making alliances with the Iroquois who could supply pelts either as trappers or as "middlemen" between the English and the tribes still further west (Nash 1974:93, 99).

The showdown between France and England came during the French and Indian War, which was fought mainly between 1754 and 1761. During the first years of this conflict, the Iroquois stood primarily neutral. However, after the English attacked with a large fighting force, the Iroquois threw their full weight to the side of the English (Nash 1974:267–268). When the war ended, an avalanche of new settlers poured into the Ohio Valley.

At this time, an Ottawa chief, Pontiac, and an Indian evangelist, Delaware Prophet, attempted to convince the Indians that they should give up the White man's trade goods, return to the old ways, and create an intertribal military organization to combat the Whites (Josephy 1961:110–112). Pontiac gained the support of many tribes, and starting with a siege of Fort Detroit in May 1763, warriors from many tribes attacked the English. As the fighting spread, the frontier was hurled back toward the Atlantic coast. When Pontiac learned that the French, Spanish, and English had signed a treaty in Europe, he sued for peace. In 1769, Pontiac was killed by a Peoria Indian whom he believed to be a friend (Josephy 1961:128).

The Proclamation of 1763

Pontiac's uprising failed to drive the English out of North America, but it served as a final argument for those in England who believed the colonies should follow a uniform policy toward the Indians. Such a policy, the Proclamation of 1763, promulgated by the English king, declared that (1) all land west of the crest of the Appalachian mountains was "Indian Country"; (2) any settlers west of the Appalachians who had not acquired a legal title to their land from the Indians must return to the colonies; and (3) all future land purchases from the Indians must be conducted in public meetings attended by representatives of the king (McNickle 1973:43). This policy recognized that the government of England must attempt to control trade between the Indians and the colonists and, in particular, must prevent the swelling colonial population from invading Indian Country. But there was no way for the English to prevent the colonists from moving onto Indian lands and taking possession of them by fair means or foul.

In 1787, the famous Northwest Territory Ordinance promised that, "The utmost good faith shall always be observed toward the Indians; their lands and property shall never be taken from them without their consent: and their property, rights, and liberty, they shall never be invaded or disturbed, unless in just and lawful wars authorized by Congress" (Jackson and Galli 1977:3). Congress, however, was no more successful in regulating contacts with the Indians than the English had been. George Washington lamented that the frontiersmen, "in defiance of the proclamation of Congress roam over the Country on the Indian side of the Ohio, mark out Lands, Survey, and even settle them. This gives great discontent to the Indians" (Prucha 1962:35).

Enforcing the Treaties

President George Washington attempted to establish "a firm peace" based on the "principles of justice and moderation" (Prucha 1962:41). His main tools were the Trade and Intercourse Acts, a series of laws enforcing the existing treaties with the major tribes of the North and South as well as future treaties. Existing treaties were widely violated. For example, following the Greenville Treaty (1795) 12 Indian tribes ceded around 50 million acres of Ohio to the United States. As usual, the Indians received a certain quantity of goods and a promise of future annual payments for their land; a line was also drawn on the map to separate Indian Country from White Country. As the White population in the Ohio Valley grew, however, many traders and settlers tried to gain concessions from the Indians beyond the established frontier line. Huge quantities of liquor were given to the Indians in return for their land and other possessions. The effects were devastating. Josephy (1961:147) stated that "almost overnight large segments of once proud and dignified tribes became demoralized in drunkenness and disease."

At this time a new leader, Tecumseh, and his brother, Tenskwatawa (the Shawnee Prophet), resumed Pontiac's call for the Indians to turn away from the White man's way, reject the trade goods that destroyed their independence, and unite to prevent the Whites from acquiring any more land. In a meeting with Governor (later president) William Henry Harrison, Tecumseh argued: "No tribe has a right to . . . sell a country! Why not sell the air, the clouds and the great sea, as well as the earth?" (Josephy 1961:155). Harrison made it clear that he would continue to make treaties and acquire Indian lands.[2] Tecumseh, therefore, continued to meet with the leaders of other tribes to urge them to join him in a pan-Indian uprising against the United States. Although Tecumseh was eloquent, most of the older chiefs were not convinced they should now become the allies of their traditional Indian enemies.

Soon after a battle between Tecumseh's warriors and Harrison's forces on Tippecanoe Creek, the War of 1812 between England and the United States began. Tecumseh supported the English. If the English won the war, he reasoned, then the rights of the Indians would be respected; but if the United States won, he believed, ". . . it will not be many years before our last place of abode and our last hunting ground will be taken from us, and the remnants of the different tribes . . . will all be driven toward the setting sun" (Josephy 1961:163). The English lost the war; Tecumseh lost his life in battle; and the Indians never again had the active support of a European power against the United States.

 Indian Removal

Legal Issues

In 1802, the state of Georgia ceded the western portion of its lands to the United States in return for a promise that the federal government would extinguish the land claims of the Cherokee Indians in Georgia (Hagan 1971:54). To fulfill the agreement, the federal government, through a series of treaties, forced the Cherokees to give up almost 60 million acres of land despite the fact that the Cherokees were celebrated as one of the most "civilized" of all the tribes. The Cherokees were organized as a loosely federated republic with a written constitution, a bicameral legislature, and an appellate judiciary. One of their members, Sequoyah, devised a system based on syllables that permitted the Cherokee language to be written; and this invention led to the spread of literacy among them (Spicer 1980a:84). Nevertheless, in 1828–1829, on the basis of the agreement of 1802, Georgia annexed the Cherokees' land. The Cherokees protested Georgia's claim to jurisdiction over their tribe in two cases argued before the U.S. Supreme Court: *Cherokee Nation v. Georgia* (1831) and *Worcester v. Georgia* (1832). The judgments in these cases, with Chief Justice John Marshall speaking for the Court, established the basic principles that have guided the Indian policies of the United States ever since (McNickle 1973:52).

These cases dealt with the issue of sovereign Indian nations. The main issue in *Cherokee Nation* was whether an Indian tribe, like foreign nations, has the constitutional right to bring a court action against a state. The U.S. Supreme Court ruled that the Cherokee tribe was not a foreign nation and, therefore, could not sue Georgia. Chief Justice Marshall stated that Indians "are acknowledged to have an unquestionable . . . right to the lands they occupy" but concluded that Indian tribes "may more correctly . . . be denominated domestic dependent nations" (Chaudhuri 1985:24).[3] This ruling, while agreeing that Indian tribes are **sovereign nations,** nevertheless placed limits on their sovereignty.

The main issue in *Worcester* was whether Georgia could pass laws that superseded the laws of the Cherokees. On this point, the Court ruled in favor of the Indians. "The Cherokee Nation," Marshall wrote, "is a distinct community, occupying its own territory . . . in which the laws of Georgia can have no force" (Bordewich 1996:46). This decision established the principle that although tribal sovereignty has limits, the remaining sovereignty is great indeed. Tribal powers included the right to make treaties, to be protected from state encroachments, and to enjoy certain basic immunities with respect to the United States (Chaudhuri 1985:23, 26). Taken together, the *Cherokee Nation* and *Worcester* rulings conveyed a view of the limits of tribal authority that has continued down to the present.

The Indian Removal Act.   Even though the Cherokees won in *Worcester,* President Andrew Jackson favored a policy of forcing the Indians to move west of the Mississippi, and he sponsored the Indian Removal Act of 1830. This act was designed to force all of the Indians in the southeastern states to move west of the Mississippi. Jackson ignored the U.S. Supreme Court's rulings and made it clear that he would enforce the Indian Removal Act. During the next 6 years, Jackson concluded 94 treaties with the Indians to induce them to move to Indian Territory (now Oklahoma) in order to make room for White settlers who were eager to move onto Indian lands. All of the usual tactics, including bribery, threats, and misrepresentation, were employed by the Whites to bring these treaties into existence. Even though many friends of the Indians' saw removal as a way to protect the Indians from the Whites, the Indians no longer believed the government's promises (Lurie 1982:138).

The Indians were given no choice. The removal process, which continued into the 1840s, is widely regarded as one of the most dishonorable chapters in American history. Removal shattered the lives of tens of thousands of Indians who owned their own homes, earned their living through farming, and sent their children to school as did their White neighbors. Despite this level of cultural assimilation, they did not receive the protection of the federal government. The Indians felt that the United States had violated basic principles of fairness and justice. One appeal to the conscience of the citizens of the United States read as follows: "Our cause is . . . the cause of liberty and justice. It is based upon your own principles, which we have learned from yourselves; for we have gloried to count your Washington and your Jefferson our great teachers" (Josephy 1961:179).

The Trail of Tears

Faced with the calamity of losing their ancestral grounds, some Indians decided to fight; others sought protection through the courts; but in the end, nearly all of them were moved hundreds of miles along what has become known as The Trail of Tears.[4] After lengthy negotiations, further legal battles, promises of "perpetual" land grants in Indian Territory, and agreed annual payments, four of the Civilized Tribes—the Choctaws, Creeks, Chickasaws, and Cherokees—moved to Indian Territory.[5]

The fifth Civilized Tribe—the Seminoles—refused to move. They had fought against the United States in the War of 1812 and again in 1818 when Andrew Jackson invaded Florida in a move against the Spanish. The Seminoles were angry over the deceptive practices that had been used in attempting to arrange their removal to the West. Another source of resistance stemmed from the fact that many Black slaves had fled from the United States and were now living among the Seminoles. Consequently, in 1835, the Seminole War erupted. The war lasted nearly 7 years, led to the deaths of between 1,500 and 2,000 American soldiers, and cost the United States at least $20 million (Josephy 1968:324).

By the early 1840s, approximately 100,000 Indian people, from southeastern and northeastern areas of the United States, had been moved from their homes east of the Mississippi into Indian Territory. The great influx of people into Indian Territory created numerous new problems. The United States had pledged to provide rations, weapons, and tools; but these necessities frequently did not arrive as promised. The United States had guaranteed protection against the "wild tribes" who already lived in or near Indian Territory, and this promise also was not kept. The Comanches, Osages, and Pawnees, for example, were outraged when the newcomers competed with them for resources. As the buffalo became more difficult to find, these Plains tribes raided the livestock of the Indian refugees, and the newcomers were forced to defend themselves (Hagan 1971:85–87).

By the late 1840s, only scattered fragments of many tribes remained east of the Mississippi River. After gold was discovered in California, the tribes could not be protected from westward movement. The idea of drawing a line on the map giving the eastern portion of the country to the Whites and the western portion to the Indians could not work. White traders, hunters, trappers, farmers, ranchers, and miners crossed the frontier line. The resistance of many western Indian tribes provided much of the imagery, romance, legend, and tragedy associated with the saga of "the winning of the West." But behind the saga lies the reality. Treaties with individual tribes were followed by the encroachments of White frontiersmen. The encroachments led to attacks, and the attacks led to retaliation. No matter how valiantly the Indians fought, they were outnumbered and outgunned. In a span of less than four decades, the experience of the western tribes recapitulated that of the eastern tribes.

 Plains Wars and Reservations

Increased Warfare

The familiar image of the Indian warrior derives principally from the cultures of the Plains tribes, especially those of the Sioux (Dakota or Lakota). These cultures, including certain styles of dancing and singing, have been most influential in the popular pan-Indian culture of modern Indian Americans (Wax 1971:149).

The development of the horse–buffalo and war complexes is well illustrated by the Arapahos, Blackfeet, Cheyennes, Comanches, and Crows, among others; but no tribes exceeded the Sioux as examples of the new lifestyle that developed on the Plains. The Lakotas became the dominant people of the northern plains and the most thoroughly adapted as horse-riding buffalo hunters. Various bands among the Tetons were particularly respected for their horsemanship and feared for their fighting abilities.

When the Whites began to cross the Plains, these tribes were "in the very midst of their great cultural fluorescence and were formidable and enthusiastic warriors" (Lurie 1982:139). But the Whites' diseases immediately took a terrible toll. In 1837, the population of the Mandans, one of the few farming tribes of the Plains, fell from around 1,600 to less than 100 (Hagan 1971:94; Wax 1971:32–33). Over a period of years, cholera and smallpox took about one-half of the Crow tribe's 4,000 people (Spicer 1980a:93); and in 1849, the Pawnees lost one-fourth of their population to diseases (Hagan 1971:94). These catastrophes were intensified by the rapid depletion of the buffalo. White hunters slaughtered the herds, making it much more difficult for the Indians to maintain a proper diet.

Soon after the signing of the Treaty of Guadalupe Hidalgo, Oregon, New Mexico, Utah, Kansas, and Nebraska were organized as territories, and California was admitted to the Union as the thirty-first state. Each of these steps stimulated traffic across Indian Country, bringing about increasing contacts and conflicts between Indian and White people. To regulate these interactions, the U.S. Army quickly extended to the western Indians the tried-and-true system of treaties and reservations that had been so successful in dispossessing the Indians of the East. In 1851, the Santee Sioux ceded most of their territory in return for a guaranteed reservation on the Minnesota River (Josephy 1968:336). Shortly thereafter, several other Plains tribes ceded over 90 percent of their lands and accepted reservations (Hagan 1971:98).

Violations of the Treaties

The U.S. government failed to prevent violations of the treaties by Whites and did not provide the rations and supplies guaranteed to the Indians. The 30-year period during and following the Civil War was a time of frequent, widespread warfare between Indians and Whites. Chiefs such as Red Cloud, Sitting Bull, Gall, Crazy Horse, Spotted Tail, Chief Joseph, Little Crow, Cochise, Geronimo, Little Wolf, and Quanah Parker and White military leaders such as Kit Carson, Philip Sheridan, William Sherman, George Crook, Alfred Terry, O. O. Howard, John Gibbon, and George Custer are reminders of the blood that was spilled across the West during these years.

The end of the Civil War brought a renewed effort by the Whites to build roads and railroads across Indian Country. The federal government attempted to complete a treaty with the Sioux that would grant a trainload of presents and an annual payment of supplies in return for safe passage of caravans through the Sioux lands. At the very time the treaty was being negotiated, however, the army sent a regiment of troops into Sioux country to build a chain of forts along the Powder River. The Sioux, led by the Oglala Chief Red Cloud, were enraged by this action and broke off the negotiations. Red Cloud gathered warriors, and after several months of guerrilla warfare, a small group led by Crazy Horse lured a detachment of soldiers under Captain William Fetterman into a trap. All 81 soldiers were slain.

This battle, called the Fetterman Massacre by the Whites, caused the U.S. government to send several commissions to meet with Red Cloud and the other Sioux chiefs.

Red Cloud refused to meet with the commissions and demanded that the soldiers be withdrawn from the forts. Finally, in 1868, the forts were abandoned and both sides promised to keep the peace. The Treaty of 1868 established the Great Sioux Reservation, comprising most of what is now North and South Dakota.

The Battle of Little Bighorn

The peace did not last long. White miners violated the Treaty of 1868 by moving into the *sacred* Black Hills to mine gold. The Sioux were infuriated by this renewed invasion of their land. They protested strongly to Washington and refused to permit mining on any basis. Tribes in the area were ordered to report to the reservation agencies; but large groups of Sioux led by Sitting Bull, Crazy Horse, and their allies refused to report. Generals Crook and Terry and Colonels Gibbon and Custer were ordered into Sioux country to deal with the hostile Indians. On June 25, 1876, Custer marched on a Sioux and Cheyenne encampment.[6] The Indians, however, had amassed an army of between 1,000 and 2,500 warriors. The warriors led by Crazy Horse, Two Moon, and Gall surrounded Custer's detachment.[7] Every member of Custer's group was killed, and the remaining two groups of the Seventh Cavalry suffered heavy losses.

The stunning victory of the Indians over the U.S. army on the Little Bighorn River was, in fact, one of the last gasps of a people fighting frantically to preserve their independence. The news of "Custer's last stand" spread quickly and stirred anger among Whites. The federal government claimed the Indians had violated the Treaty of 1868 and must now cede to the Whites all rights to the Black Hills and the Powder River country. The Indians were told if they did not agree their rations would be discontinued and they would be sent south to Indian Territory. Reluctantly, Red Cloud and Spotted Tail signed the agreement and were then placed under virtual arrest on their reservations in Nebraska.

With the surrender of Crazy Horse and, later in the same year, the surrender of Chief Joseph and his Nez Perces, armed Indian resistance to American dominance in the territory acquired from Mexico had nearly ended. Several other famous confrontations occurred during the next 10 years, including an "escape" by the Northern Cheyennes from Indian Territory, the "Ute War," and the last-ditch efforts of the Apaches in the Southwest. The words of Chief Joseph's widely publicized surrender speech reflected the situation in eloquent, tragic phrases: "Our chiefs are killed. It is cold and we have no blankets. The little children are freezing to death. Hear me, my chiefs. I am tired; my heart is sick and sad. From where the sun now stands, I will fight no more forever" (Josephy 1961:339–340).

 From Separatism
to Anglo Conformity

From the earliest days of the American republic, the primary thrust of the official policy of the U.S. federal government embodied the idea that Indians and Whites should be kept apart. This policy resulted in the sharp distinction that was created between Indian Country and White Country and the great expansion of the reservation system. Throughout this time, however, many people doubted the wisdom of separatism and urged that the Indians be assisted to become "civilized"; consequently, a secondary, contradictory official policy embodied the idea that the Indians could "be absorbed into American society" if they were given the tools, animals, seeds, and information needed to become farmers (Prucha 1962:214). The Indian Trade and Intercourse Act of 1793 empowered the president to "promote civilization" among "friendly Indians" and to expend $20,000 a year for 2 years for this purpose (Jackson and Galli 1977:63). Various additional laws continued this policy until 1819, after which time the amount of the annual "civilization fund" was reduced to $10,000; but the payment was then placed on a permanent basis.

The Bureau of Indian Affairs

The work of administering activities relating to the Indians had been entrusted to the Secretary of War in 1789. Secretary John Calhoun, in 1824, created a new agency named the Bureau of Indian Affairs (BIA). Among the duties of the bureau was "the administration of the fund for the civilization of the Indians" (Jackson and Galli 1977:43). In the Trade and Intercourse Act of 1834, the BIA was authorized, and the Commissioner of Indian Affairs was placed atop an organization that has exercised "immense power . . . over the lives and property of the Indian people" from that time to today (Deloria 1972:52).[8]

As increasing numbers of Indians became dependent on the BIA and its agents, the question of the relationship between the federal government and the Indian tribes grew more perplexing. The idea that the tribes were separate nations and could remain so began to give way to the idea that the Indians were "wards" of the government, and the government was their "guardian." Simultaneously, the idea that no further treaties should be signed with Indian tribes grew in popularity.

The End of Treaty Making

A rider to the Appropriations Act of 1871 stated that Indian tribes would no longer be recognized as powers "with whom the United States may contract by treaty" (Hertzberg 1971:3–4). All treaties previously established would continue in force. All new arrangements between the federal government and the tribes would be decided by Congress through legislation rather than by negotiation.

This sweeping change in the legal status of the Indian tribes greatly strengthened the hand of those who thought the government's traditional separatist policy should be discontinued. If Indian tribes were not sovereign nations and could not negotiate treaties, then why should they continue to live on reservations apart from other people? Land speculators and potential settlers wondered why the Indians should continue to occupy more land than they were "using." Political conservatives, forgetting the agreements to pay the Indians for their earlier land cessions, wondered why the government should continue to pay out "doles" to support the Indians. Reformers wondered if the "civilizing" process would not be hastened if the reservations were divided up so each family would have its own specific plot of land. Thus, both greed and humanitarian concern combined in support of legislation to break up the reservations, end the established policy of separatism, and institute a policy of Anglo conformity.

Critics who opposed dividing the land into individual allotments argued that it would "despoil the Indians of their lands and . . . make them vagabonds" (McNickle 1973:81). Advocates of the plan, in contrast, argued that the allotment of reservation lands to individuals would help instill in the Indians a pride of ownership, encourage them to give up their tribal past, and adopt the American way of life.

The Dawes Act

In February, 1887, the passage of the **Allotment (Dawes) Act** provided for surveying the reservations and dividing the land into tracts to be allotted to the members of the tribes. Any land left over after each tribal member had received his or her allotment would be declared "surplus" and could be sold. The money a tribe received for the sale of surplus land would be held in trust by the U.S. Treasury with interest from the funds used to support activities to move the tribes toward Anglo conformity. If, after a 25-year trial period, an individual allottee proved to be capable of managing his or her own affairs, that person could receive a "certificate of competency," a title to his or her land, and citizenship. At this point, presumably, the Indian would have become a well-motivated, self-reliant farmer and no longer a ward of the federal government (McNickle 1973:82–83). If the plan worked, the tribal life of the Indians would be disrupted, and the individual members of the tribes would be transformed into American citizens.[9]

Did the Indians who received individual land parcels adopt the White model and become self-sufficient farmers? Generally, they did not. The main effect of the Dawes Act was to transfer most of the land held by individual Indians into the hands of White people. As the opponents of the Dawes Act feared, the desire for land and the Indians' ignorance of American law led to widespread deceit and fraud in real estate transactions. Between 1887 and 1934, the Indians lost over 87 million acres of land—approximately two-thirds of their collective holdings before the passage of the Dawes Act (Jackson and Galli 1977:95).

Another important effect of the Dawes Act was to increase the power of the BIA and its control over the Indian people. The BIA hired more people and intruded in unprecedented detail into the lives of the Indians. For instance, the BIA developed membership rolls for the recognized tribes to determine who was and was not eligible for government services (Snipp 1989:33). The BIA also contracted for irrigation systems needed by the allottees to farm their land and arranged for the lease of lands not used for farming and for the investment of the collected funds. Thus, the agents of the BIA exercised decision-making powers that traditionally had been the prerogatives of the chiefs and the tribal councils. Even the rations to which the Indians were entitled could be withheld if BIA agents felt the Indians were not moving satisfactorily toward Anglo conformity.

The Dawes Act became the centerpiece of the effort to bring Indians into the mainstream of American society. The act was passed during the early period of the second immigrant stream, with its heightened nativism and renewed emphasis on Anglo conformity. The Dawes Act strengthened U.S. policies designed to promote the culture of the dominant group and, at the same time, to destroy Indian cultures.

Indian Education

The attempt to "civilize" the Indians included educational programs. Schools for this purpose had been established in colonial times. As the Indians increasingly were confined to reservations, building and operating Indian schools became an important function of the BIA. At first, the BIA established two kinds of reservation schools—day schools and boarding schools. Students who did well in the day schools, which were located near the students' homes, became candidates for "advancement" out of their homes and into the boarding schools. The boarding schools removed Indian children from their families and from the reservation as well and increased their exposure to the English language and Anglo American ways.

The Carlisle School in Pennsylvania, authorized by the BIA and founded in 1879 by Richard H. Pratt, an army officer, definitely demonstrated the Anglo-conformity ideology. Pratt believed the Indians' heritage should be replaced with the skills and attitudes of the larger society. The best way to do this, he thought, was to permanently remove Indian children from their tribal surroundings (Hertzberg 1971:16–17; Hoxie 1984:54–60). Pratt also developed the "outing system." Under this system, students from Carlisle attended the public schools while living in the homes of selected American families. In this way, each Indian child might be separated not only from his or her family and tribe, but from all other Indians as well.

In the decades following the passage of the Dawes Act, the BIA expanded the off-reservation boarding school system. These schools represented an intensive effort to transform Indian children into assimilated citizens of the United States.

The Ghost Dance and Wounded Knee

Attempts to "civilize" Indians through education were intimately bound up with programs to Christianize them. By 1819, the missionary effort was so well established that when Congress appropriated the "civilization fund" the president approved grants to some missionary societies to assist in their educational work (Jackson and Galli 1977:69). The primary effort of the missionary schools was not simply to teach the Indians but also to convert them to the Christian religion. This goal of the missionary schools was also adopted by the government-supported schools as a part of their general Anglo-conformity policy.

The Whites' fear of a resurgence of Indian religious beliefs and practices was revealed by a tragic and infamous episode in the winter of 1890. During the latter part of the 1880s, a religious revival called the *Ghost Dance* swept over the Plains. This religion, like several others of the time, promised the Indians that by practicing certain rituals, dances, and songs, they could harness the supernatural power of their ancestors and cause the White people to vanish from the earth.

The Ghost Dance quickly spread on the reservations and became so common that "almost all other activities came to a halt" (Brown 1973:409). The strange behavior of the Indians frightened the Whites. Calls went out for military protection and the arrest of the Ghost Dance leaders. One of the leaders to be arrested was Sitting Bull, the famous medicine chief of the Hunkpapa Sioux. Sitting Bull had become a celebrity while touring with "Buffalo Bill" Cody's Wild West Show, and was now living with his people at the Standing Rock Reservation. Shortly after the order went out, Sitting Bull was arrested and, in a tragic sequence of events, was killed by two of the Indian officers who took him into custody.

When the news of Sitting Bull's death reached Big Foot, a Miniconjou leader, he and about 350 others, most of whom were women and children, fled toward Red Cloud's Pine Ridge Reservation. On the way, Big Foot was apprehended by the Seventh Cavalry (Custer's former regiment) and was ordered to go to Wounded Knee Creek, South Dakota. The Indians camped that night at Wounded Knee. The next morning the army commanders ordered the warriors, most of whom wore ceremonial Ghost Shirts, to turn in their guns and other arms. According to some reports, one young warrior raised his rifle over his head and fired. The reaction of the soldiers was immediate. A withering blast of gun fire cut through the surrounded and defenseless Indians (Brown 1973:413–418). At the end of the "battle," 40 percent of the Indians were dead (Spicer 1980a:93).

The death of Sitting Bull and the U.S. army's actions at Wounded Knee snuffed out the Ghost Dance religion and with it the hope of the rebirth of tribal independence. The carnage at Wounded Knee, which occurred in the year that the frontier was officially declared closed, has served as a symbol of the appalling quality of European–Indian relations in the period from 1607 to 1890. For almost three centuries, the White people had encroached upon the Indians' lands and had insisted that the Indians either be driven away or made over in the image of White people. The Indians' resistance to either of these demands led to increased attempts to annihilate them.

Cycling between Anglo Conformity and Cultural Pluralism

As the twentieth century approached, the policy of Anglo conformity held firm. The Indian population had declined to less than 240,000, their lands were being allotted and sold, and many thought the "Indian problem" was solved. One conspicuous legal barrier, however, prevented Indians from participating fully in the mainstream. Since few Indians were citizens, they were in legal limbo. They "were prisoners of war when no state of war existed" (McNickle 1973:91). In gratitude to the thousands of Indians who had volunteered to fight in the American armed forces in World War I, Congress passed the Indian Citizenship Act in 1924. Many Indians feared, however, that this was yet another attempt to escape treaty obligations and detribalize the Indians.

Some Indian voters, nevertheless, became involved in politics and helped initiate an analysis of the effects of the federal government's trusteeship of the Indian people. The results of this analysis showed in detail that the land allotment policy had failed.[10] Most Indian allottees had lost control of their lands and, in the process, their best chance to become self-sufficient.

The Indian Reorganization Act

The Meriam Report came at a time when many people were calling for a radical change in the government's approach to Indian affairs. The 1934 Indian Reorganization Act (IRA), or the Wheeler–Howard Act, answered this call. By this act, the federal government abandoned the effort to require the Indians to adopt the Anglo lifestyle and embraced instead a pluralist policy. The new policy sought to assist (not force) the Indians to "lead self-respecting, organized lives in harmony with their own aims and ideals, as an integral part of American life" (McNickle 1973:93). The IRA restored the right of the Indian tribes to govern themselves *provided* they were willing to adopt the American model of representative democracy. The IRA also permitted Indian tribes to organize as corporate business enterprises.

In addition to stimulating democratic self-government and active participation in the U.S. business economy, the IRA also aimed to encourage Indians to maintain and develop their identities as Indians. Under the policies of the Dawes Act, all things Indian had been suppressed. Indian children in the government schools had not been permitted to wear long hair, to dress in tribal costumes, to engage in tribal rituals, or to speak their native languages. The new policy no longer viewed Indian tribal life as incompatible with contemporary American life. Indians were encouraged to develop their languages, renew their skills in arts and crafts, revive and transmit their ancient rituals and ceremonies, and participate in community life on an equal footing with other Americans.

The reorganization of most of the Indian tribes under the provisions of the IRA did not launch a dramatic increase in their educational level and standard of living; however, the management of Indian affairs definitely took a new direction. Programs were initiated to enable the Indians to recover some of their lost lands. Loan funds were established to help finance a college education for qualified Indian students and to help new Indian corporations develop and market new products or exploit the reservations' natural resources. More than in any previous period of life on the reservations, Indians began to participate in the planning and execution of the programs intended to assist them.

Throughout this period of reform, the BIA was still very much in control of reservation life. The Bureau still received the annual appropriations from Congress; and its scope expanded to include new duties such as assisting the tribes to organize representative governments, some of which appeared to represent the interests of the BIA more than those of the tribes. The BIA also continued to play a strong role in the determination of tribal memberships and the administration of justice; consequently, many Indians disliked the IRA and the way it was administered. Despite the efforts of many people, a large discrepancy remained between the ideals of the IRA and the realities of Indian life.

The "Termination" Policy

Champions of Anglo-conformity policy regained dominance during the two administrations of President Eisenhower. In 1953, Congress adopted a resolution, House Concurrent Resolution 108 (HCR 108), declaring that Indians "should be freed from Federal supervision and control" (Bahr, Chadwick, and Day 1972:485). HCR 108 suggested that all laws and treaties then binding the United States to the Indians should be nullified. This new policy, known as **termination,** seemed to be a direct assault on the idea that the Indians were entitled to payments and services for the land they had ceded to the government through treaties.[11] The Indians viewed this change as another shocking example of a unilateral action by the government to avoid completing its part of the treaty bargains (Svensson 1973:32).[12]

Congress hoped the termination policy would get the government "out of the Indian business" (Spicer 1980b:119). Termination of services to a tribe could occur only if the tribe were sufficiently assimilated, willing to sever its ties with the federal government, and able to survive economically with local and state help. Few tribes met these standards.

The termination experience of the Klamath tribe of Oregon illustrates why the policy was so unpopular among Native Americans. The Klamaths, with a tribal membership of around 2,000 people, owned nearly 1 million acres of land containing forests valued at approximately $50,000 per person (McNickle 1973:106). The government's plan gave the tribal members, many of whom did not understand the alternatives, no more than 3 years to decide what to do with their collective wealth. They could either form a corporation to manage their property or they could sell the land and timber and divide the money among the members of the tribe. Either way, the government's trusteeship would be terminated.

A tribal vote resulted in favor of selling and dividing the money. The Klamaths expected the federal government to buy their land, establish a national forest, and pay each member of the tribe $43,500. As matters developed, the government disbanded the Klamath Tribal Council and ended the trust relationship but certified only a fraction of the tribe's members as "competent." Ten years later over one-half of the members had not received their payments and continued to be wards of the government. The main result of termination for them was the destruction of tribal government and the disorganization of tribal life (Spicer 1980a:106). This policy, according to a U.S. Senate report (McNickle 1973:107), increased poverty and deepened the Indians' distrust of the federal government in general and the BIA in particular. The experience of many other "terminated" tribes paralleled that of the Klamaths (Peroff 1981).[13]

By the end of the second Eisenhower administration, it became apparent that the termination policy, as had been true of the earlier allotment policy, would not liberate the Indians to participate fully in the mainstream of American life. Both the termination policy and the allotment policy sought to end abruptly the special relationship of Indians to the U.S. government; instead, the policies took from the Indians the resources they needed to create the very independence the policies tried to enforce.

Resistance of the American Indians to the termination policy did not mean they wished to continue as dependents of the federal government. Most Indians endorsed the IRA goal of "the ultimate disappearance of any need for government aid or supervision" (McNickle 1973:93) and wished to be free of the interference and regulation of the BIA. But, in addition to the fear that termination would deny them treaty entitlements, there was the even greater fear that an abrupt end to special status would mean an end to tribal life and their existence as Indians. The policy of termination did not take into account the strong wish among American Indians to fashion a mode of participating in American society that would not sacrifice their distinctiveness as Indians.

Governmental actions to effect termination reached a standstill by 1961. One hundred and nine bands and tribes had been terminated by this time (O'Brien 1985:44). As the War on Poverty came into being, Indians began to participate in new government programs designed to expand their role in planning and controlling their own destiny. Near the end of the decade, President Johnson affirmed the right of Indians "to remain Indians while exercising their rights as Americans" (McNickle 1973:124); and in 1968, the Indian Civil Rights Act was passed. President Nixon, in 1970, attacked the idea that the federal government had the right to terminate unilaterally its special relationship with American Indians. The goal of national policy, Nixon said, must be to encourage self-determination among the Indians and "to strengthen the Indian's sense of autonomy without threatening his sense of community" (Jackson and Galli 1977:134). Congress enacted the intent of this presidential message into law in 1975 with the passage of the Indian Self-Determination and Educational Assistance Act. This act established a new relationship between the tribes and the federal government that, Olson and Wilson (1984:204) stated, represents "the greatest victory for pan-Indian activists in American history." In 1978, the U.S. Congress adopted the Federal Acknowledgment Program allowing terminated and unrecognized tribes to apply for federal recognition.

Pan-Indian Responses and Initiatives

Protest Organizations

After the federal government terminated its Anglo-conformity policy and returned to the pluralist policy of self-determination, American Indian political activism reached an unprecedented level. Throughout history, Indians generally were not organized at a level above the tribe, and when they were—as in the Powhatan, Wampanoag, and Iroquois Confederations—the organizations were loose. Loyalty to the tribe remained primary. Indians, nevertheless, did realize the advantages of acting together in broader groups. The efforts of men such as Metacom, Pontiac, Tecumseh, and Sitting Bull remind us that organizing to resist the common foe is not new. Still, intertribal enmities and factionalism within various tribes prevented these efforts from achieving lasting success. Gradually, the Indians were divided, defeated, and concentrated on reservations. By the time the Indians' treaty-making powers were revoked in 1871, the federal government had assumed complete control of their lives.

As previously self-sufficient tribes were forced onto the reservations, various "friends of the Indians," mostly Christian groups, began to work on their behalf. The Women's National Indian Association protested the forced removal of the Ponca Indians to Indian Territory. The Indian Rights Association instituted a series of annual conferences to coordinate various efforts to assist the Indians (Hertzberg 1971:20). The ideas of these groups of White Americans concerning what would be good for the Indians molded the various programs and projects undertaken by the groups.

Activities of similar well-meaning groups and individuals were partly responsible for the passage of the Dawes Act in 1887. At a time when the Anglo-conformity ideology was gaining greater strength, the idea that the Indians could best be assimilated by forcing them to abandon their ancient heritages and adopt the culture of the dominant society seemed to many of the White supporters of the Indians to be quite humane and sensible. Few Whites thought to consult the Indians to see what *they* thought or wanted, but the Indians did have opinions. The Five Civilized Tribes led a lobbying effort to prevent the passage of the Dawes Act and managed to limit its application for a time.[14]

The Society for American Indians.   Over time, a comparatively large group of highly educated Indians developed. These Indians moved easily between the White and Indian worlds. Many Indians in this bicultural position believed their people must recognize that the White-dominated industrial American society would destroy all things Indian unless the Indians joined together, accepted the reality of changed conditions, and fashioned a new "Indian identity beyond the tribe and within the American social order" (Hertzberg 1971:300). Representatives from this Indian elite came together to attempt to devise a plan through which Indians could become full participants in American society. In 1911, on Columbus Day in Columbus, Ohio, an organization was founded exclusively by and for Indians. The Society for American Indians (SAI) adopted a constitution to promote "the advancement of the Indian in enlightenment," "citizenship among Indians," and "the right to oppose any movement which may be detrimental to the race" (Hertzberg 1971:80).

Among the leaders of the new organization were several people who were well known and respected by both Indians and Whites. Dr. Charles Eastman (Ohiyesa), a Sioux, learned to read both English and Lakota as a child. He graduated from Dartmouth and Boston University Medical School and was a physician at the Pine Ridge Reservation at the time of the Wounded Knee Massacre. Dr. Carlos Montezuma (Wassaja), the fiery Apache, worked his way through the University of Illinois and the Chicago Medical College. He practiced medicine at several Indian reservations, at Carlisle, and in Chicago. Dr. Arthur Parker (Gawasowannah), a Seneca, graduated from high school in White Plains, New York, and was educated as a Presbyterian minister and as an anthropologist. He became famous for his studies of the Iroquois. Although the leaders of the SAI shared the stated objectives of the organization, they differed in certain ways. Like many other Americans of the period, the SAI leaders spoke in terms of the melting pot metaphor. Their opinions ranged, in fact, between pluralism and Anglo conformity (Hertzberg 1971:39–57, 63, 156, 195).

The SAI, which was active for about 13 years, gradually came to represent two principal goals: the abolition of the BIA and the extension of citizenship to all Indians. The first goal seemed nearly impossible to many of the members; so it became a point of vigorous disagreement. The citizenship goal was attained in 1924. The importance of the SAI, however, went beyond its specific accomplishments. The SAI demonstrated that Indians could organize to pursue group goals within the framework of American society, and it became a foundation for intertribal cooperation and pan-Indian identity.

After the decline of the SAI and the passage of the IRA, pan-Indian organization at the national level weakened. The experiences of many Indians during World War II, however, and the gradual rise in congressional opposition to the pluralist philosophy underlying the IRA, led once again to the formation of a national pan-Indian organization.

The National Congress of American Indians (NCAI).   A group of World War II veterans formed the NCAI in 1944. Like Mexican and Black American veterans, these men were exposed to many different influences as they traveled around the country and abroad in the military. They came to believe that, as citizens of the United States who had risked their lives defending the country, they were entitled to equal treatment and a "fair shake" in economic matters. They were not willing to return to the reservations to live under the authority of the BIA or to be relegated to the slums of the cities.

The NCAI promoted the interests of all Indians but, simultaneously, encouraged each tribe to pursue its own particular objectives within the framework of its agreements with the United States. When the termination policy was initiated, the NCAI was in the forefront of the opposition. They did not like the BIA's interference in their lives, yet they feared that any marked change was likely to make matters worse. The fight against termination, therefore, became a focal point of NCAI activities during the 1950s.[15]

This was a time of intellectual and spiritual ferment among American Indians. War veterans and their children completed high school and entered college in unprecedented numbers (Steiner 1968:31). As had been true a half-century earlier for the founders of the SAI, these new young intellectuals were uncertain of their place in American society. Must they leave their tribal lives irrevocably behind to enter the American mainstream? What opportunities awaited them if they returned to the reservations after completing formal education?

The New Tribalism

In 1954, a small group of American Indian university students struggled to formulate a new policy in Indian affairs (Steiner 1968:33). They desired to complete their formal education and bring their knowledge back to the reservations. The new policy they created—variously called the **new tribalism,** tribal nationalism, or Red Power—emerged in 1961 following a very influential gathering, the American Indian Chicago Conference. Shortly after the conference, the Youth Caucus met again—this time in New Mexico— and established a new pan-Indian organization, the National Indian Youth Council (NIYC). The NIYC, made up mostly of young, urban Indians, became the first of the Indian activist organizations formed during the civil rights era. The group's slogan "For a Greater Indian America" reflected its intertribal and Indian nationalist stance (Nagel 1996:129). As a part of the new policy, the underlying issue of Indian sovereignty has been debated in many court cases relating to tribal land claims, water rights, fishing and hunting rights, religious and burial rights, and contract disputes (*NARF Legal Review* 1994, 1995). In some cases the Indians have won; in other cases they have lost; and many cases are still in the courts.

The Declaration of Indian Purpose stressed the Indians' "right of sovereignty," agreement with Chief Justice Marshall's view that treaties with Indian tribes are binding, a determination to maintain Indian identity, and a need for technical assistance to regain "the adjustment they enjoyed as the original possessors of their native land" (Bahr, Chadwick, and Day 1972:485–486). The younger leaders, considered their fight to be in some ways a part of the larger fight between the dominant society and all other oppressed groups; and they argued that, along with other non-White groups, "Indians must exercise their rights" (Steiner 1968:304).

The American Indian Movement.   In 1964, the Supreme Court of the state of Washington nullified 11 federal treaties that guaranteed the fishing rights of Indians in that state. The Makah tribe called on the NIYC to organize a protest of the loss of these fishing rights. Overriding the concerns of conservative tribal leaders who feared that going to jail was "undignified" and "not the Indian way," several hundred Indians representing different tribes gathered for a "fish-in" on the Quillayute River.

The fish-ins were the precursors of the national Red Power movement. Legal issues protested in the fish-ins continued into the 1990s in court battles. In addition to forcing an eventual legal victory for Native American fishing rights, the fish-in movement provided training for Red Power activists in other parts of the United States and also taught the Indian activists that an alliance of tribal and pan-Indian organizations and collective action could be quite powerful in redressing grievances (Nagel 1996:162). The next several years were marked by a sharp increase in organized Indian actions to protest various conditions or violations of civil rights. Most of these actions were conventional, nondisruptive efforts to improve the lives of American Indians; however, the number of actions involving direct nonviolent confrontations increased dramatically. For example, in 1969, a group of 89 young Indians, identifying themselves as "Indians of all Tribes," seized Alcatraz Island in an effort to "hold on to the old ways" (*Indians of All Tribes* 1971:200; James 1986:230; Nagel 1996:131–141).

Although the demonstration did not achieve the avowed purposes of reclaiming Indian land and establishing title and a pan-Indian cultural center, the occupation of Alcatraz did succeed "in dramatizing the Native American demand for self-determination, tribal lands, and tribal identities" (Olson and Wilson 1984:170). Many Indians saw the occupation of Alcatraz and the steps that followed as a major turning point in awakening Indian ethnic pride and restoring dignity to a people who had been depicted as powerless and subjugated victims of history (Nagel 1996:133).

Propelled by the events at Alcatraz, the American Indian Movement (AIM) was established in Minneapolis, Minnesota, in 1970. This militant new body quickly grew into a national organization that argued for Indian sovereignty, insisted on the protection of the Indians' treaty rights, and challenged the validity of the tribal governments formed under the IRA (Bonney 1977:215). AIM's first major action, organized in 1972 in cooperation with some other Indian groups, was a protest march in Washington, D.C., called "The Trail of Broken Treaties."

Throughout the 1980s and into the 1990s, AIM remained a force in American Indian activism, organizing and participating in protests over land and grazing rights, the rights of tribes to sell cigarettes without state or federal taxes, and over athletic team Indian mascots, gestures, logos, and slogans. Although the tradition of active protest fostered by AIM has remained a salient force in the struggle for Indian civil rights, many of the AIM leaders either have been repressed by local and federal law enforcement agencies or their proposals have been incorporated into official policies. The result has been less direct-action protest and more attention to legal action.

Games of Chance.   An illustration of the jurisdictional conflicts between particular Indian tribes and outside legal entities concerns the operation of games of chance. During the past two decades, Indians increasingly turned to **gaming** as a source of income (*Americans Before Columbus* 1992:3); and as matters developed, by 1994 there were more than 160 tribes throughout the country with gambling businesses that were generating an estimated $6 billion per year (Bordewich 1996:108). The gaming industry thus has become a very important source of money and jobs on many Indian reservations and has been referred to as "the new buffalo economy."

A conflict developed when federal legislation, the Indian Gaming Regulatory Act, stated that certain types of gambling could be offered on the Indian reservations only if they were legal in the state outside of the reservation. One of the difficulties the Indians faced was that in many instances the state officials were unwilling to grant the permission needed to operate specific games. Officials in the state of Arizona, for instance, refused to permit the Yavapai-Apache Indians to continue offering some popular games that had been producing an estimated $1.4 million per year in revenue for the tribe. The Indians refused to discontinue the games on the ground that the state had refused to negotiate in good faith (*Americans Before Columbus* 1992). Mr. Tim Giago, the editor of *The Lakota Times,* was quoted as saying, "The Indian nations are sick and tired of being treated like children. Why in hell should these lands need the state's permission[?]" (Johnson 1994).

Sovereignty for Alaskan Tribes.   For three decades, the Alaskan Indians, with the legal assistance of the Native American Rights Fund, tried to convince the federal government that Alaskan Indians should have tribal status, as do many other U.S. Indians. The state of Alaska and various oil companies opposed this designation, claiming that Indian Country was terminated by the passage of the Alaska Native Claims Settlement Act in 1971. The Alaskan Indians sought tribal status because it would allow them to tax nonmembers and corporations on tribal land and give the tribes the authority to exercise the governing powers needed to provide social services and keep the peace. It also would entitle them to a government-to-government relationship with the United States and eligibility for various federal services. The Alaskan Indians had little doubt that the 226 tribes in Alaska could provide proof that they are "modern-day successors to historically sovereign bands of Native Americans," which is required for tribal status. In 1993, the Assistant Secretary of the Interior for Indian Affairs, Ada Deer, a Menominee Indian woman, published a list that recognized that Alaskan tribes had the same status as Indian tribes in the other states (*NARF Legal Review* 1994).

The U.S. Supreme Court Case, *Alaska v. Native Village of Venetie Tribal Government* (1998) cast some doubt on the sovereign status of Alaskan villages.[16] In a major victory for Alaskan state authorities and a blow to the sovereignty of the village of Venetie, Justice Clarence Thomas, speaking for a unanimous Court, held that Venetie's 1.8 million acres of fee-simple lands did not qualify as "Indian Country" because they had not been set aside by the federal government for tribal use and were not "under federal supervision."

Thus, the tribal government lacked the authority to tax and called into question the political status of these villages (Wilkins 2001, 2002).

Issues and incidents such as these have served to heighten the American Indians' awareness of their shared characteristics and, thus, to promote the emergence of a new concept of "Indianness." This sense of common purpose has enabled Indians to act together to protect their treaty rights and enlarge the powers of their tribal governments.[17] Many of the reservations hold some of the richest resources in the United States, including coal, oil, gas, forests for logging, and water rights. In the past, the tribes have gotten only minimal profits from leases or contracts for rights to these resources negotiated on behalf of the Indians by the BIA. Many tribes have banded together to hire their own lawyers, to negotiate more profitable contracts, or to form companies of their own to extract the resources on their reservations themselves.

Immigrant or Colonized Minority?

Is there any basis whatsoever for considering American Indians to be similar to the immigrant minorities? An attempt to apply the immigrant model to Indians may be farfetched. The possibility of such an application rests on the consequences of rural-to-urban migrations. In 1887, when the Dawes Act was passed, nearly all Indians lived on the reservations or in rural communities. By 1980, more than half of the Native Americans had left the reservations and were living in cities and towns. By 1990, however, all of the 15 largest reservations, with the exception of Pine Ridge (which is one of the poorest places in the nation), had experienced increases in population growth that exceeded what is possible from natural increases. Some of the largest reservations experienced substantial growth— with the Navajo reservation up almost 37 percent, Fort Apache up 43 percent, the Osage and Blackfeet reservations up 38 percent, and Fort Peck up 35 percent (Snipp 1992:19). These population increases suggest in-migration to the reservations. The net result is that there are still proportionally fewer Americans in Indian Country—reservations, trust lands, Alaska Native villages and lands near reservations—than there are in cities and urban areas; but the patterns indicate that an increasing number of Indians are returning to their cultural heritage.

Since the Dawes Act caused many Indians to lose their land, they frequently had little alternative but to move to nearby towns or more distant cities. That process weakened ties with those who remained on the reservations. Many were forced to take urban jobs, usually as unskilled workers, and they were required to take into account in their daily lives the language, ideas, manners, and ways of acting that predominated in the urban centers. Under such circumstances, some Indians, especially those who had attended the boarding schools, moved rapidly in the direction of cultural and secondary assimilation. Many others clustered together in small enclaves at the bottom rung of the economic ladder. In both cases, however, urban Indians experienced the same broad forces of modernization as their contemporaries who immigrated to the cities from Europe, Asia, Mexico, and the rural South.

Until the onset of World War II, the proportion of Indians who lived mainly or permanently in urban centers was comparatively small; however, during the war, the number of Indians moving to towns and cities increased sharply. Approximately 40,000 Indians were attracted to the cities, primarily on the West Coast, by the new employment opportunities created by the war. The migration was stimulated, too, because many of the approximately 25,000 Indians who were drafted into the armed forces were stationed in or near cities (Stewart 1977b:524). The most famous of these were the Navajo "code talkers" whose native languages were not understood by enemy interceptors (Jacobson 1984:167). At the end of World War II, approximately 80,000 Indians lived in urban places (Spicer 1980b:110).

The unemployment rates of Indians remaining on the reservations continued to be extremely high, but rather than attempting to develop the reservations more vigorously and strengthen tribal life, the BIA launched a new program to help Indians "relocate" in cities. This kind of assistance to Indians was by no means new, but the effort became much more important after 1950 when Dillon S. Meyer, the man who directed the program to relocate the Japanese and Japanese Americans during World War II, became the Commissioner of Indian Affairs (Officer 1986:122). In 1952, the relocation idea became the foundation for a greatly expanded nationwide effort called the Voluntary Relocation Program.

The relocation program included job training, counseling, and job creation. Indians selected for the program were provided transportation to a designated Employment Assistance Center in cities such as Chicago, Los Angeles, and Denver; and since the program's directors wished to make it difficult for the Indians to return home, they usually were sent to cities fairly far from their reservations. The idea of solving the "Indian Problem" by forcing the Indians into the mainstream again became dominant. The message communicated to the Indians was "either conform to the Anglo way and move several hundred miles away from the reservation or stay and live at substandard levels" (Bahr 1972:408). Between 1953 and 1972, more than 100,000 American Indians were settled in American cities under the relocation program. In addition, during the same period of time, more than 200,000 other Indians moved away from their reservations without help from the program.

The tremendous growth of the urban American Indian population within the last 5 decades affords a basis for arguing that, like Mexican Americans and Black Americans, Indians, too, are now on the road to higher levels of assimilation. Implied also is the belief that as Indians become more urbanized they will move more fully into the mainstream. Price (1972:438) stated the case in this way: "Conditions in the city lead the Indian away from tribal patterns. The reservation offers a very narrow range of occupational, religious, political, and recreational alternatives. The range of possible choices is vastly increased in the city."

The urban areas also offer many more opportunities for Indians to assimilate than do the rural reservations; however, one additional point concerning the urban experience of Indian Americans should be mentioned. Many Indians who *reside* in cities do not, in a certain social sense, *live* there. Some Indians, as Bahr (1972:408) expressed it, are only temporary migrants who "raid" the city, "take" city resources, and then return to the reservation or small off-reservation community to "live." This mode of adaptation resembles that of the "birds of passage," "sojourners," and "transnationalists" we have noted among various American immigrant groups. The nearness of the reservations and the strength of the tribal ties, however, may mean that the intention to return home is more easily put into practice by Indians than by the members of most other groups. This may especially be the case of the urban Indians who plan to return to the reservations when they retire from their city jobs. Even Indians who are not temporary migrants or do not plan to return to the reservation permanently may still maintain a strong sense of Indian identity and may do everything in their power to relate themselves to urban life as Indians.

Although research has shown shifts to English language usage, growing urbanization, and rising levels of education and income—all classic indicators of assimilation—researchers also have reported evidence of ethnic resurgence. There has been an increase in the extent to which people select an Indian ethnic identification in U.S. Bureau of the Census counts; Indian ethnic organizations have grown in number and have been increasingly active in civil rights litigation; and there have been social and cultural revitalizations on the reservations as well as in urban Indian communities. These points and others are amplified in our consideration of the extent to which American Indians have been affected by the main subprocesses of assimilation.

Native American Assimilation

Throughout American history, federal Indian policy has shifted between the desire to segregate the Indian people and the desire to assimilate them. How successful have the various assimilationist efforts been in promoting the cultural and structural assimilation of Native Americans?

The struggles of the American Indians have occurred in the reverse order from that of nearly all other American ethnic groups (Rothenberg 1995:290–294). Groups who came from overseas, whether voluntarily or involuntarily, started with no political or cultural rights and mainly have attempted to gain political and cultural equality with the majority. Indians, in contrast, started with their own nations and have gradually lost much of what they had to the advancing Anglo American group. Since most Indian tribes have long been separate political entities, they have been forced to struggle to maintain their own institutions and beliefs in the face of tremendous racism and, during certain periods, governmental policies of forced assimilation.

Despite the pressures, the levels of each form of assimilation among American Indians are, in general, comparatively low. Indians have clung tenaciously to their tribal heritages and presently are struggling to amplify a pan-Indian identity and to renew tribal sovereignty. Also suggested in the previous discussion of the migration of Indians to urban areas is the view that the reservations are the repositories of the traditional cultures and that the Indians who remain on the reservations are likely to live in a more traditional way and to be more successful in preserving their tribal heritages than are off-reservation Indians. Ideally, to assess the levels of cultural, secondary structural, primary structural, and all of the other forms of assimilation among the American Indians, one would wish to be able to state the current level of each type of assimilation among each of the distinct Indian groups and, also, to take into account the differences between reservation and off-reservation residents within each tribe. Such a complete approach cannot be attempted here. Rather we must rely on general comparisons that tend to submerge the important differences that exist among the tribes and a few examples chosen to illustrate some contemporary variations among the tribes.

Cultural Assimilation

Who is an Indian? The issues raised by the efforts to identify Native Americans are complex. Tribal classifications are important because they have been used over the years to decide who was entitled to government rights and privileges and who was not (Barringer 1993).

For many years, the federal government attempted to define the American Indian population based on the concept of **blood quantum.**[18] In the nineteenth century, scientific ideas concerning race and racial differences were based on the ancient belief that "races" are sharply distinguishable genetic categories and that both physical and cultural traits are transmitted "through the blood" from one generation to the next. The presumed "amount" of blood that a person possessed from a particular race determined the degree to which that person would resemble and behave like others of similar biological background. For example, full-blood Indians were presumed to have the full measure of physical and social characteristics ascribed to Indians. Individuals with one White and one Indian parent were "half breeds" or mixed-bloods. BIA officials used this blood quantum method to identify members of the Indian population and calculated that if both parents were "pure" Indian, the blood quantum of their children was 100 percent. The children of racially mixed marriages were presumed to have some calculable fraction of "Indian blood," such as three-fourths, one-half, or one-eighth.

The blood quantum method is still used in some situations. For example, a one-fourth blood quantum is the minimal requirement for receiving some government services, such as medical care on the reservations. A large number of tribal governments use one-sixteenth to one-half blood quantum criteria for determining tribal membership (Snipp 1989:34). As the relationship between the blood quantum approach and the ideas of scientific racism have been clarified, Native American activists increasingly have challenged the racist assumptions underlying blood quantum tests of Indianness (Nagel 1996:244). Indeed, the terms *full-blood* and *mixed-blood* frequently refer to a person's cultural commitment rather than to some presumption concerning his or her biological ancestry.

Amid controversies over how to determine who is a member of the various ethnic and racial groups, the federal government adopted **self-identification** as the method of classification for the U.S. Bureau of the Census and for most other agencies. As a result, changes in the ways that Native Americans have classified themselves are believed by demographers to be among the most important sources of the rapid growth of the Indian population. For example, the Indian population counted in the census increased more than fivefold in the three decades following 1950 (Passel and Berman 1986). Eschbach (1995) carefully analyzed birth and death rates and migration patterns and determined that the unexpected growth in the Native American population indicated that a large proportion of persons of mixed descent are now identifying themselves as Indian. The reality that the population has not diminished as tribal members have learned English and intermarried has challenged the idea based on the assimilation models that the Indian population would decrease over time.

Nagel and Snipp (1993) proposed that ethnogenesis is occurring among Native Americans.[19] They argued that in response to reduced numbers and various threats to their survival, some tribes have combined, resulting in the disappearance of some groups, the growth of other groups, and the creation of multitribal composite communities. The formal recognition of some groups and not others as Indian tribes by the federal government has also forced Indians to reorganize, with some reservation tribes adopting tighter, more exclusionary membership rules and nonreservation tribes adopting looser, more inclusionary rules. For many Indians, the process of ethnogenesis has meant that the pan-Indian "nationality," has become a new ethnic identity. Nagel and Snipp (1993:212) found that in 1910 only 8 percent of American Indians failed to report a tribal affiliation, but by 1980 almost one-quarter of the Americans who identified themselves as Indian failed to designate a tribe. Some of this ethnogenesis has occurred because federal policy makers tend to treat the culturally varied Native American groups simply as "Indians." The increasing urbanization of the American Indian population also has provided a basis for pan-Indian identification. Eschbach (1995) suggested that having an Indian heritage has come to convey a positive status that it formerly did not have, which has encouraged many people of mixed descent now to claim their Indian heritage.

The experiences of the Native Americans provide good examples of the complexities of the processes of assimilation. This group referred to as Native Americans or American Indians represents almost 550 diverse cultural tribes and officially recognized groups that have survived wars and policies aimed at their annihilation. According to the 2000 U.S. Census data on the American Indian and Alaska Native population, American Indian tribal groupings with 100,000 or more people or responses were Cherokee, Navajo, Latin American Indian, Choctaw, Sioux, and Chippewa. These six tribal groups accounted for about 40 percent of those reporting themselves to be American Indian. Others reported mixed identities. For example, there were an additional 448,000 people who reported Cherokee with at least one other racial identity or another American Indian tribal grouping. Seventy-four percent of those reporting American Indian in the 2000 census identified a tribe. The processes through which the Indians have moved toward becoming sovereign states and toward developing a pan-Indian identity illustrate the changing nature and dynamics of ethnic relations in the United States. Let us look more closely at the operation of these processes.

Language Maintenance.   At the time of first contact with Europeans, perhaps as many as 1,200 languages and dialects were spoken by the Native American tribes. By 1990, less than one-third of those identifying themselves as American Indians spoke a language other than English, and fewer than 3 percent spoke no English. Although some of the tribes have managed to maintain their languages and are teaching them in reservation schools, many Indian languages are now extinct. In addition to the languages that are no longer used, several other Indian languages may be nearing extinction. The Sac and Fox Indians of Oklahoma, for instance, are mainly English speakers. Among the Omahas, less than 10 percent of those under the age of 40 speak only the native tongue. By 1980, in fact, in only one census region of the country (the Mountain States) did a majority of the Indians (62 percent) speak their native language in the home (Snipp 1989:176).

Even though for the most part Indian children have been forced to learn English, and many of the Indian languages have disappeared as the elders of the tribe die, a number of different Indian languages are used in varying degrees on a daily basis. In some cases, these languages are spoken by a majority of the tribal members who usually also speak English, Spanish, or French. For example, most Iroquois, Penobscots, and Oklahoma Cherokees are bilingual. Many Indians also speak more than a single Indian language or Indian dialect. Among the Navajos—the largest reservation tribe in the United States—a majority of those on the reservation use the mother tongue in the home. Now that the Indians have control of the curriculum in the schools on the reservations, Navajo is also a language of instruction in the Rough Rock School and the Navajo Community College. Among the Apaches and many other tribes there is a renewed interest in learning and using the mother tongue (Olson and Wilson 1984:202–204; Nagel 1996:194–198).

What, then, are the general prospects for the survival and growth of the Indian languages? Since a language community is easier to maintain in comparative isolation, we should expect Indian languages to fare better on or near reservations; and since children are more likely to be affected by exposure to different languages than are adults, we should expect older people to report a greater use of an Indian language. Snipp's (1989:178) analysis confirmed that native language speakers are generally found in nonmetropolitan and reservation areas. For instance, in the east south-central region of the country, around 90 percent of the Indians living on or near a reservation speak a native language in the home, whereas in the same region only about 5 percent of those in metropolitan areas do so. Snipp (1989:180) also reported some interesting findings concerning age differences in language use. Among those between the ages of 61 and 70, for instance, around 5 percent spoke little English. Among those between the ages of 11 and 20, less than 2 percent spoke little English. These data suggest that, although those who live on or near reservations and in nonmetropolitan areas are more likely to have an Indian mother tongue than those who live in metropolitan areas, English is nevertheless the primary language of most American Indians. They also indicate that approximately 25 percent of the Indians are fluent in both English and a native language, and that younger people are more likely to be bilingual than the older. As far as languages alone are concerned, then, the Indian cultures seem very unlikely to disappear within the next generation or two. The actual conditions among American Indians may well be more nearly consistent with the pluralist conception of cultural assimilation (i.e., by language addition) than with the Anglo-conformity conception (i.e., by language substitution). The critical point here, of course, is the extent to which American Indians continue to become or remain bilingual and multilingual.

Although language is an extremely important part of culture, there also are other significant cultural elements that may be affected by assimilation processes. For example, religious preferences and ceremonies, housing styles, hair and dress styles, recreational patterns, and so on also reveal whether, or to what extent, one way of life has been added to or exchanged for another.

Indian Religious Freedom.   Historically, an enormous effort has been made by many different religious bodies to Christianize Native Americans. The resulting pattern of religious affiliations is very complex. Many American Indians have accepted Christian beliefs, many practice both Christian rites and an Indian religion, and many adhere solely to an Indian religion. In the Ghost Dance religion, for example, some elements of Christianity also were included. In many cases, an adherence to Christian or native religious ways parallels a person's general level of "Indianness," which, in turn, tends to be related to whether a person is considered to be a "full-blood" or "mixed-blood."

Probably the best known and the most controversial of the Indian religions is practiced by members of the Native American Church (NAC). The NAC is a pan-Indian religious movement that is closely related to traditional tribal life (Hertzberg 1971:239). Its religious beliefs are compatible in several important respects with those of most Christian denominations. The controversial element, however, arises from the ritual use by NAC members of peyote as a formal part of the sacrament. A number of state governments have declared the use, possession, or transportation of peyote by Indians for traditional religious purposes illegal. The NAC prohibits recreational use of the drug (Wax 1971:142–144), but numerous Indians practicing this religion have been arrested for their religious use or possession of peyote.

In addition to the NAC, a variety of Christian denominations and native religions may be found among most Indian tribes. For example, the Comanches are mainly members of the Methodist and Dutch Reformed churches, but a substantial number also belong to the NAC or practice their tribal religion; the Kiowas are divided among the Catholic, Methodist, Episcopal, and Baptist churches, as well as the NAC; and the Sioux are mainly Episcopalians, Catholics, or members of the Church of God. They, too, include many members of the NAC and their tribal Yuwipi cult. In many cases, individual American Indians belong to more than one religious organization (Spicer 1980a:88–92). This crisscross pattern of religious experiences and affiliations frequently has been the basis of conflict within some tribes. In a unique blending of traditions, Our Lady of Guadalupe Church on the Zuni Indian Reservation has combined the religious icons of the Catholic religion with large murals of more than two dozen life-sized kachinas, the spirit beings of Pueblo culture. The Catholic church has officially acknowledged a need to respect the cultural traditions of the Zuni who want to worship God in a way that is familiar to them (Niebuhr 1995).

For many Indians, even those who are Christians, traditional religion and ceremonies are the essence of Native American culture. Congress passed a joint resolution called the American Indian Religious Freedom Act in 1978, but the U.S. Supreme Court ruled in 1990 that the First Amendment of the Constitution does not protect the religious use of peyote by Indians. This situation led to a pan-Indian effort in support of new legislation to guarantee religious freedom to Indians. In 1994, Senator Inouye of Hawaii introduced The Native American Cultural Protection and Free Exercise of Religion Act. The legislation allowed the religious use of peyote by Indians and offered protection for Native American cultural and religious sites, the cultural and religious rights of Native American prisoners, and the cultural or religious use of eagle feathers and other animals or plants by Native Americans in religious ceremonies.[20]

The legislation required federally funded institutions and government agencies to return Indian skeletons, grave goods associated with Indian burials, and other sacred and culturally significant articles to those Indian tribes and individuals with a justified claim to them. Opponents of the legislation requiring the return of Indian remains argued that because of emerging techniques for analyzing skeletal material, scientific knowledge of early American diseases, diet, and settlement patterns would be lost if the artifacts were not available for study. Some compromises have been reached; many of the artifacts have been returned to the proper tribes; and an increasing number of Indian scholars have assumed important roles in museums that were formerly Anglo dominated (Washburn 1995:252–256).

Traditions.   The variety and complexity that exist among American Indians in regard to language and religion extend to every other sphere of life. In many cases, the members of a given tribe may live in a manner largely indistinguishable from that of their White neighbors, although even in such cases of high cultural assimilation, certain distinctive Indian elements may still be present. For example, Lorraine Canoe, a Mohawk Indian, has lived in Brooklyn for more than 35 years; but she considers the Mohawk reservation her real home.[21] She takes a 9-hour bus trip to the reservation for about half of the 13 annual ceremonies and spends her summer breaks there. She owns a house on the reservation where her two grown daughters live. She cooks traditional boiled corn bread and brings one of her favorites—deer meat—back from the reservation. Although her daughters grew up in New York, they moved back to the reservation because they preferred the more traditional life and relaxed pace there.

The split lives of urban Indians and the variety of cultural "mixes" also extends to differences within various tribes. Consider the Oklahoma Cherokees, for example. This nonreservation group is located principally within a five-county region of northeastern Oklahoma, and the people who consider themselves to be Cherokees vary markedly in culture. The Cherokee tribe, with over 300,000 members in 1990, was the largest American Indian tribe (U.S. Bureau of the Census 1996:50). Wax (1971:92–93) distinguished broadly between the "tribal Cherokees" and those "of Cherokee lineage." The tribal Cherokees live in old, distinctively Cherokee communities that have Cherokee names, and among these groups the main language of the home and church is Cherokee. Those of Cherokee lineage, however, may maintain only the most superficial connection with their heritage. They may have no social relationships with the tribal Cherokees, may live entirely in the White way, and may be unable to speak Cherokee. This same general pattern of variation within specific tribes may be found throughout the United States.

Consider the case of the Pequots, a 260-member Connecticut tribe. After 350 years of dispersion, most of its language, important ceremonial dances, and other traditions have disappeared. After the tribe introduced big-stakes gambling, it became enormously wealthy. In an effort to reconstruct an Indian culture, the tribe used some of its millions in profits to stage a major powwow that drew about 1,200 American Indians from all over North America to compete for prizes in sharing their traditional dances, skills, and songs (Johnson 1993:16). The Pequots planned to borrow and adapt what they could in an effort to construct a culture of their own.

What, then, can we conclude concerning the cultural assimilation of American Indians? First, all tribal cultures have been drastically changed by their long period of contact with the dominant American culture; hence, a large majority of American Indians today speak English as one of their languages and exhibit greater or lesser degrees of acceptance of Anglo American ways. Second, the number of people who bear a particular Indian culture has, in many cases, either stabilized or now is increasing. Third, in addition to the maintenance and elaboration of the many tribal cultures, pan-Indian culture continues to develop.

American Indian Ethnic Renewal.   There are many forces both inside and outside the American Indian communities that have promoted pan-Indian identity. Many have objected to the emergence of "Indian" as an ethnic group identifier, arguing that it reduces the experiences of Native Americans, who are tribal sovereign nations, to the status of immigrant ethnic groups who have no rights to sovereignty or nationhood (Nagel 1996:8). The activism of the 1960s convinced many Indian leaders that they had much in common with other minority groups. They increasingly thought of themselves as "Indians," as well as members of their tribal groups. Ironically, many of the policies aimed at assimilation, such as Indian education, political and economic development of the reservations, urban relocation, and settlement of land claims, led instead to increases in Indian ethnic identification and an Indian ethnic resurgence (Nagel 1996:115). Let us look at some of those processes.

Pan-Indian Identity.   The boarding schools often provided young Indians with their first opportunities to interact with members of other tribes and to identify similarities in values. The Carlisle School in Pennsylvania tried to bring students from different tribes together to teach them English and citizenship skills. In doing so, English became a language Indian students could use across tribes. The school also produced marriages across tribes, which strengthened mixed tribal identity. Indians educated in these schools became some of the first pan-Indian leaders (Nagel 1996:116). Pan-Indian values—which Steele (1982:287) called "the informal credentials of 'Indianness'"—included things such as an acceptance of obligations to the extended family, the importance of mutual aid among Indians, noninterference in the affairs of others, a reverence for nature, and pride in a knowledge of Indian languages.

Service in the military also contributed to both the assimilation of Indians into U.S. society and to the development of a pan-Indian identity. To others in the military who knew little about tribal differences, the Pequots, Sioux, Navajos, Cherokees, and Mohawks became simply "Indians." After World War II, many Indians used their G. I. benefits to pursue additional education and, in the process, gained a better understanding of the common Indian problems of poverty and unemployment.

When tribes pursued legal claims in court, many of the petitions involved more than one tribe and required many occasions of intertribal contact and cooperation. Additionally, the publicity of the Red Power civil rights movement and the political organization required to participate in the massive federal programs of the Great Society in the 1960s combined to mobilize members of many different tribes as "American Indians." As the urban Indian population grew, pan-Indianism increased in importance. Active all-Indian associations formed in the urban areas with large Indian populations. The Bay Area American Indian Council of San Francisco, representing around 100 tribes, and the Chicago American Indian Center, also representing nearly 100 tribes, became prominent examples of this trend (Spicer 1980a:113). Additionally, numerous all-Indian powwows, dances, and ceremonies, such as the annual American Indian Exposition at Anadarko, Oklahoma, encouraged American Indians to travel and associate with one another.

Maintenance of tribal cultures and the development of a pan-Indian culture both serve to ensure that the American Indians will have the option to remain American Indians even as they continue to assimilate the dominant culture. As Stewart (1977a:521) observed, "eventually, Indian cultures may fade away"; but, in the meantime, "Indians believe they can function with competence in modern society as Indians."

Secondary Structural Assimilation

The long period of conflict with the dominant society, the unwillingness of most tribes to adopt the dominant American ways, and the continuation of prejudice and discrimination into the present all have conspired to keep the Indians from participating equally in the educational, occupational, and financial systems of American society; consequently, they have long been "the poorest of the poor" (Josephy 1971:15).

No simple statistical accounting can do justice to the suffering and pain the Indian peoples have indured. As the members of a U.S. Senate Special Subcommittee on Indian Education stated in 1969, the statistics they had gathered could not ". . . tell of the despair, the frustration, the hopelessness, the poignancy, of children who want to learn but are not taught" or of "families which want to stay together but are forced apart" or of "children who want neighborhood schools but are sent thousands of miles away to remote and alien boarding schools" (Josephy 1971:168).

Education.   Let us consider the matter of schooling. First, there have been some definite increases in the educational levels of Indians during recent years; but, second, their educational attainments still lag noticeably behind those of Whites. For example, by 1989 more than 65 percent of all Indians over the age of 24 had completed 12 years or more of schooling; at the same time, more than 79 percent of the comparable White population had completed the same level of education (U.S. Bureau of the Census 1996:48, 50). Following a cohort of students from eighth to twelfth grade through 1992, the National Center for Education Statistics (1994) found that Native Americans had a 19.9 percent dropout rate compared to a 12.7 percent rate for Hispanics, a 9.6 percent rate for Blacks, and a 6.1 percent rate for Whites. As we have seen in some of our comparisons of Mexican and Black Americans with Whites, the rates of increase in college attendance have been higher among Indians than among Whites, but the absolute size of the gap between the groups has grown. The high percentages of high school and college dropouts among the Indian population has lowered young people's expectations of completing school. Bordewich (1996:286) quoted the dean of students at Haskell College at Lawrence, Kansas (formerly the Indian School, Haskell Institute), as saying, "Not long ago a kid came to me and said he wanted to drop out of school. I asked him why. He said, 'Because that's what Indians do.'"

As emphasized previously, the range of social variation among Indians is wide and this point certainly applies to differences in educational attainment. Probably the most noticeable differences are between those who live in nonmetropolitan or reservation areas and those who live elsewhere; but there also are large differences between the young and the old. In general, for both sexes, those who live in cities and are young attain the highest average levels of education.

There are substantial educational differences, too, among those who are over the age of 24 and reside on one of the 16 largest reservations. To illustrate, in 1970 about 36 percent of those over age 24 on the Wind River Reservation (WY) graduated from high school, whereas less than 13 percent graduated on the Papago Reservation (AZ). In 1980, these levels were over 39 and 25 percent, respectively. During the decade, however, the relative ranking of the reservations changed. In 1980, the Fort Peck Reservation (MT) had the highest proportion of graduates (almost 50 percent), whereas the Rosebud Reservation (SD) had the lowest (almost 20 percent) (Snipp 1989:202–203).

We referred earlier to the schools operated by the BIA and their role in the attempt to force the Indians to adopt Anglo conformity. Now, however, over two-thirds of the Indian children attend public schools, and the role of some of the government-operated schools has changed markedly. Many Indians now view the BIA reservation schools as their best chance to mold Indian education along the lines they desire and, in some instances, when the BIA has attempted to close reservation schools, the Indians have protested and stopped the closings (Washburn 1973:103–104). Nevertheless, the lack of adequate funding has seriously threatened the ability of the reservation schools to provide an adequate education and some reservation Indian parents have placed their children in public schools. The parents want their children to learn the best of both worlds—the reservation culture and "the English way." But those who enroll their children outside the reservation fear that the tribal elders will later retaliate for their "disloyalty" and deny them petitions for land or a building permit or a job with the tribal government. They also worry that they are going against tribal traditions that have kept the community intact over the years through wars, displacement, and Anglo intrusion.

The trend toward greater tribal control of the content and style of their children's education has extended into higher education. Among the colleges that have been established are the Navajo Community College, the Lakota Higher Education Center, Sinte Gleska College (*Newsweek* 1973:71–72), and Little Big Horn College (Bordewich 1996:286). The first tribal college opened on the Navajo reservation in Arizona in 1968, and in 1994 throughout the United States there were 26 reservation colleges enrolling more than 16,000 Indian students. These tribal institutions began as community colleges granting associate degrees; but now three of them, including Sinte Gleska, offer four-year bachelor's programs and have recently expanded to offer master's degrees. Although the continued movement of the American Indians toward higher levels of educational attainment seems almost certain, one may well doubt whether the remaining gap between the Indians and the dominant group will close rapidly.

Occupations and Incomes.   Along with higher levels of education, the jobs of Indians who are employed have become more like those of the dominant group; but, both on and off the reservations, unemployment among Indians is high and economic hardship is common. The overall unemployment rates among males and females between the ages of 21 and 25, for instance, have crossed 18 percent and 14 percent, respectively; and these rates are substantially below the rates for males and females between the ages of 16 and 20 (more than 25 and 21 percent, respectively). The levels of unemployment on the reservations are even more unfavorable than the overall pattern. To illustrate, at the Pine Ridge Reservation (SD), the unemployment rate rose between 1970 and 1980 from over 16 percent to nearly 36 percent. The reported level of unemployment on the Pine Ridge Reservation in 1995 was an appalling 75 percent and Shannon County, South Dakota, where the Pine Ridge Reservation is located, was the poorest county in the nation (Brooke 1995). These increases in unemployment occurred during a period when the number of people in the labor force also was increasing, suggesting that the increasing education and skill levels of the Indians were not matched by employment opportunities on the reservations (Snipp 1989:220, 226, 227).

One way many tribes have created jobs, as mentioned earlier, is through the establishment of casinos and gaming on the reservations. Their advantage in this area is sovereignty. The degree of sovereignty enjoyed by Indian tribes includes the suspension of many local, state, and federal laws on Indian territory. Reservations have no sales or property tax; so they can sell cigarettes, gasoline, and other items for low prices and can offer activities, such as gambling, that are not permitted off the reservations. Gaming, in fact, has been described as "the best thing to happen to New Mexico Indians in four centuries of Spanish and American Dominance" (Johnson 1996b:24).

The success of gambling initiatives, such as that of the Oneida Indian Nation of New York, helped solve unemployment problems and allowed the tribes to invest in other tribal businesses. Their Turning Stone Casino Resort, 30 miles east of Syracuse, New York, has thousands of square feet of gambling space, several golf courses, hotels, shops, and a music hall. It is estimated to have brought in $232 million for the tribe's 1,000 members in 2001. The tribe has used some of the money to buy additional land parcels and surrounding gasoline and convenience stores; and it has given away millions of dollars to educational, civic and charitable organizations, and local government agencies. Casino money has paid for new town offices, a water system, and a wastewater treatment plant. Still, relations between the tribes and local governments remain tense and largely negative. Local residents are angry over rising property taxes and revenues lost on properties and businesses bought by the Oneidas (Peterson 2003). Non-Indian shop owners claim they have been put out of business by the Indian businesses, which do not have to pay sales taxes. These jurisdictional conflicts, and other similar events, illustrate the efforts of the tribes to define and enlarge the area within which they may determine the direction of their own lives.

Consider, also, the experiences of some other tribes with gaming. The Eastern Band of Cherokees earned about $850,000 per year between 1982 and 1992 and spent the money on government services for tribal members. The Santee Sioux helped tribal members buy homes or cars or go back to school. The casino of the Yankton Sioux employed over 175 tribal members, about 80 percent of whom were previously unemployed (*Americans Before Columbus* 1992). The Oneidas of Wisconsin spent $9 million to extend the Green Bay, Wisconsin, water and sewer system to the reservation (Bordewich 1996:109). The Morongo reservation just north of Palm Springs, California, employed more than 140 people in their bingo business and planned to develop a major desert resort. The 200 members of the Shakopee Mdewekantan tribe expected 1994 payments to exceed $500,000 for each member (Johnson 1994). And the Pequots have employed 11,000 workers and made sufficient profits to fund 16 restaurants, two hotels, a museum, a theater, and a second casino. Additionally—for all who can demonstrate they are at least one-sixteenth Pequot—guaranteed employment, health care, childcare, and educational expenses from kindergarten through graduate school (Pollack 1996).

Not all tribes have been successful in their gaming businesses, however. Many who have attempted gaming have struggled with conflicts among tribe members who oppose it because of its social impact. For example, some Oglalas oppose a casino because the gaming compact with the state gives South Dakota criminal jurisdiction over nontribe members on the reservation. That, traditionalists argued, was an issue of treaty rights that Sioux warriors died for (Judson 1994). Other tribes have been exploited when they contracted with outside companies to run their gambling enterprises. As more tribes initiate gaming businesses, they sometimes end up competing with one another. Still, the opportunity to become economically successful in the gaming business has made it possible for some tribes to buy back sacred lands they lost years ago and for others to invest in housing, hospitals, schools, roads, and other social services lacking on the reservations.

The gaming income also has allowed tribes to accumulate capital to diversify reservation economies that have long relied on government payments and subsidies. The Indian Business Association, a tribal trade group, now represents some 5,000 companies (Johnson 1994:10). The Southern Utes in Colorado have bought a gas-drilling company so they can extract their own gas resources rather than leasing the land to non-Indian businesses. The Navajos have organized an oil company. The Sioux on the Cheyenne River Reservation have begun raising bison, which are lower in fat and cholesterol than beef, and have found a market outside the reservation among health-conscious non-Indians. Indians have also financed Indian-run radio stations. Along the same lines, the Pine Ridge Sioux have published the first national Indian newspaper, *Indian Country Today*, that has a circulation of over 20,000. The newspaper employs 30 full-time employees, most of them Indian.

Tribes such as the Arapaho on the Wind River Reservation in Wyoming, where there are not enough customers to make gaming work, have turned to tourism (McInnis 1994:4F). In 1988, the Arapaho placed several tribal businesses into a trust. The small businesses—including a convenience store, a truck stop, a laundromat, and a construction company—provide 85 jobs and generate $7.5 million in annual revenues. The tribe also has plans for a reservation tour service. The Nez Perce Indians, who were forced from their land in Joseph, Oregon, in 1877, now are seen by the White residents of the area as a potent economic resource (Egan 1996). The area has suffered economically as timber mills have shut down and the cattle industry has declined. Indian cultural events, such as powwows, have become a big tourist attraction, and the White town leaders have joined with tribal leaders to invest in a Nez Perce cultural center. The tribe has also bought 10,000 acres of land along a creek in the area where their famous chief, Young Joseph, was born. The tribe will manage the land for hunting and fishing. Egan notes that the Whites see the return of the tribe as an economic plus, but the tribe sees it as a homecoming.

An obstacle to entrepreneurship among the Native Americans has been the lack of a capitalist tradition, which was seen as an "Anglo way of doing things." Until recently, there have been few residents on the reservations with experience as business managers and few with college experience (McInnis 1994:4F). That pattern seems to be changing. The number of Indian-owned businesses increased 64 percent between 1982 and 1987 (Fost 1996). For example, the Laguna Indians in New Mexico have started manufacturing plants on the reservations. Laguna Industries employs 350 people and has contracts with the U.S. Department of Defense as well as several large companies. Although tribal elders hope that opportunities for jobs on the reservations will encourage young people to stay, these industries have not solved all the problems on the reservations. Unemployment continues to run as high as 35 percent on the Laguna Reservation.

Among those Indians who have jobs, the pattern of employment has become more similar to the dominant White pattern. In 1970, for instance, roughly 64 percent of White females and 43 percent of Indian females were employed in nonmanual jobs. By 1980, these figures had become 70 percent and 56 percent, respectively. Among males, the comparable figures were 41 percent and 22 percent (1970) and 45 percent and 28 percent (1980). We should also note that employed female and male Indians in both 1970 and 1980 were more likely to hold nonmanual jobs than were Black Americans (Snipp 1989:231).

Although Indians still are plagued by high unemployment and the accompanying economic hardships, and although their general pattern of employment more nearly resembles that of Blacks than of Whites, there is clear evidence that their increasing educational levels do lead to higher-paying, higher-prestige jobs. In 1980, for example, 59 percent of Indian females and 55 percent of Indian males who had received a college education were employed in managerial and professional jobs, while an additional 28 percent of the females and 18 percent of the males in this group held technical, sales, and administrative support jobs (Snipp 1989:246). It is true, nonetheless, that Indians have much more difficulty translating high school graduation into college attendance than do Whites. Snipp (1989:190) calculated that among every additional 100 White high school graduates, an additional 41 people graduate from college; but among Indians, 100 additional high school graduates produces only 12 additional college graduates. Furthermore, there is some evidence that the probability that an Indian between the ages of 25 and 30 will have completed four or more years of college is now *lower* than for those between the ages of 31 and 70 (Snipp 1989:200).

The improved educational and employment levels of Indians have been accompanied by some improvement in their overall income levels. As an example, in 1970, on average, for each dollar earned by White families, Indian families received 57 cents, which was less than 90 percent of the comparable figure for Black Americans (U.S. Bureau of the Census, *American Indians* 1973); but, by 1979, on average, Indian family income had risen to 66 cents for each dollar earned by Whites, which was, at that point, slightly *higher* than the median family income of Blacks compared to Whites (60 cents per dollar). The proportion of Indian families below the poverty line (27 percent) also has declined to a point below that of Blacks (31 percent), but both of these groups still have much larger proportions of poor families than do Whites (9.4 percent) (U.S. Bureau of the Census 1996:48, 50).

Still, by many measures American Indians are one of the poorest ethnic groups in the country (Johnson 1994). Of the 10 poorest U.S. counties in the 1990 census, four were Indian lands in South Dakota. Many Indian families on the reservations still live in shacks and must haul water in pickup trucks. Sandefur and Sakamoto (1988:79) noted that American Indians may appear to have a higher average income than Blacks; however, since Indians are more likely to live in traditional family households (couples with children) than either Blacks or Whites, their higher family income may reflect the efforts of more wage earners.

Life Chances.   Health care is an area in which the efforts to close the gap between Indians and Whites appears to be having marked success. To illustrate, consider the change in the infant mortality rates among American Indians. From 1950 to 1983, this sensitive indicator of the general health level of a population declined from an extremely high 82 infant deaths per 1,000 Indian births per year to about 11 deaths per 1,000 births (Snipp 1989:352).[22] This large decline within such a short period of time is remarkable. Not only was the American Indian infant mortality rate rapidly approaching the White level (9.7 per 1,000 in 1983), it had fallen below the rate for Black Americans in 1992 (16.8) (U.S. Bureau of the Census 1996:91).

The improvement in infant mortality, as important as it is, does not mean that the general health and mortality experience of American Indians is no longer a matter of concern. Indians still are much more likely than all Americans combined to die fairly early in life. Davis, Hunt, and Kitzes (1989:271) reported that in 1982, 37 percent of the deaths among American Indians occurred before age 45, compared with 12 percent of deaths in the same age group in the U.S. population. Indians also still suffer a disproportionate number of deaths from causes that reflect broader problems faced by Indians. For example, although accidental deaths among them have declined dramatically since 1970, Indians still are roughly twice as likely to die in an accident as are members of the general population; and suicide rates among Indians, though also lower than in 1970, are still roughly 25 percent higher than the rate for all Americans (U.S. Department of Health, Education and Welfare 1980:12, 16); and Indian teenagers are about four times as likely to attempt suicide as are other teens (Brasher 1992). Indians also are about twice as likely to be murdered, four times as likely to die of alcoholism, and nine times as likely to die of tuberculosis as are other Americans (Snipp 1989:355–358). As is true of the American population as a whole, however, Indians are more likely to die of heart disease than of any other single cause (Rhoades et al. 1988:622).

The statistics concerning the status of American Indians in various areas of life may be viewed, from different perspectives, either as encouraging or discouraging. If emphasis is placed on the recency of serious attention to the development of the reservations and to integrating Indians into urban life and industrial occupations, then the size of the "lags" in these areas may be viewed in some ways as being relatively low. But when the "lags" are seen absolutely—in terms of life chances and human privation—it is evident that much remains to be done. Even though it may now be true, after many decades of effort, that Indians, collectively, are no longer the "poorest of the poor," it also is true that they still are far from having the standard of living enjoyed by other ethnic groups in the United States and still "are one of the most disadvantaged racial/ethnic groups in the United States" (Sandefur and Scott 1983:44).

Primary Structural Assimilation

The low levels of primary assimilation among the Indians of the past have been extended into the present. Reservation Indians, both by choice and circumstance, are unlikely to have very many contacts with non-Indians. According to the 2000 U.S. Census (2001), four out of 10 American Indians lived in the Western region of the United States where the major reservations are located. California and Oklahoma combined included about 25 percent of the total American Indian population. Urban Indians, in contrast to those on the reservations and in rural areas, may have numerous opportunities to form friendships with non-Indians in schools and colleges, at work, in various social organizations, and in their neighborhoods. Of all places in the United States with 100,000 or more population, the New York City and Los Angeles areas had the largest American Indian populations.

Ablon (1972) studied American Indians living in the San Francisco Bay area who had come to the area under the BIA's relocation program. She interviewed 53 Indians concerning many aspects of their lives in the city, including things such as who their early social contacts in the city were, how those contacts were made, whether they preferred Indian or White friends, how they felt about themselves, and so on. She found, first, that the Indians most frequently established their social contacts at gatherings sponsored by various intertribal organizations founded by or for Indians. The next most common form of early contacts was with friends or relatives from the reservations. The Indians reported that after they had been in the city for a while, they had an increasing proportion of their social contacts with people from work and in their neighborhoods. Most of the Indians stated they had White friends as well as Indian friends; however, in all of these contexts, their friendships with Whites tended to be superficial. Only three of 54 Indians who participated in the study stated they had more White than Indian friends.

Aside from reasons for wishing to avoid Whites, Indians have a strong, positive wish to be with other Indians. This view accords with One Feather's (1986:171) observation that "the people who moved to urban areas formed their own Indian communities." Indian centers became a focal point for the people that lived in cities. Behavior patterns, of course, vary among the tribes. In a study of Indians in Los Angeles—the city containing the largest American Indian population—Price (1972) compared the members of the three major tribal groups in the city (the Navajo, Sioux, and Five Civilized Tribes). He found that the Navajo were least likely to establish extratribal ties to life in the city, and the members of the Five Civilized Tribes were the most likely to do so. The Sioux were intermediate (Price 1972:437). In general, the Navajo also maintained the strongest ties to the reservations, while the members of the Five Civilized Tribes maintained the weakest ties. From these findings, Price (1972:436) argued that the Navajos probably would "shift over time to patterns of life exemplified by the Five Civilized Tribes."

While the occurrence of such a shift would imply a parallel increase in primary assimilation for those involved, there is little reason to suppose that urban American Indians will soon reach a point at which associations with other Indians will become unimportant. Liebow (1989:67) found in Phoenix, for instance, that the Indians there—representing many tribes—"have set about self-consciously creating a collective identity that is primarily tied to their adoptive metropolitan home." As Price (1972:439) noted, "the great majority of Indians in the city clearly are ideologically and emotionally affiliated with pan-Indianism." The maintenance or growth of this commitment among American Indians may well exert a continuing pressure against full primary assimilation.

Marital Assimilation

Although we lack the information needed to discuss marital assimilation precisely in the present, much less in the distant past, it appears that until recently the levels of marital

assimilation among Indians have been low. This condition is what we would have expected on the basis of the generally low levels of primary assimilation.

Various circumstances have produced higher levels of intermarriage at some times
and places than others. For example, during the early years in the southern colonies,
where White women were scarce and Indian women were plentiful, there were numerous
White male–Indian female marriages. After the American Revolution, Indians struggled
to survive as communities in the face of prejudice and legal and economic discrimination. Indians and other people of color lived and worked separated from Whites and
often met and married (Mandell 1998). As in the case of Black Americans, of course, the
actual levels of sexual relations between Indians and Whites and Indians and Blacks always have been higher than the rates of legitimate intermarriage; consequently, the level
of intermixture after almost four centuries of contact is quite high. The proportion of
Indians who were considered to be full-bloods in the 1980s varied among the tribes and
was, in general, higher on the reservations than in the cities. In both locations, however,
only a minority among the American Indians now qualify as full-bloods, and many millions of Americans who do not profess an Indian identity claim some degree of Indian
ancestry. We should note again that the terms *full-blood* and *mixed-blood* frequently refer
to cultural commitment rather than to biological ancestry. Our claim that, in the past,
the levels of Indian–White intermarriage have been low, therefore, is based only on those
marriages in which one of the partners considers himself or herself to be an Indian.
Most instances in which one partner reports some degree of mixed ancestry are not
counted as examples of Indian–White intermarriage.

Roy (1972:233), for instance, found that among 28 Spokane Indian couples living
on a reservation, 20 marriages in which both partners were Indians included at least one
member who was not considered to be a full-blood.[23] Eschbach (1995:95–96) found that
the highest proportion of those who were intermarried occurred in states with large Indian populations that lived in enclave communities. The range of Indians in mixed marriages varied from 16 percent in the Southwest to 82 percent in the Midwest. The
younger Indians generally had higher intermarriage rates than older Indians, but the
same regional differences persisted for the young couples.

One of the dilemmas in intermarriages is whether the children will be identified as
Indian or non-Indian. Nationally, only 47 percent of the children in intermarried families are assigned the race of their Indian parent. The assignment of identity to children
also varies by region. Seventy three percent of the children born to intermarried couples
in Oklahoma are assigned Indian descent, but only 33 percent of the children born to intermarried couples in the Northeast are assigned Indian descent at birth. Eschbach
(1995:96) speculates that whether parents in mixed marriages assign Indian descent to
their children depends on the political and economic importance of Indian identity in
the area and the amount of discrimination and ethnic conflict between Indians and others the parents have experienced. Eschbach concludes that Indians in mixed marriages
will continue to identify as Indian as long as that identity is available to them *and* is socially valuable.

Despite the paucity of research on Indian intermarriage, we do know that the levels of marital assimilation among Indians appear to have risen sharply in recent times.
Between 1960 and 1970, the proportion of Indian husbands who married non-Indian

wives rose from 15 percent to 33 percent, and the proportion of Indian wives who married non-Indian husbands rose from over 24 percent to 39 percent (Heer 1980:519). By 1990, Eschbach (1995:93) found that nationally 59 percent of married Indians were married to non-Indians.

Taken at face value, these findings suggest a strong surge among American Indians toward the mainstream of society. Given all of our other findings, however, it seems possible that the apparently large increase in intermarriage may be "related to an increased desire among persons with mixed-White and Indian ancestry to identify themselves as Indian Americans" (Heer 1980:519). Adding to this view are the finding that as many as 358,000 people in the United States changed their self-identification from White to Indian during the 1970s (Sandefur and McKinnell 1986:348). Bordewich (1996:66) quoted an administrator of the BIA as saying, "There are a lot of just plain old Americans who want to belong to an ethnic group of some kind. . . . [A]t this point in time a lot of people want to be Indian."

Many tribes have been forced to expand their definition of who is an Indian because of the increased rate of outmarriage (Nagel 1996:245). For example, Sandefur and McKinnell (1986:357) showed that in states that traditionally have had large numbers of people who define themselves as Indian (states in which pressures toward marrying within the ethnic group, presumably, are strong), 37 percent of the Indian men marry women of different ethnicities. Out-marriage is even higher in states that traditionally have had comparatively small Indian populations. In these states, about 62 percent of the Indian men marry women of other ethnicities.

These broad generalizations, of course, leave many questions unanswered. Are the rates of intermarriage among some tribes remaining steady or falling in contrast to the general trend? Are the rates of intertribal intermarriage increasing and, if so, what is the social and cultural significance of these changes? Are many of these intermarriages with spouses of non-White ethnic groups, such as Hispanic, Asians, and Blacks? These and other questions invite further study.

Other Forms of Assimilation

Our discussion of the Native American experience in the United States illustrates that what it means to be Indian has varied according to the social, economic, political, and cultural contexts this group experienced over time. The role of women in maintaining traditional practices and resisting assimilation is important, especially as rates of intermarriage with non-Indians increase. A study of Navajo women (Schulz 1998) illustrates these patterns clearly. Schulz concluded that the women's strategies of negotiating Indian and Navajo identities were "everyday acts of political resistance" against continued pressures toward Anglo assimilation. In interviews with Navajo women of different generations Schulz found a central theme that cut across the different age groups—the feeling of being "different." Many of the older generation remembered feeling that their group was devalued. Part of their Indian identity meant countering these negative associations. The younger generation, who attended Indian schools and experienced the civil rights movements of the 1960s and 1970s, saw "Indian" as a positive identity, but their Navajo identity had to be consciously acquired. They struggled to learn the Navajo language and culture.[24] For these women the politics of identity involved not simply defining the meanings associated with being Indian and Navajo, but also the politics of determining who had a right to assume those identities. Indeed, there is enormous controversy among native people about who should be considered an Indian for purposes of receiving tribal services, federal benefits, affirmative action consideration, or rights to participate in tribal governments (Nagel 1999; Wilkins 2001, 2002).

Despite an increasing acceptance of Indian identities, in the broader society there are still high levels of prejudice against Indians, especially on the edges of Indian reservations. A study published by the U.S. Bureau of Justice Statistics in the Justice Department, and reported in the *New York Times* (Butterfield 1999), found that Indians are victims of crime at a rate more than twice the U.S. average. Using data gathered from 1992 to 1996, the study found that Indians are more likely than Whites or Blacks to be the victims of violent crimes committed by members of a race other than their own. As Indian groups have been successful in land-claim disputes and Indian-owned businesses, peaceful coexistence of Indians and Whites has been shattered. For example, the Oneida Indian Nation's casino created thousands of jobs and generated wealth, and they used their profits to challenge the legality of New York state and local government acquisitions of Oneida lands in the 1700s and 1800s. When the U.S. Supreme Court upheld the Oneidas' argument, threats of violence, boycotts of Indian businesses, and expressions of jealousy over the success of the Oneida Indian Nation and resentments of their tax-exempt status emerged (Chen 1999).

Many Indian leaders face continual challenges to their traditional Indian beliefs and lifestyles. As the Indian people seek sufficient education, well-paying jobs, modern health services, updated housing, and adequate food supplies, there are increasing demands for cultural change. For example, Indian rights to water, the right to hunt and fish, rights of land ownership, and mineral rights have all been contested in the courts. The growing demands for coal, oil, and water have forced tribal leaders into economics and law. They must deal with energy companies, the federal government, and their own tribal councils. To lead their tribes successfully in the modern era, the Indian leaders have had to comply with the "white man's" methods and practices. In the area of education, the Native American Preparatory School in Rowe, New Mexico, a boarding school founded in 1995 and modeled after East Coast boarding schools, is preparing gifted Indian students for Ivy League colleges.[25] The goal is to prepare the students to be successful in both worlds, tribal and mainstream academic.

In the legal area, tribal leaders have gone to court to protest that the royalty payments from natural resources leases are too low and the tribes are locked into poorly negotiated leases for long periods of time. The tribes have alleged that the U.S. government misadvised them about the advantages and disadvantages of the leases and have charged the Secretary of the Interior with violating the National Environmental Policy Act. In 1999, a Federal judge held two U.S. Cabinet Secretaries who oversee Indian trust accounts in contempt of court because of mismanagement of Indian trust funds. The trust accounts date to the 1880s when the government tried to break up tribal land ownership and awarded individual allotments of 80 to 160 acres of land per Indian. The Indians charged the U.S. government with improper accounting and mismanagement of the trust funds, which may have cost Indians over $10 billion in lost income over the last century. These efforts have required many Native Americans to adapt to modern American society's norms. The tribes and their leaders have had to learn to think and function like members of the mainstream society. According to Fixico (1998), this requires adopting the values of the free enterprise system of American capitalism. With the accumulation of wealth, tribes have had financial resources to improve the livelihood of their people, but this involves changing the culture of the tribes, which do not stress the accumulation of wealth. The tribal leaders have also had to educate themselves in the law in order to defend their natural resources and represent their tribal interests. Fixico (1998:202) predicted that in coming years, tribal leaders will "wage the most significant battles since the nineteenth century for the existence of their people and the protection of their homelands."

 # American Indian "Success"

In the twenty-first century, perhaps more sharply than previously, we see an illustration of the close link between a group's ideology and the question of assessing its success within American society. Even though the tribes have varied in their willingness to accept certain elements of White culture, there can be little doubt that the central impulse among the Indians has been to resist being drawn into American society. From this perspective, any step toward assimilation that involved the substitution of White for Indian ways has represented some measure of failure. The Indians' conviction that their way is best has been bolstered by the increasing problems confronting industrial civilization. Problems relating to air and water pollution, soil erosion, energy exhaustion, ecological imbalance, and widespread feelings of loneliness and powerlessness are all interpreted by many Indians, and some non-Indians as well, as signs of the impermanence and inferiority of White culture. Deloria (1972:506) argued the point as follows: "At the present time everyone is watching how mainstream America will handle the issues of pollution, poverty, crime and racism when it does not fundamentally understand the issues. . . . It just seems to a lot of Indians that this continent was a lot better off when we were running it."

As tribal economic and legal resources increase and Indian groups win their battles in the courts, they are assuming greater responsibility for managing land and natural resources, which are much in demand by the larger society. In doing this, Indian traditional values will be severely tested. The outcome of the American Indians' struggle against the worldly success of White society is presently unclear. Many hope that "tribalism can be incorporated with modern technology in an urban setting" (Deloria 1972:506). This hope is counterbalanced, however, by the unquenched fear that the ancient tribal values will be lost before they can become ascendant. As Deloria (1981:149) stated subsequently: "While tribal traditions provide a bulwark against the consumer society, continued contact may well mean the end of Indian uniqueness in a world increasingly homogenized. The pervasive fear of Indians is that they will in the years ahead move from their plateau of small nationhood to the status of another ethnic group in the American melting pot."

Reality Check

INTERVIEW WITH JEAN WILMA

Jean Wilma's mother was Pawnee and her father was Choctaw and Irish. She is married to a member of the Rappahanock Indian tribe in Virginia, a state-recognized tribe of 500 to 800 people. Her husband's tribe is part of the tribal associations lobbying the federal government for federal recognition. Jean Wilma grew up in Oklahoma.

How do you refer to yourself?
I grew up calling myself American Indian, and then in the 1960s we changed it to Native Americans. We were the original Americans, original to the land. I say Native American Indian. I use my tribal identity only when I am around other Indians. There is an ethnic identity that goes with that.

When did you first become aware of your ethnic background?
First grade, 'cause when you go to a boarding school, that's all Indian. Then from the boarding school we went to school downtown. They were always the "car students." We knew we were Indians. They had their families, that's one thing. They were living in a home, in a family. It didn't really make a big difference until we were high school age and we liked boys and they weren't looking at us, the Indian girls. I went one semester to college right after I graduated from high school and then joined the Air Force.

We spent the school year at the boarding school and went home once a month. When I was six, I hated boarding school because I wanted to be with my parents. But as I got older I realized it offered me more opportunities than I would have if I was at home, so when my father wanted to take us out of boarding school we didn't want to go home. My oldest sister and I went together. We were separated by grade, not age. Usually after school we ran up to each other and said, "Hello, how are you doing?"

Most people my age have had some experiences in boarding school. It was common practice for the government social workers to take us from our homes and put us in boarding school because they were trying to civilize us. They were trying to teach us and assimilate us into the American society.

What courses did you take in high school?
There was nothing about Indians. You heard about Pocahontas, that's about it. The teachers were White. I was not encouraged to really plan a career. I was told to learn to type and take home economics. But that could be because I was a woman not an Indian. We were not allowed to speak Indian languages until I graduated in 1969. Then it became OK to speak and teach others and remember your traditions, but until then if we called each other by Indian nicknames we were told not to do that.

What is most important to you about your ethnic background?
There's a community feeling whenever you are around Native Americans, no matter if you just met or if you have known them all your life. It's like a brotherhood, a sisterhood. It doesn't matter if you are from another tribe, it's just two brown people.

My grandfather was full Choctaw. His father did not allow the six boys in the family to learn Choctaw because he wanted them to speak like the White Men, to be able to get along in the world like the White Men. When they privatized the Indian's lands, each was given 360 or 320 hectares. My father had his land, plus he bought some from other people so he was fairly wealthy. My father and mother divorced when I was five and we grew up with my father's mother. We were raised basically Irish.

The boarding school was really good for me because it offered me opportunities that were not available to other children, even poor White children. I feel like the school gave me a very good educational background, so I've been able to compete.

My father's brother was the chief of the Choctaws for 26 years. It was a time when the Native Americans were struggling with getting recognition, getting paid back for broken treaties. My uncle, being a former lawyer and school teacher, was very good at getting that done. But once the 1960s hit and became ethnic, they didn't consider my uncle Indian enough, so then he wasn't reelected. That's how my father was, too. We can be around Indians, but he was always identified as being White. They would always say, "that White man." For me, he wasn't White, he was dark skin and dark hair, but he acted White.

Are your friends from ethnic groups other than your own?
I have a mix of friends because I am in the military. Usually my friends are not White. I haven't been able to find any Indian people to meet. I just spent a week at the Gathering of Nations Powwow in New Mexico. It is supposed to be the biggest in the world. I see my mother and her family at the July Pawnee Homecoming Powwow. My sister and I usually try to make that one. I don't really know my Indian background. At least there I know the ceremonies, the songs, the dances. I just feel like being part of that.

Have you ever experienced an uncomfortable situation because of your ethnic background?
Many, many times. Not overseas. If you tell someone you are Native American they just love you right away, It's like "Oh! A Real Indian!" And Americans are that way, too. Indians do very well in the military. You already got the dormitory life down. But boarding school had bad things, too, in that you never get the grown-up nurturing that a child should have. You get nurturing from your friends, but they don't know any more than you. You are separated from your family.

(continued)

How does being a member of an Indian tribe affect you?
I am enrolled under the Pawnee because that is what my mother was. I used to get a check every year for $13. I haven't got it during the last few years. I don't know if we run out of money or what. They have a small clinic and nursing care for the elderly and they are trying to get more. But we are not a tribe that has a casino, so we don't have the money. Choctaws in Oklahoma are fairly wealthy. They have done a lot to bring up the tribe. If I would enroll with the Choctaws, but you are supposed to enroll with only one tribe, I would get medical care. Our Pawnee tribe is very small. I would say at the most 500. The Choctaw tribe is a little more than 8,000.

 Discussion Questions

What key factors account for the resilience of Native Americans as an ethnic group?

In what ways did the boarding school and military experiences encourage Jean Wilma's assimilation? In what ways has she maintained her Indian identity?

Why have U.S. government policies toward the Native Americans cycled between assimilation and separation? Which policies have been most effective in promoting the incorporation of Native Americans into U.S. society?

In what ways will gaming change the lives of Indians? What are the arguments for and against gaming on the reservations?

What are the advantages and disadvantages of pan-Indian identity versus tribal identity?

Should the Indian tribes be allowed to maintain tribal sovereignty? Who should make final decisions when tribal laws conflict with state laws?

Why has the federal government been so lax in the management of Indian leases and trusts? What, if anything, should be done to compensate for this lax management?

What would the larger society be like if traditional Indian values regarding wealth, natural resources, and land were to become dominant?

 Key Ideas

1. France, England, Spain, and Holland each attempted to gain control of portions of North America. Indian tribes became the allies of various countries. The greater

numbers of the English and the timely support of the Iroquois led to the defeat of France and her allies.

2. Pontiac led an intertribal effort to stop the westward expansion of Anglo American society. The power of a concerted Indian resistance led the King of England to issue the Proclamation of 1763. This important document laid the foundation for the separatist Indian policies adopted later by the new American republic.

3. Land-hungry traders, settlers, and politicians devised numerous methods to persuade the Indians to sell or cede their lands, some in good faith but many involving deception and fraud. The pressure of the Whites on the Indians led to continuous friction and the transfer of enormous tracts of land to the Whites.

4. Tecumseh attempted to form a pan-Indian military alliance to stop the advance of the Whites. It was the most ambitious military effort ever attempted by the Indians.

5. The Indian Removal Act led to the forced evacuation to Indian Territory of most of the Indians east of the Mississippi River. The removal of the eastern Indians to Indian Territory and the movement of White Americans across the Plains precipitated several decades of bitter, tragic, and widely publicized warfare between the western Indians and the Americans.

6. In 1871, Congress declared that the United States would honor all existing treaties but would no longer recognize the tribes as treaty-making powers. By this time, most of the tribes had been assigned to reservations and placed under the direct supervision of the BIA.

7. Through the General Allotment (Dawes) Act of 1887, the federal government abandoned its long-standing policy of separatism and adopted a policy of Anglo conformity. The main effects of the act were to place most of the Indians' lands in the hands of White people and to increase the levels of poverty among the Indians.

8. The Indian Reorganization Act of 1934 replaced the Dawes Act and was based on the ideology of cultural pluralism. It encouraged Indians to remain Indians and to participate fully in the life of the broader society. The Reorganization Act reaffirmed tribal autonomy and encouraged Indian tribes to form their own democratic governments, organize tribal business enterprises, and revive tribal religions, languages, and cultures. The "termination" policy of the 1950s represented a brief return to the Anglo-conformity policy. The Indian Self-Determination Act of 1975 marked the resumption of a policy of cultural pluralism.

9. A number of national pan-Indian organizations have been formed to promote the interests and welfare of American Indians. In general they have expressed the wish that the American Indians be permitted to retain their cultural heritages.

10. Many groups of Native Americans have actively worked to renew their status as recognized tribes and have taken legal steps to affirm their tribal sovereignty. The emphasis on sovereignty and self-determination has resulted in conflicts between

tribal and state governments over the power to control fishing rights, taxes, gaming, and liquor trafficking.

11. Since the middle of the twentieth century, American Indians have migrated in large numbers to urban areas, and they are now predominantly an urban people. The urban Indians appear to be moving more rapidly toward cultural assimilation than are those on the reservations.

12. The Indian population is increasing in number, contrary to what each of the assimilation models would predict. This may be due to an increasing number of persons of mixed Indian heritage identifying themselves as Indian.

13. The movement of American Indians toward secondary assimilation in education, occupations, incomes, and health care has been very rapid during recent decades, especially among urban Indians. Despite the rapid rates of change, however, the Indian averages still lag behind those of American society in general, and many reservations have high levels of poverty and unemployment.

14. Tribal sovereignty has given American Indians opportunities to create their own laws, schools, and businesses on the reservations. Gaming has brought increased wealth to a number of reservations and has allowed them to use the profits to diversify the economies on the reservations, promote traditional cultures, and challenge land ownership rights and government management of Indian affairs.

15. Historically, primary and marital assimilation of the Indians into White society have been low, although the levels of primary assimilation may be rising somewhat faster in the cities than on the reservations.

16. Since the end of official separatism in the nineteenth century, the dominant society has alternated between Indian policies of Anglo conformity and cultural pluralism. Throughout this time, Indian tribes have largely rejected the dominant culture and have defined success mainly in terms of tribal and cultural survival. From the perspective of an ability to maintain identities, cultures, and forms of organization that are distinct from that of the dominant group, the American Indians have been very successful. As tribal groups succeed in using mainstream strategies to improve the lives of tribal members (e.g., the legal system and capitalism), Indian values and cultures will be severely challenged.

Key Terms

Allotment (Dawes) Act   The process of assigning parcels of Indian community land to individual land owners.

blood quantum   Indicates the degree to which a person is of Indian ancestry and is a key concept used historically as well as currently in administrative definitions of who is an American Indian. The concept was based on the ancient idea that hereditary characteristics are transmitted through the blood and, therefore, that the "amount of blood" a person possessed from a particular race determined physical characteristics and social behavior. This concept was central in the eugenics movement.

gaming   A broad term that encompasses a number of forms of gambling, including such things as bingo, slot machines, and card and dice games.

new tribalism   An emerging sense of identification with Indian tribes among young, educated American Indians. This conception often includes panethnic collaboration to protest violations of Indian rights.

relocation   A voluntary program initiated by the BIA in 1952. The aim of the program was to encourage Indians to move from the reservations to the cities and to adopt Anglo conformity.

self-identification   Allows individuals to determine their own racial or ethnic identification. Self-identification is now used in federal census counts and is believed to be a factor in the rapid growth of the Indian population.

sovereign nations   The Indian tribes have a government-to-government relationship with the U.S. government. Possessing sovereignty gives Indian tribes special privileges, such as making tribal laws, not paying federal or state taxes, establishing their own schools, and forming their own governments. Court rulings have limited tribal powers, and conflicts have arisen over relationships between tribal governments and state governments.

termination   The process by which the U.S. government declared that Indian groups that were sufficiently assimilated would no longer be considered Indian tribes. Terminated tribes no longer qualified for payments and services for the land they had given up to the government under treaties.

Notes

1. The Indian population of the United States may be defined as people who identified their race as American Indian, Eskimo, or Aleut in the census (Snipp 1989:58).

2. During the entire treaty-making period, which lasted for nearly a century, the White Americans concluded 645 treaties with various Indian tribes (Jackson and Galli 1977:26).

3. Justice Marshall went on to describe the relation of the Indians to the United States as "that of a ward to his guardian" (Jackson and Galli 1977:59). The use of the term *ward*, with its implication of dependency and close supervision, later created numerous problems for the Indians.

4. The term *The Trail of Tears* originally applied specifically to the removal experience of the Cherokees. Since then it has become generalized to describe the entire removal process.

5. About 1,000 Cherokees fled from Georgia to North Carolina where they established a separate tribe. The contemporary Eastern Band of the Cherokees, their descendants, still live in North Carolina.

6. Custer's command included about 650 cavalrymen, 145 infantrymen, and 40 "Ree" (Arikara) Indian Scouts (Connell 1984:383).

7. Some other chiefs present at the battle were Low Dog, Crow King, Hump, and Iron Thunder. Sitting Bull was a medicine chief

rather than a war chief, so he was not on the battlefield.

8. The BIA was transferred in 1849 from the War Department to the Department of the Interior.

9. The Five Civilized Tribes organized Indian protests against the Dawes proposal and, as a result, the Dawes Act was not applied to them, to the tribes of Indian Territory, or to the New York Indians (Hoxie 1984:72). Later, in the Curtis Act, the government dissolved the governments of the tribes that had refused allotment.

10. See Meriam et al. (1928).

11. The ominous word *termination* does not appear in the resolution (Officer 1986:114).

12. Public Law 280, passed during the same summer, also had an important effect on the status of American Indians. PL 280 extended to certain states jurisdiction over civil and criminal matters on federal Indian reservations, thus attacking the principle of sovereignty established in *Worcester* (Svensson 1973:33–34).

13. The Menominees were restored to their tribal status in 1974 through the passage of the Menominee Restoration Act.

14. A council of Indians representing 19 tribes in Indian Territory sent the president of the United States a resolution attacking the Dawes Act as follows: "Like other people, the Indian needs ... some governmental organization of his own ... in order to make true progress in the affairs of life" (Hertzberg 1971:9).

15. An important legislative victory for the NCAI was the establishment of an Indian Claims Commission in 1946 to hear cases involving damages to Indian tribes. By the time this program ended in 1978, 285 tribal claims had been settled among 850 filed (Olson and Wilson 1984:137, 142).

16. The issue of sovereignty has raised concerns about individual rights. Bordewich (1996:314) quoted Ramon Roubideaux, a lawyer who is a member of the Rosebud Sioux Tribe, as arguing that sovereignty "is just a mask for individuals who rob people of their rights as U.S. citizens."

17. In the matter of gambling casinos, however, there is intertribal and intratribal conflict as well as conflict between the tribes and state and federal officials (*Americans Before Columbus* 1992).

18. For an excellent discussion of the "blood quantum" approach to racial identification, see Snipp (1989).

19. Nagel and Snipp (1993) used the term *ethnic reorganization* to describe the process whereby an ethnic minority redefines its ethnic group boundaries and social structure.

20. See *NARF Legal Review* (Summer/Fall 1994).

21. See the *New York Times* article by Kleinfield (1995:A9).

22. These figures reflect only the experiences of the approximately 850,000 American Indians who in 1980 lived within the boundaries of the 88 service units of the Indian Health Service (IHS).

23. Roy did note, however, that "people with a high percentage of Indian ancestry tended to select mates with a high percentage of Indian ancestry," suggesting some relationship between the Indians' cultural and presumed biological identities. A subsequent study of the Spokane Indians by White and Chadwick (1972:246) found that urban Indians were more likely than reservation Indians to consider their identities to be mainly a matter of ancestry. An explanation of this finding may be that urban Indians suffer more discrimination because of their physical appearance and, therefore, feel "Indian" if they look "Indian."

24. All the women took pride in maintaining the Navajo language, spiritual beliefs and practices, kinship patterns, and connection to the land as important aspects of being Navajo.

25. The school's curriculum includes American Indian perspectives, and half of the faculty are Indian. The students in American history classes read both Tocqueville and speeches by Indian leaders who influenced democracy.

Japanese
Americans

The Japanese in America have faced severe racism. This family's home in Seattle, Washington was defaced while they were detained in a relocation center during World War II. However, the history of the Japanese Americans generally supports the idea that disadvantages based on racial distinctiveness are not necessarily permanent in American society.

*I am proud that I am an American citizen of Japanese
ancestry. . . . Because I believe in America. . . . I pledge
to do her honor in all times and all places.*

—Mike Masaoka

*To create a truly fulfilling identity, Asian Americans realize they must
redefine and articulate Asian American identity on their own terms.*

—Amy Tachiki

Our discussions of immigration to America, nativism, and racism showed that the less
the members of a group resembled the Anglo American ideal of an "American," the less
acceptable they were to the dominant group and the more prejudice and discrimination
they suffered. Groups that are socially, culturally, and physically most "distant" from the
dominant group's notion of the ideal American were considered to have the lowest "assimilative potential."

Of all the factors that affect a group's prospects, being classified by the dominant
group as "non-White" has been the most troublesome. During the colonial period,
Africans and American Indians were defined as standing outside of the developing Anglo
American society. As other physically distinctive groups entered the territory of the
United States, they also were viewed as being too distant from the American ideal to be included as full members of American society. They were subjected, therefore, to levels of
prejudice and discrimination resembling those directed toward African and Native Americans. Even though the Japanese immigration to America was comparatively small, many
factors combined to create the impression that the United States was in grave danger of
being overrun by "hordes" of "Mongolians" and must be constantly on guard against
"the yellow peril."[1]

An irony in the situation stemmed from the fact that certain actions of the U.S. government and various business interests had contributed directly to the beginnings of the
Japanese immigration, as they had previously helped stimulate Chinese immigration.
Japan had been ruled for many centuries by powerful military families whose leaders
(*shoguns*) established a feudal system and limited the imperial court to ceremonial functions. By the early seventeenth century, this system had become very rigid and the *shoguns*
had grown increasingly suspicious of all external influences. As a result, Japan's doors
were closed to the outside world until 1854. In that year, through intimidation and a skillful display of Western products, the American naval officer Matthew C. Perry negotiated a
treaty establishing trade relations between America and Japan.

Within a few years, the great powers of Europe also demanded similar trading
privileges. These changes in Japan's foreign relations accompanied the decline of the
power of the *shoguns*. In 1868, the emperor Matsuhito successfully challenged the rule of
the Tokugawa family and became once again the true head of government. Matsuhito

took the name "Meiji" (enlightened government), renounced the isolationist policies of the past, and launched a new policy of westernization and industrialization.

Japanese Immigration and Native Reactions

Anti-Japanese Protest

Before 1868, the Japanese government did not permit its citizens to emigrate, and laborers ordinarily did not receive permission to travel abroad until 1884 (Ichihashi 1932: 6). Those granted passports before 1884 were mainly students who were expected to seek knowledge and come back home "so that the foundations of the Empire may be strengthened" (Ichihashi 1932:3). In 1890 there were only 2,039 Japanese in the entire United States, but in 1891 about 1,500 Japanese immigrants reached the country. This small but rapid increase, following as it did some 40 years of anti-Chinese agitation, attracted the unfavorable attention of the San Francisco *Morning Call*. The *Call* launched a "crusade against Japanese contract labor" (Daniels 1969:20), claiming that Japanese immigrants were taking work away from Americans. By 1905, anti-Asian hostility was focused on the Japanese. In that year, a war between Russia and Japan ended in a resounding victory for Japan. For the first time since the Europeans began colonizing the world during the fifteenth century, a "non-White" nation had defeated a "White" nation. In so doing, Japan established a reputation as a first-rank military power. The belief that the United States was in imminent danger of being swamped in a sea of human waves from the East was revived, and the hostility among California's working people that previously had been directed at the Chinese was now aimed at the Japanese.

The first large anti-Japanese protest meeting in California, organized in 1900 after labor unions gained partial control of the San Francisco city government (tenBroek, Barnhart, and Matson 1954:35), featured prominent figures of the day such as J. D. Phelan (later a U.S. senator) and E. A. Ross, a sociology professor at Stanford University. Phelan declared that "these Asiatic laborers will undermine our civilization" (tenBroek, Barnhart, and Matson 1954:35). He stated also, in a conspicuous display of poor judgment, that "the Chinese and Japanese are not the stuff of which American citizens can be made" (Daniels 1969:21). Ross advanced the familiar claim that Japanese immigration undercut native labor, a sentiment echoed in that election year by the platforms of both major political parties.

Five years later a sustained campaign against the Japanese was launched. The most conspicuous forces initiating this campaign were, as in 1892, a newspaper and, as in 1900, organized labor. The newspaper was the respected *San Francisco Chronicle*. For nearly a year, the *Chronicle* ran "scare" headlines and page-one articles attacking Japanese immigration. In its first broadside, the headline read "The Japanese Invasion, the Problem of the Hour"; another headline said "The Yellow Peril—How Japanese Crowd Out the White Race" (Daniels 1969:25). The paper repeated the claim that the Japanese immigration would become a "raging torrent" that would inundate the West Coast and pose an economic threat to native laborers.

The anti-Japanese barrage led to the formation of the Asiatic Exclusion League (ten-Broek, Barnhart, and Matson 1954:35). This group, comprised primarily of labor union representatives, listed both economic and racial reasons for exclusion. The combined agitations of the *Chronicle* and the League were followed by a rapid increase in the number of incidents of interracial violence in San Francisco. Individual Japanese were attacked. Rocks and rotten eggs were thrown into Japanese places of business, and a boycott instituted against Japanese restaurants ended only after the restaurant owners agreed to pay for "protection." These incidents were accompanied by periodic demands that the board of education implement a school segregation plan. A year and a half after the League began its agitation, the board of education ordered all Japanese, Chinese, and Korean pupils to attend a separate school for Orientals.

The School Board Crisis

Since school segregation in San Francisco affected only a small number of pupils in only one city, we might expect that there would have been little more than local interest in it. Strangely, though, this conflict spiraled into a tense confrontation between the governments of the United States and Japan. After the segregation order went into effect, various reports concerning it were published in Tokyo newspapers, and the Japanese government filed an official complaint with President Theodore Roosevelt. President Roosevelt quickly announced his concern about the situation and authorized the use of armed forces, if necessary, to protect the Japanese. A few weeks later, the president moved to prevent local mobs from committing acts "which would plunge us into war" (Daniels 1969:39).

The school board crisis set into motion a long and complicated series of negotiations between the governments of the United States, Japan, and California. President Roosevelt wanted a solution that was not insulting to Japan and, at the same time, would restrict Japanese immigration. A compromise was achieved in two main steps during 1907 and 1908. In the first step, the school board repealed the school segregation resolution as the president issued an executive order to limit the entry of Japanese workers into the United States through Mexico, Canada, or Hawaii (Ichihashi 1932:244–245).

The second part of the compromise was the celebrated **Gentlemen's Agreement.** The agreement stated that beginning in 1908, the government of Japan would issue passports to the United States only to nonlaborers; laborers who lived in America but had been visiting Japan; the wives, parents, and children of those who had settled in America; and those who owned an interest in an American farm enterprise (Ichihashi 1932:246; Petersen 1971:43). Additionally, on its own initiative, the Japanese government curtailed the issuance of passports to Hawaii (which was now a U.S. possession) and to Mexico. Thus, about 18 months after the school crisis had erupted, the Gentlemen's Agreement appeared to have limited the further immigration of the Japanese without insulting Japan.[2]

The Gentlemen's Agreement led to sharp reductions in the number of Japanese admitted to the United States and Hawaii; and, for awhile, departures actually exceeded admissions (Petersen 1971:197). These drastic changes ended what has been called the "frontier period" of the Japanese experience in America (LaViolette 1945:10).

The "Picture-Bride Invasion"

As has been true of the vanguard of many immigrant groups, most of the Japanese who came to America before 1908 were single male sojourners who wished to "build a nest-egg" and return to the homeland (Montero 1980:104). The census of 1900 found that of the 24,326 resident Japanese, 985 were women (Glenn and Parreñas 1996:126); so the Japanese community in America at this time contained few families and the bare beginnings of ordinary institutional life. Since the Gentlemen's Agreement permitted those who were the wives of residents of the United States to enter, many of the men who decided to stay sent home to Japan for wives. This action was completely consistent with the Gentlemen's Agreement, but many Americans nevertheless saw it as treachery.

In Japan, marriages were more a union of two families than of two individuals and were arranged by a go-between who was respected by both families (Ichihashi 1932:293). Under normal circumstances the partners would meet at a specified place and time, and the wedding would be conducted. But what was to be done when the partners were, literally, an ocean apart? A solution to this problem was the "picture-bride marriage" (Miyamoto 1972:226) whereby the prospective bride and groom exchanged photographs and, after the go-between's work was done, were married in a legal proxy ceremony. The bride then would sail for America to join her husband.

The emigration of Japanese women to the United States was greatly accelerated by this method. Glenn and Parreñas (1996:128) reported that "Between 1909 and 1923, 45,706 Japanese women entered the United States, of whom 32,678 . . . were listed as wives." Although many of these newcomers were not enthusiastic about their new lives, they had little to say in the matter (Chow 1994:186). A Mrs. Takagi, for instance, stated: "They just pick out your husband and tell you what to do" (Glenn and Parreñas 1996:129). Also, the brides often were so dismayed on meeting their husbands that they vowed to go "back on this very boat" (Glenn and Parreñas 1996:130). Additionally, most of the women found that their husbands lived in rural areas, frequently under harsh conditions (Gee 1994:56; Kikumura 1994:149). In these circumstances, the picture brides often led hard and lonely lives (Glenn and Parreñas 1996:131).

In any event, the arrival of so many women enabled the Japanese in America rapidly to establish families and communities. The ratio of Japanese men to Japanese women dropped from over 24 to 1 in 1900 to less than 2 to 1 in 1920 (Glenn and Parreñas 1996:132). As a result, most Japanese men were able to marry and thereby to gain not only wives but also extra adult laborers to help them make a living. As Glenn and Parreñas (1996:132) observed, any Japanese "woman arriving in the United States could expect to pull her weight economically." The main forms of employment outside the home were in agriculture and, as was true of Irish women, domestic service.

The "picture-bride invasion" angered many natives who believed the whole process was contrary to the Gentlemen's Agreement and that many more Japanese were arriving (and staying) than really were. In fact, during the 1911–1920 period, a large number of

Japanese left the country (Ichihashi 1932:292). The arrival of the picture brides did, however, greatly reduce the imbalance between the sexes within the Japanese community in America and create the conditions necessary for building families and developing institutionally complete communities. By 1920, the Japanese, like so many other immigrant groups, had formed numerous small communities and subcommunities that recreated, in many ways, the institutions and culture of the homeland.

The Japanese Family and Community in America

Family and Community Cohesion

Many immigrant groups have been cohesive, had families that (at least formally) were dominated by the father, attached great importance to age, gave preference to male children (especially the first born), and experienced a marked split between the first and second generations. But this cluster of characteristics was especially pronounced among the Japanese.

Consider the split between the generations. The different Japanese and Japanese American generations were so distinct from one another that they were identified by different names. The first-generation immigrants, the **Issei**, were those who arrived before the legal exclusion of 1924. The second generation, the **Nisei**, were American-born citizens who generally reached adulthood by the outbreak of World War II. The third generation, the **Sansei**, were born mainly following World War II; and the **Yonsei**, the fourth generation, are the children of the Sansei.[3]

The distinctiveness of the Japanese generations resulted primarily from the interruption of the immigrant flow caused by the Gentlemen's Agreement and then, later, by exclusionary legislation. After 1924, the Issei did not continue to increase in numbers through the arrival of more newcomers from Japan. Since nearly all young people of Japanese descent in America were Nisei, the peer and youth groups established within Japanese communities were comprised almost exclusively of youngsters who had been born in the United States; hence, the Nisei seldom encountered people who were recent migrants from the old country, and the old-country ways of the Issei stood in sharp contrast to the American ways of the Nisei.

The two-stage process through which the Issei immigration was halted generated special problems for them but did not prevent them from developing in America, as in Japan, highly interdependent and cohesive communities. Within the ethnic community, a person could receive help in locating a job, finding a place to live, or starting a business. One could also speak the native language, eat familiar foods, and relax among relatives and friends. The ethnic community also provided the Japanese some protection from the hostility of the surrounding society. As was true for other immigrant groups, the ethnic community was simultaneously a tool to assist the immigrant to adjust to the demands of the new setting and to sustain and embellish the way of life that had been left behind.

Several aspects of Japanese family and community life are of special importance in understanding their adjustment in America. As noted earlier, the traditional Japanese marriage was primarily a union of two families. The extended family unit thus created was, in turn, connected in numerous ways through other marriages to the larger community. An important effect of this pattern of interrelationships was that everyone in the community had important obligations to many others within the community. The Issei identified strongly with their homeland and were eager to reestablish this traditional pattern of family and community relationships and to transmit its sustaining values to the Nisei. Their open affection for Japan was frequently used against them in later years.

The Nisei were taught Japanese etiquette, which involved a high regard for obligation and authority. Children were expected to understand that they were members of a family and community and that each member had numerous duties and responsibilities. The parents were obligated to the children, but the children were expected to reciprocate. In this way, the children learned that the acts of each individual were of significance to the entire group (LaViolette 1945:19; Miyamoto 1972:228–229). In addition to the importance of politeness, respect for authority, attention to parental wishes, and duty to the community, the Issei also emphasized the importance of education, hard work, and occupational success. The main links between the extended family and the community grew out of the fact that people from the same areas of Japan tended to settle near one another in the United States. **Kenjin**—those from the same province—felt especially close to one another and were preferred as friends, neighbors, business associates, and marriage partners. These bonds were so strong that associations based on them, called **kenjinkai**, often were formed. But the purposes of the kenjinkai went far beyond social, business, and recreational activities. They published newspapers, acted as employment agencies, provided legal advice, gave money to needy members, and paid medical and burial expenses (Light 1974:283). They also frequently sponsored a form of financial assistance known as the **tanomoshi**. The tanomoshi was an organization through which money was pooled and then loaned in rotation to various members entirely on mutual trust (Light 1974:283; O'Brien and Fugita 1991:6).[4] The success of the tanomoshi illustrates the point that the Japanese brought with them "specific principles for creating social organizations" that were of great value in developing strong communities and pursuing worldly success (O'Brien and Fugita 1991:3).

Many of the functions of the kenjinkai were formalized in the Japanese Association, which "was the most important Issei group" (Kitano 1969:81). The Japanese Association provided numerous social and benevolent services, but its main objective was the protection of the Japanese community. The Issei worked through this association to keep the Japanese community "in line" and, thereby, to reduce friction with the Americans. They also used the association to obtain legal services and police assistance. Whenever the police were unresponsive, the Japanese Association could ask the Japanese consul to intervene in their behalf. Everything considered, the Japanese Association played an important role in establishing and maintaining traditional Japanese ways of life within the American setting and, consequently, of resisting cultural, primary, and marital assimilation (Kitano 1969:81–82).

Another important community-building association established by the Issei was the Japanese Language School (Kitano 1969:24–25; Petersen 1971:54–58). The Issei, like the parents in many other ethnic groups, believed that successfully transmitting the ideals of their culture required that their children understand the language of the old-country; so the main purpose of these schools was to teach Japanese to the Nisei. Although the schools were not very effective in their efforts to transmit the Japanese language, they did symbolize the desire of the Issei to assure their children a Japanese education and, simultaneously, to prevent them from becoming "too American" (Sone 1994). The schools also brought the Nisei together after public school hours and on Saturdays, thereby strengthening the social ties among them and decreasing their contacts with non-Japanese American children.

All of these factors combined to accentuate the differences between the Issei and Nisei. Each of the two generations was unusually homogeneous with respect to age, background, and general life experiences. The center of gravity within the Issei generation was the old country and its traditions; the Nisei, like most other second-generation groups, sought increasingly to break with the old ways.

Japanese Occupations and the Alien Land Laws

The first Japanese who came to America with their government's permission, the so-called "school boys," took part-time jobs to help pay the costs of their stay here. Most of these students worked as domestic servants; however, when the main body of Japanese immigrants began to arrive during the 1890s, these newcomers took a wide variety of jobs in railroad construction, canning, lumbering, mining, fishing, and seasonal farm labor. During the first decade of the twentieth century, however, the Japanese moved increasingly into agriculture, especially in California where they were most numerous. By 1908, agriculture was the leading form of employment among them (Ichihashi 1932:162–163).[5]

As the Japanese became more conspicuous in agriculture, native Americans began to complain that the Japanese were acquiring too much land and were "taking over" food production. As usual, a persuasive charge against the Japanese was that they did not compete fairly. They were willing to work for less than White laborers and, occasionally, preferred payment in land rather than in wages. In this way, they were gradually gaining strength in agriculture and driving some of the natives out of farming.

The fear that the efficient Japanese would gradually acquire all of the farming land of California led to the passage of the Alien Land Law of 1913. This law did not specifically mention any nationality group. Instead, it prohibited ownership by those who were "ineligible to citizenship." This curious phrase rests on some equally curious facts about American naturalization law. When the first naturalization act was written in 1790, citizenship was made available to any "free white person." The Japanese initially were denied citizenship because when Hawaii was annexed in 1898, the United States recognized as citizens only people who had been citizens of Hawaii; and the Japanese had been denied citizenship in Hawaii (Petersen 1971:47). This denial of citizenship by the United States was challenged by Takao Ozawa, who described himself as "a true American," chose a wife educated in America, and spoke only English at home so his children would not learn Japanese (Takaki 1989:208). In 1916, Ozawa applied for American citizenship and his application was denied; so he appealed to the U.S. Supreme Court. In 1922, in *Ozawa v. United States,* the Court ruled that although Ozawa had many fine qualifications he, nevertheless, was not White and not eligible for citizenship.

The discriminatory intent of the Alien Land Law was readily apparent in Japan and, once again, the Japanese government entered a vigorous official protest. As matters developed, the Alien Land Law had little effect on either the development of Japanese agriculture or the relations of the United States and Japan. The Issei soon learned to evade the law by registering their land in the names of their children or trusted American friends. More important, though, was that the outbreak of World War I (in which the United States and Japan were allies) sharply increased the need for agricultural workers. The Japanese were admirably suited to meet this sudden high demand. As a result, overt anti-Japanese activities in California were reduced. The traditional Japanese techniques of farming served them well. "Their skill and energy," wrote Iwata (1962:37), "helped to reclaim and improve thousands of acres of worthless lands throughout the state . . . and made them fertile and immensely productive." Even though they controlled only about 1 percent of California's agricultural land, the crops they produced were valued at about 10 percent of the state's total (Iwata 1962:37).

By 1920, it was obvious that the Gentlemen's Agreement had not stopped the growth of the Japanese population and that the Alien Land Law had not prevented them from increasing their land holdings. As agricultural products again became plentiful, the agitation against the Japanese (whether Issei or Nisei) again increased.

Exclusion

The exclusionists now shifted their attention to immigration restriction at the national level. And, as discussed in Chapter 5, the time was ripe for a national approach. The doctrine of White supremacy had become increasingly popular throughout the United States, as had the demand that the United States be protected against "the rising tide of color" through some form of federal restriction on immigration.

The main thrust of the national movement was toward a quota system rather than a system of exclusion. The Emergency Quota Act of 1921 not only established a quota for many countries but also recognized the validity of the Gentlemen's Agreement and exempted Japan from the system. Nevertheless, when the Immigration Quota Act of 1924 was passed, the Gentlemen's Agreement was unilaterally repudiated and Japan was denied a quota. These actions were taken even though the Japanese government was willing to accept a quota (since it applied to many other nations as well). The number of Japanese who would have been eligible for admission each year under the quota system was 100 (Daniels, Taylor, and Kitano 1991:xv).

Why did the United States single out Japan for international humiliation instead of assigning it a tiny quota? In a letter that summarized the understandings of the Gentlemen's Agreement, the Japanese government expressed its willingness to modify the agreement but warned that excluding the Japanese would be "mortifying . . . to the people of Japan" and would have "grave consequences" (Daniels 1969:101). U.S. Senator Henry Cabot Lodge viewed the latter phrase as a "veiled threat" against the United States and led the drive for an exclusion provision in the new immigration law.

The Japanese were very angry. The United States had, in their view, violated its own principles of equality and justice as well as the Gentlemen's Agreement. While it is impossible to weigh fully the consequences of these events, some scholars have suggested that it was an important link in the chain of events leading to the Japanese attack on Pearl Harbor in 1941 (Kitano 1969:28).

The Second-Generation Period

The cessation of Japanese immigration to the United States in 1924 and the continuing status of the Issei as noncitizens left them in a strange position. Like many others, they had come to America, established homes, started families, and filled various niches in the American economy. Indeed, in the latter respect, they had made quite a name for themselves. They were extremely industrious and by transferring many old-country skills had become prominent in agriculture and landscape gardening. But despite their obvious ability to adapt to American conditions, even in the face of the exaggerated hostility of the natives, their standing in this country at the end of the 1907–1924 "settlement period"[6] was anything but secure. The second-generation period was one in which the Issei continued to build on the economic and community foundations established during the frontier and settlement periods.

By now many Issei men and women had established small businesses to serve other members of the Japanese community. Issei wives had assisted in these businesses and also found work in such jobs as food processing and garment making (Glenn and Parreñas 1996:133). As the Japantowns grew in San Francisco, Seattle, Los Angeles, and other cities, some professional jobs in midwifery and teaching also became available to Issei women. The goal of the Issei was to assist the Nisei to achieve the standing in American society to which their citizenship entitled them and also to adopt and exemplify the traditional virtues of Japanese society.

The Issei strongly approved of the Nisei attendance at public schools and constantly urged them to study hard and bring honor to the family name. The Nisei were encouraged to participate in American-style youth organizations through the formation of Japanese Boy and Girl Scout troops, YMCAs and YWCAs, and all-Japanese baseball and basketball leagues. Also, as the Issei themselves underwent some degree of cultural assimilation, American ways of doing things were introduced into the home, the kenjinkai, and the Buddhist church. As the Nisei grew older, they frequently were embarrassed by their parents' English and were often ashamed of their own Japanese appearance and manners. They, of course, resented being teased by other American children about their physical features and were hurt and angered when they were called "Japs." As the Nisei became aware that their parents were not and could not become citizens, they sometimes used this point to emphasize the difference between themselves and their parents (Ichihashi 1932:350).

As the Nisei reached adulthood, many of them felt that the older organizations established by the Issei did not meet their special needs. Even though they were Americans, they faced the same sort of prejudice and discrimination that was directed against their parents. Job discrimination was a particularly galling source of worry and frustration (Hosokawa 1969:191, 489). During the 1920s, the Nisei began to establish protective groups similar to the Japanese associations founded by the Issei leading, by 1930, to an umbrella organization of Nisei—the Japanese American Citizen's League (JACL) (Hosokawa 1969:194). The JACL represented the Nisei's determination to rise in American society and be accepted as equals. In addition to combating discrimination, the JACL gave attention to such conventional matters as getting out the Nisei vote, electing Japanese Americans to public office, and working to gain citizenship for the Issei (Hosokawa 1969:197–200). These efforts were not very effective; nevertheless, the JACL provided an important rallying point for the Nisei and accelerated their cultural assimilation (Kitano 1969:82).

By 1941, the Japanese American community had been developing for about 50 years. The Issei had been notably successful economically and in raising their families, despite the special hardships created by immigration restrictions and the denial of citizenship. The Nisei had undergone a high degree of cultural assimilation (mainly by substitution) and were striving for secondary assimilation. Some members of the third generation, the Sansei, were now on the scene. It is true that anti-Japanese activities continued to exist, especially during election years. But neither these hostile activities nor any of those prior to this period may easily be compared to the events in the months following December 7, 1941.

 # War, Evacuation, and Relocation

The aerial attack on Pearl Harbor led to a declaration of war against Japan, to the establishment of martial law in Hawaii, and to the quick arrest of 1,002 German, 169 Italian, and 370 Japanese "suspicious aliens" (Taylor 1993:45). It also provoked a renewed attack in many newspapers against all of the Japanese, aliens and citizens alike. Many of the old hate slogans were revived (e.g., "once a Jap, always a Jap") and there were rumors that the Japanese were planning extensive sabotage. It was said that the language schools had indoctrinated the Nisei in favor of Japan and that the other Japanese community organizations were fronts for Japanese patriotic fanaticism (tenBroek, Barnhart, and Matson 1954:93–94).[7] In the face of growing fears of an invasion of the West Coast, of espionage, and of sabotage, President Franklin Roosevelt issued Executive Order 9066 in February 1942 authorizing the military commanders as a national-defense measure to prescribe military areas and to impose restrictions on the movements of all persons within those areas. Under this authority (supported by an act of Congress in March), Lt. Gen. John L. DeWitt, the commander of the Western Defense Command, issued a series of public proclamations and civilian exclusion orders beginning in March 1942. General DeWitt argued that the entire Pacific Coast was particularly vulnerable to attack, invasion, espionage, and sabotage, and that, for these reasons, certain groups of people would be excluded from some designated military areas as a matter of "military necessity." Under these orders, all people of Japanese ancestry, whether aliens or citizens, were required to leave the prohibited areas.[8]

The first destination of the evacuees was a group of 15 "assembly centers." From the assembly centers, the evacuees were transferred to 10 "relocation centers." This movement was started in March 1942 and was completed in November. In the process, more than 110,000 people of Japanese ancestry—over 70,000 of whom were American citizens—were forced from their homes and imprisoned without warrants or indictments.[9] All of this presumably was required by "military necessity." The individuals involved were not accused of any specific acts of disloyalty or tried for any crime in a court of law. Why, then, was the mass evacuation and internment of the Japanese and Japanese Americans a "military necessity"?

One of the most revealing commentaries on this subject was General DeWitt's explanation of the decision to evacuate. The general wrote as follows:

> In the war in which we are now engaged racial affinities are not severed by migration. The Japanese race is an enemy race and while many second and third generation Japanese born on United States soil, possessed of United States citizenship have become "Americanized," the racial strains are undiluted. . . . It therefore allows that along the vital Pacific Coast over 112,000 potential enemies, of Japanese extraction, are at large today. There are disturbing indications that these are organized and ready for concerted action at a favorable opportunity. The very fact that no sabotage has taken place to date is a disturbing and confirming indication that such action will be taken. (quoted by Rostow 1945:140)

DeWitt's argument that the absence of sabotage was evidence that it surely would occur was advanced also by the famous "liberal" columnist Walter Lippmann and the "liberal" Attorney General of California (and later Supreme Court Chief Justice), Earl Warren (Walls 1987:145–146). It appears, therefore, that a very large group of people—most of whom were citizens of the United States—were arrested and imprisoned without trials purely and simply because of their race. It was assumed that whereas people from other nations may become Americans, those of Japanese ancestry remain forever Japanese.

The national security questions raised here are complex. As we have seen, the Issei and Nisei were a highly organized, cohesive group. They had worked hard to maintain the Japanese language and traditional forms of family and community life. And since the Issei were ineligible for American citizenship, their ties with Japan were quite strong. Consequently, one may agree that the military threat to the West Coast in 1942 was real and that reason and prudence required that those of Japanese ancestry should be regarded in a special light. However, even if one were to agree that considerations of this type are reasonable, does it follow that the evacuation and relocation program was a suitable response?

Consider, for instance, the situation in Hawaii. There the Japanese population comprised over 37 percent of the total population, as compared to less than 2 percent of the population of the West Coast (Ogawa and Fox 1991:136). After a period of investigation, 1,118 Issei and Nisei were sent to the mainland for internment (Daniels 1991a:74). Those taken into custody in Hawaii, however, were arrested on the basis of individual actions and charges. There was no program to take people into custody on the basis of their racial or ethnic identity.

Consider, too, the way this problem was handled among the more than one million aliens of German and Italian descent. People included in this category had to abide by certain security regulations. They could not enter military areas, own or use firearms, or travel without a permit. If German or Italian aliens were suspected of disloyal acts or violated a regulation, they could be arrested. After a hearing, they could be interned, paroled, or released. As in Hawaii, cases were treated individually. Of even greater significance is that the security regulations did not apply in any way to *citizens* of German and Italian descent. It is difficult to escape the conclusion that "the dominant element in the development of our relocation policy was race prejudice, not a military estimate of a military problem" (Rostow 1945:142).

The Relocation Program

Approximately 10 weeks after the attack on Pearl Harbor, the evacuation of the Japanese and Japanese Americans from the West Coast began. In January, Attorney General Biddle established zones that were prohibited to enemy aliens but stated there would be no "wholesale internment, without hearing and (consideration of) the merits of individual cases" (Leighton 1946:17). Throughout this period, numerous acts of hostility against the Japanese and Japanese Americans were reported: jobs were lost, credit was discontinued, signs appeared saying, "No Japs Allowed," and Japanese women were attacked by men pretending to be FBI agents. Despite these problems, the government apparently still did not intend to carry out a mass evacuation. Even after General DeWitt proclaimed portions of California, Oregon, Washington, and Arizona to be military areas, he was quoted as saying that "no mass evacuation is planned for Japanese" (Leighton 1946:34). Only a short time later, a mass evacuation was underway.

Understandably, many Japanese Americans could hardly believe it. Everything they had been taught about the American system of democracy argued against such a possibility. Even if every member of a person's family were convicted felons, each person still must be regarded as innocent until proven guilty. The strong belief in the American system and the disillusionment that accompanied the evacuation are reflected in the following comments by a farmer's son (Leighton 1946:27): "I was very confident that there would be no evacuation on a major scale . . . the American system of education . . . gave me faith that our government would not be moved by economic pressure and racial prejudice." The anguish and sense of betrayal expressed by this young man was shared, and possibly accentuated, among the Japanese who had been drafted for military service, as may be seen in a Nisei soldier's comment: "They are evacuating all the Japanese from the Coast and even trying to take away our citizenship. I don't know why I am in the Army. I want to see democracy as it is supposed to be, but this is getting just as bad as Hitler" (Leighton 1946:27).

The evacuation proceeded in two main stages spread over a period of approximately 7 months. The first stage removed people from their homes to hastily prepared assembly centers in racetracks, fair grounds, and livestock exhibition halls (tenBroek, Barnhart, and Matson 1954:126). Japanese and Japanese Americans of both sexes and all ages were required to leave behind everything they could not carry. Many people sold their homes, businesses, and other possessions at "panic-sale" prices. Others stored their goods or simply left everything in locked houses hoping that they would be safe until their return. Both the economic costs and the costs in human misery and humiliation were staggering. Probably only those who have experienced it can appreciate fully the emotional impact that is created when proud families who are leading productive lives and planning for the future are forced from their homes, assigned identification numbers, and placed under guard with hundreds of others.

The experiences of the members of the Japanese communities of San Francisco and the Bay area were typical. Most members of these communities were moved by buses to the Tanforan racetrack located south of San Francisco (Taylor 1993:61).[10] Even if the planned modifications of the racetrack had been completed, it was hardly a fit place to house the nearly 7,800 people who were there at one time. They lived in barracks and horse stalls with little privacy. The new residents were shocked by the primitive conditions and the high fences, and many of them "stated later that their experiences at Tanforan were the most disturbing of the whole relocation period" (Taylor 1993:63–64).

Most of those detained in the assembly centers gradually were moved to one of the relocation centers. These centers were placed away from the coastal areas and in climates that were "either too hot or too cold, too wet or too dry" (Hosokawa 1969:352). They were in California (Manzanar and Tule Lake), Arizona (Poston and Gila River), Arkansas (Rohwer and Jerome), Idaho (Minidoka), Utah (Topaz), Wyoming (Heart Mountain), and Colorado (Granada).[11] The camps were not finished when the first evacuees arrived; so, in addition to facing various kinds of shortages and physical discomforts, the internees also had to do a substantial share of the construction work needed to complete the camps. Since the camps' officials were eager to distinguish the relocation program from the concentration camp and forced-labor programs of the Nazis, much of the official language was euphemistic. The internees were referred to as "residents," their barracks were called "apartments," and the term "relocation center" was a euphemism for concentration camp (Tussman 1963:210).

Let us briefly consider life in the camps, giving special attention to what was intended to be the largest of the camps (Poston), which was located near Parker, Arizona.[12]

Life in the Camps

The camps' administrators attempted to organize the camps along the lines of a typical, self-governing, American community. They hoped in this way to reassure the friendly aliens and, especially, the loyal citizens that the U.S. government recognized their rights and was concerned about their welfare. It was hoped, too, that the camp communities would soon be able to support themselves through farming and also to serve as an example of the differences between authoritarian and democratic responses to internal and external threats.

The evacuees at Poston faced numerous problems related to housing, water, food, and other necessities. The "apartments" were flimsily constructed and small. Sometimes as many as eight people lived in one room and were often humiliated by the lack of privacy (Houston 1994:168–169; Sone 1994:167–168). There was hardly any furniture. Mattresses were made of cloth bags stuffed with straw. The heat was intense in the summer, while winter temperatures occasionally fell below freezing. And then there were the armed guards and the barbed-wire fences. It is little wonder that many people felt betrayed at having been sent to such a place and, therefore, either actively resisted or failed to cooperate fully with the administration's plans. Nevertheless, a newspaper, police force, and fire department were established. A community council was elected, an irrigation canal was completed, gardens were planted, and various social activities were organized. By the end of August 1942, Poston's population had reached its peak of 17,814 people (Daniels, Taylor, and Kitano 1991:xxi). By then, the more optimistic members of the administration were hoping that Poston soon would approximate a typical American community.

There were still many underlying problems, however. For example, there were internal divisions within the administrative group. And among the evacuees there existed a strong difference of opinion concerning the desirability of cooperating with the administration. The conservatives, most of whom were Issei, did not trust the administration and resented having the Nisei in positions of authority. The liberals, most of whom were Nisei, were impatient with those who did not try to prove their Americanism. Many in this group were enjoying the new responsibilities and experiences camp life had made possible. As tensions mounted, there was an increase in stealing, name-calling, and violence. Some evacuees believed there were FBI informers among them, and some of the suspected informers were assaulted. By the middle of November 1942, distrust and anger were widespread among the residents of Poston. The dissatisfaction of the residents culminated in a demonstration and general strike in one of Poston's three units. After several days of negotiations, the Emergency Executive Council (comprised almost entirely of Issei) agreed to end the strike in return for the release of a man who had been arrested.

Although the strike in Poston ended on a cooperative note, many officials were discouraged by the course of events in Poston and in most of the other camps as well. For example, several weeks after the Poston strike, a riot at Manzanar resulted in the killing and wounding of some of the evacuees (Daniels, Taylor, and Kitano 1991:xx); and early in 1943, the evacuees at Topaz were incensed when a soldier on guard duty shot and killed James Wakasa, a man who had lived in America for 40 years and had himself served in the army during World War I (Taylor 1993:136–137). Consequently, the officials abandoned the idea of developing the camps as model communities. The decision was made, rather, to resettle all "loyal" evacuees outside the camps as soon as possible.

This new plan was strengthened when the War Department reversed an earlier stand regarding military service for the Nisei by announcing its intention to form an all-Nisei combat team. Eventually, over 20,000 Japanese and Japanese American men and women were inducted following this change of policy. Many Nisei served in the Pacific theater as interpreters, interviewers of prisoners, code breakers, and translators (Johnson 1995). These young Americans, recruited mainly from the camps, were " 'the eyes and ears' of the Allied Forces in the Pacific" (O'Brien and Fugita 1991:65). Most of the rest served in the 100th Battalion and the 442nd Regimental Combat Team. These units compiled an outstanding battle record in the European theater.[13]

The decisions to resettle the evacuees and to enlist the Nisei for military duty led to a program of clearance and recruitment. Each evacuee was asked to answer a questionnaire concerning his or her background and loyalty to the United States. This program came as a surprise to the evacuees and resulted in anxiety, confusion, and controversy throughout the camps. The focus of controversy—around which several important issues revolved—was question 28: "Will you swear to abide by the laws of the United States and to take no action which would in any way interfere with the war effort of the United States" (Broom and Kitsuse 1956:28)?[14] Many internees were unsure how to answer this question. They wondered how a simple "yes" or "no" answer would be interpreted. A "yes" answer might mean that they, or some member of their family, would be drafted into military service; a "no" might mean they would be sent to a special prison camp for disloyals.

These issues clouded the government's plan to grant leave clearances to the "loyal" Japanese (i.e., those who answered "yes") and to segregate the "disloyal" Japanese in a special camp (Tule Lake). For example, by November 1943—less than a year after the Poston strike—over 18,000 people had been segregated at Tule Lake; however, there was ample reason to believe that many of those were not really disloyal.[15] Indeed, some loyal Japanese felt it was their duty as Americans to protest the violation of their rights by refusing to cooperate with the effort to draft them (O'Brien and Fugita 1991:67). Many loyal Japanese also refused to cooperate with the government's effort to release them from the camps. At first, thousands of internees, mostly Nisei, did leave when they were cleared; but the number who chose to leave rapidly declined. Newspaper reports of violence against some of those who had resettled caused many others to refuse to leave; hence, at the beginning of 1945, nearly 80,000 people remained in the camps. About half that number were still in the camps as the government moved to close them in the summer of 1945. It seems reasonable to conclude, as a government report did, that the treatment of the Japanese in the United States during World War II had tended "to disintegrate the fiber of a people who had previous to evacuation, been unusually self-reliant, sturdy, and independent" (War Relocation Authority 1946; quoted by Broom and Kitsuse 1956:32).

Legal Issues

The primary legal issues raised by the evacuation and relocation program were addressed by the U.S. Supreme Court in three different cases. The first of these, *Hirabayashi v. United States*, reached the Court in June, 1943, over a year after the relocation program was set into motion.

Gordon Hirabayashi was arrested, convicted, and jailed for violating General DeWitt's curfew order to stay in his place of residence between the hours of 8:00 P.M. and 6:00 A.M. Hirabayashi's appeal to the Supreme Court maintained that the curfew order represented an unconstitutional delegation of congressional authority to the military and that it should have applied to all citizens within the military areas, not just to those of Japanese ancestry (Ball 1991:176). In an unanimous opinion, the Court stated: "Distinctions between citizens solely because of their ancestry are by their very nature odious to a free people" (Tussman 1963:190) but ruled, nevertheless, that because the danger was great the curfew order had been appropriate (Tussman 1963:192). Although the opinion upholding the curfew was unanimous, Justice Murphy noted that the restriction on the Japanese Americans "bears a melancholy resemblance to the treatment accorded to members of the Jewish race in Germany" (Tussman 1963:197).

The second case, *Korematsu v. United States,* concerned primarily the constitutionality of the evacuation of the Japanese Americans from the West Coast. Fred Korematsu had been born in the United States, had never been out of the country, did not speak Japanese, and was not suspected of disloyalty. He attempted to avoid the order to leave his home, was convicted, and was given a suspended sentence. The Supreme Court upheld Korematsu's conviction. Justice Douglas concurred but "was distraught by his vision of thousands of citizens incarcerated without benefit of loyalty hearings" (Ball 1991:180). Unlike in *Hirabayashi,* however, the decision was not unanimous. Justice Roberts argued that Korematsu's constitutional rights had been violated. Justice Murphy stated that the exclusion was not a military necessity and fell "into the ugly abyss of racism" (Tussman 1963:213). Justice Jackson rejected the idea that a given act (in this case, refusing to leave home) could be a crime if committed by a citizen of one race but not by a citizen of another.

The reservations that plagued the Court's members in their deliberations concerning the curfew and the evacuation reached full force in their consideration of *Ex Parte Endo.* Like Fred Korematsu, Mitsuye Endo had been born in the United States, did not speak Japanese, and had committed no specific act of disloyalty. Endo challenged the right of the government to imprison her and other loyal Japanese Americans; and all of the justices agreed with her. Ms. Endo and all other loyal Americans were to be set free unconditionally. Justice Murphy, who had reluctantly agreed to the curfew and had rejected the evacuation, stated that the relocation program had been discriminatory and was "utterly foreign to the ideals and traditions of the American people" (Petersen 1971:90). In one critic's opinion, "One hundred thousand persons were sent to concentration camps on a record which wouldn't support a conviction for stealing a dog" (Rostow 1945:146).

The full effects on the Japanese and Japanese Americans of the devastating experience of evacuation, relocation, and resettlement are beyond exact calculation. No meaningful estimate may be made of the emotional costs suffered by the thousands of people who saw their hopes and aspirations destroyed and their families broken;[16] and although no one knows exactly the extent of the monetary losses, there can be no doubt that they were enormous. When in 1948 the Evacuation Claims Act was passed, the internees were paid about $37 million as restitution for their losses (Taylor 1991:166). A debate concerning the adequacy of this payment commenced, however; and in 1983 the Commission on Wartime Relocation and Interment of Civilians (CWRIC) issued a report stating that the total losses were "between $810 million and $2 billion in 1983 dollars" (quoted by Taylor 1991:166).[17] In 1988, after a long campaign for redress spearheaded by the JACL (Tateishi 1991), Congress passed a bill stating that a "grave injustice was done to both citizens and permanent resident aliens of Japanese ancestry" by the relocation program and that the relocation was a result of "racial prejudice, wartime hysteria, and a failure of political leadership" (Daniels, Taylor, and Kitano 1991:226). The bill agreed to award each of over 60,000 surviving detainees a tax-free payment of about $20,000 dollars. The payments, accompanied by a formal apology by President George H. Bush, commenced in a public ceremony on October 9, 1990 (Daniels 1991b:219).[18]

Another form of restitution also occurred during the decades following World War II. In 1983, Fred Korematsu was formally cleared of the charges leveled against him in 1942. Accordingly, his conviction for refusing to obey a military order was over-turned. Judge Marilyn Hall Patel, who presided, stated "that the government knowingly withheld information from the courts" and relied "on unsubstantiated facts, distortions and representations of at least one military commander whose views were seriously in-fected by racism" (Minami 1991:201). Then, in 1986, Gordon Hirabayashi won a court case establishing that government officials had withheld vital information during his trial in 1942. The court agreed that the government's claim that people of Japanese an-cestry had been a threat to national security was false (Howery 1986:9).

From the vantage point of the present, we may see that by the end of the second-generation period the Nisei were, in general terms, more assimilated into American soci-ety than were the Issei. Many of them embraced the goals of cultural and secondary assimilation, and perhaps some embraced all the other forms of assimilation described in Chapter 2; however, in the aftermath of the attack on Pearl Harbor, they and their families suddenly were forced out of their homes and normal pursuits, transported to prisons, and incarcerated. What were the effects of these catastrophic events on their subsequent assimilation into American society? The evidence we review concerning this question is generally based on systematic, although not necessarily representative, stud-ies of small samples; we also refer to some results based on national samples.

Japanese American Assimilation

Cultural Assimilation

We saw in Chapter 1 that among the factors that may influence the course of assimila-tion are the size of the immigrant group, the social distance between the immigrants and the host society, whether the group entered voluntarily, the timing of the immigration, and the goals of the immigrants. In the case of the Japanese in America, the factor of in-tergenerational differences also assumed an unusual importance.

Intergenerational Differences.   As is usually true of first-generation groups, the Issei limited their contacts with people outside of the group mainly to economic matters; they also wished to maintain and transmit their heritage to the Nisei. The Japanese Lan-guage Schools were designed to achieve these goals but, as noted previously, the Nisei's contacts with English-speaking children in the public schools influenced them to move toward cultural assimilation. Although the Nisei were restrained and "Japanesey" in the home, they favored the American pattern of behavior in school and other public set-tings. Additionally, although the Issei were "ineligible to citizenship," the children with whom the Nisei mainly associated were, like themselves, born in America. The halt in the flow of Japanese immigrants combined with these factors to create an unusually wide cultural gap between the Issei and Nisei.

Little has been said so far concerning the Sansei; but this third generation is of spe-cial importance in any effort to assess the rate of assimilation among Japanese Americans. According to Anglo conformity theory, the Sansei should be more assimilated than the

Nisei and both should be more assimilated than the Issei. The cultural assimilation of the Sansei should occur by substitution and should be close to the Anglo American pattern.

Several studies have found evidence that is consistent with the expectation that each succeeding generation will be more assimilated culturally. Connor (1974:161), in his study, found that the Issei were most likely to agree with statements reflecting traditional child-rearing ideas (e.g., "Parents can never be repaid for what they have done for their children"), the Nisei were intermediate in agreement, and the Sansei were least likely to agree. In a comparison of Nisei with Sansei, Feagin and Fujitaki (1972:18) found that although an individual's religious affiliation is a complicating factor, with Buddhism serving to support the traditional culture, some evidence showed that the Sansei were more culturally assimilated than the Nisei. The Nisei were more likely to be comfortable speaking Japanese and to do so regularly in the home than were the Sansei. They also felt more strongly than the Sansei the importance of maintaining Japanese customs and traditions. Matsumoto, Meredith, and Masuda (1973) found the general pattern of increasing cultural assimilation by generation among Japanese Americans in Honolulu and Seattle, although the strength of the pattern in the two cities was not identical. Kitano (1969:156–157) examined answers given by the members of the three generations to statements such as "Once a Japanese, always a Japanese" and, as expected, found that the Issei were most likely and the Sansei least likely to agree with the statements. In regard to some aspects of traditional beliefs, however, the expected pattern either was weak or did not appear. Finally, based on an analysis of data from a comprehensive national survey of the Issei, Nisei, and Sansei[19]—the Japanese American Research Project (JARP)—Woodrum (1978:80) found that in terms of proficiency in English and religious affiliation, the Nisei were more culturally assimilated than the Issei.

The findings of these studies are not totally consistent, but they strongly suggest—as expected under assimilation theory—that cultural assimilation was low among the Issei, higher among the Nisei, and highest among the Sansei.

The Sansei.   Are the Sansei "completely Americanized" as many Issei have said (Connor 1974)? Only two of the studies cited contain pertinent information. Connor (1974) found much less acceptance of traditional Japanese ideas among the Sansei than among the members of the other two generations, but he also found more acceptance of these ideas among the Sansei than among a sample of Anglo Americans. Kitano also found noticeable differences between the Sansei and the Anglo Americans in regard to certain beliefs and attitudes.

A revival of cultural nationalism among the Sansei, beginning during the 1960s, affords some further evidence that they have not completely abandoned their Japanese heritage and, at the same time, that the process of ethnogenesis may be at work. A major theme of this revival is that Japanese Americans should reject the Anglo conformity of the Nisei and actively promote some form of cultural pluralism in which the valued traditions of Japan, as modified by the American experience, may be sustained and elaborated (Takahashi 1997:160). Those who champion this view are extremely critical of the older generations' willingness to "make the most of a bad situation and push ahead" (Fujimoto 1971:207) or, even worse, to focus attention on the presumably beneficial effects of the wartime relocation. They view the historical experience of the

Japanese minority in America as being essentially like that of the Chinese, Koreans, and Filipinos and quite similar to that of Black Americans, Mexican Americans, and American Indians. As Ichioka (1971:222) stated in a critical review of Hosokawa's book *Nisei: The Quiet Americans,* "In this time of political, social, and moral crisis in America, old and new problems demand radical approaches, not tired orations. . . . We bid the old guard to retire as 'quiet Americans.'" Nevertheless, the nationalist tone of the 1960s and 1970s had subsided sufficiently by the mid-1980s to permit Kitano and Daniels (1988:71) to remark that "the Sansei and Yonsei . . . are the most 'American' of any Japanese group; many of them have never faced overt discrimination, and some have never had close ethnic ties or ethnic friends." In Spickard's (1996:151) opinion the Sansei generation has become "ever more like other Americans, while not losing entirely its distinctive ethnic identity."

On the basis of our observations concerning the Sansei, we offer the following generalization: Their level of cultural assimilation by substitution is higher than that of the two preceding generations, but they still exhibit some elements of the traditional culture of Japan and are, in some cases, actively attempting either to revive their ancient heritage or to construct a specifically Japanese American identity.[20]

Given the comparatively high degree of cultural assimilation by substitution among the Nisei and Sansei, how far have these groups moved toward the American pattern in terms of the other main subprocesses of assimilation? We saw previously that the Japanese Americans have attained in some respects a high degree of secondary structural assimilation (e.g., in education, occupation, and income). We turn now to some further evidence on secondary assimilation.

Secondary Structural Assimilation

Education, Occupation, and Income.   Japanese Americans are highly assimilated in terms of their average educational, occupational, and income levels. For instance, the average (mean) number of years of education among Japanese Americans exceeds the level attained by White Americans and by other Asian groups (Hirschman and Wong 1985:296; U.S. Bureau of the Census 1993:4). Similarly, among employed Americans, Japanese American men are more likely than White American men to be in occupations classified as "professional, technical, and kindred workers" and Japanese American women are more likely than White American women to hold such jobs. Consider, too, the matter of incomes. The average (mean) income for Japanese Americans is higher than for their majority-group counterparts and the highest of all Asian origin groups (Hurh and Kim 1989:523; U.S. Bureau of the Census 1993:7). An even larger gap favoring Japanese Americans exists between the average family incomes of the two groups. This gap may reflect a larger average number of wage earners among Japanese American families, although Japanese American families are among the least likely of Asian origin families to have three or more workers in the labor force (Hurh and Kim 1989:519; U.S. Bureau of the Census 1993:6). Japanese Americans also display one of the lowest poverty rates among Asian origin groups, half that of all Asian origin Americans (U.S. Bureau of the Census 1993:7).

Organizational Membership.   In addition to a group's levels of education, occupation, and income, another indicator of secondary assimilation is membership in nonethnic formal organizations. Excellent evidence on organizational memberships for the Japanese Americans may be found in several studies based on the data gathered in the JARP. For example, Levine and Rhodes (1981:78–79) found that most Nisei belonged to a Japanese organization, although many did not. The level of participation was lower still among the Sansei. Most of those in the third generation were not members of a Japanese organization. Montero's (1980:60) analysis showed that although a majority of both the Nisei and Sansei who belong to groups cite a non-Japanese group as their "favorite organization," this answer was most common among the Sansei.

In a different study, Fugita and O'Brien (1985:989) reported that excluding church membership, over 69 percent of their sample belonged to non-Japanese organizations. Fugita and O'Brien believed, however, that the level of Japanese American participation in ethnic organizations (53 percent) was still high in comparison to most other ethnic groups, especially "in areas with a lower density of fellow ethnics." They suggested that Japanese Americans made a special effort to be involved in the community (O'Brien and Fugita 1991:102).

Residential Assimilation.   As discussed in Chapter 7, sociologists frequently use indexes of dissimilarity to study residential assimilation and segregation. Recall that when the focus of study is the extent to which a residential area is segregated, an index value of 0 means there is no segregation and an index value of 100 means there is complete segregation.[21]

Jiobu (1988b:114) presented some valuable information on the residential segregation of Japanese Americans and the members of six other ethnic groups (each compared with Whites) in the 21 Standard Metropolitan Statistical Areas (SMSAs) in California.[22] For the Japanese Americans, the average (mean) level of segregation (dissimilarity) was a moderate 46. The levels of Japanese segregation in the various SMSAs ranged from a high of 65 (in Visalia) to a low of 29 (in San Jose). In the largest SMSA, Los Angeles, the index for Japanese Americans was 54. The average level of segregation in the 21 SMSAs for Koreans, by comparison, was 69, and for Vietnamese the average was 76. In fact, the average level of segregation for the Japanese was the lowest among the seven groups included in the study. These findings indicate that Japanese Americans in California were more assimilated residentially than the members of the other comparison groups but were still moderately segregated from the dominant group.

Some additional information presented by Farley and Allen (1987:145) indicated that residential segregation among the Japanese is moderate throughout the United States. These researchers examined 16 of the largest metropolitan areas in the United States and found that the average level of residential segregation in 1980 for all Asians combined was 43, ranging from a high of 54 in New Orleans to a low of 31 in Washington. Denton and Massey (1988) studied the relationship of residential segregation to educational, occupational, and income levels among the 20 SMSAs in the United States that contained the largest populations of Asians in 1980. The results, for all Asian groups combined, showed that as these groups have risen in socioeconomic status, the levels of segregation have been substantially and uniformly higher among the least educated than among the most educated members of the Asian groups (Denton and Massey 1988:811).

White, Biddlecom, and Guo (1993) examined a special census file to study the residential assimilation of seven Asian groups living in the 50 largest SMSAs in the United States. The results of this study confirmed that higher levels of education were linked to higher levels of residential assimilation among all of the groups. They also found that all of the Asian groups tended to live in neighborhoods comprised primarily of Anglo Americans.[23]

Taken together, we conclude that these studies of organizational participation and residential segregation are largely consistent with our earlier conclusion based on Japanese attainment in income, education, and occupation. By each of these measures, a substantial amount of secondary assimilation has occurred among Japanese Americans.

Primary Structural Assimilation

If the Japanese Americans are participating more in "mixed" organizations (including schools and businesses) than in all-Japanese organizations, and if they live in relatively mixed neighborhoods, then presumably a foundation has been laid for the more "social" activities that indicate the occurrence of primary structural assimilation. The studies based on the national data from the JARP provide important evidence concerning the extent to which the Nisei and Sansei interact with people of Japanese and non-Japanese ethnicity. For instance, in answer to questions concerning their two closest friends, a majority of the Nisei (53 percent) and a large majority of the Sansei (74 percent) reported that at least one of their two closest friends was non-Japanese (Montero 1980:60; see also Fugita and O'Brien 1985:993).

Do Japanese Americans visit their neighbors more freely if they live in a mostly Japanese neighborhood? According to Levine and Rhodes (1981:83), "the Nisei are neighborly folk. Whatever the composition of their environs, about seven of every ten are on visiting terms with three or more neighbors." These findings suggest that the Nisei have reached a fairly high level of primary assimilation and (given the findings on the friendship patterns of the Sansei) that the Sansei have moved even further in that direction. This conclusion also is supported by the finding that 75 percent of the Nisei and 80 percent of the Sansei want their children to associate actively with Whites rather than sticking "pretty much with Japanese Americans" (Levine and Rhodes 1981:115).

Marital Assimilation

Intermarriage is of special importance "because it can be understood as both an indicator of the degree of assimilation of ethnic and racial groups and an agent itself of further assimilation" (Lieberson and Waters 1988:162). Those who intermarry contribute to the blurring of ethnic boundaries. They increase the diversity of their respective ethnic groups and increase the range of ethnic identities that their children may assume.[24]

Although the importance of studying ethnic intermarriage is clear, the solution to some research problems is less so; and the interpretation of statistics on intermarriage requires caution. For example, when a marriage occurs between a member of the majority group and a member of a minority group, we ordinarily consider this to be evidence of marital assimilation by the partner from the minority group; however, if the friends of the married couple are drawn mainly from the minority group, if the couple lives in a neighborhood composed primarily of others in the minority group, and if the children of the marriage are raised in the culture of the minority group, are we still to call this assimilation? Consider, also, this situation: Minority-group members who marry-out frequently select partners from other minority groups. Does this represent assimilation? "Does a woman," Spickard (1989:17) asked, "cease to be black or brown or yellow or white if she marries someone of another color?" Moreover, what constitutes an out-marriage? Is a marriage of a person who is part Irish and part German to a person who is part Irish and part Italian an in-marriage or an out-marriage? Finally, what conclusion should be drawn when the children of out-marriages identify themselves as members of two or more ethnic groups (Stephan and Stephan 1989)? With these questions in mind, let us examine the results of some studies on intermarriage among the Japanese.[25]

Except in Hawaii, interracial marriages of all kinds in the United States have been low. This is due in large part to the fact that many laws have defined the boundaries of races in terms of the criteria commonly used in the community—as distinct from direct evidence on genotypes—and prohibited marriages across those lines. Burma (1963) studied all forms of interethnic marriage in Los Angeles between 1948 and 1959 by analyzing information gathered from marriage licenses. The period studied by Burma was chosen because, before 1948, the laws of California prohibited intermarriages of Whites with members of another race (defined largely by color); and during 1959, it became illegal to require a marriage license to show an applicant's race.[26] The data of the study, therefore, reflect what was happening during a crucial time span in an area possessing a comparatively large Japanese American population. Of more than 375,000 marriage applications, Burma (1963:163) counted over 3,000 that were interracial; and of these, 600 involved Japanese applicants. His data showed that out-marriages involving Japanese Americans approximately doubled between 1949 and 1959.[27]

Based on studies in Fresno and San Francisco, reported by Tinker (1973), the trend in intermarriages between White Americans and Japanese Americans noted by Burma apparently continued, especially among the Sansei. Tinker found that in Fresno in 1969–1971, half of all marriages involving Japanese Americans were out-marriages. A similar level of out-marriage also was discovered by Kikimura and Kitano in Hawaii for 1970 and in Los Angeles for 1971 and 1972. These authors concluded that various reports strongly suggest that out-marriages have become so frequent among Japanese Americans that the Sansei are as likely to marry outside the group as within it (see also Spickard 1996:146). Finally, Parkman and Sawyer (1967:597) compared intermarriage rates during the years 1928–1934 with those of 1948–1953 and found that the rate of Japanese out-marriage roughly tripled between the two periods.

The trend toward increasing marital assimilation among the Japanese Americans found in these geographically limited studies is generally confirmed by two broader studies. On the basis of JARP's national sample, Woodrum (1978:80) found that out-marriage became more common with each succeeding generation. Similarly, on the basis of a national public-use sample prepared by the U.S. Bureau of the Census, Gurak and

Kritz (1978:38) analyzed intermarriage statistics for 35 ethnic groups and found that the Nisei have married-out more frequently than the Issei.[28] They also found, however, that the Nisei who married-out were less likely to marry a member of the Anglo American core group than were the Issei. Finally, Hwang, Saenz, and Aguirre (1997:766), using a later national public-use sample, reported that people of Japanese ancestry were far more likely to intermarry than were the members of five other Asian ethnic groups.

Other Forms of Assimilation

Much of the evidence we have reviewed suggests that complete or practically complete Anglo conformity assimilation awaits Japanese Americans. Kitano and Daniels (1988:73) state that the Sansei and later generations "overwhelmingly" accept interracial marriage and that this belief "adds to the possible acceleration of assimilation" (Kitano and Daniels 1988:73). Nevertheless pluralist goals appear to be gaining adherents within their community. Family and community ties among them still appear to be strong and, especially among the Sansei, there has been a resurgence of pride and interest in their ethnic heritage (Spickard 1996:148; Takahashi 1997:195). And although the participation of Japanese Americans in the political process indicates they have reached a high level of civic assimilation, in many cases their political activities focus on a defense of their ethnic group or, in some cases, all people from Asia or all people of color (Spickard 1996:152; Takahashi 1997:205). For these reasons, the prediction that Japanese Americans will continue on the path toward Anglo conformity may be incorrect. As Levine and Montero (1973:47) stated, "there is little evidence that the subculture will soon wither away."

 Japanese American "Success"

The educational and socioeconomic success of the Japanese in American society has caused many people to ask how they were able to overcome the stigma of a non-White identity and to do so in a comparatively short time against such great odds. We consider briefly some leading cultural and structural answers to this question.

The Cultural View

We stressed earlier that the Issei brought with them the traditional values of Japan. They believed, as have the members of many other groups, in the importance of hard work, thrift, education, occupational success, the pursuit of long-range goals, politeness, respect for authority, mutual trust, perseverance, and duty to one's parents and community. The latter belief was at the center of family life. Marriages created not just unions of couples but unions of families. The extended family units that were formed thereby were connected, in turn, in numerous ways to the larger community. An important effect of this pattern of interrelationships was that everyone in the community had important obligations to many others within the community. Each of the individual families was embedded within a highly solidary network. Various traditions of organization, such as those leading to the formation of rotating credit groups, afforded a "cultural blueprint" that helped create community solidarity (O'Brien and Fugita 1991:3).

The high degree of cohesion in the Japanese community gave powerful assistance to the efforts of individual parents to transmit their traditional values to the Nisei and to do so despite the Issei–Nisei generation gap and the intergenerational conflict it produced. For this reason, Miyamoto (1939, 1972) and Petersen (1971) argued that the transmission of the traditional values to the Nisei and Sansei was accomplished by the entire Japanese community. According to Miyamoto (1972:218), "the Japanese minority maintained a high degree of family and community organization in America, and these organizations enforced value conformity and created conditions and means for status achievement."

The emphasis on community cohesion in the transmission of values directs our attention to the high frequency with which other people in the Japanese community supported the efforts of particular parents. Kitano (1969:68) illustrated this point in a story of a Nisei child who broke his arm in an athletic contest. The child was told by a series of Japanese adults, including his scoutmaster, his parents, his doctor, and his schoolteacher, that "Japanese boys don't cry"; and he was praised when he did not cry. Incidents of this sort were a daily reminder to the Nisei that they were Japanese and that the entire community expected them to behave as their parents had instructed. From this perspective, the entire community molded the Nisei and prepared them for success in school and later life.

Has the Japanese American family continued to place a high value on education or has cultural assimilation served to reduce education's importance? Research by Schneider and others strongly supported the view that the value of educational achievement has continued at a high level among the children and grandchildren of the Nisei. In a preliminary study of East Asian students of Chinese, Japanese, and Korean heritage, Schneider and Lee (1990:360) combined information on the students' economic and cultural histories with information concerning their personal interactions with their parents, teachers, and other students. Based on in-depth interviews, Schneider and Lee (1990:370, 374) found that "East Asian parents tended to have clearer and higher educational expectations for their children than Anglo parents" and that these expectations "are transmitted through a cultural context in which education is highly valued."

In a later study comparing the educational achievements of over 24,000 East Asian American and White American students, Schneider, Hieshima, Lee, and Plank (1994) specifically explored Japanese American values using evidence from in-depth interviews with Sansei parents and their Yonsei children. These authors found that in some respects the Yonsei were more similar to White students than to Chinese and Korean students, but they also found that "Japanese Americans, like other East-Asian groups, place a high intrinsic value on education" (1994:347). The authors argued that the emphasis on education among Japanese Americans has been transmitted through the close relations of family members even though the families have become Americanized in some other respects.

We turn now to the structural view, which, as explained earlier, attempts to explain group differences in terms of specific "material factors."

The Structural View

Discussions concerning the success of the Issei frequently note that despite their initial poverty they rapidly became established as the independent owners or operators of many small businesses and farms. Bonacich and Modell (1980:37–43) cited several studies showing that by 1930, even in the face of vigorous discrimination, the Japanese were concentrated in small, family-owned businesses, both as owners and employees.

How did the Issei become established in businesses? Several noncultural answers to this question have been proposed. Ikeda (1973:498), for instance, argued that the Japanese who came from the less impoverished districts of Japan and had the highest literacy levels were the most successful in America. Daniels (1969:11–12) stated that the hostility of the Americans toward the Japanese made their employment prospects so uncertain that the Japanese were practically forced into independent businesses. Still another suggestion was that the Japanese reached the West Coast just in time to fill some empty niches in the economy of a rapidly expanding new region (Modell 1977). Lieberson (1980:381–382) argued that the cessation of immigration from Japan decreased direct competition between the natives and Japanese and created the opportunity for the latter gradually to occupy special economic niches.

Another noncultural explanation of Japanese success is that they formed a middleman minority, as described in Chapter 7. As required by middleman minority theory, the Japanese were sojourners who concentrated in commerce and trade; and they created an ethnic economy. Their solidarity enabled them to cut costs in a number of ways and thereby to compete effectively not only with other small businesses but even with the giant firms that dominated the "center" of the American economy. Typically, the entire family worked long hours in the business without pay, and all earnings except those that were essential to life and health were "plowed back" into the business (Bonacich and Modell 1980:47). The businesses developed along these lines soon were able to provide employment for other Japanese who also were willing to work long hours at low pay; such employees commonly accepted room and board as a part of their pay, which further reduced the cost of running the business. Community solidarity also led to cooperative agreements with kinsmen that created both vertical and horizontal integration. Through thrift and cooperation, the business holdings of the Japanese grew at a very rapid rate.

Still another structural view argues that the socioeconomic achievement of the Japanese Americans is more adequately explained in terms of ethnic-enclave theory (Portes and Zhou, 1996). Portes and Bach (1985:340) argued, for instance, that "the middleman theory 'fits awkwardly' as a description of the experience of the Japanese Americans." Although they were sojourners and their economy was based on community solidarity, they did not act as intermediaries between the upper and lower reaches of the general economy. From this perspective, the Japanese American ethnic economy resembled that of a middleman economy but did not function as one.

Consequences of Issei Success

We have seen that the Japanese business economy was destroyed by the relocation program during World War II and, although it was rebuilt in a modified form after the war, many of the Nisei found careers outside of the ethnic community. The high level of education among the Nisei opened up many opportunities within the mainstream economy; but then the Nisei were torn between their loyalty to the ethnic community and their desire to "get ahead" within the majority society (Montero 1980:85–86; 1981:835). There is some irony in the fact that the educational achievement that was so encouraged by the Issei and made possible by the solidarity of the Japanese community also has made it possible for the Nisei to leave the ethnic community entirely (Bonacich and Modell 1980:152). On the other hand, as Butler (1991:244) proposed, the Issei's hope that their children would experience economic mobility in the broader society may have been an important reason for the parents' great efforts in business. Indeed, this pattern appears to be typical of entrepreneurial minorities. Portes and Bach (1985:346) concluded in this regard that the progress made by the immigrants is "consolidated into educational and occupational mobility, within and outside the ethnic enclave, by later generations."

In keeping with this view, the trend toward increased occupational assimilation appears to be marked among the Sansei, though they still are prominent as entrepreneurs (O'Hare 1992:34; Taylor 1993:276–277). O'Brien and Fugita (1991) argued, however, that the increasing independence of the Sansei from the ethnic enclave does not necessarily mean that their Japanese ethnicity is of diminished importance to them. More likely, these changes may mean that the basis of ethnic identification has shifted from one of economic cooperation to one of psychological support; therefore, we should not conclude that the continued upward mobility of the Japanese necessarily will lead to the complete loss of Japanese identity and culture.

A Comparison of Success Theories

Our discussion has revealed a variety of factors that may help to explain the worldly success of the Japanese in America. They have lived by a code of values that encourages achievement; they have exhibited a high degree of community solidarity that may be rooted in the traditions of Japan and also in their economic adaptation to American society; and they have used skills learned in Japan to fill special niches in the American economy. Each of these (and other) factors must be considered in an adequate explanation of Japanese achievement.

We must neither ignore nor exaggerate the role of culture in our attempt to understand the Japanese experience in America. An exclusive emphasis on cultural factors, as noted earlier, tends to promote "self-congratulatory sentimentalism" (Steinberg 1989:87); but it also is true that situational and other "material" factors may be overemphasized. Most theorists agree that the success values and group pride of the Japanese have played an important role in the outcome. As Hirschman and Wong (1986:4) stated, "The introduction of structural determinants does not eliminate the role of cultural influences."

The facts of Japanese success in education, occupational standing, and income levels, if not their causes, are generally uncontested; but some Japanese American militants have expressed doubts about the human meaning of their success. Is the material success that has always lain at the center of the values of American society really a worthwhile goal for human beings (Takagi 1973:151)? In the view of some Japanese Americans, the answer to this question is "no!" Okimoto (1971:17) put it this way: "I doubt whether we have succeeded in any but the narrowest materialist definition of the word."

Evidently, these questions and observations plunge us headlong into the arena of conflicting value premises. They also illustrate in concrete terms the conflict between the ideology of Anglo conformity and such alternatives as cultural pluralism and separatism. Whether one prefers or rejects Anglo conformity, however, it is generally agreed that the experience of the Japanese Americans confirms the rule that non-White groups are especially subject to severe discrimination in the United States.

Even though the evidence shows that the main trend for the Japanese Americans is toward full Anglo conformity, it still is possible that the contemporary revitalization of ethnic consciousness among the Japanese is more than a passing fad (Levine and Rhodes 1981:152–154). This conjecture seems even more plausible when one considers that over one-quarter of a million "New Issei" have been added to the American population since 1965 (Table 11.1). Some form of pluralism, which previously was most popular among the "Old Issei," has found new adherents among the Sansei and Yonsei. This trend appears to have been strengthened also by the arrival of hundreds of thousands of other "new" immigrants from a number of other Asian countries and by the concomitant rise in Asian American identity.

The "Model Minority" Stereotype

Because the Japanese Americans have been so successful *materially speaking,* they frequently have been singled out as "proof" that racially distinctive groups can succeed in America even in the face of high levels of discrimination. In terms of the main dichotomy of competing explanations of ethnic group differences in worldly success discussed in Chapter 7, this approach focuses only on differences in the levels of effort put forth by various groups. Although this way of framing the issue fails to consider the many other factors that affect the extent to which the members of different ethnic groups are able to, or wish to, achieve "success," it does highlight a widespread and persistent point of view.

Many writers have proclaimed the Japanese Americans to be a "model minority," a non-White group that has overcome all obstacles through hard work and determination (Hosokawa 1969; Petersen 1971). In McWilliams's (1949:155) opinion, "no other immigrant group ever faced such difficulties as the Japanese encountered in this country" and "no group ever conducted themselves more creditably." This view, however, has been the focus of considerable criticism by Japanese Americans and, also, by members of other Asian American groups. We mention here only four among the many criticisms that have been offered.

The first, and central, criticism of this stereotype is that its primary purpose is to support and strengthen the belief that the main cause of economic and social problems among racial minorities in America is a lack of effort on their part, rather than discrimination. It is, in Kim's (2001:35) words, "the racial trump card" which lauds Asian Americans as "exemplars for other . . . minorities, especially Blacks." As such, it is an "ideological strategy" (Palumbo-Liu 1999:396) or self-serving stereotype that may be seen as part of an ef-

Table 11.1   Japanese Immigration to the
United States, 1861–2000

Years	Number
1861–1870	186
1871–1880	149
1881–1890	2,270
1891–1900	25,942
1901–1910	129,797
1911–1920	83,837
1921–1930	33,462
1931–1940	1,948
1941–1950	1,555
1951–1960	46,250
1961–1970	39,988
1971–1980	49,775
1981–1990	47,085
1991–2000	67,942
Total	530,186

Source: U.S. Immigration and Naturalization Service, *Statistical Yearbook of the Immigration and Naturalization Service, 1998,* 2000:20–22; U.S. Immigration and Naturalization Service, *Statistical Yearbook of the Immigration and Naturalization Service, 2000,* 2002:7–10.

fort by White elites to prove that the problems of African Americans, Hispanic Americans, and American Indians are due to a lack of effort rather than to discrimination.

An implication of this view, and our second criticism, is that the model minority stereotype also assists to align racial minority groups against one another and, thus, to impede efforts on their part to unite on issues when it may be in their interest to do so. For example, some Asian Americans have voiced strong support for affirmative action programs while others have voiced strong opposition; however, the views of Asian Americans who oppose affirmative action have sometimes been "appropriated by White elites determined to silence Black claims and grievances" (Kim 2001:36). For example, in *Ho v. San Francisco Unified School District,* Chinese American plaintiffs challenged school admissions rules that required Chinese American students to score higher than Whites, as well as Blacks and Latinos, in order to be admitted to the leading academic high school in the city. Although this case has been interpreted by some as showing that the Chinese American plaintiffs were rejecting affirmative action, they, instead, were objecting to a requirement that their children had to score higher than Whites in order to be admitted (Hing 2002:20). Narasaki (2003:21A) reported the results of a national poll of Asian Americans in which 72 percent of those polled "said affirmative action was a 'good thing.' . . ." She also stated that "we are tired of opponents of affirmative action cynically attempting to use Asian-American students in their cause" (2003:21A).

A third criticism of the model minority stereotype is that while it celebrates the worldly success of certain segments of the Asian American population, it diverts attention away from those who have been downwardly mobile or have encountered various forms of personal hardship. This point will take on added force as we present information in Chapter 12 concerning socioeconomic diversity among several Asian American groups. The impression that all members of these groups have "made it" in America is flawed.

The fourth criticism of the model minority stereotype is that it distracts attention from the fact that Japanese and other Asian Americans are still the victims of various forms of discrimination. Even though racism against Japanese Americans now appears to be comparatively low and identificational assimilation among them is high, O'Brien and Fugita (1991:104) found that over half of their Sansei sample believed that Japanese Americans continue to face discrimination. Kitano and Daniels (1988:74), in a similar vein, noted that Japanese Americans are still physically visible and, therefore, are subject to certain kinds of limitations. For example, in television, movie, and stage productions, even Sansei who are highly assimilated may still find they are asked to play roles such as an enemy soldier, a gardener, or a cook. Evidently, "the desired body type and physical image in America remains that of a Caucasian" (Kitano and Daniels 1988:74). Moreover, numerous contemporary incidents continue to remind us that it is incorrect to believe Asian Americans have been insulated from racial discrimination by worldly success. Not only is anti-Asian discrimination easily provoked in day-to-day encounters and by tensions in international affairs, but it also may exist even where it seems to have been eliminated.

Consider, for instance, this important question: Do the higher incomes of Japanese Americans mean that they no longer face significant discrimination in the job market? Some scholars argue that, given their higher average levels of education, the earnings advantage of Japanese Americans should be even greater than it is. Hurh and Kim (1989:523) found when a number of relevant factors were taken into account that Japanese Americans received 93 percent as much income as similarly qualified White Americans. Hirschman and Wong (1984) found, however, that by 1976 Japanese American men earned more than similarly qualified White American men. Chiswick (1983:210–211) found, in contrast, that when adjustments were made for group differences in education, experience, and the number of weeks worked per year, the annual earnings of White and Japanese American men were roughly equal. In the 1990s, however, several studies found that the average earnings advantage of Japanese American men and women had reached a level that was either equal to or slightly more than would be expected on the basis of their educational levels and other pertinent qualifications (e.g., Barringer, Gardner, and Levin 1995; Iceland 1999; Sakamoto and Furuichi 1997; Sakamoto, Liu, and Tzeng 1998).

These criticisms of the model minority stereotype do not, of course, alter or diminish the underlying achievements of the Japanese in America. As a group, they have indeed reached high levels of educational, occupational, and civic attainment in the face of high levels of discrimination; and the reality of these achievements has provided the foundation for, and sustains, the stereotype. This reality also has provided the foundation for speculations and theories concerning how it was possible for the Japanese Americans to overcome the stigma of a non-White identity and to do so in a comparatively short time against such great odds.

The term *model minority* was first used to refer to the Japanese Americans. Subsequently, however, several other ethnic groups also have been considered by some commentators to be model minorities, including four other large Asian groups—Chinese Americans, Korean Americans, Filipino Americans, and Asian Indian Americans.[29] Although each of these groups has been represented in the American population since the beginning of the twentieth century, each remained small until after World War II; but these groups have grown rapidly in recent decades and have been a prominent part of the new immigration. Chapter 12 is devoted to brief discussions of each of these four groups.

Discussion Questions

What is your opinion of the idea that the Japanese Americans are a "model minority"? Why is this debate important?

What factors contributed to the distinctiveness of the Japanese American generations?

Why were the Japanese and Japanese Americans interned during World War II? What were some of the social and legal consequences of the internment?

How well does the three-generations idea of assimilation fit the experience of the Japanese Americans?

What kinds of factors or processes are included under the heading of "cultural"? Of "structural"? Which of these factors are most useful in understanding the worldly success of the Japanese Americans?

Which ideas concerning the assimilation of immigrant minorities receive the most support from the experiences of the Japanese Americans?

How have the Japanese Americans achieved a high level of worldly success in the face of high levels of discrimination?

Key Ideas

1. Even though they have experienced unusually high levels of prejudice and discrimination, the Japanese Americans are an exception to the generalization that non-White minorities in the United States have not attained high levels of education, occupation, and income.

2. An analysis of a group that has not responded to very high levels of prejudice and discrimination in the usual ways may afford clues concerning why the usual responses arise and how prejudice and discrimination may be prevented.

3. The Japanese family and community in America have been highly cohesive.

4. Despite vigorous efforts to stop them, the Issei were very successful in small business enterprises, particularly in agriculture.

5. When Japanese nationals within the United States experienced discrimination, they could—and often did—turn to the Japanese government for assistance.

6. The Japanese generations in America have been unusually distinctive. This distinctiveness is largely due to restrictions on immigration in the Gentlemen's Agreement and the Immigration Act of 1924.

7. The evacuation and relocation program during World War II resulted in the imprisonment of over 70,000 American citizens of Japanese origin and also about 40,000 legal resident alien Japanese without any charges, trials, or criminal convictions.

8. An effort was made to organize the Relocation Centers along the lines of a typical American community. This largely unsuccessful attempt widened further the gap between the Issei and Nisei but also increased both generations' familiarity with community organization and political participation.

9. Cultural assimilation has been comparatively low among the Issei, high among the Nisei, and higher still among the Sansei.

10. The Sansei have not completely replaced Japanese culture with Anglo American culture. Some evidence supports the idea that pluralism is gaining in popularity among them.

11. The Nisei and Sansei have moved substantially in the direction of secondary, primary, marital, and all other forms of assimilation.

12. More frequently than the Nisei, the Sansei have openly raised questions concerning the human costs of the worldly success of their group.

13. The history of the Japanese Americans generally supports the idea that disadvantages based on racial distinctiveness are not necessarily permanent in American society.

14. The cultural view of Japanese success in America stresses the role of their value system and traditional group solidarity.

15. The structural view of Japanese success in America stresses the importance of various noncultural factors such as the kinds of skills they possessed, their level of literacy, the level of economic development on the West Coast at the time of their arrival, their role as a middleman minority, and their ability to establish ethnic enclaves and, through them, become dominant in certain markets.

16. An adequate explanation of any group's worldly success requires a consideration of both cultural and structural factors.

 Key Terms

Gentlemen's Agreement   An agreement between the United States and Japan in 1908 concerning the kinds of emigrants the Japanese government would permit to leave the country.

Issei The first generation of Japanese immigrants.

kenjin Japanese people from the same province.

kenjinkai Associations based on provinces of origin.

Nisei The Japanese American children of the Issei; the second generation of people of Japanese origin.

Sansei The Japanese American children of the Nisei; the third generation of people of Japanese origin.

tanomoshi An organization through which money is pooled and then loaned in rotation to various members.

Yonsei The Japanese American children of the Sansei; the fourth generation of people of Japanese origin.

 Notes

1. The "yellow peril" originally referred to the alleged intention of the Chinese to conquer the United States through "peaceful invasion" (tenBroek, Barnhart, and Matson 1954:19–29).

2. A Canadian branch of the Asiatic Exclusion League was formed in Vancouver, B.C. in 1907. Later Canada concluded a gentlemen's agreement with Japan similar to Japan's agreement with the United States (Sugimoto 1972).

3. Another frequently used generational term is *Kibei*—Nisei who were sent to Japan as children to receive a traditional Japanese upbringing. The term *Nikkei* refers to all people of Japanese ancestry.

4. The Chinese called rotating credit associations *hui* or *woi*. The Japanese also used the names *ko* and *mujin* (Light [1972]1994:84–85).

5. The Japanese also had become prominent in rice farming in Texas (Walls 1987: 39–80).

6. Marumoto (1972:220–221) called the period 1907–1924 the settlement period and the period 1924–1941 the second-generation period.

7. The Nisei were vulnerable to the charge because Japan granted citizenship on the basis of kinship (the principle of *jus sanguinis*). The United States grants citizenship to those born within the country (the principle of *jus soli*).

8. For the effects of these orders on Italian Americans see Fox (1990).

9. In 1940, there were about 127,000 Japanese and Japanese Americans in the United States. Of these, 47,000 were aliens and 80,000 were American citizens. Almost 90 percent of the total lived in California, Arizona, Oregon, and Washington (Thomas 1952:3).

10. Before the evacuation, Japanese people were urged to leave the military areas voluntarily. About 5,000 people did (Taylor 1993: 60–61).

11. The Immigration and Naturalization Service also maintained at least 15 "internment camps" in eight states. These smaller camps were designed to hold "potentially dangerous enemy aliens," among whom were included some Japanese (Walls 1987:175–176; Daniels, Taylor, and Kitano 1991:xvii).

12. The discussion of life in the Poston Relocation Center is based on the excellent study by Leighton (1946).

13. For a discussion of the role of Japanese Americans in World War II, see Hosokawa (1969:393–422). The 100th Battalion and the 442nd, the "Go For Broke" regiment, "received more than 18,000 individual and unit citations" (O'Brien and Fugita 1991:66).

14. Question 28 initially was: "Will you swear unqualified allegiance to the United

States of America and . . . foreswear any form of allegiance to the Japanese emperor?" (Thomas and Nishimoto 1946:47). A "yes" answer to this question was impossible for most Issei because it would have left them "people without a country." Similar issues were raised by question 27, which asked if the respondent would be willing to serve in the armed forces.

15. Over 8,500 of those incarcerated at Tule Lake eventually were cleared.

16. For the human costs of these events see Maki, Kitano and Berthold (1999), Mass (1991), and Taylor (1993).

17. Taylor (1991:166) stated that a study commissioned by the CWRIC placed the losses, adjusted for inflation, at between $2.5 billion and $6.2 billion.

18. The initial payments were made "to a group of the oldest survivors, five of whom were over 100 years of age" (Daniels 1991b:220).

19. An important purpose of this study, sponsored by the JACL and directed by Gene N. Levine of UCLA, was to understand how the successive generations of Japanese and Japanese Americans have adapted to American society. The researchers initially (1962–1966) gathered data on about 18,000 Issei living in the continental United States. Subsequently (1966–1967), Nisei and Sansei participants received mailed questionnaires or were interviewed by telephone.

20. This revitalization effort also involves constructing a broader identity that relates Japanese Americans to all other Asians and other non-White minorities.

21. If 25 percent of the people in a given city were Japanese Americans, and if 25 percent of the people in each part of the city were Japanese Americans, this group would not be residentially segregated and the index of dissimilarity would be zero. On the other hand, if all of the city's Japanese Americans lived together, and there were no other ethnic groups represented among them, there would be complete segregation and the index of residential segregation would be 100.

22. The seven groups were Black, Chinese, Filipino, Japanese, Korean, Mexican, and Vietnamese. An SMSA consists of the population of a city containing at least 50,000 residents plus all contiguous, functionally related, nonagricultural counties.

23. They did not find, as Jiobu had for California, that the Japanese had the highest level of residential assimilation among these groups. After taking into account a number of factors, White, Biddlecom, and Guo (1993:110–111) concluded that the groups that had been in the United States longest (Japanese, Chinese, and Filipinos) were somewhat less assimilated residentially than the more recent arrivals, which may have reflected the earlier experiences of these groups in America.

24. Some important factors that increase the rate of out-marriage are small group size, spatial nearness to other ethnic groups, low social distance between ethnic groups, a long period of time in the United States, and religious similarity (Alba and Golden 1986; Stevens and Swicegood 1987).

25. Problems may arise from the way intermarriage rates are reported. Suppose that of 10 marriages, there are six in which both partners are Catholic and four in which only one partner is Catholic. Since four of the 10 marriages are mixed, the rate *for marriages* is 40 percent; however, since only four of 16 individual Catholics are in a mixed marriage, the rate *for individuals* is 25 percent (Rodman 1965:776–778).

26. The races listed were Chinese, Filipino, Indian, Japanese, Negro, White, and Other (Burma 1963:158).

27. They rose from about 11 percent of all out-marriages to nearly 23 percent. Calculated from Table 6 in Burma (1963:163).

28. Gurak and Kritz (1978) found that 31 of the 35 groups in the analysis had higher out-marriage rates than the Nisei.

29. See, e.g., Light (1972), Portes and Bach (1985), McDowell (1996), Moskos (1980), Steinberg (1989), Rosen (1959), and Min (1996), respectively.

Chinese, Korean, Filipino, and Asian Indian Americans

Millions of Asians have immigrated to the United States since the end of World War II. This massive immigration has included many refugees and undocumented people. Here, a boatload of Chinese are denied entry into the United States.

. . . race matters because it shapes every aspect
of my life—and everyone else's.

—Frank Wu

. . . Western peoples are brought up to regard Orientals
or colored peoples as inferior. . . .
I was completely disillusioned when
I came to know this American attitude.

—Carlos Bulosan

Jesus could not get into America because. . . . He would be an Asiatic.

—Sir Rabindranath Tagore

In Chapter 11 we saw some examples of the prejudice and discrimination directed toward the Japanese in America. We also glimpsed some of the struggles of the members of that group to make a place for themselves within American society. In the present chapter we continue to explore these themes through brief discussions of four additional Asian American groups.[1] Three of these—the Chinese, Korean, and Filipino Americans—originated in the Far East, and one—the Asian Indian Americans—originated in South Asia. Each of these groups was represented in the American population by 1910; but, as discussed previously, the ebb-and-flow of immigration since that time has paralleled the changes brought about by American immigration and naturalization laws during the nineteenth and twentieth centuries.

The Chinese Exclusion Act of 1882, the establishment of the Asian "barred zone" in 1917, and the Immigration Quota Act of 1924 combined to reduce immigration from China, Japan, and Korea to a trickle. A law curbing Filipino immigration was passed in 1934. During and following World War, special laws were passed concerning Chinese, Filipino, and Japanese naturalization. Additional laws, noted in previous chapters, concerned Japanese citizenship, war brides, family members, and orphans. These laws revived Asian immigration to a small extent; but the historically large flow we have called the Third Great Immigrant Stream began with the passage of the Immigration and Nationality Act Amendments (INAA) of 1965. These legal changes stimulated three discernible periods of immigration to the United States within each of the Asian groups discussed in this chapter.

In addition to changes in American immigration laws, the global expansion of capitalism and colonialism played an important role in Asian emigration. As the European powers competed for economic advantages in Asia during the nineteenth century, the United States also attempted to capture portions of the newly "opened" markets. The emigration of people from these Asian countries was, therefore, partly a consequence of the social and economic dislocations created by the global reach of Western economic and colonial power.

Chinese Americans[2]

Recall that the first large immigration of Chinese people to America began as a part of the California gold rush of 1849. The exciting news of the gold strikes in California led people to dream of the enormous fortunes that might await those who could make the perilous journey to work in the mines. Declining living standards and social turmoil in China also stimulated the desire to emigrate, particularly from the southeastern part of China. Historically, China had been a self-sufficient country with greater interest in maintaining its ancient social structure and its dominant position in Asia than in trading with nations outside its sphere of influence. By the beginning of the nineteenth century, however, the Manchu (*Qing*) dynasty, in power since 1644, had become weak and corrupt. Rebellions broke out against the ruling class (Takaki 1998:32–33; Tong 2000:18). These conditions assisted the Western powers to force China to open its markets to foreign trade.

Britain, for example, was exporting opium grown in India and wished to continue selling it in China. After Chinese officials destroyed British opium cargos in the harbor of Canton, the two countries went to war. China was defeated in the Opium War of 1839–1842 and then reluctantly signed a treaty agreeing to accept shipments of British opium. China also was required to pay the costs of the war and to cede Hong Kong to Britain. This "unequal treaty" was soon followed by similar treaties granting trading privileges to France and the United States.

The lure of riches in America and the declining living standards in China were joined by still another powerful force encouraging Chinese people to cross the Pacific. In 1862 the U.S. Congress authorized the construction of a transcontinental railroad and, in 1868, approved the Burlingame Treaty between the United States and China.[3] The building of the railroad required large numbers of laborers to do hard and dangerous work for low wages; and so the Central Pacific Company recruited Chinese immigrant workers. Uncounted numbers of these workers lost their lives in the process of building the railroad. Jiobu (1988a:35) quoted the historian Alexander Saxton as saying that "No man who had any choice would have chosen to be a common laborer on the Central Pacific during the crossing of the High Sierra." The journey of over 100,000 Chinese to America during the 1850s and 1860s was—as we have seen for other immigrant groups—a result of both push factors in the homeland and pull factors in the country of destination (see Table 12.1).

It is one thing, of course, to wish to emigrate and quite another to be able to do so. The vast movement of people out of China during these years, mainly to places other than the United States, was conducted in various ways. Large numbers of poor people were tricked or forced into the slavelike "coolie" trade. These practices inflamed the fears of American workers and led, with only a few exceptions, to a prohibition on the entrance of additional Chinese people. Because of a previous treaty between the United States and the Kingdom of Hawaii, which was not yet a part of the United States, many Chinese people were able to enter Hawaii to work as contract laborers on sugar plantations. A few of these people later paid their own way to the American mainland. The great majority,

**Table 12.1   Chinese Immigration to the
United States, 1820–2000**

Years	Number
1820–1850	46
1851–1860	41,397
1861–1870	64,301
1871–1880	123,201
1881–1890	61,711
1891–1900	14,799
1901–1910	20,605
1911–1920	21,278
1921–1930	29,907
1931–1940	4,928
1941–1950	16,709
1951–1960	9,657
1961–1970	34,764
1971–1980	124,326
1981–1990	346,747
1991–2000	419,114
Total	1,333,490

Source: U.S. Immigration and Naturalization Service, *Statistical Yearbook of the Immigration and Naturalization Service, 1998,* 2000:20–22; U.S. Immigration and Naturalization Service, *Statistical Yearbook of the Immigration and Naturalization Service, 2000,* 2002:19–22.

though, came under a form of sponsorship called the "credit ticket system" (Kitano and Daniels 2001:23; Takaki 1998:35). In this system, migrants would receive loans with which to pay the costs of the trip. In the typical case, the borrowers would later repay the lenders the original amount along with a substantial amount of interest.

The Chinese immigrants who came to America were similar in some respects to other immigrants we have considered. For one thing, the vast majority of these immigrants were men and, in most of the groups we have discussed, women did not emigrate as freely as men. In most cases, both wives and single women of good reputation generally were expected to remain at home; however, in the case of the Chinese, American laws and policies were expressly intended to keep Chinese women out (Takaki 1998:40; Tong 2000:28). Another resemblance between the Chinese and other immigrants is that, generally, these Chinese men did not intend to remain in the United States. They planned to go to *Gam Saan* (the "Gold Mountain") and return home with their riches (Takaki 1998:31–36). As was true of many second-stream immigrants from Europe who reached

America's East Coast during the latter half of the nineteenth century, the Chinese reaching the West Coast at this time were largely "birds of passage" or sojourners.

As noted in Chapter 5, residents of the West Coast greeted the arrival of the Chinese with various forms of hostility. After the completion of the Central Pacific Railroad in 1869, thousands of men (most of whom were Chinese) were thrown out of work and into direct competition with native workers for other jobs.[4] Hundreds of Chinese people were harassed, expelled, and sometimes killed—all of which went largely unpunished (tenBroek, Barnhart, and Matson 1954:15). In Los Angeles in 1871, anti-Chinese violence resulted in the deaths of as many as 21 Chinese (Daniels 1988:59). As the Chinese population spread out of California into other Western states, even more deadly assaults occurred. In Rock Springs, Wyoming, in 1885, 28 Chinese were killed; and 2 years later in the mines along the Snake River, another 31 Chinese were killed. General expulsions of Chinese people took place in many locations throughout the West, including Canada and Alaska; and, along with the loss of lives, millions of dollars of property were confiscated or destroyed.[5]

Throughout this period, and especially during the 1880s, the Chinese received little help from U.S. law officers and courts. Even when law officers arrested suspects, those arrested were seldom convicted (Daniels 1988:58–66). Understandably, then, large numbers of Chinese decided to leave the United States after the exclusion law went into effect. As a result, between 1882 and 1943, even with the addition of small numbers of Chinese people admitted as exceptions to the exclusion law, the Chinese population in America gradually declined.

Those who remained, or were later admitted, increasingly protested exclusion and the other forms of discrimination in the United States. Chinese people made speeches, published newspaper articles, and enlisted support from their friends in China to put pressure on the American government to improve their condition in the United States. They also filed court cases, some of which had important consequences for the developing Chinese American community. For example, in *United States v. Gue Lim* (1900) the U.S. Supreme Court ruled that, under the Burlingame Treaty, the Exclusion Act's prohibition did not apply to teachers, students, and merchants and their families, among others (U.S. Immigration and Naturalization Service 1943). Additionally, Chinese merchants were permitted to bring their wives and minor children to join them (Kitano and Daniels 2001; Lai 1980:223). This and other rulings increased to some extent the number of Chinese wives and children in the United States—an increase that was crucial to family and community development.

Roots of the Chinese American Family and Community

When exclusion went into effect, Chinese men in the United States greatly outnumbered Chinese women. Although this situation was common among other immigrant groups in America, it was more pronounced among the Chinese. The numerical imbalance between the sexes gradually declined after 1882, as did the total Chinese population, because as many Chinese men left the country, additional Chinese women were admitted.

Also, as time passed, increasing numbers of Chinese American women reached marriageable age. Still, the decline in the sex ratio was painfully slow. For instance, in 1890 the sex ratio was almost 27 Chinese males to each Chinese female. Fifty years later, even though the sex ratio had declined markedly, there were still nearly three times as many Chinese males as females in the United States (Daniels 1988:69; Kitano and Daniels 2001:25).

These adverse sex ratios slowed family formation (Hing 1993:54) and led at first to the establishment of a "bachelor society" in which families were rare.[6] The pace of family formation was slowed further by the prohibition in some states of intermarriage between Chinese and Whites (Lai 1980:223). These factors, along with the general unfamiliarity of the Chinese with American culture and the extreme hostility of Americans toward Chinese people, led to the creation of "Chinatowns" that were segregated from the life of the surrounding communities.

The Chinese in America at this time were mainly from the southeastern Chinese province of Guangdong (Kwangtung). Most of the people were of the same ethnicity, spoke the Cantonese dialect, and were peasants and wage laborers.[7] When they reached the United States, most of the immigrants settled mainly in rural areas where they could find jobs. Many of the immigrants staked claims to gold mines and continued as mine workers even after they were forced by rival American miners and anti-Chinese legislation to give up ownership. They also continued in railroad work after the Central Pacific was completed; and they gradually moved into various kinds of farm work. Those who were able to find spouses married, had children, and began the work of creating Chinese American institutions. Chinese women often combined working at home and raising a family with outside employment, typically as domestic servants (Chow 1996:116).

The relative isolation of the Chinese, the hostility directed toward them, and their intention eventually to return to China combined to discourage them from attempting to adopt American models of community organization (Nee and Wong 1998:1). Chinese communities in America, therefore, followed the traditional patterns of China and were based on kinship and regional ties. People who had the same last names and were presumably related organized family associations. People who came from the same districts of Guangdong Province formed district associations.

The district associations, or "companies," formed a still more general organization called the Chinese Consolidated Benevolent Association (CCBA),[8] which, as the name implies, attempted to help its members in numerous ways. The CCBA helped people to maintain their contacts with China, to arrange funerals, and to find jobs, medical care, and housing. In general, the CCBA served the same welfare functions we have observed among the community organizations of other immigrant groups (Kitano and Daniels 2001:27–30; Lai 1980:218; Takaki 1999:38).[9] In addition, however, the CCBA represented the community in its political and legal interactions with the Anglo American community and maintained order within the Chinatowns (Daniels 1988:24).[10] Until the first Chinese legation was established in the United States in 1878, the CCBA acted as an unofficial diplomatic agency for the Chinese (Tong 2000:49).

The formation of Chinese families, businesses, and community associations moderated the excesses of the bachelor society and laid the foundations of cultural and secondary assimilation among the small American-born portion of the population (Kitano and Daniels 2001:27). Some associations were formed expressly to encourage these forms of assimilation. For instance, in 1895 a group of Chinese Americans in San Francisco formed an association that during the next 20 years developed into the Chinese American Citizens Alliance (CACA).[11] The members of this organization felt that the commitment of the CCBA to China and traditional Chinese culture was not the best model for American citizens to follow (Tong 2000:53). Moreover, Chinese Americans were often ridiculed by traditionalists because "of their lack of knowledge and appreciation of traditional Chinese culture" (Chung 1998:152), which only strengthened the resolve of the CACA members to stress that they were Americans, albeit of Chinese ancestry. The traditionalists' charge of cultural assimilation indicates these processes were occurring among the second generation. As the CACA matured, it aimed to strengthen the ties among Chinese Americans, to fight all forms of anti-Chinese discrimination, to elevate the members' moral standards, to encourage education, to enlarge and protect legal rights, and to encourage assimilation into American society (Chung 1998:154–157).

When the CACA was organized, the Chinatowns were still dominated by Chinese men and the CCBA; nevertheless, important changes in Chinese American society were underway. By 1900 about 11 percent of the people were American-born (Tong 2000:53). Throughout the period of Chinese exclusion, most of the Chinese American population lived in the western states, especially in California; but this figure declined steadily. For example, in 1880 almost 97 percent of the Chinese population of the United States was located in the West and 71 percent were in California. By 1940 these figure had declined to about 60 and 51 percent, respectively (Daniels 1988:73). New York by then had the second largest Chinese-ancestry population (Lai 1980:224). Along with this geographical dispersion, the Chinese increasingly moved from rural settings and lines of work into urban areas. For example, the proportion of Chinese people living in cities rose from about 22 percent in 1880 to about 71 percent in 1940 (Daniels 1988:69).

Important changes in international affairs, however, presaged later improvements in the status of Chinese Americans. In 1912, the Chinese overthrew the dynasty that had ruled China since 1644 and adopted a republican form of government (Chen 1961:388). Then in 1931, Japan attacked and invaded China. Tensions between the United States and Japan had been building for many years and American sympathy for China's plight rose sharply. Simultaneously, American stereotypes of Chinese people became more favorable.[12] When Japan attacked Pearl Harbor, China and the United States became military allies; so, in addition to the glaring contradiction that already existed between American's national ideals and their treatment of the Chinese, a new contradiction now arose. On the one hand, there was increasing praise in our country for the resistance of the brave Chinese people and their leaders against the aggression of the Japanese; but, on the other hand, the Chinese exclusion laws remained in effect.

By 1943, the idea of repealing the Chinese Exclusion Act had gained substantial backing, and congressional hearings on the matter took place. President Franklin D. Roosevelt, a number of leading congressmen, a committee comprised of influential people,[13] and a number of businessmen who either already had ties with China or who hoped to have access to China's markets after the war, all favored repeal (Chung 1998:162; Kitano and Daniels 2001:41). On December 17, 1943, following a debate in

Congress, all of the previous acts that had established and supported exclusion were repealed.[14] For the first time, the Chinese were given a quota under the Immigration Act of 1924. And, also for the first time, Chinese immigrants and legal residents became eligible for citizenship (U.S. Immigration and Naturalization Service 1943). Nevertheless, Chinese immigration rose only modestly in the two decades immediately following the repeal of the Exclusion Act.[15]

World War II brought labor shortages that permitted Chinese workers to fill jobs that previously had been off-limits. Unlike the Japanese Americans, Chinese Americans were not forced into internment camps and were immediately eligible to serve in the armed forces.[16] Additionally, in 1946, the War Brides Act and, in 1947, the G.I. Fiancées Act permitted the admission of women outside the quota limit, thus accelerating the balancing of the sex ratio among Chinese Americans (Posadas 1999:28).[17] These changes helped consolidate the position of the Chinese family and community in America. As conditions improved for Chinese Americans there was a gradual exodus of people from the Chinatowns, leaving them with a dwindling population of aging, still predominantly male, residents. These communities had assisted sojourners to settle, establish families, and prepare children for a new life in American society; but they now seemed destined to become only honored remnants of the past. Instead, as large numbers of new Chinese immigrants entered the United States after 1965, the Chinatowns participated in a broad process of Chinese American cultural renewal.

Chinese American Assimilation

The upsurge of Chinese immigration after 1965 created a greatly enlarged and more variegated Chinese American community. Of the more than 1.3 million Chinese immigrants counted between 1820 and 2000, about two-thirds have arrived since 1965.[18] This rising immigration also has created a far more complicated pattern of Chinese American assimilation than existed previously. Some Chinese Americans now may trace their ancestry through as many as six generations while many others are part of a new first or second generation.

We are restricted here to presenting only a few illustrations of the workings of certain aspects of some of the assimilation subprocesses. In particular, we focus on cultural assimilation, as indicated by English-language proficiency; secondary assimilation, as indicated by education, occupation, and income; marital assimilation, as indicated by outmarriage; and identificational assimilation, as indicated by levels of naturalization. As we have pointed out previously, assimilation may occur differently among different population segments, and the main trends that may be seen within a given ethnic group may not be occurring in some segments of it. These divergences from the expectations of classical assimilation theory are the subject of scholarly debate (Zhou 1997).

The recent groups of Chinese immigrants differ from the earlier groups of immigrants in a number of sociocultural respects. The earlier immigrants were male, usually illiterate and unskilled sojourners who came from a single province on boats. The new immigrants typically come on airplanes, bring their families with them, are highly literate and skilled workers, and have come from Hong Kong, Taiwan, various parts of mainland China, or various Chinese communities in other countries (Tong 2000:100; Zhou and Cai 2002:420–421). The early immigrants were mainly Cantonese speakers who concentrated in Chinatowns in San Francisco, Los Angeles, and New York City. The new immigrants speak a variety of languages and dialects but use Mandarin (China's official language) as a common language. They have settled in large numbers both within and outside of the old Chinatowns and, also, in a number of large cities and states beyond the traditional ones. To illustrate, in 1998 California and New York were still the top two destinations for Chinese immigrants, receiving 27 and 24 percent of the newcomers, respectively; but also in that year over 49 percent of the new arrivals went elsewhere. Illinois, Massachusetts, New Jersey, and Texas each received around 3 percent (U.S. Bureau of the Census 2001:12). Still, the metropolitan areas of the traditional "gateway cities," such as San Francisco and New York, continue to house the largest Chinese populations (Zhou and Cai 2002:422–423).

These contrasts between the earlier and more recent Chinese immigrants are important for our assessment of the processes of assimilation. As we have noted, many obstacles to assimilation were faced by Chinese people in America during the first and second periods of immigration, and these obstacles delayed or prevented most members of the first generation from becoming fluent in English and from adopting other aspects of American culture.[19] The second generation, however, attended American public schools, learned English, played American sports, and were exposed to American mass media—even though many of their activities, including school attendance and sports participation—were carried out in segregated settings (Tong 2000:65). As a result, they were far more assimilated culturally, by substitution, than were their parents and gradually became the leaders of the Chinese community. Many Chinese Americans then sought to move outside the ethnic communities and into the mainstream of American society.

A key idea of classical assimilation theory we have analyzed in this book assumes that, among assimilation subprocesses, cultural assimilation typically commences first and develops more rapidly than the other subprocesses. It prepares the way for each of the other forms of assimilation, all of which have been set into motion simultaneously. Among many of the post-1965 Chinese, however, there appears to be an anomaly. Since so many of the new Chinese immigrants are highly educated and skilled people when they arrive, they often go directly into professional, technical, and managerial positions, rather than going first through a lengthy period of cultural adjustment. For example, 42 percent of the foreign-born Chinese in 1990 had more than 4 years of college education (compared to 21 percent of non-Hispanic Whites in the United States) and 35 percent also held professional jobs (compared to 27 percent of non-Hispanic Whites).[20] At the same time more than 80 percent of the foreign-born stated they speak Chinese at home and 60 percent stated they do not speak English "very well" (Zhou and Cai 2002:422–423). The ability of highly-educated Chinese immigrants to achieve rapid occupational assimilation, even though they sometimes may have only limited proficiency in English, may be due to their concentration in fields requiring mainly technical expertise.

Taken together these facts suggest that secondary assimilation may be occurring more rapidly among the newcomers than is cultural assimilation (Tong 2000:99); and, if true, that situation presents a startling contrast to the experiences, not only of the earlier

Chinese immigrants but, also, to the experiences of most other immigrant groups in American history as well. This conclusion may be premature, however, because highly educated immigrants may have a greater grasp of American culture than is readily apparent. Additionally, professionals must often first accept jobs beneath their levels of qualification and may face slower advancement even when they do move into the fields of their choice. Still further, they may then face income ceilings (Tong 2000:108). Those having lower qualifications than is typical for the group face the prospect of dead-end jobs, downward mobility, and a form of segmented assimilation in which they take on the characteristics of the working class African and Hispanic Americans in the communities where they live (Zhou 2002:89).

Consider another contrast between the occupational experiences of the earlier and more recent Chinese immigrants: entrepreneurship. Since the workers of the earlier groups were generally forced into less desirable occupations, few were able to amass the funds needed to start large, competitive, businesses. Many did, however, establish small, family business enterprises that required little capital and could be maintained by hard work, long hours, and low profit margins—such as garment factories, laundries, grocery stores, and restaurants. The initial funds used to found these businesses often were accumulated by rotating credit associations or *woi,* resembling the Japanese *tanamoshi* (Takaki 1998:241). Wealthier Chinese entrepreneurs also started larger businesses in the oil, automotive, cannery, banking, and shipping businesses, though most of these did not survive (Lai 1980:224). Still, the Chinese immigrants in America gradually became well known as entrepreneurs.

A number of the new Chinese immigrants have gained prominence as professionals and in business; and, unlike their earlier Chinese predecessors, they have not been restricted to small ethnic economy businesses in Chinatowns. They have rapidly established large businesses that cater to a broad market outside of the Chinese community, are well capitalized with both foreign and domestic funds, and have important transnational connections (Tong 2000:112–113).[21] By 2000, business ownership among Chinese Americans had become so widespread that there was about one Chinese-owned business for every 10 Chinese Americans.[22] Moreover, the reduction of anti-Chinese discrimination during the last century suggests there now appears to be a better chance than earlier that these business ventures will continue to succeed.

These indications that cultural and secondary assimilation are rapidly taking place among at least some segments of the Chinese American population give us reason to suppose that various members of this ethnic group also participate in a broad range of social interactions with non-Chinese Americans. Friendships formed in this way may lead them to select non-Chinese American spouses.[23] We now consider briefly some findings from a study of Asian American intermarriage that included information on all four of the ethnic groups of interest to us and also distinguished between the foreign-born and the American-born within each group.

The study, conducted by Liang and Ito (1999), was based on U.S. Census data for the New York City Region.[24] The researchers found, overall, that the average level of out-marriage among Chinese, Korean, Filipino, and Asian Indians of both sexes who were born in America was quite high (about 48 percent). In each of the four ethnic groups, out-marriage was very much higher among those who were American-born than among those who were foreign-born.[25] In regard to Chinese Americans, the study showed that about 33 percent of the American-born Chinese men in the New York Region had married out of their ethnic group. Moreover, this was the lowest percentage of out-marriage among either the males or females of the four American-born Asian groups we are comparing. The level of out-marriage among Chinese American women (45 percent), although higher than for the men, was still the lowest among all of the American-born Asian women studied (Liang and Ito 1999:885).[26]

The researchers considered various possible explanations of these findings and found that (1) the main factor affecting intermarriage is a similarity in levels of education and (2) the Chinese were "polarized" in that respect. The Chinese group included the second highest number of Ph.D. holders studied; but, the average level of education among the entire Chinese group was the lowest (13.3 years) of those considered (Liang and Ito 1999:883).

The marriage of a minority-group person to a majority-group person is an example of the formation of an especially important interethnic primary relationship. It also suggests, though not necessarily so, that the minority-group spouse may be moving toward identificational assimilation. Naturalization, on the other hand, is strong evidence of an increase in a person's identification with the United States and other Americans. A study by Yang (2002) showed that the average (mean) level of naturalization between 1961 and 1998 among the Chinese, Korean, Filipino, and Asian Indian Americans was very high (58 percent), with a range of 49 to 68 percent.[27] By contrast, the average level of naturalization among immigrants from Europe has steadily declined, averaging about 19 percent from 1961 to 1998 (U.S. Immigration and Naturalization Service 2000:170). Among the Asian groups, the naturalization of Chinese immigrants equaled the overall average of 58 percent. To help explain why naturalization levels vary among groups, the researcher examined several factors, including the length of time people have lived in the United States, their language proficiency, the number and density of immigrants in their present community, and the gross national product of their countries of origin. He concluded that three categories of factors—conditions in the home country, the number and density of coethnics in a person's present community, as well as a person's individual characteristics—largely explain why immigrants do or do not choose to become U.S. citizens (Yang 2002:380). Other factors, such as the citizenship requirement that one must learn English or must possess certain legal documents, may also hinder naturalization.

The balance between a second-generation person's identification as Chinese or American also reflects the opinions of their parents and other family members. A study by Kibria (2002:299–300) of ethnic identity among second-generation Chinese Americans found that many of those in her study sample spoke of "belonging to the 'Chinese race' . . ." and that this idea of a "primordial" or blood tie was transmitted by parents and the immigrant community. If one accepts this view, then identifying oneself as an American poses a special problem. How can one "choose" to be an American if she or he *is* Chinese "by blood?" Kibria (2002:301) stated that the second-generation members of her sample held the idea of a "blood tie" in an "uneasy and unresolved tension with more individualistic ones" and were aided in maintaining this contradiction by "their recognition of the significance of race in the United States."

On average, the Chinese Americans have rapidly achieved educational and occupational "success" in pursuit of the American Dream. Their attainments lend support to the view that in American society those who work hard and persevere may overcome many obstacles to worldly success. As a result, this group has been called a "model minority," as have the other three groups discussed in this chapter. But as discussed in Chapter 11, this view is freighted with political overtones, distracts attention from the condition of those portions of the group that are downwardly mobile, conceals continuing discrimination against even those who are most successful, and is deservedly controversial. We return briefly to one aspect of this issue in the closing section of this chapter.

Korean Americans

The Korean peninsula extends approximately 600 miles from the Northwest Coast of the mainland of Asia, separates the Yellow Sea and the Sea of Japan,[28] connects in the north to China, touches Russia to the northeast, and is separated from Japan to the south by the narrow Korean Strait. The proximity of China, Russia, and Japan has influenced the development of the distinctive culture and society of Korea for millenia.

The influence of China has been of the greatest importance among these countries (Hu 1961:292). During the Silla Unification Period (668–892), Korea's rulers installed tax systems and civil service exams that were similar to those used in China. Later, during the Koryŏ Dynasty (918–1392),[29] Confucianism supplanted Buddhism as the chief ethical system and guide to correct living among most Koreans. Later still, during the Yi Dynasty (1392–1910), Confucianism was adopted as the Korean state creed (Wagner 2002:551).[30]

Japanese influence in Korea began to increase over 400 years ago when the Japanese invaded the Korean peninsula. The Chinese joined the Koreans in their resistance to Japan, and the combined armies and navies expelled the invading forces after a long struggle.[31] The Koreans subsequently drove the Chinese army out of their country and, except for a continuing tributary relationship to China, Korea was largely isolated from world events for about 300 years. It became the "Hermit Kingdom" (Wagner 2002:551).

During the last half of the nineteenth century, however, the world knocked on Korea's door. In 1866, some French priests were killed there, and France sent an invasion force to retaliate. Shortly afterward, an American warship was sunk in Korean waters, and the Americans also retaliated. Then, in 1876, after Japan forced Korea to sign a commercial treaty with them, the United States and Korea concluded a treaty in 1882. Subsequently, several European powers also signed similar treaties (Hu 1961:296; Wagner 2002:552). Because of Korea's long period of self-imposed isolation, only a few Koreans had either been permitted to travel or wished to travel abroad; but the political and economic turmoil created by the conflicts on the peninsula encouraged departures. Following the treaty with the United States, the efforts of some American missionaries created the possibility of travel to the United States. Between 1885 and 1905, some 67 Koreans— 64 of whom were students—came to the United States (Kim 1980:602).

Americans also played key roles in the migration of a group of Korean laborers to Hawaii. The United States annexed Hawaii in 1898, extending the reach of the Chinese Exclusion Act and halting the flow of Chinese labor to the islands. The sugar planters in

Hawaii then became interested in Korea as a new source of workers. After some negotiations, the Korean emperor permitted 7,226 Korean immigrants, including 637 women and 541 children, to go to Hawaii, beginning in 1903.

Japan's increasing power in the region heightened the rivalry between Japan, China, and Russia for control of the Korean peninsula. In successive wars, Japan defeated both China (1894–1895) and Russia (1904–1905); so by 1905 Korea became, in effect, an occupied colony of Japan. In 1905, the Japanese cancelled the arrangement permitting workers to go to Hawaii and stopped the further migration of Koreans (Hurh and Kim 1984:39). Nevertheless, the foundation was laid for a Korean community in Hawaii; and over a thousand of the Koreans in Hawaii later migrated to the U.S. mainland (Takaki 1998:270). In 1910, Japan formally annexed Korea and ruled the country harshly until the end of World War II.

The Gentlemen's Agreement between the United States and Japan, discussed in Chapter 11, affected the lives of Korean immigrants as well as those of Japanese immigrants. Since Japan now ruled Korea, the provisions of the Gentlemen's Agreement included Koreans. The United States no longer permitted the entry of people with Korean passports and, as agreed, the Japanese limited the issuance of passports to both Japanese and Koreans. Additionally, a number of the Korean immigrants who had come previously to the United States returned to Korea. The combined effect of these changes was to limit the growth of the Korean population in Hawaii and on the mainland for the next four decades. Only two significant additions to these populations took place during those 40 years. The provisions of the Gentlemen's Agreement permitted the entry of women who were the wives of U.S. residents or were to be married as picture brides, and a group of young political activists who were fleeing from Japanese rule were admitted as "students." Altogether, 1,100 Korean picture brides and over 500 political refugees were permitted to enter Hawaii and the United States prior to the further restrictions imposed by the immigration act of 1924 (Hurh and Kim 1984:42).

Given America's anti-Asian laws and the small number of Koreans who reached the United States during the nineteenth and early twentieth centuries, official statistics on their arrival were not listed separately. Americans' attitudes toward Koreans were illustrated in 1941 after the Japanese attack on Pearl Harbor. Even though Koreans were unwilling subjects of Japan, made no secret of their hatred of the Japanese, and very strongly supported America's effort to defeat Japan, they were nevertheless classified as enemy aliens and subjected to the regulations entailed by that status (Kim 1980:603).

At the end of World War II, Japan was forced to relinquish control of Korea. The United States and the Soviet Union agreed that the Americans would occupy the Korean peninsula up to the thirty-eighth parallel while the Russians occupied the country north of that line. Subsequent efforts to agree on a unified Korean government for the entire peninsula failed; so in 1948, an election was held in the south under American auspices and the government of the Republic of Korea (ROK) was established. A few months later, the Democratic People's Republic of Korea (DPRK) was established in the north under Russian auspices (Henderson 2002:552–553). Each of the two new Korean governments proclaimed itself to be the rightful ruler of the entire peninsula. These competing claims escalated into the conflict that became the Korean War (1950–1953).[32]

This war abruptly brought together the affairs of the United States and South Korea. The United States and other members of the United Nations sent a large expeditionary force to Korea, beginning in 1950; and when a truce was declared in 1953, a large contingent of American forces remained in Korea. The continuing presence of U.S. military forces in Korea has stimulated innumerable interactions and exchanges between the peoples of the two countries for more than a half a century. Early effects of the Korean War included changes in America's official views of Korean immigrants. These changes, in turn, stimulated a second period of Korean immigration to America that reinforced and enlarged the population created during the first period of settlement. This second period merged into the much larger post-1965 period (see Table 12.2).

Roots of the Korean American Family and Community

Immigrants from many countries have centered their initial organizational efforts on their religious faiths, and this was true also of the first Koreans in Hawaii. Since Protestant missionaries had played an important part in arranging the migration, a number of Koreans who made the journey had already been baptized as Christians. Many others attended Protestant, primarily Methodist, services after arrival and, eventually, nearly all of the early immigrants became Christians (Hurh and Kim 1984:47; Melendy 1977:139). They generally used the churches, not only for religious needs but, also, as cultural centers and language schools. Additionally, they organized for self-defense against Anglo

Table 12.2   Korean Immigration to the
United States, 1941–2000

Years	Number
1903–1905	7,226
1910–1924	1,100
1941–1950	107
1951–1960	6,231
1961–1970	34,526
1971–1980	267,638
1981–1990	333,746
1991–2000	164,166
Total	814,740

Source: U.S. Immigration and Naturalization Service, *Statistical Yearbook of the Immigration and Naturalization Service, 1998,* 2000:20–22; U.S. Immigration and Naturalization Service, *Statistical Yearbook of the Immigration and Naturalization Service, 2000,* 2002:19–22; Hurh 1998:33.

Americans and the members of the Chinese and Japanese communities that already existed in Hawaii. They organized also to regulate the social interactions of their group's members with one another and with outsiders (Kim 1980:603). Although the group of Koreans who reached the mainland was even smaller than the group in Hawaii, they, too, founded some churches and language schools.

Some of the initial circumstances of the Korean immigrants' lives did not favor the formation of families and communities. In the first place, the sex ratio among Korean immigrants was highly unbalanced, as it was among those from China and Japan. In addition, even when families were formed, family members had to struggle to maintain the family relationships prescribed by the Confucian ethic. These prescriptions include observing the specific duties and responsibilities of the father and son, husband and wife, elder and younger brother, and friend and friend (Min 1988:207–208). Like the Japanese and Chinese, the first Korean immigrants planned to return to Korea. They, therefore, did not initially view themselves as permanent residents of the host country. Nevertheless, the arrival of picture brides assisted in the formation of families. Moreover, because Korea was being taken over by Japan, the immigrants knew they could not return to their home country until Japan's domination ended (Kitano and Daniels 2001:123). As a result, the political situation in the mother country became the primary focus of family and community life among the Korean immigrants. Their sense of Korean identity was increased, and they formed political associations with the purpose of assisting to free their country from Japan (Kim 1980:603).

As matters developed, three of the 64 Korean students who came to the United States before 1905—Syngman Rhee, Pak Yong-man, and Ahn Chang-ho—became outstanding political leaders, first in the immigrant communities and, later, in Asia.[33] Different views concerning the independence of Korea existed among Koreans, however, and discord was evident in the competing strategies favored by the organizations established by the three young patriots. The work of each helped the Korean immigrants to maintain high morale and mobilize the resources needed to keep alive their hope of independence for their country.

In the early years though, while Korean immigrants in the United States organized and tried to devise ways to attain Korea's freedom, the immigrants also had to take care of the day-to-day tasks of working and—when possible—starting families and raising children. Those who worked on the sugar plantations in Hawaii spent long hours at hard labor, and most of what they earned was used to provide life's necessities and the repayment of the money they had borrowed to pay for the tickets to Hawaii. Koreans on the mainland worked mainly as field hands or as domestic servants. They were unable in either location to gain access to higher paying jobs because of widespread discrimination against Asians. Under these circumstances, most immigrants could save little from their wages.[34] Some individuals, nevertheless, accumulated enough capital to establish various businesses. Others were able to fund businesses through participation in a rotating credit association or *kye* (Light, Kwuon, and Zhong [1990]1998:132). For instance, Kim Hyong-soon and Kim Ho formed a fruit wholesaling company that expanded to include orchards and packing houses. They also developed new types of fruit, including the nectarine. The business of another farming entrepreneur, Kim Chong-nim, was so successful as a producer of rice that he became known as the "rice king" (Kim 1980:604; Takaki 1998:276).

Throughout the first period of Korean immigration to America (up to 1948), the ratio of males to females continued to be unbalanced. Although the picture brides who were admitted during the 1910–1924 period did enable many men to head families in which both spouses were Korean, many other men did not have that option. Instead, they were forced either to remain bachelors or to marry non-Korean women.[35] This situation was eased somewhat by the admission of more Korean women in the period during and following the end of the Korean War (1950–1953), though many of these women were the wives of U.S. servicemen. In addition, the Korean American population increased prior to 1965 by the admission of over 6,000 orphans of the Korean War and also of about 6,000 students (Hurh and Kim 1984:50–51). Altogether, during the first two periods of Korean immigration to the United States (1885–1948 and 1948–1965), 22,353 Koreans had been counted as admittees to the United States.

Korean American Assimilation

Between 1965 and 2000, 784,061 Koreans were admitted to the United States; and over 20 percent of this large group entered the country after 1990. The recency of the arrival of these immigrants is reflected in the fact that by the late 1990s more than 70 percent of the Korean Americans were first-generation immigrants (Hurh 1998:80).

More Koreans live in the western states (44 percent) than in any other region of the country, but each region is home to a sizable segment of this group's population. About 23 percent of the Koreans live in the Northeast; 21 percent live in the South; and the remaining 12 percent live in the Midwest. The new Korean immigrants, as a group, differ from the Korean settlers of the first period of immigration in many respects. They are much more likely than their predecessors to come from an urban area, to be highly educated, to be trained as professional, technical, and managerial workers, and to come as family units. To illustrate, studies of Korean Americans in Los Angeles and Chicago by Hurh and Kim (1984) found that among the most recent arrivals from Korea, almost 78 percent were graduates of Korean colleges. In a subsequent study in Chicago, these researchers found that almost 50 percent of the sample members had held professional/technical and administrative/managerial jobs in Korea (Hurh 1998:42–43). Their geographical dispersion in America and their urban backgrounds spurred the development of large Koreatowns in Los Angeles, New York City, Chicago, San Francisco, and Washington, D.C. (Min 1988:205). The largest of these, in Los Angeles, has been officially dedicated by the city as "Koreatown" (Hurh 1998:119, 163).

These characteristics favor cultural assimilation among those who wish to adopt American ways. There is evidence that the Koreans favor cultural assimilation by addition rather than substitution (Hurh 1998:79), and that their transnational ties and cultural homogeneity increase the feasibility of this mode of adaptation (Min [1991]1998:226; Min 2002:141–144). Another fact favoring cultural assimilation among Koreans is that a majority of them are Protestants. A special problem of adaptation among Korean Americans, however, is that their acquisition of and proficiency in English has been lower than among the other main Asian American groups. For instance, about two-thirds of the Korean participants in the Los Angeles sample studied by Hurh and Kim (1984:215) rated themselves as not being either "fluent" or "moderately fluent" in speaking, reading, or writing English. The respondents in the two Chicago samples rated themselves more highly in speaking ability but only about 40 percent considered their English to be "good" or "fluent" (Hurh 1998:42).

Another indication that English-language proficiency may be a problem among first-generation Korean Americans is that, in general, their jobs in the United States have not been commensurate with their educational and occupational backgrounds. For instance, in a 1986 study, Hurh and Kim (Hurh 1998:43) found that of the 45 percent of those sampled who had held high-status jobs in Korea, only 28 percent held such jobs in the United States. The researchers also found that more than twice as many Koreans in their sample made their living as owners of small, labor-intensive retail and service businesses than had done so in Korea. These are the kinds of businesses that have been available to the impoverished and uneducated early settlers from many different ethnic groups who faced discrimination in the workplace (Min 2002:288–289). In addition, Hurh and Kim (1984:117) found in a previous study that those employed in the White community were likely to be segregated at work. The extent to which such circumstances may be traced to language difficulties or to discrimination or both is unclear; but, in any event, by 2000 a higher proportion of Korean Americans were business owners than was true for any other American immigrant group. At that time, there was about one Korean-owned business for every eight Korean Americans.

Liang and Ito (1999:885) also have found evidence showing that first-generation Korean men were less likely than the men of the Chinese, Filipino, or Asian Indian groups to have spouses of European descent. First-generation Korean women, however, were more likely than Chinese or Asian Indian women to have married outside their ethnic group. The higher proportion of out-marriages among first-generation Korean women may stem from the presence of American troops in Korea since 1950. The situation among second-generation Korean Americans, however, was quite different. Sixty-three percent of the men and 45 percent of the women married outside their group.[36] These figures suggest a rapid movement of Korean Americans toward marital assimilation. This movement may come at an emotional price to those experiencing it, however. Kibria's (2002) findings concerning the "blood tie" idea are again pertinent. One of her informants, Sandra, stated that "Koreans are very nationalistic, they want to keep the Korean blood pure" and that her father had told her "it was unacceptable for me to marry a non-Korean" (Kibria 2002:301).

The general findings concerning marital assimilation among second-generation Korean Americans suggest, nevertheless, that they are accepting and being accepted by other members of American society and may be moving toward a strong identification with America. A high level of naturalization among Koreans strengthens this impression. Yang (2002:380) reported that over 56 percent of the Korean immigrants in his national sample had become U.S. citizens.

 Filipino (Pilipino) Americans[37]

The Philippine Islands lie between 300 and 750 miles off the eastern mainland of Asia and span a distance of about 1,150 miles from northeast to southwest. The islands were populated primarily by various groups of Malay people who migrated from more southerly portions of the Malay Archipelego. These were joined much later by a small number of Chinese people who originally came as traders. Later still, during the twelfth and thirteenth centuries, Arab missionaries reached the Philippines and converted the Moros of the southern island of Mindanao to Islam (Melendy 1980:355).

The first Europeans arrived in the Philippines in 1521 when Magellan's Spanish expedition sailed into the islands and claimed them for Spain. Twenty-one years later the leader of another Spanish expedition named the islands *Las Islas Filipinas* in honor of King Phillip II. During the 1570s, Spanish colonies were established on Cebu and also on the main island of Luzon. From these islands the Spanish extended their control, as well as their efforts to convert the native population to Christianity. These efforts were largely successful except in the southern and southwestern islands where Islam remained dominant.[38] Spanish rule was never welcomed, however, and the Filipinos made frequent efforts to regain their independence. Altogether, Spain's rule continued over 300 years until the final years of the nineteenth century (Fifield and Romulo 1962:333, 341). This long period of Spanish domination established the Spanish language and culture as markers of elite social status in the Philippines (Melendy 1980:355).

Recall that the doctrine of White supremacy flourished during the nineteenth and early twentieth centuries. Americans spread westward across North America under the banner of Manifest Destiny. At the same time, the major European countries continued to move aggressively to subjugate indigenous populations in other parts of the world, establishing far-flung colonial empires. Before the Spanish–American War, the United States took several steps toward becoming a "Great Power" in the Pacific, thrusting itself into the internal affairs of Japan, China, and Korea. The biggest imperialist move by the United States in the Pacific during the nineteenth century, however, began in February, 1898, when America declared war on Spain.[39] In June of that year Filipinos, led by Emilio Aguinaldo, declared independence and joined with American forces to invade the island of Luzon and capture the city of Manila.

The rebels believed that if the United States won the war, they would be granted immediate independence; but instead, in the concluding treaty, Spain agreed to cede the Philippines to the United States. President William McKinley explained that it was the "duty" of the United States to assume control of the islands. We could not in good conscience, he stated, avoid the task of "educating," "uplifting," and "civilizing" the Filipinos (Faulkner 1948:568). A "special relationship" was thus formed between the United States and the Philippines through which the Americans exercised colonial rule over the islands for 48 years (Posadas 1999:1). The Americans promised to set the Philippines free when they were deemed "ready" to govern themselves. Aguinaldo and his rebels felt betrayed, again declared independence, and resumed fighting—this time against the Americans. After two more years of fighting for Philippine independence, Aguinaldo was captured and required to sign an oath of allegiance to the United States (Fifield and Romulo 1962:341).[40]

A five-man Philippine Commission, led by future president of the United States William Howard Taft, was appointed to govern the islands; and Taft was selected to be the first American civil governor. The colony that Taft governed, and attempted to Americanize, consisted of about 7,100 islands clustered in three main groups. The largest island in the northern group is Luzon, where Manila is located; the southern group centers on the even larger island of Mindanao, which is the center of Islamic culture. Between these two large island groups lie the Visayans, which include the most densely populated islands of the country. The people of these many islands speak at least 80 different dialects. Communication among the different groups is fairly easy, though, because most people speak one or more of several languages belonging to the Malayo–Polynesian group of languages (Fifield and Romulo 1962:442; Melendy 1980:355).

To pursue the goals set forth by U.S. President McKinley, the Philippine Commission conducted general elections, and the first elected Filipino national assembly was seated in 1907. Also new public schools were opened in which the children were taught the English language and American ideas of democracy. Between 1900 and 1921, the number of children enrolled in the primary schools rose from 150,000 to more than 1 million (Posadas 1999:9). In addition, Governor Taft started an educational program through which several hundred young Filipino men, called *pensionados,* were sent to the United States to attend colleges and universities.[41] Between 1903 and 1910, several hundred students received training in this program and then returned to the Philippines. Many members of this group later became political and economic leaders. Their example and experiences in America encouraged many others also to cross the Pacific.

Although the free elections pleased most Filipinos, as did the colonial government's initiatives in education, the people were far from pleased to have traded Spanish for American rule. For instance, even though the members of the national assembly were elected, this body held only limited powers. Moreover, the American system left in place the social and political elite that existed under the Spanish (Posadas 1999:9). As a result, the political party that opposed U.S. rule and favored independence, the *nacionalista,* was the most popular party in the country and dominated national elections for decades.

The war with Spain had further consequences that are pertinent here. In addition to bringing American control and ideas to the Philippines, it also converted the Filipinos into American nationals (but not citizens) who could travel freely between the islands and the United States. Additionally, the American public's enthusiasm for the war provided an opportune moment to annex Hawaii to advance further the military and commercial strength of the United States in the Pacific. These changes and the discontinuation of the supply of Korean and Japanese workers to both Hawaii and the mainland, led the sugar planters of Hawaii to actively recruit Filipinos.

The first recruiting efforts centered on the populous island of Cebu and the city of Manila on Luzon. Most of the workers from these areas spoke the Tagalog (Pilipino) language and the Cebuano dialect of the Visayan language. Later on, recruitment focused on people who spoke the Ilocano language because the members of this group were poor and eager to find work. Between 1909 and 1931, over 113,000 Filipinos went to Hawaii. As usual, a large majority of these immigrants (about 87 percent) were sojourning men, 55,000 of whom eventually became permanent residents of Hawaii. About one-third of the other 58,000 eventually moved to the mainland, and the rest returned to the Philippines (Fifield and Romulo 1962:341–342; Melendy 1980:356–357).

In addition to the *pensionados* and those who migrated from Hawaii to the mainland, thousands of other Filipinos, again mostly men, went directly to the mainland from the Philippines, especially to California. The main surge of this second group of immigrants took place after World War I and, by 1930, around 45,000 Filipinos were living in the United States (Kitano and Daniels 2001:92). About 30,000 of these migrants lived in California working mainly in agricultural jobs, but many found work in other states across the country and in a wide range of other jobs. Some worked in post offices; others joined the navy; still others worked in restaurants, homes, factories, the merchant marine, and hotels (Melendy 1980:359–360).

In the meantime, the U.S. government was unsure what to do with the Philippines and Filipino immigrants; consequently its official policy toward the territory vacillated. Even though the immigrants were American nationals, often imbued by American teachers and missionaries with idealistic visions of equal participation in American society, on the mainland they met the same hostility and discrimination that had greeted the Chinese, Japanese, and Koreans. They were labeled with negative stereotypes, called names, blocked from the best jobs, denied access to public accommodations, and attacked by White workers (Takaki 1998:324–326). Those who had come to America to receive an education sometimes were unable to find jobs in their chosen fields. Thousands of Filipino men recruited into the U.S. Navy learned that they were restricted to being servants and entertainers (Posadas 1999:20, 23).

Finally, in 1934, the Tydings–McDuffie Bill elevated the Philippines from territorial to commonwealth status within the American political system and set a date for independence. Under the provisions of this bill, the Filipinos adopted a constitution and elected a president. In 1946, after the end of World War II, the Philippine Islands finally became an independent country. The Tydings–McDuffie Bill also, however, exacted a price: In return for independence Filipinos were reclassified as aliens and placed under the quota limitations of the Immigration Act of 1924 (Takaki 1998:332). These changes brought a sharp drop in Filipino immigration (Melendy 1980:361). Not until the passage of the INAA in 1965 did Filipino immigration reach, and then exceed, the earlier levels (see Table 12.3).

Roots of the Filipino American Family and Community

Filipinos had even more difficulty forming families and communities in America than the other Asian groups we have discussed, although many of the obstacles they faced were not unique. For instance, Filipinas were scarce, and the immigrants confronted high levels of discrimination in all areas of life; and, as was true for the other Asian groups, Filipinos were viewed as representatives of an "alien" race who threatened to undermine the standard of living of the American worker. Also, even though they were American nationals, they—like all other Asians—were ineligible for citizenship.

The circumstances of Filipino life in Hawaii and on the mainland during the period before World War II did not encourage immigrants to reproduce the sociocultural patterns of the home islands. In the islands both culture and religion had supported the importance of family unity, loyalty, and reciprocity; and of vital importance within the

Table 12.3 Filipino Immigration to the United States, 1931–2000

Years	Number
1931–1940	528
1941–1950	4,691
1951–1960	19,307
1961–1970	98,376
1971–1980	354,987
1981–1990	548,764
1991–2000	503,945
Total	1,530,598

Source: U.S. Immigration and Naturalization Service, *Statistical Yearbook of the Immigration and Naturalization Service, 1998,* 2000:20–22; U.S. Immigration and Naturalization Service, *Statistical Yearbook of the Immigration and Naturalization Service, 2000,* 2002:19–22.

family system was the tradition of *compadrinazgo* (ritual co-parenthood). This tradition created and maintained an interclass and intercultural network of fictive kinsmen and affected practically all activities in Philippine society, but that network was difficult to re-create in America.

A unique problem of the Filipinos, however, arose from an ironic source. Since they were American nationals, rather than resident aliens, their orientation toward life on the U.S. mainland was generally different from that of the other Asian ethnic groups. They often believed initially that they would be well received and would have a realistic chance of participating in American life on a nearly equal footing. Also since they could move back-and-forth freely between their homeland and the United States, they saw little reason to construct large, distinctive ethnic enclaves possessing permanent social and economic institutions along the lines followed by most other immigrant groups.[42] The Little Manilas, therefore, remained small and inconspicuous (Yu [1980]1998:103) and that situation, in turn, meant it was generally not profitable to start businesses to serve other Filipinos. Most Filipinos found they could satisfy their needs by shopping at the many Chinese and Japanese businesses that already existed. As a result, unlike the Chinese, Japanese, and (at a later time) Korean immigrants, Filipinos did not develop a distinctive merchant class (Yu [1980]1998:108).

The absence of large concentrations of Filipinos in distinctive ethnic enclaves impeded the development of the mutual benefit and protective associations that have been founded in other immigrant communities. Also, until after 1965, Filipinos started comparatively few newspapers that might have helped to stimulate community development and keep the group's members informed about events in the United States and in the homeland. The main force drawing Filipinos together into loosely organized communities were shared languages, with Cebuano, Tagalog, and Ilocano (in that order) being spoken by about 85 percent of the Filipino American population (Melendy 1980:355, 360).

The most volatile problem arising from the Filipinos' status as American nationals concerned interracial dating, sex, and marriage. Recall that before 1948 the laws of California prohibited intermarriage between a White person and any person defined as non-White. Such laws were passed because of the widespread racist belief and fear that non-White men would "mongrelize" and "pollute" the "pure white race." Under these circumstances, any behavior that seemed to Whites to suggest that a non-White man might be making "improper advances" to a White woman was likely to stir up great resentment and, in many cases, provoke retaliation for violations of the etiquette of race relations.[43] Since most Filipinos were descendants of the Malay peoples of the islands, rather than of people who were referred to in the law as "Mongolians," there was no valid legal barrier to Filipino–White relationships. Filipino men, therefore, departed from the pattern of men in the other Asian groups, refused to accept their "place," and openly associated with White women, especially prostitutes and those who worked in what were known as "taxi" dance halls (Takaki 1998:338–340). In such establishments, a man could purchase a single dance for 10 cents and then publicly embrace his partner for the short period of the dance. Since large numbers of Filipino men patronized the taxi dance halls, this form of Filipino recreation drew the attention of news reporters and led to racist, anti-Filipino headlines in many newspapers (Kitano and Daniels 2001:92).

The outrage of Whites over having Filipino men dance with White women was surpassed by the further fact that the associations between these men and women sometimes led to lasting relationships and, in some cases, marriages. Nativists proposed and supported legal measures to close this loophole in the intermarriage laws and, in 1933, California extended its legal prohibition on intermarriages to include unions between Whites and "Malays" (Kitano and Daniels 2001:93). The Tydings–McDuffie Bill, passed soon afterward, limited further immigration by Filipinos to the United States. In the following years, 12 other states also passed laws prohibiting Filipino–White intermarriages (Takaki 1998:330).

The combined effects of racist policies, discriminatory actions, negative racial stereotypes, an unfavorable balance of males and females, and an ambiguous legal status established and reinforced a pattern of transient employment among Filipino men and, thus, interfered with the development of well-organized and distinctive Filipino American communities. Indeed, after the quota principle was extended to Filipinos in 1934, their aging population went into a period of decline. Nevertheless, as time passed some Filipinos did settle down, get married, raise children, create neighborhoods and civic organizations, join labor unions, and help to introduce various elements of Filipino culture into American life (Posadas 1999:24).

With the onset of World War II and the Japanese conquest of the Philippines, one of America's important wartime goals became to recover the islands and fulfill the promise of granting them independence. The islanders strongly supported the American war effort, and thousands of Filipinos living in the United States volunteered to serve in the armed forces. Thousands of noncitizen Filipinos volunteered for service, and a policy that barred Filipinos from service was quickly changed to permit them to enlist. The First and Second Filipino Infantry Regiments were formed, and thousands of these men served in the Pacific and in Europe (Posadas 1999:26; Yu [1980]1998:106). The right to become a citizen was extended to these servicemen in 1943; but not until 1946 did all Filipino nationals become eligible for naturalization (Melendy 1980:361).

Family and community formation among Filipino Americans was accelerated by a sharp increase in the Filipina American population after the War Brides and Fiancées Acts were passed. To illustrate, in 1930 less than 3,000 (6.5 percent) of the 45,208 Filipinos in California were women; by 1960, of 114,179 Filipinos in the United States, 67,435 (37.1 percent) were women. In addition to the women who came as war brides and fiancées, others were married to men who were recently naturalized and had returned to the islands to find a wife. Still another important impetus to Filipina immigration was the Information and Education Exchange Act of 1948 (EVA). This act created opportunities for additional training and work in the United States for foreign nursing students. A large number of those who came were from the Philippines (Posadas:1999:30). Thus, many factors stemming from the "special relationship" created between the Philippines and the United States during the American colonial period helped spark a massive Filipino immigration in the post-1965 period.

Filipino American Assimilation

The post-1965 period has produced a much larger and more diverse Filipino American population than existed previously, although the Filipino American group was substantially larger than the immigration statistics of Table 12.3 indicate. Since Filipinos at first were American nationals, they were not counted as immigrants until after 1934. By then, thousands of Filipinos had come to Hawaii and the mainland. The Filipino American population grew also by natural increase, and by 1950 the total Filipino American population exceeded 120,000 (Kitano and Daniels 2001:92). Since 1960, however, that population has increased twelvefold through immigration alone.

The educational and occupational skills levels of the new Filipino immigrants, like those of the other Asian American groups discussed, generally have been very high—and very much above those of the earlier Filipino arrivals. For instance, Yang (2002:388) found in an analysis of U.S. Census data that 40 percent of the Filipino immigrants had Bachelor's degrees or higher and that 68 percent of them held professional and managerial jobs. In addition, the new Filipino immigrants typically possessed a higher level of proficiency in English than their predecessors, with 94 percent saying they spoke English "well" or "very well." Still further, Filipino immigrants typically have arrived with a working knowledge of American culture. These characteristics are assets to those who wish to assimilate culturally, either by addition or substitution.

Unlike the Filipino immigrants of the earlier period, who were prominent in farm work and military service, the post-1965 Filipino immigrants are much more likely to work in the professions.[44] Probably the most noticeable occupational concentration of the new Filipino immigrants is in the health care industry. This development was fostered by the opportunities offered to foreign students of nursing under the EVA. Because many Filipinas who participated in the program already spoke English and, also, had been trained in American-style nursing programs, they were especially welcomed in American hospitals and other health care settings. This new avenue of upward social mobility encouraged many young women in the Philippines to enter nursing programs;

and between 1948 and 1953, the number of nurses in the Philippines increased from 7,000 to 57,000. By 1973, over 12,000 of these nurses had migrated to the United States (Posadas 1999:30). Filipino doctors and other kinds of health care workers have followed the path pioneered by the student nurses. By 1990, 20 percent of employed Filipino Americans over age 16 were working in some form of health care, though it is unclear how many of these workers were in professional-level jobs (Posadas 1999:78).

We stated earlier that during the first and second periods of Filipino immigration to America, the Filipinos were the least entrepreneurial of the four Asian American groups discussed in this chapter. This difference among the groups has continued into the contemporary period. In 2000, there were about 22 Filipino Americans for each Filipino-owned business. The comparatively low level of business activity among Filipinos has not prevented them from attaining a high level of household income through other lines of work. Indeed, as a group, Filipinos rank near the top of the average income list among various ethnic groups. For instance, among 60 ethnic groups in America in 1989, the median household income of Filipinos ranked third. At the same time, the median income of households headed by native-born Filipinos was about 16 percent lower than of those headed by Filipino immigrants (Posadas 1999:82–83).

Liang and Ito (1999:885) found that among the Chinese, Korean, Filipino, and Asian Indian American groups we are discussing, Filipinas were more likely to marry outside their ethnic group than either the women or the men in any other group. This was true among both the foreign-born and the native-born groups, with nearly three-fourths of the American-born Filipinas marrying out. These findings probably reflect the fact that Filipinas have immigrated in large numbers. They also may reflect the rise of the mail-order bride business through which non-Asian American men may acquire Asian brides (Kitano and Daniels 2001:199). Overall, Filipino men still were more likely to marry outside their group than were Chinese, Korean, or Asian Indian men; however, in a comparison of the American-born Asian men in the study, the Filipino men ranked second among the four groups studied.

Given the historical relationship of the Philippines and the United States and the high levels of marital assimilation among Filipino immigrants, we should expect that their rates of naturalization also would be high. That, in fact, is the case. Among the four groups in our comparison, Yang (2002:380) found that Filipino immigrants had the highest level of naturalization (68 percent) among Asian Americans. The English-language proficiency of the Filipino Americans, their familiarity with American culture, their level of educational and occupational attainment, and their high rates of out-marriage and naturalization all indicate a rapid adaptation to American society. There is some evidence, though, that many second-generation Filipino youths still identify themselves more strongly as *Filipino* Americans than as Americans (Wolf 2002:263).

Asian (East) Indian Americans

Europeans had known for many centuries of the existence and riches of India through the reports of adventurers, merchants, and soldiers. The Europeans' ability to exploit India's riches, however, was severely limited by the fact that several Muslim powers controlled the overland trade routes running from the eastern end of the Mediterranean Sea to India. Portuguese explorer Vasco da Gama's discovery of an uncontrolled sea route in 1498 set into motion a vast expansion of European commercial, military, and colonial activities in Asia.

India's people at the beginning of the sixteenth century comprised, as they do today, an intricate cultural mosaic created through a long and tumultuous history. The various empires and dynasties that have existed in India over a period of several millenia left diverse cultural imprints. Here we note a few of the major features of the sociocultural setting into which the Portuguese thrust themselves.

The two main families of Indian languages originated with very early peoples known as Dravidians and Indo-Iranians (or Indo-Aryans). During a long period, beginning over three thousand years ago, a flourishing Dravidian civilization in the valley of the Indus river was disrupted by invading tribes of people from the northwest. The invaders spoke what are now called Indo-European languages—the language group that contains Hindi, the official language of the modern Republic of India (Bharat).[45] Most of the Dravidians were gradually driven south into the great peninsula below the Vindhya Mountains. This region, referred to as the Deccan because it contains the large Deccan Plateau, comprises roughly one-half of the contemporary Republic of India. The conquering fair-skinned Indo-Iranians established a social barrier between themselves and the darker-skinned Dravidians, thus initiating an hereditary caste system that became increasingly elaborate with the passage of time.[46] The importance of this social system increased and became more rigid as the Indo-Iranians incorporated it into the developing Hindu religion. Hinduism itself developed slowly over a long period of time and is the most prevalent religion of India. This ancient religion's sacred scriptures (written mainly in the Sanskrit language) had no single founder, but many religious reform groups have been started by individual Indians who disagreed with some or many of the doctrines of Hinduism (Mayhew 1961:225; Brown 2002:869).[47]

The second most prevalent religion in India, Islam, was brought into the country forcibly by Mahmud of Ghazni in the year 1000 following a long period of internal conflicts in India.[48] As had been true of the Indo-Iranians previously, groups of Islamic warriors came into India through the northwestern mountain passes connecting India and Afghanistan. The descendants of these groups dominated India for the next four centuries; but even though Mongol invaders supplanted this dominant group, the new Mogul[49] Sultans and Shahs were also Muslims whose leadership continued to foster the spread of Islam (Majumdar 2002:945).

This process was far advanced by the time Vasco da Gama reached India's southwest coast. Although da Gama was courteously received by the Hindu Raja of Malabar who offered "cinnamon, cloves, pepper, and precious stones" as trade goods (Durant 1954:613), local Muslim merchants had sufficient power to disrupt da Gama's effort to negotiate a trade agreement. Two years later another Portuguese expedition tried to establish trade relations but, again, could not overcome the opposition of the Muslim merchants. In 1502 da Gama returned with an armed fleet of 14 vessels, bombarded the coast, and destroyed a fleet the Muslims sent against him. This show of force led to a long-lasting Portuguese trade monopoly, and the establishment of Portuguese bases and colonies on the Malabar Coast.

During the sixteenth century, the maritime power of Spain and Portugal enabled those countries to explore widely and to invade other people's homelands, subordinate them, and establish foreign colonies. During the seventeenth century, however, the dominance of these powers in the Far East was successfully challenged by Holland, England, and France, beginning in each case with the establishment of an East India Company.

As we saw in Chapter 3, these companies were commercial enterprises chartered by their respective governments and given certain rights to establish and manage trade in the East Indies.[50] Early in the seventeenth century, the English and Dutch companies cooperated to some extent in their efforts to undermine the power of Portugal; but the alliance withered as the Dutch took control of the Malay Archipelago and the Moluccas (the "Spice Islands") and drove the English out.[51] The English East India Company then concentrated its efforts on India. By 1620, the English company had established ties with the Mogul emperor, defeated the Portuguese, and set up trading posts in the Indian provinces of Madras and Bombay. Throughout the remainder of the century, the company expanded its bases and territories to other parts of India and, by 1700, the British government had given the company the authority to rule the colonies as well as to carry on trade.

During the first half of the seventeenth century, the French East India Company also established bases in Bombay Province and on the Coromandel Coast. Both the English and French sought alliances with native princes and both enjoyed some success. The competition of these two colonial powers, not only in India but also in America, led to a long conflict that circled the globe.[52] When the fighting subsided in 1763, the French relinquished nearly all of their possessions in India. The English, therefore, continued to expand their presence in India until—over rising native opposition to numerous forms of oppression, bribery, and theft—they controlled the entire Indian subcontinent, including what later became Pakistan and Bangladesh. After some of the Indian troops employed by the English East India Company rebelled in 1857,[53] the British government relieved the company of its ruling authority; and, until 1947, India was governed as a British Royal Colony.

The British Raj (rule) built roads, railways, telegraph and telephone systems, factories, schools, universities, and a unifying bureaucracy; but the accompanying oppression and conflicts led to widespread political unrest and an increase in nationalistic sentiments among the Indians. The Indian National Congress was founded in 1885 to bring Hindus and Muslims together and to unify the country in opposition to the British. Many manifestations of hostility toward Britain followed.[54] Some Muslims, however, feared that an independent Hindu-ruled India would lead to the oppression of Muslims; so the Muslim League was formed in 1906 to oppose the Indian National Congress.[55]

Earlier in the nineteenth century, as the African slave trade declined, plantation owners in various parts of the world turned to India for replacement workers; hence Indian coolie laborers were sent to such places as the West Indies and Africa (Melendy 1977:184). Hawaiian sugar planters also considered the possibility of using Indian workers but, as we have seen, were able to recruit workers from China, Japan, Korea, and the Philippines. On the American mainland, however, Asian Indians were still needed to fill jobs for the railroads, in lumbering, and in agriculture; so during the first two decades of the twentieth century, almost 6,800 Asian Indians were admitted to the United States (see Table 12.4). A small group of these entrants were students who attended American universities and became vocal advocates of Indian independence (Melendy 1977:185).

Table 12.4   Asian Indian Immigration to
the United States, 1820–2000

Years	Number
1820	1
1821–1830	8
1831–1840	39
1841–1850	36
1851–1860	43
1861–1870	69
1871–1880	163
1881–1890	269
1891–1900	68
1901–1910	4,713
1911–1920	2,082
1921–1930	1,886
1931–1940	496
1941–1950	1,761
1951–1960	1,973
1961–1970	27,189
1971–1980	164,134
1981–1990	250,786
1991–2000	363,060
Total	818,776

Source: U.S. Immigration and Naturalization Ser-
vice, *Statistical Yearbook of the Immigration and
Naturalization Service, 1998,* 2000:20–22; U.S. Im-
migration and Naturalization Service, *Statistical
Yearbook of the Immigration and Naturalization
Service, 2000,* 2002:19–22.

Roots of the Asian Indian American Family and Community

As was true of the other Asian groups we have discussed, the Asian Indian immigrants were overwhelmingly men who initially intended to sojourn in America, make money, and return to their homes in India. Most of the immigrants were poor, illiterate farmers who in India had lived in crowded areas where making a living was very difficult. Some of these men also had previously served overseas in the British army or police forces and were unhappy with their lives after they returned to India; but these men had the advantage of being able to speak, read, and write English (Jensen 1980:298). All of these immigrants believed they could earn enough on the Pacific Coast to live well when they returned to India; so, using methods resembling the Chinese credit-ticket system, they headed for San Francisco and Vancouver, B. C. (Kitano and Daniels 2001:105; Melendy 1977:185–186).[56]

Since this first sizable group of Asian Indian immigrants reached America during a peak period of anti-Asian hysteria, they too suffered the same sort of hostility, discrimination, and humiliation faced by Chinese, Japanese, Korean, and Filipino immigrants.[57] Although the Indians had Caucasian features, their Asian origin, religious observances, dark skin, and exotic costumes (especially the turbans) marked them as beyond the acceptable limits for newcomers. Each of these traits became focal points of unfavorable criticism and attack. In addition to racial epithets, the Asian Indians were generally referred to as "Hindus" or "Hindoos" even though very few members of the initial group actually were Hindus.[58] These immigrants were overwhelmingly from the state of Punjab in northwest India.[59] Panjabi, not Hindi, was their main language. Approximately two-thirds of them were Sikhs,[60] and about one-third were Muslims (Sheth 2001:17; Takaki 1998:295).

The anti-Asian groups who clamored for the exclusion of all Asian immigrants added the Asian Indians to their list for specific abuse. Samuel Gompers, president of the American Federation of Labor, attacked the "Hindus," as well as the Chinese and Japanese, for undermining the standards of American laborers. The Asiatic Exclusion League stated that the "Hindoos" were "undesirable" because, among other charges, they were unclean and insolent to women, sentiments that were echoed in some official documents of California and the federal government. Physical, as well as verbal assaults, also occurred in Bellingham and Everett, Washington, near Portland, Oregon, and in the Sacramento Valley of California, among other places (Melendy 1977:192–195; Takaki 1998:296–297).

This campaign of vitriol and violence was rewarded by several governmental actions. Immigration officials increasingly denied Asian Indians admission to the United States; and when Congress created the "barred zone" in 1917, Asian Indians were named as a barred group (Takaki 1998:297). Moreover, when some Asian Indians were denied the right to become naturalized citizens of the United States and took their cases to court, they were rebuffed after a few successes. Some lower-court decisions held that since Asian Indians were Caucasians, they were also "white persons" and, on this basis, over 100 Asian Indians became naturalized citizens. Nevertheless, in *U.S. v Bhagat Singh Thind* (1923), the U.S. Supreme Court overturned these decisions. The Court reasoned that even though Asian Indians might be Caucasians they were not White within the meaning of the naturalization law of 1790 (Kitano and Daniels 2001:107; Takaki 1998:298–299).[61] Finally, the Immigration Act of 1924 stopped the further immigration of Asian Indian workers.[62]

As we have seen in our discussions of the other Asian immigrant groups, the effects of sojourning, an unbalanced ratio of the sexes, and official and unofficial discrimination combined to impede the formation of Asian Indian families and communities in America. The small number of Asian Indian immigrants and the transient nature of agricultural work prevented the development of permanent and distinctive Indiantowns; and under the Alien Land Laws, Asian Indians were prevented from buying and owning land. Moreover, there were virtually no Asian Indian women available as marriage partners to help found families. By 1914, according to various reports, there were as few as 12 and no more than 30 Asian Indian women in the United States.

In order to start families and circumvent the land laws, skilled and hardworking Punjabi farm workers—who were outstanding producers of rice, fruits, nuts, vegetables, and cotton—selected wives from other ethnic groups, particularly Latinas, and with their savings were able to buy or lease farmland (Sheth 2001:19; Takaki 1998:309–311).[63] The first Punjabi–Mexican marriage took place in the Imperial Valley in southern California in 1916; and, by 1949, around 300 Punjabi–Mexican families had been established in the area. Since the men in this community may have constituted as much as one-third of the total Asian Indian population of California, it is an important example of early Asian Indian family and community life in America (Leonard 1997:49–51).

The small Asian Indian community in the United States at this time was not totally confined to the West Coast. A few hundred educated, mainly Hindu, Asian Indians who left India mainly for political reasons lived in eastern and midwestern states. Most of these individuals vigorously advocated freedom for India; and the Sikh merchant J. J. Singh founded the India League of America to promote peaceful methods of gaining independence (Kitano and Daniels 2001:109). Indian nationalists also operated on the West Coast. Taraknath Das, a student at the University of Washington who soon became a U.S. citizen, published the newspaper *Free Hindustan;* and Har Dayal, a lecturer at Stanford University, founded the Hindu Association of the Pacific Coast. Dayal also joined Das, Ram Chandra, and others to found the revolutionary Ghadar (Mutiny) Party. The leaders included Sikhs, Muslims, and Hindus. During World War I, the U.S. government suspected the Ghadar party of plotting revolution, and 17 Asian Indians, including Ram Chandra, were arrested. Of these, 14 were convicted (Jensen 1980:298; Melendy 1977:210–211).

Following the *Thind* decision, officers of the federal and some state governments began an effort to rescind the U.S. citizenship that had already been granted to a number of Asian Indians and, also, to deprive them of lands they had purchased. In addition, some highly educated Asian Indian professionals were threatened with the loss of licenses and jobs. These actions led to numerous law suits and protests that, in some cases, succeeded in stopping the citizenship reversals (Melendy 1977:219–222). The discrimination suffered by Asian Indians, regardless of education or social standing in Indian society, encouraged the cause of Indian independence by weakening regional, linguistic, and caste lines among the Asian immigrants (Jensen 1980:298). During the period of the global Great Depression and World War II, the idea of American citizenship for Asian Indians gained support. In 1946, people from India received the right to become American citizens and, also, a small admissions quota (Kitano and Daniels 2001:110). During the interim between the end of World War II and the passage of the INAA, Asian Indian immigration began slowly to rise.

Asian Indian American Assimilation

Fewer than 14,000 Asian Indians came to the United States before 1960, and almost half of those came between 1900 and the establishment of the Asian "barred zone" in 1917. As late as 1965, the Asian Indian American population may have reached no more than 20,000 people (Sheth 2001:33). In the remaining years of the twentieth century, however, more than 800,000 additional Asian Indians entered the United States. Over one-third of that number arrived between 1991 and 2000.

Before the new immigration of Asians began, second- and third-generation Americans of Asian Indian ancestry had reached a high average level of cultural and secondary assimilation. To illustrate, in 1980 over one-half of the members of this group were college graduates, and their annual average household incomes exceeded the U.S. national average (Sheth 2001:31). Although the Asian Indian newcomers did not markedly alter these aspects of the picture, the contemporary portrait of Asian Indian Americans now reflects overwhelmingly the characteristics of the new immigrant population. The newcomers brought with them a high level of English language proficiency. Like Filipino immigrants, Asian Indian immigrants come from a society in which English is a commonly used language; and like Filipinos, over 90 percent of them report that they speak English well or very well (Yang 2002:388).

The secondary assimilation of the new Asian Indians also appears to be taking place rapidly. At least 55 percent of the members of this group hold a Bachelor's degree or higher; and around two-thirds of the Asian Indians employed in the United States hold professional, managerial, or white-collar jobs (Leonard 1997:79; Sheth 2001:31; Yang 2002:388). In addition, more Asian Indians have gone into business (Leonard 1997:83). By 2000, there was about one business owned by Asian Indians for every 10 members of the group. Probably the most widely noticed example of business success among Asian Indians has been the work of a group of entrepreneurs who came to America from the state of Gujarat. Starting with a small, leased hotel in San Francisco, a cohesive group of people named Patel,[64] with support from various segments of the Asian Indian American community, undertook the development of a motel/hotel chain that now extends throughout the United States (Sheth 2001:287–304).[65]

Given the English-language proficiency of Asian Indian Americans and the rapidity with which cultural and secondary assimilation appear to be taking place among them, one might expect the members of this group to be especially likely to marry outside their ethnic group. That expectation was not supported by Liang's and Ito's (1999:885) study of intermarriage. Although the level of out-marriage among the American-born Asian Indian men surely may be described as high (45 percent), comparable Korean and Filipino American men had still higher levels. Additionally, marrying outside the group was lower among American-born Asian Indian women (about 24 percent) than among any of the other groups analyzed in this study.

A similar placement of Asian Indian Americans among the four groups discussed in this chapter also was revealed by Yang's (2002:380) study of naturalization. Although each of the four groups had very high rates of naturalization when compared to all immigrants from Europe since 1970,[66] the Asian Indian Americans' level of 49 percent, though high, still ranked fourth among the four Asian groups.[67]

Findings from interview studies of second-generation immigrants show that balancing Asian Indian identity and American identity may create personal dilemmas for the individual. For instance, Levitt (2002:132–133) learned in interviews with Priti, a 27-year-old Asian Indian who had been in the United States for 20 years, that Priti felt she had led a "double life" as a child. While doing her best to "fit in" with her peers at school, she was surrounded at home by Indian family members and friends. When Priti was about age 14, her father joined the Swadhyay spiritual movement and required Priti to attend the youth meetings. Although at first she hated attending the meetings, she gradually came to value what she was learning and felt strengthened by it. She stated that she no longer cares about "... 'being brown' because I am a Swadhyayee. . . ." She now has traveled to India and is proud of her Indian heritage.

Some Additional Observations on Asian American Assimilation

We have examined various studies showing the rates at which the Chinese, Korean, Filipino, and Asian Indian American groups experienced cultural, secondary, marital, and identificational assimilation during the last third of the twentieth century.[68] The members of all four groups have moved with remarkable speed to adopt American culture, often by addition, and to enter into the mainstream of American society. The transformation of these groups from despised and hated foreigners during their early years in the United States to their present status as "model minorities" could not have occurred without substantial reductions in the anti-Asian prejudices and discriminatory actions and laws that existed in America prior to 1965.

Substantial reductions in prejudice and discrimination, however, do not mean that barriers to further assimilation among those who choose that option have disappeared. Asian Americans frequently write and speak about the many daily experiences that remind them of that fact. A common theme in personal reports is that, unlike European immigrants who are regarded as White, Asian Americans—no matter how American they may feel—still are identified by their phenotype and are frequently thought to be foreigners. Racial, not ethnic, identification often takes precedence as a regulator of their interactions with other Americans.[69] It seems to many Asian Americans that they may remain "forever foreigners" (Tuan 1998).

We cannot safely assume that the most significant current forms of anti-Asian prejudice and discrimination center primarily on signs of disrespect for, or misunderstanding of, Asian Americans by dominant-group members. Consider, for instance, the U.S. government's handling of an investigation of missing secret documents at the Los Alamos Laboratories. Dr. Wen Ho Lee, an American citizen of Chinese descent, was the only scientist to be investigated for espionage even though dozens of other scientists of European ancestry had had the same level of access to nuclear secrets as had Lee. When no evidence of spying was uncovered, Lee was charged with "mishandling classified information," a charge that had never been used before (Zia 2002:6). Recall, too, the violent attacks on Korean merchants in Los Angeles in 1992, discussed in a previous chapter. Asian Americans are well aware of the dangers of complacency in the face of such events; indeed, these concerns serve as stimulants for the pan-Asian ethnic movement and for active participation in conventional party politics.

Within this context, we briefly consider one further question of great practical, as well as theoretical, importance: Is the current level of anti-Asian prejudice and discrimination still high enough to prevent Asian Americans from receiving "equal pay for equal work?" A number of excellent sociological studies have concluded that the answer to that question is "yes." The central pertinent finding of many studies has been that even Asian Americans who were receiving pay that was equal to, or higher than, non-Hispanic Whites in the same jobs were still underpaid when their levels of education and experience were taken into account. The difference between what highly trained workers *ought* to receive, according to their qualifications, and the amount that they *actually* receive, even if that amount is relatively high, may plausibly be attributed to discrimination.

Iceland (1999) conducted a carefully designed and executed study to see whether the earlier findings were still valid. His study was based on a large, nationally representative sample that included employed Chinese, Korean, Filipino, and Asian Indian men and women, as well as a large comparison group of White men and women.[70] The study's findings present strong evidence that, at this time, it is no longer true that employed Asian American men and women typically suffer discrimination in the pay they receive for their work. Iceland did find that foreign-born Asian men were at a disadvantage and, further, that the amount of disadvantage varied according to the men's countries of origin. He emphasized, too, that since most of the Asian ancestry people in America today are foreign-born that the problem of discrimination toward them is a large and important one. Nevertheless, it now may be true that American-born people of Asian ancestry may invest in education and job training with the realistic expectation that they may look forward to receiving pay in the workplace that is in line with their qualifications. If this finding is confirmed, it is important evidence that the principle of achievement is not an empty ideal.

We note in closing that much of the information presented in this chapter concerns group averages. A full interpretation of these facts must focus also on the large numbers of people in these ethnic groups, even among the American-born, who still face serious problems of employment, acceptance, and social welfare in our society.

Chapter 13 briefly discusses Vietnamese Americans, a group originating in Southeast Asia, and Arab Americans, a group originating initially in the opposite corner of Asia, the Middle East. Although the Arab Americans have been represented in the U.S. population for a much longer period of time than have the Vietnamese Americans, the immigration of most members of each ethnic group was stimulated by European and American economic, political, and military activities in their homelands.

 Discussion Questions

How did European and American economic expansion during the nineteenth century contribute to the emigration to the United States of people from China, Korea, the Phillipines, and India?

How did incentives provided by American laws and businesses contribute to the decisions of people from the four countries discussed to come to the United States?

How were the Asian immigrants received in America during the nineteenth and early twentieth centuries? Has discrimination affected their upward mobility? How?

What factors impeded the formation of families among the Asian immigrants of the nineteenth and early twentieth centuries?

What are the social characteristics of the Asian immigrants of the second great immigrant stream and the third great immigrant stream and how are they different? Similar?

What are some of the reasons that the four groups discussed in this chapter may have been characterized as "model minorities?" What are the limitations of this characterization in regard to each of these groups?

 # Key Ideas

1. The global economic expansion of Europe and America during the nineteenth century contributed to disorder and unrest in the countries of the Far East and South Asia, stimulating emigration from China, Korea, the Philippines, and India. These emigrants went to many different countries, including the United States.

2. American businessmen in Hawaii and on the West Coast—especially sugar planters and railway owners—needed large numbers of low-wage workers. The efforts of the agents of those business groups helped recruit successive waves of Chinese, Korean, and Filipino workers. Some Asian Indians were also attracted, though the members of this group were not specifically recruited.

3. The members of each of the four groups discussed in this chapter encountered high levels of hostility, rejection, and violence in America. Anti-Chinese sentiment led to a generalized anti-Asian sentiment, and the legislative program of the supporters of Chinese exclusion was generalized to all Asian peoples.

4. The obstacles impeding the settlement of Asian people in America curtailed the growth of these populations. Each group declined in size between 1924 and World War II.

5. Changes in American immigration and naturalization laws affecting Asians between World War II and 1965 included the repeal of the Exclusion laws, the assignment of small immigration quotas, the extension of citizenship eligibility, and the admission over the quota limits of wives and family members.

6. In 1965, the INAA overhauled and liberalized America's immigration laws, setting into motion the Third Great Immigrant Stream. By 2000, this new immigration had exceeded in absolute numbers each of the previous two great streams.

7. The post-1965 Asian immigrants and their children are, as a whole, highly educated and skilled. They have moved rapidly toward the adoption of American

culture, by substitution and addition, and have enjoyed a high level of worldly success in work and business. The American-born segments of these populations are still, overall, smaller than the foreign-born segments; but the American-born have high rates of marital assimilation. The foreign-born members of these groups have high levels of naturalization and, presumably, identificational assimilation.

8. The rapid overall adaptation of the members of these groups to U.S. society has led each group to be called a "model minority." The critique of this concept as it applies to Japanese Americans, presented in Chapter 11, is also applicable in the case of Chinese, Korean, Filipino, and Asian Indian Americans.

Notes

1. The term *Asian American* has been used increasingly since the 1960s. It usually refers to "Everyone with origins east of Afghanistan" (Zhou and Gatewood 1999:8). Officially, it refers to anyone with origins in any one of 29 countries listed by the U.S. Census Bureau (Hurh 1998:137). Asian Indians are also referred to as East Indians.

2. Included under this rubric are immigrants from mainland China, Taiwan, Hong Kong, and people of Chinese ancestry from communities throughout the world.

3. The Burlingame Treaty permitted Chinese laborers to enter the United States with the same rights and protections as other aliens. The treaty was amended in 1880 to permit the United States to "regulate, limit, or suspend" but not "absolutely prohibit" the entrance of Chinese people (U.S. Immigration and Naturalization Service 1943).

4. Takaki (1998:85) states that "The construction of the Central Pacific Railroad line was a Chinese Achievement."

5. Among authors recounting these assaults and depredations are Crane and Larson ([1940] 1978:47); Daniels (1978); Daniels (1988:62–64); Karlin ([1940] 1978a), ([1954] 1978b); Locklear ([1960] 1978:244); Lynwood ([1961]1978); Tsai (1986:70–71).

6. Many of the immigrants were married, and they were expected to send money home for their family's support. The households of these men are often referred to as "mutilated" or "split" (Wong 1988:234).

7. Many of these laborers came from a single county (Tong 2000:24).

8. The CCBA was known informally as the Six Chinese Companies because the first CCBA, formed in San Francisco, consisted of six district associations (Kitano and Daniels 2001:28; Lai 1980:222).

9. Small Chinatowns were often dominated by a single clan (Daniels 1988:81; Kitano and Daniels 2001:27).

10. The main internal challenge to the authority and power of the CCBA within the Chinatowns were the secret societies (*tongs*). These societies were both criminal and political organizations (Daniels 1988:26; Lai 1980: 222).

11. The CACA was modeled after the White organization the Native Sons of the Golden West and originally was named the United Parlor of the Native Sons of the Golden State (NSGS). The name was changed in 1915 to permit an expansion to Boston, Chicago, Detroit and a number of other cities (Chung 1998:154–155).

12. One factor contributing to a rapid change in Chinese stereotypes was the acclaimed novels of Chinese life by Pearl S. Buck and the movies based on them (Kitano and Daniels 2001:39). Another factor was the popularity among Americans of Madame Chiang Kai-shek (Mei-ling), the Chinese leader's wife, who was fluent in English, a persuasive public speaker, and a graduate of Wellesley College (Taylor 1961:335).

13. The Citizens Committee to Repeal Chinese Exclusion was led by Richard J. Walsh, the husband of Pearl S. Buck. Chung (1998:176) cites a study by Fred W. Riggs that "attributes the repeal . . ." to the influence of this group.

14. Among the arguments presented for repeal were that it would strengthen the support of Chinese Americans for the war, combat Japanese propaganda that (correctly) claimed Chinese people in America were mistreated, help boost morale in China, and bring American practices into line with our professed beliefs. The opponents of repeal argued that we should not debate divisive issues during wartime and that it would lead to an "invasion" of Chinese workers.

15. China's quota was only 105 people per year. Anyone of Chinese descent was counted against the quota limit.

16. Kitano and Daniels (2001:42–43) report that during the period 1940–1946, nearly 16,000 Chinese Americans served in the U.S. armed forces.

17. Over 11,000 Chinese were admitted between 1945 and 1953. Of these, 90 percent were female (Kitano and Daniels 2001:42).

18. Chinese immigration rates have remained high, and the Chinese American population has continued to grow rapidly; but, by 2000, the foreign-born portion of this population of over 2.4 million had declined to about 45 percent (calculated from tables in U.S. Census Bureau 2001:24, 45).

19. Important exceptions to these generalizations include Yung Wing, the first Chinese graduate of an American college (Yale 1854), and Sun Yat-Sen, considered the founder of the Chinese Republic (Lai 1980:225).

20. There are wide differences among Chinese immigrants from the Mainland, Hong Kong, and Taiwan. The Taiwanese are the most highly educated, followed by those from Hong Kong, and then by those from the Mainland. The same ordering is found also among those holding professional jobs (Chen 1998:202; Zhou and Cai 2002:422).

21. Although the extent of transnational ties today greatly exceeds the earlier period of immigration, transnationalism is not a new phenomenon (see, e.g., Hsu 2000).

22. The comparable figures for Latinos and Black Americans were about 29 and 42 percent, respectively. These and subsequent figures concerning the number of businesses per capita were calculated from tables in U.S. Census Bureau (2001:24, 487).

23. Many Chinese have chosen to move into suburban areas, including largely Chinese suburban neighborhoods (Zhou and Cai 2002:423). This choice may promote residential assimilation and increase the chances, especially among children, of developing primary relationships with non-Chinese people outside of the home or workplace. Increasing primary assimilation may include marital assimilation and, also, stimulate other processes of assimilation.

24. The New York City Region includes areas of Connecticut and New Jersey. The data for this study were taken from a 5 percent, nationally representative public use microdata sample (PUMS) gathered in 1990 by the U.S. Census Bureau. Despite some shortcomings, these data are among the best available because they contain sufficiently large samples for the analysis of each Asian American group. They also contain a wide range of social and cultural variables that researchers may use to investigate many questions of interest.

25. Since the total number of foreign-born people within each ethnic group was greater than the total number of those who were American-born, the overall amount of out-marriage was much lower (15 percent) than among the American-born portion alone.

26. Another study, by Hwang, Saenz, and Aguirre (1997), focused on competing explanations of ethnic and gender variations in out-marriage but, also, presented some pertinent descriptive statistics. They found that for the entire country, Filipino and Asian Indian men were the most likely to marry outside their group and, among women, that Filipinas and Korean women were the most likely to marry outside their group.

27. This study was based on two sets of data, one from a special longitudinal study

conducted by the U.S. Immigration and Naturalization Service between 1977 and 1995 and another from the 1990 PUMS collected by the U.S. Census Bureau.

28. Many Koreans prefer to call this body of water either the East Sea or the Korean Sea.

29. From which Korea's present name derives. Many Koreans, however, believe the correct spelling is Corea.

30. During the Yi Dynasty, and also during ancient times, Korea was known as Choson.

31. Admiral Yi Sun-sin's naval victories included the use of his invention the "turtleboat"—the first ironclad ship (Wagner 2002:551).

32. Russian and American troops were withdrawn soon after North and South Korea were established (Hu 1961:296). When the North invaded the South in 1950, the United Nations asked its member countries to help South Korea. The United States and at least 15 other countries sent a large body of troops to join in the defense of the South.

33. In the United States, the order of Korean names is often reversed and, also, may be Anglicized. Rhee Syngman, thus, became Syngman Rhee; and Pak was called Young Man Park. Ahn Chang-ho is also known by the pseudonym Do-San. Rhee earned a doctorate from Princeton in 1910 and, in 1948, became South Korea's first president. Rhee and Pak Yong-man split over strategies to gain independence, with Rhee favoring education and diplomacy and Pak favoring a military solution (Takaki 1998:282). Ahn Chang-ho's approach resembled Rhee's (Kim 1980:603).

34. Even so, they sent money to their families in Korea when they could.

35. Because there was little out-marriage, approximately one-half of the Korean men remained bachelors (Hurh and Kim 1984:42–43).

36. In sharp contrast to the earlier period of immigration, Korean women now outnumber men, increasing the probability of out-marriage by women (Min 1988:216).

37. Pilipino is pronounced Filipino. It refers to both the people and the official language of the Philippines.

38. Posadas (1999) reports that about one-twelfth of the population presently are Islamic.

39. John Hay described this conflict as "a splendid little war" (Nasaw 2002:13).

40. Although American forces defeated Aguinaldo's forces, the Moros in the southern islands continued fighting for an additional 12 years (Melendy 1980:356).

41. Small Philippine communities had previously been established in the Louisiana bayou country and in New Orleans, possibly by Filipino sailors who left their ships (Melendy 1980:359; Posadas 1999:14).

42. In Hawaii, the situation was more favorable for family and community formation. The sex ratio there was much lower than on the mainland, and Filipino men were able to marry women from other non-White groups more easily (Melendy 1980:358).

43. For descriptions of an assault on Filipinos in Watsonville, California, see Melendy (1977:54–55); Posadas (1999:20), and Takaki (1998:327–328).

44. In the decade after 1965, Asia replaced Europe as the main source of professional immigration to the United States (Yu [1980]1998: 106).

45. English is an associate official language. There are 15 national languages and at least 800 languages and dialects, 30 of which have more than one-half million speakers. Both Indo-Iranian and Dravidian languages are spoken throughout the country, though Hindi is the main language; and nearly three-fourths of the population speaks some Indo-Iranian language. The main Dravidian languages are most often used within the Deccan (Jensen 1980:297; Thieme 2002:882).

46. The castes that developed, in order of their social importance, were the (1) Brahmans (priests), (2) Kshatriyas (warriors), (3) Vaisyas (merchants), and (4) Sudras (artisans, peasants). Below these castes were those having no caste, that is, the outcasts or "Untouchables" (Mayhew 1961:225). India's constitution now forbids discrimination on the basis of caste, but the movement to create equality and assimilation of Untouchables is still underway (Leonard 1997:7, 31–32).

47. Outstanding among these are the founder of Buddhism, Gautama Buddha (c. 500 B.C.); the founder of Jainism, Mahavira (c. 500 B.C.); and the founder of Sikhism, Guru Nanak (1469–1538). Buddhism was the leading religion of India for about a century, beginning with the reign of Asoka (273–232 B.C.). Hinduism is noted for its tolerance of diversity of thought and many of its precepts are present also in the reform religions.

48. Ghazni was a small state in eastern Afghanistan.

49. Mogul is often spelled Mughal. Both terms are derivatives of Mongol.

50. The term *East Indies* may be used in a wide sense to include India and all of Southeast Asia. More narrowly it refers to the islands of the Maylay Archipelego (van der Kroef 1961:22).

51. This was the conflict in which the English occupied New Amsterdam in America.

52. The American phase of this conflict was the French and Indian War.

53. The rebellion of the *Sepoys* (Indian soldiers in the Bengal Army) spread throughout northern India and lasted until 1859.

54. Despite the many legitimate grievances of the Indians against Britain, large numbers of Indians were loyal to the Empire. At the beginning of World War I, Gandhi urged his countrymen to support Britain, saying that "We are, above all, British citizens of the Great British Empire" (Ferguson 2003:23). Over 1 million Indians answered the call to arms.

55. When India and Pakistan became independent nations in 1947, the subcontinent was partitioned along religious lines with predominantly Hindu areas being allocated to India and predominantly Muslim areas being allocated to Pakistan. Pakistan's areas were on both the east and west sides of India; so the two provinces of East and West Pakistan were established as a single Muslim nation. Soon after the partition, violence erupted and millions of refugees fled India for Pakistan and vice versa; but many people of each religion remained in each country. In 1971, East Pakistan broke away from West Pakistan and became the new country of Bangladesh (Morse and Hendelson 1972a: 258–261).

56. The Asian Indians received hostile receptions in both the United States and Canada. A special problem for the Canadians was that both they and the Indians were subjects of the British Empire (Melendy 1977: 187–191).

57. Among the few who were received favorably was Swami Vivekananda, a Hindu guru who appeared unexpectedly at the Chicago World's Fair in 1893. According to Durant (1954:618), Vivekananda "captured everyone by his magnificent presence (and) his gospel of the unity of all religions. . . ." Melendy (1977:184) states that Vivekananda established societies for the study of Vedantic philosophy "throughout the United States."

58. The titles of two publications in 1910 were "The Tide of Turbans" and "The Hindu Invasion" (Sheth 2001:35).

59. A few of the immigrants were from Uttar Pradesh, Bengal, and Gujarat (Melendy 1977:185).

60. Sikhs are disciples of Guru Nanak whose religious doctrine of universal brotherhood is prominent in the Punjab region of India.

61. Thind had received citizenship after being drafted, serving, and being honorably discharged from the U.S. Army (Melendy 1977:218). The Court's decision in *Thind* narrowed still further the interpretation of the meaning of "White" given in *Ozawa* (1922).

62. Students and merchants were still permitted to enter.

63. A study by La Brack and Leonard of nearly 400 early Asian Indian families found that these marriages were not very successful (cited by Kitano and Daniels 2001:108). Sheth (2001:19) suggests that "cultural factors" were largely responsible for the problems in these marriages.

64. By 1994, Asian Indian Americans owned or leased some 20,000 motels and hotels. Gujaratis, such as the Patels, have a long history of entrepreneurial success. Gujaratis now comprise more than 40 percent of the Asian Indian American population (Sheth 2001:287, 307).

65. This mode of business development has been called the "Patel-motel model." About 10 percent of the members of the Asian American Hotel Owners' Association are Korean or Chinese. Of the remaining 90 percent, the majority are Gujaratis, and most of these are named Patel (Sheth 2001:287).

66. U.S. Immigration and Naturalization Service (2001:170).

67. The high rates of naturalization among Asian Americans are even more remarkable when we consider that the advantages of citizenship—as compared to those of permanent residency—have declined. Many social services are now open to people of both categories (Schneider 2001:188).

68. Some evidence suggests that the members of the new first generation of Asians who hold jobs in multiethnic settings generally work amicably with other Americans but socialize mainly with co-ethnics.

69. When Asian Americans meet non-Asian Americans and are asked "Where are you from?" the question is often asked with the expectation that the answer will be the name of a foreign country rather than some U.S. state or city.

70. This study was based on the 1990 5 percent PUMS of Asian Americans and, also, the one in 1,000 PUMS for non-Hispanic Whites. It is the most comprehensive study of this important issue to date.

Vietnamese Americans, Arab Americans, and Resurgent Racism

Global conflicts and turmoil have forced many people to flee their homelands and go to other countries, including the United States. Global conflicts also have fueled terrorism and racism. Here people protest stereotyping of Arab Americans.

It doesn't take much to become a refugee.
Your race or beliefs can be enough.
—UNCHR wall poster, Bangkok

Ethnic diversity is an opportunity, rather than a problem.
—Andrew M. Greeley

The American way of life is based on fairness, justice,
and liberty for all. All of these virtues are at risk. . . .
—Imad Hamad

The experiences of the Native Americans, African Americans, Mexican Americans, Asian Americans, and Puerto Rican Americans we have discussed reveal some of the social consequences of the main types of intergroup contact occurring at different periods in American history. Native Americans were subjected to the rule of Europeans and their descendants over a long period of time. African Americans were a part of the colonial immigration but, since the overwhelming majority came as slaves, they certainly did not enter the country voluntarily. The Mexican American ethnic group, initially created through conquest, has increased through voluntary immigration in the second and, especially, the third great immigrant streams. The Puerto Rican American group also was created through conquest, but its members have generally been American citizens before they reached the mainland. Even though each of the Asian American groups participated in various degrees to the second immigrant stream, their immigration was halted or severely restricted at various points. They were able to resume immigration after World War II and have been prominent members of the third great stream. The various sequences through which each of these groups has travelled to become a part of American society has played an important role in their members' tendencies to adopt or reject one or another of the ideologies of intergroup relations discussed in Chapter 2.

We turn in the present chapter to brief discussions of two additional American ethnic groups—first, to the Vietnamese Americans, who have emigrated from Southeast Asia and, second, to the Arab Americans, who have emigrated from the Middle East and North Africa. Vietnamese immigrants were not counted separately until after 1952; and, prior to 1971, only 4,675 Vietnamese had been admitted to the United States (see Table 13.1). As the United States became more deeply involved in the Vietnamese War between 1961 and 1970, the number of people who were driven from their homes and forced to flee rose dramatically. These refugees sought sanctuary in many countries, including the United States. Because of the circumstances of the war, a substantial effort was made to assist the Vietnamese refugees to adjust to American life. For that purpose, a number of analyses of their experiences were conducted, and these form the basis of our description of the early stages of Vietnamese American assimilation.[1]

TABLE 13.1   Vietnamese Immigration to the United States, 1951–2000

Years	Number
1951–1960	335
1961–1970	4,340
1971–1980	172,280
1981–1990	280,782
1991–2000	286,145
Total	744,422

Source: U.S. Immigration and Naturalization Service, *Statistical Yearbook of the U.S. Immigration and Naturalization Service, 1998*, 2000:20–22; U.S. Immigration and Naturalization Service, *Statistical Yearbook of the U.S. Immigration and Naturalization Service, 2000*, 2002:19–22

Refugees: An International Issue

The expulsion of people from their lands of residence is nothing new, of course; but the problems associated with international refugee movements have increased steadily since the seventeenth century. As the world became organized into nation-states and the human population skyrocketed, governments increasingly sought to control the composition of their populations by welcoming the members of some groups and driving out others. This tendency increased until, by the twentieth century, the problem of what to do with the rising number of refugees became an important international question. The "refugee problem" of the latter half of the twentieth century has been created by internal and international conflicts in which millions of people have fled from their homelands fearing for their lives. These people have sought to resettle in other countries primarily because they believed it was necessary to avoid execution, imprisonment, or persecution for political reasons rather than to improve their economic or religious opportunities.

Many people who were displaced by World War II or were refugees from communist countries were admitted to the United States under provisions of the Displaced Persons Act of 1948, which created 220,000 spaces above the immigration quotas for European victims of the ravages of the war. Additional numbers of nonquota immigrants were permitted under the Refugee Relief Act of 1953 (Abrams 1984:109). After the Hungarian Revolution of 1956, large numbers of the defeated anticommunist "freedom fighters" sought admission to the United States. President Eisenhower set a precedent by admitting thousands of Hungarians above Hungary's quota by granting them asylum under the "parole" authority (Reimers 1985:26).

The parole provision also was used by President John F. Kennedy in 1961 to allow the entry above the quota of the anticommunist Cuban refugees who fled following Fidel Castro's revolution (Reimers 1985:27). Additionally, following the failed Bay of Pigs invasion of Cuba, the Migration and Refugee Assistance Act of 1962 granted refugee status to resident Cubans and provided financial and other assistance to aid in their resettlement within the United States. During the remainder of the 1960s and throughout the 1970s, wars in Vietnam and other parts of Indochina created millions of new refugees who sought to establish new lives in other countries. The Refugee Act of 1980 aimed to establish a "systematic procedure for the admission and effective resettlement of refugees of special humanitarian concern to the United States" (U.S. Immigration and Naturalization Service 1996:A.1–18). Altogether, more than 780,000 Cubans and 725,000 Indochinese whose lives were disrupted by military and political upheavals have become a part of the population of the United States (Kitano and Daniels 1988:138; U.S. Immigration and Naturalization Service 1996:28). During the 1990s, wars in the former Soviet Union, Bosnia, Rwanda, and other locations throughout the world continued to displace people from their homes and create new refugees, many of whom have sought asylum in the United States.

The staggering increases in the numbers of refugees in the world and the efforts of displaced people to gain admission to the United States have generated serious tensions between Americans' desire to limit immigration, on the one hand, and the traditional idea that the United States is an asylum for oppressed people, on the other (Bernard 1980:495).[2] The periodic admission of refugees outside of the normal quota limits has left us uncertain whether such additional newcomers demonstrate, in Glazer's (1985:3) words, "our openness and generosity, or our simple incapacity to forge a national policy on the key question of who shall be allowed to become an American."

Vietnamese Americans

We noted that the third immigrant stream has contained a disproportionately large share of refugees. Thousands of Hungarian and Cuban refugees were admitted to the United States during the 1950s, but only 335 emigrants from Vietnam entered during that period (U.S. Immigration and Naturalization Service 1996:27). However, the situation changed noticeably between 1961 and 1970 as America became more deeply involved in the war in Vietnam; and it increased dramatically after 1975 when American participation in the war ended (see Table 13.1).

Vietnam's contact with the West began in the sixteenth century when Vietnam was an independent country. Three centuries later, in 1863, it became an unwilling colony of France (Montero 1979:16; Morse and Hendelson 1972a:262–263). Our previous discussions of the relationship between colonized minorities and dominant invaders would lead us to expect that the French invasion probably resulted in long-term conflict, and it did. Following World War I, two opposing groups of Vietnamese nationalists were organized, one communist and the other anticommunist; but both groups aimed to end foreign domination of Vietnam (Morse and Hendelson 1972a:263).

The Thirty Years War in Vietnam: 1945–1975

France lost control of Vietnam during World War II; but after the war, with U.S. and British support, the French came back. Eight years of bitter struggle led to the end of French rule and the Geneva Agreements of 1954 whereby Vietnam was partitioned into North and South Vietnam at the seventeenth parallel. People were allowed to choose whether they wished to live in the North or the South. In response, between 800,000 and 1 million Vietnamese (most of whom were Catholics) migrated from the North to the South (Kelly 1977:13; Morse and Hendelson 1972b:317).

After South Vietnam was established as a separate republic (with U.S. backing), a group called the National Liberation Front (the Vietcong) launched a guerrilla war within South Vietnam, supported by North Vietnam. As the United States continued to support South Vietnam, President Lyndon Johnson ordered a military buildup in 1963 that led the United States into a full-scale war with both the Vietcong and the regular military forces of North Vietnam (the Vietminh).

Although the war centered on Vietnam, it also included Cambodia (Kampuchea) and Laos. In the process, hundreds of thousands of people were uprooted. Rumbaut (1996:318) stated that in South Vietnam "about a third of the population was internally displaced during the war," in Laos "about a third of the Hmong population had been uprooted by combat," and in Cambodia "as many as a quarter of its people may have died." Villages became battlefields, and the residents fled to escape death or mutilation (Kelly 1977:13). In the United States, the combined effects of the civil rights protests, antiwar protests, and opposition to the protesters produced turmoil. In 1969, President Nixon began to withdraw U.S. troops. Nevertheless, U.S. participation in the war dragged on for another 6 years. It ended suddenly in 1975 when the South Vietnamese army collapsed within the space of a few weeks under the combined attacks of the Vietcong and Vietminh (Wright 1980:509).

The War and the Boat People

The fighting in Southeast Asia continued after the Americans left with increasing numbers of people searching for places of refuge. Communist governments were established in Vietnam and in Laos. The new Laotian government waged war against the Hmong people of the mountain regions and harassed the Chinese Laotians who dominated the merchant and professional occupations. As a result, thousands of Laotians fled to neighboring Thailand.

At the same time, an insurgent group in Cambodia toppled the American-backed Cambodian government. Cambodia had been heavily bombed by Americans during the early 1970s and hundreds of thousands of people had been driven from their homes. Now, on top of that tragedy, the new ruler of Cambodia, Pol Pot, instituted a shocking relocation and slaughter, which, in the words of Kitano and Daniels (1988:147), "ended with the murder of at least one million Cambodians by Cambodians and the forced relocation of many others." This carnage ranks among the leading disasters of human history. More than 100,000 Cambodians fled to Thailand and were joined later by an additional 150,000 Cambodians who were victims of famine. Most of these people were jammed into refugee camps that the Thai government had erected along the border (Strand and Jones 1985:19–21, 34).

Conditions in Vietnam were still very unsettled. The government of Vietnam was involved in the conflicts in Cambodia and Laos and also was engaged in border conflicts with China. In addition, Vietnam was pressing to restructure its economy along communist lines. As a part of the latter effort, large numbers of people who were engaged in private business or the professions (including many of the ethnic Chinese) were subjected to various reprisals[3]; consequently, tens of thousands of people were gripped by panic and fled from the country by sea in frail, untrustworthy boats.

Thousands of people had used small boats in 1975 to reach rescue vessels waiting off the coast of Vietnam. But this time there were no rescue vessels waiting, and the refugees were far from certain they would arrive safely at any destination. Many overloaded boats were swamped; the motors on many others failed at sea; and perhaps as many as 80 percent of the boats were attacked by pirates (Kitano and Daniels 1988:141). Even the refugees who succeeded in reaching land often were physically attacked, killed, or forced back to sea (St. Cartmail 1983:87–97).

There is no exact count of the Boat People. St. Cartmail (1983:89–90) estimated that by 1982, more than 493,000 people had arrived by boat in countries of first asylum. More than 200,000 more may have drowned or died of other causes in their attempt to find safety. Some 300,000 were accepted, temporarily, by Malaysia, Hong Kong, Indonesia, and Thailand. By 1981, at least 197,000 of the Boat People had been accepted by the United States (Strand and Jones 1985:9); but many thousands of other people were still awaiting new homes.

Roots of the Vietnamese American Family and Community

Refugee Resettlement.   Most of those coming to America during the 1960s were the wives and children of U.S. citizens; but as the end of the war approached, the U.S. government announced that some refugees from Vietnam would be evacuated and resettled in the United States. As the communist troops approached Saigon in April 1975, a hastily arranged and panicky evacuation of more than 60,000 Vietnamese was set into motion. Most refugees were flown to the Philippines and then to a holding center at Guam (Kelly 1977:30). Amidst the chaos of the evacuation, an additional 70,000 Vietnamese people left the country on their own initiative (Wright 1980:509). One way or another, approximately 130,000 refugees quickly reached U.S. territory. These were only the vanguard of the more than 2 million refugees who have fled from Vietnam, Cambodia, and Laos since then (Rumbaut 1996:316).

The United Nations High Commission for Refugees (UNHCR) mobilized to assist in solving the human problems generated by the crisis in Southeast Asia. Several countries agreed to accept refugees, but the countries that agreed to receive the largest number were those believed to be most responsible for the debacle—the United States and France. By 1992, more than 1 million Southeast Asian refugees "had been resettled in the United States, 750,000 in other Western countries" while many thousands were still in refugee camps in Asia (Rumbaut 1996:319).

The first refugees to reach the United States were admitted under the federal government's parole authority, which had been used earlier for Hungarian and Cuban refugees. The existing laws and authority were supplemented in 1975 by the Indochina Migration and Refugee Assistance Act, which provided funds to pay for the transportation and resettlement of the refugees. A permanent Refugee Resettlement Program was put into place in the Refugee Act of 1980.

President Gerald Ford assigned the responsibility for managing the evacuation to the Interagency Task Force for Indochinese Refugees (IATF). The IATF set up the initial receiving station at Guam and four mainland refugee camps in California (Camp Pendleton), Pennsylvania (Fort Indian Town Gap), Arkansas (Fort Chafee), and Florida (Eglin Air Force Base) to carry out the task of assisting the refugees to begin life anew in the United States. The main purpose of the camps was to assist the newcomers, in Kelly's (1977:2) phrase, to make "the transition from refugee to immigrant."

The Refugee Camps.   In the camps, the refugees received security interviews and physical examinations and were assigned to living quarters in a tent or barracks. Then they were registered with one of nine voluntary agencies that had contracted with the IATF to find individual or group sponsors who would "assume fiscal and personal responsibility for the refugee families for a period of up to two years" (Montero 1979:26). The average cost of resettling a family was around $5,600, most of which was borne by the refugees' sponsors (Montero 1979:24, 28).[4] For this reason, most refugees were sponsored by groups rather than by individual Americans.

The first of the four original mainland refugee centers, at Camp Pendleton, California, opened on April 29, 1975, the day before Saigon fell. By December of that year, approximately 130,000 people had been released from the reception centers into the United States. Over 121,000 of these had been matched with sponsors through the efforts of the voluntary agencies, while the remainder had been released after proving they did not require assistance (Strand and Jones 1985:33). The camps provided temporary shelter, food, clothing, and medical care for the refugees. They also provided childcare classes, college placement services, English language training, and instructions concerning how to handle some typical problems the refugees would encounter in their new home. Later on, the various sponsors of the refugees continued to provide life's necessities, help them find jobs, and enroll their children in schools (Kelly 1977:83–89; Montero 1979:27).

In this way, Vietnamese refugees were dispersed (though unevenly and in the face of some criticism) to every state in the United States. California received more than one-third of the refugees, while Texas, Pennsylvania, Louisiana, Virginia, Washington, and Florida (in that order) together received another one-third. The remaining refugees were scattered throughout the country, ranging from a few thousand in Illinois, New York, and Minnesota, to less than a hundred in Vermont and Wyoming (Montero 1979:8).

Has this massive program of evacuation and resettlement succeeded in enabling the Vietnamese to become established in America?

Vietnamese American Assimilation

Recall that among the most important factors that may influence the rate of assimilation for a particular group are its members' command of English, their educational levels, their work skills, the extent to which the group organizes along family and ethnic lines for mutual aid and support, and the economic conditions in the host society at the time the group arrives. Although all of these factors may come into play simultaneously, they represent different aspects of the assimilation process and will be more or less prominent at various times. Our very brief summary only illustrates the refugee's experiences and begins, as before, with cultural assimilation.

Cultural Assimilation.   The extent to which English is used and understood by the members of an immigrant group is the key indicator of the occurrence of cultural assimilation within the group. Immigrants need to know the language to communicate effectively with those around them, find and keep jobs, arrange for places to live, and, in general, negotiate their way through a new and strange society. The central questions to be raised here, then, are: How proficient were the Vietnamese refugees in the English language at the time of their arrival? To what extent has their level of English proficiency risen since then? Information concerning the Vietnamese refugees' command of English was gathered in several studies of differing scope. We draw on two of these to illustrate the main points.

The *first study*, by Montero (1979), described and analyzed a series of studies conducted under the sponsorship of the U.S. Department of Health, Education, and Welfare (HEW) following the opening of the four mainland resettlement camps in 1975. The HEW reports included data on the entire population of refugees who went through the camps between 1975 and 1977 and from five special surveys that were conducted to ascertain how well the refugees were adapting to American life.[5]

In four surveys, the participants were asked whether the members of their household could understand, speak, read, and write English "not at all," "some," or "well." For example, one survey[6] revealed that among the refugees who were released from the resettlement camps within a few months, around 18 percent said they could understand, speak, read, and write English "well"; another 9 percent said they could not do these things "at all."[7] It appears, therefore, that the majority of people between these extremes (roughly 73 percent) had "some" ability to understand, speak, read, and write English.

The English proficiency of the resettled Vietnamese apparently rose rapidly within the first 2 years after their arrival. Survey five, conducted in 1977, found that those reporting they could understand or speak English "well" had risen to 34 percent and those reporting they could read or write English "well" had risen to about 30 percent. At the same time, those saying they could not understand, speak, read, or write English "at all" had fallen to between 2 and 4 percent; hence, it seems that between one-fifth and one-third of the Vietnamese refugees who fled to the United States after the fall of Saigon either had a good command of English or rapidly acquired it.

The *second study,* conducted by Caplan, Whitmore, and Choy (1989:39), focused on two sample surveys of Boat People from Cambodia, Laos, and Vietnam. The sample contained 690 Vietnamese households in five locations within the United States.[8] The initial and current levels of the refugees' competence in English were assessed by using three measures of reading, speaking, and performance. The researchers found that in more than one-third of the Vietnamese households "the majority of adults knew at least some English when they arrived" (Caplan, Whitmore, and Choy 1989:31). By the time the interviews were conducted, there had been substantial improvements in the ability of the refugees to conduct their daily affairs in English.[9] Although the two studies we have cited concerning the English language skills of the Vietnamese are not strictly comparable, a cautious reading of the combined findings of these studies suggests that no less than one-third of the Vietnamese refugees, and possibly more, were fairly proficient in speaking English within 5 years of their arrival in the United States.

Secondary Structural Assimilation.   Our principal indicators of secondary assimilation among Vietnamese Americans are education, occupation, income, and residential segregation. We examine each of these briefly.

Information on the *educational level* of the Vietnamese refugees was gathered as a routine part of each person's induction into the resettlement camps. The general result of the statistics released by the federal government shows that "nearly 50 percent of the heads of household have at least a secondary school education, and more than 25 percent are college and university graduates." The average (median) educational level of the Vietnamese refugees by 1980 was approximately 14 years (Jiobu 1988a:92), which equaled the educational level of White Californians. Recall, however, that the refugees who arrived in the United States immediately following the evacuation in 1975 were more highly educated on average than the Boat People who came after 1978 (Caplan, Whitmore, and Choy 1989:24).

Of special interest in regard to educational assimilation, however, is the experience of the children of the refugees. Caplan, Whitmore, and Choy (1989:70) found that almost three-fourths of the Vietnamese refugees' children had overall grade point averages in the A or B grade range; and on the standardized California Achievement Test, over 60 percent scored in the top half. Zhou and Bankston (1998) found, in addition, that Vietnamese children who had a strong commitment to traditional values and a high level of participation in community activities were more likely than other children to receive high grades. These findings suggest that the secondary assimilation of the second generation should be comparatively rapid.

What *jobs* did the Vietnamese perform in their homeland? As one might expect of the members of the first wave, there was a strong representation of doctors, managers, and other professionals. Indeed, the largest single category was comprised of those who engaged in professional, technical, and managerial pursuits (24 percent) (Montero 1979:23). In this regard, the first-wave refugees compared favorably with the other main Asian groups and exceeded the level of White Americans (Barringer, Gardner, and Levin

1995:198–199). Montero (1979:43–44) showed that the employment rate among male heads of household rose from 68 to 95 percent between surveys one and five, while the employment rate among female heads of household rose from 51 to 93 percent. Caplan, Whitmore, and Choy (1989:53) found that unemployment declined rapidly from about 88 percent shortly after the refugees' arrival to about 28 percent after 40 months in the United States. These findings suggest rapid secondary assimilation.

Another point of note, which we already have encountered, is that the occupational talents and skills exercised by the refugees in their native land frequently did not carry over directly into the American setting. The fifth HEW survey, for instance, showed that although 95 percent of the male heads of household and 93 percent of the female heads of household had found some kind of employment, the kinds of jobs they held often were of lower pay and prestige than the jobs they had held in Vietnam (Montero 1979:38–44).[10] Moreover, refugees were consistently less likely to be in the labor force than were most Americans (Bach and Carroll-Seguin 1986:401).

It is not surprising, therefore, to find that the *incomes* of the Vietnamese were not as high as those of workers in many other groups and that they considered money problems to be of special importance. Strand and Jones (1985:134–135) reported that among 20 problem areas, the Vietnamese ranked "not enough money" as of greatest importance. Montero (1979:51) found that the annual median incomes of refugee households was about 70 percent that of the U.S. average. Barringer, Gardner, and Levin (1995:266) stated that the "Vietnamese consistently displayed incomes as low as, or lower than, blacks and Hispanics." By 1990, however, the labor force participation level of the Vietnamese was almost equal to that of the United States as a whole (Rumbaut 1996:324). It appears, therefore, that the Vietnamese have found a place in the American occupational structure and have achieved a fairly high level of economic self-sufficiency.[11]

The last of the four indicators of secondary assimilation under review is *residential assimilation*. As noted in Chapter 11, Jiobu (1988a:107–148) presented a thorough analysis of ethnic group residential assimilation. The main finding of this study for our present purpose is simply that the Vietnamese were highly segregated. Their average level of residential segregation was 76. For comparison, the level of the Japanese, was 46 (Jiobu 1988a:114).

Primary Structural Assimilation.   We noted previously that immigrant groups to America commonly have considered the welfare of the family to be more important than the freedom and development of the individual. Discussions of the Vietnamese have emphasized that the family is "an entity by itself, an irreducible value and the only way of life for the Vietnamese" (Phung thi Hanh, quoted by Haines 1988:3). This value has been apparent in the efforts made by the resettled Vietnamese to maintain contacts with family members and compatriots in other parts of the country. In many cases, they have moved from their initial locations to other places having larger Vietnamese populations, particularly to California. While family reunification provided the primary impetus for this migration, some of the movement has been stimulated by the efforts of Vietnamese leaders to help reorganize the community within the new social context (Kelly 1977:202). This regrouping to achieve family and community cohesion has resembled the earlier formation of ethnic enclaves by Chinese and Japanese immigrants of the late nineteenth and early twentieth centuries (Montero 1979:61) and of Cubans in the last half of the twentieth century.

The focus of the Vietnamese on the maintenance and reunification of their families and community, along with the great demands of cultural and secondary assimilation, presumably has left them with little time or inclination to establish and develop primary relationships with native Americans; but little systematic information concerning this process is available. The Vietnamese have associated closely with their resettlement sponsors, of course, and an unknown number of lasting friendships may have emerged from these relationships. The relationship between the American sponsors and the Vietnamese, however, was mainly one in which the dominant Americans were working to bring an end to the financial responsibilities of sponsorship (Kelly 1977:159). Such arrangements did not encourage the formation of the friendly, equalitarian types of relationships that we have described as primary.

Marital Assimilation.   Given the brief period of time the Vietnamese have been in the United States, the extent to which they arrived in family groups, and their apparently low level of primary assimilation, there is little reason to expect a high level of marital assimilation among them. It is true that many of the first Vietnamese to come to the United States during the 1960s were the spouses of Americans; but this group is now a very small proportion of the total Vietnamese American population. Our interest centers on how much out-marriage has occurred among the entire group.

Excellent evidence on this point comes from Jiobu's (1988a:159–162) analysis of 241,102 couples. Of the eight ethnic groups represented in this study,[12] the Vietnamese had a very low rate of intermarriage and the lowest rate observed in the comparisons. We conclude, therefore, that the rate of out-marriage among these refugees within the United States has been, so far, extremely low.

Conclusion.   The Vietnamese appear to be undergoing fairly rapid cultural assimilation. Their knowledge of the English language and of American society appears to have been high at the time they arrived (though much lower than that of the Filipinos and Asian Indians) and to have increased noticeably during their early years here. Moreover, their rates of naturalization are substantially higher than the average among all immigrants (58 versus 46 percent) and equal to the rate among Chinese immigrants (Yang 2002:380). Of special importance is that the children of the Boat People are reported to be succeeding very well in American schools (Caplan, Choy, and Whitmore 1992).

The high initial educational and occupational levels of the Vietnamese adults did not, however, prevent them from undergoing rapid downward mobility as they moved into American society; consequently, their income levels have been comparatively low. Residential segregation among the Vietnamese has been high despite the efforts of the American government to disperse them throughout the population. Indeed, the Vietnamese, like so many before them, have worked hard to construct their own distinctive communities and institutions; and they may have done this in the face of above-average levels of psychological distress and family conflict.[13] Primary and marital assimilation among the Vietnamese Americans appear still to be low.

On the basis of the available evidence—and despite the unquestionably unique experiences of this group of people—the Vietnamese appear to be following a sequence of adaptation to the American setting that will produce results resembling those found among the other Asian American groups we have considered.

The unfolding experience of the Vietnamese in America has much to teach us about the human meaning of immigration and adaptation to new circumstances. It invites us to examine the skills and resources of new immigrants, which we have done in a cursory fashion. The Vietnamese experience gives us an occasion to reflect on America's responsibilities to refugees from countries in which we have engaged in military conflict, such as Vietnam, and also on our willingness to continue to serve as a place of asylum for dispossessed people. These issues are brought to the forefront also by America's military involvement in the Middle East and the large number of people who have been displaced by wars in that region of the world.

Arab Americans[14]

At least 200 million Arabs now live in the Middle East and North Africa and constitute the center of "the Arab World." Although these millions share a language, a cultural heritage and, to a large extent, the religion of Islam,[15] they also live in many different countries, speak various arabic dialects, and adhere to differing interpretations of the Islamic faith. The countries of the Arab world contain numerous ethnically distinct peoples who adhere to other religions; and, although Islam began among the Arabs, by the end of the twentieth century fewer than one-half of the world's Muslims were Arabs (Russell 2003).

Arab civilization grew out of the lives and cultures of nomadic peoples who lived in the Arabian peninsula. The birth and life of the Arab prophet Muhammed, who was born in Mecca, led to the religious and political unification of Arabia and the expansion of Arab culture beyond the peninsula. Following a profound religious experience, Muhammed revealed the basic tenets and laws of a new religion, Islam, presented in written form as the Koran. Converts to the new religion accepted Muhammed as the final member of the line of prophets listed in the Bible. During the following century, Muhammed and his successors (*caliphs*) spread Muslim rule and Islam throughout the Near East but were tolerant of Judaism and Christianity within their subject populations. By 750 they had extended their control westward across North Africa to the Atlantic Ocean and eastward through Iran, initiating an efflorescence of Arab civilization and a five-hundred-year period of Arab rule (Naff 1980:128; Russell 2003).

European countries came into contact with the expanding Arab civilization through commerce, armed resistance to Arab conquest, and—in the case of the Crusades—religiously inspired counterattack. Since the Arabs at this time were more advanced in many arts and sciences than the Europeans, these contacts led to the diffusion of Arab learning among the scholars and peoples of Europe and laid the groundwork for the Renaissance.

From its formative years, Arab civilization faced internal challenges. Early schisms resulted in civil war and the establishment of two major sects of Islamic belief and practice—the Sunni and the Shi'a—as well as a number of minor sects and subsects (Naff 1985:23–24). Then, after 7 centuries of development and expansion, Turkish–Mongolian invaders, who previously had converted to Islam, supplanted the ruling Arabs and created the Ottoman Empire. This empire lasted until 1918, but during the final century of its rule, resentment of Turkish control rose among many Arab groups and fueled nationalism and the desire for independence.

In World War I the Central Powers, including Turkey, were defeated; and the Ottoman Empire was dismembered. The lands of the Middle East were reorganized, under the aegis of the League of Nations. The League created the Republic of Turkey and established the boundaries for several territories that were slated to become independent nations at some unspecified date in the future. Different Allied countries received mandates to supervise these territories until the League deemed each territory to be "ready" to become independent. The announced purpose of the League's plan was to prevent the victors from establishing permanent new colonies in the former territories of the defeated Central Powers. Nevertheless, the mandates clearly reflected the preexisting interests of the Allied Powers.

Consider the mandate France received to supervise the province known under the Ottoman government as Greater Syria. This area, which included the lands of Syria, Lebanon, and Palestine has long contained rival religious sects that have made war on one another. For example, in 1860, a massacre of Maronite Christians by members of the Islamic Druze sect led the French to invade Lebanon and force the Ottoman government to convert the area into an autonomous administrative district known as Mount Lebanon. France became Mount Lebanon's unofficial protector. During World War I, French and British troops occupied Greater Syria and, after Turkey's defeat, the League of Nations approved the French mandate of Mount Lebanon and Syria. After 24 years of Arab protests, and civil turbulence, French troops withdrew and Lebanon and Syria became separate independent countries.[16]

American involvement in Greater Syria during the nineteenth century came, in one form, through the work of American Protestant missionary groups. They established schools in both Mount Lebanon and Syria and, in 1866, founded the Syrian Protestant College. Another form of American involvement in Greater Syria came through labor recruitment, as both American employers and steamship companies encouraged emigration. Ten years after the Syrian Protestant College was founded, some Christian traders from Syria attended an American centennial celebration in Philadelphia and were enthusiastic about the economic opportunities that existed there. Their reports helped set into motion an emigrant stream from Mount Lebanon to America. The letters and return visits of the first immigrants confirmed that they had, indeed, found economic opportunities, leading others to follow the same path (Naff 1980:129–130).

The economic pull of America was not, however, the only reason for the Arab immigration. Deteriorating economic and social conditions in the Ottoman Empire during the nineteenth century provided strong incentives for many poor people to look elsewhere for opportunities to make a living; and they looked to South, as well as to North, America. Conflicts between Turkey and Russia created a massive flow of Muslim refugees out of the Crimea and the Balkans and into Turkey and Greater Syria. Among the effects of this population shift were that the Christians of Greater Syria, and particularly of

Mount Lebanon, became a minority, suffering losses of political power and income in the process. In addition, the opening of the Suez Canal in 1869 and the destruction of the Lebanese vineyards by disease added to the economic misery (Haddad 1984:301). In time, Eastern-rite Catholic Christians from Mount Lebanon, who were mainly Maronite, Greek (Eastern) Orthodox, and Melkite, comprised the overwhelming majority of the emigration (Naff 1985:2). However, there is disagreement concerning the proportion of the total that were Muslims.[17]

This first period of immigration of Arabs to America stretched from the late 1870s to the passage of the Immigration Quota Act of 1924.[18] During this period, Arabic-speaking immigrants were commonly referred to as "Syrians" regardless of their actual birthplaces. At first, the Syrians' sense of collective identity seldom extended beyond their village, tribe, or family, as was also true of many other American ethnic groups. Indeed, they often saw themselves as Maronite, Melkite, or Orthodox people, rather than as members of an ethnic group (Kayal 1973:411). Later, as many decided to remain in the new country, they accepted the term *Syrian* and gradually viewed themselves as Syrian Americans.

Roots of the Arab American Family and Community

During the early years, most of the Arab immigrants were unmarried men whose journeys frequently were financed by their families. Their main intention was to earn money to improve the circumstances of their families when they returned home, so we may say they were sojourners. Unlike the sojourning groups of Far Eastern Asians who also entered the United States at this time, however, the sex ratio among the Syrians did not remain so severely unbalanced for so long. Many of the Syrian men could, and did, return to their homes to bring wives and other family members back to America with them. Naff (1980:130) reports that between 1899 and 1915, women comprised about 47 percent of the Arab immigration; hence, within a comparatively short period of time, the members of this ethnic group were poised to establish families and move into the mainstream of American life. Also during this time, the immigration of Muslims increased, especially of Shi'a and Druze (Haddad 1984:102).

Since the Syrians were mainly Christians of a Caucasian racial type, government officials did not classify them as being ineligible for citizenship; and naturalization among them began as early as the 1880s. Nonetheless, Arabic speakers were a segment of the rising numbers of the second great immigrant stream and were viewed, along with Jews, Italians, and Slavs as "undesirables." To begin with, their skin color often raised the question of their racial classification. In addition, their language, dress, cuisine, modes of religious observance—all of the many cultural items that increase a group's visibility—were objects of ridicule. They were, in Samhan's (1987:13) words, ". . . qualified for nativist prejudice on every score. . . ." Moreover, many people assumed that these immigrants were enemies of Christianity despite the fact that most of them *were* Christians and the further fact that all of them were, as noted previously, from societies with histories of tolerance toward Christians (Suleiman and Abu-Laban 1989:5). Samhan

(1987:12) concluded that, even though the Arab immigrants of the early period were "victims of generalized racist attitudes and policies . . . ," the average level of discrimination against them was comparatively low and, therefore, "did not retard their assimilation . . ." nor promote a "unified ethnic identity."

During one period, however, Arabic speakers did face a serious threat to their opportunities—an attack on their right to become citizens. Since the highest levels of Syrian immigration came during the first decade of the twentieth century, Syrians too became targets of the virulent hatred of nativists for groups who originated in Asia. In 1909, the naturalization petition presented by C. J. Najour of New York was challenged on the ground that he was Asian rather than a "free white person" as required by the law. The Syrian community of New York joined together in the Association for Syrian Unity to support a rehearing. On appeal, the earlier decision was overturned; but rejections of petitions by Syrians continued, particularly in the South and Midwest (Naff 1985: 255–256).

A crucial case for Syrians was *Dow v. United States* in 1915. George Dow was described in a previous South Carolina case as a "Syrian of Asiatic birth" and was denied naturalization because Syrians, the judge said, "are not white" (Hassan 2002). On this ruling, a large segment of the Arabic-speaking population of America was mobilized in opposition. The Association for Syrian Unity sent a delegation to Washington, D.C. to present evidence favoring the continuation of naturalization for Syrians. Dow's denial of citizenship was reversed on appeal; but his experience had aroused, at least briefly, a sense of Arab identity that crossed traditional regional and religious lines (Bragdon 1989:84; Suleiman and Abu-Laban 1989:1–2).

By the 1920s, a second generation of Syrian Americans had been born, and assimilation among them was taking place "at every level" (Samhan 1987:15). Arab communities had developed all across America, but mainly in urban centers, and were modeled along the traditional community, family, and religious lines of the homeland. Although they possessed, on the average, a higher level of skills than other immigrants of the time, the principal type of work they adopted initially was "pack peddling," which Naff (1985:128) identified as "The most fundamental factor in the assimilation of Syrians in America . . . ," although many also chose to work in factories, mining, and agriculture. Syrian Muslims, for example, generally preferred to seek jobs building automobiles in Detroit or Toledo or to work in the steel mills of Pennsylvania. For many, however, peddling served the Syrians, as it has many other groups, as an entryway into the American economy, "as a stepping stone on the . . . path to success . . ." (Naff 1985:150). Peddling is hard work requiring thrift and long hours; but, among other advantages, it requires little in the way of training and equipment, the profits are usually satisfactory and, if it leads to an established business, many members of a family can play a role in the enterprise. In addition, those who live by peddling infrequently concentrate in large numbers in ethnic communities and seldom compete directly with natives for jobs. They are, therefore, less likely than others to arouse extreme levels of native hostility.

The first large Syrian community developed in New York City, and a second grew in Boston. The New York community served as a supply depot for a network of peddlers, many of whom arrived from the homeland with "a stock of carpets or other craftworks" to sell (Karpat 1985:180). They then fanned out all across the country. To illustrate, by

1910 there were over 1,000 Syrians living in at least 11 cities and towns of Texas (Bragdon 1989:87). As peddlers became established in different locations and saved some money, many enlarged and stabilized their businesses by setting up small stores and becoming retail merchants and suppliers for later Syrian immigrants. Whether by peddling or other forms of labor, Syrian American neighborhoods were founded in many different parts of America. Communities grew in Pennsylvania, Michigan, Alabama, California, North Dakota, Florida, and other states. The members of these communities established schools, churches (overwhelmingly Christian),[19] and formal organizations that served to foster social interactions among people in neighborhoods that were widely separated geographically (Bragdon 1989:90–93). A similar pattern of penetration, disperson, and settlement occurred in every region of the country within a strikingly short period of time; by the beginning of World War I, peddling among the Syrians had largely given way to stable businesses in settled communities.

During the years between 1924 and the end of World War II, few Arabs were admitted to the United States under the allotted quotas. By the onset of World War II, most Arab Americans were pursuing some ideal of assimilation into American society—whether it was Anglo conformity, the melting pot, or pluralism. As was true of the European immigrants of the second stream, they had not forgotten their cultural heritage. Their expressions of it, however, were increasingly limited to the home, church, and social gatherings of co-ethnics; and it was not transmitted systematically to their children. Given a continuation of this set of sociocultural conditions, it seems likely that the levels of prejudice and discrimination faced by Syrian Americans would have continued to decline and would today have been hardly distinguishable from that facing their European contemporaries. Indeed, it is possible that Syrian Americans, in Naff's (1985:330) words, "might have assimilated themselves out of existence." But transformations in both international and domestic relations greatly altered the social composition of the participants in the second period of Arab immigration to America, producing marked contrasts between them.

Arab Immigration between 1948 and 1965

Four main differences distinguished the first period of Arab immigration (up to 1948) from the second period (1948–1965):

1. The immigrants of the first period were primarily from the Mount Lebanon portion of Greater Syria, while the immigrants of the second period came from Arab countries all over the Middle East and North Africa.
2. The earlier immigrants generally had been poor and uneducated people, while the second period included a large proportion of highly educated and professional people.
3. The first-period immigrants were predominantly Christians, while the second period included a high proportion of Muslims.
4. The earlier immigrants favored small towns and villages, while the second-period immigrants favored large urban centers. (Nigem 1986:631–632; Orfalea 1988:140–141)

Some events contributing to the second period of Arab immigration occurred during the final years of the Ottoman Empire. As noted previously, European Jews were severely persecuted at that time, especially in Russia, and were emigrating in large numbers to other countries. In response to the persecutions, a Zionist plan to establish a Jewish homeland in Palestine gained increasing support[20] and was backed by Great Britain in the Balfour Declaration of 1917. In 1922, both the plan and the Balfour Declaration were adopted by the League of Nations. The indigenous Arabs felt increasingly threatened by rising Jewish immigration, and conflict between the two groups escalated. Following World War II, Jewish immigration to Palestine resumed, as did Jewish–Arab hostilities. In 1948, a United Nations plan to end the dispute failed.[21] The British then left Palestine, the Jews established Israel as an independent state, and the United States immediately recognized the new country.

Throughout the years between the two world wars (1918–1939), increasing numbers of Palestinian Arabs fled the violence in their homeland; and after Israel was established, the emigration of Palestinians increased sharply. Many of the emigrants went directly or indirectly to the United States.[22] During this second period of Arab emigration (1948–1965), Palestinians were a conspicuous, and perhaps the largest, component; but Arabs from a number of other countries—including many newly independent states (such as Egypt, Lebanon, and Syria)—also emigrated at this time. Many, if not most, of the Palestinian and other Arab immigrants were Muslims. During the period between the two world wars, Syrians had mainly centered on their lives in America, rather than on the politics of the homeland. Even though some Syrian Americans had given attention to the events in the Middle East, raised funds for Middle Eastern causes, and tried to influence the policies of the U.S. government, they were by 1948 highly assimilated. They did not, therefore, instantly view the Arab newcomers—so different from themselves in many ways—as co-ethnics.

The term *Arab American* had not yet come into use, and the former Syrians and the new Arab immigrants remained apart rather than combining in a new, reinvigorated, Arab community (Orfalea 1988:141). But the Arab immigration of the second period was reenforced and enlarged by the onset of a third, larger, post-1965 immigration. Additionally, further conflicts between Arabs and Israelis in the Middle East, as well as intra-Arab conflicts, encouraged the development of political consciousness and an international outlook among people of Arab ancestry, including many Syrian Americans. Moreover, the civil rights protests of the 1960s in America and the increased advocacy of pluralist ideologies of assimilation created a wider awareness of the duality of ethnic identity and the options that existed for people who considered themselves to be both Americans and members of a particular ethnic group.

Arab American Assimilation

The increase in Arab immigration after 1965 mirrored the general increase of the third great immigrant stream. The enlarged Arab immigration reflected not only the changes in America's immigration laws but also people's increasing dissatisfaction with life in their home countries. The Arab–Israeli War of 1967, the Lebanese Civil War of 1975, the

Israeli invasion of Lebanon in 1982, the long war between Iraq and Iran in the 1980s, and the ongoing Palestinian–Israeli conflict each triggered additional Arab emigration.

In general, the third-period Arab arrivals to the United States have continued and magnified, rather than altered, the main sociocultural traits of the second-period Arab immigrants. The third-period arrivals, like those of the second period, have been disproportionately highly educated people representing various countries throughout the Arab world; and the visibility of Arab Muslims has been heightened by the increasing migration of Muslims from both Arab countries and Islamic countries beyond the Arab world. For these reasons, the post-1965 immigration may be viewed as a continuation and intensification of the post-1948 immigration. These two periods have led to a greater variety in America of countries and cultures representing the Arab world, a large increase in the proportion of Muslims (from Arab lands and elsewhere), and a sharp rise in prejudice and discrimination directed toward Arab Americans and Muslims of all nationalities.

We have noted previously that the official statistics for Arab Americans are deemed by many scholars to be unreliable and, therefore, that different individuals and organization who study the social and economic characteristics of this population present different estimates.[23] For example, Nigem (1986:632) reported that, in the early 1980s, the estimates of various organizations and scholars indicated the total Arab American population to be between 1 and 3 million people; however, during the same period, the U.S. Census's count was only 660,000. Nigem (1986:632) also stated, however, that despite the shortcomings of official statistics (particularly undercounts), they still are an important source of information concerning the social characteristics of Arab Americans.

The Arab American population has always been a comparatively small American ethnic group; however, a study by Kulczycki and Lobo (2001:459) showed that between 1980 and 1990 the group increased 42 percent to more than 1 million people.[24] Moreover, in the authors' opinion, the actual number was almost certainly higher.[25] In 1990, the following ancestry groups comprised over 80 percent of the Arab American population: Lebanese, Syrian, Egyptian, Palestinian, Moroccan, and Jordanian. The Lebanese and Syrians, who were predominantly native-born, comprised almost 60 percent of the total. As in the past, Arab Americans were distributed across all regions of the country, though over one-half of them were concentrated in five states[26] and nearly one-third lived in three cities (Detroit/Dearborn, 8 percent; New York, 7 percent; Chicago, 4 percent).

By 2000, the Arab American population of Los Angeles may have surpassed that of Detroit and Dearborn; however, the Detroit/Dearborn Arab American community is still the focus of much scholarly and media attention. Some reasons for this focus are the community's age (over a century), its size (approximately 300,000), its mix of Arab-ancestry groups, its many Arab-owned businesses, and its mix of different Christian Arab and Muslim Arab groups (see, e.g., Abraham and Shryock 2000). In addition, many valuable studies and commentaries exist concerning a large number of other Arab communities in North America.[27]

Kulczycki and Lobo (2001:466) presented findings showing that Arab American cultural assimilation—especially among the native-born—had reached a high level.[28] For instance, native-born Arab Americans, when compared to all Americans, reported more frequently that they had a strong command of English; and there was evidence that English proficiency was increasing among recently arrived Arabs.[29] In regard to the use of a language other than English in the home (presumably Arabic), however, there was a large difference between the native- and foreign-born groups. Sixteen percent of the natives and 87 percent of the foreign-born said they used a language other than English at home.

Comparisons of educational levels produced strong evidence of secondary assimilation among Arab Americans. To illustrate, among adult Arab Americans who had received some education beyond the Bachelor's degree, the percent of Arab American men and women—both native- and foreign-born—exceeded the average of all American adult men and women. The average level for each group of women was lower than among their male counterparts, though among Arab Americans the native-born women ranked above the foreign-born, while the reverse was true among men.[30]

When the average (median) household incomes of Arab Americans were compared to those of American households in general, Kulczyki and Lobo (2001:468) found a more complex pattern. The household incomes of native-born Arab Americans were substantially higher than the American average, while those of the foreign-born were only slightly higher. In regard to the median earnings of individuals, both male and female Arab Americans reported higher earnings than the respective averages for all male and female Americans. In each comparison, men earned more than women; and the native-born Arab Americans earned more than the foreign-born. Nevertheless, comparisons of group difference in poverty rates showed that the native-born, but not the foreign-born, Arab Americans were less likely than the average to be living in poverty.[31]

Additional evidence of secondary assimilation was found in the analysis of occupations. Arab Americans, both native- and foreign-born and both men and women, are more likely to hold managerial and professional jobs than the average of all Americans. Specifically, native-born Arab American men are more likely to be managers and professionals than are foreign-born Arab American men, who, in turn, are more likely to hold such positions than the average of all American men. The same pattern of differences existed among the women; however, native-born Arab American women are much more likely than the average for women to hold such positions, while foreign-born Arab American women are only slightly above the average.[32]

In regard to marital assimilation, Elkholy (1988:443–444) stated that neither Christian nor Muslim Arabs consider intermarriage to be desirable but that resistance is greater among Muslims. Nevertheless, among native-born Arab Americans, over 80 percent have married out (Kulczyki and Lobo 2002:206), and Elkholy reported that since so many of the recent Muslims were unmarried when they arrived, about two-thirds of them have married-out. He noted, though, that community pressures and cultural differences do place special strains on such marriages. For those who wish to live as Muslims, though, the contemporary immigrants have a great advantage over the earlier Muslim arrivals. The earlier immigrants were placed in a largely Christian society in which there were no mosques or Islamic institutions. Even most of their coethnics were Christians. The post-1965 Muslim immigrants, however, may now be welcomed into a developed Muslim community in which they can live and, if they wish, effectively resist many aspects of assimilation (Abu-Laban 1989:56).

The main contemporary obstacle to Arab American identificational assimilation—as well as being a precipitating cause of prejudice and discrimination against them—lies in the political realm. We have noted that although the immigrants of the early period did encounter some prejudice and discrimination, including stereotyping and attacks on their right to naturalize, their assimilation prospects were not seriously impeded. The comparatively small size of the Syrian immigration, their wide dispersal across the country, and their principal mode of making a living made them a relatively invisible and nonthreatening minority. Even though they founded many ethnic associations and were well organized along religious lines, they were not strongly united ethnically across their many divisions.

The extent of the Syrians' interest in the increasing influence of Zionists in Palestine during this period is a subject of debate. The founding of an independent Israel, however, combined with the increasing immigration of Arabs to America from newly independent nations, greatly increased the visibility of the Arab Americans. These changes heightened their sense of Arab identity and, simultaneously, increased their desire to play a larger role in the formation of the U.S.'s foreign policy decisions.

Problems of discrimination against Arab Americans and of their identificational assimilation into American life became more salient in the decades following the Arab–Israeli war of 1967. As Arab countries increasingly used their oil as a bargaining tool and Islamic extremist groups reacted to Western support for Israel, the level of prejudice in the United States toward people of Arab ancestry rose. Negative images of Arabs that had long been present within American culture were reactivated and made explicit in interpersonal interactions and the remarks of some public officials.[33] The attention given by the U.S. government to politically active Arab Americans also rose. Operation Boulder, for example, was a "wide-scale, centrally-coordinated operation . . . to monitor the Arab community, and take measures to diminish their political effect" (Fischbach 1985:89). This federal operation, which began in 1972, was opposed by members of the Arab American community and was terminated in 1975. According to Fischbach (1985:90), not a single instance was found "of the violation of a U.S. law . . ." by an Arab American.[34] Nevertheless, in Samhan's (1987:17) opinion, Operation Boulder set a precedent for government intimidation of Arab American leaders and stamped them with a "stigma of complicity" in alleged "terrorism."[35]

The conflicts in the Middle East, the presence of many groups of new Arab and Muslim immigrants in America, the endemic xenophobia and nativism among Americans, and the increases in individual and official hostility toward the new immigrants helped stimulate efforts among Arab Americans to organize and unify. For example, in 1967 an influential segment of the Arab population founded the Association of Arab-American University Graduates (AAUG), with the purpose of speaking for the whole group and of serving as a source of information concerning the Arab view of the Palestinian question (Suleiman and Abu-Laban 1989:6). The publications of the AAUG have served for decades to help inform Americans about the Arab world.

Three other important national Arab American organizations formed during this time are the National Association of Arab Americans (NAAA), the American-Arab Anti-Discrimination Committee (ADC), and the Arab American Institute (AAI). Each of these organizations serves, with different emphases, to disseminate information about Arab Americans and to encourage political participation. For instance, the NAAA and ADC have worked to further Arab American interests in Congress and to fight discrimination. The AAI works to stimulate Arab American political participation by organizing Republican and Democratic clubs and by assisting Arab Americans who run for political office (Suleiman and Abu-Laban 1989:6). The combined effects of these organizations have been such that by 1988, Arab Americans were playing important roles in the presidential campaigns of both Democrats and Republicans. In 2003, the FBI created an Arab American Advisory Committee to improve relations between federal law enforcement officers and the Arab community (Arab American Institute 2003). In addition to national organizations, Arab Americans also have formed local organizations to increase the numbers of people who participate in electoral politics (Terry 1999).

During the 1980s, however, after several terrorist acts against Western targets were traced to extremist Islamic groups, both individual Americans and official agencies of the federal government were increasingly hostile toward Arabs and Muslims. The terrorist acts appeared to lend credence to stereotypes of Arabs and Muslims as dangerous and fanatical people and, thereby, to foster other Americans' suspicions about them (Akram 2002:67).[36] Individual discrimination, including the murder and bombing, of people who "looked Arab" increased; and the American government responded, in part, by increasing the level of surveillance of Arab Americans and the interrogation, arrest, and deportation of noncitizen Arabs and Muslims.

The levels of anti-Arab and anti-Muslim sentiment in the United States increased still further during the first Gulf War. In the months preceding Iraq's invasion of Kuwait in 1990, the ADC recorded five anti-Arab hate crimes. In the following 6 months, they recorded 86 instances in which Arab community organizations and businesses were bombed, vandalized, or destroyed (Akram 2002:67). When the Murrah Federal Building in Oklahoma City was destroyed by a bomb in 1995, killing 168 people, many citizens and police officials immediately assumed the attack was the work of Islamic terrorists. Through the process of guilt by association, the entire Arab and Muslim population fell under suspicion. According to one report, over 200 hate crimes were committed against Arab and Muslim Americans within the next three days (Public Broadcasting System 2003).

Arab Americans have reacted to the problems they have faced by becoming more organized, more conscious of their civil rights, and more experienced as participants in the American political system. Despite their increasing civic assimilation, however, anti-Arab hostility has been widely prevalent. Moreover, in addition to rising anti-Arab hostility, there also has been a rise of White supremacist organizations such as the Ku Klux Klan, the National Alliance, the Aryan Nations, the Christian Identity Movement, various "skinhead" groups, and literally hundreds of others. These groups espouse White supremacy and hatred toward all minorities and immigrants.

These sociocultural conditions caused some observers to wonder whether America had truly learned the lessons of the Japanese American internment in World War II.[37] Might we again use a national crisis as a pretext for condemning and persecuting an entire ethnic group? This question moved to the forefront in the aftermath of the tragic attacks on the World Trade Center and the Pentagon on September 11, 2001.

 # Resurgent Racism

We saw in previous chapters that native resistance to immigration rose as the volume of each of the first two great immigrant streams increased. During both periods, many natives feared the country was in danger of being "taken over" or "inundated" by "hordes" of foreigners. During the period of the first immigrant stream, nativists backed legal restrictions on the rights of the foreign-born, promoted anti-Catholic prejudice, and subscribed to the racist idea that the Irish were an inherently inferior people.

During the second stream, nativist xenophobia, bolstered by the White supremacy theories and arguments of scientific racism, led to the exclusion of Asians and the creation of immigration quotas aimed particularly at southern and eastern Europeans. Nativists feared the economic impact of the immigrants and were concerned that the country might not be able to absorb the newcomers.

As America's immigration policies after World War II permitted a renewal of immigration, we appeared to move toward a greater acceptance of newcomers. With the increasing and diversified immigrant flow of the third stream and the general social turbulence of the 1960s, however, ethnic awareness was heightened and the apprehension of natives began to rise. Public opinion polls conducted between the 1960s and 1990s showed a steady increase in the percentage of those who believed that immigration into the United States should be decreased (Mydans 1992:14). Hate crimes against the members of several minority groups increased during this period, and during the 1990s, hate crimes against some groups were reported to be at record levels. Many accounts revealed harassment, vandalism, and assaults aimed at Jews, Latinos, and various Asian groups. Although these incidents often involved attacks on minority-group members by majority-group members, many of them were instances in which members of minority groups attacked the members of other minority groups or members of the majority.

The Southern Poverty Law Center (2003:35–37), an organization that monitors hate group activity, reported that "academic racists, those who promote racial theories of intelligence and a return to the once discredited 'science' of eugenics" are doing well. Several foundations fund journals, such as *Occidental Quarterly* and *American Renaissance Magazine,* that publish nativist and racist material. The Southern Poverty Law Center identified over 700 active hate groups in the United States in 2002. The neo-Nazis, with 220 organizations, and the KKK, with 133 organizations, led the list of groups that promote marches, rallies, speeches, meetings, leafleting, the publication of racist material, or various criminal acts. California and Texas had the greatest numbers of active hate groups with 48 each in 2002.

Antiimmigrant groups have benefited from Americans' worries about foreign terrorism, and they have lobbied for closing U.S. national borders. Several vigilante groups have participated in roundups of illegal migrants in Arizona and allegedly have been associated with the murders of other immigrants as they attempted to cross the border. The Southern Poverty Law Center (2003:35) reported that a group called "The League of the South" described the terrorist attacks of September 11, 2001, as "the fruit of multiculturalism." The Southern Poverty Law Center also identified a growing number of active hate Internet Web sites (443 in 2002), some of which actively promote hate actions going beyond the publication of Internet material. In the wake of 9/11, David Duke, a KKK leader who in 1991 won 55 percent of the White vote in the gubernatorial race in Louisiana, appeared on the Arab satellite TV network and urged Christians and Muslims to work together against the Jewish archenemy. His actions prompted a protest by the U.S. Department of State (Southern Poverty Law Center 2003:59).

In the weeks following September 11, 2001, Arabs and Muslims (as well as people who resembled them) became the primary focus of xenophobic resentments. Consider a few of the many instances.[38] Within 10 days, at least three Arab or Muslim Americans were murdered in hate attacks; and within 9 weeks, the ADC had received over 600 reports of violent incidents and direct threats of violence. In several cities, Arabs and Muslims were forced to leave airplanes after they had cleared the security checkpoints and been seated. ADC recorded 60 such instances in which either other passengers or members of the plane's crew refused to fly if those "suspected" of being Arabs or Muslims remained on board.

Soon after the attack on New York's World Trade Center, the Islamic Institute of New York received a phone call threatening "to paint the streets with (Muslim) children's blood." A Lebanese American man who was searching for survivors in the rubble of the World Trade Center was cursed and told to "go back to your country." In Laramie, Wyoming, the members of a Muslim family were harassed outside a Wal-Mart store and were told to "go back to your country." A mosque in Denton, Texas, was firebombed; another in Cleveland, Ohio, was damaged when a car was driven into it. In Huntington, New York, a man attempted to run over a Pakistani woman in a parking lot. In Seattle, Washington, a man approached a mosque, doused a parked car with gasoline, and tried to shoot the car's owner.

The anger, though not the violence, directed toward Muslims and symbols of Islam was manifested also in the intensification of a movement among evangelical Christians to convert Muslims to Christianity and brand Islam as an "evil" faith. Minister Franklin Graham, for instance, was quoted as saying that Islam is "a very evil and wicked religion"; and Ministers Pat Robertson and Jerry Falwell have voiced other criticisms. According to Reverend Richard Cizik of the National Association of Evangelicals, a group representing 43,000 congregations, "Muslims have become the Modern-day equivalent" of Communism and, hence, of a new "Evil Empire" (cited in Goodstein 2003:A22). Most Christian denominations, however, responded to the 9/11 attacks by sponsoring various interfaith meetings and efforts to show solidarity with Arab and Muslim Americans.

Hate attacks following 9/11 were generalized to include any person whom the perpetrators in some way associated with Arabs and Muslims. For instance, in Richmond Hill, New York, an elderly Sikh man was beaten with a baseball bat. In San Diego, California, two men attacked a Sikh woman, shouting, "This is what you get for what you've done to us." Sikhs may have been targeted because of the men's turbans and beards. Two Spanish-speaking women in Los Angeles were attacked and told, "You foreigners caused all this trouble." In Minneapolis, Minnesota, three young men punched an Asian Indian woman in the stomach and told her, "This is what you people deserve." The National Asian Pacific American Legal Consortium (NAPALC) compared their records of past violence against Asian Americans with the number of attacks occurring during the first 3 months after 9/11 and found that the rate of hate crimes against Asian and Pacific Island peoples had approximately doubled.[39]

These incidents suggest something of the character and extent of the backlash in interpersonal relations that erupted nationwide in the days and months following the tragedies of 9/11. A more general view of the reaction was suggested by an ABCNews/ *Washington Post* poll (American Broadcasting System September 13, 2001). The results showed that a sizable minority of the respondents (43 percent) were "personally more suspicious" of people who looked Arab or Muslim than they had been before. Another poll conducted by Zogby International (2001) among Arab Americans a month after 9/11 found that nearly one-half of the respondents knew "someone of Arab ethnicity or Arab-speaking background who (had) experienced discrimination since the September 11 attacks."

The violent attacks we have described occurred despite an energetic effort by Arab and Muslim Americans to demonstrate their patriotism and loyalty to America and despite some timely efforts by federal and local officials to prevent such attacks. Arab and Muslim American organizations moved quickly to condemn the 9/11 attacks and to make clear that Arab Americans also had lost relatives and friends in the attacks. They joined all other Americans in mourning and stated their hope that those responsible for the attacks would be found and held responsible. They also urged their fellow Americans, as stated in an AAI press release on 9/11, not to "rush to judgment" and place collective blame on any ethnic or religious community (Arab American Institute 2002:2). Similar statements were issued by the Coalition of Chicago Arab Organizations, by Arab American and American Muslim leaders meeting in Washington, D.C., and by the ADC. In addition to their own grief and expressions of solidarity with other Americans, Arab American police officers, firefighters, and members of the national guard were among those who were at work in the rescue efforts at Ground Zero in New York. Still further, Arab and Muslim groups throughout the country donated hundreds of thousands of dollars to the Red Cross Disaster Relief Fund, the Twin Towers Relief Fund, and other groups engaged in bringing help to those most directly affected by the attacks (Arab American Institute 2002:2–5).

The actions of federal and local officials to prevent violence, reported by the Arab American Institute (2002:6–8), included the following: On September 12, 2001, the U.S. Congress adopted a resolution stating "that the civil rights and civil liberties of all Americans . . . should be protected" and condeming "any acts of violence or discrimination against any Americans. . . ." President George W. Bush reminded the nation that Arab and Muslim Americans also love their country and deserve to be treated with respect. Robert Mueller, the Director of the FBI, stated on September 17 that the FBI already had "initiated 40 hate crime investigations" concerning attacks on Arab Americans and their institutions. In addition, mosques and Islamic centers in several cities were given 24-hour police protection. Although it is not possible to know the exact effects of these official efforts to curb the backlash, Ibish (2003) reported that about 9 weeks after 9/11 the rate of individual attacks against Arab and Muslim people "declined rapidly." Ibish also expressed the opinion that the swift and reassuring actions of the president and other officials may well have prevented even more violence. He added, however, that there was a sharp rise in the firing of Arab workers and that the level of employment discrimination remained high.

The attacks—primarily on Arabs and Muslims, but also on Asians, Latinos, and others—showed that racism and xenophobia remain alive and could surge in a crisis situation.[40] At the same time, however, there was an outpouring of sympathy and concern for Arab and Muslim Americans. Many American individuals and groups found ways to express their support, including posting signs in their yards urging tolerance toward Arab and Muslim Americans and conveying their sentiments directly through phone calls and e-mail messages. In one instance, the congregations of a mosque and a synagogue in Albuquerque, New Mexico, organized a peace pilgrimage. Eight hundred participants walked over 6 miles through downtown Albuquerque praying and chanting "peace and unity," while displaying signs saying "Salam and Shalom" (Public Broadcasting System 2003).

Federal officials also issued statements asking all Americans to draw a clear distinction between assigning collective and individual guilt—between blaming the many patriotic Arab and Muslim Americans who were in no way connected to the 9/11 attacks and the few Arab Muslims who actually were responsible for them. Nonetheless, several subsequent official actions, such as the mass interrogations of young Arab men, strongly suggested that the government assumed Arab and Muslim Americans were "by definition, suspicious and possibly dangerous" (Hamad 2001). Such actions also aroused the fears of many people that America's democratic institutions might fail in this crisis to protect the civil rights not only of the Arab and Muslim minorities, but of all other Americans as well.

Two leading sources of concern have been the effects of the USA Patriot Act of 2001, which was passed "to deter and punish terrorist acts" in the United States and elsewhere, and various administrative policy changes. The USA Patriot Act grants law enforcement officers broad new powers to detain noncitizens indefinitely without due process and, also, reduces the standards that officers must meet to conduct searches, seizures, and surveillance. The main concern in the area of administrative policy has been that the government may try accused people in military tribunals, deny them counsel, hold them incommunicado and indefinitely, and eavesdrop on client–attorney communications (American-Arab Anti-Discrimination Committee 2002).

Whether these changes in laws and policies actually increase the nation's ability to fight terrorism and, therefore, increase collective safety or are themselves the more serious threats to American liberty are hotly debated questions. Most Americans probably accept that in times of great peril some special powers must temporarily be granted to government officials. When specific racial or ethnic groups are targeted for scrutiny, however, the danger is great that official actions may reflect the racism that has accompanied the development of our country since its very founding. Many people believed in 1942 that the Japanese internment was a matter of "military necessity," but this rationale was later revealed to be only a thin veil covering the interlocking assumptions of racist and nativist thought. Great care must be exercised in the present crisis to prevent "national security" from also acting as a veil for discrimination and, once again, propelling our country into "the ugly abyss of racism."[41]

 Reality Check

INTERVIEW WITH THU

Thu is a freshman college student. Her parents are Vietnamese refugees but Thu and her sister were born in the United States. Her grandfather was a political leader in Vietnam and fled with his family when the war ended. Thu's parents both have a college education. She grew up in a small Gulf Coast town in which many of the Vietnamese refugees work as shrimp fishermen.

How do you refer to yourself in terms of racial or ethnic identity?
Asian American. As I've grown up I really didn't have that many Vietnamese friends. I use Asian because it's more general. There are a lot of groups like Chinese and Japanese and it's just more of a general name.

How does your ethnic background affect your daily life?
I don't think it has a huge impact on my daily life because I'm a student. You go to school, you come home and eat. You study. That's basically our routine. Other than the student organizations you join, I don't really think that my background has much of an impact on my daily life. My grandfather had to leave Vietnam because if he didn't leave the next day then they were going to be killed and they had no other choice but to leave.

When did you first become aware of your ethnic or racial background?
In daycare you really don't notice those differences. I would say elementary. In the school I went to, everybody was a minority. There was a small population of Caucasians but everybody else was African American, Mexican. Just me and another guy were the only Asian people. I knew that there was a difference but it never really mattered because we were all friends. I transferred to another school that was a majority Caucasian and I kind of felt like I didn't really belong, although I never had any problems making friends. I adjusted but I was scared about it.

Have you ever experienced an uncomfortable situation because you were Vietnamese?
There wasn't anything major. Whenever I go to Vietnam, it seems like I don't fit into the Vietnamese population there either. I was raised differently. I went to a different school and the way I talk, who my friends are, it just seemed like I was totally different from the other Vietnamese. I never really felt like I fit in with the Vietnamese people. But then I didn't really fit in with American people.

How do you family members identify themselves?
I guess my sister would say Asian or American. I think my parents, however would say that they are Vietnamese. My sister graduated last December as a social worker. All through college, she's always been doing Asian things. I think one of the reasons she became a social worker was to help the Vietnamese population. My sister

is the really active one in Asian issues and I talk to her about our identity. Most of the conversations I've had are with her.

Tell me about your friends.
I have a few friends who are American and a few who are Mexican. I think the majority are Vietnamese basically because I've joined the Vietnamese Student Association and we do activities together. I've never had Vietnamese friends, so I thought it would be beneficial because it would be easier to make friends and I would get to know more about my culture.

Is marriage or a romantic relationship with someone outside your ethnic group acceptable?
Right now my sister is dating a Caucasian guy. I dated outside of my race and generally my mom had problems with me dating period. It's not about race but any guy period. I don't think it's a major problem because I have another cousin who is married to a White guy. I think it would be nice to marry a Vietnamese person but you never know.

Did you speak a language other than English when you first went to school?
My mom and dad would talk to me in Vietnamese but I would respond to them in English. I can understand Vietnamese but I have problems answering. I can't read or write Vietnamese. I could read but not tell you what I'm reading. I can just sound words out and don't know their meaning. Basically it was just English. My mom and dad know French.

Tell me about your high school.
It was a small town and there wasn't a very big population of Asians. It was predominantly Caucasian and then Vietnamese and Mexican American and then Mexican and then Indian. Lately there has been more Vietnamese and more minorities coming into the school. As time passes, it will be more like that. I hung out with American people, but I knew I was Vietnamese. I knew I was a minority but I had American friends.

Discussion Questions

How did the refugee status of the Vietnamese affect their entrance into American society?

How would you describe the level of assimilation of the Vietnamese at the present time? What is your forecast for their future?

In what ways did Thu's family's status as refugees affect her incorporation into American society?

Why does Thu believe her ethnic background has little impact on her daily life? Are there structural factors that she is not aware of that may affect her opportunities to succeed?

What are the major differences between the Arab immigrants who came during their first period of immigration (1870s–1920s) and those who have come since 1948?

Among the major differences between the Arab immigrants of the pre- and post-1948 periods, which differences have had the most significant effects on their reception by Americans?

How have these differences affected the course of the immigrants' assimilation into American society?

How would you compare the resurgence of racism in the United States since about 1980 with the racism of the period between 1880 and 1924?

What are the long-range effects of 9/11 on American racism?

 # Key Ideas

1. The Vietnamese have been an especially visible refugee group, both because they were the largest refugee group of the twentieth century and because of the U.S. military involvement in Vietnam leading up to the flight of the refugees.

2. Although the war in Southeast Asia was centered in Vietnam, hundreds of thousands of people in Cambodia and Laos were displaced by fighting and were forced to flee to neighboring countries. Many of these refugees later came to the United States from their countries of first refuge.

3. The sudden emigration of the Vietnamese combined with the U.S. government's resettlement program created a unique immigration experience for this group's people.

4. The cultural assimilation of the Vietnamese immigrants appears to have taken place rapidly. The secondary assimilation of the first generation has been difficult, though fairly successful; and that of the second generation has been highly successful. Primary and marital assimilation appear to be low.

5. The first period of Arab immigration to America consisted primarily of Christians from present-day Lebanon. These immigrants were called "Syrians" regardless of their actual land of origin. Although the "Syrians" at first identified themselves in terms of their religious group affiliations, they accepted "Syrian" as a group identifier.

6. The Arab immigrants of the post-1948 period differ from the earlier immigrants in a number of ways: They are more highly educated, more skilled, more likely to come from countries throughout the Arab World, and more likely to be Muslims.

7. The diversity of the new Arab immigrants and the involvement of the United States in Middle Eastern affairs have increased the level of hostility toward Arab and Muslim peoples—both among individual Americans and by the American government.

8. Arab Americans responded to hostility by establishing several national organizations that seek to promote group unity, help inform other Americans about Arab American life, combat discrimination, and encourage political participation.

9. A sharp increase in the number of assaults against the members of various racial and ethnic groups occurred during the last two decades. At the same time, White supremacist organizations proliferated. These groups established strong links with other groups who expressed anger over immigration policies or who organized "patriotic" militia groups that promoted hatred or "race war."

10. The terrorist attacks of September 11, 2001, focused racist sentiments in America on Arab Americans and people who may be mistaken for Arabs, especially Asian and Latin Americans. Interpersonal violence escalated in the immediate post-9/11 period but subsided within a few weeks. Employment discrimination and government scrutiny of Arab men continued.

 Notes

1. Rumbaut (1996:320) stated that "the 1975 refugees . . . may be the most closely studied arrival cohort in U.S. history."

2. This tension was illustrated also in a pathetic incident, known as "the Voyage of the Damned." Over 900 Jews attempted to escape from Germany in 1939 aboard a cruise ship bound for Havana. After the ship was denied permission to dock in Havana, it attempted to land in Florida. The United States enforced its quota law, and the ship returned to Germany. Most of the Jews on board lost their lives in Nazi concentration camps.

3. For example, "reeducation programs," confiscations of property, and conscriptions to forced labor.

4. These grants provided $2,500 or more to assist in the resettlement of most families (Kelly 1977:133).

5. The sample surveys were conducted in five waves by telephone with random samples of Vietnamese household heads in various American communities (Montero 1979:33–55). The household heads reported information on all of the members of their households (Montero 1979:35).

6. This was the second survey. It was based on interviews of a national probability sample "of all refugees who had left the camps on or before October 15, 1975" (Montero 1979:35).

7. Calculated from Table 4.6 in Montero (1979:48).

8. The five locations were Boston, Chicago, Houston, Orange County (California), and Seattle.

9. For example, the percent of refugees who felt able to use English to shop for food rose from 32 to 92 percent and to be a salesperson

rose from 6 to 23 percent (Caplan, Whitmore, and Choy 1989:220).

10. Vietnamese workers were substantially less likely than Filipino, Chinese, Korean, and Japanese workers to hold the types of jobs held by White workers (Jiobu 1988a:87).

11. Caplan, Whitmore, and Choy (1989:77) found that "arrival English" played a very important role in economic advancement.

12. The eight groups were: Black, Chinese, Filipino, Japanese, Korean, Mexican, Vietnamese, and White.

13. Studies focusing on the psychological and interpersonal consequences for the Vietnamese created by the shock of a rapid, unplanned entry into the United States and a sharp downturn in economic standing have found widespread psychological distress, depression, and marital conflict among the refugees (see, e.g., Rumbaut 1996:328–330).

14. *Arab Americans* refers to people whose origins lie in any of the 22 countries comprising the contemporary League of Arab States (the Arab League). The extent to which the people from these different countries accept or use the panethnic identifier, Arab Americans, is highly variable.

15. *Islam* means submission to one God. Muslims, like Jews and Christians, are monotheists.

16. Britain received a mandate to supervise the territories of Iraq and Palestine. The British already had commercial interests in the region, including concessions to develop oil fields in Iraq. During World War I, Britain gained Arab support for Allied military operations against Turkish forces with a promise that the Arabs would be granted independence at the end of the war, and, by 1918, British forces occupied all of Mesopotamia. The British mandate led to a troubled military occupation. Iraq was established as an independent monarchy in 1932, and Israel was established as a republic in 1948.

17. Karpat (1985:177–183) argued that many more Muslims came to America than is usually supposed, comprising possibly 15 to 20 percent of the total. Some pretended to be Christians to decrease hostility toward them

and, also, to deceive Ottoman authorities. Naff (1985:112) stated, in contrast, that 90 to 95 percent were Christians who came from Mount Lebanon, while the remainder were Sunni or Shi'a Muslims, while a few were Druze.

18. Systematic data distinguishing the various Arab countries of today were not gathered until 1979 (Nigem 1986:630). Until after 1924 separate immigration records for Syria were not kept (U.S. Bureau of the Census 1961:58); and all Arabs were recorded, along with some others, as being from "Turkey in Asia" (Karpat 1985:181; Naff 1980:128). Most estimates place the number of Arab immigrants before 1924 at between 200,000 and 250,000 people.

19. Elkholy (1988:438) stated that at the beginning of World War II, Christians outnumbered Muslims nine to one. The first Muslim mosque probably was not built before the 1920s or 1930s (Haddad 1984:103; Orfalea 1988:95). By 2003, there were around 130 mosques in New York City alone.

20. There have been many shades of Zionist opinion. While some advocates sought only a homeland, others sought an independent state.

21. In 1939, Britain adopted a policy intended to limit the Jewish population of Palestine to make it a permanent minority, but many Jews entered Palestine in defiance of the policy. In 1947, the United Nations voted to partition Palestine into two independent states, but the Arabs rejected the plan.

22. Official U.S. statistics show that 4,806 Palestinians were admitted between 1948 and 1967, but nearly all observers agree this is an undercount. Orfalea (1988:140) estimated that altogether 750,000 Palestinians were displaced from their homes. He stated that "tens of thousands more immigrated [to the United States] from other lands of first refuge" and noted the irony of people immigrating "to the country that most supported" their eviction.

23. There are no official statistics on the number of Arab Americans who are Muslims nor on the number of American Muslims. Kulczyki and Lobo (2001:462) cite estimates stating that, by 1980, less than one-half of the Arab

Americans were Muslims and that, by 2000, there may have been 5.5 million American Muslims. Kang (2001:46), on the other hand, presents a "ball park" figure of "at least 10 million" Muslims. Most foreign-born American Muslims are from Iran, Turkey, Pakistan, and India. In addition, there is a large and growing population of Black American Muslims.

24. In 2000, the U.S. Census found that the Arab American population exceeded 1.2 million people (U.S. Census Bureau 2000).

25. The U.S. Census Bureau collected ancestry information on Arab Americans for the first time in a Current Population Survey in 1979. Nigem (1986) presented analyses based on U.S. Census data for 1980 and, also, for 1979. Kulczycki and Lobo (2001) compared U.S. Census data on Arab Americans for 1980 and 1990. Their data were drawn from the 5 percent PUMS samples for both years. They defined as "Arab" anyone who chose an Arab state (either first or second) as their place of ancestry or said they were born in an Arab state. No study of Arab Americans comparable to Kulczyki and Lobo's (2001) that uses data for 2000 is yet available.

26. These are: California, New York, Michigan, Florida, and New Jersey.

27. See, e.g., Abu-Laban and Suleiman (1989); Hooglund (1985); Orfalea (1988: 224–311); Suleiman (1999); and Zogby (1984).

28. All of the subsequent information based on this study reflect the data reported for 1990.

29. There are differences in attainment among the Arab groups as well as between them and other Americans. El-Badry and Poston (1990) showed that in 1980 both male and female Egyptian immigrants surpassed Syrians, Lebanese, and all other Middle East immigrants in earnings and education.

30. The levels of graduate education among native-born and foreign-born Arab American men were 15.5 percent and 20.0 percent, respectively, compared to 8.7 percent for all American men. The respective figures for native-born Arab women were 10.4 percent; for foreign-born Arab women, 8.8 percent; and for all American women, 6.0 percent.

31. The figures, respectively were 10 percent, 17.6 percent, and 13.1 percent.

32. About 39 percent of the native-born and 36 percent of the foreign-born Arab American men were in managerial and professional positions, compared to about 26 percent for the American average. The comparable figures for women were about 41 percent, 31 percent, and 29 percent (Kulczyki and Lobo 2001:469).

33. For example, one highly assimilated Jordanian American high-school student reported that he "was constantly referred to as sand-nigger and camel jockey" (Daoud 1989:173). Suleiman and Abu-Laban (1989:5) reported that Ralph Nader was referred to by a member of the U.S. Federal Trade Commission as "a dirty Arab." For analyses of images of Arabs in Western newspapers, magazines, and movies, see Abu-Laban and Zeady (1975) and Shaheen (2001).

34. One high-profile case involved the government's harassment of Abdeen Jabara. Jabara filed suit against the FBI in 1972 on the ground that his rights of free speech and privacy had been violated. The case lasted 12 years and was settled out of court in 1984 (Fischbach 1985:91).

35. For a penetrating consideration of the meaning of *terrorism,* see Gibbs (1990).

36. We have focused in this book primarily on dominant-subordinate group relations, but we have noted that important rivalries and conflicts also exist between or among American ethnic groups. The existence of such conflicts has been brought into sharp relief by the charges, countercharges, and efforts to influence American policy that have taken place among Jewish and Arab American organizations.

37. See, e.g., Kang (2001).

38. A number of organizations and individuals compiled lists of the violent incidents that were reported during the weeks following 9/11. Unless otherwise noted, the information concerning the incidents cited in this and the next four paragraphs were drawn from the following sources: the American-Arab Anti-Discrimination Committee (2002); the American Broadcasting System (2001); the Arab

American Institute (2002); Ibish (2003); Idupuganti (2001); the Public Broadcasting System (2003); United Methodist Women (2003); and Zogby International (2001).

39. The organizations comprising NAPALC are the Asian Pacific American Legal Center, the Asian Law Caucus, and the Asian American Legal Defense and Education Fund.

40. Sanchez (1997) argued that the surge of nativism in the late twentieth century derived partially from the traditional sources of native hostility but also expressed a new strain of American racism and, thus, is not identical with the earlier surges.

41. For two pertinent commentaries by legal scholars, see Kang (2001) and Yamamoto and Serrano (2001).

The Future of Ethnicity

These students at the University of Texas at San Antonio (UTSA) are studying about racial and ethnic relations. UTSA has a total student population of 18,700 which is 45 percent Anglo American, 44 percent Hispanic, 5 percent African American, 3.5 percent Asian, 0.5 percent American Indian, and 2 percent international students.

*For the third generation, the . . . ethnic cultures . . . are now only an
ancestral memory . . . to be savored once in a while
in a museum or at an ethnic festival.*

—Herbert J. Gans

*The American nationality is still forming. Its processes are mysterious, and
the final form, if there is ever to be a final form, is as yet unknown.*

—Nathan Glazer and Daniel P. Moynihan

The social changes triggered by the civil rights movement and the ethnic diversity of the third great immigrant stream have combined to increase sharply the ethnic-group consciousness of people throughout the United States. These social forces have stimulated a renewed national debate over cooperation and conflict among people of different racial and ethnic backgrounds and, also, over the future of intergroup relations in America. Have the White ethnics of the first and second immigrant streams been absorbed into the mainstream of American society? Will non-White Americans and immigrants of the third stream follow the path of the colonial White immigrants? As the second generation of contemporary immigrants comes of age, into what social structures will they assimilate? Will some form of pluralism be accepted by all groups, including the Anglo Americans?

We touch on some of the issues raised by these questions through brief discussions of (1) the present status of the descendants of the earlier immigrant groups, (2) an alternative to the immigrant and colonial models, and (3) a few examples of racial and ethnic relations in some other countries of the world.

Further Reflections on Assimilation and Ethnicity

At the outset of our analysis, we pointed out that many people accept the idea that newcomers should follow the path of Anglo conformity assimilation and, ideally, to be fully incorporated into American society within three generations. Our review has shown, however, that very few, if any, American groups have reached full Anglo conformity assimilation in the expected period of time. Even the colonial Scotch–Irish and Germans did not undergo complete primary and marital assimilation within three generations.[1] Indeed, it still may be possible early in the twenty-first century to find some distinctive patterns of behavior among the descendants of these colonial immigrants. For example, a number of people in the United States, including some of the students whose interviews appear in this text, still report that they are of Scotch-Irish or German ancestry and that this identity continues to play some role in their lives. These groups, therefore, may be said to have at least a nominal sense of ethnic identity other than American and may be said to "persist" as distinctive ethnic groups (Lieberson and Waters 1988:13–14).[2]

Even if ethnicity among Europeans and their descendants is moving toward, or has reached, a point beyond which it no longer will serve reliably as an authentic basis for group cohesion and economic support, valued ethnic identities nevertheless may serve as social insulation—what Handlin called "contexts of belonging." Identity as a member of an ethnic group may serve to prevent the anonymity that frequently develops among people within urban-industrial settings. What may survive is a new form of ethnicity that Gans (1985) referred to as **symbolic ethnicity.** Symbolic ethnicity arises "as the functions of ethnic cultures and groups diminish and identity becomes the primary way of being ethnic" (Gans 1985:434). Gans predicted that this form of ethnicity may easily persist into the fifth and sixth generations and beyond.

Waters (1998) suggested two other reasons for the persistence of symbolic ethnicity. First, it assists people in enjoying a sense of community as well as expressing their individuality. Second, it provides an ideological "fit" with contemporary racist beliefs. It is "a sad irony," Waters stated, that the enjoyment and individual character of their own ethnicity contribute to the thinking that makes some middle-class Whites oppose programs designed to foster a pluralist society in which all Americans may enjoy their heritages in a similar way.

In Retrospect

The Colonial Immigrants.   It is true that the present levels of merger between the colonial immigrant groups and the American core are so high as to be virtually complete. Since the colonial Scotch–Irish and Germans began entering in force during the early part of the 1700s, we may say that the full Anglo conformity assimilation of a northwestern White European group in America may occur in less than 200 years, possibly in less than 150 years. Although this estimate extends the three-generations idea to as many as six or eight generations, it gives evidence that for all practical purposes, an Anglo conformity merger of some groups does occur, as Park said, "eventually." Moreover, if the cultural pluralists' definition of full assimilation is adopted, it is likely that the colonial immigrants approximated that goal in three generations.

The First-Stream Immigrants.   Turning from the colonial immigrants to those who formed the first immigrant stream, we find little to alter the conclusions just reached. Many of the descendants of these immigrants have been in this country for as long as six generations, and very few have been here less than three. The levels of cultural and secondary assimilation that have occurred between them and the Anglo American core are unquestionably high, although not necessarily as high as those of the colonial immigrants. The first-stream immigrant Irish and Germans in New York, for instance, may be more distinguishable than their colonial counterparts (Glazer and Moynihan 1964); but there is every reason to suppose that with the passage of time these nineteenth-century immigrants will move toward higher levels of Anglo conformity. Again, this judgment must be tempered by the realization that a number of events could revive and strengthen the ethnic bonds that still exist. As the concept of ethnogenesis reminds us, if the conditions were right, it is possible that even symbolic ethnicity could serve as the foundation for ethnic-group revival or mobilization. In addition, various groups that now are considered distinctive might seek a broader, overarching identity. We have seen, for example, that many Native Americans prefer a pan-Indian identity and many Mexican Americans and Puerto Ricans prefer the pan-ethnic terms Hispanic or Latino.

The Second-Stream Immigrants.   As discussed in Chapter 4, the Italian immigrants of the second stream did not seem to be good prospects for Anglo conformity assimilation. They were, comparatively speaking, poor, illiterate, unskilled sojourners. Their continued allegiance to the family and the Italian community, their suspicion of American education, and the high levels of discrimination they encountered all combined to maintain a high level of ethnic distinctiveness well beyond the decline in immigration after 1924. As Alba (1988:141) stated: "By the end of the 1930s . . . the group's . . . cultural and occupational background would seem to have doomed Italian Americans to a perpetual position of inferiority and separateness in American society."

The changes that have taken place since then, however, have not confirmed that expectation. In regard to cultural differences, for instance, Alba (1985:135; 1988:146–147) marshaled evidence from the General Social Surveys of the NORC for the years 1975–1980 to compare certain values of the Italian Americans with those of a group of White Anglo-Saxon Protestants. When factors such as the respondents' sex and age, the education and occupation of their parents, and the region of the country in which they now live or were raised were taken into account, Italian Americans were found to be very similar to the Anglo group. In Alba's (1988:153) opinion, "among virtually all White ethnic groups, one can observe a progressive, if gradual, dampening of cultural distinctiveness." Alba (1999a, b) noted that assimilation need not be a one-sided process. The various ethnic groups also influence the core culture. Moreover, assimilation takes place, whether or not immigrants want it to occur, because it is an unintended by-product of their efforts to better their lives.

Some Other Indications of Assimilation.   Our previous discussions showed that factors such as the skills immigrants brought with them, their time of arrival in the United States, and the geographic location of their points of entry resulted in concentrations of different groups in particular communities and occupations. Lieberson and Waters (1988:127) found in a study of 13 European ethnic groups that earlier ". . . immigrant occupational patterns still have significant vestiges 80 years later." Alba (1985: 122–123), however, found that when the groups were matched for age, place of residence, and family background, no significant differences in occupational patterns remained. Research on group differences in education, income, and occupational opportunities have produced similar results. As expressed by Alba and Nee (1997:841), "There is abundant evidence that assimilation has been the master trend among the descendants of the immigrants . . . who mainly came from Europe . . . before 1930" and that there has been "a broad convergence toward the life chances of the 'average' white American."

There are also high levels of marital and civic assimilation among the descendants of European ethnic groups. Among all White groups, the number of interethnic marriages has grown steadily larger (Alba 1988:149–152), as has the number of people of mixed European ancestry; and today there appears to be very little discrimination against individuals of European ancestry simply because they are members of a particular ethnic group.

Consider again the experience of the Irish in America. In his book *How the Irish Became White*, Ignatiev (1995) described how the Catholic Irish, an oppressed group in Ireland, became part of an oppressing "White race" in America. The Irish who came to America in the eighteenth and nineteenth centuries came to a society in which color was important in determining social status. The Irish found themselves among the lowest in status, living among other poor immigrants and African Americans. Many of the histories of this time note widespread animosity between the Irish and African Americans. To "become White," the Irish had to distinguish themselves from Black workers and compete successfully for jobs with other White workers. Becoming accepted as White was a strategy the Irish pursued to distance themselves from Blacks and secure advantages in a competitive society. Ignatiev documented how the Irish did this by not speaking against slavery, by joining White labor unions that excluded Blacks, and by supporting political parties that took positions favoring Whites.

White Ethnic Identity

The experiences of the Irish and Italians are consistent with the view we have expressed previously that the concept of race (and also of national origin, nationality, and racial and ethnic identity) is not fixed by nature but is socially constructed; consequently, in the United States, the meaning of the term *White* and the consequences of being classified as White have changed over time. For instance, in a study of the implementation of the system of national-origin quotas required by the Immigration Act of 1924, Ngai (1999) presented examples showing that "Whiteness" was negotiated in various legal cases as the members of some ethnic groups attempted to become citizens.

For example, in the court case *Ozawa v. United States* (1922), discussed in Chapter 11, the Supreme Court ruled that Ozawa could not become a U.S. citizen because he was not White. The Court conceded that skin color alone could not be the determining criterion because many "non-White" people have skins of a lighter color than many "White" people; but the Court held that the term *White,* under the naturalization law of 1790, was equivalent to the term *Caucasian* and that Ozawa was not Caucasian. Ozawa argued that in 1790 the term *White* meant anyone who was not African or Indian; but the Court ruled that since Ozawa was not Caucasian, he also was not White and, therefore, could not become a citizen. In another official negotiation, the 1930 census enumerated Mexicans as members of a separate, non-White, race. The "Mexican race" was defined as a residual category comprised of persons who "are not definitely white, Negro, Indian, Chinese, or Japanese" (Ngai 1999:92).

Because of the historical sharpness of the social and legal boundaries between races in America, and because of continued residential segregation, it is possible even today for third- and fourth-generation White children to interact only, or almost only, with others who are White. Since the U.S. core culture is centered around White norms, White people rarely are forced to think about having a **White ethnic identity.** It is possible, therefore, that many, perhaps most, of these White children may grow up without ever giving much thought to the fact or meaning of their *whiteness.* It is mainly when Whites come into contact with members of some other racial or ethnic group that whiteness becomes an issue (Helms 1993). In general, most White people do not talk much about racism or their own racial identity, do not recognize the existence of institutional discrimination, and feel personally threatened even by the mention of racism (Sleeter 1997).

A growing number of scholars who study White racial identity (Tatum 1992; Fine, Weis, Powell, and Wong 1997; McIntyre 1997) have argued that many White people who reject the idea that they are racists, nevertheless subscribe to racist ideas and engage in (mostly subtle) racist actions. This point is illustrated by the idea that many White people who say they favor some form of equality—for instance, school desegregation—may nevertheless reject all practical steps that may be proposed to achieve that end. They also may reject all implications that they bear any responsibility for the regrettable conditions within many segregated schools or that they may have benefited economically and socially by their unearned membership in a privileged group.[3] Bobo, Kluegel, and Smith (1997) refer to this cluster of beliefs and acts as **laissez-faire racism.**

Laissez-faire racism contributes to the tendency of many White people to underestimate the importance of the status of being White in American society and to rationalize their own opposition to social change in ways that may contribute to the continuation of racial oppression. Although laissez-faire racism refers specifically to anti-Black attitudes, the general point is applicable also to the situation of other non-White groups such as Asians, African Americans, Latinos, and Native Americans. These considerations seem to imply that racism is primarily a White problem that needs to be addressed by the White community (Myrdal 1964; Feagin and Vera 1995; hooks 1994; Sleeter 1997).

Increasingly, due to high rates of out-marriage, it is apparent that most people are descended from multiple, not single, ethnic sources. Most Scandinavian Americans have some German relatives, and most African Americans are part European American and Native American. Few White American extended families exist today without at least one member who has married or cohabited across ethnic lines (Spickard and Fong 1999). As noted in Chapter 1, people of mixed ancestry increasingly have begun to claim both or several parts of their ancestry and identify themselves as multiethnic persons.[4] The U.S. census of the year 2000 allowed multiracial categories of enumeration. Thus, as Americans select multiple identities, the idea of assimilation becomes even more complex. The idea that it is necessary to choose one identity and give up all others is no longer the only option.

An Interpretation. On the basis of these considerations, the following speculations about the White ethnic experience seem reasonable. White ethnics of the second and third immigrant streams have not disappeared in three generations, but neither did the colonial or first-stream immigrants.[5] As Neidert and Farley (1985:849) concluded, "if assimilation means that third-generation ethnic groups will be indistinguishable from the core English group" then these groups still have not assimilated; however, they went on to say, "if assimilation means that ethnic groups are neither favored nor at a disadvantage in the process of occupational achievement, then there is strong evidence to support the theory."[6]

Although three generations may be long enough to permit a high degree of cultural and secondary assimilation among White European groups, the remaining forms of assimilation may take much longer. Even when the host and immigrant groups are similar in race and culture, full Anglo conformity assimilation may require as many as eight generations. On the assumption that the members of the second immigrant stream are moving toward an Anglo conformity merger with the dominant group, they should become less distinctive as time goes on. Perhaps, given a few generations beyond three, they may be no more distinctive than the colonial Irish and Germans are now. In short, the sheer fact that the second-stream groups are in some respects still distinguishable after three generations is not really too surprising. Since the speed of Anglo conformity assimilation among the colonial and first-stream immigrants has been much slower than is generally recognized, the belief that the merger of the second-stream immigrants with the host group is unusually slow has not yet been put fully to the test. Indeed, on the basis of the evidence we have reviewed, it can be argued that the speed with which the second-stream Europeans have assimilated culturally and in the secondary arena constitutes, in Greeley's (1985) phrase, an "Ethnic Miracle!" Somewhat paradoxically, pluralist *principles* appear to have been gaining force as actual *ethnic differences* among Whites have been, as Steinberg (1989:254) argued, "on the wane." In his view, the United States has "never before . . . been closer to welding a national identity out of the melange of ethnic groups that populated its shores."

Waters (1990:166) argued that symbolic ethnicity "will continue to characterize the ethnicity of later-generation whites." In her view, symbolic ethnicity has a strong appeal to White Americans because identification with an ethnic group carries for Whites many rewards and few penalties; for non-Whites, however, "the consequences of being Asian or Hispanic or black are not symbolic. . . . They are real and hurtful" (Waters 1990:156).[7] Whether the continuation of White ethnic distinctiveness and identity will be the central focus of everyday life or an expression of "a nostalgic allegiance to the culture of the immigrant generation" (Gans 1985:435) remains to be seen. Either way, however, the expectation is for a continued prominence of White ethnicity in American life for at least one or two more generations and a continued or growing acceptance of cultural pluralism as the principal view of the way immigrants and their descendants should become Americanized.

The Non-White Experience

Although this conclusion seems reasonable in regard to the White ethnics, how well does it fit the situation of non-White Americans? Recall that some observers have interpreted the conflict between the Anglo American and non-White American ethnic groups in terms of the colonial model. Under this interpretation, the initial relations between a dominant group and a colonized group establishes a pattern that does not lead toward conformity to the dominant group's way of life. Rather, this pattern leads to attempts by the minority to end colonization through the establishment of a separate nation, either by overthrowing the dominant (usually invading) group or by leaving the territory altogether. The dominant group, for its part, prefers either that the colonized minority leave the territory or assimilate culturally while remaining apart and subordinate in all other ways. Because, in this view, both the dominant group and the colonized minority resist the full merger of the groups, the continuation of friction among them would be expected, resulting, after numerous conflicts, either in separation or secession.

The main criticisms of the colonial model rest on efforts to show that some non-White groups (e.g., Japanese Americans) have achieved a high level of cultural and secondary assimilation and that the recent historical experiences of Mexican, Black, and Indian Americans resemble in some essential ways those of the second-stream immigrants from Europe. This argument—based on the immigrant model—does not claim that the immigration experience of the Japanese and the migration experiences of the other groups are identical to that of European immigrants. The non-White groups have faced, as Kristol (1972:205) conceded, "unique and peculiar dilemmas of their own"; whereas Lieberson (1980:383), in an extensive analysis of the differences between Blacks and second-stream immigrants, concluded that "the situation for new Europeans in the United States, bad as it may have been, was not as bad as that experienced by blacks at the same time."

From this standpoint, most Blacks in the northern cities have not yet been there more than three generations; and although they have met less favorable conditions and greater discrimination there than previous immigrants, their future experiences may nevertheless, in highly important ways, resemble those of the White ethnics. Indeed, we saw evidence in Chapter 7 that many Black Americans, following the expansion of opportunities beginning in the 1960s, already have attained practically the same average levels of education as Whites. This finding suggests the interesting (if debatable) idea that Black Americans who have reached maturity since the 1960s have only recently been accorded the levels of opportunities that were available to European immigrants a century ago.

The immigrant model does not deny the validity of the colonial model as an interpretation of some of the experiences of non-Whites in America (e.g., slavery; the conquest of the Indians, Mexican Americans, and Puerto Ricans; the Japanese internment). It does assert, however, that in different ways the non-Whites are moving toward some form of assimilation, perhaps cultural pluralism, and are moving away from separatism and secession. From the standpoint of national unity, the immigrant model is evidently more optimistic than the colonial model. Which of these views, then, gives us the best basis for forecasting the probable course of race relations in the United States? As we have seen, the answer to this question is still a matter of keen debate. But it is possible, as frequently happens, that the wrong question has been asked. Since the histories of Black, Mexican, Puerto Rican, Japanese, and Indian Americans contain certain elements that may justify either the colonial or the immigrant view, we may conclude (as people frequently do in such arguments) that both views are to some extent correct. Let us consider an alternative view that may help place the facts of conquest and assimilation in a new light.

Consequences of Colonization and Immigration: An Alternative View

We have stressed that the conditions surrounding the initial contact between groups are extremely important in understanding the subsequent course of their relations. In general (1) a conquered minority is likely to be hostile for a long period of time and to have separatist and secessionist tendencies, and (2) an immigrant minority is likely to exhibit hostility for a shorter period of time and to prefer some form of assimilation. There is a substantial amount of evidence, drawn from racial and ethnic contacts throughout the world, to support these basic generalizations. It is their strength, indeed, that sustains the debate over the colonial and immigrant models. The alternative view we consider does not question the accuracy of these basic generalizations. It emphasizes, instead, (1) some differences in the social characteristics of colonized and immigrant minorities during the early stages of their formation, (2) that the basic generalizations refer to probabilities rather than to certainties, and (3) that assimilation processes include a dynamic merger of elements found in the immigrant and colonial models.

Early Stages of Ethnic-Group Formation

Consider the hypothetical (but realistic) situation of the people living in a small, independent, society that is soon to be conquered by an invading power. They have their own set of social institutions for dealing with life's problems: their own forms of government, religion, making a living, conducting family life, and raising children. They do not seek, wish, or need to join, or become part of, some other society. These circumstances provide the motive force for prolonged resistance to an invader.

If such a society is invaded and overpowered by outsiders, it may be taken into the invading society as an entire unit. If so, it is no longer an independent society; it is now a *colonized group* within an alien society. Because such groups already are complete social units at the time they enter the host society, their relationship to the host is mainly political. The group's members may "remain firmly embedded . . . in a web of familiar relationships" (Francis 1976:169).[8] This new ethnic group is a "viable corporate unit" (Francis 1976:397) that is able—if permitted to do so—to "continue functioning in the host society in much the same way" as it had before being conquered (Francis 1976:170). The members resent being subordinate and, rather than seeking equal treatment with the majority, wish to restore their former existence as a separate group. They, therefore, are more likely to resist vigorously any efforts the host society may make to bring about any aspect of assimilation. Their primary goal is to escape the unsought and unwanted control of the invaders.

Immigrant Groups.   The conditions leading to the formation of an ethnic group by immigrants are quite different. The members of this type of ethnic group are, at the outset, completely dependent on the host society for the satisfaction of all their needs, economic as well as social. There are no established ethnic institutions; therefore, there is no existing web of familiar relationships. Although a group of people sharing similar cultural characteristics has assembled in the same location, a community of people who possess a sense of common ethnicity remains to be formed within the host society. The group's potential members possess little in the way of resources and cannot continue to function as they did in their previous society. The social pattern the immigrant group develops represents a mixture of the cultures of the parent society and the host society. It is identical to neither but is a variety of each (Francis 1976:223).[9] The members of an immigrant ethnic group are less likely than those in a colonized group to resent the majority and are more likely to seek to be treated as equal to the majority. They, therefore, are more likely to be willing than those of a colonized ethnic group to undergo at least some aspects of assimilation (Francis 1976:397).

An Important Implication.   Because ethnic groups that come into being as a result of conquest and colonization often are complete social units from the beginning,[10] an important objective of such groups generally is to hold what they still have while attempting to recover what has been lost. This is why the *relationship of the colonized minority* to the society's majority is *likely* to be adversarial and characterized by vigorous resistance to assimilation. Because the main concerns in this type of relationship of the dominant and subordinate groups center on preventing the society from flying apart, we refer to it as a **centrifugal relationship.** In contrast, ethnic groups that come into being as a result of immigration usually are formed within the host society and must rely to a considerable extent on the social institutions they find there. An important goal of the immigrant ethnic group, therefore, is to organize for mutual assistance and protection to assist its members to combat discrimination and gain equality with the majority in important areas such as jobs, education, and political participation. The *relationship of the immigrant minority to* the host society, therefore, is *likely* to be one of resistance to some aspects of assimilation combined with active efforts to achieve secondary assimilation. Because the main concerns in this type of relationship of the dominant and subordinate groups usually center on finding mutually satisfactory ways to bring the groups together, we refer to it as a **centripetal relationship.**

A Dynamic View of the Colonial and Immigrant Models

The distinction we have drawn between two types of relationships that may develop between ethnic groups and dominant groups (centrifugal and centripetal) helps to clarify another point that is hidden in the debate over the colonial and immigrant models. Regardless of the type of relationship that is formed at the time of the original contact between two groups, this situation is not necessarily fixed for all time. The concept of ethnogenesis, which we have encountered at various points in our analysis, directs attention to an extraordinarily important phenomenon: Although the boundaries between racial and ethnic groups may appear to be highly stable lines that signify fixed, naturally occurring biological and cultural differences among groups, the importance of these boundaries may wax or wane depending on many factors.

As the members of immigrant groups become more numerous or more highly concentrated in a particular area, for instance, competition arises between the natives and the newcomers for "the same valued resources (e.g., housing, schools, jobs, other kinds of rewards)" and this situation is likely to lead members of both groups to organize to further their own interests (Olzak 1986:18). Such situations may cause people whose ethnic identities and attachments originally were weak to place a higher value and emphasis on them than in the past. A strong line of division may develop between "them" and "us" where no line or only a weak line previously existed. Conversely, strong lines of division may weaken when some external factor, perhaps an attack from outside that threatens the survival of both groups, alters the situation.

These considerations support the idea that the boundaries of racial and ethnic groups that are accepted at any given time may be altered by changing circumstances. See (1986:224) has stated the matter succinctly: "the salience of ethnic identity is situationally determined." The groups of people who are thought of as "them" or as "us" may form and re-form, join and split, depending on the situation; hence, a centrifugal relationship may, at a later time, be transformed into a centripetal relationship. In addition, regardless of the original contact situation, many groups seek, or have thrust on them, broad identities that previously did not exist. This aspect of ethnogenesis may be seen in the emergence of new identities such as Asian, Hispanic, or Latino, and, from an earlier time, American Indian, that bring together groups with separate identities that may vary widely in sociocultural characteristics. Striking examples of this phenomenom occurred during the period immediately following 9/11 as Americans of all ethnicities displayed a sense of pride in being Americans as well as members of their specific ethnic groups. The alternative view of the long-range outcomes of contact between dominant and subordinate groups, therefore, is more dynamic than the view of either the colonial or immigrant models.

Some Applications of the Alternative View

Mexican Americans, Puerto Rican Americans, and Native Americans

The Mexican American, Puerto Rican American, and Native American groups were each created through conquest. The fact of conquest itself, however, is not so crucial to our understanding of the present and future condition of these dominated groups as is a consideration of the institutions that existed within them at the time of conquest. Before they were colonized, each of these groups possessed fully developed sets of social institutions and did not depend on the institutions of the dominant society for the satisfaction of life's needs; consequently, their initial relationship to the colonizing society was centrifugal.

As the forces of industrialization, urbanization, and bureaucratization gained strength, however, each of these groups has been drawn increasingly into the larger American and global economies. These vast social changes do not mean that these groups have somehow stopped being colonized minorities or that their history of conquest by the dominant group can be disregarded. The changes mean, rather, that these groups have undergone—but have not necessarily completed—a prodigious transformation from a centrifugal to a centripetal relationship with the dominant group. Despite the efforts of many members of each group to resist this transformation, the main trend throughout the past century has been toward the groups' gradual incorporation into the larger society. The members of these groups increasingly have accepted their status as American citizens and have demanded that they be accorded all the rights and privileges of citizens. In short, their relationship to the dominant group is now largely centripetal, and their main goal frequently is described as achieving "the best of both worlds." This statement of the groups' goal is somewhat vague, but the specific demands presented in its behalf (even by militants) generally imply an acceptance of cultural pluralism.[11]

This conclusion must be accepted only tentatively. Consider, for instance, that the proximity of Mexico, the debate over statehood for Puerto Rico, and the continued discrimination of the United States against people of Mexican and Puerto Rican origin are forces favoring the possibility that they will give up on assimilationist goals and seek some other social arrangement. For instance, those who seek the complete separation of Puerto Rico from the United States may gain support for that goal. Another possibility is that the increasing concentration of Mexican Americans and Mexicans in the American Southwest may produce demands for regional autonomy or separation (Kennedy 1996:68). Still another possibility is that Mexican and Puerto Rican Americans may merge with some or all of the other Hispanic groups into a large pan-ethnic Latino group that will greatly increase their political and economic power within the American framework. Finally, the transnationalist goal of maintaining a foot in both the home and American societies appears to be an increasingly attractive and feasible option.

As was true for Mexican and Puerto Rican Americans, the various American Indian societies were viable social units before they were conquered and offer myriad illustrations of the formation of centrifugal relationships. Native Americans neither sought nor desired to become citizens of the expanding United States. They preferred instead to be left alone to reconstruct their own independent societies. Most tribes have steadfastly resisted assimilation into the dominant society for more than three centuries. Since they became citizens in 1924, however, the Indians have shown increasing signs of being transformed into one loosely federated, ethnic group with a centripetal relationship to the majority. As with most other Americans, they have been unable to resist completely the pressures of urbanization, industrialization, bureaucratization, and assimilation. Large numbers of Indians have moved into urban centers in search of employment. They have not, though, readily broken their ties to the reservations or to other members of their tribes within the cities. In general, their movement toward the status of a typical immigrant group has not been rapid. The tribes generally are quite cool toward the prospect of full Anglo conformity; they continue to be ambivalent about secondary assimilation, and they continue to resist all efforts to terminate their treaty rights. Nonetheless, as they have tried to protect their resources and improve the lives of tribal members, they have had to participate in mainstream institutions and take on some of the ways of Anglo capitalism. They seem to continue to move toward the goal of being admitted into American society on an equal footing with other citizens while maintaining the right to live as Indians.

Unless the citizens of each of these groups are permitted to advance (as compared to the dominant group) in income, education, access to jobs, political participation, health care, police protection, and housing, they may at some point reject pluralism and seek separatist or secessionist solutions instead. Still, it seems improbable that antiassimilationist forces will prevail. Even less probable, however, is that Mexican, Puerto Rican, and Native Americans will soon embrace Anglo conformity. Kasinitz, Waters, and Mollenkopf (1999) point out that early immigrants assimilated into an easily identifiable Anglo core society, but Anglo conformity is not as dominant in the twenty-first century. The "core society" of the United States that groups are assimilating into today is much more ethnic and diverse. Thus, there is every reason to believe that these groups will remain, and will wish to remain, distinctive ethnic groups within American life for several generations to come.[12]

African Americans

African Americans were not conquered in their homeland, as were Mexicans, Puerto Ricans, and Native Americans. Nevertheless, there can be little question that the cruel treatment and suffering they endured under slavery fostered social relationships with the members of the dominant group that were in many ways comparable to those usually created through conquest. In this regard, we may view African Americans as a colonized minority; however, and this is crucial, *they did not form a centrifugal relationship with the dominant group.* At the time of enslavement, they represented many different nationalities and did not share a common culture or set of social institutions. In America, they were not independent of the host society; they were heavily dependent on it. Indeed, even the formation of an inclusive ethnic group and culture was greatly hindered by the slave system, with its deliberate interference with the efforts of the slaves to communicate with each other and to organize. Only slowly and with great effort were the African slaves able to construct institutions of their own within the host society. This process, if not its rate of change, resembled the experience of many other immigrant groups.

With all due respect to Garveyism, we may say that during most of the past century, Blacks have been divided mainly between cultural pluralism and Anglo conformity (Jaynes and Williams 1989:195). The NAACP, the Urban League, CORE, the March on Washington movement, SCLC, and many other organizations have centered their efforts on improving jobs, education, income, housing, health care, and so on (i.e., on increasing secondary assimilation). Because these goals are common to both Anglo conformity and cultural pluralism, it is not clear which of these ideologies has been most favored.

The decade of the 1960s brought about noticeable changes in the perspectives of Black Americans. They increasingly doubted that Anglo conformity was a desirable goal and that cultural pluralism was feasible; separatist ideas again gained support. Separatist sentiments seemed to decline during the 1970s and 1980s, but some signs of a revival began to appear in the 1990s. The continued inability of many Black Americans to gain better jobs, housing, police protection, and representation in government—especially among the urban poor described by Wilson (1987)—is sure to strengthen the hand of separatists (Lieberson and Waters 1988:155; Neidert and Farley 1985:848). Even among the middle class, there are doubts about the goals of assimilation. A June 7, 1999 *Newsweek* survey found that Black income was at its highest level ever and unemployment among Blacks was lower than it had been in a quarter of a century, yet many successful African Americans still felt it was "impossible to feel truly accepted in America" (Cose 1999). In any event, African Americans will continue to be a distinctive group within American society for many additional generations.

This conclusion has been strengthened by the increasing numbers of Black immigrants who have arrived as a portion of the third immigrant stream. These newcomers are from Jamaica, Trinidad, Haiti, the Dominican Republic, and countries in Africa. The second-generation Black immigrants challenge the racial patterns of exclusion of America's non-White peoples. The children of Black immigrants face a choice about whether to identify as Black Americans or to maintain an ethnic identity reflecting their parents' national origins. First-generation Black immigrants have tended to distance themselves from American Blacks and have stressed their national origins and ethnic identities, but they face many pressures in the United States to identify only as "Blacks" (Waters 1999a).[13]

 # Some Tentative Conclusions about Racial and Ethnic Relations in the United States

Given these interpretations, we offer the following tentative conclusions. The main ideological debate among Whites concerns cultural pluralism. The strength of Anglo conformity is greater among White Anglo Saxon Protestants, whereas the strength of pluralism is greater among the White descendants of the second immigrant stream. Support within either group for separatism or secessionism is low, although there are some signs of rising support.

The picture is different when Whites are compared with non-Whites, but not drastically so. Alba (1999a, b) concluded that the three-generations model holds for the majority of contemporary immigrants, particularly when English language use is taken as evidence of assimilation. Asian groups are 90 to 95 percent English dominant or English monolingual as adults. For Latino groups the issue is less clear. Spanish shows more staying power than other languages in the United States, especially for Cubans in Miami and Mexicans growing up along the United States–Mexico border where there is community support for Spanish. Children growing up away from the border are more likely to be English dominant. Alba cautioned that English dominance may be even more prevalent than surveys show because respondents are asked to indicate their own language abilities and it is not clear to what extent those who profess to be so are truly bilingual; thus, estimates of bilingualism among second- and third-generation immigrants are probably overstated. The motivation for assimilation is the desire to improve the circumstances of one's life, and opportunities to do so are often greater outside of immigrant communities than in ethnic enclaves. In the more diverse U.S. society of today, assimilation is likely to occur in many different forms, but it does not require the extinction of ethnic differences.

There is definitely some support within both White and non-White groups for separatism, with the strongest support being among the Whites. For instance, many Whites want Blacks to be kept out of their neighborhoods and feel they have the right to keep them out (Schuman, Steeh, and Bobo 1985:97; Taylor, Sheatsley, and Greeley 1978: 269). Despite a general decline in racial intolerance and prejudice and laws passed as a result of the civil rights movements of the 1960s, there are still sizable segments of the U.S. population that do not want their children to go to school with Black children, do not want to be led by Black leaders, and do not want relatives to be married to a Black person (Herring and Amissah 1997). Also, during the 1990s, White separatist propaganda proliferated, coinciding with an increasingly visible tendency among separatists to talk of establishing an "Aryan homeland" (Reiss 1995:A11). Within both the White and non-White groups, however, the predominant preference of each group in regard to the other group appears to be a pluralist arrangement, although controversy surrounding residential desegregation is intense.[14]

The generally high support for cultural pluralism among both Whites and non-Whites with respect to the other suggests that a foundation is being constructed for a broad agreement on ethnic-group goals. Although the popularity of separatism may not be ignored, pluralism has emerged as the chief alternative to Anglo conformity in American thought concerning racial and ethnic relations. This point is frequently obscured by criticisms of assimilationist theory. For example, many critics conclude their attacks on assimilationist theory by advocating cultural pluralism. Despite its rejection of full Anglo conformity, cultural pluralism (we have tried to show) is best understood as a form of assimilation that is competing for acceptance within American society as a legitimate and equivalent alternative goal.

To insist that Anglo conformity and cultural pluralism are both legitimate forms of assimilation, however, may obscure another important point. We must emphasize again that the differences between these two forms are by no means trivial. Quite different social policies and tactics of change are suggested by these two assimilationist ideologies. One of the clearest illustrations of this point is the example of bilingual–bicultural education. Most people who favor Anglo conformity are opposed to programs of bilingual–bicultural education. Pluralists, on the other hand, want to pass on their family's language and culture; and they want the public schools, which they help support, to assist in their efforts.

The Future of Ethnicity in the United States

Social policy preferences of Anglo conformists and cultural pluralists do indeed differ—and in ways that most Americans consider to be of great importance; however, their disagreements, although large and significant, take place primarily within a mutually accepted economic and political framework. This does not mean that cultural pluralists are uncritical of the American economic and political system, nor does it mean that the conflicts arising between Anglo conformists and pluralists in this connection are minor. What it does mean is that cultural pluralists believe the operating principles of American life afford, in Glazer's (1972:174) words, "enormous scope for group diversity."

It is true, as our historical review illustrates, that official discrimination has occurred against many ethnic groups in the United States, especially against the non-White groups. But our courts and legislatures have declared (even if slowly) that all of these acts are opposed to America's basic principles. Slavery was, at last, ended; the relocation of the Japanese was declared illegal; African, Native, and Japanese Americans have become citizens; and discrimination on the basis of race, color, and national origins has been declared unconstitutional (Glazer 1972:175). The basic faith of the cultural pluralists is that the consensus on the principles of American economic and political life does not require a capitulation to the will of the dominant group. Even though the amount and severity of dominant-group discrimination in our history must give even an optimist pause, the main ethnic-group conflicts of the past have been settled on the side of the rights of minorities. Stated differently, the "tyranny of the majority," which Tocqueville ([1835]1988:250) warned might be the fatal flaw of democracy, has, so far, been forestalled; and cultural pluralists believe the institutions of this nation are sufficiently flexible to permit this pattern of intergroup acceptance to continue.

The right to maintain a pluralist pattern, however, does not ensure a group's actual success in doing so. Regardless of the desire of a group's members to have "the best of both," it may still be that time will gradually erode the distinctiveness of the ethnic groups in American society. The complexity of U.S. society has made it extremely difficult for ethnic groups to maintain or revive a centrifugal relationship with the majority. During the twentieth century, Mexican Americans came to resemble an immigrant minority more than a conquered minority. Because of the sovereignty rights guaranteed to many American Indian tribes by treaties, they are in a stronger position than any others to resist assimilative pressures and to maintain an unusually high level of separation, if they so desire. Even so, many individual Native Americans have married out of their ethnic group and have moved into the mainstream of the society; even though there have been patterns of movement from urban areas back to the reservations, those who live on the reservations increasingly live in a manner that resembles the main forms of American life.

Although many groups have undergone a high degree of cultural and secondary assimilation within three generations, the third and subsequent generations frequently have experienced a renewed interest in revitalizing their ethnic heritages and ties. In some cases in which individual ethnic heritage identifications have declined, larger pan-ethnic identities have allowed groups to combine and increase their political and social power. Given sufficient time, nevertheless, the maintenance of the levels of separation endorsed by pluralists may succumb to the homogenizing pressures of an advanced industrial, information age society. No one knows how long such an outcome might take; but unless there are catastrophic changes in the world order, it seems almost certain that ethnic distinctions among Whites will disappear earlier than the distinctions between Whites and non-Whites. Taking history as our guide, and given the continuous possibility of ethnic rejuvenation under favorable circumstances, some of the White groups could sustain themselves for many additional generations, especially symbolically. Additionally, given the high levels of continued discrimination in neighborhoods, the labor market, and societal institutions, the disappearance of the sociocultural distinctions between Whites and non-Whites could take centuries.

These two conclusions suggest a third. Although the continued existence of racial and ethnic minorities may occasionally pose problems for national unity, a more pressing problem is posed by the continuing failure to afford an equal opportunity for secondary assimilation to every American who wishes it. Increasing the individual's opportunities to leave the ethnic community or remain within it, as he or she chooses, requires further genuine reductions in the existing levels of racism. Steps in this direction would honor the best traditions and highest aspirations of the American people.

Across National Boundaries

As we have mentioned at various points throughout this book, the United States is not alone in its struggle to incorporate different racial and ethnic groups. Indeed, multi-ethnic countries are typical in the modern world, and many of the peoples who comprise those countries favor increasing the political independence of their own ethnic group. Serious tensions exist even within some countries that are celebrated as examples of ethnic harmony—Sweden, for example.

Sweden

In the late 1930s Gunnar Myrdal, a famous social scientist, was invited to come from Sweden to the United States to lead the research team that produced the pathbreaking book *An American Dilemma.* Myrdal was selected to conduct the research in part because as a citizen of a country with no history of colonialism or interracial conflict, he could perhaps view American race relations through eyes untainted by racism.

This presumption was backed by the fact that Sweden has long had a strong political commitment to create an equitable society and has been kind to newcomers. It has been generous to refugees from countries with political dictatorships, and it has maintained a policy of trying to incorporate guest workers into its society rather than returning them to their native countries after their jobs ended. But today Myrdal's own nation has seen its centuries-old homogeneous population become 10 percent non-Nordic, and the nation is struggling with the assimilation of newcomers and the acceptance of diversity. Hoge (1998) noted "It's very hard for people who don't have white skins and blond hair to be accepted in Sweden. If you look different you are called an immigrant."

Sweden has altered its approach to assimilation over time, first embracing what we might call Swedish Conformity and, then, moving gradually to a pluralist policy that encourages distinct cultures and equality of opportunity. When the government discovered that some immigrants, even after more than three decades in the country, could speak no Swedish, the Swedish government offered intensive, free, language instruction. In 1986 the government created a new position whose incumbent's job is to fight discrimination.

In addition to immigration, economic restructuring also created some problems of incorporation. In a pattern common to other industrialized countries, factories closed or left the country, taking unskilled work opportunities with them. Gains in productivity further reduced the total number of jobs across the whole economy, which led to high rates of unemployment and heightened tensions between the local and foreign populations. In some cities, such as Rinkeby, a small town near Stockholm, immigrants make up an overwhelming majority of the population. Neighborhoods that were primarily Swedish are increasingly immigrant neighborhoods. As a result of the slow rates of assimilation, Swedish policymakers have begun to refer to "third generation immigrants" (Hoge 1998).

South Africa

South Africa is in the midst of the massive task of incorporating the Black majority population that was for decades kept segregated under a legal system called **apartheid.** Under apartheid, Whites, who make up about 12 percent of the population, controlled the majority of the wealth of the nation, the good jobs, and the government. At the same time, 70 percent of all Black people were below the poverty line and about 50 percent were illiterate. Schools, neighborhoods, transportation, health care, and almost everything else were legally segregated. The vast majority of the nation's citizens were systematically denied adequate education and jobs. Following a quarter century of incarceration, Nelson Mandela, the popular leader of the African National Congress, was released from prison and was elected President of South Africa. The Black majority now controls the South African government and apartheid has been dismantled. The incorporation of this large Black population (previously a minority in terms of power) is a challenge to the very survival of South Africa as a multiracial society. Having to make up for many years of extensive injustice under apartheid, Blacks are infuriated that Whites are not embracing programs such as affirmative action to redress inequality (Daley 1997).

South Africa also has to deal with tensions created by a flood of undocumented immigrants (Daley 1998). When it was ruled by Whites, South Africa strictly controlled the number of immigrants allowed in as cheap labor; borders were patrolled, mined, and protected with high-voltage electric fences set to kill those who crossed. Mandela's government has eased such restrictions because, in the past, many of the neighboring countries had supported their antiapartheid struggles and welcomed South African immigrants, refugees, and exiles. This new policy has attracted large numbers of undocumented immigrants from all over Africa, many of them destitute.[15] Despite a booming economy, Mandela's government has not been able to produce enough housing, health clinics, and good schools to serve a population long denied such services. Antiforeign attitudes, particularly against undocumented Black immigrants, are widespread, and violence against all immigrants is growing.

Several human rights reports have condemned South Africa's increasing abuses of immigrants, including beatings, arbitrary arrests, and escalating deportations. Although most residents of South Africa have little contact with the undocumented immigrants, who end up at the lowest rungs of the economy and live together in their own neighborhoods, increasing numbers think the government should place strict limits on the number of foreigners allowed into the country. Both Black and White South Africans exhibit an increasing xenophobia.

Canada

Canada, our neighbor to the north, has struggled since the 1960s with a strong secessionist movement (DePalma 1998) seeking the independence of Quebec, a French-speaking province. Montreal and cities along the U.S. border have many English- and French-speaking families who have long lived side by side. The streets in those areas often have bilingual signs and many of the residents are bilingual in French and English; but, because of the conflicts over the status of Quebec, many of the English speakers have left the province.

The secessionist movement is comprised of Quebecers who take great pride in their French heritage and, in many cases, speak only French. In 1995, a referendum held on the question of independence for Quebec almost succeeded. Had it done so, Canada and Quebec would have been faced with issues such as deciding the new nation's share of the Canadian national debt and its payment for the federal properties taken over by Quebec. They would have had to decide what to do with those territories of Quebec that did not want to leave Canada, including particularly the northern areas settled by Cree Indians (who voted overwhelmingly against secession) and the eastern townships that were settled by Loyalist families who fled the United States during and after the Revolutionary War.

Canada, like the United States, also has problems concerning immigration. Canada accepts about 200,000 legal immigrants a year, but has had to tighten its regulations on undocumented immigrants and refugees. On the West Coast, Canadian authorities have had to deal with large numbers of undocumented Chinese immigrants who have been smuggled into the country (DePalma 1999). Some of the immigrants told authorities they paid smugglers as much as $38,000 for the trip. In July 1999, a ship carrying 122 immigrants without identification papers, all but 18 of them women, was taken into custody by Canadian authorities and detained. If the detainees claim to be refugees, they will have to prove they would be persecuted if they returned to China. If they do not qualify for refugee status, they will be subject to deportation. The increasing numbers of immigrants who are allowed to stay may change the balance in the debate over the status of Quebec.[16]

Brazil

Brazil is similar in size to the United States and also experienced a history of slavery, but there are notable differences in race relations in the two countries (Degler 1971). Both countries have large Black populations, but in Brazil, during the colonial era, much of the population was both colored and slave and there was never a systematic separation of races; thus there was much more intermarriage between Whites and Blacks. As a result, Brazilians did not develop a full-blown defense of slavery such as was elaborated in the South in the United States, and there has been a wider recognition and acceptance of racial mixing in Brazil. For example, a Mulatto in Brazil was recognized as a person of mixed race, but in the United States legal definitions made persons with any Black heritage a Black person. Brazilians have long recognized that Blacks have been a part of their history and culture, whereas the United States was late in recognizing the role of Blacks in its history, literature, and culture.

For these reasons, many Brazilian and other Latin American scholars have argued that their countries have few racial conflicts and that social class lines, rather than racial or ethnic background, represent the dominant divisions in their societies. Although many in Brazil deny the existence of racism, a 1989 U.S. State Department report noted that Blacks and Mulattos in Brazil receive less income and education than Whites and encounter discrimination in housing and services (cited in Jalali and Lipset 1998:320).

Degler (1971) compared race relations in Brazil and the United States and speculated, in accordance with theories of group conflict, that the emphasis on competition in U.S. society caused greater discrimination against people of color. He speculated further that as Brazil becomes more industrialized and competition for jobs and housing spreads, discrimination will increase there, too. Degler noted that the U.S. Civil Rights movement heightened people's awareness of racial discrimination in Brazil as well as in the United States, but argued that the aggressive protests of Blacks for equal rights have been more effective in the United States. He acknowledged that the United States has made much progress in reducing the legal, social, and political barriers to equality of opportunity, but concluded that no biracial society in which Whites dominate has created a nation in which Blacks and Whites live together in mutual respect, with equal justice.[17]

Among scholars of race relations in Brazil, as well as in the United States, questions of what to emphasize—the role of history, social class, culture, or prejudice and discrimination—in accounting for economic and other forms of deprivation among people of color remain a prominent issue. The Brazilian experience suggests that prejudice and discrimination do not just disappear as a consequence of intergroup association. For instance, in the United States, even with the active efforts that have been made to expand opportunities for Blacks, Hispanics, and other ethnic groups and to draw them into the mainstream of economic and social life, these groups are not yet fully incorporated. In Brazil, in spite of a professed ethnic pluralism, stratification is still correlated with racial ancestry (Jalali and Lipset 1998). The privileged classes are largely of European background and/or of lighter skin color than the less affluent classes. In both Brazil and the United States there continues to be a discrepancy between the creeds of democracy and the everyday deeds of social life.

Kosovo

A dramatic example of the failure of ethnic inclusion occurred in the 1990s in Kosovo, a former province of Yugoslavia. Ninety percent of the population of Kosovo was ethnic Albanian, many of whom were Muslim. For many years Serbs and Albanians lived side by side, although separated socially, in a "sullen apartheid" (Gall 1999). Ethnic Albanians and ethnic Serbs conducted their lives almost entirely within their own ethnic groups, with each group insisting on speaking only its native language.

In 1989, Serbs, under the direction of President Slobodan Milosevic, began attacking Albanians in what was described in the U.S. media as an "ethnic cleansing." Serbian authorities expelled Albanian teachers and professors from schools and the state-run university in 1990. The pattern was repeated in all state institutions, from hospitals to factories. In 1998 Serbs destroyed Albanian villages, murdered civilians, and drove hundreds of thousands of Albanian people into the surrounding mountains. As the violence continued, large numbers of ethnic Albanians fled their country as refugees. The United States joined with its European allies in the North American Treaty Organization (NATO) to try to stop the violence. For 3 months, NATO bombed suspected Serbian military locations, supplies, and supply routes. The groups involved finally worked out a plan to stop the violence and return the Albanian refugees to their homes. Despite the occupation of NATO troops whose mandate was to keep the peace, violence continued to erupt between the two ethnic groups. For example, in August 1999, Albanian rebels forced Serbs out of the village of Zitinje, near the Macedonian border, where only a year earlier the Serbs had forced Albanians to leave their homes (Erlanger 1999). NATO troops continued to occupy Kosovo in 1999 hoping to keep peace amid continued ethnic hatred on both sides.

Kumovich (1999) studied the reasons for the unwillingness of various ethnic groups in this geographic area to extend economic, political, and social rights to other groups. He concluded that ethnic intolerance was not just a result of differences in religious beliefs or intolerant attitudes toward others, but arose, rather, because competition and conflict for scarce resources led to a polarization of the groups into rigid categories of "them" and "us."

These are only a few brief examples of the complex patterns of racial and ethnic relations that exist around the world. Learning more about problems of racial and ethnic relations in other countries may help us to understand better such problems in the United States. Canada's situation, for example, demonstrates that the strong sense of ethnic identity that attaches to language may be maintained over many generations. The delicate balance between pluralism and separatism in Brazil's experiences shows that the blending of ethnic and racial groups through intermarriage does not, in itself, offer a definitive solution to racial and ethnic problems. Both Kosovo's and Sweden's experiences illustrate how difficult it is to overcome or prevent racism based on differences in appearance, culture, religion, and history that lead to intergroup competition. And South Africa's experience shows that when given power, even previously powerless groups may behave xenophobically.

Mere association between groups over time will not ensure equality of treatment or of opportunity. Recognizing that discrimination is an ever-present tendency in any society in which there are identifiable racial or ethnic groups is a first step in promoting positive racial and ethnic relations. It is important to note, too, that the values of a society can signal that discrimination is not acceptable; and a society's laws and policies can help prevent the damaging self-fulfilling prophecies that accompany prejudice and discrimination. However, the members of each new generation have to learn anew to recognize the often irrational bases of their stereotypes and the injustices of racism. To prevent the perpetuation of racism, the members of all groups must take action against intolerance. As Degler reminds us, "We have to recognize that the price of equality in pluralism, like the price of liberty, is eternal vigilance" (Degler 1971:292).

Discussion Questions

How does symbolic ethnicity enter into contemporary American racial and ethnic relations?

What are some of the structural changes in U.S. job markets that have affected the assimilation processes experienced by the children of the immigrants who have come to the United States in the third immigrant stream?

Why might immigrant youths choose to assimilate to the culture of low-income, inner-city youths instead of White middle-class culture?

What exactly does it mean to be White in U.S. society?

Why do some cases of interethnic contact generate conflict and others do not?

What factors explain the timing and nature of modern ethnic conflicts?

In societies in which ethnic tensions are high, what can be done to minimize conflicts?

The theory of economic competition suggests that conflicts based on ethnic boundaries occur when competition for jobs, housing, and other valued resources increases. What kinds of policies might a government implement to reduce high levels of competition for scarce resources? What kinds of policies might encourage political mobilization or conflicts linked to ethnic differences?

Do intense ethnic loyalties in a multiethnic society endanger democracy? Why or why not?

The text presented a critique of the colonial and immigrant models' analyses of the sociological consequences of intergroup contact and offered an alternative view. What is your critique of this alternative interpretation?

 Key Ideas

1. Full Anglo conformity assimilation has been much slower to occur than the "three-generations" theory would suggest. Although many *individuals* have achieved this type of merger with the dominant group within three generations, very few groups have done so; however, a virtually complete merger has occurred for practically all White ethnic groups over a longer time period. Groups from the countries of the second immigrant stream are unlikely to disappear entirely for perhaps four additional generations and may continue symbolically for many years to come.

2. Since no non-White group has experienced full Anglo conformity assimilation, no one knows whether this process can occur; however, some non-White immigrant groups (e.g., Japanese Americans) have experienced high levels of pluralism, especially at the cultural and secondary structural levels. This shows that under some circumstances this assimilationist goal may be approximated by non-Whites within three generations.

3. Colonized and immigrant minorities typically establish different types of relationships with dominant groups. Colonized minorities usually have arisen from previously intact societies and typically have sought to maintain their group's distinctiveness and independence rather than to be accepted as equal members of the dominant society. Ethnic groups within the host society serve, among other things, to assist the group's members to attain equal treatment.

4. Researchers who have studied immigrants from the third stream have changed the conceptualization of assimilation. As various members of the second stream have become part of the core society, it is less Anglo and more diverse. Newcomers may also assimilate into ethnic communities already established in U.S. urban areas and may have very little contact with Anglo Saxon Protestant Americans. Intermarriages have resulted in multiple ethnic or racial identities.

5. The concept of ethnogenesis may help to explain why heavily oppressed groups such as African Americans, Mexican Americans, Native Americans, and Puerto Ricans, whose initial contacts with the dominant American society were, or were similar to, those of classic colonialism, may nonetheless adopt cultural pluralism or Anglo conformity as goals. Although the initial relationship of each of these groups to the majority group arose through conquest, their subsequent experiences have, for the most part, transformed them into the type of ethnic group that typically arises through immigration. However, even though cultural pluralism is

now widely accepted among members of these groups, the continuation of discrimination against them could fuel separatist tendencies.

6. Mexican Americans, Puerto Ricans, and Indian tribes were conquered and initially formed a centrifugal relationship to the majority. Although there has been substantial variation among these groups, they have shown a definite movement toward the acceptance of cultural pluralism. An increased resistance to this movement by the dominant group, however, could easily halt it and strengthen the movement for greater autonomy.

7. Whites are likely to express a higher level of separatist sentiment with respect to non-Whites than with respect to other Whites. The main line of division within the White and non-White groups with respect to the other group lies between those who favor cultural pluralism or some alternative.

8. In many cases, Anglo conformity and cultural pluralism, although both ideologies of assimilation, lead to noticeably different social policies and tactics of change. America's shift from an agrarian to an urban-industrial society and then to a technology-based, global economy has made it extremely difficult for ethnic groups to maintain or restore a centrifugal relationship with the majority. A pluralist pattern of life, however, may persist within contemporary American society for many generations.

9. The failure to grant equal opportunity to achieve secondary assimilation is a far more serious problem for America than the existence of ethnic divisions. The emergence of a White ethnic identity can result in increased separatism or, if Whites recognize the privilege associated with being White and work to reduce inequities, can result in a pluralistic democracy. Higher levels of secondary assimilation among minorities require further reductions in the levels of prejudice and discrimination.

10. Although the maintenance of ethnic groups may pose a problem for national unity, they also give meaning and purpose to people's lives. Racial and ethnic differences have not disappeared in any country and may, in fact, have become more distinct. Maintaining some form of pluralism that does not erupt in conflict and separatism remains a challenge to countries throughout the world.

⦿ Key Terms

apartheid   An official system of racial segregation implemented by the Republic of South Africa to maintain White domination.

centrifugal relationship   The type of relationship that usually is formed between a conquered group and the conquering group. It is characterized by conflict and by efforts on the part of the subordinate group to free itself from the dominant group.

centripetal relationship   The type of relationship that usually is formed between an immigrant group and the host society. It is characterized by a desire on the part of the subordinate group to achieve equality with the dominant group in the secondary structural sphere coupled with restrained resistance to some forms of assimilation.

laissez-faire racism   This ideology attributes Black disadvantages to supposed characteristics of Blacks themselves, such as lack of attachment to the work ethic, and denies the power of structural determinants of conditions in Black communities.

symbolic ethnicity   An ethnic identity that does not serve as an organizing focus for an individual's life or livelihood and does not require frequent interactions with, or deep commitments to, co-ethnics. This form of ethnicity arises "as the functions of ethnic cultures and groups diminish and identity becomes the primary way of being ethnic."

White ethnic identity   A sense of group or collective identity based on an individual's perception that he or she shares a common racial heritage with a White racial group.

 Notes

1. The Germans, in particular, maintained their language and other cultural elements well beyond that time (see Chapter 3).

2. Whether people who report a particular ancestry actually are of that ancestry is, of course, a different issue (see, e.g., Lieberson and Waters 1988:22–25).

3. Tatum (1992) proposed six stages that Whites may go through as they come to recognize that being White places them in a privileged class. Tatum posited that these processes are not linear; there may be back and forth movements between the stages, with one's vantage point changing with each step.

4. The American golf professional Tiger Woods, for instance, has described himself as a "Cablinasian"—a term he used to embrace his Caucasian, Black, Indian, and Asian identities.

5. Many *individuals* have lost their ethnic identities. The speculations here refer entirely to groups.

6. See also Sakamoto, Wu, and Tzeng (2000).

7. Waters (1990:155–164) argued further that people who experience ethnicity as a trait that they may either choose to ignore or to accentuate may greatly underestimate the extent to which an ethnic identity creates obstacles in American society for those who are racially distinctive. As a result, being "an ethnic" may reduce, rather than increase, a White person's understanding of the problems facing non-Whites.

8. Francis refers to this type of ethnic group as a primary ethnic group.

9. Francis refers to this type of ethnic group as a secondary ethnic group.

10. In cases in which the invader has conquered only a portion of the conquered group's territory, the members of the invaded group who are now cut off from the main body of the society may still possess a full complement of institutions and be able to continue as if they were a whole society.

11. For example, the list of priorities adopted by La Raza Unida Party included

improvements in jobs, education, housing, health care, and justice, as well as community control of the schools, economy, and law enforcement (Forbes 1973:292–294).

12. Kasinitz, Waters, and Mollenkopf (1999) found that a substantial number of immigrants send money home at least once or twice a year, although remittances drop off significantly in the second generation.

13. Waters (1999) found that first-generation Black immigrants tend to emphasize their identities as immigrants, and that second-generation Black immigrants use ethnic identity as a way to distance themselves from poor native-born Blacks.

14. Bobo and Zubrinsky (1996:904) suggested that high levels of Black residential seg-regation are likely to continue even in large, ethnically diverse urban areas because many Latinos and Asians also hold negative stereotypes of Blacks and, like Whites, resist residential desegregation.

15. Estimates of the illegal immigrant population in South Africa vary widely from two million to eight million.

16. Immigrants tend to oppose secession.

17. Degler did not address questions related to the growing complexity of racial and ethnic relations in the United States as Hispanics surpass African Americans in numbers and the immigrant populations become increasingly diverse.

Appendix 1

A Chronology of Selected Federal Immigration Laws, 1875–1996

Year	Law	Major Provisions
1875	Immigration Act	Barred "undesirables."
1882	Chinese Exclusion Act	Suspended immigration of Chinese workers; declared the Chinese ineligible for citizenship. (The suspension of immigration became "permanent" in 1904.)
1917	Immigration Act	Required immigrants to take a literacy test. Created an Asian barred zone.
1921	Immigration Act (Johnson Act)	Set a quota of 3 percent of the number of foreign born of each nationality counted in the census of 1910.
1924	Immigration Act (Johnson–Reid Act)	Reduced quota to 2 percent of the number of foreign born of each nationality counted in the census of 1890; set the total at 165,000; created "national-origins" approach; excluded the Japanese.
1929	Implementation of "national-origins" provisions of 1924	Replaced 2 percent quota with the percentage of people of each nationality in 1920; set the total at 150,000.
1943	Repeal of the Chinese Exclusion Act	Gave the Chinese a quota under the "national-origins" provision.
	Braceros Act	Permitted Mexican laborers to enter the United States on a temporary basis.
1948	Displaced Persons Act	Permitted "nonquota" entrance of refugees from Europe.
1952	Immigration and Nationality Act (INA) (McCarran–Walter Act)	Continued the quota principle; gave Japan a quota; introduced special preference categories; created parole power for the president.
1953	Refugee Relief Act	Permitted 189,000 nonquota refugee admissions.
1965	Amendments to the INA (Hart–Cellar Act)	National-origins quota principle abolished; annual ceiling raised to 290,000; limit of 120,000 set on the Western Hemisphere; set limit of 20,000 for each country of the Eastern Hemisphere; created seven-tiered preference system.

Year	Law	Major Provisions
1976	Western Hemisphere Act	Set limit of 20,000 for each country of the Western Hemisphere.
1980	Refugee Act	Regulated refugee policy; established for the first time grants of asylum under U.N. criteria.
1986	Immigration Reform and Control Act (IRCA) (Simpson–Rodino Act)	Provided legalization procedures, employer sanctions, and rules for foreign agricultural workers.
1990	Immigration Act	Raised annual ceiling to 700,000; revised naturalization requirements and enforcement procedures.
1996	Illegal Immigration Reform and Immigrant Responsibility Act	Increased border enforcement and penalties for illegal entry; placed new restrictions on federal public benefits for immigrants.

Appendix 2
Reducing
Prejudice and
Discrimination

Our review of theories of prejudice and discrimination (Chapter 5) showed that many people assume prejudice is either the sole or the principal cause of discrimination and that to reduce discrimination the causes of prejudice must be altered. Our review also showed, however, that discrimination has additional roots. For example, if a person is unjustly denied a college education, then that person's lack of qualifications will later provide a seemingly "fair" basis for refusing to hire him or her for a job requiring a college education. Although the prospective employer may harbor little prejudice, the employer has nevertheless become a part of a chain of discrimination. Discrimination of this type is unlikely to be reduced by attacking the prejudice of particular individuals. This example suggests that prejudice and discrimination are not simply connected to one another but are embedded within a larger sociocultural system that operates to produce them both.

 Theory and Practice

Theories of prejudice and discrimination are important sources of ideas for attacking these problems. There is not, however, a simple one-to-one correspondence between theories and strategies of social change. Moreover, people differ in the priority they assign to reducing prejudice or discrimination and, consequently, may differ in their theoretical preferences. A cultural-transmission theory of prejudice, for instance, may suggest that a high priority be given to removing ethnic stereotypes from children's schoolbooks; but the same theory may also suggest that prejudice may be reduced more effectively by requiring children from different groups to attend the same schools. If a person has little faith in attempting to alter prejudices, however, she or he may prefer to attack discrimination more directly, perhaps through litigation.

Broadly speaking, people who prefer consensual approaches to solving social problems are likely to focus on the reduction of prejudice and to select strategies suggested by cultural-transmission, group-identification, and personality theories. People who prefer conflict approaches to solving social problems are likely to focus on the reduction of discrimination and to select strategies suggested by situational-pressures, group-gains, and institutional-discrimination theories. Most Americans appear to fall into the first group and to emphasize courses in schools to combat group stereotypes, sensitivity training for professionals who deal with different racial and ethnic groups (e.g., teachers, police officers), books and films that promote understanding of the plight of oppressed peoples, personal counseling for people who are filled with ethnic hatreds, and opportunities that enable the members of different groups to become acquainted. A more vigorous consensual approach may promote information concerning public affairs so that minority groups may know which political candidates to support and how to participate effectively in the political life of the country.

Many Americans, however, have little faith in direct efforts to alter prejudices. They prefer to focus, instead, on the reduction of discrimination (rather than prejudice) through methods derived mainly from the situational-pressures, group-gains, and institutional-discrimination theories. They are likely to advocate litigation to force changes in unfair laws and organizational rules, organizing and participating in militant political groups, and, if these steps fail, engaging in organized protest. Discrimination, they argue, can be reduced effectively only by changing the society's organization—its structure—and to accomplish that, it is necessary to use group power and confrontation. These advocates tend to prefer legal, political, and protest methods that promise rapid social changes even though the risk of intergroup conflict may increase.

We illustrate these issues through brief discussions of educational, legal, and political approaches.

 The Educational Approach

Cognitive Approach

Many people believe that individual prejudice and discrimination reflect a lack of knowledge and, therefore, that everyone should receive more education. This view rests on the belief that the more education people receive, the less likely they are to accept ethnic stereotypes or to wish to hold people of a different ethnicity at a great social distance. Fortunately for all who favor rational discourse in the treatment of human problems, there is considerable evidence to back up this belief. In general, the more educated people are, the lower their prejudice levels appear to be. Regrettably, however, the beneficial effects of cognitive approaches in decreasing intergroup hostility may easily be overestimated.

To illustrate, if the cognitive approach is a powerful method of reducing prejudice, then we would expect that in settings in which large numbers of highly educated people come together—such as in colleges and universities—there would be high levels of interethnic harmony. However, as minority enrollments in American colleges and universities rose during the 1980s and 1990s, so did the levels of interethnic hostility on many campuses. The faculties and students at a large number of colleges and universities were embroiled in often bitter debates concerning things such as the introduction of new courses focusing on racial and ethnic relations, recruitment of minority faculty members, new facilities to accommodate the growing numbers of students representing one ethnic group or another, and the creation of new departments and programs focusing on ethnic studies. And, as we discuss later, hostilities were increased over affirmative action in hiring and admissions. In addition, there were numerous incidents on campuses in which students exchanged ethnic slurs (or "hate speech"), defaced one another's property, and, occasionally, engaged in open confrontation and conflict. Various political disagreements erupted. Such disappointing evidence of the limited tolerance of ethnic-group differences existing among these young, well-educated people probably came as no surprise to the many scholars whose research had shown that although high levels of education and low levels of prejudice were correlated, the connection was not usually strong (see, e.g., Taylor, Sheatsley, and Greeley 1978:45) and that "stereotypic beliefs are extremely resistant to change" (Pettigrew and Martin 1989:186; Stephan 1999).

Although the cognitive approach is useful, and may become more so as more is learned about how to implement it, many researchers and practitioners feel that it must be supplemented by noncognitive methods such as the vicarious experience approach.

Vicarious Experience Approach

Instead of simply imparting specific facts to people, a program of intergroup education may be based on films, plays, television productions, biographies, novels, and other modes of communication that present the members of all groups in a positive way (Allport 1958:454). This approach attempts to "speak to the heart rather than to the head." The underlying premise is that exposure to such materials may help people recognize and appreciate the humanness of the members of all groups and, thus, reduce the tendency for people to draw sharp boundaries between "them" and "us." Participants in such programs are encouraged to "take the role of the other," or to "walk awhile in the other person's shoes." Such a vicarious experience, it is assumed, should lead prejudiced people—members of minority groups as well as the majority—to see the world through the eyes of others and, thereby, to stimulate changes in attitudes and behavior.

Several criticisms of the vicarious experience approach have been advanced. Prejudiced people frequently do not accurately interpret a film or book that runs counter to their prejudices. They may pay more attention to side issues and ignore the central point. Also the effectiveness of a film or some other dramatic presentation in reducing prejudice depends greatly on the skill with which the "message" of tolerance is presented. Some presentations actually create a "boomerang" effect in which prejudices are heightened instead of diminished (Brown 1986:224). And it may reasonably be argued that it is unrealistic to assume that something as superficial as a film or a book may seriously disrupt a deep-seated ethnic prejudice or lead to tolerant behavior.

Intergroup Contact

So far, we have considered two main approaches to increasing the intercultural knowledge of prejudiced people: (1) exposing them to accurate information, especially concerning ethnic out groups and (2) assisting them "to place themselves in the other person's shoes."

So far as change in attitude is concerned, the informational approach generally appears to be weaker than the more emotional approach using novels, plays, films, and so on; but little evidence exists that either approach leads to permanent reductions in prejudice or to much change in behavior. It seems that other methods are required if much change is to be effected.

One of the most common suggestions for improving intergroup relations is that people should "get together" so they may establish communications, participate in various joint activities, discuss their differences, and learn to judge the members of other groups on their merits rather than on the basis of stereotypes. The contact hypothesis argues that "contact, particularly close and sustained contact, with members of different racial and ethnic groups promotes positive, tolerant attitudes toward those groups" (Ellison and Powers 1994:385).

Studies of intergroup contacts have been conducted in various social settings, and numerous factors have been shown to influence the outcome of contacts between the members of dominant and subordinate groups. For example, declines in prejudice are most probable if the people involved are of equal social status, if they are working cooperatively on something, if their activity is supported by people in positions of authority, and if the activity involves a relatively high level of intimacy (Stephan 1987:14; 1999: 46–50). Intergroup contacts occurring under other circumstances, in contrast, may leave prejudices unchanged or intensify them. For example, children involved in school-desegregation programs may become more prejudiced unless parents, teachers, school administrators, and local elected officials make strong public declarations supporting desegregation (Robinson and Preston 1976:911) and classroom activities are organized appropriately (Aronson and Gonzalez 1988:304–307).

Intergroup Contact in Schools.   Studies of intergroup contact in schools have been concerned with a number of topics such as academic achievement and self-esteem, as well as with interracial attitudes and behavior. Although the effects of contact in each of these respects is a matter of considerable practical importance, we are interested here in interracial attitudes and behavior.

One important review of evidence relating to the contact hypothesis in desegregated schools was conducted by St. John (1975). St. John's (1975:67–68) summary stated that "for either race positive findings are less common than negative findings. . . . Sometimes desegregation is reported to have ameliorated the prejudice of Whites but intensified that of Blacks, sometimes the reverse." She noted, however, that the conditions under which contact was theoretically expected to lead to changes in attitudes were seldom fully realized in actual desegregation programs; and that when such conditions were met, the results were more promising.

This conclusion received general support from the results of subsequent studies of the long-term effects of desegregation (Hawley and Smylie 1988:284–285; Stephan 1986:196; 1988:19). Gerard and Miller (1975), conducted a well-designed study of approximately 20,000 children's choices of friends, school-work partners, and play partners in the elementary schools of Riverside, California. Although the observed attitude changes led to "little or no real integration . . . during the relatively long-term contact situation" (Gerard, Jackson, and Conelley 1975:237), studies covering still longer periods of time have shown that Blacks who have attended desegregated schools are more likely than other Blacks to attend college, to work in integrated settings, and to live in desegregated housing (Stephan 1999:52).

The results of studies of the type reviewed so far suggest that more attention should be given to the classroom conditions under which children meet. For instance, even when children are assigned cooperative tasks in small groups, the status rankings of the larger society are imported into the groups. As a result, White children are often more active and influential in classroom projects than are minority-group children (Cohen 1980:253–256; Schofield 1995). For this reason, several techniques have been developed to foster interdependence among students in the classroom (Brown 1986: 615–620; van Oudenhoven 1989:208–213). Methods in which a task can be completed only when the specific contribution of each member is included have been found to be effective ways to reduce status inequalities in classrooms (Jaynes and Williams 1989: 81).

Efforts have been made also to understand to what extent interracial contact encourages the formation of cross-race friendships. In a study of cross-race friendship pairs, Hallinan and Williams (1989:76) found that children who form such friendships are likely to be in frequent contact and to be similar in their attitudes, values, and statuses. Other factors, such as language, group loyalties, and peer responses also may come into play.

Surveys.   In an analysis of a biracial national survey, Sigelman and Welch (1993: 792–793) found that Blacks who had interracial friendships and Whites with interracial neighborhood contacts experienced a decrease in the extent to which they perceived hostility between the races. And in a study based on a national sample of Black Americans, Ellison and Powers (1994:395) found that "blacks who report having close white friends express more favorable views of whites and race relations that those who lack such friends." They concluded that although casual interracial contacts have little direct effect on Black's opinions of Whites, such contacts are nevertheless important because they increase the chance that close interracial friendships may develop (Ellison and Powers 1994:396).

Herring and Amissah (1997), using the 1990 General Social Survey, found that despite the supposed declines in racial intolerance and prejudice, there are still greater negative attitudes toward African Americans than toward any other group. Sizable segments of the U.S. population did not want their children to go to school with Black children, did not want to live in the same neighborhoods with Black people, did not want to be led by Black leaders, and definitely did not want their relatives to be married to a Black person. African Americans were more tolerant and open to interaction with other groups than were all other racial and ethnic groups.

Although the evidence is mixed, the main point of the contact hypothesis has been supported: Under appropriate conditions, personal contacts between majority- and minority-group members can lead to reductions in prejudice (Stroessner and Mackie 1993:83). The method seems to work best when people are "in the same boat"; but even under typical conditions, contact sometimes leads to reduced antipathy (Amir 1976; Ellison and Powers 1994; Stephan 1999).

 The Legal Approach

The Laws and the Mores

Opponents of the legal approach to improving intergroup relations often point out that such attempts may inadvertently make matters worse. For instance, prohibiting the manufacture, sale, and use of alcoholic beverages in America seemed to have increased each of these activities. Similar results have accompanied legal efforts to control the use of other drugs and to control other types of social problems.

Opponents of the legal approach also often echo the argument that "legislation cannot make mores" (Sumner [1906] 1960:8); however, despite appearances, Sumner believed that if laws were skillfully framed and rationally planned, some portions of conduct could be altered; and he believed that if conduct were altered, changes in thought and feeling would follow (Ball, Simpson, and Ikeda 1962).

There certainly is a large element of good sense in this argument. Quite clearly, as Sumner emphasized, the "stroke of the pen" does not produce changes in the morality of people; however, an important reservation should be noted. This viewpoint assumes that attitudes (e.g., prejudice) are the wellspring of action; however, new ways of acting may lead people to new ways of thinking (Pettigrew 1971:279). Additionally, the law seldom is required to stand alone against a monolithic set of opposing mores. More often, the law chooses between competing sets of mores and may tip the balance one way or another (Berger 1968:219).

The effort to desegregate public schools is a prominent example of the use of laws to choose between moral codes. Jim Crow segregation came into being in the South following *Plessy v. Ferguson* in 1896, and the majority of White Americans openly supported this racist system. Nevertheless, many Americans believed, in contrast, that our nation's commitment to equality required that public facilities and institutions should be equally available to all citizens. By the 1930s, the National Association for the Advancement of Colored People (NAACP), the League of United Latin American Citizens (LULAC), and other organizations had selected the desegregation of education as the primary target of their efforts to expand civil rights to include minority citizens. By the late 1960s, busing children to school had become the most prominent method used to achieve this goal.

School Busing

A series of court victories concerning segregation in graduate and professional education led to *Brown I* and the end of legal school segregation, although not to actual school desegregation. A number of school districts in the South and the District of Columbia did begin to comply in 1955, but "massive resistance" to desegregation in some states followed *Brown II* in which the Supreme Court stated that compliance must take place "with all deliberate speed." Consequently, "ten years after *Brown* only 1.2 percent of the nearly 3 million Black students in the 11 Southern States attended school with White students" (U.S. Commission on Civil Rights 1976:4).

The turmoil surrounding school desegregation may seem to show the futility of a legal approach to social change. Consider, however, that the *Brown* decision led not only to a national effort to desegregate schools but also to the much more sweeping task of desegregating every institution in American life. Moreover, many people believed the Court's ruling in *Brown* had infringed on Congress's legislative authority and that the ruling was illegal until Congress passed the Civil Rights Act of 1964. Consider, too, that once the U.S. Supreme Court had the backing of Congress, it moved swiftly to desegregate schools. The Court ruled that school systems must be desegregated, that busing might be used to attain that end, and that busing might be used to bring about school desegregation outside of the South. But is it true that the orders of the courts and the federal government have "failed"?

A federal judge ruled in 1999 that forced desegregation was no longer necessary in the Charlotte–Mecklenburg School District (Yellin and Firestone 1999). This decision had enormous symbolic significance for the institution of court-ordered busing because it was in a 1971 ruling on desegregation in the Charlotte-Mecklenburg district that the United States Supreme Court first approved busing for desegregation nationwide. In the 1990s many busing plans have been dismantled by the same courts that imposed the plans, declaring that the schools have been officially desegregated.

· The U.S. Commission on Civil Rights (1976:77–88) analyzed the role of the courts and the responsible executive agency (HEW) in effecting desegregation. The Commission's study found that among 615 school districts, 84 percent were desegregated between 1966 and 1975. Some 59 percent of the districts reported that either the courts or HEW had provided the most important impetus to desegregate. During the period of heaviest intervention by legal bodies (1968–1972), the racial segregation of school children declined sharply in the South (to 46 percent) while remaining nearly constant in the North and West (29 percent) (Farley 1978; Jaynes and Williams 1989:75). By 1980, 70 percent of Black students were attending schools in which at least 5 percent of the students were White (Stephan 1988:8). It is evident that although many children still attended predominantly segregated schools in 1980, a substantial amount of desegregation of the public schools had taken place. It also is clear that most of this change occurred after 1967, mainly as a result of court orders and busing (Farley 1975:22; Orfield 1982:1). By the school year 1990–1991, only four of the nation's 44 largest urban school districts "had *not* implemented a school desegregation plan" (Heise 1996:1095). Armor's (1995) review of the evidence (cited by Heise 1996:1100) showed that mandatory desegregation plans generated more racial balance than voluntary plans.

Racial balance, of course, is not the only test of the success of school desegregation. For instance, does placing children of different races within the same school necessarily lead to declines in racial prejudice among children? Apparently, this change may or may not occur, depending on other factors (St. John 1975; Stephan 1999). Additionally, it is possible that placing minority children in schools where the majority is White may actually be harmful to the minority children. Indeed in Wilkinson's (1996b:27–28) view, forced "public school integration and the associated demolition of the black school has had a devastating impact on" the "self-esteem, motivation to succeed . . . respect for adults and academic performance" of African American children.

Those who believe, nevertheless, that the patterns of school desegregation created through busing are on balance desirable, must face another question: Can school desegregation be maintained in the face of continued resistance to residential desegregation?

For decades Whites have moved more rapidly to the suburbs than Blacks and other minorities. A part of this movement is due to the "normal" forces of spatial mobility, but a part of it reflects so-called "White Flight." Studies of the problem of housing desegregation show that White residents begin to leave a neighborhood if the proportion of Black residents exceeds 8 percent of the total and that nearly all White residents will leave if the proportion of Black residents reaches 20 percent (Hacker 1992:37). As long as these trends continue, the large increases in school desegregation that have been achieved may be reversed by resegregation in housing. At this time, the courts appear to accept the claims of suburban school systems that school resegregation is largely a reflection of voluntary, individual, and family residential decisions rather than a result of discriminatory administrative policies (Kunen 1996; Orfield and Eaton 1996).

This discussion of legal approaches to the reduction of prejudice and discrimination has focused exclusively on formal laws and court decisions. Of great importance also are the many rules that govern the operation of the large bureaucracies of modern societies. Procedures for hiring and firing, admission into prestigious colleges and professional programs, and eligibility for various licenses and certificates play vital roles in the lives of everyone in our society. Increasing the fairness of the way these many procedures operate is essential for decreasing discrimination and may be necessary before there can be further decreases in prejudice. For a broader discussion of these issues, refer to the discussion of affirmative action in Chapter 7.

 # Political Participation

Consensus Approach: Electoral Politics

Consensus theorists believe an effective way to reduce prejudice and discrimination is to participate in electoral politics. Citizens are urged to inform themselves, vote in elections, lobby legislators, join political parties, and become candidates for office. For 25 years after the Civil War, African Americans participated in elections and held many political offices; but during the period between *Plessy* (1896) and the end of World War II, their participation fell sharply in the South. In the late 1940s, however, returning African, Mexican, and Native American war veterans began organizing to attain equal rights and full participation in American society. Since then, many minority-group members have held positions in the U.S. Congress, the President's cabinet and staff, and as governors of states, members of state legislatures, mayors of cities, members of city councils, and members of school boards, among other posts.

An indication of the magnitude of the increase in minority-group participation in electoral politics in general is revealed by examining some of the changes among African

Americans, as presented by Jaynes and Williams (1989:230–244). For example, the percent of Southern Blacks who were registered to vote rose dramatically from about 3 percent in 1940 to about 67 percent in 1970. For the next 18 years, the level of Southern Black registration ranged between 53 and 67 percent. As Black voter registration rose, so did the number of Black elected officials—and much more in the South than in the other regions of the country. In 1941, there were 33 elected Black officials in the United States, and 20 of those were in the North Central region. By 1985, there were 6,016 elected Black officials, and over 63 percent of these (3,801) were in the South. During those same years, the number of Black members in the U.S. House of Representatives rose from 1 to 20, the number of state senators rose from 3 to 90, and the number of state representatives rose from 23 to 302. Between 1941 and 1986, the number of Black Judges in the United States rose from 10 to 841. As their voting mass has grown, African Americans have become the swing vote in numerous local, state, and federal elections. President Bill Clinton, for example, was elected in 1992 with less than 45 percent of the popular vote nationally but with more than 90 percent of the African American vote. Reverend Jesse Jackson's efforts to register Black voters and his extraordinary performance as a vote-getting presidential candidate in 1980 and 1984 helped, in 1992, to elect 40 African Americans to the U.S. Congress (Dentler 1996:33).

Mexican Americans, too, have always been active politically in mutual aid societies, trade union movements, and political clubs; but their relative concentration in the southwestern United States has affected their political visibility and has led policymakers to think of Hispanic concerns as simple variations of Black problems (Moore and Pachon 1985:176). The Voting Rights Act passed in 1975 extended to Hispanics the protection and benefits that the 1965 Act provided to Blacks. Throughout the 1980s, as court cases replaced at-large elections with single-member districts, major voter registration drives increased the number of Mexican American voters and increased their voting-bloc strength. Still, much of the research on Hispanic voting patterns shows that the majority of the Hispanic adults do not participate in electoral politics (Tomás Rivera Center 1996:21). Many Hispanics are foreign born or recent immigrants who lack citizenship and cannot vote or participate politically. Recent elections, however, have shown that Hispanic voters can be mobilized around issues of importance to them or in support of Hispanic candidates. Hispanic voting participation and the number of Hispanic elected officials have both increased sharply.

All minority groups have shown an increased reliance on bureaucracies and the courts to achieve their political goals. There is a growing influence of Washington-based Asian, African American, Mexican American, and Native American lobby groups and a growing representation of these groups in national policy debates affecting their communities. Even though minorities still are underrepresented in many important decision-making positions, there can be little doubt that their ability to affect public policy in important ways has increased substantially since 1945.

Conflict Approach: Organized Social Protest

The various methods of reducing prejudice and discrimination considered thus far have rested mainly on the assumptions of consensus theory. Those who favor education, intergroup contact, the passage of laws, and fair organizational rules assume that the majority will gradually, and for the most peacefully, become more tolerant and inclusive. As opportunities for minority-group members are created, intergroup tensions gradually will be reduced with only moderate conflicts along the way. This assumption, which is consistent with the expectations of the ideologies of Anglo conformity, the melting pot, and cultural pluralism, has been sharply challenged by conflict theorists, among whom minority-group members may be highly represented.

Although nonviolent public protest also, strictly speaking, is consistent with the three assimilation ideologies, subscribers to assimilationist views tend to frown on such actions and to emphasize that other approaches are likely to be more successful. Conflict theorists, in contrast, consider such actions to be absolutely necessary. It is argued that equality will never be given freely by the majority. The majority is much more likely, in this view, to reduce its levels of discrimination in the face of a boycott, a strike, a sit-in, or an outburst of violence than in response to the usual kinds of educational programs or even to laws prohibiting discrimination. Indeed, the majority may be unwilling to adopt laws of this type unless it is pressured to do so by organized protest groups.

From this vantage point, it is possible to claim that whenever the legal approach does succeed it is largely due to the power of protest groups, often groups comprised of minority-group members. Although educational programs, interracial contacts, and antidiscrimination laws may be desirable, from the conflict perspective these steps must always be only a part of a larger program consisting of militant ethnic organizations that pose a constant threat of confrontation with the majority.

Although it is crucial to distinguish between nonviolent and violent protest, the distinction sometimes breaks down as nonviolent efforts inadvertently spill over into violence—often when nonviolent protesters themselves are attacked. Whether the nonviolent or violent forms of protest are the most effective in gaining concessions from the majority represents an important theoretical dividing line. Many who accept nonviolent conflict as a necessary part of social change are totally opposed to the use of violence and believe that it is, in fact, counterproductive. For example, even though the ultimate goals sought by Martin Luther King, Jr. and Malcolm X were similar, these men disagreed sharply on what methods were most likely to succeed. King believed that violence was always wrong and would impede the progress of those who use it. Malcolm X, in contrast, strongly supported "defensive" violence and, at times, seemed to endorse "offensive" violence as well. This kind of division almost surely may be found among the conflict theorists within every minority group in America.

All efforts to reduce discrimination and to attain a social standing that are acceptable to the minority, conflict theorists believe, must involve some intergroup disharmony, tension, and open protest of some kind. Even the most educated Black Americans, Hacker (1996:29) asserted, "have no illusions that bias has been eradicated and they know that without external pressure they would not be where they are."

References

Ablon, Joan. "Relocated American Indians in the San Francisco Bay Area: Social Interaction and Indian Identity." In Howard M. Bahr, Bruce A. Chadwick, and Robert C. Day, eds., *Native Americans Today*, 412–428. New York: Harper & Row, 1972.

Abraham, Nabeel, and Andrew Shryock, eds. *Arab Detroit: From Margin to Mainstream*. Detroit, Mich.: Wayne State University, 2000.

Abrams, Franklin. "Immigration Law and Its Enforcement: Reflections of American Immigration Policy." In Roy Simon Bryce-Laporte, ed, *Sourcebook on the New Immigration*, 27–35. New Brunswick, N.J.: Transaction Books, 1980.

———. "American Immigration Policy: How Strait the Gate?" In Richard R. Hofstetter, ed., *U.S. Immigration Policy*. Durham, N.C.: Duke University Press, 1984.

Abu-Laban, Baha, and Michael W. Suleiman, eds. *Arab Americans: Continuity and Change*. Belmont, Mass: Association of Arab-American University Graduates, 1989.

Abu-Laban, Baha, and Faith T. Zeady, eds., *Arabs in America: Myths and Realities*. Wilmett, Ill.: The Medina University Press International, 1975.

Abu-Laban, Sharon. "The Coexistence of Cohorts: Identity and Adaptation among Arab-American Muslims." In Baha Abu-Laban and Michael W. Suleiman, eds., *Arab Americans: Continuity and Change*, 45–63. Belmont, Mass.: Association of Arab-American University Graduates, 1989.

Acuña, Rodolfo. *Occupied America*, 2nd ed. New York: Harper & Row, 1981.

Adamic, Louis. *A Nation of Nations*. New York: Harper and Brothers, 1944.

Adams, Romanzo. "The Unorthodox Race Doctrine of Hawaii." In E. B. Reuter, ed., *Race and Culture Contacts*, 143–160. New York: McGraw-Hill, 1934.

Adorno, T. W., Else Frenkel-Brunswik, Daniel J. Levinson, and R. Nevitt Sanford. *The Authoritarian Personality*. New York: Harper and Brothers, 1950.

Akram, Susan M. "The Aftermath of September 11, 2001: The Targeting of Arabs and Muslims in America." *Arab Studies Quarterly* 24 (Spring–Summer 2002): 61–119.

Alba, Richard D. *Italian Americans*. Englewood Cliffs, N.J.: Prentice-Hall, 1985.

———, ed. *Ethnicity and Race in the U.S.A.* New York: Routledge, 1988.

———. "Italian Americans: A Century of Ethnic Change." In Silvia Pedraza and Rubén G. Rumbaut, eds., *Origins and Destinies: Immigration, Race, and Ethnicity in America*, 172–181. Belmont: Wadsworth Publishing Company, 1996.

———. "Immigration and the American Realities of Assimilation and Multiculturalism." *Sociological Forum* 14 (March 1999a):3–25.

———. "Reflections on Assimilation and Immigration." Paper presented at the Annual Meeting of the American Sociological Association, Chicago, 1999b.

————. "To the Editor." *The New York Review of Books* (May 23, 2002):84.

Alba, Richard D., and Reid M. Golden. "Patterns of Ethnic Marriage in the United States." *Social Forces* 65 (September 1986): 202–223.

Alba, Richard D., and Victor Nee. "Rethinking Assimilation Theory for a New Era of Immigration," *International Migration Review* (Winter 1997):826–874.

Alba, Richard, and Victor Nee. *Remaking the American Mainstream*. Cambridge, Mass.: Harvard University Press, 2003.

Allen, Walter R., and Joseph O. Jewell. "The Miseducation of Black America: Black Education Since *An American Dilemma*." In Obie Clayton, Jr., ed., *An American Dilemma Revisited: Race Relations in a Changing World,* 169–190. New York: Russell Sage Foundation, 1996.

Allport, Gordon. *The Nature of Prejudice*. Garden City, N.Y.: Doubleday, 1958.

Allsup, Carl. *The American G.I. Forum: Origins and Evolution*. Center for Mexican American Studies Monograph no. 6. Austin, Tex.: University of Texas Press, 1982.

Alvarez, Rodolfo. "The Psycho-Historical and Socioeconomic Development of the Chicano Community in the United States." In Rodolfo O. de la Garza, Frank D. Bean, Charles M. Bonjean, Ricardo Romo, and Rodolfo Alvarez, eds., *The Mexican American Experience,* 33–56. Austin, Tex.: University of Texas Press, 1985.

Alvírez, David, and Frank D. Bean. "The Mexican American Family." In C. H. Mindel and R. W. Habenstein, eds., *Ethnic Families in America: Patterns and Variations,* 271–292. New York: Elsevier North-Holland, 1976.

American-Arab Anti-Discrimination Committee. "ADC Fact Sheet: The Condition of Arab Americans Post 9/11," March 27, 2002. http://www.adc.org.

American Broadcasting System. ABCNews/*Washington Post* Poll, September 13, 2001. http://abcnews.go.com.

Americans Before Columbus. Albuquerque, N.Mex.: National Indian Youth Council, 1992.

Amir, Yehuda. "The Role of Intergroup Contact in Change of Prejudice and Ethnic Relations." In P. A. Katz, ed., *Toward the Elimination of Racism,* 245–308. New York: Pergamon Press, 1976.

Anderson, Robert N., and Rogelio Saenz. "Structural Determinants of Mexican American Intermarriage, 1975–1980." *Social Science Quarterly* 75 (June 1994): 414–429.

Appiah, K. Anthony, and Amy Gutman. *Color Conscious: The Political Morality of Race*. Princeton, N.J.: Princeton University Press, 1996.

Arab American Institute. *FBI Forms First Arab Advisory Committee*, 2003. http://aaiusa.org.

Armor, David J. *Forced Justice: School Desegregation and the Law*. New York: Oxford University Press, 1995.

Aronson, Elliot, and Alex Gonzalez. "Desegregation, Jigsaw, and the Mexican-American Experience." In Phyllis A. Katz and Dalmas A. Taylor, eds., *Eliminating Racism,* 301–314. New York: Plenum Press, 1988.

Ayres, B. Drummond, Jr. "Fighting Affirmative Action, Leader's Race Looms Large." *New York Times* (April 18, 1996): A1.

Bach, Robert L., and Rita Carroll-Seguin. "Labor Force Participation, Household Composition and Sponsorship among Southeast Asian Refugees." *International Migration Review* 20 (Summer 1986): 381–404.

Badar, Christine Velez, Clifford L. Broman, Janet L. Bokemeier, and Maxine Baca Zinn. "Labor Force Participation Among Mexican and Mexican American Women in the Rural and Urban Southwest: A Comparative Study." *Latino Studies Journal* 6 (January 1995): 68–91.

Bahr, Howard M. "An End to Invisibility." In Howard M. Bahr, Bruce A. Chadwick, and Robert C. Day, eds., *Native Americans Today,* 404–412. New York: Harper & Row, 1972.

Bahr, Howard M., Bruce A. Chadwick, and Robert C. Day, eds., *Native Americans Today*. New York: Harper & Row, 1972.

Baker, Ross K., ed. *The Afro-American*. New York: Van Nostrand Reinhold Company, 1970.

Baker, Susan Gonzales, Robert Cushing, and Charles Haynes. "Fiscal Impacts of Mexican Migration to the United States." In Frank D. Bean, Rodolfo O. De La Garza, Bryan R. Roberts, and Sidney Weintraub, eds., *At the Crossroads: Mexico and U.S. Immigration Policy,* 145–176. New York: Rowman and Littlefield, 1997.

Balderrama, Francisco E. *In Defense of La Raza: The Los Angeles Mexican Consulate and the Mexican Community, 1929 to 1936,* 58–61. Tucson, Ariz.: University of Arizona Press, 1982.

Baldwin, John R. "Tolerance/Intolerance: A Multidisciplinary View of Prejudice." In Michael L. Hecht, ed., *Communicating Prejudice,* 24–56. Thousand Oaks, Calif.: Sage Publications, 1998.

Ball, Harry V., George Eaton Simpson, and Kiyoshi Ikeda. "Law and Social Change: Sumner Reconsidered." *American Journal of Sociology* 57 (March 1962): 532–540.

Ball, Howard. "Judicial Parsimony and Military Necessity Disinterred: A Reexamination of the Japanese Exclusion Cases, 1943–44." In Roger Daniels, Sandra C. Taylor, and Harry H. L. Kitano, eds., *Japanese Americans: From Relocation to Redress,* rev. ed., 72–74. Seattle, Wash.: University of Washington Press, 1991.

Baltzell, E. Digby. *The Protestant Establishment*. New York: Vintage Books, 1964.

Bardolph, Richard. *The Negro Vanguard*. New York: Vintage Books, 1961.

Baron, Harold M. "The Web of Urban Racism." In Louis L. Knowles and Kenneth Prewitt, eds., *Institutional Racism in America,* 134–176. Englewood Cliffs, N.J.: Prentice-Hall, 1969.

Baron, Robert A. *Human Aggression*. New York: Plenum Press, 1977.

Barrera, Mario. *Race and Class in the Southwest*. South Bend, Ind.: University of Notre Dame Press, 1979.

———. *Beyond Aztlan: Ethnic Autonomy in Comparative Perspective*. South Bend, Ind.: University of Notre Dame Press, 1988.

Barringer, Felicity. "Ethnic Pride Confounds the Census." *New York Times* (May 9, 1993): E3.

Barringer, Herbert R., Robert W. Gardner, and Michael J. Levin. *Asian and Pacific Islanders in the United States*. New York: Russell Sage Foundation, 1995.

Bean, Frank D. "Immigration Combatants Overlook the New Reality." *Houston Chronicle* (August 29, 1993): F1, F5.

Bean, Frank D., Jorge Chapa, Ruth Berg, and Kathryn Sowards. "Educational and Sociodemographic Incorporation Among Hispanic Immigrants to the United States." In Barry Edmonston and Jeffrey S. Passel, eds., *Immigration and Ethnicity: The Integration of America's Newest Arrivals,* 73–100. Washington, D.C.: Urban Institute Press, 1994.

Bean, Frank D., and Marta Tienda. *The Hispanic Population of the United States*. New York: Russell Sage Foundation, 1987.

Beck, E. M. "Discrimination and White Economic Loss: A Time Series Examination of the Radical Model." *Social Forces* 59 (September 1980): 148–168.

Beck, E. M., and Stewart Tolnay. "The Killing Fields of the Deep South: The Market for Cotton and the Lynching of Blacks, 1882–1930." *American Sociological Review* 55 (August 1990): 526–539.

Bennett, Lerone, Jr. *Before the Mayflower,* rev. ed. New York: Penguin Books, 1964.

Benokraitis, Nijole V., and Joe R. Feagin. *Affirmative Action and Equal Opportunity: Action, Inaction, Reaction*. Boulder, Colo.: Westview Press, 1978.

Berelson, Bernard, and Patricia J. Salter. "Majority and Minority Americans: An Analysis of Magazine Fiction." *Public Opinion Quarterly* 10 (Summer 1946): 168–190.

Berger, Morroe. *Equality by Statute,* rev. ed. Garden City, N.Y.: Doubleday, 1968.

Berkowitz, Leonard, ed. *Roots of Aggression: A Re-examination of the Frustration-Aggression Hypothesis.* New York: Atherton Press, 1969.

———. "Frustration-Aggression Hypothesis: Examination and Reformulation." *Psychological Bulletin* 106 (July 1989): 59–73.

Bernard, William S. "Immigration: History of U.S. Policy." In Stephan Thernstrom, Ann Orlov, and Oscar Handlin, eds., *Harvard Encyclopedia of American Ethnic Groups,* 486–495. Cambridge, Mass.: The Belknap Press, 1980.

Billingsley, Andrew. *Black Families in White America.* Englewood Cliffs, N.J.: Prentice-Hall, 1968.

Blassingame, John W. *The Slave Community: Plantation Life in the Antebellum South.* New York: Oxford University Press, 1972.

Blauner, Robert. *Racial Oppression in America.* New York: Harper and Row, 1972.

———. "Colonized and Immigrant Minorities." In Ronald Takaki, ed., *From Different Shores: Perspectives on Race and Ethnicity in America,* 2nd ed., 149–160. New York: Oxford University Press, 1994.

———. "Talking Past Each Other: Black and White Languages of Race." In Karen E. Rosenblum and Toni-Michelle C. Travis, eds., *The Meaning of Difference,* 167–176. New York: McGraw-Hill, 1996.

Blee, Kathleen M. *Women of the Klan: Racism and Gender in the 1920s.* Berkeley, Calif.: University of California Press, 1991.

Bobo, Lawrence. "Group Conflict, Prejudice, and the Paradox of Contemporary Racial Attitudes." In Phyllis A. Katz and Dalmas A. Taylor, eds., *Eliminating Racism,* 85–114. New York: Plenum Press, 1988.

Bobo, Lawrence, and James R. Kluegel. "Status, Ideology, and Dimensions of Whites' Racial Beliefs and Attitudes: Progress and Stagnation." In Steven A. Tuch and Jack K. Martin, eds., *Racial Attitudes in the 1990s: Continuity and Change,* 93–120. Westport, Conn.: Praeger Publishers, 1997.

Bobo, Lawrence, James R. Kluegel, and Ryan A. Smith. "Laissez-Faire Racism: The Crystallization of a Kinder, Gentler, Antiblack Ideology." In Steven A. Tuch and Jack K. Martin, eds., *Racial Attitudes in the 1990s: Continuity and Change,* 15–42. Westport, Conn.: Praeger Publishers, 1997.

Bobo, Lawrence, and Camille L. Zubrinsky. "Attitudes on Residential Integration: Perceived Status Differences, Mere In-Group Preference, or Racial Prejudice?" *Social Forces* 74 (March 1996): 883–909.

Bodnar, John. *The Transplanted.* Bloomington, Ind.: Indiana University Press, 1985.

Bogardus, Emory S. "A Social Distance Scale." *Sociology and Social Research* 17 (January–February 1933): 265–271.

Bolino, August C. *The Ellis Island Source Book.* Washington, D.C.: The Catholic University of America, 1985.

Bonacich, Edna. "A Theory of Ethnic Antagonism: The Split Labor Market." *American Sociological Review* 37 (October 1972): 547–559.

———. "A Theory of Middleman Minorities." *American Sociological Review* 38 (October 1973): 583–594.

———. "Abolition, the Extension of Slavery, and the Position of Free Blacks: A Study of Split Labor Markets in the United States, 1830–1863." *American Journal of Sociology* 81 (November 1975): 601–628.

———. "Advanced Capitalism and Black/White Race Relations in the United States: A Split Labor Market Interpretation." *American Sociological Review* 41 (February 1976): 34–51.

Bonacich, Edna, and John Modell. *The Economic Basis of Ethnic Solidarity*. Berkeley, Calif.: University of California Press, 1980.

Bonney, Rachel A. "The Role of AIM Leaders in Indian Nationalism." *American Indian Quarterly* (Autumn 1977): 209–224.

Bordewich, Fergus M. *Killing the White Man's Indian*. New York: Doubleday, 1996.

Borjas, George J. *Friends or Strangers: The Impact of Immigration on the U.S. Economy*. New York: Basic Books, 1990.

———. "The New Economics of Immigration." *The Atlantic Monthly* (November, 1996): 72–80.

———. *Heaven's Door: Immigration Policy and the American Economy*. Princeton: Princeton University Press, 1999.

Boston, Thomas D. *Race, Class, and Conservatism*. Boston: Unwin Hyman, 1988.

Boswell, Terry E. "A Split Labor Market Analysis of Discrimination Against Chinese Immigrants, 1850–1882." *American Sociological Review* 51 (June 1986): 352–371.

Bowen, William G., and Derek Bok. *The Shape of the River*. Princeton, N.J.: Princeton University Press, 1998.

Bowman, Phillip J. "Joblessness." In James S. Jackson, ed., *Life in Black America*, 156–178. Newbury Park, Calif.: Sage Publications, 1991.

Boyd, Robert L. "A Contextual Analysis of Black Self-Employment in Large Metropolitan Areas, 1970–1980." *Social Forces* 70 (December 1991): 409–429.

Bradshaw, Benjamin S., and Frank D. Bean. "Intermarriage Between Persons of Spanish and Non-Spanish Surnames: Changes from the Mid-Nineteenth to the Mid-Twentieth Century." *Social Science Quarterly* 51 (September 1970): 389–395.

Bragdon, Ann Louise. "Early Arabic-Speaking Immigrant Communities in Texas." In Baha Abu-Laban and Michael W. Suleiman, eds., *Arab Americans: Continuity and Change*, 83–101. Belmont, Mass.: Association of Arab-American University Graduates, 1989.

Brasher, Philip. "High Risk of Suicide Found in Native American Youths." *Austin American-Statesman* (March 25, 1992): A4.

Brigham, Carl C. *A Study of American Intelligence*. Princeton, N.J.: Princeton University Press, 1923.

———. "Intelligence Tests of Immigrant Groups." *Psychological Review* 37 (March 1930): 158–165.

Brimelow, Peter. "Time to Rethink Immigration?" *National Review* 44 (June 22, 1992): 30–46.

———. *Alien Nation*. New York: Random House, 1995.

Brisbane, Robert H. "Black Protest in America." In Mabel M. Smythe, ed., *The Black American Reference Book*, 537–579. Englewood Cliffs, N.J.: Prentice-Hall, 1976.

Brooke, James. "In the Budget Talk from Washington, Indians See the Cruelest Cuts of All." *New York Times* (October 15, 1995): 10.

Broom, Leonard, and Norval D. Glenn. "When Will America's Negroes Catch Up?" *New Society* (March 25, 1965): 6–7.

Broom, Leonard, and John L. Kitsuse. *The Managed Casualty*. Berkeley, Calif.: University of California Press, 1956.

Brown, Roger. *Social Psychology*, 2nd ed. New York: The Free Press, 1986.

Brown, W. Norman. "India." *Encyclopedia Americana* 14 (2002): 864–865.

Bryan, Samuel. "Mexican Immigrants on the Labor Market." In Wayne Moquin and Charles Van Doren, eds., *A Documentary History of the Mexican Americans*, 333–339. New York: Bantam Books, 1972.

Bryson, Bill. *The Mother Tongue: English and How It Got That Way*. New York: William Morrow and Company, Inc., 1990.

Bullard, Sara, ed. *The Ku Klux Klan: A History of Violence and Racism*, 4th ed. Montgomery, Ala.: Klanwatch, The Southern Poverty Law Center, 1991.

Bunche, Ralph J. "The Programs, Ideologies, Tactics, and Achievements of Negro Betterment and Interracial Organizations," Unpublished Memorandum, 1940. In August Meier, Elliott Rudwick, and Francis L. Broderick, eds., *Black Protest Thought in the Twentieth Century*, 2nd ed., 122–131. Indianapolis, Ind. and New York: Bobbs-Merrill, 1971.

Burma, John H. "Interethnic Marriage in Los Angeles, 1948–1959." *Social Forces* 42 (December 1963): 156–165.

Burner, David, Elizabeth Fox-Genovese, and Virginia Bernhard. *A College History of the United States*, Vol. 1. St. James, N.Y.: Brandywine Press, 1991.

Burns, W. Haywood. *The Voices of Negro Protest.* New York: Oxford University Press, 1963.

Burr, Jeffrey A., Omer R. Galle, and Mark A. Fossett. "Racial Occupational Inequality in Southern Metropolitan Areas, 1940–1980: Revisiting the Visibility-Discrimination Hypothesis." *Social Forces* 69 (March 1991): 831–850.

Butler, John Sibley. *Entrepreneurship and Self-Help Among Black Americans.* Albany, N.Y.: State University of New York Press, 1991.

———. "Myrdal Revisited: The Negro in Business, the Professions, Public Service, and Other White Collar Occupations." In Obie Clayton, Jr., ed., *An American Dilemma Revisited: Race Relations in a Changing World*, 138–168. New York: Russell Sage Foundation, 1996.

Butler, John Sibley, and Kenneth L. Wilson. "The American Soldier Revisited: Race Relations in the Military." *Social Science Quarterly* 59 (December 1978): 451–467.

———. "Entrepreneurial Enclaves: An Exposition into the Afro-American Experience." *National Journal of Sociology* 2 (Fall 1988): 127–166.

Butterfield, Fox. "Indians are Crime Victims at Rate Above U.S. Average." *New York Times* (February 15, 1999): A12

Cafferty, Pastora San Juan, Barry R. Chiswick, Andrew M. Greeley, and Teresa A. Sullivan. *The Dilemma of American Immigration.* New Brunswick, N.J.: Transaction Books, 1983.

Camarillo, Albert M., and Frank Bonilla. "Hispanics in a Multicultural Society: A New American Dilemma?" In Charles A. Gallagher, ed., *Rethinking the Color Line: Readings in Race and Ethnicity*, 509–533. Boston: McGraw Hill, 2004.

Cancio, Silvia A., T. David Evans, and David J. Maume, Jr. "Reconsidering the Declining Significance of Race: Racial Differences in Early Career Wages." *American Sociological Review* 61 (August 1996): 541–556.

Caplan, Nathan, Marcella H. Choy, and John K. Whitmore. *Children of the Boat People: A Study of Educational Success.* Ann Arbor, Mich.: University of Michigan Press, 1992.

Caplan, Nathan, John K. Whitmore, and Marcella H. Choy. *The Boat People and Achievement in America.* Ann Arbor, Mich.: University of Michigan Press, 1989.

Carmichael, Stokely, and Charles Hamilton. *Black Power.* New York: Vintage Books, 1967.

Carter, Deborah J., and Reginald Wilson. *Minorities in Higher Education. 1992 Eleventh Annual Status Report.* Washington, D.C.: American Council on Education, 1993.

Cavalli-Sforza, L. Luca, Paolo Menozzi, and Alberto Piazza. *The History and Geography of the Human Gene.* Princeton, N.J.: Princeton University Press, 1994.

Celis, William 3rd. "The Answer Is Either 'Si' or 'No Way.'" *New York Times* (October 15, 1995a): 5.

———. "Study Finds Rising Concentration of Black and Hispanic Students." *New York Times* (December 14, 1995b): A1.

Chaudhuri, Joyotpaul. "American Indian Policy: An Overview." In Vine Deloria, Jr., ed., *American Indian Policy in the Twentieth Century*, 15–33. Norman, Okla.: University of Oklahoma Press, 1985.

Chen, David W. "Begrudging the Neighbors' Luck: Newly Rich Oneidas' Land Claim Stirs Other Resentments." *New York Times* (January 22, 1999): A23.

Chen, Shyh-Jer. "Characteristics and Assimilation of Chinese Immigrants in the U.S. Labour Market." *International Migration Review* 36 (June 1998): 187–210.

Chen, Theodore H. E. "China." *World Book Encyclopedia* 3 (1961): 291.

Chiswick, Barry R. "An Analysis of the Earnings and Employment of Asian-American Men." *Journal of Labor Economics* 1 (April 1983): 197–214.

Chow, Esther Ngan-Ling. "Family, Economy, and the State: A Legacy of Struggle for Chinese American Women." In Silvia Pedraza and Rubén G. Rumbaut, eds., *Origins and Destinies: Immigration, Race, and Ethnicity in America,* 110–124. Belmont, Calif.: Wadsworth Publishing Company, 1996.

———. "The Feminist Movement: Where Are All the Asian American Women?" In Ronald Takaki, ed., *From Different Shores: Perspectives of Race and Ethnicity in America,* 2nd ed. New York: Oxford University Press, 1994.

Chung, Sue Fawn. "The Chinese American Citizen Alliance: An Effort in Assimilation, 1895–1965." In Franklin Ng, ed., *Asians in America: The Peoples of East, Southeast, and South Asia in American Life and Culture,* 150–177. New York: Garland Publishing, 1998.

Church, George J. "The Fire This Time." *Time* (May 11, 1992): 18–25.

Clark, Kenneth B. *Prejudice and Your Child,* 2nd ed. Boston: Beacon Press, 1963.

Clark, Kenneth B., and Mamie K. Clark. "The Development of Consciousness of Self and the Emergence of Racial Identification in Negro Preschool Children." *Journal of Social Psychology* 10 (November 1939): 591–599.

———. "Racial Identification and Preference in Negro Children." In Eleanor E. Maccoby, Theodore M. Newcomb, and Eugene L. Hartley, eds., *Readings in Social Psychology,* 602–611. New York: Henry Holt, 1958.

Clark, W. A. V., and Milan Mueller. "Hispanic Relocation and Spatial Assimilation: A Case Study." *Social Science Quarterly* 69 (June 1988): 468–475.

Clemetson, Lynette, and Steven Holmes. "Old Dream and New Issues 40 Years After Rights March." *New York Times* (August 24, 2003): A1.

Cobb-Clark, Deborah A., and Sherrie A. Kossoudji. "Mobility in El Norte: The Employment and Occupational Changes of Unauthorized Latin American Women." *Social Science Quarterly* 81 (March 2000): 311–324.

Cohen, Elizabeth G. "Design and Redesign of the Desegregated School." In Walter G. Stephan and Joe R. Feagin, eds., *School Desegregation,* 251–280. New York: Plenum Press, 1980.

Cole, K. C. "Innumeracy." In Russell Jacoby and Naomi Glauberman, eds., *The Bell Curve Debate: History Documents, Opinions,* 73–80. New York: Times Books, 1995.

Cole, Stewart G., and Mildred Wiese Cole. *Minorities and the American Promise.* New York: Harper and Brothers, 1954.

Collison, Michele N.-K. "A Seldom-Aired Issue: Do Black-Student Groups Hinder Campus Integration?" *Chronicle of Higher Education* 35 (October 5, 1988): A35.

Connell, Evan S. *Son of the Morning Star.* San Francisco: North Point Press, 1984.

Connerly, Ward. "Up From Affirmative Action." *New York Times* (April 29, 1996): A11.

Connor, John W. "Acculturation and Family Continuities in Three Generations of Japanese Americans." *Journal of Marriage and the Family* 36 (February 1974): 159–165.

Conzen, Kathleen Neils. "Germans." In Stephan Thernstrom, Ann Orlov, and Oscar Handlin, eds., *Harvard Encyclopedia of American Ethnic Groups,* 405–425. Cambridge, Mass.: The Belknap Press, 1980.

Cook, James. "The American Indian Through Five Centuries." *Forbes* (November 1981).

Cose, Ellis. "The Good News About Black America: (And Why Many Blacks Aren't Celebrating)." *Newsweek* (June 7, 1999): 29–40.

Cotter, David, Joan M. Hermsen, Seth Ovadia, and Reeve Vanneman. "The Glass Ceiling Effect." *Social Forces* 80 (December 2001): 655–682.

Crane, Jonathan. "Race and Children's Cognitive Test Scores: Empirical Evidence That Environment Explains the Entire Gap." Paper presented to the Seminar on Meritocracy and Equality, University of Chicago, May 26, 1995.

Crane, Paul, and Alfred Larson. "The Chinese Massacre." In Roger Daniels, ed., *Anti-Chinese Violence in North America*, 47–55. New York: Arno Press, 1978.

Crawford, James. "Congress Hears English-only Legislation." *News Reports and Analyses.* University of California, Santa Barbara: UC Linguistic Minority Research Institute, December 1995.

Crevecoeur, J. Hector St. John. "Welcome to My Shores, Distressed European." In Moses Rischin, ed., *Immigration and the American Tradition.* Indianapolis, Ind.: Bobbs-Merrill, 1976.

Cronon, Edmund David. *Black Moses.* Madison, Wis.: University of Wisconsin Press, 1969.

Crosby, Alfred W., Jr. *The Columbian Exchange.* Westport, Conn.: Greenwood Press, 1972.

Cross, Harry (with Genevieve Kenney, Jane Mell, and Wendy Zimmerman). *Employer Hiring Practices: Differential Treatment of Hispanic and Anglo Job Seekers.* Washington, D.C.: Urban Institute Press, 1990.

Cuéllar, Alfredo. "Perspective on Politics." In Joan W. Moore, ed., *Mexican Americans,* 137–156. Englewood Cliffs, N.J.: Prentice-Hall, 1970.

Curran, Thomas J. *Xenophobia and Immigration.* Boston: Twayne Publishers, 1975.

Daley, Suzanne. "Reversing Roles in a South Afrian Dilemma." *New York Times* (October 26, 1997): WK5

———. "New South Africa Shuts the Door on Its Neighbors." *New York Times* (October 19, 1998): A6.

Daniels, Roger. *The Politics of Prejudice.* New York: Atheneum, 1969.

———. *Asian America: Chinese and Japanese in the United States Since 1850.* Seattle, Wash.: University of Washington Press, 1988.

———. *Anti-Chinese Violence in North America.* New York: Arno Press, 1978.

———. "The Forced Migrations of West Coast Japanese Americans, 1942–1964: A Quantitative Note." In Roger Daniels, Sandra C. Taylor, and Harry H. L. Kitano, eds., *Japanese Americans: From Relocation to Redress,* rev. ed., 72–74. Seattle, Wash.: University of Washington Press, 1991a.

Daniels, Roger, Sandra C. Taylor, and Harry H. L. Kitano, eds. *Japanese Americans: From Relocation to Redress,* rev. ed., Seattle, Wash.: University of Washington Press, 1991.

Daoud, Mojahid. "Growing Up Arab in America." In Baha Abu-Laban and Michael W. Suleiman, eds., *Arab Americans: Continuity and Change,* 173–179. Belmont, Mass.: Association of Arab-American University Graduates, 1989.

Darder, Antonia, Rodolfo D. Torres, and Henry Gutiérrez, eds. *Latinos and Education: A Critical Reader.* New York: Routledge, 1997.

Davidson, Lawrence. "Debating Palestine: Arab-American Challenges to Zionism 1917–1932." In Michael W. Suleiman, ed., *Arabs in America,* 227–240. Philadelphia: Temple University Press, 1999.

Davie, Maurice R. *Negroes in American Society.* New York: McGraw-Hill, 1949.

Davis, Sally M., Ken Hunt, and Judith M. Kitzes. "Improving the Health of Indian Teenagers—A Demonstration Program in Rural New Mexico." *Public Health Reports* 104 (May–June 1989): 271–278.

Deaux, Kay, Anne Reid, Kim Mizrahi, and Kathleen A. Ethier. "Parameters of Social Identity." *Journal of Personality and Social Psychology* 68 (February 1995): 280–290.

DeFleur, Melvin L., and Frank B. Westie. "Verbal Attitudes and Overt Acts." *American Sociological Review* 23 (December 1958): 667–673.

Degler, Carl N. *Neither Black Nor White: Slavery and Race Relations in Brazil and the United States.* Madison, Wis.: University of Wisconsin Press, 1971.

———. "Slavery and the Genesis of American Race Prejudice." In Donald L. Noel, ed., *The Origins of American Slavery and Racism,* 61–80. Columbus, Ohio: Charles E. Merrill, 1972.

del Castillo, Richard Griswold. *The Treaty of Guadalupe Hidalgo: A Legacy of Conflict.* Norman, Okla.: University of Oklahoma Press, 1990.

de La Garza, Rodolpho O., Frank D. Bean, Charles M. Bonjean, Ricardo Romo, and Rodolfo Alvarez, eds., *The Mexican American Experience.* Austin, Tex.: University of Texas Press, 1985.

Delgado, Melvin, and Sharon L. Tennstedt. "Making the Case for Culturally Appropriate Community Services: Puerto Rican Elders and Their Caregivers." *Health and Social Work* 22 (November 1997): 246–255.

Deloria, Vine, Jr. *Custer Died for Your Sins.* New York: Avon Books, 1969.

———. "This Country Was a Lot Better Off When the Indians Were Running It." In Howard M. Bahr, Bruce A. Chadwick, and Robert C. Day, eds., *Native Americans Today,* 498–506. New York: Harper & Row, 1972.

———. "Native Americans: The Indian American Today." *The Annals: America as a Multicultural Society* 454 (March 1981): 139–149.

Dennis, Henry C. *The American Indian 1492–1976.* Dobbs Ferry, N.Y.: Oceana Publications, 1977.

Dent, David J. "The New Black Suburbs." *New York Times Magazine* (June 14, 1992): 18–25.

Dentler, Robert A. "The Political Situation and Power Prospects of African Americans in Gunnar Myrdal's Era and Today." In Obie Clayton, Jr., ed., *An American Dilemma Revisited: Race Relations in a Changing World.* New York: Russell Sage Foundation, 1996.

Denton, Nancy A., and Douglas S. Massey. "Residential Segregation of Blacks, Hispanics, and Asians by Socioeconomic Status and Generation." *Social Science Quarterly* 69 (December 1988): 797–817.

DePalma, Anthony. "Vote in Quebec May be Last Fling with Secession" *New York Times* (November 25, 1998): A1–A10.

———. "Canada Seizes Chinese Boat Smuggling in 100 Immigrants." *New York Times* (July 22, 1999): A6.

Diner, Hasia. "Erin's Children in America: Three Centuries of Irish Immigration in the United States." In Silvia Pedraza and Rubén G. Rumbaut, eds., *Origins and Destinies: Immigration, Race, and Ethnicity in America,* 161–171. Belmont, Calif.: Wadsworth Publishing Company, 1996.

Dinnerstein, Leonard, and Frederic Cople Jaher, eds. *The Aliens.* New York: Appleton-Century-Crofts, 1970.

Dinnerstein, Leonard, and David M. Reimers, eds. *Ethnic Americans.* New York: Dodd, Mead, 1975.

Dobzhansky, Theodosius. *Mankind Evolving.* New Haven, Conn.: Yale University Press, 1962.

Dollard, John. *Caste and Class in a Southern Town,* 3rd ed. Garden City, N.Y.: Doubleday, 1957.

Dollard, John, Leonard Doob, Neal Miller, O. H. Mowrer, and R. R. Sears. *Frustration and Aggression.* New Haven, Conn.: Yale University Press, 1939.

Donato, Rubén. *The Other Struggle for Equal Schools: Mexican Americans During the Civil Rights Era.* Albany: State University of New York Press, 1997.

Donohue, John J., III, and Peter Siegelman. "The Changing Nature of Employment Discrimination Litigation." *Stanford Law Review* 43 (May 1991): 983–1033.

Dovidio, John F., and Samuel L. Gaertner. "Stereotypes and Evaluative Intergroup Bias." In Diane M. Mackie and David L. Hamilton, eds., *Affect, Cognition, and Stereotyping,* 167–193. San Diego, Calif.: Academic Press, 1993.

Doyle, Bertram W. *The Etiquette of Race Relations in the South.* Chicago: University of Chicago Press, 1937.

Drury, D. W. "Black Self-Esteem and Desegregated Schools." *Sociology of Education* 53 (April 1980): 88–103.

Du Bois, William E. B. *The Souls of Black Folk* [1903]. Reprinted in *Three Negro Classics.* New York: Avon Books, 1965.

Ducas, George, ed., with Charles Van Doren. *Great Documents in Black American History.* New York: Praeger, 1970.

Dunn, L. C., and Theodosius Dobzhansky. *Heredity, Race and Society.* New York: The New American Library, 1964.

Dunne, John Gregory. *Delano.* New York: Farrar, Straus & Giroux, 1967.

Durant, Will. *Our Oriental Heritage.* New York: Simon and Schuster, 1954.

Easterbrook, Gregg. "Blacktop Basketball and *The Bell Curve.* In Russell Jacoby and Naomi Glauberman, eds., *The Bell Curve Debate:* 30–43. New York: Times Books, 1995.

Easterlin, Richard A. "Immigration: Social Characteristics." In Stephan Thernstrom, Ann Orlov, and Oscar Handlin, eds., *Harvard Encyclopedia of American Ethnic Groups,* 476–486. Cambridge, Mass.: The Belknap Press, 1980.

Eckberg, Douglas Lee. *Intelligence and Race.* New York: Praeger, 1979.

Edwards, R. C., Michael Reich, and David M. Gordon, eds. *Labor Market Segmentation.* Lexington, Mass.: D. C. Heath, 1975.

Egan, Timothy. "Expelled in 1877, Indian Tribe Is Now Wanted as a Resource." *New York Times* (July 22, 1996): 1, A9.

———. "Indians Win Round in Fight On Trust Funds: 2 Cabinet Secretaries Are Held in Contempt." *New York Times* (February 23, 1999): A1.

Eggebeen, David J., and Daniel T. Lichter. "Race, Family Structure, and Changing Poverty Among American Children." *American Sociological Review* 56 (December 1991): 801–817.

Eichenwald, Kurt. "Texaco Executives, On Tape, Discussed Impending Bias Suit." *New York Times* (November 4, 1996): A7.

Ehrlich, Howard J. *The Social Psychology of Prejudice.* New York: Wiley, 1973.

Ehrlich, Howard J., and James W. Rinehart. "A Brief Report on the Methodology of Stereotype Research." *Social Forces* 44 (December 1965): 171–176.

Ehrlich, Paul R., and S. Shirley Feldman. *The Race Bomb.* New York: Ballantine Books, 1977.

El-Badry, Samia, and Dudley L. Poston, Jr. "Fitting In: Socio-Economic Attainment Patterns of Foreign-Born Egyptians in the United States." *Sociological Inquiry* 60 (May 1990): 142–157.

Elkholy, Abdo A. "The Arab American Family." In Charles Mindel, Robert W. Habenstein, and Roosevelt Wright, Jr., eds., *Ethnic Families in America: Patterns and Variations,* 3rd ed., 438–455. New York: Elsevier, 1988.

Elkins, Stanley M. *Slavery,* 2nd ed. Chicago: University of Chicago Press, 1968.

Ellis, David. "L.A. Lawless." *Time* (May 11, 1992): 26–29.

Ellison, Christopher G., and Daniel A. Powers. "The Contact Hypothesis and Racial Attitudes among Black Americans." *Social Science Quarterly* 75 (June 1994): 385–400.

Ellison, Ralph. *Shadow and the Act.* New York: Random House, 1964.

Elson, R. M. *Guardians of Tradition.* Lincoln, Nebr.: University of Nebraska Press, 1964.

Embree, Edwin R. *Indians of the Americas.* New York: Collier Books, 1970.

Erlanger, Steven. "Despite the G.I.'s, Kosovo Town Is Purged of Serbs." *New York Times* (August 1, 1999): A1.

Eschbach, Karl. "The Enduring and Vanishing American Indian: American Indian Population Growth and Intermarriage in 1990." *Ethnic and Racial Studies* (January 1995): 89–107.

"Excerpts from Justices' Opinions on Michigan Affirmative Action Cases." *New York Times* (June 24, 2003): A26–A27.

Falcoff, Mark. "Our Language Needs No Law." *New York Times* (August 5, 1996): A11.

Farley, Reynolds. "Racial Integration in the Schools: Assessing the Effect of Governmental Policies." *Sociological Focus* 9 (January 1975): 3–26.

———. "School Integration in the United States." In Frank D. Bean and W. Parker Frisbie, eds. *The Demography of Racial and Ethnic Groups,* 15–50. New York: Academic Press, 1978.

———. "Three Steps Forward and Two Back? Recent Changes in the Social and Economic Status of Blacks." In Richard D. Alba, ed., *Ethnicity and Race in the U.S.A.,* 4–28. New York: Routledge, 1988.

———. The New American Reality: *Who We Are, How We Got Here, Where We Are Going.* New York: Russell Sage Foundation, 1996.

Farley, Reynolds, and Walter R. Allen. *The Color Line and the Quality of Life in America.* New York: Russell Sage Foundation, 1987.

Farley, Reynolds, and William H. Frey. "Changes in the Segregation of Whites from Blacks During the 1980s: Small Steps Toward a More Integrated Society." *American Sociological Review* 59 (February 1994): 23–45.

Farmer, James. *Freedom—When?* Reprinted in August Meier, Elliott Rudwick, and Francis L. Broderick, eds., *Black Protest Thought in the Twentieth Century,* 2nd ed., 183–202. Indianapolis, Ind. and New York: Bobbs-Merrill, 1971.

Faulkner, Harold Underwood. *American Political and Social History,* 5th ed. New York: Appleton-Century-Crofts, 1948.

Feagin, Joe R. "Indirect Institutionalized Discrimination." *American Politics Quarterly* 5 (April 1977): 177–200.

Feagin, Joe R., and Nancy Fujitaki. "On the Assimilation of the Japanese Americans." *Amerasia Journal* 1 (February 1972): 13–30.

Feagin, Joe R., and Harlan Hahn. *Ghetto Revolts.* New York: Macmillan, 1973.

Feagin, Joe R., and Melvin P. Sikes. *Living with Racism: The Black Middle-Class Experience.* Boston: Beacon Press, 1994.

Feagin, Joe R., and H. Vera. *White Racism.* New York: Routledge, 1995.

Featherman, David L., and Robert M. Hauser. *Opportunity and Change.* New York: Academic Press, 1978.

Feldstein, Stanley, and Lawrence Costello, eds. *The Ordeal of Assimilation.* Garden City, N.Y.: Anchor Press/Doubleday, 1974.

Ferguson, Niall. "The Jihad of 1914." *New York Review of Books* (February 13, 2002): 21–23.

Ferguson, Ron F. "Shifting Challenges: Fifty Years of Economic Change Toward Black-White Earnings Equality." In Obie Clayton, Jr., ed., *An American Dilemma Revisited: Race Relations in a Changing World,* 76–111. New York: Russell Sage Foundation, 1996.

Fifield, Russell H., and Carlos P. Romulo. "Philippines." *The World Book Encyclopedia,* vol 14, 332–344. Chicago: Field Enterprises Educational Corp., 1962.

Fine, Michelle, Lois Weis, Linda C. Powell, and L. Mun Wong, eds. *Off White: Readings on Race, Power, and Society.* New York: Routledge, 1997.

Firebaugh, Glenn, and Kenneth E. Davis. "Trends in Antiblack Prejudice, 1972–1984: Region and Cohort Effects." *American Journal of Sociology* 94 (September 1988): 251–272.

Fischbach, Michael R. "Government Pressures against Arabs in the United States." *Journal of Palestine Studies* 14 (Spring 1985): 87–100.

Fischer, C. S., Michael Hout, Martín Sánchez Jankowski, Samuel R. Lucas, Ann Swidler, and Kim Voss. *Inequality by Design: Cracking the Bell Curve Myth.* Princeton, N.J.: Princeton University Press, 1996.

Fix, Michael, and Jeffrey S. Passel. *Immigration and Immigrants: Setting the Record Straight.* Washington, D.C.: The Urban Institute, May 1994.

Fixico, Donald. *The Invasion of Indian Country in the Twentieth Century: American Capitalism and Tribal Natural Resources.* Niwot, Col.: University Press of Colorado, 1998.

Fligstein, Neil, and Roberto Fernandez. "Educational Transitions of Whites and Mexican-Americans." In George J. Borjas and Marta Tienda, eds., *Hispanics in the U.S. Economy,* 161–192. Orlando, Fla.: Academic Press, 1985.

Flores, Juan. "Pan-Latino/Trans-Latino: Puerto Ricans in the 'New Nueva York.' " *CENTRO Journal of the Center for Puerto Rican Studies* 8 (Spring 1996): 171–186.

Flynn, James R. "Massive IQ Gains in 14 Nations: What IQ Tests Really Measure." *Psychological Bulletin* 101 (March 1987): 171–191.

Fogel, Robert W. *Without Consent or Contract.* New York: W. W. Norton and Company, 1989.

Fogel, Robert William, and Stanley L. Engerman. *Time on the Cross: The Economics of American Negro Slavery.* Boston: Little, Brown, 1974.

Footnotes. "ABS Statement Assails Book by Wilson." (December 1978): 4.

Forbes, Jack D. *Aztecas Del Norte.* Greenwich, Conn.: Fawcett, 1973.

Fost, Dan. "American Indians in the 1990s." In John A. Kromkowski, ed., *Annual Editions: Race and Ethnic Relations 96/97,* 101–105. Guilford, Conn.: Dushkin Publishing Group, 1996.

Fox, Stephen. *The Unknown Internment: An Oral History of the Relocation of Italian Americans during World War II.* Boston: Twayne Publishers, 1990.

Francis, E. K. *Interethnic Relations.* New York: Elsevier, 1976.

Franklin, John Hope. *Reconstruction.* Chicago: University of Chicago Press, 1961.

Franklin, John Hope, and Alfred A. Moss, Jr. *From Slavery to Freedom,* 6th ed. New York: Alfred A. Knopf, 1988.

Frazier, E. Franklin. *The Negro in the United States,* rev. ed. New York: Macmillan, 1957.

Fredrickson, George M. "Toward a Social Interpretation of the Development of American Racism." In Nathan I. Huggins, Martin Kilson, and Daniel M. Fox, eds., *Key Issues in the Afro-American Experience,* 240–254. New York: Harcourt Brace Jovanovich, 1971.

Frethorne, Richard. "The Experiences of an Indentured Servant, 1623." In Frederick M. Binder and David M. Reimers, eds., *The Way We Lived,* 35–37. Lexington, Mass.: D. C. Heath, 1988.

Fuchs, Lawrence H. "Reactions of Black Americans to Immigration." In Virginia Yans-McLaughlin, ed., *Immigration Reconsidered: History, Sociology, and Politics,* 293–314. New York: Oxford University Press, 1990.

Fugita, Stephen S., and David J. O'Brien. "Structural Assimilation, Ethnic Group Membership, and Political Participation Among Japanese Americans: A Research Note." *Social Forces* 63 (June 1985): 986–995.

Fujimoto, Isao. "The Failure of Democracy in a Time of Crisis." In Amy Tachiki, Eddie Wong, Franklin Odo, and Buck Wong, eds., *Roots: An Asian American Reader,* 207–214. Los Angeles: The Regents of the University of California, 1971.

Furstenberg, Frank, J., Jr., T. Hershberg, and John Modell. "The Origins of the Female-Headed Black Family: The Impact of the Urban Experience." *Journal of Interdisciplinary History* 6 (Autumn 1985): 211–233.

Gall, Carlotta. "How They Live Squeezed Together, Separately." *New York Times* (March 8, 1999): A3.

Gallagher, Charles A., ed. *Rethinking the Color Line: Readings in Race and Ethnicity,* 2nd ed. Boston: McGraw Hill, 2004.

Galton, Francis. *Hereditary Genius.* London: Macmillan, 1869.

Gans, Herbert J. "Symbolic Ethnicity: The Future of Ethnic Groups and Cultures in America." In Norman R. Yetman, ed., *Majority and Minority,* 4th ed., 429–442. Boston: Allyn and Bacon, 1985.

Garcia, John A. "Yo Soy Mexicano . . . : Self-Identity and Sociodemographic Correlates." *Social Science Quarterly* 62 (March 1981): 88–98.

Garcia, Mario T. *Mexican Americans.* New Haven, Conn. and London: Yale University Press, 1989.

Garvey, Amy Jacques. *Garvey & Garveyism.* London: Collier-Macmillan Ltd., 1970.

Garvey, Marcus. "An Appeal to the Conscience of the Black Race." In Gilbert Osofsky, ed., *The Burden of Race,* 290–295. New York: Harper & Row, 1968a.

Gee, Emma. "Issei Women: 'Picture Brides' in America." In Maxine Schwartz Seller, ed., *Immigrant Women,* rev., 2nd ed., 53–59. Albany, N.Y.: State University of New York Press, 1994.

Genovese, Eugene D. *Roll, Jordan, Roll.* New York: Pantheon Books, 1974.

Gerard, Harold B., and Norman Miller. *School Desegregation: A Long-Term Study.* New York: Plenum Press, 1975.

Gerard, Harold B., Terrence D. Jackson, and Edward S. Conelley. "Social Contact in the Desegregated Classroom." In Harold B. Gerard and Norman Miller, eds., *School Desegregation: A Long-Term Study,* 211–241. New York: Plenum Press, 1975.

Geschwender, James A., Rita Carroll-Seguin, and Howard Brill. "The Portuguese and Haoles of Hawaii: Implications for the Origin of Ethnicity." *American Sociological Review* 53 (August 1988): 515–527.

Gibbs, Jack P. *Control: Sociology's Central Notion.* Urbana, Ill. and Chicago: University of Illinois Press, 1989.

———. "Conceptualization of Terrorism." *American Sociological Review* 54 (June 1989): 329–340.

Glazer, Nathan. "America's Race Paradox." In Peter I. Rose, ed., *Nation of Nations,* 165–180. New York: Random House, 1972.

———, ed. *Clamor at the Gates.* San Francisco: Institute for Contemporary Studies, 1985.

Glazer, Nathan, and Daniel Patrick Moynihan. *Beyond the Melting Pot,* 1st and 2nd eds. Cambridge, Mass.: MIT Press, 1964 and 1970.

Glenn, Evelyn Nakano, and Rhacel Salazar Parreñas. "The Other Issei: Japanese Immigrant Women in the Pre-World War II Period." In Silvia Pedraza and Rubén G. Rumbaut, eds., *Origins and Destinies: Immigration, Race, and Ethnicity in America,* 125–140. Belmont, Calif.: Wadsworth Publishing Company, 1996.

Glenn, Norval D. "White Gains from Negro Subordination." *Social Problems* 14 (Fall 1966): 159–178.

Glickstein, Howard A. "Discrimination in Higher Education." In Barry R. Gross, ed., *Reverse Discrimination,* 14–18. Buffalo, N.Y.: Prometheus Books, 1977.

Goff, Regina. "Educating Black Americans." In Mabel M. Smythe, ed., *The Black American Reference Book,* 410–452. Englewood Cliffs, N. J.: Prentice-Hall, 1976.

Gold, Steven J., and Bruce Phillips. "Mobility and Continuity among Eastern European Jews." In Silvia Pedraza and Rubén G. Rumbaut, eds., *Origins and Destinies: Immigration, Race, and Ethnicity in America,* 182–194. Belmont, Calif.: Wadsworth Publishing Company, 1996.

Gómez-Quiñones, Juan. "The First Steps: Chicano Labor Conflict and Organizing, 1900–20." In Manuel P. Servín, ed., *An Awakening Minority: The Mexican Americans,* 2nd ed., 79–113. Beverly Hills, Calif.: Glencoe Press, 1974.

Gonzalez-Ramos, Gladys, Luis H. Zayas, and Elaine V. Cohen. "Child-Rearing Values of Low-Income, Urban Puerto Rican Mothers of Preschool Children." *Professional Psychology, Research and Practice* 29 (August 1998): 377–382.

Goodstein, Laurie. "Seeing Islam as 'Evil' Faith, Evangelicals Seek Converts." *New York Times* (May 27, 2003): A1, A22.

Gordon, Milton M. *Assimilation in American Life.* New York: Oxford University Press, 1964.

———. *Human Nature, Class, and Ethnicity.* New York: Oxford University Press, 1978.

Gossett, Thomas F. *Race: The History of an Idea in America.* Dallas, Tex.: Southern Methodist University Press, 1963.

Gould, C. W. *America, A Family Matter.* New York: Scribner's, 1922.

Gould, Stephen Jay. *The Mismeasure of Man.* New York: W. W. Norton & Company, 1981.

———. "Curveball," *The New Yorker* (November 28, 1994): 139–149.

Graham, Hugh Davis. "The Origins of Affirmative Action: Civil Rights and the Regulatory State." In Harold Orlans and June O'Neill, eds., *Affirmative Action Revisited, The Annals* (September 1992): 50–62.

Grebler, Leo, Joan W. Moore, and Ralph C. Guzman. *The Mexican-American People.* New York: The Free Press, 1970.

Greeley, Andrew M. *Why Can't They Be Like Us?* New York: E. P. Dutton, 1971.

———. *That Most Distressful Nation: The Taming of the Irish Americans.* Chicago: Quadrangle Books, 1975.

———. "The Ethnic Miracle." In Norman R. Yetman, ed., *Majority and Minority,* 4th ed., 268–277. Boston: Allyn and Bacon, 1985.

Grenier, Gilles. "Shifts to English as Usual Language by Americans of Spanish Mother Tongue." In Rodolfo O. de la Garza, Frank D. Bean, Charles M. Bonjean, Ricardo Romo, and Rodolfo Alvarez, eds., *The Mexican American Experience,* 346–358. Austin, Tex.: University of Texas Press, 1985.

Gross, Andrew B., and Douglas S. Massey. "Spatial Assimilation Models: A Micro-Macro Comparison." *Social Science Quarterly* 72 (June 1991): 347–360.

Gurak, Douglas T., and Mary M. Kritz. "Intermarriage Patterns in the U.S.: Maximizing Information from the U.S. Census Public Use Samples." *Public Data Use* (March 1978): 33–43.

Gutiérrez, David G. *Walls and Mirrors: Mexican Americans, Mexican Immigrants, and the Politics of Ethnicity.* Berkeley and Los Angeles: University of California Press, 1995.

———. *Between Two Worlds: Mexican Immigrants in the United States,* xviii. Wilmington, Del.: Scholarly Resources Inc., 1996.

Gutman, Herbert G. *The Black Family in Slavery and Freedom, 1750–1925.* New York: Pantheon Books, 1976.

Guzmán, Hector R. Cordero. "The Structure of Inequality and the Status of Puerto Rican Youth in the United States." In Antonia Darder, Rodolfo D. Torres, and Henry Gutiérrez, eds., *Latinos and Education: A Critical Reader,* 80–94. New York: Routledge, 1997.

Hacker, Andrew. *Two Nations.* New York: Charles Scribner's Sons, 1992.

———. "Goodbye to Affirmative Action?" *New York Review of Books.* (July 11, 1996): 21–29.

Haddad, Yvonne, "Arab Muslims in America: Adaptation and Reform." In James Zogby, ed., *Taking Root, Bearing Fruit,* 101–105. Washington, D.C.: ADC Research Institute, 1984.

Hagan, William T. *American Indians.* Chicago: The University of Chicago Press, 1971.

Hagopian, Elaine. "Minority Rights in a Nation State: The Nixon Administration's Campaign Against Arab-Americans." *Journal of Palestine Studies* 5 (Autumn, 1975–Winter, 1976): 97–114.

Haines, David W. "Kinship in Vietnamese Refugee Resettlement: A Review of the U.S. Experience." *Journal of Comparative Family Studies* 19 (Spring 1988): 1–16.

Hakuta, Kenji. *Mirror of Language: The Debate on Bilingualism.* New York: Basic Books, 1986.

Hallinan, Maureen T., and Richard A. Williams. "The Stability of Students' Interracial Friendships." *American Sociological Review* 52 (October 1987): 653–664.

———. "Interracial Friendship Choices in Secondary Schools." *American Sociological Review* 54 (February 1989): 67–78.

Hamilton, Alexander, James Madison, and John Jay. *The Federalist Papers.* New York: New American Library, 1961.

Hamilton, David L., and Tina K. Trolier. "Stereotypes and Stereotyping: An Overview of the Cognitive Approach." In John F. Dovidio and Samuel L. Gaertner, eds., *Prejudice, Discrimination, and Racism.* Orlando, Fla.: Academic Press, Inc., 1986.

Hamad, Imad. "Anti-Terrorism Law." Op-Ed, *Detroit Free Press,* November 23, 2001.

Handlin, Oscar. *Boston's Immigrants, 1790–1865: A Study in Acculturation.* Cambridge, Mass.: Belknap Press, 1941.

———. *Race and Nationality in American Life.* Garden City, N.Y.: Doubleday, 1957.

Hansen, Marcus Lee. *The Problem of the Third Generation Immigrant.* Rock Island, Ill.: Augustana Historical Society, 1938.

———. *The Atlantic Migration 1607–1860.* Cambridge, Mass.: Harvard University Press 1945.

Harris, David R., and Jeremiah Joseph Sim. "Who is Multiracial? Assessing the Complexity of Lived Race." *American Sociological Review* 67 (August 2002): 614–627.

Harrison, Roderick J., and Daniel H. Weinberg. "Changes in Racial and Ethnic Residential Segregation, 1980–1990." U.S. Bureau of the Census, Racial Statistics Branch, Population Division, 1992 (mimeographed).

Hassan, Salah D. "Arabs, Muslims and Race in America." *Middle East Report* 224 (Fall 2002). http://www.merip.org.

Hatchett, Shirley J., Donna L. Cochran, and James S. Jackson. "Family Life." In James S. Jackson, ed., *Life in Black America,* 46–83. Newbury Park, Calif.: Sage Publications, 1991.

Hauser, Robert M. "The Bell Curve." *Contemporary Sociology* 24 (March 1995): 149–153.

Hawley, Willis D., and Mark A. Smylie. "The Contribution of School Desegregation to Academic Achievement and Racial Integration." In Phyllis A. Katz and Dalmas A. Taylor, eds., *Eliminating Racism,* 281–297. New York: Plenum Press, 1988.

Hazuda, Helen P., Michael P. Stern, and Steven M. Haffner. "Acculturation and Assimilation Among Mexican Americans: Scales and Population-Based Data." *Social Science Quarterly* 69 (September 1988): 687–706.

Hecht, Michael L., and John R. Baldwin. "Layers and Holograms: A New Look at Prejudice." In Michael L. Hecht, ed., *Communicating Prejudice,* 57–84. Thousand Oaks, Calif.: Sage Publications, Inc., 1998.

Heer, David M. "Negro-White Marriage in the United States." *Journal of Marriage and the Family* 28 (August 1966): 262–273.

———. "Intermarriage." In Stephan Thernstrom, Ann Orlov, and Oscar Handlin, eds., *Harvard Encyclopedia of American Ethnic Groups,* 513–521. Cambridge, Mass.: The Belknap Press, 1980.

Heise, Michael. "Assessing the Efficacy of School Desegregation." *Syracuse Law Review* 46 (1996): 1093–1117.

Heiss, Jerold, and Susan Owens. "Self-evaluation of Blacks and Whites." *American Journal of Sociology* 78 (September 1972): 360–370.

Helms, Janet E. *Black and White Racial Identity: Theory, Research, and Practice*. Westport, Conn.: Praeger, 1993.

Herberg, Will. *Protestant-Catholic-Jew*. Garden City, N.Y.: Doubleday, 1960.

Herring, Cedric, and Charles Amissah. "Advance and Retreat: Racially Based Attitudes and Public Policy." In Steven A. Tuch and Jack K. Martin, eds., *Racial Attitudes in the 1990s: Continuity and Change*, 121–143. Westport, Conn.: Praeger, 1997.

Herrnstein, Richard J. "IQ." *Atlantic Monthly* 228 (September 1971): 43–64.

Herrnstein, Richard J., and Charles Murray. *The Bell Curve: Intelligence and Class Structure in Amercan Life*. New York: The Free Press, 1994.

Hewstone, Miles. "Intergroup Attribution: Some Implications for the Study of Ethnic Prejudice." In Jan Pieter van Oudenhoven and Tineke M. Willemsen, eds., *Ethnic Minorities*, 25–42. Amsterdam: Swets & Zeitlinger B.V., 1989.

Higham, John. *Strangers in the Land: Patterns of American Nativism 1860–1925*. New York: Atheneum, 1963.

Hijab, Nadia. Preface to "Arab-Israeli Conflict and the Association of Arab-American University Graduates." *Arab Studies Quarterly* 19 (Summer 1997): 3–5.

Hill, Robert B. *The Strengths of Black Families*. New York: Emerson Hall Publishers, 1971.

Hing, Bill Ong. *Making and Remaking Asian America Through Immigration Policy, 1850–1990*. Stanford, Calif.: Stanford University Press, 1993.

Hing, Bill Ong. "Asians without Blacks and Latinos in San Francisco: Missed Lesson of the Common Good." *Amerasia Journal* 27:2 (2001)/28:1 (2002): 19–27.

Hirschman, Charles. "America's Melting Pot Reconsidered." In Ralph Turner and James F. Short, Jr., eds., *Annual Review of Sociology*, 397–423. Palo Alto, Calif.: Annual Reviews, 1983.

Hirschman, Charles, and Morrison G. Wong. "Socioeconomic Gains of Asian Americans, Blacks, and Hispanics: 1960–1976." *American Journal of Sociology* 90 (November 1984): 584–607.

———. "Trends in Socioeconomic Achievement among Immigrant and Native-Born Asian-Americans, 1960–1976." In Norman R. Yetman, ed., *Majority and Minority*, 4th ed., 290–304. Boston: Allyn and Bacon, 1985.

———. "The Extraordinary Educational Attainment of Asian-Americans: A Search for Historical Evidence and Explanations." *Social Forces* 65 (September 1986): 1–27.

Hochschild, Jennifer L. *Facing Up to the American Dream: Race, Class, and the Soul of the Nation*. Princeton, N.J.: Princeton University Press, 1995.

Hoffman, Abraham. *Unwanted Mexican Americans in the Great Depression: Repatriation Pressures 1929–1939*. Tucson, Ariz.: University of Arizona Press, 1974.

Hoge, Warren. "A Swedish Dilemma: The Immigrant Ghetto." *New York Times* (October 6, 1998): A3.

Holmes, Steven. "A Matter of Perspective in a Lending-Bias Suit," *New York Times* (October 11, 1995): C1.

Holt, Jim. "Skin-Deep Science." In Russell Jacoby and Naomi Glauberman, eds., *The Bell Curve Debate*, 57–60. New York: Times Books, 1995.

Holzer, Harry J. "Racial Differences in Labor Market Outcomes Among Men." In Neil J. Smelser, William Julius Wilson, and Faith Mitchell, eds., *America Becoming: Racial Trends and Their Consequences*, Volume II, 98–123. National Research Council, Commission on Behavioral and Social Sciences and Education. Washington, D.C.: National Academy Press, 2001.

Hondagneu-Sotelo, Pierrette. *Gendered Transitions: Mexican Experiences of Immigration*. Berkeley, Calif.: University of California Press, 1994.

Hood, Lucy. *Immigrant Students, Urban High Schools: The Challenge Continues*. New York: Carnegie Challenge, Carnegie Corporation of New York, 2003.

Hooglund, Eric, ed. *Taking Root: Arab-American Community Studies.* Washington, D.C.: ADC Research Institute, 1985.

hooks, bell. *Teaching to Transgress: Education as the Practice of Freedom.* New York: Routledge, 1994.

Horn, Miriam, "The Return to Ellis Island." *U.S. News & World Report* (November 21, 1988): 63.

Horowitz, Donald L. *Ethnic Groups in Conflict.* Berkeley, Calif.: University of California Press, 1985.

Horton, John. "Order and Conflict Theories of Social Problems as Competing Ideologies." *American Journal of Sociology* 71 (May 1966):701–713.

Hosokawa, Bill. *Nisei: The Quiet Americans.* New York: William Morrow, 1969.

Houston, Jeanne Wakatsuki. "Shikata Ga Nai—This Cannot Be Helped." In Maxine Schwartz Seller, ed., *Immigrant Women,* rev., 2nd ed., 167–171. Albany, N.Y.: State University of New York Press, 1994.

Howery, Carla B. "Update on Human Rights Cases." *Footnotes,* American Sociological Association (November 1986): 9.

Hoxie, Frederick E. *A Final Promise: The Campaign to Assimilate the Indians, 1880–1920.* Lincoln, Nebr.: University of Nebraska Press, 1984.

Hsu, Madeline Y. *Dreaming of Gold, Dreaming of Home: Transnationalism and Migration Between the United States and South China, 1882–1943.* Stanford: Stanford University Press, 2000.

Hu, Charles Y. "Korea." *World Book Encyclopedia* 10 (1961): 292–296.

Huddle, Donald. *The Costs of Immigration.* Carrying Capacity Network. Revised July, 1993.

Hughes, Michael and Steven A. Tuch. "Gender Differences in Whites' Racial Attitudes: Are Women Really More Tolerant?" Mimeographed paper presented at the Annual Meetings of the American Sociological Association, Chicago, 1999.

Hunt, Larry L. "Hispanic Protestantism in the United States: Trends by Decade and Generation." *Social Forces* 77 (June 1999):1601–1623.

Hurh, Won Moo. *The Korean Americans.* Westport, Conn.: Greenwood Press, 1998.

Hurh, Won Moo, and Kwang Chung Kim. *Korean Immigrants in America: A Structural Analysis of Ethnic Confinement and Adhesive Adaptation.* New Jersey: Fairleigh Dickenson University Press, 1984.

———. "The 'Success' Image of Asian Americans: Its Validity and Its Practical and Theoretical Implications." *Ethnic and Racial Studies* 12 (October 1989): 512–537.

Hwang, Sean-Shong, Steven H. Murdock, Banoo Parpia, and Rita R. Hamm. "The Effects of Race and Socioeconomic Status on Residential Segregation in Texas, 1970–80." *Social Forces* 63 (March 1985): 732–747.

Hwang, Sean-shong, Rogelio Saenz, and Benigno E. Aguirre. "Structural and Assimilationist Explanations of Asian American Intermarriage." *Journal of Marriage and the Family* 59 (August 1997): 758–772.

Hyman, Herbert H., and Paul B. Sheatsley. "Attitudes Toward Desegregation." *Scientific American* (July 1964): 16–23.

Ibish, Hussein. "Analysis: Experience of Arab Americans since 9/11." National Public Radio, March 11, 2003. http://ww.npr.org/programs/totn/transcripts/2003/mar/030311/ibish.html.

Iceland, John. "Earnings Returns to Occupational Status: Are Asian Americans Disadvantaged?" *Social Science Research* 28 (March 1999): 45–65.

Ichihashi, Yamato. *Japanese in the United States.* Palo Alto, Calif.: Stanford University Press, 1932.

Ichioka, Yuji. "Nisei: The Quiet Americans." In Amy Tachiki, Eddie Wong, Franklin Odo, and Buck Wong, eds., *Roots: An Asian American Reader,* 221–222. Los Angeles: Regents of the University of California, 1971.

Idupuganti, Anura. "Lists of Racist Attacks Across the Country Since 9/11." September 20, 2001. http:// www.incite-national.org/issues/attacks.html.

Ignatiev, Noel. *How the Irish Became White.* New York: Routledge, 1995.

Ikeda, Kiyoshi. "A Different 'Dilemma.'" *Social Forces* 51 (June 1973): 497–499.

Indians of All Tribes. "We Must Hold on to the Old Ways." In Alvin M. Josephy, Jr., ed., *Red Power,* 197–201. New York: American Heritage Press, 1971.

Institute for the Study of Social Change. *The Diversity Project: Final Report.* Berkeley, Calif.: University of California, November 1991.

Iwata, Masakazu. "The Japanese Immigrants in California Agriculture." *Agricultural History* 36 (January 1962): 25–37.

Jabara, Abdeen M. "A Strategy for Political Effectiveness." In Baha Abu-Laban and Michael W. Suleiman, eds., *Arab Americans: Continuity and Change,* 201–205. Belmont, Mass.: Association of Arab-American University Graduates, 1989.

Jackson, Curtis E., and Marcia J. Galli. *A History of the Bureau of Indian Affairs and Its Activities Among Indians.* San Francisco: R & E Research Associates, Inc., 1977.

Jackson, James S., ed., *Life in Black America.* Newbury Park, Calif.: Sage Publications, 1991.

Jacobs, Paul, and Saul Landau, eds., *To Serve the Devil,* vol. 1. New York: Vintage Books, 1971.

Jacobson, Cardell K. "Internal Colonialism and Native Americans: Indian Labor in the United States from 1871 to World War II." *Social Science Quarterly* 65 (March 1984): 158–171.

Jacobsen, Michael Frye. *Whiteness of a Different Color: European Immigrants and the Alchemy of Race.* Cambridge, Mass.: Harvard University Press, 1998.

Jalali, Rita, and Seymour Martin Lipset. "Racial and Ethnic Conflicts: A Global Perspective." In Michael W. Hughey, ed., *New Tribalisms: The Resurgence of Race and Ethnicity,* 317–343. New York: New York University Press, 1998.

James, Lenada. "Activism and Red Power" (comment). In Kenneth R. Philp, ed., *Indian Self-Rule,* 229–231. Salt Lake City, Utah: Howe Brothers, 1986.

Jasinski, Jana. "Beyond High School: An Examination of Hispanic Educational Attainment." *Social Science Quarterly* 81(March 2000): 276–290.

Jaynes, Gerald David, and Robin M. Williams, Jr., eds., *A Common Destiny.* Washington, D.C.: National Academy Press, 1989.

Jencks, Christopher. "Who Should Get In?" *The New York Review of Books,* November 29, 2001a, 57–63.

———. "Who Should Get In? Part II" *The New York Review of Books,* December 20, 2001b, 94–102.

Jencks, Christopher, and Meredith Phillips, eds. *The Black-White Test Score Gap.* Washington, D.C.: Brookings Institution Press, 1998.

Jensen, Arthur R. "How Much Can We Boost IQ and Scholastic Achievement?" *Harvard Educational Review* 39 (Winter 1969): 1–123.

———. "Race and the Genetics of Intelligence: A Reply to Lewontin." In N. J. Block and Gerald Dworkin, eds., *The IQ Controversy,* 93–106. New York: Pantheon Books, 1976.

Jensen, Joan M. "East Asians." In Stephan Thernstrom, Ann Orlov, and Oscar Handlin, eds., *Harvard Encyclopedia of American Ethnic Groups,* 296–301. Cambridge, Mass.: The Belknap Press, 1980.

Jiobu, Robert M. *Ethnicity and Assimilation.* Albany, N.Y.: State University of New York Press, 1988a.

———. "Ethnic Hegemony and the Japanese of California." *American Sociological Review* 53 (June 1988b): 353–367.

Johnson, Dirk. "Mob Violence Continues in Las Vegas." *New York Times* (May 19, 1992): A10.

————. "Economies Come to Life on Indian Reservations." *New York Times* (July 3, 1994): 1,10,11.

————. "A Migration Created by Burden of Suspicion." *New York Times* (August 14, 1995): A6.

Johnson, George. "Indians Take On the U.S. in a 90's Battle for Control." *New York Times* (February 11, 1996a): 6E.

————. "Indian Casino in New Mexico Is Forced to Close." *New York Times* (September, 26, 1996b): A12.

Johnson, James Weldon. "Description of a Race Riot in Chicago." In Gilbert Osofsky, ed., *The Burden of Race*, 304–309. New York: Harper and Row, 1968.

Johnson, Kirk. "Rich, but Not in History, Connecticut Pequots Sponsor Cultural Powwow." *New York Times* (September 19, 1993): 16.

Jones, James M. *Prejudice and Racism*, 2nd ed. New York: McGraw-Hill, 1999.

Jones, Maldwyn Allen. *American Immigration*. Chicago: The University of Chicago Press, 1960.

————. *Destination America*. New York: Holt, Rinehart and Winston, 1976.

————. "Scotch-Irish." In Stephan Thernstrom, Ann Orlov, and Oscar Handlin, eds., *Harvard Encyclopedia of American Ethnic Groups*, 895–908. Cambridge, Mass.: The Belknap Press, 1980.

Jordan, Winthrop D. "Modern Tensions and the Origins of African Slavery." In Donald I. Noel, ed., *The Origins of American Slavery and Racism*, 81–84. Columbus, Ohio: Charles E. Merrill, 1972.

Jordan, Winthrop D., and Leon F. Litwack. *The United States*, 6th ed., vol. 1. Englewood Cliffs, N.J.: Prentice-Hall, 1987.

Josephy, Alvin M., Jr. *The Patriot Chiefs*. New York: Viking Press, 1961.

————. *The Indian Heritage of America*. New York: Alfred A. Knopf, 1968.

Judson, George. "Not 'The Last' But an Official Tribe, Mohegan Indians Now Want Casino." *New York Times* (March 24, 1994): A12.

Jussim, Lee, Thomas E. Nelson, Melvin Manis, and Sonia Soffin. "Prejudice, Stereotypes, and Labelling Effects: Sources of Bias in Person Perception." *Journal of Personality and Social Psychology* 68 (February 1995): 228–246.

Kamin, Leon. "Lies, Damned Lies, and Statistics." In Russell Jacoby and Naomi Glauberman, eds., *The Bell Curve Debate: History Documents, Opinions*, 81–105. New York: Times Books, 1995.

Kamphoefner, Walter D. "German Americans: Paradoxes of a 'Model Minority.'" In Silvia Pedraza and Rubén G. Rumbaut, eds., *Origins and Destinies: Immigration, Race, and Ethnicity in America*, 152–160. Belmont, Calif.: Wadsworth Publishing Company, 1996.

Kandel, William, and Douglas S. Massey. "The Culture of Mexican Migration: A Theoretical and Empirical Analysis." *Social Forces* 80 (March 2002): 981–1004.

Kang, Jerry. "Thinking Through Internment: 12/7 and 9/11." *Amerasia Journal* 27:3 (2001)/28:1 (2002): 42–50.

Karlin, Jules Alexander. "The Anti-Chinese Outbreak in Tacoma, 1885." In Roger Daniels, ed., *Anti-Chinese Violence in North America*, 271–283. New York: Arno Press, 1978a.

————. "The Anti-Chinese Outbreaks in Seattle, 1885–1886." In Roger Daniels, ed., *Anti-Chinese Violence in North America*, 103–129. New York: Arno Press, 1978b.

Karlins, Marvin, Thomas L. Coffman, and Gary Walters. "On the Fading of Social Stereotypes: Studies in Three Generations of College Students." *Journal of Personality and Social Psychology* 13 (September 1969): 1–16.

Karpat, Kemal H. "The Ottoman Emigration to America, 1860–1914." *International Journal of Middle East Studies* 17 (May 1985): 175–209.

Kasinitz, Philip. *Caribbean New York: Black Immigrants and the Politics of Race*. Ithaca, N.Y.: Cornell University Press, 1992.

Kasinitz, Philip, Mary C. Waters, and John H. Mollenkopf. "Assimilation into What?: The Second Generation Comes of Age in Contemporary New York." Paper presented at the Annual Meeting of the American Sociological Association, Chicago, 1999.

Katz, Daniel, and Kenneth W. Braly. "Racial Stereotypes of One Hundred College Students." *Journal of Abnormal and Social Psychology* 28 (October–December 1933): 280–290.

Kayal, Phillip M. "Religion and Assimilation: Catholic 'Syrians' in America." *International Migration Review* 7 (Winter 1973): 409–425.

Kazal, Russell A. "Revisiting Assimilation: The Rise, Fall, and Reappraisal of a Concept in American Ethnic History." In Norman R. Yetman, ed., *Majority and Minority: The Dynamics of Race and Ethnicity in American Life,* 6th ed., 285–311. Boston: Allyn & Bacon, 1999.

Keefe, Susan E., and Amado M. Padilla. *Chicano Ethnicity.* Albuquerque, N. Mex.: University of New Mexico Press, 1987.

Keely, Charles. "Immigration Policy and the New Immigrants, 1965–1975." In Roy Simon Bryce-Leporte, ed., *Sourcebook on the New Immigration,* 15–25. New Brunswick, N.J.: Transaction Books, 1980.

Keita, S. O. Y. and Rick A. Kittles. "The Persistence of Racial Thinking and the Myth of Racial Divergence," *American Anthropologist* 99 (No. 3, 1997): 534–544.

Kelly, Gail Paradise. *From Vietnam to America.* Boulder, Col.: Westview Press, 1977.

Kennedy, David M. "Can We Still Afford to Be a Nation of Immigrants?" *Atlantic Monthly* 278 (November 1996): 52–68.

Kennedy, Randall. "Racial Trends in the Administration of Criminal Justice." In Neil J. Smelser, William Julius Wilson, and Faith Mitchell, eds., *America Becoming: Racial Trends and Their Consequences,* Volume II, 1–20, National Research Council, Commission on Behavioral and Social Sciences and Education. Washington, D.C.: National Academy Press, 2001.

Kennedy, Ruby Jo Reeves. "Single or Triple Melting-Pot? Intermarriage Trends in New Haven, 1870–1940." *American Journal of Sociology* 49 (January 1944): 331–339.

Kerr, Louise Año Nuevo. "Mexican Chicago: Chicano Assimilation Aborted, 1939–1952." In Melvin G. Holle and Peter d'A. Jones, eds., *The Ethnic Frontier: Group Survival in Chicago and the Midwest,* 293–330. Grand Rapids, Mich.: Eerdmans, 1977.

Kibria, Nazli. "Of Blood, Belonging, and Homeland Trips: Transnationalism and Identity among Second-Generation Chinese and Korean Americans." In Peggy Levitt and Mary C. Waters, eds., *The Changing Face of Home,* 295–311. New York: Russell Sage Foundation, 2002.

Kikumura, Akemi. "Once You Marry Someone It Is Forever." In Maxine Schwartz Seller, ed., *Immigrant Women,* rev., 2nd ed., 149–154. Albany, N.Y.: State University of New York Press, 1994.

Kim, Claire Jean. "Playing the Racial Trump Card: Asian Americans in Contemporary U.S. Politics." *Amerasia Journal* 26:3 (2001): 35–65.

Kim, Hyung-chan. "Koreans." In Stephan Thernstrom, Ann Orlov, and Oscar Handlin, eds., *Harvard Encyclopedia of American Ethnic Groups,* 601–606. Cambridge, Mass.: The Belknap Press, 1980.

King, James C. *The Biology of Race.* New York: Harcourt Brace Jovanovich, 1971.

King, Martin Luther, Jr. "The Case Against 'Tokenism.' " *The New York Times Magazine* (August 5, 1962): 11ff.

———. *Why We Can't Wait?* New York: New American Library, 1964.

———. "Our Struggle for an Interracial Society Based on Freedom for All." In August Meier, Elliott Rudwick, and Francis L. Broderick, eds., *Black Protest Thought in the Twentieth Century,* 2nd ed., 291–302. Indianapolis, Ind. and New York: Bobbs-Merrill, 1971a.

———. "We Still Believe in Black and White Together." In August Meier, Elliott Rudwick, and Francis L. Broderick, eds., *Black Protest Thought in the Twentieth Century,* 2nd ed., 584–595. Indianapolis, Ind. and New York: Bobbs-Merrill, 1971b.

Kitano, Harry H. L. *Japanese Americans.* Englewood Cliffs, N.J.: Prentice-Hall, 1969.

Kitano, Harry H. L., and Roger Daniels. *Asian Americans.* Englewood Cliffs, N.J.: Prentice Hall, 1988.

———. *Asian Americans: Emerging Minorities,* 3rd ed., Upper Saddle River, N.J.: Prentice-Hall, 2001.

Kleinfield, N. R. "Urban Indians Yearn for Lives They Left Behind." *New York Times* (January 3, 1995): A9.

Klineberg, Otto. "Mental Tests." *Encyclopedia of the Social Sciences,* vol. 10, 323–329. New York: Macmillan, 1937.

———. "Pictures in Our Heads." In Edgar A. Schuler, Thomas Ford Hoult, Duane L. Gibson, and Wilbur B. Brookover, eds., *Readings in Sociology,* 5th ed., 631–637. New York: Thomas Y. Crowell, 1974.

Kloss, Heinz. *The American Bilingual Tradition.* Rowley, Mass.: Newbury House Publishers, Inc., 1977.

Kluegel, James R. "Trends in Whites' Explanations of the Black-White Gap in Socioeconomic Status, 1977–1989." *American Sociological Review* 55 (August 1990): 512–525.

Kohn, Howard. "Service with a Sneer." *New York Times Magazine* (November 6, 1994): 43–81.

Kramer, Michael. "What Can Be Done?" *Time* (May 11, 1992): 41.

Kraut, Alan M. *The Huddled Masses: The Immigrant in American Society, 1880–1921.* Arlington Heights, Ill.: Harlan Davidson, Inc., 1982.

Kristol, Irving. "The Negro Today Is Like the Immigrant of Yesterday." In Peter I. Rose, ed., *Nation of Nations,* 197–210. New York: Random House, 1972.

Krysan, Maria, and Reynolds Farley. "The Residential Preferences of Blacks: Do They Explain Persistent Segregation?" *Social Forces* 80 (March 2002): 937–980.

Kulczycki, Andrzej, and Arun Peter Lobo. "Deepening the Melting Pot: Arab Americans at the Turn of the Century." *Middle East Journal* 55 (Summer 2001): 459–473.

———. "Patterns, Determinants, and Implications of Intermarriage Among Arab Americans." *Journal of Marriage and the Family* 64 (February 2002): 202–210.

Kumovich, Robert M. August. "Conflict, Religious Identity, and Ethnic Intolerance in Croatia." In *Sociological Abstracts.* Abstracts of papers presented at the 94th Annual Meeting of the American Sociological Association, Chicago, 1999.

Lacayo, Richard. "Between Two Worlds: African American Middle Class." *Time* (March 13, 1989): 58–68.

———. "Anatomy of an Acquittal." *Time* (May 11, 1992): 30–32.

———. "A New Push for Blind Justice." *Time* (February 20, 1995): 39–40.

Lai, H. M. "Chinese." In Stephan Thernstrom, Ann Orlov, and Oscar Handlin, eds., *Harvard Encyclopedia of American Ethnic Groups,* 256–261. Cambridge, Mass.: The Belknap Press, 1980.

Lamont, Michele, ed. *The Cultural Territories of Race: Black and White Boundaries.* Chicago: The University of Chicago Press, 1999.

Lapham, Susan. "Census Bureau Finds Significant Demographic Differences Among Immigrant Groups." In John A. Kromkowski, ed., *Annual Editions: Race and Ethnic Relations 96/97,* 55–59. Guilford, Conn.: Dushkin Publishing Group, 1996.

LaPiere, Richard T. "Attitudes vs. Actions." *Social Forces* 13 (December 1934): 230–237.

LaViolette, Forrest E. *Americans of Japanese Ancestry.* Toronto: Canadian Institute of International Affairs, 1945.

Lawson, Stephen F. *Black Ballots: Voting Rights in the South, 1944–1969.* New York: Columbia University Press, 1976.

Laycock, Douglas. "The Supreme Court's Decisions on Consideration of Race in Admissions." Report prepared for the University of Texas System Office (July 3, 2003).

Lea, Tom. *The King Ranch*, vol. 1. Boston: Little, Brown, 1957.

LeBlanc Flores, Judith. "Facilitating Postsecondary Outcomes for Mexican Americans." *EDO-RC-94-4* (September 1994).

Leighton, Alexander. *The Governing of Men*. Princeton, N.J.: Princeton University Press, 1946.

Lemann, Nicholas. "The Other Underclass." In Christopher G. Ellison and W. Allen Martin, eds., *Race and Ethnic Relations in the United States: Readings for the 21 Century*, 71–78. Los Angeles, Calif.: Roxbury Publishing Company, 1999.

Leonard, Karen Isakson. *The South Asian Americans*. Westport, Conn.: Greenwood Press, 1997.

Lerner, Richard M., and Christie J. Buehrig. "The Development of Racial Attitudes in Young Black and White Children." *Journal of Genetic Psychology* 127 (September 1975): 45–54.

Levine, Gene N., and Darrel M. Montero. "Socioeconomic Mobility among Three Generations of Japanese Americans." *Journal of Social Issues* 29, no. 2 (1973): 33–47.

Levine, Gene N., and Colbert Rhodes. *The Japanese American Community*. New York: Praeger, 1981.

Levine, Lawrence W. *Black Culture and Black Consciousness*. New York: Oxford University Press, 1977.

Levitt, Peggy. "The Ties That Change." In Peggy Levitt and Mary C. Waters, eds., *The Changing Face of Home*, 123–144. New York: Russell Sage Foundation, 2002.

Levitt, Peggy, and Mary C. Waters "Introduction." In Peggy Levitt and Mary C. Waters, eds., *The Changing Face of Home*, 1–30. New York: Russell Sage Foundation, 2002.

Leyburn, James G. "Frontier Society." In Leonard Dinnerstein and Frederick Cople Jaher, eds., *The Aliens*, 65–76. New York: Appleton-Century-Crofts, 1970.

Liang, Zai, and Naomi Ito. "Intermarriage of Asian Americans in the New York City Region: Contemporary Patterns and Future Prospects." *International Migration Review* 33 (Winter 1999): 876–900.

Lieberson, Stanley. *A Piece of the Pie*. Berkeley, Calif.: University of California Press, 1980.

Lieberson, Stanley, and Glenn V. Fuguitt. "Negro-White Occupational Differences in the Absence of Discrimination." *American Journal of Sociology* 73 (September 1967): 188–200.

Lieberson, Stanley, and Mary C. Waters. *From Many Strands*. New York: Russell Sage Foundation, 1988.

Liebow, Edward R. "Category or Community? Measuring Urban Indian Social Cohesion with Network Sampling." *Journal of Ethnic Studies* 16 (Winter 1989): 67–100.

Light, Ivan H. "Kenjin and Kinsmen." In Rudolph Gomez, Clement Cottingham, Jr., Russell Endo, and Kathleen Jackson, eds., *The Social Reality of Ethnic America*, 282–297. Lexington, Mass.: D. C. Heath and Co., 1974

Light, Ivan, Im Jung Kwuon, and Deng Zhong. "Korean Rotating Credit Associations in Los Angeles." In Franklin Ng, ed., *Asians in America: The Peoples of East, Southeast, and South Asia in American Life and Culture*, 129–148. New York: Garland Publishing, 1998.

Lincoln, C. Eric. *The Black Muslims in America*. Boston: Beacon Press, 1961.

Linton, Ralph. *The Study of Man*. New York: Appleton-Century-Crofts, 1936.

Lippmann, Walter. *Public Opinion*. New York: Harcourt, Brace, Jovanovich, 1922.

Lipset, Seymour Martin. *The First New Nation*. New York: W. W. Norton & Co., 1979.

Littlefield, Alice, Leonard Lieberman, and Larry T. Reynolds. "Redefining Race: The Potential Demise of a Concept in Physical Anthropology." *Current Anthropology* 23 (December 1982): 641–655.

Litwack, Leon F. *Been in the Storm So Long: The Aftermath of Slavery*. New York: Vintage Books, 1979.

Lobel, Sharon Alisa. "Effects of Personal Versus Impersonal Rater Instructions on Relative Favorability of Thirteen Ethnic Group Stereotypes." *Journal of Social Psychology* 128 (February 1988): 29–39.

Locklear, William R. "The Celestials and the Angels." In Roger Daniels, ed., *Anti-Chinese Violence in North America*, 239–256. New York: Arno Press, 1978.

Loehlin, John C., Gardner Lindzey, and J. N. Spuhler. *Race Differences in Intelligence*. San Francisco: W. H. Freeman, 1975.

Lohman, Joseph D., and Dietrich C. Reitzes. "Note on Race Relations in Mass Society." *American Journal of Sociology* 57 (November 1952): 240–246.

Lopez, Manuel Mariano. "Patterns of Interethnic Residential Segregation in the Urban Southwest, 1960 and 1970." *Social Science Quarterly* 62 (March 1981): 50–63.

Lopreato, Joseph. *Italian Americans*. New York: Random House, 1970.

———. *Human Nature and Biocultural Evolution*. Boston: Allen & Unwin, 1984.

Lurie, Nancy Oestreich. "The American Indian: Historical Background." In Norman R. Yetman and C. Hoy Steele, eds., *Majority & Minority*, 3rd ed., 131–144. Boston: Allyn and Bacon, 1982.

Lutz, Donald S. "The Changing View of the Founding and a New Perspective on American Political Theory." *Social Science Quarterly* 68 (December 1987): 669–686.

Lynwood, Carranco. "Chinese Expulsion from Humboldt County." In Roger Daniels, ed., *Anti-Chinese Violence in North America*, 329–340. New York: Arno Press, 1978.

Majumdar, R. C. "India: Ancient and Medieval India." *Encylopedia Americana* 14 (2002): 940–947.

Maki, Mitchell T., Harry H. L. Kitano, and S. Megan Berthold. *Achieving the Impossible Dream: How Japanese Americans Obtained Redress*. Urbana, Ill.: University of Illinois Press, 1999.

Malcolm X, and James Farmer. "Separation or Integration: A Debate." In August Meier, Elliott Rudwick, and Francis L. Broderick, eds., *Black Protest Thought in the Twentieth Century*, 2nd ed., 387–412. Indianapolis, Ind. and New York: Bobbs-Merrill, 1971.

Maldonado, Lionel, and Joan Moore, eds., *Urban Ethnicity in the United States*, 51–71. Beverly Hills, Calif.: Sage Publications, 1985.

Mandell, Daniel R. "Shifting Boundaries of Race and Ethnicity: Indian-Black Intermarriage in Southern New England, 1760–1880." *The Journal of American History* 85 (September 1998): 466–501.

Marumoto, Masaji. " 'First Year' Immigrants to Hawaii & Eugene Van Reed." In Hilary Conroy and T. Scott Miyakawa, eds., *East Across the Pacific*, 5–39. Santa Barbara, Calif.: American Bibliographical Center-CLIO Press, 1972.

Marquez, Benjamin. "The Politics of Race and Class: The League of United Latin American Citizens in the Post–World War II Period." *Social Science Quarterly* 68 (March 1987): 84–101.

Mass, Amy Iwasaki. "Psychological Effects of the Camps on Japanese Americans." In Roger Daniels, Sandra C. Taylor, and Harry Kitano, eds., *Japanese Americans: From Relocation to Redress*, rev. ed., 159–162. Seattle, Wash.: University of Washington Press, 1991.

Massey, Douglas S. "Dimensions of the New Immigration to the United States and the Prospects for Assimilation." In Ralph J. Turner and James F. Short, Jr., eds., *Annual Review of Sociology* 7 (1981): 57–85.

Massey, Douglas S., Gretchen A. Condran, and Nancy A. Denton. "The Effect of Residential Segregation on Black Social and Economic Well-Being." *Social Forces* 66 (September 1987): 29–56.

Massey, Douglas S., and Nancy A. Denton. "Trends in the Residential Segregation of Blacks, Hispanics, and Asians: 1970–1980." *American Sociological Review* 52 (December 1987): 802–825.

———. *American Apartheid: Segregation and the Making of the Underclass*. Cambridge, Mass.: Harvard University Press, 1993.

Massey, Douglas S., and Zoltan L. Hajnal. "The Changing Geographic Structure of Black-White Segregation in the United States." *Social Science Quarterly* 76 (September 1995): 527–542.

Matsumoto, Gary M., Gerald M. Meredith, and Minoru Masuda. "Ethnic Identity: Honolulu and Seattle Japanese-Americans." In Stanley Sue and Nathaniel Wagner, eds., *Asian-Americans,* 65–74. Ben Lomand, Calif.: Science and Behavior Books, 1973.

Mayhew, George Noel. "Hindus." *World Book Encyclopedia* 8 (1961): 224–225.

Mazon, Mauricio. *The Zoot Suit Riots: The Psychology of Symbolic Annihilation.* Austin, Tex.: The University of Texas Press, 1984.

McAdam, Doug. *Political Process and the Development of Black Insurgency, 1930–1970.* Chicago: University of Chicago Press, 1982.

McCarthy, John, and William Yancey. "Uncle Tom and Mr. Charlie: Metaphysical Pathos in the Study of Racism and Personal Disorganization." *American Journal of Sociology* 76 (January 1971): 648–672.

McConahay, J. B. "Modern Racism, Ambivalence, and the Modern Racism Scale." In Dovidio and Gaertner, eds., *Prejudice, Discrimination, and Racism,* 91–125. Orlando, Fla.: Academic Press, 1986.

McCone, John A. "The Watts Riot." In Gilbert Osofsky, ed., *The Burden of Race,* 608–621. New York: Harper & Row, 1968.

McDaniel, Antonio. "The Dynamic Racial Composition of the United States." In Obie Clayton, Jr., ed., *An American Dilemma Revisited: Race Relations in a Changing World,* 269–287. New York: Russell Sage Foundation, 1996.

McDermott, Monica. *Black Like Who? African and Haitian Immigrants and Urban American Conceptions of Race.* Unpublished paper used by permission of the author, 2003.

McFee, Malcolm. "The 150% Man, A Product of Blackfeet Acculturation." In Howard M. Bahr, Bruce A. Chadwick, and Robert C. Day, eds., *Native Americans Today,* 303–312. New York: Harper & Row, 1972.

McInnis, Doug. "At Wind River, Cautious Steps Toward Capitalism." *New York Times* (November 6, 1994): 4F.

McIntyre, Alice. *Making Meaning of Whiteness: Exploring Racial Identity with White Teachers.* Albany: State University of New York Press, 1997.

McKinnon, Jesse. *The Black Population in the United States: March 2002.* Current Population Reports. U.S. Department of Commerce, U.S. Census Bureau, April 2003.

McMillen, Marilyn M., Phillip Kaufman, and Summer D. Whitener. *Dropout Rates in the United States: 1993.* U.S. Department of Education, National Center for Education Statistics, Office of Educational Research and Improvement NCES 94–669. Washington, D.C.: U.S. Government Printing Office, 1994.

McNeill, William H. *Plagues and Peoples.* Garden City, N.Y.: Anchor Books, 1976.

McNickle, D'Arcy. *Native American Tribalism.* London: Oxford University Press, 1973.

McWilliams, Carey. *Brothers Under the Skin.* Boston: Little, Brown, and Co., 1945.

———. *California: The Great Exception.* New York: A. A. Wyn, 1949.

———. "Getting Rid of the Mexicans." In Wayne Moquin and Charles Van Doren, eds., *A Documentary History of the Mexican Americans,* 383–387. New York: Bantam Books, 1972.

———. *North from Mexico.* New York: Greenwood Press, 1973.

Mead, George Herbert. *Mind, Self, and Society.* Chicago: University of Chicago Press, 1934.

Meier, August, Elliott Rudwick, and Francis L. Broderick, eds., *Black Protest Thought in the Twentieth Century,* 2nd ed. Indianapolis, Ind. and New York: Bobbs-Merrill, 1971.

Meister, Richard J., ed., *Race and Ethnicity in Modern America.* Lexington, Mass.: D. C. Heath, 1974.

Melendy, Howard Brett. *Asians in America: Filipinos, Koreans, and East Indians.* Boston, Mass.: Twayne, 1977.

————. "Filipinos." *Harvard Encyclopedia of American Ethnic Groups*, 354–362. Cambridge, Mass.: Belknap Press, 1980.

Meriam, Lewis, et al. *The Problem of Indian Administration.* Washington, D.C.: Brookings Institution, 1928.

Merton, Robert K. *Social Theory and Social Structure*, rev. ed. Glencoe, Ill.: The Free Press, 1957.

Middlekauff, Robert. "The Assumptions of the Founders in 1787." *Social Science Quarterly* 68 (December 1987): 656–668.

Miller, Adam. "Professors of Hate." In Russell Jacoby and Naomi Glauberman, eds., *The Bell Curve Debate.* New York: Times Books, 1995.

Miller, Neal E. "The Frustration-Aggression Hypothesis." *Psychological Review* 48 (July 1941): 337–342.

Mills, C. Wright. *The Power Elite.* New York: Oxford University Press, 1956.

Min, Pyong Gap. "The Korean American Family." In Charles H. Mindel, Robert W. Habenstein, and Roosevelt Wright, Jr., eds., *Ethnic Families in America,* 3rd ed., 199–229. New York: Elsevier, 1988.

————. "Cultural and Economic Boundaries of Korean Ethnicity: A Comparative Analysis." In Franklin Ng, ed., *Asians in America: The Peoples of East, Southeast, and South Asia in American Life and Culture,* 225–241. New York: Garland Publishing, 1998.

———— ed. *Mass Migration to the United States: Classical and Contemporary Periods.* Walnut Creek, Calif.: AltaMira Press, 2002.

Minami, Dale. "*Coram Nobis* and Redress." In Roger Daniels, Sandra C. Taylor, and Harry H. L. Kitano, eds., *Japanese Americans: From Relocation to Redress,* rev. ed., 200–202. Seattle, Wash.: University of Washington Press, 1991.

Mindel, Charles H., Robert W. Habenstein, and Roosevelt Wright, Jr., eds. *Ethnic Families in America,* 3rd ed. New York: Elsevier, 1988.

Mittlebach, Frank G., and Joan W. Moore. "Ethnic Endogamy—The Case of Mexican Americans." *American Journal of Sociology* 74 (July 1968): 50–62.

Miyamoto, S. Frank. *Social Solidarity Among the Japanese of Seattle.* Seattle, Wash.: University of Washington Press, 1939.

————. "An Immigrant Community in America." In Hilary Conroy and T. Scott Miyakawa, eds., *East Across the Pacific,* 217–243. Santa Barbara, Calif.: American Bibliographical Center-CLIO Press, 1972.

Modell, John. *The Economics and Politics of Racial Accommodation: The Japanese of Los Angeles, 1900–1942.* Urbana, Ill.: University of Illinois Press, 1977.

Mogelonsky, Marcia. "Asian-Indian Americans." In John A. Kromkowski, ed., *Annual Editions: Race and Ethnic Relations 96/97,* 132–138. Guilford, Conn.: Dushkin Publishing Group, 1996.

Monahan, Thomas P. "An Overview of Statistics on Interracial Marriage in the United States, with Data on Its Extent from 1963–1970." *Journal of Marriage and the Family* 38 (May 1976): 223–231.

Monk, Maria. "Few Imaginations Can Conceive Deeds So Abominable as They Practiced." In Moses Rischin, ed., *Immigration and the American Tradition.* Indianapolis: Bobbs-Merrill, [1836] 1976.

Monsho, Kharen. "Kwanzaa Celebrates Community of Blacks." *Austin American-Statesman* (December 16, 1988): F2.

Montero, Darrel. *Vietnamese Americans: Patterns of Resettlement and Socioeconomic Adaptation in the United States.* Boulder, Colo.: Westview Press, 1979.

————. *Japanese Americans: Changing Patterns of Affiliation Over Three Generations.* Boulder, Colo.: Westview Press, 1980.

————. "The Japanese Americans: Changing Patterns of Assimilation over Three Generations." *American Sociological Review* 46 (December 1981): 829–839.

Moore, Joan W. *Mexican Americans,* 1st and 2nd eds. Englewood Cliffs, N.J.: Prentice-Hall, 1970 and 1976.

Moore, Joan W., and Harry Pachon. *Hispanics in the United States.* Englewood Cliffs, N.J.: Prentice-Hall, 1985.

Moquín, Wayne, and Charles Van Doren, eds. *A Documentary History of the Mexican Americans.* New York: Bantam Books, 1971.

Morganthau, Tom, Marcus Mabry, Frank Washington, Vern E. Smith, Emily Yoffe, and Lucille Beachy. "Losing Ground." *Newsweek* (April 6, 1992): 20–22.

Morison, Samuel Eliot. *The Oxford History of the American People,* vol. 1. New York: New American Library, 1972.

Morris, Aldon. *The Origins of the Civil Rights Movement: Black Communities Organizing for Change.* New York: The Free Press, 1984.

Morse, Joseph Laffan, and William H. Hendelson, eds. "Indochina." *Funk & Wagnalls New Encyclopedia* 13 (1972a): 262–268.

————. "Vietnam." *Funk & Wagnalls New Encyclopedia* 24 (1972b): 317–326.

Morse, Samuel F. B. "Riot and Ignorance in Human Priest-Controlled Machines." In Moses Rischin, ed., *Immigration and the American Tradition.* Indianapolis, Ind.: Bobbs-Merrill, [1835] 1976.

Moskos, Charles C., Jr. *Greek Americans.* Englewood Cliffs, N.J.: Prentice-Hall, 1980.

Moskos, Charles C., Jr., and John Sibley Butler. *All That We Can Be: Black Leadership and Racial Integration the Army Way.* New York: Basic Books, 1996.

Moynihan, Daniel Patrick. *The Negro Family.* Washington, D.C.: U.S. Department of Labor, 1965.

Mukhopadhyay, Carol C., and Yolanda T. Moses. "Reestablishing 'Race' in Anthropological Discourse," *American Anthropologist* 99 3 (1997): 517–533.

Mulroy, Kevin. *Freedom on the Border: The Seminole Maroons in Florida, the Indian Territory, Coahuila, and Texas.* Lubbock, Tex.: Texas Tech University Press, 1993.

Muller, Thomas, and Thomas J. Espenshade. *The Fourth Wave: California's Newest Immigrants.* Washington, D.C.: The Urban Institute Press, 1985.

Murguía, Edward. *Chicano Intermarriage.* San Antonio, Tex.: Trinity University Press, 1982.

————. *Assimilation, Colonialism, and the Mexican American People.* Lanham, Md.: University Press of America, 1989.

Murguía, Edward, and Tyrone Forman. "Shades of Whiteness: The Mexican American Experience in Relation to Anglos and Blacks." In Woody Doane and Eduardo Bonilla-Silva, eds., *Whiteout: The Continuing Significance of Racism,* 63–79. New York: Routledge, 2003.

Murguía, Edward, and W. Parker Frisbie. "Trends in Mexican American Intermarriage: Recent Findings in Perspective." *Social Science Quarterly* 58 (December 1977): 374–389.

Myrdal, Gunnar. *An American Dilemma,* 2 vols. New York: McGraw-Hill, 1964.

Naber, Nadine. "Ambiguous Insiders: An Investigation of Arab American Invisibility." *Ethnic and Racial Studies* 23 (January 2000): 37–61.

Naff, Alixa. *Becoming American: The Early Arab Immigrant Experience.* Carbondale, Ill.: Southern Illinois Press, 1985.

————. "Arabs." In *Harvard Encyclopedia of American Ethnic Groups,* 128–136. Cambridge, Mass.: Belknap Press, 1980.

Nagel, Caroline. "Constructing Difference and Sameness: The Politics of Assimilation in Arab Communities." *Ethnic and Racial Studies* 25 (March 2002): 258–287.

Nagel, Joane. *American Indian Ethnic Renewal: Red Power and the Resurgence of Identity and Culture.* New York: Oxford University Press, 1996.

———. "American Indian Ethnic Renewal: Politics and the Resurgence of Identity." In Charles A. Gallagher, ed., *Rethinking the Color Line: Readings in Race and Ethnicity,* 73–85. Mountain View, Calif.: Mayfield Publishing Company, 1999.

Nagel, Joane, and C. Matthew Snipp. "Ethnic Reorganization: American Indian Social, Economic, Political, and Cultural Strategies for Survival." *Ethnic and Racial Studies* (April 1993): 203–235.

Narasaki, Karen K. "Debunking a Myth: Asians for Affirmative Action." *Houston Chronicle* (April 7, 2003): 21A.

NARF Legal Review. "Indian Religious Freedom Bills Near Passage," (Summer/Fall 1994): 1–7.

Nasaw, David. "First Great Triumph." *New York Times Book Review* (November 24, 2002): 13.

Nash, Gary B. *Red, White, and Black.* Englewood Cliffs, N.J.: Prentice-Hall, 1974.

National Advisory Commission. *Report of the National Advisory Commission on Civil Disorders.* New York: New York Times Co., 1968.

National Center for Education Statistics. *Dropout Rates in the United States: 1993.* Washington, D.C.: U.S. Department of Education, 1994.

Nee, Victor, and Herbert Y. Wong. "Asian American Achievement: The Strength of the Family Bond." In Franklin Ng, ed., *Asians in America: The Peoples of East, Southeast, and South Asia in American Life and Culture,* 1–26. New York: Garland Publishing, 1998.

Neidert, Lisa, and Reynolds Farley. "Assimilation in the United States: An Analysis of Ethnic and Generation Differences in Status and Achievement." *American Sociological Review* 50 (December 1985): 840–850.

Newman, William M. *American Pluralism.* New York: Harper & Row, 1973.

New York Times. "F.B.I. Agents Raid Casinos on 5 Indian Reservations." (May 13, 1992): A8.

———. "Of 58 Riot Deaths, 50 Have Been Ruled Homicides." (May 17, 1992): A17.

———. "Coroner Drops Toll in Los Angeles Riot to 51 After Review." (August 13, 1992): A11.

Newsweek. "For Indians, by Indians." In Herbert L. Marx, ed., *The American Indian,* 108–110. New York: H. W. Wilson, 1973.

Ngai, Mae M. "The Architecture of Race in American Immigration Law: A Reexamination of the Immigration Act of 1924." *The Journal of American History* 86:1 (June 1999): 67–97.

Niebuhr, Gustav. "Zunis Mix Tribe Spirit with Icons of Church." *New York Times* (January 29, 1995): A8.

Nieto, Sonia. "Fact and Fiction: Stories of Puerto Ricans in U.S. Schools." *Harvard Educational Review* 68 (Summer 1998): 133–163.

Nigem, Elias T. "Arab Americans: Migration, Socioeconomic and Demographic Characteristics." *International Migration Review* 20 (Autumn 1986): 629–649.

Nisbett, Richard E. "Race, Genetics, and IQ." In Christopher Jencks and Meredith Phillips, eds., *The Black-White Test Score Gap,* 86–102. Washington, D.C.: Brookings Institution Press, 1998.

Noel, Donald L. "A Theory of the Origin of Ethnic Stratification." *Social Problems* 16 (Fall 1968): 157–172.

Nostrand, Richard L. " 'Mexican American' and 'Chicano': Emerging Terms for a People Coming of Age." *Pacific Historical Review* 62 (August 1973): 389–406.

Novotny, Ann. *Strangers at the Door.* Toronto: Bantam Pathfinders Edition, 1974.

O'Brien, David J., and Stephen S. Fugita. *The Japanese American Experience.* Bloomington, Ind.: University Press, 1991.

O'Brien, Sharon. "Federal Indian Policies and the International Protection of Human Rights." In Vine Deloria, Jr., ed., *American Indian Policy in the Twentieth Century,* 35–61. Norman: University of Oklahoma Press, 1985.

O'Hare, William. "Reaching for the Dream." *American Demographics* (January 1992): 32–36.

O'Hare, William P., Kelvin M. Pollard, Taynia L. Mann, and Mary M. Kent. "African Americans in the 1990s." *Population Bulletin* 46 (Washington, D.C.: Population Reference Bureau, July 1991): 29–30.

O'Hare, William, and Margaret L. Usdansky. "What the 1990 Census Tells Us about Segregation in 25 Large Metros." *Population Today* 20 (September 1992): 6–7.

Officer, James E. "Termination as Federal Policy: An Overview." In Kenneth R. Philp, ed., *Indian Self-Rule,* 114–128. Salt Lake City, Utah: Howe Brothers, 1986.

Ogawa, Dennis M., and Evarts C. Fox, Jr. "Japanese Internment and Relocation: The Hawaii Experience." In Roger Daniels, Sandra C. Taylor, and Harry H. L. Kitano, eds., *Japanese Americans: From Relocation to Redress,* rev. ed., 135–138. Seattle, Wash: University of Washington Press, 1991.

Ogunwole, Stella U. "The American Indian and Alaska Native Population: 2000." Census 2000 Brief. U.S. Department of Commerce, U.S. Census Bureau, February 2002.

Okimoto, Daniel. "The Intolerance of Success." In Amy Tachiki, Eddie Wong, Franklin Odo, and Buck Wong, eds., *Roots: An Asian American Reader,* 14–19. Los Angeles: Regents of the University of California, 1971.

Olson, James S., and Raymond Wilson. *Native Americans in the Twentieth Century.* Urbana, Ill. and Chicago: University of Illinois Press, 1984.

Olzak, Susan. "A Competition Model of Ethnic Collective Action in American Cities, 1877–1899." In Susan Olzak and Joane Nagel, eds., *Competitive Ethnic Relations,* 17–46. Orlando, Fla.: Academic Press, 1986.

Olzak, Susan, and Joane Nagel. "Introduction, Competitive Ethnic Relations: An Overview." In Susan Olzak and Joane Nagel, eds., *Competitive Ethnic Relations,* 1–14. Orlando, Fla: Academic Press, 1986.

Olzak, Susan, and Suzanne Shanahan. "Deprivation and Race Riots: An Extension of Spilerman's Analysis." *Social Forces* 74 (March 1996): 931–961.

One Feather, Gerald. "Relocation" (comment). In Kenneth R. Philp, ed., *Indian Self-Rule,* 171–172. Salt Lake City, Utah: Howe Brothers, 1986.

Orfalea, Gregory. *Before the Flames: A Quest for the History of Arab Americans.* Austin, Tex.: The University of Texas Press, 1988.

Orfield, Gary. *Must We Bus.* Washington, D.C.: Brookings Institution, 1978.

———. *Desegregation of Black and Hispanic Students from 1968 to 1980.* Quoted in Mary Swerdlin, ed., *Education Daily* 15 (September 10, 1982): 1–2.

Orfield, Gary, and Susan E. Eaton. *Dismantling Desegregation: The Quiet Reversal of Brown v. Board of Education.* New York: The New Press, 1996.

Osofsky, Gilbert, ed., *The Burden of Race.* New York: Harper & Row, 1968.

Pabon, Edward. "Hispanic Adolescent Delinquency and the Family: A Discussion of Sociocultural Influences." *Adolescence* 33 (Winter 1998): 941–955.

Pachon, Harry P., and Joan W. Moore. "Mexican Americans." *The Annals* 454 (March 1981): 111–124.

Padilla, Felix M. *Latino Ethnic Consciousness: The Case of Mexican Americans and Puerto Ricans in Chicago.* Notre Dame, Ind.: University of Notre Dame Press, 1985.

Palumbo-Liu, David. *Asian American's Historical Crossings of a Racial Frontier.* Stanford, Calif.: Stanford University Press, 1999.

Papademetriou, D. G. "The Immigration Reform and Control Act of 1986: America Amends Its Immigration Law." *International Migration* 25 (September 1987): 325–334.

Paredes, Américo. *With His Pistol in His Hand: A Border Ballad and its Hero.* Austin, Tex.: University of Texas Press, 1958.

Park, Robert E. "Our Racial Frontier on the Pacific." *Survey Graphic* 56 (May 1926): 192–196. In Robert E. Park, ed., *Race and Culture,* 138–151. New York: Free Press, 1964.

———. *Race and Culture.* New York: Free Press, 1964.

Parkman, Margaret A., and Jack Sawyer. "Dimensions of Ethnic Intermarriage in Hawaii." *American Sociological Review* 32 (August 1967): 593–607.

Pascoe, Peggy. "Miscegenation Law, Court Cases, and Ideologies of 'Race' in Twentieth-Century America." *The Journal of American History* 83 (June 1996): 44–69.

Passel, Jeffrey S. *Immigrants and Taxes: A Reappraisal of Huddle's "The Cost of Immigrants."* Washington, D.C.: The Urban Institute, PRIP–U1–29, January 1994.

Passel, Jeffrey S., and Patricia Berman. "Quality of 1980 Census Data for American Indians." *Social Biology* 3 1986: 163–182.

Patterson, Orlando. *Rituals of Blood: Consequences of Slavery in Two American Centuries.* Washington, D.C.: Civitas Counterpoint, 1998.

Pedraza, Silvia, and Rubén G. Rumbaut, eds. *Origins and Destinies: Immigration, Race, and Ethnicity in America,* 43–59. Belmont, Calif.: Wadsworth Publishing Company, 1996.

Peñalosa, Fernando. "The Changing Mexican-American in Southern California." In John H. Burma, ed., *Mexican Americans in the United States,* 41–51. Cambridge, Mass.: Schenkman, 1970.

———. *Chicano Sociolinguistics: A Brief Introduction.* Rowley, Mass.: Newbury House Publishers, 1989.

Perez, Lisandro. "Cubans." In Stephan Thernstrom, Ann Orlov, and Oscar Handlin, eds., *Harvard Encyclopedia of American Ethnic Groups,* 256–261. Cambridge, Mass.: The Belknap Press, 1980.

Peroff, Nicholas G. "Termination Policy and the Menominees: Feedback of Unanticipated Impacts." In John G. Grumm and Stephen L. Wasby, eds., *The Analysis of Policy Impact,* 123–131. Lexington, Mass.: Lexington Books, 1981.

Petersen, William. *Japanese Americans.* New York: Random House, 1971.

———. "Concepts of Ethnicity." In Stephan Thernstrom, Ann Orlov, and Oscar Handlin, eds., *Harvard Encyclopedia of American Ethnic Groups,* 234–242. Cambridge, Mass.: Belknap Press, 1980.

Peterson, Iver. "1993 Deal for Indian Casino Is Called a Model to Avoid." *New York Times* (July 30, 2003): A16.

Pettigrew, Thomas F. *Racially Separate or Together?* New York: McGraw-Hill, 1971.

———. *Racial Discrimination in the United States.* New York: Harper & Row, 1975.

Pettigrew, Thomas F., and Joanne Martin. "Shaping the Organizational Context for Black American Inclusion." In George Levinger, ed., *Black Employment Opportunities: Macro and Micro Perspectives,* special issue. *Journal of Social Issues* 43, no. 1 (1987): 41–78.

———. "Organizational Inclusion of Minority Groups: A Social Psychological Analysis." In Jan Pieter van Oudenhoven and Tineke M. Willemsen, eds., *Ethnic Minorities,* 169–200. Amsterdam: Swets & Zeitlinger B.V., 1989.

Piore, Michael J. *Birds of Passage: Migrant Labor and Industrial Societies.* New York: Cambridge University Press, 1979.

Pollack, Denan. "Mashantucket Pequots: A Tribe That's Raking It In." *U.S. News and World Report* (January 15, 1996): 59.

Portes, Alejandro. "Modes of Structural Incorporation and Present Theories of Immigration." In Mary M. Kritz, Charles B. Keely, and Sylvano M. Tomasi, eds., *Global Trends in Migration,* 279–297. Staten Island, N.Y.: CMS Press, 1981.

Portes, Alejandro, and Robert L. Bach. *Latin Journey.* Berkeley, Calif.: University of California Press, 1985.

Portes, Alejandro, and Lingxin Hao. "*E Pluribus Unum:* Bilingualism and Loss of Language in the Second Generation." *Sociology of Education* 71 (October 1998): 269–294.

Portes, Alejandro, and Ruben G. Rumbaut. *Immigrant America: A Portrait.* Berkeley and Los Angeles: University of California Press, 1990.

Portes, Alejandro, and Richard Schauffler. "Language Acquisition and Loss Among Children of Immigrants." In Silvia Pedraza and Rubén G. Rumbaut, eds., *Origins and Destinies: Immigration, Race, and Ethnicity in America,* 442–443. Belmont, Calif.: Wadsworth Publishing Company, 1996.

Portes, Alejandro, and Min Zhou. "Self-Employment and the Earnings of Immigrants." *American Sociological Review* 61 (April, 1996): 219–230.

Posadas, Barbara M. *The Filipino Americans.* Westport, Conn.: Greenwood Press, 1999.

Poston, Dudley L., Jr., and David Alvírez. "On the Cost of Being a Mexican American Worker." *Social Science Quarterly* 53 (March 1973): 697–709.

Poston, Dudley L., Jr., David Alvírez, and Marta Tienda. "Earnings Differences between Anglo and Mexican American Male Workers in 1960 and 1970: Changes in the 'Cost' of Being Mexican American." *Social Science Quarterly* 57 (December 1976): 618–631.

Pottinger, J. Stanley. "The Drive Toward Equality." In Barry R. Gross, ed., *Reverse Discrimination,* 41–49. Buffalo, N.Y.: Prometheus Books, 1977.

Prewitt, Kenneth. "Race in the 2000 Census." In Joel Perlmann and Mary C. Waters, eds., *The New Race Question: How the Census Counts Multiracial Individuals,* 354–361. New York: Russell Sage Foundation, 2002.

Price, John A. "The Migration and Adaptation of American Indians to Los Angeles." In Howard M. Bahr, Bruce A. Chadwick, and Robert C. Day, eds., *Native Americans Today,* 428–439. New York: Harper & Row, 1972.

Prucha, Francis Paul. *American Indian Policy in the Formative Years.* Cambridge, Mass.: Harvard University Press, 1962.

Public Broadcasting System. "Caught in the Crossfire," 2003. http://www.pbs.org/itvs/caught inthecrossfire.

Quillian, Lincoln, and Mary E. Campbell. "Beyond Black and White: The Present and Future of Multiracial Friendship Segregation." *American Sociological Review* 68 (August 2003): 540–566.

Quint, Howard H., Milton Cantor, and Dean Albertson, eds. *Main Problems in American History,* vol. 1, 4th ed. Homewood, Ill.: Dorsey, 1978.

Rainwater, Lee, and William L. Yancey. *The Moynihan Report and the Politics of Controversy.* Cambridge, Mass.: MIT Press, 1967.

Ramirez, Roberto R., and G. Patricia de la Cruz. *The Hispanic Population in the United States: March 2002.* U.S. Department of Commerce, U.S. Census Bureau, June 2003.

Randolph, A. Philip. "Address to the Policy Conference." In August Meier, Elliott Rudwick, and Francis L. Broderick, eds., *Black Protest Thought in the Twentieth Century,* 2nd ed., 224–233. Indianapolis, Ind. and New York: Bobbs-Merrill, 1971a.

———. "A. Philip Randolph Urges Civil Disobedience Against a Jim Crow Army." In August Meier, Elliott Rudwick, and Francis L. Broderick, eds., *Black Protest Thought in the Twentieth Century,* 2nd ed., 233–238. Indianapolis, Ind. and New York: Bobbs-Merrill, 1971b.

Rawick, George P. "From Sundown to Sunup: Slavery and the Making of the Black Community." In Silvia Pedraza and Rubén G. Rumbaut, eds., *Origins and Destinies: Immigration, Race, and Ethnicity in America,* 60–72. Belmont, Calif.: Wadsworth Publishing Company, 1996.

Reimers, David M. *Still the Golden Door.* New York: Columbia University Press, 1985.

Reinhold, Robert. "Police Are Slow to React as the Violence Spreads." *New York Times* (May 1, 1992): A1, A12.

Reisler, Mark. *By the Sweat of Their Brow: Mexican Immigrant Labor in the United States, 1900–1940.* Westport, Conn.: Greenwood, 1976.

Reiss, Tom. "Home on the Range." *New York Times* (May 26, 1995): A11.

Rhoades, Everett R., Russell D. Mason, Phyllis Eddy, Eva M. Smith, and Thomas R. Burns. "The Indian Health Service Approach to Alcoholism Among American Indians and Alaska Natives." *Public Health Reports* 103 (November–December 1988): 621–627.

Richardson, Chad. *Batos, Bolillos, Pochos, and Pelados: Class and Culture on the South Texas Border.* Austin, Tex: University of Texas Press, 1999.

Riesman, David, Nathan Glazer, and Reuel Denney. *The Lonely Crowd.* New Haven, Conn.: Yale University Press, 1950.

Riis, Jacob A. *How the Other Half Lives.* New York: Hill and Wang, [1890] 1957.

Robinson, J. W., and J. D. Preston. "Equal-Status Contact and Modification of Racial Prejudice: A Re-examination of the Contact Hypothesis." *Social Forces* 54 (1976): 911–924.

Robinson, William L., and Stephen L. Spitz. "Affirmative Action: Evolving Case Law and Shifting Philosophy." *The Urban League Review* 10 (Winter 1986–87): 84–100.

Rodman, Hyman. "Technical Note on Two Rates of Mixed Marriage." *American Sociological Review* 30 (October 1965): 776–778.

Rodriguez, Clara. *Puerto Ricans Born in the U.S.A.* Boulder, Colo.: Westview Press, 1991.

———. "Challenging Racial Hegemony: Puerto Ricans in the United States." In Roger Sanjek and Steven Gregory, eds., *Race,* 131–145. New Brunswick, N.J.: Rutgers University Press, 1994.

Róman, Miriam Jiménez. "Un hombre (negro) del pueblo: José Celso Barbosa and the Puerto Rican 'Race' Toward Whiteness." *Centro,* VIII (Spring 1996): 8–29.

Romano, Octavio Ignacio. "The Anthropology and Sociology of the Mexican Americans." *El Grito* 2 (Fall 1968): 13–26.

Romo, Harriett D., and Toni Falbo. *Latino High School Graduation: Defying the Odds.* Austin, Tex.: University of Texas Press, 1996.

Romo, Ricardo. *East Los Angeles: History of a Barrio.* Austin, Tex.: University of Texas Press, 1983.

Romo, Ricardo, and Harriett Romo. "Introduction: The Social and Cultural Context of the Mexican American Experience in the United States." In Rodolfo O. de la Garza, Frank D. Bean, Charles M. Bonjean, Ricardo Romo, and Rodolfo Alvarez, eds. *The Mexican American Experience: An Interdisciplinary Anthology,* 317–333. Austin, Tex.: University of Texas Press, 1985.

Roosevelt, Franklin D. "Executive Order 8802." In Gilbert Osofsky, ed., *The Burden of Race,* 400–401. New York: Harper Torchbooks, 1967.

Rosenbaum, Robert J. *Mexican Resistance in the Southwest: "The Sacred Right of Self-Preservation."* Austin, Tex.: University of Texas Press, 1981.

Rosenberg, Morris, and Roberta Simmons. *Black and White Self-Esteem: The Urban School Child.* Washington, D.C.: American Sociological Association, 1972.

Rosenberg, Morris, Carmi Schooler, Carrie Schoenbach, and Florence Rosenberg. "Global Self-Esteem and Specific Self-Esteem: Different Concepts and Different Outcomes." *American Sociological Review* 60 (February 1995): 141–156.

Ross, Sonya. "More Blacks Get College Degrees But They Still Receive Lower Pay." *Austin American-Statesman* (September 16, 1993).

Rostow, Eugene V. "Our Worst Wartime Mistake." *Harper's Magazine* (September 1945): 193–201.

Rothenberg, Paula S. *Race, Class, and Gender in the United States: An Integrated Study.* New York: St. Martin's Press, 1995.

Roy, Prodipto. "The Measurement of Assimilation: The Spokane Indians." In Howard M. Bahr, Bruce A. Chadwick, and Robert C. Day, eds., *Native Americans Today,* 225–239. New York: Harper & Row, 1972.

Rubenstein, Richard E. *Rebels in Eden.* Boston: Little, Brown, 1970.

Rumbaut, Rubén G. "A Legacy of War: Refugees from Vietnam, Laos, and Cambodia." In Silvia Pedraza and Rubén G. Rumbaut, eds., *Origins and Destinies: Immigration, Race, and Ethnicity in America,* 315–333. Belmont, Calif.: Wadsworth Publishing Company, 1996.

Russell, Mona L. "Arab Civilization." *Encyclopedia Americana.* Grolier Online, 2003. http://ea-ada.grolier.com.

Rustin, Bayard. "A Workable and Christian Technique for the Righting of Injustice." In August Meier, Elliott Rudwick, and Francis L. Broderick, eds., *Black Protest Thought in the Twentieth Century,* 2nd ed., 233–238. Indianapolis, Ind. and New York: Bobbs-Merrill, 1971.

Ryan, Alan. "Apocalypse Now." In Russell Jacoby and Naomi Glauberman, eds., *The Bell Curve Debate,* 12–29. New York: Times Books, 1995.

Ryan, William. *Blaming the Victim.* New York: Vintage Books, 1971.

Sakamoto, Arthur, and Satomi Furuichi. "Wages Among White and Japanese-American Male Workers." *Research in Stratification and Mobility,* vol 15, 177–206. Greenwich, Conn.: JAI Press, Inc., 1977.

Sakamoto, Arthur, and Jessie M. Tzeng. "A Fifty-Year Perspective on the Declining Significance of Race in the Occupational Attainment of White and Black Men." *Sociological Perspectives* 42 (Summer 1999): 157–179.

Sakamoto, Arthur, Jeng Liu, and Jessie M. Tzeng. "The Declining Significance of Race Among Chinese and Japanese American Men." *Research in Stratification and Mobility,* vol 16, 225–246. Greenwich, Conn.: JAI Press, Inc., 1998.

Sakamoto, Arthur, Huei-Hsai Wu, and Jessie M. Tzeng. "The Declining Significance of Race Among American Men During the Latter Half of the 20th Century." *Demography* 37 (February 2000): 41–51.

Salzman, Jack, ed., *Bridges and Boundaries: African Americans and American Jews.* New York: The Jewish Museum, 1992.

Samhan, Helen Hatab. "Politics and Exclusion: The Arab American Experience." *Journal of Palestine Studies* 16 (Winter 1987): 11–28.

San Miguel, Guadalupe, Jr. *"Let All of Them Take Heed": Mexican Americans and the Campaign for Educational Equality in Texas, 1910–1981.* Austin, Tex.: University of Texas Press, 1987.

Sanchez, George I. "Pachucos in the Making." In Wayne Moquín and Charles Van Doren, eds., *A Documentary History of the Mexican Americans,* 409–415. New York: Bantam Books, 1972.

———. *Becoming Mexican American: Ethnicity, Cluture and Identity in Chicano Los Angeles, 1900–1945.* New York: Oxford University Press, 1993.

Sanchez, George J. "Face the Nation: Race, Immigration, and the Rise of Nativism." *International Migration Review* 31 (Winter 1997): 1009–1031.

Sandefur, Gary D., and Trudy McKinnell. "American Indian Intermarriage." *Social Science Research* 15 (December 1986): 347–371.

Sandefur, Gary D., and Arthur Sakamoto. "American Indian Household Structure and Income." *Demography* 25 (February 1988): 71–80.

Sandefur, Gary D., and Wilbur J. Scott. "Minority Group Status and the Wages of Indian and Black Males." *Social Science Research* 12 (March 1983): 44–68.

Santiago-Valles, Kevin. "Policing the Crisis in the Whitest of all the Antilles." *CENTRO Journal of the Center for Puerto Rican Studies* 7 (Winter 1996): 43–55.

Schermerhorn, Richard A. *These Our People*. Boston: D. C. Heath, 1949.

———. *Comparative Ethnic Relations*. New York: Random House, 1970.

Schlesinger, Arthur M., Jr. *The Disuniting of America*. New York: W. W. Norton & Company, 1992.

Schneider, Barbara, and Yongsook Lee. "A Model for Academic Success: The School and Home Environment of East Asian Students." *Anthropology and Education Quarterly* 21 (December 1990): 358–377.

Schneider, Barbara, Joyce A. Hieshima, Sehahn Lee, and Stephen Plank. "East-Asian Academic Success in the United States: Family, School, and Community Explanations." In Patricia M. Greenfield and Rodney R. Cocking, eds., *Cross-Cultural Roots of Minority Child Development*, 323–349. Hillsdale, N.J.: Lawrence Erlbaum Associates Publishers, 1994.

Schneider, Dorothee. "Naturalization and U.S. Citizenship in Two Periods of Mass Migration (1890–1930 and 1965–2000)." In Pyong Gap Min, ed., *Mass Migration to the United States: Classical and Contemporary Periods*, 161–197. Walnut Creek, Calif.: AltaMira Press, 2001.

Schoen, Robert, and Lawrence E. Cohen. "Ethnic Endogamy among Mexican American Grooms: A Reanalysis of Generational and Occupational Effects." *American Journal of Sociology* 86 (September 1980): 359–366.

Schoen, Robert, Verne E. Nelson, and Marion Collins. "Intermarriage among Spanish Surnamed Californians, 1962–1974." *International Migration Review* 12 (1978): 359–369.

Schofield, Janet Ward. "Black-White Contact in Desegregated Schools." In Miles Hewstone and Rupert Brown, eds., *Contact and Conflict in Intergroup Encounters*, 79–92. Oxford: Basil Blackwell Ltd., 1986.

———. "Improving Intergroup Relations Among Students." In James A. Banks and Cherry A. McGee Banks, eds., *Handbook of Research on Multicultural Education*, 635–646. New York: Macmillan, 1995.

Schulz, Amy J. "Navajo Women and the Politics of Identity." *Social Problems* 45 (August 1998): 336–355.

Schuman, Howard, and Lawrence Bobo. "Survey-based Experiments on White Racial Attitudes toward Residential Integration." *American Journal of Sociology* 94 (September 1988): 273–299.

Schuman, Howard, and Shirley Hatchett. *Black Racial Attitudes: Trends and Complexities*. Ann Arbor, Mich.: University of Michigan Institute for Social Research, 1974.

Schuman, Howard, and Michael P. Johnson. "Attitudes and Behavior." In Alex Inkeles, ed., *Annual Review of Sociology*, 161–207. Palo Alto, Calif.: Annual Reviews, 1976.

Schuman, Howard, Charlotte Steeh, and Lawrence Bobo. *Racial Attitudes in America*. Cambridge, Mass.: Harvard University Press, 1985.

Schuman, Howard, Charlotte Steeh, Lawrence Bobo, and Maria Krysan. *Racial Attitudes in America: Trends and Interpretations*, rev. ed. Cambridge, Mass.: Harvard University Press, 1997.

Schwarz, Benjamin. "The Diversity Myth: America's Leading Export." *The Atlantic* (May 1995): 57–67.

Schwartz, Tony. "Is This Any Way to Run a Meritocracy?" *New York Times Magazine* (January 10, 1999): 30.

Scott, Robin Fitzgerald. "Wartime Labor Problems and Mexican-Americans in the War." In Manuel P. Servín, ed., *An Awakening Minority: The Mexican Americans*, 2nd ed., 134–142. Beverly Hills, Calif.: Glencoe Press, 1974.

See, Katherine O'Sullivan. "For God and Crown: Class, Ethnicity, and Protestant Politics in Northern Ireland." In Susan Olzak and Joane Nagel, eds., *Competitive Ethnic Relations*, 221–245. Orlando, Fla.: Academic Press, 1986.

Seller, Maxine S. "Historical Perspectives on American Immigration Policy: Case Studies and Current Implications." In Richard R. Hofstetter, ed., *U.S. Immigration Policy,* 137–162. Durham, N.C.: Duke University Press, 1984.

Shaheen, Jack. *Reel Bad Movies: How Hollywood Vilifies a People.* New York: Olive Branch Press, 2001.

Shain, Yossi. "Arab-Americans at a Crossroads." *Journal of Palestine Studies* 25 (Spring 1996): 46–59.

Sherwood, Mary. "Striving Toward Assimilation." *Corpus Christi Times-Caller* (December 29, 1988): D14–16.

Sheth, Pravin. *Indians in America: One Stream, Two Waves, Three Generations.* Jaipur, India: Rawat Publications, 2001.

Siegel, Paul M. "On the Cost of Being a Negro." *Sociological Inquiry* 35 (Winter 1965): 41–57.

Sigelman, Lee, and Susan Welch. "The Contact Hypothesis Revisited: Black-White Interaction and Positive Racial Attitudes." *Social Forces* 71 (March 1993): 781–795.

Simmons, Roberta G. "Blacks and High Self-Esteem: A Puzzle." *Social Psychology* 41 (March, 1978): 54–57.

Simpson, George Eaton, and J. Milton Yinger. *Racial and Cultural Minorities,* 4th ed. New York: Harper & Row, 1972.

Singer, Lester. "Ethnogenesis and Negro Americans Today." *Social Research* 29 (Winter 1962): 419–432.

Sklare, Marshall. "American Jewry: Social History and Group Identity." In Norman R. Yetman and C. Hoy Steele, eds., *Majority & Minority,* 2nd ed., 261–273. Boston: Allyn and Bacon, 1975.

Sleeter, Christine E. *Multicultural Education as Social Activism.* Albany: SUNY Press, 1996.

———. "Foreword." In Alice McIntyre, *Making Meaning of Whiteness: Exploring Racial Identity with White Teachers,* ix–xii. Albany: State University of New York Press, 1997.

Smith, James P. "Race and Ethnicity in the Labor Market: Trends over the Short and Long Term." In Neil J. Smelser, William Julius Wilson, and Faith Mitchell, eds., *America Becoming: Racial Trends and Their Consequences,* Volume II, 52–97. National Research Council, Commission on Behavioral and Social Sciences and Education. Washington, D.C.: National Academy Press, 2001.

Smith, James P., and Finis Welch. *Race Differences in Earnings: A Survey and New Evidence.* Santa Monica, Calif.: The Rand Corp., 1978.

———. *Closing the Gap: Forty Years of Economic Progress for Blacks.* Santa Monica, Calif.: The Rand Corp., 1986.

Smith, Jerry E. *Hopwood et al. v. Texas.* The United States Court of Appeals for the Fifth Circuit 94–50569, 1996.

Smothers, Ronald. "Restaurant Chain Promises Revolution in Race Policies." *New York Times* (January 31, 1993): 12.

Snipp, C. Matthew. *American Indians: The First of This Land.* New York: Russell Sage Foundation, 1989.

———. "American Indians Today." In *National Rural Studies Committee: A Proceedings of the Annual Meeting,* Las Vegas, Nevada, May 14–16, 1992: 16–26.

Sone, Monica. "The Stubborn Twig: 'My Double Dose of Schooling.' " In Maxine Schwartz Seller, ed., *Immigrant Women,* rev., 2nd ed., 243–248. Albany, N.Y.: State University of New York Press, 1994.

Southern Poverty Law Center. "Violent Hate Crimes Remain at Record Levels." *Intelligence Report* (March, 1994a): 1–5.

———. *Klanwatch Intelligence Report* (March 1994b).

———. "For the Record." *Klanwatch Intelligence Report* (August 1995): 13–18.

———. "Before They Were Patriots." *False Patriots: The Threat of Antigovernment Extremists.* 1996a.

———. "Bias Incidents Reported During 1995." *Klanwatch Intelligence Report* (February 1996b): 7–23.

———. "National Alliance: North America's Largest Neo-Nazi Group Flourishing." *Klanwatch Intelligence Report* (May 1996c): 5–8.

———. *Intelligence Report* 109 (Spring 2003).

Sowell, Thomas. " 'Affirmative Action' Reconsidered." In Barry R. Gross, ed., *Reverse Discrimination,* 113–131. Buffalo, N.Y.: Prometheus Books, 1977.

Sparks, Sam. *Hopwood et al. v. Texas.* United States District Court, Western District of Texas, Austin Division, No. A 92 CA 563 SS, August 19, 1994.

Spearman, Charles. "General Intelligence Ojectively Determined and Measured." *American Journal of Psychology* 15 (January 1904): 201–293.

Spencer, Robert F. "Language-American Babel." In Robert F. Spencer, Jesse D. Jennings, et al., eds., *The Native Americans,* 37–55. New York: Harper & Row, 1977.

Spencer, Robert F., Jesse D. Jennings, et al., eds. *The Native Americans,* 2nd ed. New York: Harper & Row, 1977.

Spicer, Edward H. "American Indians." In Stephan Thernstrom, Ann Orlov, and Oscar Handlin, eds., *Harvard Encyclopedia of American Ethnic Groups,* 58–114. Cambridge, Mass.: The Belknap Press, 1980a.

———. "American Indians, Federal Policy Toward." In Stephan Thernstrom, Ann Orlov, and Oscar Handlin, eds., *Harvard Encyclopedia of American Ethnic Groups,* 114–122. Cambridge, Mass.: The Belknap Press, 1980b.

Spickard, Paul R. *Japanese Americans: The Formation and Transformations of an Ethnic Group.* New York: Twayne Publishers, 1996.

———. *Mixed Blood: Intermarriage and Ethnic Identity in Twentieth-Century America.* Madison, Wisc.: University of Wisconsin Press, 1989.

Spickard, Paul, and Rowena Fong. "Pacific Islander Americans and Multiethnicity: A Vision of America's Future?" In Christopher G. Ellison and W. Allen Martin, eds., *Race and Ethnic Relations in the United States: Readings for the 21st Century,* 486–493. Los Angeles, Calif.: Roxbury Publishing Company, 1999.

St. Cartmail, Keith. *Exodus Indochina.* Auckland, New Zealand: Heinemann, 1983.

St. John, Nancy H. *School Desegregation Outcomes for Children.* New York: Wiley, 1975.

Steele, Shelby. *The Content of Our Character.* New York: St. Martin's Press, 1990.

Steinberg, Stephen. *The Ethnic Myth.* New York: Atheneum, 1989.

Steiner, Stan. *The New Indians.* New York: Harper & Row, 1968.

———. *La Raza: The Mexican Americans.* New York: Harper & Row, 1969.

Stephan, Cookie White, and Walter G. Stephan. "After Intermarriage: Ethnic Identity among Mixed-Heritage Japanese Americans and Hispanics." *Journal of Marriage and the Family* 51 (May 1989): 507–519.

Stephan, Walter G. "Intergroup Relations." In Gardner Lindzey and Elliot Aronson, eds., *Handbook of Social Psychology,* 3d ed. New York: Random House, 1985.

———. "The Effects of School Desegregation: An Evaluation 30 Years After Brown." In Michael J. Sax and Leonard Saxe, eds., *Advances in Applied Social Psychology,* 181–206. Hillsdale, N.J.: Lawrence Erlbaum, 1986.

———. "The Contact Hypothesis in Intergroup Relations." In Clyde Hendrick, ed., *Group Processes and Intergroup Relations,* 13–40. Beverly Hills, Calif.: Sage Publications, 1987.

————. "School Desegregation: Short-Term and Long-Term Effects." Paper presented in Tuscaloosa, Alabama, June 10, 1988 (mimeographed).

Stephan, Walter. *Reducing Prejudice and Stereotyping in Schools.* New York: Teachers College Press, 1999.

Stephan, Walter G., and Cookie White Stephan. "Cognition and Affect in Stereotyping: Parallel Interactive Networks." In Diane M. Mackie and David L. Hamilton, eds., *Affect, Cognition, and Stereotyping,* 111–136. San Diego, Calif.: Academic Press, 1993.

Stern, Gary M. "Hispanics Challenge Bilingual Education." *The Hispanic Outlook in Higher Education* (January 5, 1996): 6–8.

Stevens, Gillian. "The Social and Demographic Context of Language Use in the United States." *American Sociological Review* 57 (April 1992): 171–185.

Stevens, Gillian, and Gray Swicegood. "The Linguistic Context of Ethnic Endogamy." *American Sociological Review* 52 (February 1987): 73–82.

Stewart, Kenneth M. "American Indian Heritage: Retrospect and Prospect." In Robert F. Spencer, Jesse D. Jennings, et al., eds., *The Native Americans,* 501–522. New York: Harper & Row, 1977a.

————. "The Urban Native Americans." In Robert F. Spencer, Jesse D. Jennings, et al., eds., *The Native Americans,* 523–537. New York: Harper and Row, 1977b.

Strand, Paul J., and Woodrow Jones, Jr. *Indochinese Refugees in America.* Durham, N.C.: Duke University Press, 1985.

Stroessner, Steven J., and Diane M. Mackie. "Affect and Perceived Group Variability: Implications for Stereotyping and Prejudice." In Diane M. Mackie and David L. Hamilton, eds., *Affect, Cognition, and Stereotyping,* 63–86. San Diego, Calif.: Academic Press, 1993.

Suarez-Orozco, Marcelo M. "Everything You Ever Wanted to Know about Assimilation But Were Afraid to Ask." *Daedalus* 129 (Fall 2000): 1–30.

Sugimoto, Howard H. "The Vancouver Riots of 1907: A Canadian Episode." In Hilary Conroy and T. Scott Miyakawa, eds., *East Across the Pacific,* 92–126. Santa Barbara, Calif.: American Bibliographical Center-CLIO Press, 1972.

Suleiman, Michael W., ed. *Arabs in America.* Philadelphia: Temple University Press, 1999.

Suleiman, Michael W., and Baha Abu-Laban, eds. "Introduction." In Baha Abu-Laban and Michael W. Suleiman, eds., *Arab Americans: Continuity and Change.* Belmont, Mass.: Association of Arab-American University Graduates, 1989.

Sumner, William Graham. *Folkways.* New York: American Library, (1906) 1960.

Suzuki, David. "Correlation as Causation." In Russell Jacoby and Naomi Glauberman, eds., *The Bell Curve Debate: History Documents, Opinions,* 280–282. New York: Times Books, 1995.

Svensson, Frances. *The Ethnics in American Politics: American Indians.* Minneapolis, Minn.: Burgess, 1973.

Sydnor, Charles S. *American Revolutionaries in the Making.* New York: The Free Press, 1965.

Tabb, William K. "What Happened to Black Economic Development?" *The Review of Black Political Economy* 9 (Summer 1979): 392–415.

Taeuber, Karl E., and Alma F. Taeuber. "The Negro as an Immigrant Group: Recent Trends in Racial and Ethnic Segregation in Chicago." *American Journal of Sociology* 69 (January 1964): 374–394.

————. *Negroes in Cities.* New York: Atheneum, 1969.

Tajfel, Henry, and J.C. Turner. *An Integrative Theory of Intergroup Conflict.* Monterey, Calif.: Brooks/Cole, 1979.

Takagi, Paul. "The Myth of 'Assimilation in American Life.'" *Amerasia Journal* 3 (Fall 1973): 149–158.

Takahashi, Jere. *Nisei/Sansei: Shifting Japanese American Identities and Politics.* Philadelphia: Temple University Press, 1997.

Takaki, Ronald. *Strangers from a Different Shore: A History of Asian Americans.* Boston: Little, Brown and Company, 1989.

———. "At Issue: Is It Accurate to Call Asian Americans a Model Minority?" *CQ Researcher* 1 (December 13, 1991): 961.

———, ed., *From Different Shores: Perspectives of Race and Ethnicity in America,* 2nd ed. New York: Oxford University Press, 1994.

———. *Strangers from a Different Shore: A History of Asian Americans,* up. and rev. ed. Boston, Mass.: Little Brown, 1998.

Tatum, Beverly. "Talking about Race, Learning about Racism." *Harvard Educational Review* 62 (Spring 1992): 1–24.

Taylor, D. Garth, Paul B. Sheatsley, and Andrew M. Greeley. "Attitudes toward Racial Integration." *Scientific American* (June 1978): 42–49.

Taylor, George E. "Chiang Mei-ling or Mayling." *World Book Encyclopedia* 3 (1962): 335.

Taylor, Howard F. *The IQ Game.* New Brunswick, N.J.: Rutgers University Press, 1980.

Taylor, Patricia Ann. "Education, Ethnicity, and Cultural Assimilation in the United States." *Ethnicity* 8 (1981): 31–49.

Taylor, Sandra C. "Evacuation and Economic Loss: Questions and Perspectives." In Roger Daniels, Sandra C. Taylor, and Harry H. L. Kitano, eds., *Japanese Americans: From Relocation to Redress,* rev. ed., 163–167. Seattle, Wash.: University of Washington Press, 1991.

———. *Jewel of the Desert: Japanese American Internment at Topaz.* Berkeley, Calif.: University of California Press, 1993.

Telles, Edward E., and Edward Murguía. "Phenotypic Discrimination and Income Differences among Mexican Americans." *Social Science Quarterly* 71 (December 1990): 682–696.

tenBroek, Jacobus, Edward N. Barnhart, and Floyd W. Matson. *Prejudice, War, and the Constitution.* Berkeley, Calif. and Los Angeles: University of California Press, 1954.

Tenenbaum, Barbara A., ed. *Encyclopedia of Latin American History and Culture,* vol 4. London: Charles Scribner's Sons, 1996.

Terry, Don. "California Bilingual Teaching Lives on After Vote to Kill It." *New York Times* (October 3, 1998): A1.

Terry, Janice J. "Community and Political Activism Among Arab Americans in Detroit." In Michael W. Suleiman, ed., *Arabs in America,* 241–254. Philadelphia: Temple University Press, 1999.

Thernstrom, Abigail. "The Drive for Racially Inclusive Schools." In Harold Orlans and June O'Neill, eds., *Affirmative Action Revisited, The Annals* (September 1992): 131–143.

Thieme, Paul. "India: Languages." *Encyclopedia Americana* 14 (2002): 881–882.

Thomas, Dorothy Swaine. *The Salvage.* Berkeley, Calif. and Los Angeles: University of California Press, 1952.

Thomas, Dorothy Swaine, and Richard S. Nishimoto. *The Spoilage.* Berkeley, Calif. and Los Angeles: University of California Press, 1946.

Thompson, Charles H. "The Conclusions of Scientists Relative to Racial Differences." *Journal of Negro Education* 19 (July 1934): 494–512.

Thornton, Russell. "North American Indians and the Demography of Contact." In Silvia Pedraza and Rubén G. Rumbaut, eds., *Origins and Destinies: Immigration, Race, and Ethnicity in America,* 43–59. Belmont, Calif.: Wadsworth Publishing Company, 1996.

Thurstone, L. L. *The Vectors of the Mind.* Chicago: University of Chicago Press, 1935.

Tindall, George Brown. *America: A Narrative Story.* New York: W. W. Norton & Co., 1984.

Tinker, John N. "Intermarriage and Ethnic Boundaries: The Japanese American Case." *Journal of Social Issues* 29, no. 2 (1973): 49–66.

Tittle, Charles R., and Thomas Rotolo. "IQ and Stratification: An Empirical Evaluation of Herrnstein and Murray's Social Change Argument." *Social Forces* 79 (September 2000): 1–28.

Tocqueville, Alexis de. *Democracy in America,* ed. by J. P. Mayer. New York: Harper and Row, Perennial Library, (1835) 1988.

Todorovich, Miro M. "Discrimination in Higher Education." In Barry R. Gross, ed., *Reverse Discrimination,* 12–14. Buffalo, N.Y.: Prometheus Books, 1977.

Tolnay, Stewart, and E. M. Beck. "Racial Violence and Black Migration in the American South, 1910–1930." *American Sociological Review* 57 (February 1992): 103–116.

Tomás Rivera Center. *The Latino Vote at Mid-Decade.* Claremont, Calif.: Scripps College, 1996.

Tong, Benton. *The Chinese Americans.* Westport, Conn.: Greenwood Press, 2000.

Torrecilha, Ramon S., Lionel Cantú, and Quan Nguyen. "Puerto Ricans in the United States." In Anthony G. Dworkin and Rosalind J. Dworkin, *The Minority Report: An Introduction to Racial, Ethnic, and Gender Relations,* 3d ed., 230–254. Fort Worth, Tex: Harcourt Brace & Co., 1999.

Trotter, Monroe. Editorial, *Boston Guardian,* December 20, 1902. Reprinted in August Meier, Elliott Rudwick, and Francis L. Broderick, eds., *Black Protest Thought in the Twentieth Century,* 2nd ed., 32–36. Indianapolis and New York: Bobbs-Merrill, 1971.

Tsai, Shih-Shan Henry. *The Chinese Experience in America.* Bloomington, Ind.: Indiana University Press, 1986.

Tuan, Mia. *Forever Foreigners or Honorary Whites?: The Asian American Experience Today.* New Brunswick, N.J.: Rutgers University Press, 1998.

Tuch, Steven A., and Lee Sigelman. "Race, Class, and Black-White Differences in Policy Views." In Barbara Norrander and Clyde Wilcox, eds., *Understanding Public Opinion.* Washington, D.C.: CQ Press, 1997.

Tuch, Steven A., Lee Sigelman, and Jason A. McDonald. "Race Relations and American Youth, 1976–1995." *Public Opinion Quarterly* 63 (Spring 1999): 109–148.

Tuchman, Barbara W. *The First Salute.* New York: Alfred A. Knopf, 1988.

Tucker, Belinda M., and Claudia Mitchell-Kernan. "Trends in African American Family Formation: A Theoretical and Statistical Overview." In M. Belinda Tucker and Claudia Mitchell-Kernan, eds., *The Decline in Marriage Among African Americans,* 3–26. New York: Russell Sage Foundation, 1995.

Turner, Frederick Jackson. *The Frontier in American History.* New York: Henry Holt, 1920.

Tussman, Joseph, ed., *The Supreme Court on Racial Discrimination.* New York: Oxford University Press, 1963.

Ueda, Reed. "Naturalization and Citizenship." In Stephan Thernstrom, Ann Orlov, and Oscar Handlin, eds., *Harvard Encyclopedia of American Ethnic Groups,* 734–748. Cambridge, Mass.: The Belknap Press, 1980.

United Methodist Women. "Post 9/11 Hate Crimes," 2003. http://gbgm-umc.org.

U.S. Bureau of the Census. *Historical Statistics of the United States: Colonial Times to 1957.* Washington, D.C.: U.S. Government Printing Office, 1961.

———. *U.S. Census of Population: 1970,* Subject Reports. Final Report PC(2)-1F, "American Indians." Washington, D.C.: U.S. Government Printing Office, 1973.

———. *Historical Statistics of the United States, Colonial Times to 1970.* Washington, D.C.: U.S. Government Printing Office, 1975.

———. Current Population Reports, Series P-20, No. 438, *The Hispanic Population in the United States: March, 1988.* Washington, D.C.: U.S. Government Printing Office, 1989a.

———. *Statistical Abstract of the United States: 1989,* 109th ed. Washington, D.C.: U.S. Government Printing Office, 1989b.

———. Current Population Reports, Series P-20, No. 455, *The Hispanic Population in the United States: March 1991.* Washington, D.C.: U.S. Government Printing Office, 1991.

———. Current Population Reports, March 1994: Educational Attainment Level by Ethnicity; Population Age 25 and Over; Family Income in Previous Year by Race-Ethnicity; Occupation by Race-Ethnicity (http://www.census.gov/population/socdemo/)

———. *We the Americans: Asians.* Washington, D.C.: U.S. Government Printing Office, 1993.

———. *Statistical Abstract of the United States: 1995,* 115th ed. Washington, D.C.: U.S. Government Printing Office, 1996.

———. Current Population Reports, Series P60-200, *Money Income in the United States: 1997 (With Separate Data on Valuation of Noncash Benefits.)* Washington, D.C.: U.S. Government Printing Office, 1998a.

———. *Statistical Abstract of the United States: 1998,* 118th ed. Washington, D.C.: U.S. Government Printing Office, 1998b.

———. *Census Gateway American Fact Finder.* Summary File 3, OT-P13, Ancestry: 2000. http://www.census.gov/main/www/cen2000.html.

———. *Statistical Abstract of the United States: 2001,* 121st ed. Washington, D.C.: U.S. Government Printing Office, 2001.

U.S. Commission on Civil Rights. *Puerto Ricans in the Continental United States: An Uncertain Future: A Report to the United States Commission on Civil Rights.* Washington, D.C.: October 1976.

———. *Affirmative Action in the 1980s: Dismantling the Process of Discrimination.* Washington, D.C.: U.S. Government Printing Office, 1981a.

———. *Civil Rights Issues Facing Asian Americans in the 1990s.* Washington, D.C.: U.S. Government Printing Office, February 1992.

———. *Civil Rights Update* (March 1979a).

———. *Civil Rights Update* (August 1979b).

———. *Civil Rights Update* (September/October 1988a).

———. *Civil Rights Update* (November 1988b).

———. *Civil Rights Update* (March 1989a).

———. *Civil Rights Update* (June 1989b).

———. *Civil Rights Update* (March/April 1992).

U.S. Department of Commerce *NEWS.* "Updated Information on Nation's African American Population Released by Census Bureau, CB96–90, (June 11, 1996): Table 8 (Total Money Income in 1994 of Persons 15 Years Old and Over, by Sex, Region (Persons as of March 1995).

U.S. Department of Education. *Descriptive Study of Services to Limited English Proficient Students: Analysis and Highlights.* Washington, D.C.: Office of the Under Secretary, 1993.

U.S. Department of Health, Education, and Welfare. *Health, United States, 1979.* Washington, D.C.: U.S. Government Printing Office, 1980.

U.S. Immigration and Naturalization Service. *Statistical Yearbook of the Immigration and Naturalization Service, 1994.* Washington, D.C., 1996.

———. *Statistical Yearbook of the Immigration and Naturalization Service, 1996.* Washington, D.C.: U.S. Government Printing Office, 1997.

———. *News Release: INS Announces Legal Immigration Figures For Fiscal Year 1997.* Washington, D.C.: U.S. Government Printing Office, 1998.

———. *News Release: INS Announces Legal Immigration Figures for Fiscal Year 1998.* Washington, D.C.: U.S. Government Printing Office, 1999.

————. *Statistical Yearbook of the Immigration and Naturalization Service, 1998.* U.S. Government Printing Office, Washington, D.C., 2000.

————. *Statistical Yearbook of the Immigration and Naturalization Service, 2000,* 2002. http://www.immigration.gov/graphics/aboutus/statistics/ybpage.htm.

————. Bureau of Citizenship and Immigration Services. "This Month in Immigration History: December 1943." 2004. http://www.uscis.gov/graphics/aboutus/history/dec43.htm.

Vaca, Nick C. "The Mexican-American in the Social Sciences." *El Grito* 4 (Fall 1970): 17–51.

Vaglieri, Laura Veccia. "The Patriarchal and Umayad Caliphates." In P. M. Holt, Ann K. S. Lamberton, and Bernard Lewis, eds., *The Cambridge History of Islam,* Vol. 1A, 57–103. London: Cambridge University Press, 1970.

Valdez, Luis. "The Tale of the Raza." In Renato Rosaldo, Robert A. Calvert, and Gustav L. Seligman, eds., *Chicano: The Evolution of a People,* 269–272. Malabar, Fla: Krieger, 1982.

Valdivieso, Rafael, and Cary Davis. *U.S. Hispanics: Challenging Issues for the 1990s.* Washington, D.C.: Population Reference Bureau, 1988.

van den Berghe, Pierre L. *Man in Society,* 2nd ed. New York: Elsevier, 1978.

van der Kroef, James. "East Indies." *World Book Encyclopedia* 5 (1961): 22.

van Oudenhoven, Jan Pieter. "Improving Interethnic Relationships: How Effective is Cooperation?" In Jan Pieter van Oudenhoven and Tineke M. Willemsen, eds., *Ethnic Minorities,* 25–42. Amsterdam: Swets & Zeitlinger B.V., 1989.

van Oudenhoven Jan Pieter, and Tineke M. Willemsen, eds. *Ethnic Minorities.* Amsterdam: Swets & Zeitlinger B.V., 1989.

Van Valey, Thomas L., Wade Clark Roof, and Jerome E. Wilcox. "Trends in Residential Segregation: 1960–1970." *American Journal of Sociology* 82 (January 1977): 826–844.

Veltman, Calvin. *The Future of the Spanish Language in the United States.* Washington, D.C.: Hispanic Policy Development Project, 1988.

————. "The Status of the Spanish Language in the United States at the Beginning of the 21st Century." *International Migration Review* 24 (Spring 1990): 108–123.

Vernez, George, and Kevin F. McCarthy. *Meeting the Economy and Labour Needs Through Immigration: Rationale and Challenges.* Santa Monica, Calif.: N-3052-FF, RAND, June 1990.

————. *The Costs of Immigration to Taxpayers: Analytical and Policy Issues.* Santa Monica, Calif.: Rand, 1996.

Visweswaran, Kamala. "Race and the Culture of Anthropology," *American Anthropologist* 100, no. 1 (1998): 70–83

Wagley, Charles, and Marvin Harris. *Minorities in the New World.* New York: Columbia University Press, 1958.

Wagner, Edward W. "History of Korea to 1945." *Encyclopedia Americana* 16 (2002): 550–553.

Walls, Thomas. *The Japanese Texans.* San Antonio, Tex.: University of Texas, Institute of Texan Cultures, 1987.

Walsh, Catherine E. " 'Staging Encounters': The Educational Decline of U.S. Puerto Ricans in [Post]-Colonial Perspective." *Harvard Educational Review* 68 (Summer 1998): 218–243.

Warner, W. Lloyd, and Leo Srole. *The Social Systems of American Ethnic Groups,* 2nd ed., New Haven, Conn.: Yale University Press, 1946.

Washburn, Wilcomb E. "The Status Today." In Herbert L. Marx, Jr., ed., *The American Indian,* 102–104. New York: H. W. Wilson, 1973.

————. *Red Man's Land White Man's Law,* 2nd ed., Norman, Okla.: University of Oklahoma Press, 1995.

Washington, Booker T. *Up from Slavery.* New York: Bantam Books, 1959.

Waters, Mary C. *Ethnic Options.* Berkeley, Calif.: University of California Press, 1990.

———. "The Costs of a Costless Community." In Michael W. Hughey, ed., *New Tribalisms: The Resurgence of Race and Ethnicity,* 273–295. New York: New York University Press, 1998.

———. *Black Identities: West Indian Dreams and American Realism.* New York: Russell Sage Foundation, 1999.

———. "Ethnic and Racial Identities of Second-Generation Black Immigrants in New York City." In Charles A. Gallagher, ed., *Rethinking the Color Line: Readings in Race and Ethnicity,* 2nd ed., 493–508. Boston: McGraw Hill, 2004.

Wax, Murray L. *Indian Americans.* Englewood Cliffs, N.J.: Prentice-Hall, 1971.

Webb, Walter Prescott. *The Texas Rangers.* Austin, Tex.: University of Texas Press, 1987.

Weggert, Karl H. *German Radicals Confront the Common People.* Mainz: Verlag Philipp Von Zabern, 1992.

White, Lynn C., and Bruce A. Chadwick. "Urban Residence, Assimilation and the Identity of the Spokane Indians." In Howard M. Bahr, Bruce A. Chadwick, and Robert C. Day, eds., *Native Americans Today,* 239–249. New York: Harper & Row, 1972.

White, Michael J., Ann E. Biddlecom, and Shenyang Guo. "Immigration, Naturalization, and Residential Assimilation Among Asian Americans in 1980." *Social Forces* 72 (September 1993): 93–117.

Wilhelm, Sidney M. *Black in a White America.* Cambridge, Mass.: Schenkman, 1983.

Wilkerson, Isabel. "Interracial Marriage Rises, Acceptance Lags." *New York Times* (December 2, 1991): A1.

Wilkins, David E. "Governance within the Navajo Nation: Have Democratic Traditions Taken Hold?" *Wicazo Sa Review* 17 (Spring 2002): 91–129.

———. *American Indian Politics and the American Political System.* Lanham, Md.: Rowman & Littlefield, 2001.

Wilkinson, Doris Y. "Toward a Positive Frame of Reference from Analysis of Black Families: A Selected Bibliography." *Journal of Marriage and the Family* 40 (November 1978): 707–708.

———. "Gender and Social Inequality: The Prevailing Significance of Race." In Obie Clayton, Jr., ed., *An American Dilemma Revisited: Race Relations in a Changing World,* 288–313. New York: Russell Sage Foundation, 1996a.

———. "Integration Dilemmas in a Racist Culture." *Society* 8 (March/April 1996b): 27–31.

Williams, J. Allen, Jr., Peter G. Beeson, and David R. Johnson. "Some Factors Associated with Income among Mexican Americans." *Social Science Quarterly* 53 (March 1973): 710–715.

Williams, J. Allen, Clyde Z. Nunn, and Louis St. Peter. "Origins of Tolerance: Findings from a Replication of Stouffer's Communism, Conformity, and Civil Liberties." *Social Forces* 55 (December 1976): 394–418.

Williams, Norma. *The Mexican American Family: Tradition and Change.* Dix Hills, N.Y.: General Hall, Inc., 1990.

Williams, Robin M., Jr. *The Reduction of Intergroup Tensions.* New York: Social Science Research Council, 1947.

———. *Strangers Next Door.* Englewood Cliffs, N.J.: Prentice-Hall, 1964.

Wilson, Kenneth L., and W. Allen Martin. "Ethnic Enclaves: A Comparison of the Cuban and Black Economies in Miami." *American Journal of Sociology* 88 (July 1982): 135–160.

Wilson, William J. *The Declining Significance of Race,* 2nd ed. Chicago: University of Chicago Press, 1980.

———. *The Truly Disadvantaged.* Chicago: The University of Chicago Press, 1987.

———. "A Response to Critics of *The Truly Disadvantaged.*" In Robert G. Newby, ed., *The Truly Disadvantaged: Challenges and Prospects,* Special Issue, *Journal of Sociology and Social Welfare* 16 (December 1989): 133–148.

———. "Studying Inner-City Social Dislocations: The Challenge of Public Agenda Research." *American Sociological Review* 56 (February 1991): 1–14.

———. *When Work Disappears: The World of the New Urban Poor.* New York: Alfred A. Knopf, 1996.

Winegarten, Ruthe. *Black Texas Women: 150 Years of Trial and Triumph.* Austin, Tex.: University of Texas Press, 1995.

Wirth, Louis. "The Problem of Minority Groups." In Ralph Linton, ed., *The Science of Man in the World Crisis,* 347–372. New York: Columbia University Press, 1945.

Wittke, Carl. *We Who Built America,* 3d ed. Englewood Cliffs, N.J.: Prentice-Hall, 1964.

———. *The Germans in America.* New York: Teachers College Press, 1967.

Wojtkiewicz, Roger A., and Katharine M. Donato. "Hispanic Educational Attainment: The Effects of Family Background and Nativity." *Social Forces* 74 (December 1995): 559–574.

Wolf, Diane C. " 'There's No Place Like 'Home': Emotional Transnationalism and the Struggles of the Second Generation Filipinos." In Peggy Levitt and Mary C. Waters, eds., *The Changing Face of Home,* 255–294. New York: Russell Sage Foundation, 2002.

Wong, Morrison G. "The Chinese American Family." In Charles H. Mindel, Robert W. Habenstein, and Roosevelt Wright, Jr., eds., *Ethnic Families in America,* 3d. ed., 230–257. New York: Elsevier, 1988.

Wood, Peter B., and Michelle Chesser. "Black Stereotyping in a University Population." *Sociological Focus* 27 (February 1994): 17–34.

Woodrum, Eric. "Japanese American Social Adaptation over Three Generations." Ph.D. dissertation, University of Texas at Austin, 1978.

Woodward, C. Vann. *The Strange Career of Jim Crow.* New York: Oxford University Press, 1957.

Wright, Mary Bowen. "Indochinese." In Stephan Thernstrom, Ann Orlov, and Oscar Handlin, eds., *Harvard Encyclopedia of American Ethnic Groups,* 508–513. Cambridge, Mass.: The Belknap Press, 1980.

Yamamoto, Eric K., and Susan Kiyomi Serrano. "The Loaded Weapon." *Amerasia Journal* 27:3 (2001)/28:1 (2002): 51–62.

Yancy, William L., Eugene P. Ericksen, and Richard N. Juliani. "Emergent Ethnicity: A Review and Reformulation." *American Sociological Review* 41 (June, 1976): 391–403.

Yang, Philip Q. "Citizenship Acquisition of Post-1965 Asian Immigrants." *Population and Environment* 23 (March 2002): 327–404.

Yellin, Emily, and David Firestone. "By Court Order, Busing Ends Where It Began." *New York Times* (September 11, 1999): A1.

Yu, Elena S. H. "Filipino Migration and Community Organizations in the United States." In Franklin Ng, ed., *Asians in America: The Peoples of East, Southeast, and South Asia in American Life and Culture,* 102–128. New York: Garland Publishing, 1998.

Zambrana, Ruth E. *Understanding Latino Families: Scholarship, Policy and Practice.* Thousand Oaks, Calif.: Sage Publications, 1995.

Zentella, Ana Celia. "Returned Migration, Language, and Identity: Puerto Rican Bilinguals in Dos Worlds/Two Mundos." In Antonia Darder, Rodolfo D. Torres, Henry Gutiérrez, eds., *Latinos and Education: A Critical Reader,* 302–318. New York: Routledge, 1997.

Zhou, Min. "Segmented Assimilation: Issues, Controversies, and Recent Research on the New Second Generation." *International Migration Review* 31 (Winter 1997): 975–1008.

———. "The Changing Face of America: Immigration, Race/Ethnicity, and Social Mobility." In Pyong Gap Min, ed., *Mass Migration to the United States: Classical and Contemporary Periods,* 65–98. Walnut Creek, Calif.: AltaMira Press, 2002.

Zhou, Min, and Carl L. Bankston. *Growing Up American: How Vietnamese Children Adapt to Life in the United States.* New York: Russell Sage Foundation, 1998.

Zhou, Min, and Guoxuan Cai. "Chinese Language Media in the United States: Immigration and Assimilation in American Life." *Qualitative Sociology* 25 (Fall 2002): 419–443.

Zhou, Min, and James V. Gatewood, eds. *Contemporary Asian Americans: A Multidisciplinary Reader.* New York: New York University Press, 1999.

Zhou, Min, and John R. Logan. "In and Out of Chinatown: Residential Mobility and Segregation of New York City's Chinese." *Social Forces* 70 (December 1991): 387–407.

Zia, Helen. "Oh Say Can You See?" *Amerasia Journal* 27 (2002): 2–12.

Zogby International. "Arab Americans are Strong Advocates of War Against Terrorism." *Arab American Institute Poll,* October, 2001. http://www.aaiusa.org.

Zogby, James, ed. *Taking Root Bearing Fruit.* Washington, D.C.: ADC Research Institute, 1984.

Name Index

Ablon, Joan, 323
Abraham, Nabeel, 424
Abrams, Franklin, 88, 124, 125, 409
Abu-Laban, Baha, 420, 421, 425, 426, 427
Acuña, Rodolfo, 231, 232
Adamic, Louis, 63, 82
Adams, John, 67
Adams, John Quincy, 21
Adams, Romanzo, 40
Adorno, T. W., 132
Aguinaldo, Emilio, 386
Aguirre, Benigno, 358
Chang-ho, Ahn, 383
Akram, Susan, 427
Alba, Richard, 3, 90, 91, 92, 93, 107, 212, 442, 443, 452, 453
Albertson, Dean, 57
Allen, Walter, 161, 192, 193, 194, 195, 196, 197, 198, 355
Allport, Gordon, 11, 131, 469
Allsup, Carl, 243
Alvarez, Rodolfo, 6, 234, 235, 243
Alvírez, David, 273
Amherst, Sir Jeffrey, 52
Amir, Yehuda, 471
Amissah, Charles, 453, 471
Anzaldua, Gloria, 227
Appiah, K. Anthony, 212
Armor, David, 473
Arnold, Benedict, 163
Aronson, Elliot, 470
Austin, Stephen F., 229
Ayres, B. Drummond, Jr., 204
Ayres, E. D., 240

Bach, Robert, 90, 93, 96, 280, 360, 361, 416
Badar, Christine Velez, 269
Bahr, Howard, 301, 306, 309

Bakke, Allan, 204–205
Baldwin, John R., 131
Ball, Harry, 472
Ball, Howard, 350, 351
Baltzell, E. Digby, 95
Bankston, Carl, 415
Bardolph, Richard, 151
Barker, Eugene, 230
Barnhart, Edward, 123, 337, 338, 345, 347, 373
Baron, Harold, 137
Baron, Robert, 131
Barrera, Mario, 277, 280
Barringer, Felicity, 311
Barringer, Herbert, 364, 415, 416
Bean, Frank, 104, 106, 256, 257, 269, 271, 274
Beck, E. M., 135, 164
Bennett, Lerone, Jr., 150
Benokraitis, Nijole V., 204
Berg, Ruth, 271
Berger, Morroe, 472
Berkowitz, Leonard, 131
Berman, Patricia, 311
Bernard, William, 88, 410
Bernhard, Virginia, 53, 54, 63, 64, 97, 231
Biddle, Francis, 347
Biddlecom, Ann E., 356
Big Foot, 300
Billingsley, Andrew, 152, 190
Binet, Alfred, 118
Blassingame, John, 152
Blauner, Robert, 33, 34, 185, 186
Blee, Kathleen, 156
Bobo, Lawrence, 127, 129, 198, 202, 444, 453
Bogardus, Emory, 129
Bok, Derek, 209, 210
Bokemeier, Janet, 269

Bolino, August, 88
Bonacich, Edna, 135, 214, 360
Bonilla, Frank, 255
Bonney, Rachel, 306
Bordewich, Fergus, 293, 307, 317, 318, 319, 325
Borjas, George, 105, 106, 107
Boswell, Thomas, 124
Bowen, William G., 209, 210
Bowman, Phillip, 192
Boyd, Robert, 214
Bragdon, Ann Louise, 421, 422
Braly, Kenneth, 129
Brasher, Philip, 322
Brigham, C. C., 118
Brill, Howard, 93
Brimelow, Peter, 104, 106
Brisbane, Robert, 184
Broderick, Francis, 163, 164
Broman, Clifford, 269
Brooke, James, 319
Broom, Leonard, 350
Brown, Roger, 134, 299, 300, 469, 471
Brown, W. Norman, 393
Bryan, Samuel, 233
Bryson, Bill, 39
Bullard, Sara, 181
Bulosan, Carlos, 370
Bunche, Ralph, 168
Burma, John, 201, 357
Burner, David, 53, 54, 63, 64, 97, 231
Burns, W. Haywood, 180
Bush, George H., 184, 351
Bush, George W., 430
Bush, Jeb, 206
Butler, John Sibley, 154, 163, 165, 214, 215, 361
Butterfield, Fox, 326

Cafferty, Pastora San Juan, 88, 114, 125, 126
Cai, Guoxuan, 377
Calhoun, John, 297
Camarillo, Albert, 255
Campbell, Mary E., 200, 275
Cancio, Silvia, 193
Canoe, Lorraine, 315
Cantor, Milton, 57
Cantú, Lionel, 257, 259, 270, 275, 278
Caplan, Nathan, 415, 416, 417
Carmichael, Stokely, 137, 183
Caroli, Betty, 92
Carroll-Seguin, Rita, 93, 416
Carson, Kit, 295
Carter, Deborah, 272
Celis, William, 261
Chadwick, Bruce, 301, 306
Chandra, Ram, 397
Chaney, James, 181
Chapa, Jorge, 271
Chaudhuri, Joyotpaul, 293
Chavez, César, 244
Chen, Shyh-Jer, 326
Chen, Theodore H. E., 375
Chesser, Michelle, 129
Chiswick, Barry, 88, 114, 125, 126, 364
Chow, Esther Ngan-Ling, 339, 374
Choy, Marcella, 415, 416, 417
Chung, Sue Fawn, 375
Church, George, 186
Cizik, Richard, 429
Clark, Kenneth B., 171
Clark, W. A. V., 274
Clemetson, Lynette, 210
Cobb-Clark, Deborah, 270
Cochise, 295
Cochran, Donna, 190
Cody, Buffalo Bill, 300
Cohen, Elaine, 268
Cohen, Elizabeth, 471
Cohen, Lawrence, 277
Cole, K. C., 122
Collins, Patricia Hill, 179
Collison, Michele, 200
Columbus, Christopher, 258
Condran, Gretchen, 198
Conelley, Edward, 470
Connor, John, 353
Conzen, Kathleen Neils, 87
Cortina, Juan N. "Cheno," 231
Cose, Ellis, 452

Costello, Lawrence, 115
Cotter, David, 194
Cotton, Jeremiah, 273
Crazy Horse, 295, 296
Cronon, Edmund David, 166
Crook, George, 295, 296
Cross, Harary, 273
Cuéllar, Alfredo, 243
Curran, Thomas, 123–124
Custer, George, 295, 296

da Gama, Vasco, 393
Daley, Suzanne, 456
Daniels, Roger, 123, 337, 338, 343, 346, 349, 351, 354, 358, 360, 364, 372, 373, 374, 375, 383, 388, 390, 391, 392, 395, 396, 397, 410, 412
Darwin, Charles, 117
Das, Taraknath, 397
Davie, Maurice, 151, 154, 162
Davis, Kenneth E., 127
Davis, Sally, 322
Day, Robert C., 301, 306
Dayal, Har, 397
de la Cruz, G. Patricia, 255
Deer, Ada, 307
DeFleur, Melvin, 133, 134
Degler, Carl, 59, 458, 460
del Castillo, Richard Griswold, 231
Delany, Martin, 153
Delaware Prophet, 290
Delgado, Melvin, 268
Deloria, Vine, Jr., 289, 297, 327
Denney, Reuel, 41
Dent, David, 198
Dentler, Robert, 475
Denton, Nancy, 196, 197, 198, 274, 356
DePalma, Anthony, 457
DeWitt, John L., 240, 345, 346, 347
Díaz, José, 240
Díaz, Porfirio, 232
Diner, Hasia, 65, 82, 83
Dinnerstein, Leonard, 77, 85, 93
Dollard, John, 131
Donato, Katharine, 271
Donato, Rubén, 264
Douglas, William O., 351
Douglass, Frederick, 179
Dovidio, John, 127
Dow, George, 421
DuBois, W. E. B., 150, 163, 164, 203, 212
Ducas, George, 151

Duke, David, 429
Durant, Will, 393

Easterlin, Richard, 67
Eastman, Charles, 304
Eaton, Susan, 274
Egan, Timothy, 320
Eggebeen, David, 190
Ehrlich, Howard, 129
Eichenwald, Kurt, 188
Eisenhower, Dwight D., 172, 204, 301, 302, 409
Eliot, John, 21
Elkholy, Abdo, 425
Elkins, Stanley, 152, 175
Ellis, David, 186
Ellison, Christopher, 470, 471
Ellison, Ralph, 191
Endo, Mitsuye, 351
Engerman, Stanley, 152
Erlanger, Steven, 459
Eschbach, Karl, 311, 312, 324, 325
Espenshade, Thomas, 105
Evans, T. David, 193

Falbo, Toni, 272
Falcoff, Mark, 265
Falwell, Jerry, 429
Fard, W. D., 167
Farley, Reynolds, 161, 188, 190, 192, 193, 194, 196, 197, 198, 199, 355, 444, 452, 473
Farmer, James, 169, 182
Farrakhan, Louis, 167
Faulkner, Harold Underwood, 116, 155, 230, 386
Feagin, Joe, 137, 203, 204, 353, 444
Featherman, David, 216
Feldstein, Stanley, 115
Ferguson, Ron, 192, 193
Fernandez, Roberto, 272
Fetterman, William, 295
Fifield, Russell, 386, 387
Fillmore, Millard, 116
Fine, Michelle, 444
Firebaugh, Glenn, 127
Firestone, David, 473
Fischbach, Michael, 426
Fischer, C. S., 122, 138
Fix, Michael, 105
Fixico, Donald, 327
Fligstein, Neil, 272
Flores, Juan, 278
Flynn, James, 122

Fogel, Robert, 152
Fong, Rowena, 444
Forman, Tyrone, 13
Fost, Dan, 320
Fox, Evarts, Jr., 346
Fox-Genovese, Elizabeth, 53, 54,
  63, 64, 97, 231
Francis, E. K., 83, 447, 448
Franklin, Benjamin, 66, 67
Franklin, John Hope, 59, 60, 154,
  155, 165
Frazier, E. Franklin, 59, 60, 61,
  158, 161
Fredrickson, George, 55
Frenkel-Brunswick, Else, 132
Frethorne, Richard, 60
Frey, William, 197, 198
Fuchs, Lawrence, 105
Fugita, Stephen, 341, 349, 350, 355,
  356, 359, 361, 364
Fuhrman, Mark, 186
Fujimoto, Isao, 353
Fujitaki, Nancy, 353
Furstenberg, Frank, Jr., 190
Furuichi, Satomi, 364

Gaertner, Samuel, 127
Gall, 459
Gall, Carlotta, 295, 296
Galli, Marcia J., 91, 297, 298,
  299, 303
Galton, Francis, 118, 143
Gans, Herbert J., 440, 441, 445
Garcia, Macario, 239
Garcia, Mario, 262
García, John, 243
Gardner, Robert, 364, 415, 416
Garvey, Marcus, 38, 150, 165–167,
  176, 182
Gates, Henry Louis, Jr., 187
Gawasowannah, 304
Gee, Emma, 339
Gerard, Harold, 470
Geronimo, 295
Geschwender, James, 93
Giago, Tim, 307
Gibbon, John, 295, 296
Ginsburg, Ruth Bader, 209
Glazer, Nathan, 5, 40, 41, 95, 410,
  440, 441, 454
Glenn, Evelyn Nakano, 339, 344
Glenn, Norval, 134
Glickstein, Howard, 205
Goff, Regina, 195
Gold, Steven, 94, 95, 96

Goldman, Ron, 186
Gómez-Quiñones, Juan, 233, 236
Gompers, Samuel, 396
Gonzales-Ramos, Gladys, 268
Gonzalez, Alex, 470
Goodman, Andrew, 181
Goodstein, Laurie, 429
Gordon, Milton, 9, 10, 11, 15, 21,
  22, 25–27, 31, 45, 58, 64, 191
Gossett, Thomas, 54, 117
Gould, C. W., 119
Gould, Stephen Jay, 120, 122
Graham, Franklin, 429
Graham, Hugh Davis, 205
Grebler, Leo, 233, 237, 238, 239,
  275, 276
Greeley, Andrew, 63, 82, 88, 93,
  114, 125, 126, 408, 445, 451, 469
Grenier, Gilles, 260
Gross, Andrew, 196
Guo, Shenyang, 356
Gurak, Douglas, 201, 357
Gutiérrez, David G., 244, 262, 280
Gutman, Herbert, 152, 189, 190
Guttman, Amy, 212
Guzman, Ralph, 233, 237, 238,
  239, 275, 276
Guzmán, Hector R. Cordero, 272

Hacker, Andrew, 128, 194, 203,
  474, 476
Haddad, Yvonne, 420
Hagan, William, 292, 294, 295
Haines, David, 416
Hajnal, Zoltan, 198
Hakuta, Kenji, 264, 266
Hallinan, Maureen, 471
Hamad, Imad, 408, 431
Hamilton, Alexander, 68
Hamilton, Charles, 137
Hamm, Rita, 198
Handlin, Oscar, 9, 59, 60, 441
Hansen, Marcus Lee, 9, 63, 84, 85
Hao, Lingxin, 260
Harlan, John Marshall, 159
Harrison, Roderick, 197, 274
Harrison, William Henry, 292
Hassan, Salah, 421
Hatchett, Shirley, 190
Hauser, Robert, 122, 216
Hawley, Willis, 470
Heer, David, 201, 325
Heise, Michael, 473
Helms, Janet, 444
Hemings, Sally, 12

Henderson, Gregory, 381
Hendelson, William H., 410, 411
Herberg, Will, 40
Hermsen, Joan, 194
Herring, Cedric, 453, 471
Herrnstein, Richard, 120, 121, 122,
  123, 143
Hershberg, T., 190
Hertzberg, Hazel, 297, 299, 303,
  304, 314
Hieshima, Joyce, 359
Higham, John, 118
Hill, Robert, 190
Hing, Bill Ong, 363, 374
Hirabayashi, Gordon, 350, 352
Hirschman, Charles, 40, 124, 354,
  361, 364
Hochschild, Jennifer, 186, 215
Hoffman, Abraham, 238
Hoge, Warren, 456
Holmes, Steven, 188, 210
Holms, 207
Holzer, Harry, 192, 193, 195
Hondagneu-Sotelo, Pierrette, 268
Hood, Lucy, 254
hooks, bell, 444
Horn, Miriam, 88
Horowitz, Donald, 41
Hosokawa, Bill, 345, 348, 354, 362
Houston, Jeanne Wakatsuki, 348
Howard, O. O., 295, 296
Howery, Carla, 352
Hoxie, Frederick, 299
Hu, Charles, 380
Huddle, Donald, 105
Huerta, Dolores, 244
Hughes, Langston, 165
Hunt, Ken, 322
Hunt, Larry L., 277
Hurh, Won Moo, 354, 364, 381,
  382, 384, 385
Hurston, Zora Neale, 165
Hwang, Sean-shong, 198, 358
Hyman, Herbert, 127

Ibish, Hussein, 430
Iceland, John, 364, 400
Ichihashi, Yamato, 337, 338, 339,
  340, 342, 344
Ichioka, Yuji, 354
Ignatiev, Noel, 443
Ikeda, Kiyoshi, 360, 472
Inouye, Daniel, 314
Ito, Naomi, 378, 379, 385, 392, 398
Iwata, Masakazu, 343

Jackson, Andrew, 293, 294
Jackson, Curtis E., 291, 297, 298, 299, 303
Jackson, James S., 190
Jackson, Robert, 351
Jackson, Terrence, 470
Jacobs, Paul, 61, 151
Jacobson, Cardell, 309
Ja.ali, Rita, 458, 459
James I, 53
James, Lenada, 306
Jasinski, Jana, 272
Jaynes, Gerald David, 197, 199, 202, 209, 451, 471, 473, 475
Jefferson, Thomas, 12, 67, 293
Jencks, Christopher, 104, 105, 107
Jennings, Jesse, Jr., 55
Jensen, Arthur, 120, 121, 143
Jensen, Joan M., 395, 397
Jewell, Joseph, 195
Jiobu, Robert, 355, 371, 415, 416, 417
Johnson, Andrew, 154
Johnson, Dirk, 307, 319, 320, 321, 349
Johnson, George, 319
Johnson, James Weldon, 165
Johnson, Kirk, 315
Johnson, Lyndon B., 181, 203, 411
Jones, James M., 212
Jones, Maldwyn Allen, 63, 64, 67, 80, 82, 84, 87, 92, 94, 115, 116, 125
Jones, Woodrow, Jr., 412, 413, 416
Jordan, Winthrop, 54, 56, 230
Joseph, 295, 296
Josephy, Alvin, Jr., 290, 291, 292, 293, 294, 296, 317
Judson, George, 320

Kallen, Horace, 21, 31
Kamin, Leon, 122
Kamphoefner, Walter, 66
Kandel, William, 213
Kantrowitz, Barbara, 196
Karpat, Kemal, 421
Kasinitz, Philip, 217, 451
Katz, Daniel, 129
Kaufman, Phillip, 195
Kazal, Russell, 9, 10
Keefe, Susan E., 267, 268
Keely, Charles, 100
Kelly, Gail Paradise, 411, 413, 416, 417
Kennedy, David M., 107, 450
Kennedy, John F., 181, 203, 410

Kennedy, Randall, 187, 210
Kennedy, Robert F., 187
Kennedy, Ruby Jo Reeves, 9, 276
Kent, Mary, 194, 198
Kerr, Louise Año Nuevo, 236
Kibbe, Pauline, 230
Kibria, Nazli, 379, 385
Kikumura, Akemi, 339, 357
Kim, Chong-nim, 383
Kim, Claire Jean, 362, 363
Kim Ho, 383
Kim Hyong-soon, 383
Kim Hyung-chan, 380, 381, 383
Kim, Kwang Chung, 354, 364, 381, 382, 384, 385
King, Martin Luther, Jr., 38, 169, 179, 180, 181, 184, 476
King, Rodney, 185, 187
Kitano, Harry, 124, 341, 343, 344, 345, 349, 351, 353, 354, 357, 358, 359, 364, 372, 374, 375, 383, 388, 390, 391, 392, 395, 396, 397, 410, 412
Kitsuse, John, 350
Kitzes, Judith, 322
Klineberg, Otto, 118
Kloss, Heinz, 86, 262
Kluegel, James, 127, 129, 211, 444
Kohn, Howard, 188
Korematsu, Fred, 351–352
Kossoudji, Sherrie, 270
Kramer, Michael, 186
Kraut, Alan, 88, 90, 94, 96, 97
Kristol, Irving, 161, 446
Kritz, Mary, 201, 358
Krysan, Maria, 198
Kulczycki, Andrzej, 424, 425
Kumovich, Robert, 459
Kwaon, Im Jung, 383

Lacayo, Richard, 186, 203, 210
Lai, H. M., 124, 373, 374, 375, 378
Lamont, Michele, 213
Landau, Saul, 61, 151
Lapham, Susan, 104
LaPiere, Richard, 133
LaViolette, Forrest, 339, 341
Lawson, Stephen, 158
Laycock, Douglas, 207
Lazarus, Emma, 2
Lea, Tom, 231
LeBlanc Flores, Judith, 272
Lee, Sehahn, 359
Lee, Wen Ho, 399
Leighton, Alexander, 347

Lemann, Nicholas, 271
Leonard, Karen Isakson, 397, 398
Lerner, Max, 77
Levin, Michael, 364, 415, 416
Levine, Gene, 355, 356, 358, 362
Levine, Lawrence W., 189
Levinson, Daniel J., 132
Levitt, Peggy, 5, 10, 398
Liang, Zai, 378, 379, 385, 392, 398
Lichter, Daniel, 190
Lieberman, Leonard, 12
Lieberson, Stanley, 8, 91, 94, 96, 134, 201, 202, 356, 360, 441, 446, 452
Liebow, Edward, 323
Light, Ivan, 341, 383
Lim, Gue, 373
Lincoln, Abraham, 87, 114, 153, 154, 230
Lincoln, C. Eric, 165
Lindzey, Gardner, 120
Lippmann, Walter, 346
Lipset, Seymour, 458, 459
Little Crow, 295
Little Wolf, 295
Littlefield, Alice, 12
Litwack, Leon, 54, 56, 154, 230
Liu, Jeng, 364
Lobel, Sharon Alisa, 127
Lobo, Arun Peter, 424, 425
Lodge, Henry Cabot, 114, 343
Loehlin, John, 120
Logan, John, 196
Lohman, Joseph, 133
Lopreato, Joseph, 90, 92, 93
Loury, Glenn, 191
Luna, Gregory, 244
Lurie, Nancy Oestreich, 93, 293, 295

MacDonald, Jason A., 137
Macias, Reynaldo, 254
Mackie, Diane, 471
Madison, James, 68
Magellan, Ferdinand, 386
Mahmud of Ghazni, 393
Majumdar, R. C., 393
Malcolm X, 38, 167, 182, 476
Maldonado, Lionel, 100
Mandela, Nelson, 456
Mandell, Daniel, 5, 324
Mann, Taynia, 194, 198
Marín, Luis Muñoz, 259
Marquez, Benjamin, 243
Marshall, John, 292, 293, 305

Martin, Joanne, 127, 469
Martinez, José P., 242
Marx, Karl, 135
Masaoka, Mike, 336
Massasoit, 57
Massey, Douglas, 98, 104, 196, 197, 198, 213, 274, 355, 356
Masuda, Minoru, 353
Matson, Floyd, 123, 337, 338, 345, 347, 373
Matsuhito, 336
Matsumoto, Gary, 353
Maume, David, 193
Mayhew, George Noel, 393
Mazon, Mauricio, 239, 241
McAdam, Doug, 180
McCarroll, Jeanne, 203
McCarthy, Kevin F., 105, 106
McConahay, J. B., 127
McCone, John, 183
McDaniel, Antonio, 201, 202
McDermott, Monica, 218
McDowell, Jeanne, 203
McFee, Malcolm, 23
McInnis, Doug, 320
McIntyre, Alice, 444
McKay, Claude, 165
McKinley, William, 386, 387
McKinnell, Trudy, 325
McMillen, Marilyn, 195
McNeill, William H., 289
McNickle, D'Arcy, 291, 292, 298, 300, 301, 302, 303
McWilliams, Carey, 124, 238, 239, 240, 241, 262, 362
Mead, George Herbert, 130
Meier, August, 163, 164
Meister, Richard, 31
Melendy, Howard Brett, 382, 386, 387, 388, 390, 391, 394, 395, 396, 397
Meredith, Gerald, 353
Merton, Robert, 131
Metacom, 58, 303
Meyer, Dillon S., 309
Miele, Stefano, 92
Miller, Neal, 131
Miller, Norman, 470
Milosevic, Slobodan, 459
Min, Pyong Gap, 383, 384, 385
Mittlebach, Frank, 277
Miyamoto, S. Frank, 339, 341, 359
Modell, John, 190, 360
Mogelonsky, Marcia, 102
Mollenkopf, John, 451

Monahan, Thomas P., 201, 202
Monk, Maria, 115
Montejano, David, 227, 230
Montero, Darrel, 102, 339, 355, 356, 358, 361, 410, 413, 414, 415, 416, 417
Montezuma, Carlos, 304
Moore, Joan, 101, 233, 237, 238, 239, 257, 275, 276, 277, 280, 475
Moquín, Wayne, 230
Morales, Dan, 206
Morganthau, Tom, 137
Morison, Samuel Eliot, 53
Morris, Aldon, 180
Morse, Joseph Laffan, 410, 411
Morse, Samuel F. B., 115
Moskos, Charles, Jr., 154
Moss, Alfred, Jr., 59, 60, 154, 155, 165
Moynihan, Daniel P., 5, 40, 189–190, 213, 440, 441
Mueller, Milan, 274
Mueller, Robert, 430
Muhammad, Elijah, 167, 182
Muhammed, 418
Muller, Thomas, 105
Mulroy, Kevin, 62
Murdock, Steven, 198
Murguía, Edward, 13, 277
Murphy, Frank, 350, 350
Murray, Charles, 120, 121, 122, 123, 143
Músquiz, Ramón, 229
Mydans, Seth, 428
Myrdal, Gunnar, 135, 168, 195, 444, 455–456

Naff, Alixa, 418, 419, 420, 421, 422
Nagel, Joane, 9, 10, 289, 290, 305, 306, 311, 312, 313, 316, 325, 326
Najour, C. J., 421
Narasaki, Karen, 363
Nash, Gary, 56, 290
Navarro, José Antonio, 229
Nee, Victor, 3, 212, 374, 442
Neidert, Lisa, 444, 452
Newman, William, 31
Ngai, Mae M., 126, 443
Nguyen, Quan, 257, 259, 270, 275, 278
Niebuhr, Gustav, 314
Nieto, Sonia, 266
Nigem, Elias, 422, 424
Nixon, E. D., 179
Nixon, Richard, 203, 303

Noel, Donald, 134
Novotny, Ann, 90, 96, 97
Nunn, Clyde, 127

O'Brien, David, 341, 349, 350, 355, 356, 359, 361, 364
O'Brien, Sharon, 303
O'Connor, Sandra Day, 208, 209
Officer, James, 309
Ogawa, Dennis, 346
Ogunwole, Stella, 289
O'Hare, William, 194, 198, 214, 361
Ohiyesa, 304
Okimoto, Daniel, 362
Olson, James S., 303, 306, 313
Olzak, Susan, 9, 79, 136, 449
One Feather, Gerald, 323
Orfalea, Gregory, 422, 423
Orfield, Gary, 274, 473
Osofsky, Gilbert, 169, 170, 171, 181, 183
Ovadia, Seth, 194
Ozawa, Takao, 342, 443

Pabon, Edward, 268
Pachon, Harry, 237, 238, 257, 280, 475
Padilla, Amado M., 267, 268
Padilla, Felix, 260
Pak, Yong-man, 383
Palumbo-Liu, David, 362
Pantoja, Antonia, 263
Papademetriou, D. G., 104
Paredes, Américo, 231
Park, Robert E., 8–9, 15, 21, 34, 39, 45, 58, 62, 64
Parker, Arthur, 304
Parker, Quanah, 295
Parkman, Margaret, 357
Parks, Rosa, 179
Parpia, Banoo, 198
Parreñas, Rhacel Salazar, 339, 344
Passel, Jeffrey, 105, 311
Patel, Marilyn Hall, 352
Patterson, Orlando, 191
Peñalosa, Fernando, 266, 277
Perez, Lisandro, 102
Peroff, Nicholas, 302
Perry, Matthew C., 336
Pershing, John J. "Blackjack," 232
Petersen, William, 4, 11, 13, 338, 339, 341, 342, 351, 359, 362
Peterson, Iver, 319
Pettigrew, Thomas, 127, 469, 472
Phelan, J. D., 337

Phillip II, 386
Phillips, Bruce, 94, 95, 96
Hanh, Phung thi, 416
Piore, Michael, 92
Plank, Stephen, 359
Plessy, Homer, 159
Pol Pot, 411
Polk, James K., 230
Pollack, Denan, 320
Pollard, Kelvin, 194, 198
Pontiac, 290, 291, 303
Poole, Elijah, 167
Portes, Alejandro, 3, 90, 93, 96,
    102, 103, 260, 261, 262, 265, 280,
    360, 361
Posadas, Barbara, 376, 386, 387,
    388, 390, 391, 392
Poston, Dudley, Jr., 273
Pottinger, J. Stanley, 205
Powell, Linda, 444
Powers, Daniel, 470, 471
Powhatan, 56
Pratt, Richard H., 299
Preston, J. D., 470
Prewitt, Kenneth, 13
Price, John A., 309, 323
Prosser, Gabriel, 151, 166
Prucha, Francis Paul, 291, 297

Quillian, Lincoln, 200, 275
Quint, Howard, 57

Rainwater, Lee, 190
Ramirez, Roberto R., 255
Randolph, A. Philip, 166, 168,
    170, 180
Rawick, George, 61
Rawle, William, 77
Reagan, Ronald, 184
Red Cloud, 295, 296, 300
Rehnquist, William, 208
Reimers, David, 77, 85, 93, 100,
    124, 239, 410
Reinhold, Robert, 185
Reisler, Mark, 236
Reiss, Tom, 453
Reitzes, Dietrich, 133
Reynolds, Larry, 12
Rhee, Syngman, 383
Rhoades, Everett, 322
Rhodes, Colbert, 355, 356, 362
Richardson, Chad, 245
Riesman, David, 41
Riis, Jacob, 93, 97
Robertson, Pat, 429

Robinson, J. W., 470
Robinson, James R., 169
Robinson, William L., 203, 209
Rodríguez, Clara, 254, 256, 276
Róman, Miriam Jiménez, 276
Romano, Octavio Ignacio, 279
Romo, Harriett, 272
Romo, Ricardo, 240, 241
Romulo, Carlos, 386, 387
Roof, Wade Clark, 197
Roosevelt, Franklin D., 106, 169,
    204, 345, 375
Roosevelt, Theodore, 265, 338
Rosenbaum, Robert, 231
Ross, E. A., 337
Rostow, Eugene, 346, 347, 351
Rothenberg, Paula, 310
Roy, Prodipto, 324
Rubenstein, Richard E., 68, 117
Rudwick, Elliott, 163, 164
Rumbaut, Ruben, 3, 102, 103, 265,
    280, 411, 412, 413, 416
Russell, Mona, 418
Rustin, Bayard, 170
Ryan, Alan, 120
Ryan, William, 213

Saenz, Rogelio, 358
St. Cartmail, Keith, 412
St. John Crevecoeur, J. Hector, 30
St. John, Nancy, 470, 473
St. Peter, Louis, 127
Sakamoto, Arthur, 321, 364
Salzman, Jack, 164
Samhan, Helen Hatab, 420,
    421, 426
San Miguel, Guadalupe, Jr., 263
Sanchez, George I., 227, 240, 262
Sandefur, Gary, 321, 322, 325
Sanford, R. Nevitt, 132
Santa Anna, Antonio López
    de, 230
Santiago-Valles, Kevin, 256
Sawyer, Jack, 357
Saxton, Alexander, 371
Schauffler, Richard, 261, 262
Schermerhorn, Richard, 91, 92, 93,
    94, 95
Schlesinger, Arthur M., Jr., 77, 106
Schneider, Barbara, 359
Schoen, Robert, 277
Schofield, Janet Ward, 199, 200, 471
Schulz, Amy J., 325
Schuman, Howard, 127, 202, 453
Schurz, Carl, 87

Schwarz, Benjamin, 29
Schwerner, Michael, 181
Scott, Robin Fitzgerald, 242
Scott, Wilbur, 322
See, Katherine O'Sullivan, 449
Seller, Maxine, 100
Sequoyah, 292
Shanahan, Suzanne, 136
Sheatsley, Paul, 127, 451, 469
Sheridan, Philip, 295
Sherman, William, 295
Sheth, Pravin, 396, 397, 398
Shryock, Andrew, 424
Sigelman, Lee, 137, 471
Sikes, Melvin, 203
Simmons, William, 164
Simon, Thomas, 118
Simpson, George Eaton, 132, 472
Simpson, Nicole Brown, 186
Simpson, O. J., 186, 187, 203
Singer, Lester, 93
Singh, J. J., 397
Sitting Bull, 295, 296, 299–300, 303
Sklare, Marshall, 94, 95
Sleeter, Christine, 444
Smith, James P., 194, 195
Smith, Jerry E., 206
Smith, Ryan, 127, 444
Smothers, Ronald, 188
Smylie, Mark, 470
Snipp, C. Matthew, 57, 289, 298,
    308, 311, 312, 313, 318, 319,
    321, 322
Sone, Monica, 342, 348
Sowards, Kathryn, 271
Sowell, Thomas, 210
Sparks, Sam, 206
Spearman, Charles, 120, 143
Spencer, Robert, 55
Spicer, Edward, 55, 289, 290, 292,
    295, 300, 302, 309, 314, 316
Spickard, Paul, 14, 202, 354, 357,
    358, 444
Spitz, Stephen, 203, 209
Spotted Tail, 295
Spuhler, J. N., 120
Steeh, Charlotte, 127, 202, 453
Steele, Shelby, 205, 316
Steinberg, Stephen, 83, 84, 91, 92,
    218, 361, 445
Steiner, Stan, 305, 306
Stephan, Cookie White, 357
Stephan, Walter G., 357, 469, 470,
    471, 473
Stevens, Gillian, 260

Stevens, Ted, 265
Stevenson, Coke, 239
Stewart, Kenneth, 290, 309, 317
Strand, Paul, 412, 413, 416
Stroessner, Steven, 471
Suarez-Orozco, Marcelo, 5
Suleiman, Michael, 420, 421,
    426, 427
Sullivan, Teresa, 88, 114, 125, 126
Sumner, William, 54, 130, 472
Suzuki, David, 122
Svensson, Frances, 302
Sweatt, Heman M., 206
Sydnor, Charles, 68

Tabb, William, 184
Tachiki, Amy, 336
Taeuber, Alma, 196, 197
Taeuber, Karl, 196, 197
Taft, William Howard, 386, 387
Tagore, Rabindranath, 370
Tajfel, Henry, 130
Takagi, Paul, 361
Takahashi, Jere, 353, 358
Takaki, Ronald, 342, 371, 372,
    374, 378, 381, 388, 390,
    396, 397
Tateishi, John, 351
Tatum, Beverly, 444
Taylor, 230
Taylor, D. Garth, 451, 469
Taylor, Sandra, 343, 345, 348, 349,
    351, 361
Tecumseh, 291, 292, 303
tenBroek, Jacobus, 123, 337, 338,
    345, 347, 373
Tennstedt, Sharon, 268
Tenskwatawa, 291
Terry, Alfred, 295, 296
Terry, Don, 427
Thind, Bhagat Singh, 396
Thom, Melvin, 289
Thomas, Clarence, 208, 307
Thompson, Charles, 119
Thurmond, Strom, 12
Thurstone, L. L., 120
Tienda, Marta, 104, 256, 257, 269,
    273, 274
Tijerina, Pete, 244
Tindall, George Brown, 154, 155
Tinker, John, 357
Tocqueville, Alexis de, 454
Todorovich, Miro, 205
Tolnay, Stewart, 164

Tong, Benton, 371, 372, 374, 375,
    377, 378
Torrecilha, Ramon, 257, 259, 270,
    275, 278
Trotter, Monroe, 163
Truman, Harry S., 170, 176, 204
Tuan, Mia, 399
Tuch, Steven, 137
Tuchman, Barbara, 23
Turner, Frederick Jackson, 39
Turner, J. C., 130
Turner, Nat, 151, 166
Tussman, Joseph, 159, 171, 348,
    350, 351
Two Moon, 296
Tzeng, Jessie, 364

Ueda, Reed, 114

Vaca, Nick, 279
Valdez, Luis, 244
Van Doren, Charles, 230
van Oudenhoven, Jan Pieter, 471
Van Valey, Thomas, 197
Vanneman, Reeve, 194
Veltman, Calvin, 260
Vera, H., 444
Vernez, George, 105, 106
Vesey, Denmark, 151, 166
Villa, Francisco "Pancho," 232

Wagner, Edward, 380
Wakasa, James, 349
Walls, Thomas, 346
Walsh, Catherine E., 259, 266
Warren, Earl, 171, 346
Washburn, Wilcomb, 315, 318
Washington, Booker T., 150,
    162–163, 164, 166
Washington, George, 51, 67,
    291, 293
Wassaja, 304
Waters, Mary C., 5, 8, 10, 11, 91,
    94, 96, 201, 202, 213, 217, 218,
    356, 441, 445, 451, 452
Wax, Murray, 294, 295, 314, 315
Webb, Walter Prescott, 231
Weggert, Karl, 86
Weinberg, Daniel, 197, 274
Weis, Lois, 444
Welch, Finis, 194
Welch, Susan, 471
Westie, Frank, 133, 134
White, Michael J., 356

Whitener, Summer, 195
Whitmore, John, 415, 416, 417
Wilcox, Jerome, 197
Wilhelm, Sidney, 192
Wilkerson, Isabel, 202
Wilkins, David, 308, 326
Wilkins, Roy, 150
Wilkinson, Doris, 190, 473
Williams, J. Allen, 127
Williams, Norma, 267
Williams, Richard, 471
Williams, Robin M., Jr., 130,
    197, 199, 202, 209, 451, 471,
    473, 475
Williams, Roger, 57
Wilson, Kenneth, 163, 165
Wilson, Raymond, 303, 306, 313
Wilson, Reginald, 272
Wilson, William J., 191, 213, 215,
    216, 451
Wilson, Woodrow, 125, 232
Winbush, Don, 203
Winegarten, Ruthe, 151, 157, 158
Wirth, Louis, 41
Wittke, Carl, 65, 82, 86, 87, 93, 94
Wojtkiewicz, Roger, 271
Wolf, Diane, 392
Wong, Herbert, 374
Wong, Morrison, 124, 354, 361, 364
Wong, W. Mun, 444
Wood, Peter, 129
Woodrum, Eric, 353, 357
Woodward, C. Vann, 157
Wright, Mary Bowen, 102, 411, 412
Wu, Frank, 370

Yancey, William, 190
Yang, Philip Q., 379, 385, 391,
    398, 417
Yellin, Emily, 473
Yinger, J. Milton, 132
Young Joseph, 320
Yu, Elena, 389, 390

Zambrana, Ruth, 267
Zangwill, Israel, 21
Zayas, Luis, 268
Zentella, Ana Celia, 266, 267
Zhong, Deng, 383
Zhou, Min, 10, 196, 360, 376, 377,
    378, 415
Zia, Helen, 399
Zinn, Maxine Baca, 269
Zubrinsky, Camille, 129, 198

Subject Index

Achieved characteristics, 14,
  defined, 16
Adams, John Quincy, 21
Affirmative action
  Asian attitudes toward, 363–364
  criticisms of, 205
  defenses of, 205
  defined, 223
  effectiveness of, 209–210
  establishment of, 203
  growth of, 203–204
  legal challenges to, 204–205,
    207–209
  legal reaffirmation of, 205–206
  percent plans and, 206–207
  reasons for, 203, 210–211
Africa, economic issues in, 34
African Americans
  assimilation of, 6, 152, 189–203,
    451–452
  civil rights movement and,
    162–172
  in Civil War, 151
  and colonial model, 34–35
  contemporary conflicts with
    whites, 184–189
  corporate discrimination
    against, 188–189
  cultural assimilation of, 189–191
  discriminatory laws against, 6,
    156–160
  economic position of, 105,
    193–194, 214–215
  economic progress of, 194–195,
    216–217
  educational attainments of,
    194–196
  entrepreneurship among,
    214–215
  family values of, 189–191

foreign- vs. native-born,
    217–218
  friendship patterns, 200
  history of racism against, 211
  immigration of, 217–218
  and intelligence testing, 118–119
  literature of, 165
  marital assimilation of, 201–202
  in modern labor market,
    192–193
  original entry into U.S. of, 5–6,
    59–62
  political participation of, 475
  postemancipation, 154–155
  postreconstruction voting
    restrictions on, 158
  primary structural assimilation
    of, 199–201
  racial profiling against, 187
  reality check, 172–174, 219–221
  residential assimilation of,
    196–199
  secondary structural
    assimilation of, 191–199
  separatist movements of,
    165–168
  and slavery, 59–62, 150–153
  terminology of, 212
  third-stream, 452
  urbanization of, 160–162
  violence against, 164–165
  white hostility to, in post-Civil
    War period, 155–156
  in World War II, 170
Agriculture, and population
    growth, 77
Aguinaldo, Emilio, 386
Ahn Chang-ho, 383
Alaska Native Claims Settlement
    Act, 307

Alaska v. Native Village of Venetie
    Tribal Government, 307
Alaskan tribes, sovereignty for,
    307–308
Albanians, 459
Algonkian people, 55
Alien Land Laws, 342–343, 396
Allotment Act, 298,
    defined, 332
America. See United States
America, A Family Matter, 119
American ("Know-Nothing")
    Party, 115–116
American Colonization
    Society, 153
American Dilemma, An, 195, 455
American Indian Chicago
    Conference, 305
American Indian Exposition, 317
American Indian Movement
    (AIM), 306–307
American Indian Religious
    Freedom Act, 314
American Indians, 2
  Anglo conformity vs. pluralism
    for, 300–302
  assimilation of, 310–327
  and colonial model, 34–35,
    308–310
  as conquered minority, 449–451
  cultural assimilation of, 311–317
  discrimination against, 326
  diversity of, 289, 290
  economic status of, 318–321
  education programs for,
    sponsored by BIA, 299, 318
  educational attainments of,
    317–318
  educational opportunities
    for, 318

American Indians *(continued)*
effects of Anglo contact on, 291, 295
ethnogenesis among, 312, 316
and gaming industry, 307
geographic distribution of, 308–309
health issues for, 322
as immigrants, 308–310
infant mortality among, 322
language issues of, 290, 312–313
legal issues regarding, 326–327
legal status of, 300
marital patterns of, 323–325
in Mexico, 227–229
in modern labor market, 321
modern tribalism of, 305–308
and pan-Indian identity, 315–316, 323
Plains wars and, 294–295
population fluctuations of, 289–290, 308–309, 312
pre-Colonial, 55
preservation of heritage by, 5, 290, 315–316
primary structural assimilation of, 322–323
protest organizations of, 303–305
reality check, 328–330
relations with Anglo Americans, 55–58
religions of, 313–315
relocation of, 5, 309, 333
removal of, 292–294
secondary structural assimilation of, 317–322
self-identification as, 311–312
sovereignty of, 288
treaties with, 56–57, 291–292, 295–296
U.S. policies toward, 296–300
in urban areas, 309–310
warfare with Anglos, 295–296
in World War II, 316
American Renaissance Magazine, 428
American-Arab Anti-Discrimination Committee (ADC), 426
Americanization, defined, 16. *See* Assimilation
Americans. *See* United States; names of individual ethnicities and groups

Amherst, Jeffrey, 52
Amnesty and Reconstruction, Proclamation of, 154
Anglo Americans
continuing position of, 40
and indentured servitude, 59
political dominance of, 67–69
reality check, 69–71
Anglo-conformity ideology, defined, 47
Anglo-conformity model, of assimilation, 27–30
aspects of, 29
defined, 47
Antiassimilationist ideologies, 27, 33–38
defined, 47
Anticoolie clubs, 123
Anzaldua, Gloria, 227
Apartheid, 456
Appropriations Act of 1871, 297
Arab American Advisory Committee, 427
Arab American Institute (AAI), 426
Arab Americans, 103
ancestorship of, 424
assimilation of, 421, 423–428
association building by, 426–427
confusion about, 2
discrimination against, 420, 421, 426
early immigration of, 420
educational attainments of, 425
family formation among, 420
geographic distribution of, 424
hate crimes against, 427, 429–431
immigration after World War II, 422–423
income levels of, 425
in labor force, 421
marital patterns of, 425
in modern labor force, 425
obstacles to assimilation for, 426
religions of, 420–421, 424
stereotyping of, 407
Arab-Israeli War of 1967, 423, 426
Arabs
confusion about, 2
contact with Europe, 418–419
geographic distribution of, 418
nationalism among, 419
Arapaho people, 294, 320
Arizona
Indian affairs of, 307

Mexican labor in, 236
Aryans, 117
Ascribed characteristics, defined, 16
Ashkenazim, 94
Asian Exclusion League, 338
Asian Indian Americans, 102, 103
assimilation of, 397–399
discrimination against, 296
early immigration of, 394, 395–396
early occupations of, 396–397
educational attainments of, 398
marriage patterns of, 398
in modern labor market, 398
immigration figures for, 395
Asians. *See* names of individual national groups
ASPIRA, 263
ASPIRA of New York, Inc. v. Board of Education of the City of New York, 264–265
Assimilation
of Asian Americans, 399–400
attitude receptional, 25
behavior receptional, 25
civic, 25
complex nature of, 3
cultural, by addition, 47
cultural, by substitution, 47
economic conditions and, 8
effects of, 9
ethnic and racial factors affecting, 8
factors affecting, 6–8
group size and concentration and, 7–8
identificational, 24
ideologies of, 27–33
defined, 47
indications of, 442–443
marital, 24
models of, 29, 30, 32–33, 36–37
defined, 47–48
non-European instances of, 5–6
pace of, 440–441
popular view of, 3–5
process, defined, 16
segmented, 10, 25, 107
social power and, 6–7
straight line theory of, 4–5
structural, 23–24
subprocesses of, 10, 22–27
three-generations model of, 5

and voluntariness of
    immigration, 7
transnational character of, 10
Assimilation subprocesses, 22–25
    Gordon's theory of, defined, 49
Assimilation theory, 8–11
    weaknesses of, 21–22
Assimilationist ideologies, 35
Association of Arab-American
    University Graduates
    (AAUG), 426
Association of Syrian Unity, 421
Atlanta Compromise, 162
    defined, 176
Attitude receptional assimilation,
    defined, 47
Austin, Stephen F., 229
Austrians, immigration into
    U.S., 87, 88
Authoritarian personality,
    defined, 144
*Awful Disclosures of Maria
    Monk,* 115
Ayres, E. D., 240, 241

Back to Africa movement, 165–166
Bakke, Allan, 204–205
Balfour Declaration, 423
Banking industry, discriminatory
    policies in, 188
Barrios, defined, 250
Bay of Pigs, 410
Behavior receptional assimilation,
    defined, 47
Bell Curve, The, 121, 122
Bhagat Singh Thind, U.S. v.,
    396, 397
Biddle, Francis, 347
Big Foot, 300
Bilingual education, 261
    and Anglo conformity, 265–266
    controversy regarding, 261
    defined, 284
    future of, 266–267
    historical perspectives on,
        262–263
    legal issues regarding, 263–266
Bilingual Education Act
    of 1968, 264
Binet, Alfred, 118
Binet-Simon scale, 118
Birds of passage, 92
Birmingham, AL, civil rights
    protests in, 180

Birth of a Nation, 164
Black Americans. *See* African
Black Codes, 154–155
Black Eagle Flying Corps, 166
Black Muslims, 182
    founding of, 167
    goals and creed of, 167
    renewal of, 182
    success of, 167–168
Black Power, 137
Black Power movement
    emergence of, 183
    precursors of, 182–183
    reasons for, 181–182
    waning influence of, 184
Black Renaissance, defined, 176
Black Seminoles, 61–62
Blackfeet Reservation, 308
Blackfoot people, 294
Blood quantum, 311
    defined, 332
Boat People, 411–412, 415
Bok, Derek, 209
Borderlands, 227
    defined, 250
Boston, Irish in, 82
Bowen, William G., 209
Boycotts, 179
Bracero Program, 238–239, 241, 244
Braceros, defined, 250
Braceros Act, 465
Brazil
    race relations in, 458–459
    stratification in, 459
Brigham, C. C., 118–119
Britain, in opium trade, 371
*Brown v. Board of Education of
    Topeka,* 126, 171–172, 181,
    193, 196, 205
    consequences of, 472–473
    precursors of, 263
Bulosan, Carlos, 370
Bureau of Indian Affairs, 297
    powers of, 298
Burlingame Treaty, 371, 373
Bush, George H., 184, 351
Bush, George W., 430
Bush, Jeb, 206
Busing, school, 472

Calhoun, John, 297
California
    antiimmigration sentiment
        in, 278

challenges to affirmative action
    in, 204
discrimination against Mexican
    Americans in, 239–242, 263
1848 constitution of, 262
gold rush in, 123, 371
Mexican American civil rights
    efforts in, 244
Mexican labor in, 236
percent plans in, 206
statehood of, 295
Cambodia, 411
    genocide in, 411–412
Cambodian Americans, violence
    against, 185
Canada
    immigrant issues in, 457–458
    secessionist movement of, 457
Canoe, Lorraine, 315
Caribbean immigrants, 101, 103,
    217. *See also* names of
        individual countries
        of origins
Carlisle School, 299, 316
Carmichael, Stokely, 183
Carpetbaggers, 155
Carson, Kit, 295
Castle Garden, 88
Catholic Church
    attitudes toward, 82, 114–115
    and colonization of
        Americas, 228
    among Hispanics, 277–278
    among Native Americans, 314
Caucasians. *See* Whites
Causa, La, 244
Central Americans, 101
Central Pacific Company, 124, 371
Centrifugal relationship, 448
    defined, 462
Centripetal relationship, 448
    defined, 462
Chain migration, defined, 101
Chandra, Ram, 397
Chaney, James, 181
Charlotte-Mecklenburg School
    District, 473
Chavez, César, 244
Cherokee Nation v. Georgia, 292, 293
Cherokee people, 292, 293
    Eastern Band of, 319
    languages of, 313
Cheyenne people, 294
Chickasaw people, 293

Chief Joseph, 295, 296
China
   economic colonization of, 371
   history of, 375
   influence on Korea, 380
Chinatowns, 374
Chinese American Citizens
      Alliance (CACA), 375
Chinese Americans, 101
   assimilation of, 376–380
   assimilation rates of, 377–378
   associations of, 374–375
   attitudes toward, 117, 123–124,
      373, 374
   early immigration of, 123,
      371–376
   entrepreneurship of, 378
   family formation among,
      373–375
   geographic distribution of, 374
   immigration figures for, 372
   marriage patterns of, 378–379
   "model minority" stereotype
      of, 380
   in modern labor market,
      378–379
   naturalization rates of, 379
   reality check, 138–141
   recent immigration of, 377
   violence against, 373
   in World War II, 376
Chinese Consolidated Benevolent
      Association (CCBA), 374
Chinese Exclusion Act of 1882,
      123–124, 370, 373, 465
   repeal of, 375–376, 465
Choctaw people, 293
Cincinnati, Germans in, 86
Civic assimilation, 25
Civil Rights Act of 1866, 155
Civil Rights Act of 1964, 126,
      205, 473
   passage of, 181
Civil Rights Act of 1991, 184
Civil rights movement
   and Black Power movement,
      181–184
   court victories of, 170–172
   early days of, 163–164
   foci of, 451
   legislative victories of, 181
   Mexican Americans and,
      242–245
   militancy in, 179–181

nonviolent protest in,
      169–170, 179
   precursors to, 162–163
   separatist movements, 165–168
   strategies and tactics of,
      168–170
   violence against, 164–165
   violence in, 182–184
Civil War, 87, 116
   purposes of, 153–154
   Reconstruction after, 155
   and slavery issue, 151
Cizik, Richard, 429
Clinton, Bill, 475
Cochise, 295
Code switching, defined, 284
Cody, Buffalo Bill, 300
Cognitive approach, toward
      remedying prejudice,
      468–469
Collective violence theory, 136
Collins, Patricia Hill, 179
Colonial model of assimilation, 34
   criticisms of, 446
   dynamic view of, 448–449
Colonialism
   end of, 170
   internal, 33–35
   religious motives for, 228
Colonized minorities
   contrasted with immigrant
      minorities, 34, 153
   relations with majority, 448
Colorado, Mexican labor in, 236
Columbus, Christopher, 258
Comanche people, 294
   religions of, 314
Commonwealth, defined, 284
Community Service Organization
      (CSO), 243
Compensatory treatment,
      defined, 223
Conflict theory, 21
   defined, 47
   vs. assimilation theory, 21–22
Confucianism, 382
Congregation, defined, 16
Congress of Racial Equality
      (CORE), 169, 170, 180
Connerly, Ward, 204
Consensus (order) theories,
      defined, 47
Constitution
   and Anglo dominance, 68

Convention of 1787 and, 51
   and pluralism, 41
Correlation, defined, 47
Cortina, Juan "Cheno," 231
Cortina Wars, 231
   defined, 250
Cosa Nostra, 92
Crazy Horse, 295, 296
Creation generation, defined, 250
Credit ticket system, 372
Cree people, 457
Creed-deed discrepancy, 132
Creek people, 293
Crisis, The, 164
Crook, George, 295, 296
Crow people, 294
   effects of Anglo contact on, 295
Crystal City, TX, Mexican
      American political power
      in, 244
Cuba, U.S. relations with, 258
Cuban Americans, 102
   after Bay of Pigs, 410
   language issues of, 453
Cultural assimilation
   by addition, defined, 47
   as separate from other types of
      assimilation, 25–26
   by substitution, defined, 47
   in United States, 39
Cultural pluralism, 31–33, 42
   aspects of, 32
   ideology of, defined, 48
Cultural transmission theories of
      prejudice, 128–130
Custer, George, 295, 296
Cycle of race relations, 8–9, 34

da Gama, Vasco, 393
Dade County, FL, bilingual
      education experiment
      in, 264
Dakota people, 294–295
Darwin, Charles, 117
Das, Taraknath, 397
Dawes Act, 298, 304, 308
Dayal, Har, 397
De Leon, Juan Poncé, 258
Deccan, 393
Declaration of Indian Purpose, 305
Declining Significance of Race, The,
      215, 216
Deer, Ada, 307
Delany, Martin, 153

Delaware Prophet, 290
Democratic Party, and Irish, 82
Denny's, discriminatory policies
    at, 188
Desegregation, 126, 170–172,
    181–182, 198
    attitudes toward, 199–200
    distinguished from
        integration, 200
    metrics of, 473
Detroit, Michigan, 1943 riots in,
    169, 183
DeWitt, John L., 240, 345, 346,
    347, 350
Díaz, José, 240
Díaz, Porfírio, 232
Dinnerstein, Leonard, 77
Discrimination, 127, 128
    corporate, 188–189
    defined, 47
    group conflict and, 134–136
    institutional, 136–138
    legal remedies for, 472–474
    levels of, 211–212
    organized protest against,
        475–476
    political efforts to end, 474–475
    racial profiling as, 187
    reverse, 205
    situational pressures and,
        132–134
    structural view of, 213, 214–217
    studies of, 133–134
    theories of, 132–138
    See also Prejudice; Racism
Disparate impact, defined, 223
Displaced Persons Act, 100,
    409, 465
Dissimilarity, indexes of, 196,
    273–274, 355–356
    defined, 223
Diversity, increase in late 20th
    century, 2
Dominant group, defined, 16
Dominican Americans, 101, 103
Douglas, William O., 351
Douglass, Frederick, 179
Dow v. United States, 421
Downward mobility, 107
Draft Riots, 116
Dravidians, 393
DuBois, W.E.B., 150, 163–164, 203
Dutch
    colonization by, 22, 54, 394

cultural influence of, 23
Dutch West India Company, 54

East India Companies, 394
East Indian Americans. See Asian
    Indian Americans
Eastern Europeans, immigration
    into U.S., 87, 89–90
Eastman, Charles, 304
Economic slavery, 157
Edgewood v. Kirby, 245
Eisenhower, Dwight, 172, 204,
    301–302, 409
Elementary and Secondary
    Education Act of 1965, 264
Eliot, John, 21
Ellis Island, 1, 88
Emancipation Proclamation, 154
    defined, 176
Emergency Quota Act, 125, 343
Endo, Mitsuye, 351
English
    colonization by, 22, 394
    legacy of, 52–55
    relations with American
        Indians, 55–59
    See also Anglo Americans
Environmentalism, 118
    defined, 144
    rise of, 119–120
Estimates of heritability, 121
    defined, 144
Ethnic group, defined, 16
    early stages of formation of,
        447–448
Ethnic pluralism, 16
Ethnic-resource model, 190
Ethnicity
    concepts supplanting, 13–14
    defined, 17
    future of, 454–455
    symbolic, 441
    traditional concept of, 13
    transformation of, after
        immigration, 93–94
Ethnics, defined, 17
Ethnocentrism, 54, 130
Ethnogenesis, 10–11, 93
    defined, 17
Eugenics, 428
Europe, population growth in, 77
Europeans. See names of
    individual national groups
Evacuation Claims Act, 351

Ex Parte Endo, 351
Executive Order 10925,
    203, 204
Extended families, 267
    defined, 284

F (Fascism) scale, 132
Fair Employment Practices
    Committee, 169
Fair Housing Act, 198
Falwell, Jerry, 429
Familism, 267
Family, and values
    transmission, 212
Fard, W. D., 167
Farmer, James, 169
Farrakhan, Louis, 168
Federal Acknowledgment
    Program, 303
Federalist Papers, The, 68
Fetterman, William, 295
Fifteenth Amendment, 159
Filipino (Pilipino) Americans,
    101, 102
    ambiguous status of, 390
    assimilation of, 391–392
    associations of, 389
    disadvantages of, 389–390
    early immigration of,
        387–388
    family formation among, 391
    immigration figures for, 389
    marriage patterns of, 390, 392
    in modern labor market,
        391–392
    in World War II, 390–391
Fillmore, Millard, 116
First generation, defined, 17
First great immigrant stream,
    defined, 111
First stream immigrants
    assimilation of, 441–442
    Germans, 84–87
    Irish, 79–84
Florida, percent plans in, 207
Folkways, 130
Folkways, 54
Ford, Gerald, 413
Fort Apache Reservation, 308
Fort Detroit, 290
Fort Peck Reservation, 308
Forty-eighters, 86–87
Fourteenth Amendment, 155, 159
Fox people, 312

France
colonization efforts of, 394
in Middle East, 419
in New World, 290–291
rule over Vietnam, 411
Franklin, Benjamin, 66
Free-floating hostility, 131
defined, 144
Freed Blacks, defined, 176
Freedmen's Bureau, 154, 158
Freedom Rides, 180
French and Indian War, 290–291
Frethorne, Richard, 60
Frontier thesis, 39
Frustration-aggression
hypothesis, 131
Fuhrman, Mark, 186
Fundamental attribution error,
defined, 144

G.I. Fiancées Act, 376, 391
G.I. Forum, 243
Gall, 295, 296
Galton, Francis, 118
Gaming, 307, 319
Gans, Herbert, 440
Garvey, Marcus, 38, 150, 165–166,
167, 182
Gates, Henry Louis, Jr., 187
Gawasowannah, 304
Gentleman's Agreement, 338,
343–344, 381
Georgia
Indian affairs of, 292
and slavery, 61
Germans
assimilation of, 440, 441
attitudes toward, 115
colonial presence of, 65–66, 69
Jews, 94–95
language, 86
nineteenth-century
immigration into U.S., 79,
84–87
political participation by, 86–87
potato famine and, 84
in Revolutionary war, 67
Geronimo, 295
Ghadar Party, 397
Ghost Dance religion, 299–300, 314
Giago, Tim, 307
Gibbon, John, 295, 296
Ginsberg, Ruth Bader, 209
Glass ceiling effect, 194

defined, 223
Glazer, Nathan, 440
Goldman, Ron, 186
Gompers, Samuel, 396
Gone with the Wind, 61
Goodman, Andrew, 181
Gordon, Milton, 9–10, 21, 22, 25–27
Graham, Franklin, 429
Grandfather clause, 158
Gratz v. Billinger, 207–208
Great Depression, 98
effect on African Americans, 168
effect on Mexican Americans,
237–239
Great Sioux Reservation, 296
Greeley, Andrew, 408
Greensboro, NC, civil rights
protests in, 179
Greenville Treaty, 291
Griggs v. Duke Power Co., 204
Group conflict theories of
discrimination, 134–136
Group identification, and
prejudice, 130–131
Grutter v. Billinger, 207, 208
Guadalupe Hidalgo, Treaty of, 230,
231, 262, 295
defined, 251
Gue Lim, United States v., 373

Haitian Americans, 217
Hamad, Imad, 408
Handlin, Oscar, 9
Hansen, Marcus, 9
Harlan, Justice John, 159
Harrison, William Henry, 292
Hart-Cellar Act, 100, 465
Hawaii
annexation of, 380
Chinese in, 371
Filipinos in, 387–388
Japanese in, 346–347
Koreans in, 380–381, 383
Hemings, Sally, 12
Hereditarianism, 118–119
defined, 144
revival of, 120–123
Heritability, 121
Herrnstein, Richard, 120, 121–123
Hinduism, 393, 396
Hirabayashi v. United States, 350
Hirabayashi, Gordon, 350, 352
Hispanics. See Latinos; names of
individual national groups

Hmong people, 411
*Ho v. San Francisco Unified School
District,* 363–364
Hopwood v. Texas, 205–206
House Concurrent Resolution 108,
301–302
How the Irish Became White, 443
Howard, O. O., 295
Huerta, Dolores, 244
Hughes, Langston, 165
Hungarians, immigration into
U.S., 87, 88, 409–410
Hurston, Zora Neale, 165

Identificational assimilation,
defined, 48
Illegal Immigration Reform and
Immigrant Responsibility
Act, 466
Immigrant minorities
contrasted with colonized
minorities, 34, 153
defined, 48
and ethnic-group formation,
447–448
Immigrant model, 34,
232–236, 446
dynamic view of, 448–449
Immigration
changing patterns of, 87–89
economic impact of, 105–106
educational level of immigrants,
106–107
and ethnic absorption, 106–107
factors affecting, 77–79
job skills and, 102
laws regarding, 99
regulation of, 88
restrictions on, 98
voluntary vs. involuntary, 7
of women, 83–84
Immigration Act of 1875, 465
Immigration Act of 1917, 125, 465
Immigration Act of 1921, 465
Immigration Act of 1924, 123,
124–125, 237, 343, 396, 465
Immigration Act of 1990, 466
Immigration and Nationality Act
of 1952 (INA), 99, 100,
102, 465
Immigration and Nationality Act
Amendments (INAA), 99,
100–101, 102, 465
effects of, 101–102, 370, 388

Immigration Quota Act of 1924, 370, 376
Immigration Reform and Control Act (IRCA), 270, 466
In-groups, 13
Inclusion, defined, 17
Indentured servitude, 59
India
    British rule over, 394
    foreign contact with, 392–393
    foreign exploitation of, 394
    independence efforts of, 394
    languages of, 393
    Portuguese colonization of, 393–394
    religions of, 393
Indian Americans. *See* American Indians; Asian Indian Americans
Indian Business Association, 320
Indian Citizenship Act, 300
Indian Civil Rights Act, 303
Indian Country Today, 320
Indian Gaming Regulatory Act, 307
Indian League of America, 397
Indian Removal Act, 293
Indian Reorganization Act (IRA), 301, 304
Indian Rights Association, 303
Indian Self-Determination and Educational Assistance Act, 303
Indian Trade and Intercourse Act of 1793, 297
Indo-Iranians, 393
Indochina Migration and Refugee Assistance Act, 413
Indochinese, 410. *See also* Cambodian Americans; Laos; Vietnamese Americans
Information and Education Exchange Act (EVA), 391
Inouye, Daniel, 314
Institutional discrimination theories, 136–138
Integration
    distinguished from desegregation, 200
    multiracial social contacts, 200–201
Intelligence
    current controversies regarding, 120–123

heritability of, 121
scales of, 118
testing of, 118–119
Interagency Task Force for Indochinese Refugees, 413
Intergroup contact to reduce prejudice
    in schools, 470–471
    studies of, 470
    surveys regarding, 471
    theoretical underpinning of, 470
Internal colonialism, theory of, 33–35
    defined, 49
Internment of Japanese in World War II
    camp conditions, 348–350
    camp locations, 348
    discriminatory nature of, 346–347
    legal issues regarding, 350–352
    procedures for, 347–348
    protests against, 349
    rationales for, 345–346
Interracial marriage, 357
    attitudes toward, 202
    constitutional protection of, 201
    increase in late 20th century, 2, 201–202
    among second generation, 4
Irish
    assimilation of, 443
    attitudes toward, 82–83, 114–115
    colonial presence of, 63
    nineteenth-century immigration into U.S., 79–84
    political participation by, 82–83
    potato famine, 80–82
    women immigrants, 83–84
Iroquois Confederacy, 55
Iroquois people, 290, 313
Islam
    confusion about, 2
    hostility toward, 429–430
    in India, 393, 394
    origins of, 418
    in Philippines, 386
    sects of, 419
Israel
    conflict with Palestinians, 424
    formation of, 423
    and Syrians, 426
Issei, 340

cultural preservation by, 341–342, 352
    defined, 367
    new, 362
    status of, 344
    success of, 360–361
Italians
    assimilation of, 442
    demographics of immigrants, 90–92
    immigration into U.S., 87, 88
    maintenance of ethnic identity of, 93–94, 95–96
    professions of immigrants, 96, 97
    reactions to immigration of, 92–93
    women immigrants, 91–92

Jackson, Andrew, 293, 294
Jackson, Jesse, 475
James I, 53
Jamestown, VA, 22, 52–53, 56
Japan
    Gentlemen's Agreement with U.S., 338, 343–344, 381
    imperial aims of, 381
    influence on Korea, 380, 381
    opening of, to trade, 336–337
    in World War II, 375
Japanese American Citizen's League (JACL), 345
Japanese Americans
    and Alien Land Law, 342–343
    assimilation of, 352–362
    associations of, 355
    civil rights groups of, 345
    in commerce, 360
    community building among, 341–342, 359
    cultural assimilation of, 352–354
    cultural preservation among, 341
    discrimination against, 335, 337–339, 347
    early immigration of, 336–340
    economic condition of, 354, 364
    educational attainments of, 354, 359
    exclusion of, 343–344
    family formation among, 340–342, 359
    generational issues among, 340–342, 352–354
    in Hawaii, 346–347

Japanese Americans *(continued)*
  immigration rates of, 363
  internment of, during World
    War II, 347–352, 376, 431
  marital patterns of, 356–358
  "model minority" stereotype of,
    362–365
  in modern labor force, 354
  "picture-bride invasion," 339–340
  in political mainstream, 358
  primary structural assimilation
    of, 356
  relocation of, 347—348
  residential assimilation of,
    355–356
  segregation of, in schools,
    338–339
  theories of success of, 361–362
  violence against, 338
  in World War II, 345–347,
    349–350, 376
Jefferson, Thomas, 12
Jensen, Arthur, 120–121
Jews
  Ashkenazaic, 94
  German, 94–95
  Orthodox vs. Reform, 94
  professions of immigrants, 96–97
  reality check, 108–109
  Russian, 95
  Sephardic, 94
Jim Crow
  defined, 176
  effects of, 160, 162
  laws, 157–158
Johnson Act, 125, 465
Johnson, Andrew, 154
Johnson, James Weldon, 165
Johnson, Lyndon, 181, 203, 303, 411
Johnson-Reid Act. *See*
    Immigration Act of 1924

Kachinas, 314
Kallen, Horace, 21, 31
Kampuchea, 411
Kenjin, 341
  defined, 367
Kenjinkai, 341
  defined, 367
Kennedy, John F., 181, 203, 410
Kennedy, Randall, 187, 210
Kim Chong-nim, 383
Kim Ho, 383
Kim Hyong-soon, 383

King Philip (Metacom), 58, 303
King, Martin Luther, Jr., 38, 169,
    179, 180, 181, 184, 476
King, Rodney, 185–186
Kiowa people, religions of, 314
Klamath people, 302
Know-Nothing Party, 115–116
Korea, 380
  division of, 381
  Japan and, 380, 381
  nineteenth-century relations
    with west, 380
  after World War II, 381–382
  in World War II, 381
Korean Americans, 101, 102, 103
  assimilation of, 384–385
  associations of, 383
  English proficiency of, 385
  family formation among, 383
  geographic distribution of, 384
  immigrant enterprises of,
    383–384, 385
  immigration of, 381, 382
  immigration figures for, 382
  marriage patterns of, 384, 385
  in modern labor market, 384
  post-Korean War influx of, 384
  religion of, 382–383, 384
  violence against, 185
Korean War, 381, 384
Korematsu, Fred, 351
Korematsu v. United States, 351
Koryo Dynasty, 380
Kosovo, ethnic issues in, 459
Ku Klux Klan (KKK), 113, 156,
    164–165, 181
  defined, 177
  revival of, 171, 428

Labor, Department of,
    discriminatory
    policies at, 188
Labor unions, 116–117
Laguna people, 320–321
Laissez-faire racism, 444
Lakota people, 294–295
Laos, Hmong people in, 411
La Raza, 242
  defined, 250
Latinos, 450
  assimilation of, 278–280
  cultural preservation of, 279
  diversity of, 254–255
  economic situation of, 270–271

educational attainments of,
    271–273
  family dynamics of, 267–269
  friendship patterns of, 275–276
  geographic distribution of, 254,
    256–258
  language issues of, 452–453
  marital patterns of, 276–277
  in modern labor market,
    269–270, 280
  language issues of, 260–261, 279
  pan-ethnic identity of, 278
  political participation of, 475
  religions of, 277–278
  residential assimilation of,
    273–274
  stereotypes about, 279–280
Lau Task Force Remedies, 264
  defined, 285
Lau v. Nichols, 264
Lazarus, Emma, 2
League of the South, 429
League of United Latin-American
    Citizens (LULAC), 243,
    263, 472
Lebanese Civil War of 1975, 423
Lebanon, 419, 420
  Israeli invasion of, 424
Lee, Wen Ho, 399
Lemon Grove, California, 263
Lerner, Max, 77
Liberia, 153
Liberty City, FL, riots in, 185, 187
Limited English proficiency, 260
  defined, 285
Lincoln, Abraham, 87, 114, 230
  racial views of, 153–154
Lippmann, Walter, 346
Literacy tests, 158
Little Big Horn, 296
Little Crow, 295
Little Rock, Arkansas, school
    desegregation in,
    171–172
Little Wolf, 295
Lodge, Henry Cabot, Sr., 114, 343
London Company, 53
Los Angeles, CA
  1965 riots in, 182–183, 187
  1992 riots in, 185, 187
  residential segregation in,
    198–199
Lost Nation of Islam. *See* Black
    Muslims

Louisiana, postreconstruction laws of, 159
Louisiana Purchase, 229
Loury, Glenn, 191
LULAC v. Richards, 245
Luna, Gregory, 244
Lutheranism, 87
Lynchings, 164–165

Machismo, defined, 285
Macias, Reynaldo, 254
Mafia, 92
Magellan, Ferdinand, 386
Mahmud of Ghazni, 393
Majority, defined, 17
    dominant behavior of, 7–8
Makah people, 306
Malcolm X, 38, 167, 182, 476
Manchu dynasty, 371
Mandan people, 295
Mandela, Nelson, 456, 457
March on Washington movement, 168, 169, 170, 180
Marital assimilation, 24
    reality check, 42–44
Marriage
    assimilation through, 24, 42–44
    interethnic, 9
    interracial, 2, 4, 201–202, 357
Marshall, John, 292, 293, 305
Martinez, José P., 242
Marx, Karl, 135
Maryland, slave laws of, 52, 59
Masaoka, Mike, 336
Massachusetts Bay Colony, 54
Massasoit, 57
Matsuhito, 336–337
Mayflower, 54
McCarran-Walter Act, 100, 465
McKay, Claude, 165
McKinley, William, 386
Meiji empire, 337
Melting-pot ideology, defined, 48
Melting-pot model of assimilation, 30–31, 42
    defined, 48
Mendez v. Westminster School District, 263
Mennonites, 66, 69
Mestizos, defined, 250
Metacom (King Philip), 58, 303
Mexican American Legal Defense and Education Fund (MALDEF), 244–245

Mexican American Political Association (MAPA), 244
Mexican American Youth Association (MAYA), 244
Mexican Americans, 101, 102, 105, 107
    annexation into U.S. of, 230–231
    assimilation of, 6, 245–246, 278–280
    from borderlands, 227
    case studies of, 246–248, 281–282
    Civil Rights movement and, 242–245
    classification of, 256–257
    and colonial model, 34–35
    as conquered minority, 449–451
    Creation Generation of, 231
    cultural assimilation of, 259–261
    cultural preservation of, 279
    Depression and, 237–239
    discrimination against, 231, 239–245
    diversity of, 255, 257
    early immigration of, 233
    in early labor market, 236–237
    economic situation of, 270–271
    educational attainments of, 271–273
    family dynamics of, 267–268
    friendship patterns of, 275–276
    geographic distribution of, 235, 256–258
    historical relations with Anglos, 235–236
    immigration figures for, 234
    language issues of, 260–261, 266, 267, 279, 453
    legal status of, 443
    marital patterns of, 276–277
    Migrant Generation of, 235
    mixed Indian-Spanish origin of, 227–229
    in modern labor market, 269–270, 280
    political participation of, 475
    in post-Chicano era, 245–246
    religions of, 278
    residential assimilation of, 273–274
    stereotypes about, 279–280
    traditional attitudes toward, 237

20th century immigration of, 233–234
    unique situation of, 234–235
    in World War II, 242–243
Mexico
    border disputes with, 231–232
    ethnic makeup of, 229
    independence of, 228–229
    Spanish rule over, 227–228
    U.S. relations with, 229–231
Meyer, Dillon S., 309
Miami, FL, 1980s riots in, 184–185
Michigan, challenges to affirmative action in, 207–209
Middleman minority, defined, 223
Middleman minority theory, 214
    defined, 223
Miele, Stefano, 92
Migrant generation, defined, 250
Migrant workers, 236–237
Million Man March, 191
Milosevic, Slobodan, 459
Minority, working definition of, 7
Mississippi, postreconstruction laws of, 158
Model minority stereotype
    of Chinese, 380
    criticisms of, 362–364
    of Japanese, 362–365
Montejano, David, 227
Montezuma, Carlos, 304
Montgomery, AL, civil rights protests in, 179
Morales, Dan, 206
Mores, defined, 74
Morongo reservation, 319
Morse, Samuel F. B., 115
Moynihan, Daniel P., 189, 213, 440
Moynihan Report, 189–190
Mueller, Robert, 430
Muhammad, Elijah, 167, 182
Muhammed, 418
Muñoz Marín, Luis, 259
Murphy, Frank, 350, 351
Murrah Federal Building, 427
Murray, Charles, 120, 121–123
Muslims. *See* Black Muslims; Islam
Músquiz, Ramón, 229
Myrdal, Gunnar, 455

Najour, C. J., 421
Napoleonic Wars, 67
National Asian Pacific American Legal Consortium, 430

National Association for the
Advancement of Colored
People (NAACP), 164, 166
strategies of, 168, 170, 180, 472
National Association of Arab
Americans (NAAA), 426
National Congress of American
Indians (NCAI), 305
National Environmental Policy
Act, 326
National Indian Youth Council
(NIYC), 305
National Liberation Front, 411
National Negro Business
League, 162
National-origins principle, 100
defined, 111
Native American Church (NAC),
314
Native American Cultural
Protection and Free Exercise
of Religion Act, 314
Native American Party, 115
Native American Preparatory
School, 326
Native Americans. *See* American
Indians
Nativism, 114
defined, 144
revival of, 165
Nature vs. nurture, 118
Navajo people, 323
business ventures of, 320
identity of, 325–326
language of, 313
Navajo Reservation, 308
Navarro, José Antonio, 229
Neo-Nazis, 428
New Amsterdam, 22
New England
Anglo-Indian relations in, 57, 58
Scotch-Irish in, 63
settlement of, 54
New Mexico
early laws of, 262
Mexican labor in, 236
New Negro Alliance, 168
New Netherland, 22, 54
New tribalism, 305–308
defined, 333
New York
founding of, 22
Germans in, 86
immigration facilities in, 88

Irish in, 82
Italians in, 93
1964 riots in, 182
Nez Percé people, 296, 320
Niagara Movement, 163–164
defined, 177
Nisei, 340
assimilation of, 352
civil rights groups of, 345
cultural preservation by, 341, 342
defined, 367
education of, 344
military service of, 349–350
Nisei: The Quiet Americans, 354
Nixon, E. D., 179
Nixon, Richard, 303, 411
Nonviolent protest, 169–170,
179, 476
Nonwhites, 445, 446. *See also*
names of individual ethnic
and national groups
Nordics, 117–118
North Vietnam, 411
Northwest Territory Ordinance, 291

Occidental Quarterly, 428
O'Connor, Sandra Day, 208, 209
Oglala people, 320
Ohiyesa, 304
Oklahoma Cherokee people
languages of, 313
tribal vs. lineage members, 315
Oklahoma City bombing, 427
Omaha people, 312
One point five generation, 5
Oneida people, 319, 326
Operation Boulder, 426
Operation Wetback, 239
Opium War, 371
Organization of Afro-American
Unity, 182
Orthodox Judaism, 94
Osage people, 294
Osage Reservation, 308
Ottoman Empire, 419
fall of, 423
Out-groups, 13
Ozawa, Takao, 342–343
Ozawa v. United States, 343, 443

Pachucos, 239, 240–241
Pak Yong-man, 383
Palestinians
conflict with Israelis, 424

religion of, 423
Pan-ethnic identity, 278
defined, 285
Panjabi, 396
Pantoja, Antonia, 263
Park, Robert E., 8, 21, 34, 39
Parker, Arthur, 304
Parks, Rosa, 179
Parole authority, 410
Patel, Marilyn Hall, 352
Pawnee people, 294
effects of Anglo contact on, 295
Penn, William, 64
Pennsylvania
Germans (Pennsylvania Dutch)
in, 65
Scotch-Irish in, 63–64
Penobscot people, 313
Pequot people, 315, 319–320
Percent plans, 206–207
ineffectiveness of, 207
Perry, Matthew, 336
Pershing, John "Blackjack," 232
Personality
authoritarian, 132
and prejudice, 131–132
Peyote, 314
Phelan, J. D., 337
Philippine Islands, 385–386
emigration to U.S. from. *See*
Filipino (Pilipino)
Americans
foreign contact with, 386
independence efforts in, 386, 387
languages of, 387
religion in, 386
Spanish rule over, 386
United States rule over, 386–387
Picket lines, 168
Picture brides, 339–340
Pilipino Americans. *See* Filipino
(Pilipino) Americans
Plains tribes, 294
Plantation system, 60–61
Plessy v. Ferguson, 159–160, 162,
171, 472, 474
Pluralism
and assimilation, 31–33, 453
Constitution and, 41
criticisms of, 40–41
cultural, 35
reality check, 42–44
reasons for, 41–42
support for, 453

varieties of, 35–38
Plyler v. Doe, 244
Plymouth, MA, 22, 52, 53–54
Pol Pot, 411–412
Political Association of Spanish-
    Speaking Organizations
    (PASO), 244
Polk, James, 230
Poll taxes, 158
Ponca people, 303
Pontiac, 290–291, 303
Poole, Elijah, 167
Portuguese, colonization by, 22, 393
Post-Chicano era, 245–246
Postcolonial perspective, 266
Potato famine, of 1840s, 81–82
Poverty, analysis of, 213
Powhatan people, 56
Pratt, Richard H., 299
Preferential treatment, defined, 223
Prejudice, 24, 113
    cognitive remedies for, 468–469
    conscious efforts to correct,
        467–468
    cultural transmission of,
        128–130
    defined, 48
    educational approach to,
        468–471
    group identification and,
        130–131
    intergroup contact remedy for,
        469–471
    personality and, 131–132
    and racism, 127–128
    studies of, 133–134
    theories of, 128–132
    vicarious-experience remedies
        for, 469. *See also*
        Discrimination; Racism
Presbyterians, 63
Primary group relations, 26
Primary relationships, defined, 48
Primary structural assimilation, 24
Principles of achievement and
        ascription, defined, 17
Proclamation of 1763, 291
Prosser, Gabriel, 151, 166
Puerto Ricans, 255
    assimilation of, 278–280
    classification of, 256–257
    as conquered minority, 449–451
    cultural assimilation of, 259–261
    cultural preservation of, 279

discrimination against, 271
economic situation of, 271
educational attainments of,
        272–273
family dynamics of, 268–269
friendship patterns of, 275
geographic distribution of,
        256–257
immigration to mainland, 259
language issues of, 260–261,
        262, 266–267, 279
marital patterns of, 276–277
in modern labor market, 270, 280
religions of, 278
residential assimilation of,
        273–274
stereotypes about, 279–280
Puerto Rico
    current status of, 259
    independence movement of,
        253, 259
    official language of, 262
    Spanish language in, 266–267
    Spanish rule over, 258
    U.S. rule over, 258–259
Puritans, 54
    relations with American
        Indians, 57

Qing dynasty, 371
Quanah Parker, 295
Quebec, secessionist movement
    in, 457
Quota Act, 265
Quota system, 99

Race relations, cycle of, 8–9, 34
Race
    and intelligence, 119–120
    overlapping boundaries of, 12,
        117–118
    views of, 11–13
Racial group, defined, 17
Racial profiling, 187
Racial violence, 164–165
Racism
    blood quantum concept, 311
    and classism, 135
    contemporary, 126–128
    defined, 144
    economic disadvantage caused
        by, 214–215
    laissez-faire, defined, 463
    legislation of, 123–124

modern face of, 188–189
modern resurgence of, 427,
        428–431
scientific, 117–123
structural view of, 213
    See also Discrimination
Randolph, A. Philip, 166, 168, 170,
        180, 204
Rawle, William, 77
Reagan, Ronald, 184
Reconstruction, 155
Red Cloud, 295, 296
Red Power movement, 305, 306
Red Summer, 165, 169
Reform Judaism, 94
Refugee Act of 1980, 410, 465
Refugee Escape Act, 100
Refugee Relief Act of 1953, 409, 465
Refugees
    from Communism, 101, 409
    reality check, 432–433
    recent sources of, 409–410
    after World War II, 98
*Regents of the University of
        California v. Bakke,*
        204–205
Rehnquist, William, 208
Reimers, David, 77
Repatriation, 238
    defined, 250
Republican Party, and Forty-
        eighters, 87
Residential segregation, 196–199
Reverse discrimination, 205
Revolutionary War, role of recent
        immigrants in, 66–69
Rhee, Syngman, 383
Riis, Jacob, 97
Roberts, Owen, 351
Robertson, Pat, 429
Robinson, James R., 169
Rodríguez, Clara, 254
Roosevelt, Franklin D., 106, 169,
        204, 338, 375
Roosevelt, Theodore, 265
Ross, E. A., 337
Russians
    immigration into U.S., 87, 88
    Jews, 95–97

Sac people, 312
St. John Crevecoeur, J. Hector, 30
Salvadoran Americans, 103
Sánchez, George, 262

Sansei
    assimilation of, 352–354
    cultural revival among, 353
    defined, 340
Sanskrit, 393
Santa Anna, Antonio, 230
Saxton, Alexander, 371
Scalawags, 155
Scandinavians, immigration into
    U.S., 87
Scapegoat, defined, 144
Schlesinger, Arthur, Jr., 77
Schurz, Carl, 87
Schwerner, Michael, 181
Scotch-Irish, 63, 441
    assimilation of, 64–65, 440
    in Pennsylvania, 63–64
    in Revolutionary war, 67
Secession, 36
    ideology of, defined, 48
Second generation, defined, 17
Second great immigrant stream,
    defined, 111
Second stream immigrants
    assimilation of, 442
    Austrians, 87, 88
    German Jews, 94–95
    Hungarians, 87, 88
    Italians, 87, 90–97
    Russian Jews, 95–97
Secondary relationships,
    defined, 17
Secondary structural assimilation,
    defined, 48
Segmented assimilation, 10, 25,
    107
    defined, 17
Segregation, 159–160, 472
    attitudes toward, 127
    end of legal, 170–172
    in housing, 196–199
    outlawing of, 126, 181–182,
        263–264
Self-fulfilling prophesy, defined, 144
Self-identification, defined, 333
Selma, AL, civil rights protests
    in, 181
Seminole people, 294
    Black, 61–62
Seminole War, 294
Separate but equal doctrine,
    159–160
    end of, 171
Separatism, 36–37, 38, 107

Black nationalism, 182
    ideology of, defined, 48
    support for, 453
Sephardim, 94
September 11, 2001, effects of, 2,
    428, 429
Sequoyah, 292
Serbs, 459
Shakopee Mdewekantan
    people, 319
Shape of the River, The, 210
Sharecropping, 157
Sheridan, Philip, 295
Sherman, William, 295
Shoney's, discriminatory policies
    at, 188
Sikhs, 396
Silla Unification Period, 380
Simmons, William, 164
Simon, Thomas, 118
Simpson, Nicole, 186
Simpson, O. J., 186–187
Simpson-Rodino Act, 466
Singh, J. J., 397
Sioux people, 294–295, 323
    business ventures of, 320
    religions of, 314
    Santee, 319
    warfare of, 295
Sit-ins, 169, 179–180
Sitting Bull, 295, 296, 300–301, 303
Situational pressures theories of
    discrimination, 132–134
Slave patrols, 62
Slavery
    and Civil War, 151
    in colonial period, 150–151
    economic, 157
    Emancipation Proclamation
        and, 154
    harshness of, 60
    impact of, on victims, 152
    and indentured servitude, 59
    labor source of, 61
    and plantation system, 60–61
    profitability of, 152–153
    race and, 59–61
    resistance and rebellions
        against, 61–62, 151
Sleepy Lagoon Trial, 240, 241
    defined, 251
Snipp, C. Matthew, 289
Social Darwinism, 117–118
    defined, 145

20th century revival of, 122–123
Social desirability bias, defined, 145
Social distance, defined, 145
Social identity theory, defined, 145
Social self theory, defined, 145
Society for American Indians,
    304–305
Sojourners, 92
South Africa, 198
    apartheid in, 456
    immigrant issues in, 456, 457
South Carolina, slaves in, 61
South Vietnam, 411
Southern Christian Leadership
    Conference (SCLC), 179
Southern Europeans, immigration
    into U.S., 87, 89–90
Southern Poverty Law Center, 428
Southern Ute people, business
    ventures of, 320
Sovereign nations, defined, 333
    Indian tribes as, 293
Spanish
    colonization by, 22
    language, 260–262. *See also*
        Bilingual education
    in Mexico, 227–229
    in Philippines, 386
    in Puerto Rico, 258
Spanish-American War, 386, 387
Spatial assimilation, theory of, 196
    defined, 223
Spearman, Charles, 120
Split labor market theory, 135–136
    defined, 145
Spokane people, 324
Spotted Tail, 295
Stanford, Leland, 123
Stereotypes, 129, 362–365
    defined, 145
Stevens, Ted, 265
Straight line theory, 4–5
Stratification system, defined, 145
Student Nonviolent Coordinating
    Committee (SNCC), 180
*Study of American Intelligence,
    A,* 119
Subcultures, 10
Subordinate group, defined, 17
Subsocieties, defined, 18
Substitution, cultural assimilation
    by, 23
Suez Canal, 420
Sweatshops, 76

Sweatt, Heman M., 206
Sweatt v. Painter, 206
Sweden
    liberalism in, 455–456
    racism in, 456
Swift, Jonathan, 63
Symbolic ethnicity, 441
    defined, 463
Syria, 419
Syrians, 419
    assimilation of, 421–422
    discrimination against, 420, 421
    family formation among, 420
    geographic distribution of,
      421–422
    and Israel, 426
    in labor force, 421
    religion of, 420–421

Tachiki, Amy, 336
Taft, William Howard, 386–387
Tagore, Rabindranath, 370
Tanomoshi, 341, 378
    defined, 367
Tecumseh, 38, 291–292, 303
Tejanos, 229–230
    defined, 251
Tenskwatawa, 291
Termination policy, 301–303
    defined, 333
Terrorism
    effects of, 427
    efforts to fight, 431
    September 11, 2001, 2, 428, 429
Terry, Alfred, 295, 296
Testing theory, 120
Teutons, 117
Texaco, discriminatory policies
    at, 188
Texas
    affirmative action in, 205–206
    annexation of, 230–232
    border disputes of, 231–232
    early laws of, 262
    independence of, 229–230
    Mexican American civil rights
      efforts in, 244–245
    Mexican labor in, 236
    percent plans in, 206, 207
Texas Bilingual, United States
    v., 244
Theory of assimilation
    subprocesses, defined, 49
Third generation, defined, 18

Third stream immigrants
    Arabs, 103
    Asian Indians, 102, 103
    from Caribbean, 101, 103
    Central Americans, 101, 103
    Chinese, 101
    Cubans, 102
    Dominicans, 101, 103
    INAA and, 370
    Koreans, 101, 102, 103
    Mexicans, 101, 102
    from Philippines, 101, 102
    Salvadorans, 103
    settlement patterns of, 102
    time of arrival of, 102–103
    undocumented workers,
      103–104
    Vietnamese, 101, 102
    See also names of individual
      groups
Thirteenth Amendment, 154,
    155, 159
Thom, Melvin, 289
Thomas, Clarence, 208–209, 307
Three-generations model, 5
Three-generations process,
    defined, 18
Thurmond, Strom, 12
Thurstone, L. L. 120
Tijerina, Pete, 244
Time on the Cross, 152
Tippecanoe, 292
Tobacco
    and colonization, 53, 56
    and slavery, 150
Tokugawa shogunate, 336
Trade and Intercourse Act of
    1834, 297
Trail of Tears, 293–294
Transcontinental railroad, 371, 373
"Transmuting pot," defined, 49
Transnational, defined, 18
Treaty of 1868, 296
Triangle Shirtwaist Company, 97
Tribal nationalism, 305
Trotter, Monroe, 163
Truly Disadvantaged, The, 216
Truman, Harry, 170, 204
Truncated middleman minority,
    defined, 223
Turkey, 419
Turner, Frederick Jackson, 39
Turner, Nat, 151, 166
Turning Stone Casino Resort, 319

Tuskegee Institute, 162
Tydings-McDuffie Bill, 388, 390

Underground Railroad, 62, 151
Undocumented workers, 103–104
United Farm Workers (UFW), 244
United States
    absorption of immigrants into,
      106–107
    changing patterns of
      immigration in, 87–89
    Civil War of, 87, 116
    colonization of, 22–23
    cultural assimilation in, 39–40
    diversity of, 2
    early plurality of, 23
    ethnic identification in, 2
    factors affecting growth of,
      77–79
    first great immigration stream
      into, 79–87, 441–442
    German immigration into, 79,
      84–87
    immigration laws of, 465–466
    immigration rates in, 78
    Irish immigration into, 79–84
    pluralism of, 10–11
    pre-1830 immigration into, 79
    role of immigrants in life of,
      104–107
    second great immigration
      stream into, 89–98, 442
    third great immigrant stream
      into, 98–107
Universal African Legion, 166
Universal Black Cross Nurses, 166
Universal Negro Improvement
    Association (UNIA),
    165–167
Up from Slavery, 166
USA Patriot Act of 2001, 431

Vacuum domicilium doctrine, 57
Vertical social class mobility, 121
Vesey, Denmark, 151, 166
Vicarious experience approach,
    toward remedying
    prejudice, 468–469
Vietcong, 411
Vietminh, 411
Vietnam
    foreign contact with, 410–411
    French rule over, 411
Vietnam War, 411

Vietnamese Americans, 101,
102, 408
assimilation of, 414–418
educational attainments of, 415
English proficiency of, 414–415
family reunification of, 416–417
geographic dispersal of,
413–414
immigration figures for, 409
in labor market, 415–416
marital patterns of, 417
postwar resettlement of,
412–413
reality check, 432–433
refugee origin of, 409–410,
411–414
Vigilantes, antiimmigrant,
428–429
Villa, Francisco "Pancho," 232
Virginia
Anglo-Indian relations in, 57, 58
settlement of, 53
slave laws of, 60
Virginia Company, 53
Voluntary Relocation Program,
309
Voting Rights Act of 1965, 181,
205, 475
Voting Rights Act of 1975, 475

Wampanoags, 57, 58
War Brides Act, 376, 391
War of 1812, 292

War on Poverty, 303
Warren, Earl, 171, 346
Wartime Relocation and
Internment of Civilians,
Commission on, 351
Washington, Booker T., 150,
162–163, 164, 166
Washington, George, 51, 291
Washington, Indian affairs of, 306
Wassaja, 304
Waters, Mary, 217
Watts riots, 182–183, 187
West Indian Americans, 217, 218
Western Hemisphere Act, 100, 466
Wheeler-Howard Act, 301
When Work Disappears, 216–217
White Flight, 474
White supremacy, defined, 74
doctrine of, 55
restoration after election of
1876, 156–160
resurgence of, 427–428
Whites
attitudes toward racism of,
185–186, 444
conflicts with African
Americans in modern
times, 184–189
ethnic identity of, 443–445
in modern labor market, 192
pluralistic principles among,
445, 453

separatist sentiments among,
453
Wilkins, Roy, 150
Williams, Roger, 57
Wilson, William J., 215, 216
Wilson, Woodrow, 125, 232
Without Consent or Contract, 152
Woi, 378
Women's National Indian
Association, 303
Worcester v. Georgia, 292, 293
Workingman's Party, 124
World War II, 98
African Americans in, 170
and end of Depression, 168
racial tensions in, 169
reasons for, 170
refugees after, 98
Wounded Knee, 300
Wu, Frank, 370

Xenophobia, defined, 145
Yavapi-Apache people, 307

Yi Dynasty, 380
Yonsei, defined, 340
Young Joseph, 320

Zangwill, Israel, 21
Zionists, 423
Zoot-Suit Riots, 239–241
defined, 251